READING FOR THINKING

Reading for Thinking

Sixth Edition

Laraine E. Flemming

Ann Marie Radaskiewicz
Contributing Writer

HEINLE
CENGAGE Learning™

Australia • Brazil • Japan • Korea • Mexico • Singapore • Spain • United Kingdom • United States

HEINLE
CENGAGE Learning™

Reading for Thinking, Sixth Edition
Laraine E. Flemming

Executive Publisher: Patricia A. Coryell

Editor in Chief: Carrie Brandon

Sponsoring Editor: Joann Kozyrev

Senior Marketing Manager: Tom Ziolkowski

Senior Development Editor: Judith Fifer

Discipline Product Manager: Giuseppina Daniel

Senior Project Editor: Margaret Park Bridges

Senior Media Producer: Philip Lanza

Senior Content Manager: Janet Edmonds

Art and Design Manager: Jill Haber

Cover Design Director: Tony Saizon

Senior Photo Editor: Jennifer Meyer Dare

Senior Composition Buyer: Chuck Dutton

Senior New Title Project Manager: Pat O'Neill

Editorial Assistant: Daisuke Yasutake

Marketing Assistant: Bettina Chiu

Cover image: © Jupiter Images

Credits appear on pages 642–643, which constitute an extension of the copyright page.

For product information and technology assistance, contact us at **Cengage Learning Customer & Sales Support, 1-800-354-9706**

For permission to use material form this text or product, submit all requests online at **www.cengage.com/permissions** Further permissions questions can be emailed to **permissionrequest@cengage.com**

Library of Congress Control Number: 2007931299
ISBN-10: 0-618-98582-4
ISBN-13: 978-0-618-98582-1

Heinle
25 Thomson Place
Boston, MA 02210
USA

Cengage Learning is a leading provider of customized learning solutions with office location around the globe, including Singapore, the United Kingdom, Australia, Mexico, Brazil and Japan. Locate your local office at: **international.cengage.com/region**

Cengage Learning products are represented in Canada by Nelson Education, Ltd.

For your course and learning solutions, visit **academic.cengage.com**
Visit Heinle online at **elt.heinle.com**
Visit our corporate website at **www.cengage.com**

Printed in the United States of America
4 5 6 7 11 10

CONTENTS

Chapter 3 Reviewing the Essentials 98

Chapter 6   The Role of Inferences in Comprehension and Critical Reading   *318*

Chapter 7   Defining the Terms *Fact* and *Opinion*   *403*

Chapter 8   Identifying Purpose and Tone   *439*

Chapter 9   Recognizing and Evaluating Bias   477

Chapter 10   Understanding and Evaluating Arguments   520

PREFACE

As the author, I couldn't be happier that *Reading for Thinking* has earned another edition. Still, revising it was something of a balancing act. On the one hand, I wanted to keep the material from previous editions that teachers and students really liked. I wasn't about to change, for instance, the carefully structured sequence, which steadily elaborates on and refines basic comprehension skills until they become critical reading strategies. Yet while keeping what worked, I also wanted to respond to suggestions from longtime users as well as current reviewers. Then, too, I was determined to put into practice whatever new insights I had gained from recent reading research.

I think I found the right balance for this new edition. In its sixth edition, *Reading for Thinking* still draws heavily on exciting topics chosen for their ability to stimulate student interest. It also continues to model all the various skills introduced, provide numerous exercises as well as tests, and highlight the connections between reading for understanding and reading to evaluate. At the same time, there is much here that is brand new. What follows are some of the most significant new features.

New Chapter on Vocabulary Building

Rather than including just a chapter section, *Reading for Thinking* now has an entire chapter on vocabulary building (Chapter 2, "Developing an Academic Vocabulary"). As in previous editions, four common context clues are explained, illustrated, and accompanied by exercises and tests. However, the new chapter also introduces a series of words central to the study of government, psychology, and sociology. The purpose of these additions is to familiarize students with some of the words bound to appear in their textbooks. My hope is that these lists of specialized vocabulary will encourage students to start similar ones based on their reading assignments. To that end, I have included an explanation of how students can decide if a word is essential to the subject matter.

New Chapter on Organizational Patterns

Identifying organizational patterns can prove useful in two ways: (1) As soon as students recognize the organizational pattern underlying a reading, they are better equipped to separate what's especially important from what's not so significant. (2) Being able to organize new information into an overarching pattern makes it easier to store that information in long-term memory. Because the ability to recognize organizational patterns is so useful, it made sense to expand the original section on patterns into an entire chapter (Chapter 4, "Recognizing Patterns of Organization"). The new chapter covers *definition, process, sequence of dates and events, simple listing, classification, comparison and contrast,* and *cause and effect*.

Completely Revised Chapter on Study Skills

A number of instructors wrote to say that they liked the first chapter of *Reading for Thinking*, which introduces students to some basic study skills. They mentioned as well that they'd like to see the chapter enlarged to include some of the skills described later in the book, that is, annotating, underlining, and paraphrasing. In responding to those requests, I revised the chapter from beginning to end. In addition to *SQ3R*, Chapter 1 now shows students how to annotate pages, paraphrase for note-taking, summarize chapter sections, and commit new word meanings to memory. These skills are then reintroduced and refined throughout later chapters.

More on Inferences

With every edition, the material on drawing inferences seems to expand. It continues to grow because instructors consistently request more practice with inferences. But it's also true that, across the board, reading research emphasizes the role of inferences at every level of understanding. To just grasp the author's meaning, readers need to infer numerous connections and pieces of background information, which the author suggests but never states. Yet at the same time, all kinds of critical reading, such as evaluating bias, identifying tone, and recognizing purpose, rely on the reader's ability to draw appropriate inferences. Because drawing inferences is central to both comprehension and critical reading, this new edition offers a whole range of reading-related inferences, from making connections between sentences and supplying supporting details to recognizing purpose and drawing conclusions about the author's personal prejudices.

New Section on Inferences and Pronouns

Although experienced readers are likely to connect pronouns and antecedents without even noticing they are doing it, connecting pronouns to the nouns they stand for can be problematic for many readers. Thus it seemed worthwhile to spend some time on connecting antecedents to pronouns early in the book and use this instruction to underscore the importance of reader-supplied inferences.

More Attention to Paraphrasing

Paraphrasing is an essential part of comprehension. It's the only way readers can really be sure they have understood the author's meaning. Thus in every edition, I have extended the number of pages devoted to paraphrasing. The sixth edition is no exception. This time, I've tried to give paraphrasing its due by introducing it in the first chapter and then reintroducing it in later chapters.

New Criteria for Evaluating Websites

When it comes to providing students with the background knowledge for textbook assignments, the World Wide Web is an underutilized resource. For that reason, this edition of *Reading for Thinking* offers students a step-by-step system for using the Web to supplement their background knowledge about unfamiliar textbook material. The sixth edition shows students how to eliminate sites not relevant to their purpose and go directly to the sites that will give them the general background they need for efficient comprehension.

Graphical Organizers

Diagramming ideas, in addition to paraphrasing them, seems to work wonders for both understanding and remembering. For that reason, the sixth edition of *Reading for Thinking* devotes more attention than ever before to the use of diagrams as a way of understanding and representing complex material. The chapter on organizational patterns, in particular, makes heavy use of diagramming to emphasize how different kinds of texts call for different kinds of diagrams.

Focus on Allusions

The sixth edition of *Reading for Thinking* spends a considerable amount of time on allusions. At the most basic level, students learn how and why writers use allusions to convey meaning and develop tone. They learn as well a number of the most common allusions that writers employ. However, because allusions are so often tied to historical events, they also serve to enhance background knowledge. For precisely that reason, ten of the allusions introduced in Chapter 2 refer to people and events crucial to World War II and its aftermath. By learning what it means to call someone or something "Trumanesque," students also learn about an extremely influential president and the events related to his tenure. Similarly, in learning the meaning of "the iron curtain," they learn about a particularly critical juncture in the relationship between the United States and the former Soviet Union.

Synthesizing Longer Readings

Reading for Thinking has always included material on synthesizing, but in the past, most of the readings were only a paragraph or two. This new edition looks at longer readings and explains, step by step, how to synthesize, or combine, related readings under the umbrella of a more general and more inclusive statement. This is a skill students desperately need in order to read and write at an academic level, and synthesizing longer readings deserves the extra attention it now receives.

New Sample Textbook Chapter

Chapter 1 describes and models a number of different ways to read and remember textbook information. While students are expected to apply those strategies to their own texts, instructors who used *Reading for Thinking* in the past mentioned that a sample textbook chapter would be a big help to them. In response to this request, I have included a history chapter titled "America Under Stress, 1967–1976." I chose the chapter because many of the people, places, and events discussed, from the Warren Court to the Tet Offensive, have become common cultural allusions, which represent, in abbreviated form, a succession of significant events. Students who use the sample chapter to practice note-taking, paraphrasing, or *SQ3R* will also learn a good deal about recent U.S. history.

Numerous New Readings

The sixth edition contains a wide mix of readings drawn from a variety of sources—textbooks, magazines, and newspapers. As in the past, I have selected readings that I thought would arouse student curiosity and interest while keeping students abreast of crucial past and current events. The topics are as diverse as the feud between J. Robert Oppenheimer and Edward Teller over the hydrogen bomb to the current fears about bird flu. New readings address the controversial ideas of animal rights champion Peter Singer; the disappearance of honey bees; and the virtues and drawbacks asso- ciated with the online phenomenon Wikipedia. Selections excerpted from textbooks are identified by an open book icon.

Many Thanks to the Reviewers

A particular thanks to Professor Barbara Real of Rhode Island Community College, who gave me some great exercises on inferences, available on **laflemm.com**, and Professor Patricia Domenico, who encouraged me to do more with graphical organizers. As always, many thanks to Professors Joan Hellman and Dawn Sedik, who permanently influenced my thinking about reading instruction. Thanks also to the following reviewers whose suggestions I relied on to steer my way through this new revision: Susan Chainey, Sacramento City College; Frank Crayton, Palo Alto College; Nancy Davies, Miami Dade College; Janet A. Flores, St. Philip's College; Jeanne Ann Graham, Ivy Tech Community College; Denice Josten, Saint Louis Community College at Forest Park; Robbi Muckenfuss, Durham Technical Community College; Larry R. Shirk, Johnson County Community College; and Sherry Wilson, Crowder College.

Best Wishes, Laraine Flemming

Also Available in the Same Series

Reading for Thinking is the third and highest-level text in a three-part series. The two lower-level texts offer the same step-by-step approach combined with lively readings and clear explanations. *Reading for Results* concentrates mainly on comprehension skills and includes one chapter on critical thinking. The perfect precursor to *Reading for Thinking, Reading for Results* lays the groundwork for all of the skills introduced in its more advanced sister text. Instructors teaching a basic reading course, however, might prefer to start with *Reading Keys*, which offers more abbreviated explanations and more multiple-choice exercises along with more repetition and review. *Reading Keys* also introduces both concepts and skills in smaller, more incremental steps.

Companion Online Resources

Students and instructors can rely on the following online resources for additional practice and support:

- *Getting Focused*, the Web-based program for reading improvement that accompanies this textbook, helps students to review and reinforce both comprehension and critical reading skills. Please see **college.cengage.com/devenglish/flemming/getting _focused/1e/student_home.html** for more information about the program.
- Additional materials and exercises are available at Cengage Learning's student website at **college.cengage.com/pic/flemming RFT6e**.
- A complete instructor's manual is available on the password-protected instructor's website, which can be accessed through **college.cengage.com/pic/flemmingRFT6e**. Instructors who wish to can also request a hard copy of the manual from their Houghton representatives.
- More online exercises for all of the skills introduced in this text can also be found on the author's website, at **laflemm.com**.
- PowerPoint slides are available for many of the key comprehension and critical reading terms introduced in this text. The Power-Points are available at **college.cengage.com/pic/flemmingRFT6e** and **laflemm.com**.

The Online Study Center

The Online Study Center represents all of the carefully integrated, interactive, and valuable online learning content Cengage Learning has developed for its college reading programs. The Online Study Center is available in several versions across multiple platforms, including many of the most popular Course Management Systems (CMS) like Blackboard, WebCT, ANGEL, and others. All versions of The Online Study Center allow students to access a core set of valuable, text-specific, and interactive-learning content and resources. The two most popular versions of The Online Study Center are delivered via a standalone website and in Eduspace®, Cengage Learning's course-management system.

The Online Study Center in Eduspace

The Online Study Center in Eduspace contains a full set of test items that instructors can assign. And, like all course-management systems, Eduspace allows instructors to build and customize their own online courses, deliver homework and other assignments to students, and track student progress and results via a powerful gradebook. Instructors can go to **college.cengage.com/pic/ flemmingRFT6e**, for a link to The Online Study Center in Eduspace, or contact their Cengage Learning sales representative for more information.

The Online Study Center in Eduspace provides students with a wealth of learning resources to help them succeed in their course, including all of the following:

- A progressive sequence of Pre-, Practice, and Mastery Tests with instant feedback at three reading levels
- Diagnostic assessment modules that generate individualized study paths
- Interactives powered by the Associated Press
- Total Practice Zone, which includes practice with Reading, Vocabulary, Writing, and Grammar as well as access to popular programs such as VEER, Timed Readings, Reading Space, and Advanced Vocabulary
- A training module to help students develop their abilities to read online

Additional Print Supplements

***Cengage Learning Guide to Reading Textbooks,* Second Edition** This guide lets students practice their reading skills on textbook selections.

***The American Heritage College Dictionary,* Fourth Edition** With 7,500 new words and meanings, along with 2,500 new illustrations, the Fourth Edition is the most up-to-date college dictionary available.

The American Heritage ESL Dictionary The first ESL dictionary of its kind to be based on one of the most respected and authoritative English-language dictionaries available, this resource is specially designed to meet the needs of ESL students.

Words Count Also written by Laraine Flemming, this is a basic vocabulary book using a contextual approach to vocabulary building. Each chapter links new words together based on a shared theme, such as money, marriage, or friendship.

READING FOR THINKING

CHAPTER 1

Becoming a Successful Student

In this chapter, you will learn

- how to use a five-step method for comprehending textbook assignments.

- why annotating and underlining material aid both comprehension and memory.

- why paraphrasing while reading is important.

- the basic steps for writing summaries.

- how to use the World Wide Web as a source of background knowledge.

By the time you finish this textbook, you'll possess all the reading strategies you need to be a successful student. However, like most of us, you probably don't want to wait. Instead, you want more immediate results. The good news is that you can get those quick results by consistently putting into practice all the learning strategies introduced in this chapter.

1

To be sure, future chapters will further discuss the strategies and tips generally described here. But that doesn't mean you have to wait until then to start putting them into practice. On the contrary, you can begin using them right now. All that requires is your willingness to make the effort.

 # Use *SQ3R* to Complete Textbook Assignments

If you are reading a novel purely for your own pleasure, it's fine to just open the book and start reading, making little or no effort to focus or distribute your attention selectively. But if you do the same thing with a textbook assignment, it's easy to pay too much attention to the details that don't matter and miss the ones that do. Effective textbook reading requires a method.

One of the most popular methods was invented more than fifty years ago by a psychology instructor named Francis Robinson. The method is called *SQ3R*, and it reflects everything Robinson knew about the workings of the human mind. Robinson knew, for instance, that we tend to forget new information right after learning it. For this reason, *SQ3R* has a step built in to decrease forgetting right after reading. Robinson also knew that good reading comprehension relies heavily on the mind's ability to make and confirm predictions about how an author's thoughts will unfold. For that reason, his five-step system starts by giving readers a basis for making predictions, which can then be confirmed or contradicted through the actual reading of the text.

Since Robinson created *SQ3R*, other systems have come along, most of them quite similar and distinguished only by the acronym,* or initials, used to create the name. If you are familiar with one of those systems and feel that it works, then you should certainly continue to use it. But if you don't already have a method for reading textbooks and tend to read them the same way you might read an article in *USA Today*, then you should learn, adapt, and apply the steps in *SQ3R* listed below.

---

*acronym: words based on the initials of three or more words; for example, the word *scuba* is derived from the term *self-contained underwater breathing apparatus*.

A Note on Flexibility

Some people claim that *SQ3R* might be too rigid to be useful. However, I believe that claim is made by people who have never read Robinson's book, *Effective Study*. Robinson himself modifies the steps in *SQ3R* and you should do the same. If, for instance, an author opens each chapter section with a question and you feel you can use the questions to test your understanding—instead of inventing your own—follow your instincts and do just that.

S: Survey

> A quick overview orients the reader and allows him to comprehend at least partially what is to come.
>
> —Francis Robinson, *Effective Study*[†]

To survey a chapter, take a few minutes—ten or fifteen—to get an overview of the chapter's contents and organization. Although exactly what elements of the chapter you look at during a survey will vary with the textbook format, you should always read any portions of text titled *introduction*, *summary*, or *review*. Then skim the remaining pages, looking for the kinds of clues to significance listed in the following box.

Textbook Clues to Significance

1. Headings
2. Notes in the margins
3. Questions in italics appearing between chapter sections
4. Pictures, cartoons, graphs, tables, and charts, including captions
5. Words printed in boldface, colored ink, or italics
6. Icons, or symbols, used to highlight information in the text
7. Boxed statements or lists

[†]All quotations attributed to Robinson in this section come from the fourth edition of Robinson's book, *Effective Study*, published by Harper and Row in 1961.

If you've read the introduction and summary page and glanced at all the possible clues listed above and still have no idea what direction the chapter will take, read the opening sentence of every paragraph.

Q: Question

> The use of a question at the beginning of each section gives an immediate questioning attitude and a core idea around which to organize the material which follows.[†]
>
> —Francis Robinson

Headings and titles can be enormously helpful when it comes to posing questions to guide your attention while reading. Questions based on headings will lead you to central points in a chapter or an article section. For instance, the sample textbook chapter on pages 625–626 uses the heading "The Warren Court." On seeing this heading, readers should immediately pose questions like "What was the Warren Court?" and "What made the Warren Court special?"

Questions such as these determine how you distribute your attention. For instance, based on these questions, you might quickly read through the paragraph describing earlier courts but slow down to read descriptions of what judges were on the Warren Court and what the Court as a whole accomplished.

Raising and answering questions will also help you stay motivated. Each time you can answer one of your own questions, you will feel a sense of accomplishment.

R-1: Read

The first *R* in *SQ3R* stands for *Read*. However, that doesn't mean you should read a textbook chapter from beginning to end in one sitting. Instead, divide assignments into manageable chunks of fifteen to twenty pages at most. That way, you'll maintain your concentration the entire time it takes to complete that chunk of the assignment.

In addition to posing questions that focus and distribute your attention while reading, try to predict how the flow of the author's thought will develop. Then read to confirm or revise your initial prediction.

[†]Robinson's method, if consistently applied, can really boost your comprehension, but no one would ever claim he was a stylish writer.

The sample textbook chapter on pages 625–641 includes the heading "American Indian Activism." Given the chapter title, "America Under Stress, 1967–1976," a likely prediction based on the heading would be "This section will describe the rise in American Indian activism during this decade." Reading to confirm or modify this prediction will give you precisely the focused concentration that textbook reading requires.

R-2: Recall

When Robinson first created the *SQ3R* system, the second *R* meant *Recite*. Robinson's thought was that whenever students finished a chapter section, they should look away from the book and briefly recite answers to the questions they had posed initially. Recitation was a way of **monitoring**, or checking, comprehension so that students couldn't trick themselves into thinking they had understood a text they really needed to read a second time.

Because Robinson himself was inclined to modify this step, suggesting, for instance, that students write out the answers, more modern versions of *SQ3R* have broadened the meaning of the second *R*, which now usually means *Recall.*

Given the substitution of the more general term, there are now a number of different ways to fulfill this step. You can look away from the text and see if you can recite the key points of the text, as Robinson suggested. If you want, you can also write out answers to your original questions or even ask a friend or roommate to say a few key words while you respond with the words' larger meaning. Whatever method you choose, the goal is to see how much you can recall from what you've just read. If it turns out you can recall very little, then mark the chapter section for a second reading.

R-3: Review

After you finish reading the entire chapter, take a few minutes to review everything you have read. You can, for instance, list the headings and jot down a few key points about each one. You can also ask a friend or your roommate to pose questions based on the heading and then answer those questions. You might also consider making a concept map or an informal outline. Here, for example, is a concept map based on the reading that appears on pages 8–10.[†]

[†]Thanks for the concept map go to Professor Pat Domenico from Rhode Island Community College.

SQ3R Review—Concept Map

Nisei and Issei

Nisei

Issei

Second-generation Japanese, born in Hawaii, U.S. citizens.

Immigrants from Japan.

Largest ethnic group: 1/3 of population.

Strong desire to prove loyalty to U.S.

Attack on Pearl Harbor raised fear of sabotage and espionage by Hawaiians of Japanese descent.

Destroyed old books, photographs of relatives and "obi."

Encouraged their children (AJAs[†]) to become "super patriots."

But official military and administrative policy maintained traditional interracial harmony.

AJAs contributed war bonds, sponsored campaigns against Tokyo, converted Japanese religious & educational facilities into factories producing items needed for the war.

AJA's served in military campaigns as translators and interpreters.

No internment.

Contributions gave new sense of self-worth and expectation of equal opportunity and treatment.

[†]American-born Japanese Americans.

Check Your Understanding

Monitor your comprehension of this chapter section by answering the following questions.

1. *True* or *False.* The Survey step in *SQ3R* requires you to skim the entire chapter from beginning to end.

2. *True* or *False.* The questions you pose as part of *SQ3R* should all be brief ones that require only a *yes* or *no* answer.

3. *True* or *False.* Textbook assignments should usually not be completed at one sitting. They should be broken up into manageable chunks of around fifteen or twenty pages.

4. *True* or *False.* The only way to complete the second *R* in *SQ3R* is to recite aloud the key points of each chapter section.

5. *True* or *False.* While some students rely mainly on concept maps, there are a number of ways to review the chapter once you have finished reading it.

EXERCISE 1 **DIRECTIONS** *Survey* the following selection using the steps listed in the following box. When you finish, answer the questions at the end of the selection.

Survey Steps

1. Read the title and ask yourself, "What does the author want to tell readers about wartime Hawaii?"
2. Read the first paragraph and ask yourself, "What point does the author want to make in the reading?"
3. Read the headings and turn them into questions.
4. Read the first sentence of every paragraph.
5. Read the last paragraph.
6. Ask yourself whether you already know anything about wartime Hawaii that might enhance your understanding of this reading.

Wartime Hawaii

1 Much as the war came to the United States initially and most dramatically at Pearl Harbor, the outlines of an increasingly multicultural United States emerging from World War II could be seen first and most clearly in Hawaii. The nearly one million soldiers, sailors, and marines stopping in Hawaii on their way to the battlefront, as well as the more than one hundred thousand men and women who left the mainland to find war work on the islands, expected the Hollywood image of a simple Pacific paradise: blue sky, green sea, and white sand; palm trees and tropical sunsets; exotic women with flowers in their hair. They found instead a complex multiracial and multiethnic society. The experience would change them, as they in turn would change the islands.

Hawaii's Multiracial Society

2 Before December 7, 1941, few Americans knew where Pearl Harbor was or even that Hawaii was a part of their country, a colonial possession, a territory annexed by the U.S. government in 1898. Few realized that Honolulu, a tiny fishing village when Captain James Cook sailed by the difficult entrance to its harbor in 1778, had subsequently become the major maritime center of a kingdom, the seat of a territorial government, and a gritty port city that would serve as the major staging ground for the war to be waged in the Pacific. And few knew that this American outpost, as a result of successive waves of immigration beginning in the 1870s by Chinese, Portuguese, Japanese, and Filipinos, had a population in 1940 in which native Hawaiians and white Americans (called *haoles,* which in Hawaiian means "strangers") each constituted only 15 percent of the islands' inhabitants.

The Nisei and Issei

3 The approximately 160,000 Hawaiians of Japanese ancestry—including some 100,000 second-generation Japanese, or *Nisei,* who had been born in Hawaii and were therefore U.S. citizens—composed Hawaii's largest ethnic group, more than a third of the population. Japan's attack on Pearl Harbor immediately raised fears of sabotage or espionage by Hawaiians of Japanese descent. Rumors flew of arrow-shaped signs cut in the sugarcane fields to direct Japanese planes to military targets and of *Nisei* women waving kimonos to signal Japanese pilots.

4 But in stark contrast to the wholesale incarceration* of the Japanese in the Pacific coast states, where the dangers of subver-

---

*incarceration: imprisonment.

sive activities were slight in comparison to Hawaii, official military and administrative policy in the islands was to maintain traditional interracial harmony throughout the war, and to treat all law-abiding inhabitants of Japanese ancestry justly and humanely. "This is America and we must do things the American way," announced Hawaii's military governor. "We must distinguish between loyalty and disloyalty among our people." There was no mass internment of the *Nisei* and *Issei* (those who emigrated from Japan) as there was on the mainland.

5   For the *Issei,* loyalty to the United States had become an obligation, a matter of honor. To eliminate potential associations with the enemy, they destroyed old books, photographs of relatives, and brocaded *obi* (kimono sashes) and replaced portraits of the Japanese emperor with pictures of President Roosevelt. A burning desire to prove that they were true Americans prompted many of their Hawaiian-born children, often referred to as AJAs (Americans of Japanese ancestry), to become "superpatriots." AJAs contributed heavily to war-bond drives and sponsored their own "Bombs on Tokyo" campaign; they cleared areas for new military camps; and they converted the halls of Buddhist temples, Shinto* shrines and Japanese-language schools (all closed for the duration and reopened after the war) into manufactories of bandages, knit socks, sweaters, and hospital gowns (the latter sewn for the Red Cross and Office of Civil Defense). Their newly expanded contact with other Hawaiians, including *haoles*, hastened their assimilation into the larger Hawaiian society. In addition, AJAs served in the military campaigns in the Pacific as interpreters—translating, interrogating, intercepting transmissions, and cracking enemy codes; and they fought in Europe with the all-*Nisei* 442d Regimental Combat Team, the most highly decorated organization in the U.S. Army. These contributions gave the Japanese in Hawaii, as it did other ethnic groups, a new sense of their worth and dignity. The war experience aroused expectations of equal opportunity and treatment, of full participation in island politics, of no longer accepting a subordinate status to *haoles*.

Changing Attitudes Toward **Haoles**

6 In addition, the attitudes of many Hawaiians toward *haoles* changed as native islanders witnessed a large number of whites doing manual labor for the first time. Their view that whites would always hold superior positions in society—as bosses, plantation

---

*Shinto: a religion native to Japan characterized by worship of nature and ancestors.

owners, business leaders, and politicians—was turned topsy-turvy by the flood of Caucasian mainland war workers. The hordes of white servicemen crowding into Honolulu's Hotel Street vice district for liquor, for tattoos, for posed pictures with hula girls in grass skirts, for three-dollar sex at the many brothels,* and then for treatment at prophylaxis* stations to ward off venereal diseases also tarnished traditional notions of white superiority.

The Majority Becomes a Minority

7 Most of the whites who had come to Hawaii had never lived where whites did not constitute a majority and where *they* were the ones who were different. Most had never before encountered or conversed with those of African or Asian ancestry. Suddenly, they were in the midst of a mixture of ethnic and racial groups unmatched anywhere in the United States, in the midst of a society of people of diverse cultures working together for a common cause. So also were the nearly thirty thousand African-American servicemen and workers who arrived in the islands before the war's end. Having experienced nothing like the fluid and relaxed racial relations of Hawaii's multiethnic society, blacks discovered an alternative to the racist America they knew. Some chose never to go back to the mainland. Others returned home to the States to press for the rights and freedoms they had first tasted in Hawaii. In so many ways, wartime Hawaii, termed "the first strange place" by historians Beth Bailey and David Farber, would anticipate the "strangeness" of U.S. society today. (Adapted from Boyer et al., *Enduring Vision*, pp. 779a–b.)

1. The soldiers and wartime workers who came to Hawaii expected to find _____. But instead, they found _____.

2. Who composed Hawaii's largest ethnic group? _____

_____.

3. *True* or *False*. Unlike the mainland, Hawaii maintained interracial harmony throughout the war.

4. In wartime Hawaii, whites who lived there suddenly discovered what it was like to be_____.

---

*brothels: houses of prostitution.
*prophylaxis: preventive treatment for diseases.

5. In wartime Hawaii, African Americans discovered _____

_____ .

 # Underline and Annotate While Reading

In his Web column at HigherLearning.com, writer Scott McLemee describes how important it is for him to annotate and underline the books he reads. In some cases, he even buys two copies of a book, one to be left unmarked, the other to be thoroughly annotated and underlined, according to his personal system, described here: "Key passages are underscored, with lines so straight it looks as if a ruler had been used; the margins filled with cross-references; the inside covers and other blank pages turned into a *customized index.*† Often, there is a list of unfamiliar words (with the pages on which they occur) to be looked up later."‡

McLemee describes his addiction to marking books as if it were something of a personal eccentricity. But there is a good deal of evidence suggesting that for skilled readers, marginal notes and marking pages are common comprehension strategies. Taking marginal notes, along with underlining, highlighting, and annotating pages, helps these readers follow *and* remember the writer's train of thought.

Keep in mind, though, that, like reading textbooks, underlining and annotating require conscious attention and thought. Underlining without thinking about why you are marking a particular sentence or phrase is not going to improve your comprehension. Similarly, marginal comments like *Boring, Whatever,* and *Who Cares* are not going to help advance your college career. What will advance it is applying the following pointers for thoughtful annotation and selective marking of pages.

Annotating and Marking Textbook Pages

1. Underline (or highlight) sparingly, marking only those words and phrases essential to the author's meaning.

---

†customized index: McLemee's notion of a customized index is worth thinking about and applying to your own reading. To get more tips from this author, go to www.insidehighered.com/views/2005/03/01/mclemee9.

‡Some students prefer to highlight with felt-tip pen. If that's your preference, the same points apply.

2. If an entire sentence seems important, don't underline the whole sentence. Paraphrase† it in the margins, using your own words to express the author's ideas.

3. Make mini-diagrams in the margins of your textbook. For instance, draw arrows to show connections between cause and effect, generalization, and example, or claim and proof. Use chains of boxes or circles to describe a sequence or chain of events; e.g., Heavy tax collection 1786 → Shays' Rebellion 1787

4. Paraphrase the main, or central, points of chapter sections, along with one or two examples, details, studies, or statistics used to explain the key points; e.g., "Amphibia reveal environmental threat, e.g., three-legged frogs."

5. Note possible test questions; e.g., "Describe the purpose of the Federalist Papers."

6. Record ideas for term papers; e.g., "During his lifetime, J. Robert Oppenheimer went from hero to outcast."

7. Make marginal notes, **synthesizing**,‡ or combining, what you learned from lectures and outside readings with what you are discovering from the chapter; e.g., "Baylin is like Zinn in his emphasis on the economic basis for the colonists' rebellion against the British."

8. Compare and contrast the author's point of view with those of writers who agree or disagree.

9. Circle vocabulary words that seem central to the subject under discussion, jotting down brief definitions in the margin. You can also double underline the actual textbook definitions.

10. Make personal connections to movies you might have seen or novels you might have read dealing with the same or similar subjects; e.g., "*Bad Day at Black Rock* good example of author's thinking."

11. Check your underlining at the end of each chapter section to see if reading just the underlined words and phrases makes enough sense for you.

†More on paraphrasing on pages 16–20.
‡More on synthesizing on pages 270–284 in Chapter 5.

12. If you are reading a particularly difficult chapter, it's a good idea to underline in pencil first. Use pen only on the second reading.

13. Make the "customized index" McLemee refers to on page 11. Every time you see a word or an idea that is central to the discussion, list it along with the page number on one of your text's blank pages. When you are through reading, go back and add definitions.

14. Use textbook margins to create general categories that sum up portions of the text; e.g., "Causes of the Revolutionary War"; "Characteristics of Minerals"; "Effects of Acid Rain."

Symbols for Underlining and Annotating

The following chart lists symbols for underlining and annotating pages. Feel free to adapt the symbols listed here to better suit your particular needs. You can even make up your own symbols. Whichever symbols you choose, though, be sure to use them consistently so that you will remember what they represent.

Symbols for Marking Textbook Pages

Arrows to identify cause and effect relationships

Boxes to highlight names you need to remember

Charles Darwin

Cause and effect diagrams to indicate relationships

Coercive Acts → Revolutionary War

Circles to highlight key points, specialized vocabulary, key terms, statistics, dates, and unfamiliar words

(1830)

Colon to signal the simpler restatement of a complex thought

:

Cross-reference notes to compare closely related statements in the text	See p. 27 *or* Compare p. 27
Double underlining to highlight the main idea of the entire reading	═ ═ ═
Equals sign to signal a definition	=
Exclamation points to indicate your surprise at the author's statements	!
Mini-outlines to indicate relationships	*Issei* want to prove loyalty buy war bonds become superpatriots
Numbers to itemize and separate a series of statistics, studies, reasons, etc.	1, 2, 3, 4
Question marks to indicate confusion	?
Quotation marks to remind about quotes that might be effective in term papers	" "
Star to identify a crucial piece of information	★
Single underlining to highlight key ideas in paragraphs	__ __ __
Initials to identify ideas for term papers, possible sources of test questions, or passages in need of a second reading	TP, TQ, RR
Vertical lines to emphasize key passages longer than a sentence or two	‖

To illustrate what the pages of your textbook should look like when you finish underlining and annotating, here's another excerpt from the reading on page 8:

The *Nisei* and *Issei*

= born in U.S.— second generation

The approximately 160,000 Hawaiians of Japanese ancestry— including some 100,000 second-generation Japanese, or Nisei, who had been born in Hawaii and were therefore U.S. citizens— composed Hawaii's largest ethnic group, more than a third of the population. Japan's attack on Pearl Harbor immediately raised

Pearl Harbor → breeds fear of sabotage

fears of sabotage or espionage by Hawaiians of Japanese descent. Rumors flew of arrow-shaped signs cut in the sugarcane fields to direct Japanese planes to military targets and of *Nisei* women waving kimonos to signal Japanese pilots.

Contrast to internment camps in Pacific coast states

But in stark contrast to the wholesale incarceration of the Japanese in the Pacific coast states, where the dangers of subversive activities were slight in comparison to Hawaii, official military and administrative policy in the islands was to maintain traditional interracial harmony throughout the war, and to treat all law-abiding inhabitants of Japanese ancestry justly and

★★

use quotes in paper?

humanely. "This is America and we must do things the American way," announced Hawaii's military governor. "We must distinguish between loyalty and disloyalty among our people." There was no

Issei emigrated from Japan

mass internment of the *Nisei* and *Issei* (those who emigrated from Japan) as there was on the mainland.

For the *Issei*, loyalty to the United States had become an obligation, a matter of honor. To eliminate potential associations

Ways Issei tried to show loyalty

with the enemy, they destroyed old books, photographs of relatives, and brocaded *obi* (kimono sashes), and replaced portraits of the Japanese emperor with pictures of President Roosevelt. A burning desire to prove that they were true Americans prompted many of their Hawaiian-born children, often referred to as AJAs (Americans of Japanese ancestry), to become "superpatriots." AJAs contributed heavily to war-bond drives and sponsored their own "Bombs on Tokyo" campaign.

Paraphrase to Monitor Comprehension and Encourage Remembering

> What we summarize *in our own words*[†] becomes our own.
>   —Susan Wise Bauer, *The Well-Educated Mind*

The term *paraphrasing* may be familiar to you from writing courses. You know, for instance, that if you want to sum up an author's ideas in a term paper, you have to **paraphrase** them, using your words to express the same ideas.[‡] If you don't paraphrase, you can easily end up with several pages of tacked-together quotations, which is the last thing you want to hand in to your instructor.

Paraphrasing while reading, however, is a little different. While a reading paraphrase requires you to be accurate, it doesn't require you to be quite so complete. Compare, for instance, two different paraphrases of the original text shown below. The first paraphrase is for a paper. The second is a **reading paraphrase**, created solely for the purposes of monitoring comprehension or taking marginal notes.

Original

The word *irony* derives from "Eiron," who was one of the basic characters in Greek drama. Eiron is a trickster who makes fun of pretension and pomposity* by pretending he is ignorant and asking naïve questions. His seemingly ignorant questions provoke others to reveal how little they really know despite their claims to expertise. Eiron's technique, however, was not confined to the Greek stage. The Greek philosopher Socrates used a similar strategy. He would pretend complete ignorance when asking a question such as "What is truth?" His goal was to provoke the person answering into revealing ignorance or lack of depth. This technique is known as "Socratic irony."

[†]Italics are mine.

[‡]You also have to credit the person with whom the ideas originated.

*pomposity: the tendency to show off; self-importance.

Paraphrase for a Paper

Eiron was one of the staple characters in early Greek drama. He was a trickster, who acted as if he didn't know anything and encouraged others to give explanations that revealed their own ignorance. The ancient Greek philosopher Socrates used the same device. He would pose questions like "What is truth?" in a naïve and simple manner that suggested he didn't know the answer. When the person questioned responded, Socrates would make it clear that the other person's answer was poorly thought out. This pretense of ignorance in order to uncover a lack of knowledge or depth is called "Socratic irony."

Reading Paraphrase

The word *irony* comes from Eiron, a trickster in Greek plays, who asked dumb questions to reveal other people's ignorance. "Socratic irony" uses the same method of pretending ignorance to uncover superficial thinking.

As the above examples show, paraphrasing to check comprehension or take reading notes—and you should preferably do both—does not require that you recall every detail of the original text. Instead, think of a reading paraphrase as your personal answer to two questions: (1) What does the author want to tell me about some person, practice, idea, place, or event? (2) How did the author clarify, illustrate, or prove that point?

Be aware, though, that with complicated texts, you may need to ask additional and more specific questions to arrive at answers to those two questions. If the text is difficult, try asking questions such as "Who's doing what to whom?" "What event is the author describing?" "Under what conditions does this happen?" "What theory is the author explaining and what examples does he or she use to illustrate how that theory works?" If none of these questions provides you with a paraphrase, mark the passage for a second reading.

Paraphrasing in Marginal Notes

For another illustration of a reading paraphrase, study the passage and marginal notes that follow. The passage is the original text; the notes are the reader's paraphrase of that text.

Many students coping with stress or anxiety are bringing pets into class.

Officials not sure when pets are medically needed.

Across the country, a growing number of students are seeking permission to bring "psychiatric service" animals into college classrooms and dormitories. The students say the animals, which range from cats and dogs to snakes, rats, and even tarantulas, help them cope with the stress of college life. But the law is unclear on whether colleges must accommodate such animals, and many colleges have grappled with how to distinguish a student with a true need from one who simply does not want to be separated from Fluffy or Spot. (Source of information: Kelly Field, "These Student Requests Are a Different Animal," *Chronicle of Higher Education*, October 13, 2006, p. A-3.)

As they should, the marginal notes identify the author's general point: Students are asking to bring pets into classrooms in order to alleviate stress. Notice, too, that the first marginal note tells you not just who's doing what but also why they are doing it: Students want to bring animals into the classroom *because* they want help coping with psychiatric problems. The second marginal note answers the question, What are the consequences or results? Apparently college administrators are unsure as to where they should draw the line when it comes to allowing animals in the classroom.

These two brief paraphrases in the marginal notes, one of them not even a grammatically correct sentence, are all a reader would need in order to use paraphrasing as a comprehension check and memory aid. As the examples show, paraphrasing while reading does not require the same precision or completeness that paraphrasing for a paper does. Each type of paraphrasing has a different purpose.

When paraphrasing for a paper, you are showing your instructor that you have clearly understood another person's ideas in all of their complexity and detail. When you paraphrase, however, all you need to do is make sure that you have understood the meaning of the author's words. Paraphrasing while reading also gives your brain a chance to process new information for a second time. It's this second chance to process that makes paraphrasing a memory booster as well as a comprehension check.

Pointers on Paraphrasing While Reading

The more you get into the habit of paraphrasing while you read, the better you will be at it. Here are some pointers to get you started.

1. **Paraphrase only the basics.** When you are paraphrasing to check your comprehension or jot some marginal notes, your goal is to sum up in your own words the main idea or point of the paragraph along with one or two details used to explain or prove it. When you paraphrase for your own purposes, abbreviations of all kinds are allowed. After all, you are the only one reading the paraphrase. Just don't abbreviate so much that later on you don't know what the note means.

2. **Look away from the page while paraphrasing.** If you look at the paragraph while you paraphrase it, you are likely to think you have understood the material better than you do. Looking at a text while paraphrasing it encourages you to use the author's words and forget about finding your own. Put more directly, it defeats the purpose of paraphrasing.

3. **Use questions to focus your paraphrase.** If you finish a chapter section and have only a foggy notion of what the author wanted to say, don't get discouraged and give up. Force yourself to figure out answers for questions like these: What's the author's point? How does he prove or clarify it? For more complicated readings, make your questions more specific; e.g., What events does the author describe? What were the circumstances of those events? Who did what and why did they do it?

4. **Be ready to re-read.** If you pose any of the questions above and ponder them a minute or two without getting an answer, mark the passage you were trying to paraphrase for a second reading. One of the biggest misconceptions about "good readers" is that they "get" the author's point without ever having to re-read the author's words. Nothing could be further from the truth. Good readers know that difficult texts sometimes require a second, even a third reading.

Chapter 3 will give you more examples of paraphrasing for papers.

<table>
<tr><td align="center">Check Your Understanding</td></tr>
<tr><td>In your own words, why should you paraphrase while reading?

_____

_____</td></tr>
</table>

EXERCISE 2   DIRECTIONS   Read each passage. Then select the letter of the best *reading* paraphrase.

Original **1.** Erik Erikson's theory of developmental tasks appropriate to different stages of life has profoundly influenced the way many psychologists describe life. Yet because research on Erikson's stages of development would require extensive and costly long-range studies, his ideas have not been scientifically proven. (Adapted from Engler, *Personality Theories,* p. 1266.)

Reading Paraphrase

a. Theory of stages and tasks very influential but no longitudinal studies to prove it.

b. Erik Erikson's theory of developmental stages and tasks very influential despite the lack of long-term studies as proof.

c. Erikson has had a big influence on how we describe ourselves and our lives. No longitudinal studies have been done. Too expensive.

Original **2.** A 2006 survey of 1,144 doctors around the country looked at how physicians' moral or religious beliefs might affect patient care. Among those responding, 86 percent said they believed patients should be aware of all treatment options, even those that went against the doctor's personal value system. Fourteen percent of the physicians polled believed they had no obligation to mention a treatment that went against their personal moral or religious beliefs.

Reading Paraphrase

a. The 2006 survey of 1,144 doctors proves the obvious: when prescribing treatment, doctors influenced by their moral, ethical, and religious beliefs, even though they are supposed to remain objective.

b. A 2006 survey of 1,144 doctors across the country suggests majority—86 percent—don't let personal beliefs affect treatment.

c. Study of doctors shows they let personal beliefs influence treatment.

Becoming Adept at Writing Summaries

> The ability to write a summary might be the most important writing skill a college student can possess.
>
> —Drew University Online Resources for Writers[†]

There are at least three practical reasons why you should become adept at writing a summary. Instructors frequently require summaries as part of their outside reading assignments. Then, too, when you do research for a term paper, you'll need to summarize passages or articles as part of your note-taking. Finally, summaries are often part of exam questions (e.g., "Summarize Erik Erikson's developmental stages and give an example of each one").

Perhaps the most important reason, though, has been succinctly expressed by Susan Wise Bauer in her book *The Well-Educated Mind*: "To master the content of what you read, summarize." Like paraphrasing, only in a more extended form, summarizing is a way of monitoring your understanding. It's a way of telling yourself whether you have really mastered the material. Anytime you can't summarize an article or a chapter section, you know that something is missing. Either you haven't understood the overall point or you haven't grasped a key relationship.

Summarizing what you read isn't something you should do for an entire chapter assignment. Rather, it's the kind of review you should save for special chapter sections—the ones you think might be the basis for an exam question or that you might use as background or support in a term paper.

To start you on the path to regular summary writing, here are several tips. The first seven apply to all kinds of summaries, whether they are written for your own personal use or for an instructor's assignment. The last two apply mainly to summaries written for other people to read. Bear that in mind as you go through the list.

1. **Mark your text *before* you summarize.** To make sure you have thoroughly mastered the author's ideas before you try to summarize them, underline, mark, and annotate the text, indicating what's important and what's not. As you learned earlier in this chapter, underlining and marking text is a way of getting your mind in tune with the author's. Thoroughly marking up the

[†]www.users.drew.edu/~sjamieso/summary.html.

material you plan on summarizing is also a good way of deciding which sentences or passages are essential and which ones are not. In fact, some people prepare for summary writing by penciling a line through any sentences or sections they consider nonessential.

2. **Paraphrase the key point of each paragraph.** Generally, how you annotate pages should vary with the material. But if you are annotating and underlining in preparation for writing a summary, then you really should identify the key point of every paragraph in the margins. That way, when you are finished, you can go through the marginal list and put an asterisk next to the ideas essential to your summary.

3. **Use the author's main idea to guide your selection of details.** If the main idea, or central point, of the chapter section you are summarizing identifies a set number of theories, stages, studies, and so on—for example, "Erik Erikson described four stages of psychosocial development"—then your summary needs to include one of each theory, stage, or study. Skip one and you haven't fully explained the overall main idea. Where you can abbreviate is in the amount of time you spend describing each stage. Although the author might have given each stage three sentences apiece, you might settle for one or two sentences at the most.

   However, if the central point is something like "Adolescence is an especially turbulent time of life" and the rest of the chapter section describes four or five ways in which adolescence is a time of conflict and change, then it's probably safe to include only two or three of the illustrations given. After all, what makes adolescence so turbulent is, to some degree, general knowledge, even common sense. You don't need lots of examples to explain the point.

4. **Look for underlying relationships.** As you read, try to determine how the author connects ideas as he or she moves from sentence to sentence. Is the author identifying the specific causes of one event or comparing and contrasting opposing points of view on the same subject? Does he trace a series of dates and events that preceded some major social change, or is she listing the various solutions experts have proposed for a pressing problem? (For more on relationships in paragraphs, see Chapter 4.)

5. **Maintain relationships in your summary.** If the author compares and contrasts Thomas Jefferson and Andrew Jackson to illustrate how differently each president viewed the issue of government intervention, your summary should also use similari-

ties and differences to make the same overall point: The presidents differed. It should *not* summarize each man individually as if two separate portraits of two famous presidents had been the author's original **purpose**, or intention. If the material you are reading is structured by a comparison and contrast relationship, your summary should do the same. (For more on common organizational patterns, see Chapter 4. For more on purpose, see pp. 442–445.)

6. **Get right to the point.** Although textbook writers are more inclined than most to open with the central, or key, point of a chapter section, they, too, sometimes start with an introductory sentence or two. Here's an example:

> President Theodore Roosevelt was not alone in his concern that American companies were becoming monopolies* that undermined competition. Progressive* politicians had been saying for years that big industry was controlling the economic market, instead of letting it regulate itself through supply and demand. Roosevelt, however, was the first president who decided to do something about the growing power of monopolies. It was Roosevelt's attack on big business that earned him his reputation as a "trustbuster."

In this example, the author leads up to the point of the passage by telling readers how others before Roosevelt were concerned about monopolies' growing influence. But that information is purely introductory. The real focus of the passage is on what Roosevelt actually did about the problem. A summary of a passage like the one above would eliminate the introductory material and start off with the key point about Roosevelt taking action to bust up monopolies; e.g., "Theodore Roosevelt was the first president to attack the growing power of monopolies. That's what earned him the nickname 'trustbuster.'"

7. **Leave out any opinions of your own.** Whether you are summarizing for research or for an assignment, your goal is to create an accurate version of the original material, so don't distort the original by making a value judgment. A summary should be a miniature version of the author's ideas. It should express only the author's thoughts and leave out any of your own.

---

*monopolies: companies that gain complete control over the production of a product and are not subject to competition in the marketplace.
*progressive: person committed to social change.

8. **If the writing gets too choppy, connect sentences with transitions that identify relationships.** Summaries require you to **synthesize** information—to pull ideas from different sentences or paragraphs and link them together into a new whole. This can result in a summary with a disjointed and choppy style. While summaries used as chapter notes don't necessarily have to flow smoothly, it's still true that, even at a glance, you should be able to determine why one sentence follows another. The quickest way to make that happen is to use transitions like the ones listed in the following box. **Transitions** are words, phrases, even sentences that signal the relationship between sentences.

Common Transitional Signals and the Author's Intentions

Signal	Author's Intentions
For instance, As illustration, For example, To be more precise	"Here comes an example."
Consequently, Thus, Therefore, As a result, In response	"Having identified causes, I'm now listing effects."
Afterward, In the next step, At the next stage, In the following year, At this point	"I'm trying to show readers how events occur or occurred in real time."
Similarly, Likewise, In the same vein	"Here's how the two topics mentioned are similar."
In contrast, However, In opposition, Whereas	"Here's how the topics are different."

---

9. **Tell your instructor what you are summarizing.** If you are writing a summary as part of an assignment, include the author and title of the article, weaving it as gracefully as possible into the opening sentence; for instance, "Dexter Filkins in his *New York Times* appraisal of David Halberstam's career, 'A Skeptical Vietnam Voice Still Echoes in the Fog of Iraq,' points out that Halberstam refused to print uncritically what the government said about success or failure in Vietnam. Along with journalists like Neil Sheehan and Malcolm Brown, Halberstam reflected a skepticism that was, until the Vietnam War, unheard of in the American press." When you are assigned a summary to write,

always check to see if your professor has a preference as to how you include the source and author of the original text.

What follows is an excerpt from a history text along with a sample summary.

Going West

1 In nineteenth-century America, most migrants went west because the region seemed to promise a better life. Railroad expansion made remote farming regions accessible, and the construction of grain elevators eased problems of shipping and storage. As a result of population growth, the demand for farm products grew rapidly, and the prospects for commercial agriculture—growing crops for profit—became more favorable than ever.

2 Life on the farm, however, was much harder than the advertisements and railroad agents suggested. Migrants often encountered shortages of essentials they had once taken for granted. The open prairies contained little lumber for housing and fuel. Pioneer families were forced to build houses of sod and to burn manure for heat. Water was sometimes as scarce as timber. Few families were lucky or wealthy enough to buy land near a stream that did not dry up in summer and freeze in winter. Machinery for drilling wells was scarce until the 1880s, and even then it was very expensive.

3 The weather was seldom predictable. In summer, weeks of torrid* heat and parching winds often gave way to violent storms that washed away crops and property. In winter, the wind and cold from blizzards piled up mountainous snowdrifts that halted all outdoor movement. During the Great Blizzard that struck Nebraska and the Dakota Territory in January 1888, the temperature plunged to 36 degrees below zero, and the wind blew at 56 miles per hour. The storm stranded schoolchildren and killed several parents who ventured out to rescue them. In the spring, melting snow swelled streams, and floods threatened millions of acres. In the fall, a week without rain could turn dry grasslands into tinder, and the slightest spark could ignite a raging prairie fire.

4 Nature could be cruel even under good conditions. Weather that was favorable for crops was also good for breeding insects. Worms and flying pests ravaged corn and wheat. In the 1870s and 1880s, swarms of grasshoppers virtually ate up entire farms. Heralded only by the din of buzzing wings, a mile-long cloud of insects would smother the land and devour everything: plants, tree bark, and clothes. As one farmer lamented, the "hoppers left

*torrid: intensely hot.

behind nothing but the mortgage." (Adapted from Norton et al., *A People and a Nation*, pp. 492–493.)

Summary

During the 19th century, scores of men and women went west believing that farming was a way to make money and improve their lot in life. But farm life proved to be much harder than most expected. Essentials like lumber and water were hard to come by, while the weather was harsh and unpredictable. The temperature might plunge as low as 36 degrees below zero and the wind could blow at 56 miles per hour. In summer, scorching heat and drought would suddenly be followed by heavy rainstorms. Insects were an additional problem and plagues of them devoured entire farms.

EXERCISE 3 **DIRECTIONS** Read each passage. Then circle the letter of the best summary. *Note*: These would be considered note-taking summaries.

Original **1.** Obviously, a great deal of controversy continues to surround the issue of executing criminals. Researchers generally agree that if punishment is to discourage future criminal behavior, it must be swift and certain. Neither of these conditions is met by the death penalty in the United States, and few reasonable and informed people today argue that capital punishment acts as a deterrent, except in the specific case of the individual who is executed. Studies comparing homicide rates between states with and without death penalties either find no significant difference or disclose that states with capital punishment actually have higher rates of homicide. Also disturbing is the fact that personal characteristics of judges influence their decisions. Republicans are much more likely to vote for the death penalty, as are older judges and those with previous experience as a prosecutor. In this sense, the death penalty resembles a lottery. Application of the death penalty can also be shocking, in more ways than one. Florida's "Old Sparky" overheated in 1997, causing flames and smoke to erupt from a leather mask worn by the unfortunate murderer, Pedro Medina. (This gruesome scene helped to convince Florida officials to replace the chair with lethal injection in January 2000.) Perhaps most distressful of all aspects of the death penalty is the possibility that an innocent party may be executed. (Excerpted from Bowman and Kearney, *State and Local Government*, 5th ed, p. 463.)

Summary a. In the United States, the death penalty is extremely controversial, and many people oppose its use because it is said to be ineffective, unfair, and cruel. However, death-penalty opponents tend to exaggerate these so-called flaws. They also ignore the fact that execution has been a just form of punishment for hundreds of evildoers who deserved to pay the ultimate price for taking a life and, in some cases, lives.

b. In America, the death penalty is a flawed form of punishment. Not only does it fail to deter people from committing criminal acts, but it is also applied inconsistently, and judges differ in their readiness to exact the death penalty. In addition, as the 1997 Florida execution of Pedro Medina illustrates, the application of the death penalty can cause inhumane suffering to those being executed. Worst of all, the death penalty can result in the execution of wrongly convicted innocent people.

c. The case of Pedro Medina is a perfect illustration of why Americans should follow the Europeans and abolish the death penalty. Medina was executed in an electric chair so old, it was nicknamed "Old Sparky." After officials pulled the switch on Medina, the machine overheated and flames erupted from the executed murderer's head. Is it any wonder Florida officials replaced the electric chair with lethal injection?

Original **2.** Prior to the Civil War, getting a message delivered from the eastern part of the United States to a friend or relative living in the western part of the country could take months. However, the establishment of a fast, dependable mail service known as the Pony Express reduced the delivery time for mail traveling from the Atlantic to the Pacific coast to about ten days by replacing stagecoach transportation of mail with swift riders on horseback. Established in April 1860, the 1,966-mile Pony Express route roughly followed the Oregon Trail, Mormon Trail, and California Trail, crossing the plains, valleys, deserts, and mountains of Missouri, Kansas, Nebraska, Wyoming, Utah, Nevada, and California. Along this route, Pony Express stations were built in desolate areas at 10- to 12-mile intervals, the maximum distance a horse could travel at a full, 10-mile-per-hour gallop before needing to rest. A rider would place up to 20 pounds of mail in the pockets of a specially designed pouch called a *mochila*, which was thrown over his saddle and held in place by his weight. At each station, he would move the mail pouch to a fresh horse before continuing on, braving dangers like thieves, thunderstorms, and blizzards. Every 75 to 100 miles, the rider himself would be replaced by another rider. This system of mail delivery provided the fastest means of communication between the east and west until 1861, when the transcontinental telegraph line was completed, allowing messages to be sent in minutes. (Sources of information: Nancy Pope, "The Story of the Pony Express," *Enroute*, April–June 1992, National Postal Museum, www.postalmuseum .si.edu/resources/6a2b_ponyexpress.html.)

Summary

a. The horseback riders of the Pony Express significantly reduced the amount of time for transcontinental mail delivery. These horsemen would relay mail to stations set at regular intervals along the Missouri-to-California route of the Pony Express, changing mounts at each station so that horses could always travel at a full gallop. Operating from 1860 to 1861, the Pony Express ended when telegraph service began.

b. Pony Express riders were among the most courageous heroes of the American West. Riding the vast, uninhabited areas of the western states from 1860 to 1861, these men pioneered swift, regular mail service. Not only were they skilled horsemen able to ride long distances at a full gallop, they were also fearless in the face of danger. Thanks to their brave service, communication between easterners and westerners greatly improved.

c. From 1860 to 1861, the men who rode for the Pony Express would place mail in a pouch called a *mochila*, which could carry up to 20 pounds of mail. These pouches were made so that they draped over saddles, and the riders would sit on them to hold them in place. Then, traveling about 10 miles per hour at a full gallop, the riders transported the pouches to Pony Express stations spaced 10 to 12 miles apart. At each new station, the riders would switch to a fresh horse. Using this system, one rider was able to cover 75 to 100 miles of the 1,966-mile route before another rider took his mail pouch and continued on. As they moved across deserted parts of Missouri, Kansas, Nebraska, Wyoming, Utah, Nevada, and California, Pony Express riders faced hazards like robbers and blizzards.

EXERCISE 4 **DIRECTIONS** Read the chapter section titled "The Tet Offensive" on pages 634–635 of the sample chapter. Then decide which of the following summaries is the best.

Summary

a. The Tet Offensive was characterized by some of the worst fighting of the Vietnam War. During several weeks of battles, as American and South Vietnamese troops took back dozens of cities captured by the North Vietnamese army, entire cities were destroyed, and the Viet Cong suffered extremely high casualties.

Horrified by the campaign's violence, even those Americans who initially supported the war turned against it. This growing opposition in the United States forced political and military leaders to acknowledge that the conflict had resulted only in extremely high loss of life and massive amounts of property destruction.

b. The Tet Offensive of 1968 was a military defeat for the North Vietnamese and Viet Cong forces; however, this military campaign also turned out to be a defeat for South Vietnamese troops and their American allies. Even though the anti-Communist forces managed to regain control of the cities and villages captured by the Viet Cong, the Tet Offensive undermined the Johnson administration's promises of imminent victory and fueled the American antiwar movement. Two months after the campaign, President Johnson and his advisers concluded that the war could not be won and decided to pursue a diplomatic, rather than military, strategy.

c. The Tet Offensive is the name for the period of fighting in 1968 during which American and South Vietnamese forces took back 41 cities and villages captured by the North Vietnamese. Those cities included Saigon, South Vietnam's capital city, and Hue, where more than 15,000 were killed in a 24-day battle. When the Tet Offensive was over, the Communists had lost control of all cities and capitals, and more than 40,000 Viet Cong had been killed. Nevertheless, the campaign turned influential American journalist Walter Cronkite against the war, causing average citizens to oppose it, too. By March 1968, President Johnson finally admitted that the United States could not win the war and began pulling American troops out of the conflict.

 # Use the World Wide Web to Build Background Knowledge

The World Wide Web is a marvelous resource, but it also has some drawbacks. One is that it has the tendency to promote the rapid spread of misinformation. All one has to do is to put up some sloppily researched and/or incorrect data, and this will be picked up on by other persons who have no reason to believe otherwise, and who don't have the time or inclination to check their facts.

— From the unofficial Stephen Jay Gould archive,
www.stephenjaygould.org.

Reading research for the last two decades has consistently made the same point. The more background knowledge you have about the topic under discussion, the easier it is to follow the writer's train of thought. When evidence for this claim first began to emerge, it was hardly cause for jubilation. After all, if you were a student trying to master a chapter on the theory of continental drift, background knowledge on the subject was not easy to acquire. The Internet, however, has changed all that, and now you can get the background knowledge you need by logging on to the World Wide Web.

Take, for instance, some of the topics in our sample chapter on pages 625–641. Imagine you are getting ready to read the section titled "The Warren Court" and you don't have a clue what the heading means. If you have access to the Internet, you can type that phrase into the search box of a search engine like Google or Yahoo!, and you will immediately have a list of sources that would provide you with background information about Earl Warren's Supreme Court.

Here's an example from Google:

Web   Images   Video   News   Maps   Gmail   more   Sign in

| The Warren Court | | Search |

Web   Results **1- 10** of about **2,530,000** for **The** Warren Court (**0.13** seconds)

1. Supreme **Court** Cases (**Warren Court**)
   Betts v Brady - 1942 - Right To Counsel **Not a **Warren Court** case - this case
   is the precedent overturned by the following two cases; Escobedo and Gideon. ...
   www.socialstudieshelp.com/Lesson_106_Notes.htm - 80k - Cached - Similar pages

2. Supreme **Court** of the United States - Wikipedia, the free encyclopedia
   The Warren Court (1953–1969) made a number of alternately celebrated and
   controversial rulings expanding the application of the Constitution to civil ...
   en.wikipedia.org/wiki/Supreme_**Court**_of_the_United_States - 146k - Jun 2, 2007 -
   Cached - Similar pages

   3. Earl **Warren** - Wikipedia, the free encyclopedia
      In the years that followed, **the Warren Court** became recognized as a high
      point in the use of the judicial power in the effort to effect social change in
      the ...
      en.wikipedia.org/wiki/Earl_**Warren** - 73k - Cached - Similar pages
      [More results from en.wikipedia.org]

4. Earl **Warren**
   The Warren Court that is remembered today is the 1953-69 **Court**, in which a solid
   ... Earl **Warren** became well known as a "liberal" Supreme **Court** justice, ...
   www.michaelariens.com/ConLaw/justices/**warren**.htm - 15k - Cached - Similar pages

5. Harvard University Press: **The Warren Court** and American Politics ...
   The Warren Court and American Politics: by Lucas A. Powe, Jr., published by
   Harvard University Press.
   www.hup.harvard.edu/catalog/POWWAR.html - 13k - Jun 2, 2007 -
   Cached - Similar pages

6. **Warren Court**: Information from Answers.com
   This entry contains information applicable to United States law only. Related Topics
   Apportionment Baker v.
   www.answers.com/topic/**warren-court** - 50k - Cached - Similar pages

7. Impeach Earl **Warren**: **The Warren Court's** Legacy Fifty Years Later ...
   As Robert Bork has stated, "**[The Warren Court]** stands first and alone as a
   legislator of policy, whether the document it purported to apply was the ...
   www.eagleforum.org/**court**_watch/alerts/2003/feb03/02-21-03Brief.shtml - 17k -
   Cached - Similar pages

8. The Supreme **Court** Historical Society
   history of the **court the warren court**, 1953-1969 ... On May 31, 1955, Chief
   Justice **Warren** again spoke for a unanimous **Court**. The cases would go back to
   the ...
   www.supreme**court**history.org/02_history/subs_history/02_c14.html - 33k -
   Cached - Similar pages

9. Earl **Warren**, Norwegian American
   As a result of **the Warren Court's** bent, the leader of that **court** became a target of
   the right in the early to mid 1960s. Although **Warren** had been a vocal ...
   www.mnc.net/norway/**warren**.htm - 16k - Cached - Similar pages

Selecting a Site for Background Knowledge

Noting the number of entries that comes up in response to the search term "The Warren Court," you might be thinking that the Internet is not much help when it comes to having quick access to background knowledge. After all, how would you know which site to look at? Well, answering that question is not quite the mystery it might seem initially. That's because each site's heading and caption can tell you a lot about what you will find on the site itself. For example, the first site listed seems to focus on one particular case, so you would probably not even look at that one. The second and third sites belong to the popular online encyclopedia Wikipedia. The heading tells you, though, that the first Wikipedia site deals with the Warren Court as a part of a larger discussion focusing on the "Supreme Court." Because getting background knowledge for text-book assignments should not be a lengthy process of sifting and searching through numerous sources, site 3 might serve your purpose more than site 2. Hit the link for site 3 and this is what comes up on the screen.

Earl Warren

From Wikipedia, the free encyclopedia

Earl Warren (March 19, 1891 – July 9, 1974) was a California district attorney of Alameda County, the 20th Attorney General of California, the 30th Governor of California, and the 14th Chief Justice of the United States (from 1953 to 1969). As Chief Justice, his term of office was marked by numerous rulings affecting, among other things, the legal status of racial segregation, civil rights, separation of church and state, and police arrest procedure in the United States. In the years that followed, the Warren Court became recognized as a high point in the use of the judicial power in the effort to effect social progress in the U.S. and Warren himself became widely regarded as one of the most influential Supreme Court justices in the history of the United States and perhaps the single most important in the 20th century.

He also chaired the Warren Commission, which was formed to investigate the John F. Kennedy assassination.

Contents

1 Education and early career
2 Governor of California
3 Supreme Court
4 Family
5 Death
6 Honors
7 Quotations
8 See also
9 References
10 Notes
11 External links

Education and early career

Earl Warren was born in Los Angeles, California, to Methias H. Warren, a Norwegian immigrant, and Crystal Hernlund, a Swedish immigrant. Methias Warren was a longtime employee of the Southern Pacific Railroad. Earl grew up in Bakersfield, California where he attended Washington Junior High and Kern County High School (now called Bakersfield High School). It was in Bakersfield that Warren's father was murdered during a robbery by an unknown killer. Warren went on to attend the University of California, Berkeley, both as an undergraduate (B.A. 1912) in Legal Studies and as a law student at Boalt Hall earning his Juris Doctor in 1914. While at Berkeley, Warren joined the Sigma Phi Society, a fraternal organization with which he maintained lifelong ties. He was also a member of the secretive Gun Club. Warren was admitted to the California bar in 1914. Many buildings and schools have been named in Warren's honor, including Warren Hall on the Bakersfield High School campus, Warren Hall on the UC Berkeley campus, Earl Warren college at the University of California San Diego, Earl Warren Senior High School in Downey, California, Earl Warren Junior High in Bakersfield, and Earl Warren Middle School in Solana Beach, California. Earl Warren Elementary School in Lake Elsinore, California opened its doors Aug. 20, 2007.

Earl Warren

14th Chief Justice of the United States	
In office	
October 5, 1953 – June 23, 1969	
Nominated by	Dwight D. Eisenhower
Preceded by	Fred M. Vinson
Succeeded by	Warren E. Burger
30th Governor of California	
In office	
January 4, 1943 – October 5, 1953	
Preceded by	Culbert Olson
Succeeded by	Goodwin Knight
20th Attorney General of California	
In office	
January 3, 1939 – January 4, 1943	
Preceded by	Ulysses S. Webb
Succeeded by	Robert W. Kenny
Born	March 19, 1891
	Los Angeles, California
Died	July 9, 1974 (aged 83)
	Washington, D.C.
Spouse	Nina Palmquist Meyers
Alma mater	University of California, Berkeley
Religion	Protestant

Clearly, if you want to know something about the Warren Court, you've hit pay dirt with this site. Note, however, the list of contents. If you were writing a paper on Earl Warren, focusing perhaps on the contrast between the conservatism of his early career with his later, and liberal, court decisions, you might well hit the first term on the list of contents, "Education and early career." However, what we need for our purposes is general background knowledge in preparation for reading a chapter section about the Warren Court. That means you would click on item 3, "Supreme Court," and this is what you would find:

Supreme Court

In 1953, Warren was appointed Chief Justice of the United States by President Dwight D. Eisenhower, who wanted a very conservative justice and commented that "he represents the kind of political, economic, and social thinking that I believe we need on the Supreme Court ... He has a national name for integrity, uprightness, and courage that, again, I believe we need on the Court."[1] Warren resigned from the governorship shortly afterwards, replaced by Lieutenant Governor Goodwin Knight.

Warren's nomination was caused in part by his support for Eisenhower in the 1952 campaign, although whether an explicit deal was ever in place is not known. Warren stood as a "favorite son" candidate of California for the Republican nomination in 1952 but withdrew in support of Eisenhower. Warren also provided crucial campaigning service to Eisenhower in California after Vice Presidential Candidate Richard Nixon was weakened by controversy over an alleged "slush fund."

To the surprise of many, Warren was a much more liberal justice than had been anticipated. As a result, President Eisenhower is perhaps apocryphally* said to have remarked that nominating Warren for the Chief Justice seat was "the biggest damned-fool mistake I ever made."[2] Warren was able to craft a long series of landmark decisions including *Brown v. Board of Education* 347 U.S. 483 (1954), which overthrew the segregation of public schools; the "one man, one vote" cases of 1962–1964, which dramatically altered the relative power of rural regions in many states; *Hernandez v. Texas*, which gave Mexican-Americans the right to serve on juries; and *Miranda v. Arizona*, 384 U.S. 436 (1966), which required that certain rights of a person being interrogated while in police custody be clearly explained, including the right to an attorney (often called the "Miranda warning").

---

*apocryphally: not proven to be true.

> ### A Note on Wikipedia
>
> Keep in mind when using Wikipedia for background knowledge that it is what's called an "open source site," meaning volunteers write and edit the entries, using a source code to post, revise, or add to entries. The entries on Wikipedia are only as good as the volunteers who create them. For this reason, I recommend not getting background knowledge *solely* from a wiki site; I would follow up site 3 with a quick look at the information on site 4, which suggests that the Wikipedia site, in this instance, is a solid source of background information. That means you are now ready to read, with maximum efficiency and speed, the chapter section dealing with Earl Warren's Supreme Court.

Pointers on Selecting Sites for Background Knowledge

1. In general, textbook headings function quite well as search terms. However, if a heading doesn't get you the information you need, change the wording to make the search term more specific. If, for instance, the heading of the chapter section is "César Chávez" and the number of sites that comes up in response to Chávez's name is both long and not obviously useful, modify your search term to make it "César Chávez's leadership of the United Farm Workers."

2. When selecting a site to look at, remember that the first sites on the list your browser brings up are going to be the ones most directly related to your topic. Therefore, don't read three or four webpages in the hopes that the material will become more relevant. It probably won't. You would be better off revising your search term.

3. To avoid wasting your time, pay close attention to site titles and captions. They are the best indicators of what each website includes or ignores. Captions that include the exact words in your search term, particularly in the same order, all but guarantee that the website will be useful.

4. Pay particular attention to sites with a URL, or Web address, ending in *.edu*. This indicates that the site is related to an educational institution and the information on it is probably accurate because someone is double-checking it. That's not to rule out personal or organizational websites ending in *.com*, but with these, you must check the information against two, even three

other websites to authenticate the websites' accuracy. Like blogs, personal websites can be terrific sources of information, posted by people deeply interested in a particular subject and anxious to share their knowledge. But they can also be posted by prejudiced crackpots, who spout nonsense about, to take one example, NASA's faking of the moon landing. Guard against gathering such misinformation by always cross-checking at least two different sites purporting to deal with the same subject.

EXERCISE 5   **DIRECTIONS**   In preparation for reading the sample chapter, use the Web to answer the following questions. *Note*: Use words and dates in the questions to create your search terms.

1. What happened in 1963 in Crystal City, Texas?

_____

_____

_____

_____

_____

_____

2. In 1973, what happened in Wounded Knee, South Dakota?

_____

_____

_____

_____

_____

_____

_____

3. What were the Pentagon Papers?

_____

_____

_____

_____

_____

_____

_____

_____

_____

_____

_____

_____

_____

_____

_____

 For more on study skills like answering essay questions and improving reading rate, go to **laflemm.com**, click on _Reading for Thinking_: "Additional Materials," and look at the list under "Handouts."

Test 1: Using *SQ3R*

DIRECTIONS Survey the following selection using the steps listed below. When you finish, answer the questions in Part A on page 40. Then go back and read the selection from beginning to end. When you are done, answer the questions in Part B on page 41.

Survey Steps

1. Read the first and last paragraphs.

2. Use the title to pose a question.

3. Read the headings and the marginal note.

4. Read the first sentence of every paragraph.

5. Read through the questions on pages 40–41.

How the Need for Achievement Spurs Motivation

need achievement A motive for action influenced by the degree to which a person establishes specific goals, cares about meeting those goals, and experiences feelings of satisfaction by doing so.

1 Many athletes who hold world records still train intensely; many people who have built multimillion-dollar businesses still work fourteen-hour days. What motivates these people? A possible answer is a motive called **need achievement** (H. A. Murray, 1938). People with a high need for achievement seek to master tasks—such as sports, business ventures, intellectual puzzles, or artistic creations—and feel intense satisfaction from doing so. They work hard at striving for excellence, enjoy themselves in the process, take great pride in achieving at a high level, and often experience success.

2 *Individual Differences*   How do people with strong achievement motivation differ from others? To find out, researchers gave children a test to measure their need for achievement and then asked them to play a ring-toss game. Children scoring low on the need-for-achievement test usually stood so close or so far away from the ring-toss target that they either could not fail or could not succeed. In contrast, children scoring high on the need-for-achievement test stood at a moderate distance from the target, making the game challenging but not impossible (McLelland, 1958).

3 Experiments with adults and children suggest that people with high achievement needs tend to set challenging, but realistic, goals. They actively seek success, take risks as needed, and are intensely satisfied with success. Yet if they feel they have tried

their best, people with high achievement motivation are not too upset by failure. Those with low achievement motivation also like to succeed, but success tends to bring them not joy but relief at having avoided failure (Winter, 1996).

4   People with strong achievement motivation tend to be preoccupied with their performance and level of ability (Harackiewicz & Elliot, 1993). They select tasks with clear outcomes, and they prefer feedback from a harsh but competent critic rather than from one who is friendlier but less competent (Klich & Feldman, 1992). They like to struggle with a problem rather than get help. They can wait for delayed rewards, and they make careful plans for the future (F. S. Mayer & Sutton, 1996). In contrast, people who are less motivated to achieve are less likely to seek or enjoy feedback, and they tend to quit in response to failure (Graham & Weiner, 1996).

5   *Development of Achievement Motivation*   Achievement motivation tends to be learned in early childhood, especially from parents. For example, in one study young boys were given a very hard task, at which they were sure to fail. Fathers whose sons scored low on achievement motivation tests often became annoyed as they watched their boys work on the task, discouraged them from continuing, and interfered or even completed the task themselves (B. C. Rosen & D'Andrade, 1959). A different pattern of behavior emerged among parents of children who scored high on tests of achievement motivation. Those parents tended to (1) encourage the child to try difficult tasks, especially new ones; (2) give praise and other rewards for success; (3) encourage the child to find ways to succeed rather than merely complaining about failure; and (4) prompt the child to go on to the next, more difficult challenge (McClelland, 1985).

6   Cultural influences also affect achievement motivation. Subtle messages about a culture's view of the importance of achievement often appear in the books children read and the stories they hear. Does the story's main character work hard and overcome obstacles, thus creating expectations of a payoff for persistence? Or does the main character loaf around and then win the lottery, suggesting that rewards come randomly, regardless of effort? And if the main character succeeds, is it the result of personal initiative, as is typical of stories in individualist cultures? Or is success based on ties to a cooperative and supportive group, as is typical of stories in collectivist cultures? Such themes appear to act as blueprints for reaching one's goals. It is not surprising, then, that ideas about achievement motivation differ from culture to culture. In

one study, individuals from Saudi Arabia and from the United States were asked to comment on short stories describing people succeeding at various tasks. Saudis tended to see the people in the stories as having succeeded because of the help they got from others, whereas Americans tended to attribute success to the internal characteristics of each story's main character (Zahrani & Kaplowitz, 1993).

7   Achievement motivation can be increased in people whose cultural training did not encourage it in childhood (McClelland, 1985). For example, high school and college students with low achievement motivation were helped to develop fantasies about their own success. They imagined setting goals that were difficult but not impossible. Then they imagined themselves concentrating on breaking a complex problem into small, manageable steps. They fantasized about working hard, failing but not being discouraged, continuing to work, and finally feeling great about achieving success. Afterward, the students' grades and academic success improved, suggesting an increase in their achievement motivation (McClelland, 1985). In short, achievement motivation is strongly influenced by social and cultural learning experiences and by the beliefs about oneself that these experiences help to create. People who come to believe in their ability to achieve are more likely to do so than those who expect to fail (Butler, 1998; Dweck, 1998; Wigfield & Eccles, 2000). (Bernstein and Nash, *Essentials of Psychology*, pp. 274–276.)

Part A: Surveying

DIRECTIONS Answer the following questions by filling in the blanks or circling the correct response.

1. Throughout the reading, what question is the author trying to answer?

_____

2. *True* or *False*. People with high achievement needs tend to set themselves impossible goals.

3. *True* or *False*. Achievement motivation is learned during adolescence.

4. *True* or *False*. Culture affects achievement motivation.

5. *True* or *False*. Once established, a person's level or degree of achievement motivation cannot be changed or altered in any way.

Part B: Reading

DIRECTIONS Answer the following questions by filling in the blanks or circling the letter of the correct response.

6. How do people with high achievement motivation respond to failure?

   a. They get outraged and give up.

   b. They criticize the person in charge for causing their failure.

   c. If they've tried their best, they don't get too upset by failure.

   d. They refuse to quit even when everything is against them.

7. Which of the following does *not* characterize people with high achievement motivation?

   a. They prefer to get feedback from someone who won't hurt their feelings.

   b. They like to struggle with a problem.

   c. They tend to make careful plans for the future.

   d. They select tasks with clear outcomes.

8. What was the difference when individuals from Saudi Arabia and the United States were asked to comment about people in stories succeeding at various tasks?

   _____

   _____

9. Which of the following does *not* characterize the parents of children with high achievement motivation?

   a. They encourage their children to try difficult tasks, especially new ones.

   b. Even if their children perform a task poorly, the parents give high praise in an effort to bolster their children's self-esteem.

   c. They encourage their children to find ways to succeed rather than merely complaining about failure.

   d. Once their children succeed at a task, the parents encourage them to go on to the next, more difficult challenge.

10. *True* or *False*. People who believe in their ability to achieve are more likely to succeed than people who expect to fail.

Test 2: Recognizing an Accurate Paraphrase

DIRECTIONS Circle the letter of the most accurate paraphrase. *Note*: These are reading paraphrases.

 1. A *dialect* is language—including vocabulary, grammar, and pronunciation—unique to a particular group or region. Audiences sometimes make negative judgments about a speaker based on his or her dialect. Such negative judgments are called *vocal stereotypes*. (Adapted from Gronbeck et al., *Principles of Speech Communications,* p. 100.)

Paraphrase a. A *dialect* is particular way of speaking. Unfortunately, people sometimes judge others based on the way they speak. Southerners, for example, complain about being stereotyped because of their accent.

b. The term *vocal stereotypes* refers to the negative judgments people make based on dialect. A *dialect* is speech unique to a group or region, includes vocabulary, grammar, and pronunciation.

c. A *vocal stereotype* is a type of dialect. People who speak a particular dialect are critical of those who speak other dialects.

2. Because China has banned them from selling their products door to door, vendors* for companies like Amway, Mary Kay, and Avon are not very happy with the Chinese government. According to the Chinese press, such door-to-door marketing tends to foster "excess hugging" and "weird cults." ("China Slams the Door on the Avon Lady," *Newsweek,* May 4, 1998, p. 49.)

Paraphrase a. The Chinese press gave odd reason for government's ban on door-to-door salespeople selling products from companies like Avon and Amway: says that salespeople encourage "weird cults" and "excess hugging."

b. Amway, Mary Kay, and Avon stopped selling products in China because their salespeople have become the victims of stereotyping.

c. The Chinese government angry with companies who use door-to-door marketing because it says that Amway, Mary Kay, and Avon don't understand the Chinese people. Chinese are different from Americans, don't like to hug others or join cults.

3. During World War II, movies about Japan made little effort to develop a Japanese character or explain what Japan hoped to accomplish in the war. The Japanese remained nameless, faceless, and almost

*vendors: people who sell products.

totally speechless. No attempt was made to show a Japanese soldier trapped by circumstances beyond his control, or a family man longing for home, or an officer who despised the militarists* even if he supported the military campaign. This was in sharp contrast to the portrayal of German soldiers, who were often shown as decent human beings altogether different from the Nazis. (Adapted from Clayton R. Koppes and Gregory D. Black, *Hollywood Goes to War.* Berkeley: University of California Press, 1998, p. 254.)

Paraphrase

a. During World War II, Hollywood filmmakers applauded for engaging in racist propaganda. The 1942 film *Wake Island*, for example, with story of 377 Marines resisting a Japanese invasion, was smash hit despite its racial stereotypes of Japanese soldiers. Today, such movies, even during wartime, would be sharply criticized.

b. Hollywood films made in World War II portrayed Japanese soldiers like robots, who followed government orders without question. Films suggested that Japanese soldiers never experienced emotional conflict, unlike German soldiers, who were shown disagreeing with their government's inhumane course of action. Indeed, Japanese soldiers always fulfilled their duty to Japan.

c. During World War II, Hollywood filmmakers made propaganda movies, failing to distinguish between the Japanese government's war machine and the Japanese soldier caught in that machine.

4. Disco became the biggest commercial pop genre* of the 1970s— actually, the biggest pop music movement of all time—and in the end, its single-minded, booming beat proved to be the most resilient and enduring stylistic breakthrough of the last twenty years or so. (Mikal Gilmore, *Night Beat.* New York: Doubleday, 1998, p. 241.)

Paraphrase

a. In 1970s, disco challenged rock and roll's position as the music of the young. Following the success of *Saturday Night Fever,* disco died well-deserved death.

b. In the 1970s, disco the hottest dance music around; over the last two decades, pulsing beat has had real staying power.

c. No other kind of music more popular than disco in the 1970s, freshest, most upbeat type of music ever created. No wonder people still love it.

---

*militarists: people devoted to war.
*genre: type or class; a category of literature, music, or art.

5. During the nineteenth and early twentieth centuries, the South American countries of Argentina, Uruguay, and Brazil had their own homegrown cowboys called *gauchos*. Derived from the Quechua* word *wáhcha,* the word *gaucho* usually referred to cowhands or horse handlers, but it could also refer to horse thieves and mercenaries.*

Paraphrase

a. In Argentina, Uruguay, and Brazil, gauchos considered romantic figures, like America's cowboys. Heroes of movies and novels. Most famous novel was *The Four Horsemen of the Apocalypse,* also became movie.

b. During nineteenth and beginning of the twentieth centuries, American-like cowboys, called gauchos, worked the ranches of Uruguay, Argentina, and Brazil. Term *gaucho*—comes from the Quechua word *wáhcha*—means "cowboy" or "horse handler"; could also be used to refer to horse thieves and soldiers of fortune.

c. Gauchos, the nineteenth- and early twentieth-century horsemen of Argentina, Uruguay, and Brazil, tended to be lawless robbers and guns-for-hire. When their American counterparts were wreaking havoc in the Old West, these South American cowboys were causing trouble in their homeland.

*Quechua: language spoken by people belonging to the Incan Empire.
*mercenaries: soldiers for hire, soldiers of fortune.

Test 3: Recognizing an Accurate Paraphrase

DIRECTIONS Circle the letter of the most accurate paraphrase. *Note*: These are the kinds of paraphrases you would do when writing term papers.

Original **1.** In 1960, researcher Jane Goodall went to Africa's Gombe National Park to study chimpanzees. No one before her had attempted to observe the animals in their natural habitat and, initially, the chimps ran from her. However, when Goodall didn't give up, the animals gradually became used to her, letting her watch them for hours. In time Goodall's pioneering fieldwork revolutionized primate research: she was the first to observe that chimps eat meat, use tools, and engage in warfare. (Source of information: Dan Vergano, "Chimp Charmer Jane Goodall Returns to Gombe," *USA Today*, March 8, 2004, p. 8D.)

Paraphrase

a. Jane Goodall, who studied chimpanzees in 1960 in Africa's Gombe National Park, was a better researcher than anyone who had previously studied the shy animals. Unlike earlier researchers, she got the chimps to accept her. Their acceptance gave her the opportunity to observe them in the wild for long periods of time. As a result, she found out that chimps live like humans: They eat meat, use tools, and wage war.

b. In 1960, Jane Goodall became the first person to study chimpanzees in their natural habitat of Africa's Gombe National Park. After patiently overcoming the chimps' initial resistance to her presence, Goodall significantly influenced primate research by witnessing and reporting on chimpanzee behaviors such as meat eating, tool use, and warfare, none of which had been documented before.

c. If Jane Goodall hadn't gone to Africa's Gombe National Park in 1960, it's unlikely that we'd know today that chimpanzees are meat-eaters, use tools, and occasionally engage in cannibalism. Jane Goodall had a special talent for working with the animals and could communicate to them that they had nothing to fear. The chimps allowed her to get close enough to make some astonishing discoveries.

d. When Jane Goodall went to Africa's Gombe National Park in 1960, she did not know how difficult it would be to study chimpanzees in their natural surroundings. Initially, the animals would not let her approach. Goodall didn't give up, though. She kept trying, and eventually the chimps permitted her to watch them for long periods of time.

Original **2.** People can successfully perform two different activities simultaneously. However, one of the two activities has to be performed automatically and require little or no attention. For example, we can drive a car and talk at the same time because we can steer, brake, accelerate, and so on, without close attention to each individual action. The actions necessary to driving are practically automatic and require little thought once they have been thoroughly learned. We can also do two things at the same time if the tasks or activities involved require different kinds of attention. It's possible to read music and play the piano simultaneously because each activity requires a separate mode of concentration. One forces us to pay attention to incoming stimuli; the other requires us to produce a response. What's nearly impossible is having a conversation and reading at the same time because both activities rely on similar types of attention. (Source of information: Bernstein et al., *Psychology*, 6th ed., p. 177.)

Paraphrase a. To perform two activities at the same time, one of them has to be automatic. Driving, for example, is automatic, so we can usually drive while talking. When playing the piano, pressing the keys is an automatic response to reading the music. However, we cannot talk and read at the same time because we have to pay attention to both of these tasks. Neither one can be performed without thinking.

b. It is possible to do two different things at the same time. But one of those two things has to require little or no thought. It must be almost completely automatic. For instance, many people can drive while they talk because the motions of driving—steering, accelerating, braking, etc.—are automatic, so they don't require close concentration. We can also do two things at the same time if the two tasks are quite different and thus require different types of concentration. We can, for example, read music at the same time that our fingers play the piano keys. Reading the notes forces us to attend to incoming external stimuli. When we play the piano, in contrast, we are producing a response. However, we can't talk and read at the same time because those two tasks require similar kinds of attention.

c. If two tasks require different kinds of attention, then they can be performed at the same time. For example, you don't really have to pay attention when you drive a car, which leaves you free to talk to your passengers. Plus, you don't have to think about how your fingers are moving over the keyboard, so you can read music while playing a piano. But reading and talking both force you to pay attention to what you're doing. Therefore, they cannot be performed simultaneously.

d. Because the human brain allows us to divide our attention, we can often do two things at the same time. For example, we can drive and talk at the same time because one of the tasks (driving) is automatic. Also, we can read music while playing the piano because each task requires the same kind of attention.

Original 3. Local television news directors have long known that their primary goal is to attract audiences for their advertisers. However, thanks to a large increase in media choices, competition for viewers has become fiercer. Because it's difficult to write catchy stories about politics and government, many news directors have given up trying to cover that kind of news. Instead, they concentrate on TV news programs that mix action stories—short clips about murders, robberies, rapes, fires, and car accidents—with weather, sports, human interest stories, and friendly banter between the anchors. (Source of information: Turow, *Media Today: An Introduction to Mass Communication*, pp. 423–424.)

Paraphrase
a. Television news programmers know they have to draw big audiences if they are going to please their advertisers. Because audiences have many programs to choose from, local TV news directors try to attract viewers with action-oriented shows that mix stories about crimes, accidents, and disasters with news about sports and weather and the chipper chatter of the newscasters. Because it's hard to write snappy stories about government and politics, most news programs feature very little information about these kinds of topics.

b. Local TV directors know that viewers won't watch dull news programs. They also know they must provide viewers for their advertisers. For those two reasons, today's local news programs rarely include much information about boring subjects like government and politics. Instead, they tend to focus mostly on violent action. Tune in to a local TV news broadcast, and you're likely to see attractive and smiling anchormen and anchorwomen introducing videotape of mangled cars, raging fires, and storm damage, all accompanied by interviews with teary victims.

c. Local TV news directors know they have to create action-packed shows to draw in advertisers. Consequently, they have stopped covering politics and government. Most people would rather see video footage of crimes, accidents, weather forecasts, and sports events, particularly if it is interspersed with friendly conversation between the newscasters. News directors can't really be blamed for giving people what they want.

d. Local TV news directors know that advertisers prefer to place their ads in action-oriented shows with large audiences. They have given up trying to make subjects like government and politics interesting, and they put together shows filled with reports of murders, robberies, accidents, sports highlights, and weather information. They know people are interested in those subjects.

Original 4. A *class-action suit* is a case brought into a court of law by a person who wishes to sue an organization not only for himself or herself but also on behalf of everyone who has been wronged in the same way by that organization. One of the most famous class-action suits was brought in 1954 by the National Association for the Advancement of Colored People (NAACP), which sued on behalf of Linda Brown, a black girl from Topeka, Kansas, who was denied admission to a white elementary school, as well as all other children who were forced to attend segregated schools. The resulting Supreme Court decision, *Brown v. Board of Education*, led to the desegregation of public schools. (Source of information: Wilson and DiIulio, *American Government: The Essentials*, 9th ed., pp. 419–420.)

Paraphrase

a. Class-action suits are brought by people who want to sue an institution not only on their own behalf but also on behalf of anyone who might have been unfairly treated by the same institution. Perhaps the most famous class-action suit was brought by the NAACP, which sued in the name of Linda Brown, an African-American girl denied entry to an all-white elementary school. The suit also included the names of all other children excluded by the practice of segregation in the schools. This class-action suit, which the NAACP won, was the first step in the desegregation of all public schools.

b. The term *class-action suit* is applied to those cases where a group of people are suing one institution. The lawsuit that led to the desegregation of schools, *Brown v. Board of Education*, was a class-action suit filed by the NAACP.

c. The first and most famous class-action suit ever brought into court was *Brown v. Board of Education*, which was the first step in the desegregation of all public schools. The NAACP, fearing it could not win its case in the name of a single child, decided to sue on behalf of all the children who had ever been denied access to a local school because of the practice of segregation.

d. A class-action suit is brought by someone who wants to sue an institution not only in the name of himself or herself but also in the names of any others who might have been wrongly treated by the same institution. The famous lawsuit, which paved the way for desegregation, is probably the best example of a class-action suit that had important consequences not just for a single person but also for a host of people. This is typical of class-action suits brought by the NAACP.

⬛⬤ Test 4: Summarizing Chapter Sections

`DIRECTIONS` Read the original for these summaries on pages 626–629 of the sample chapter. Then circle the letter of the passage that best summarizes each chapter section.

1. The Warren Court

a. Many Americans were enraged by the decisions of the Warren Court. The law-enforcement community, for example, said that the Court's expansion of protections for defendants and people under arrest hindered efforts to combat crime. Religious Americans were infuriated when the Warren Court enforced separation of church and state and prohibited prayer and Bible reading in public schools. In protest, outraged members of Congress tried unsuccessfully to pass resolutions to reinstate both. Many people angrily accused the Court of promoting immorality by ruling that states could not block access to sexually explicit materials or contraceptives. The justices faced additional criticism for decisions prohibiting the practice of drawing voting district lines to favor one party over another. To many Americans, the Warren Court seemed determined to advance the rights of women, minorities, and other nonmainstream groups at the expense of everyone else.

b. In the 1950s, the Warren Court's decisions provided the foundation for the Civil Rights Act of 1964. In 1957, the Court's ruling in *Yates v. the United States* freed from prison American Communist Party officials who had argued for the overthrow of the government without taking any action. From 1961 to 1969, the Court ruled in more than 200 criminal-justice–related cases. Among the most noteworthy were *Gideon v. Wainwright* in 1963, *Escobedo v. Illinois* in 1964, and *Miranda v. Arizona* in 1966, which gave all defendants the right to an attorney; required that people under arrest be told of their right to remain silent, and allowed them to refrain from answering questions until their attorney was present. Prayer and Bible readings in schools ended with the Court's decisions in *Engel v. Vitale* (1962) and *Abington v. Schempp* (1963). With its rulings in *Jacobvellis v. Ohio* (1963) and *Griswold v. Connecticut* (1964), the Court established broader definitions of what constitutes "obscene" and sexually explicit materials. Finally, in the 1962 *Baker v. Carr* case, the Warren Court ruled against the practice of gerrymandering.*

---

*gerrymandering: the deliberate rearrangement of the boundaries of congressional districts to influence the outcome of elections.

c. The Warren Court advanced a liberal agenda by promoting individual rights. Its decisions laid the groundwork for legislation that affirmed the rights of black Americans and expanded the rights of those accused of crimes. For example, the Court ruled that people under arrest could refuse to answer questions without an attorney present. It also ruled that all defendants were entitled to an attorney. Other controversial decisions restored protections guaranteed to individuals by the Bill of Rights, including freedom of expression and right to privacy. Citizens jailed for exercising their right to free speech were released, and state laws that attempted to establish specific moral standards for citizens were overturned. Despite sometimes fierce opposition, the Court enforced the separation of church and state, removing prayer and Bible reading from public schools. Finally, it ended states' practice of gerrymandering and established the goal of making voting districts equal in size.

2. The Emergence of *La Causa*

a. From the 1920s to the 1960s, Mexican Americans tried unsuccessfully to get Anglo governments at the federal, state, and local levels to address Hispanic issues. Although they formed a number of different organizations in attempts to build their political power, Mexican Americans remained for decades an ignored minority. Because officials and governments refused to take their needs seriously, many Mexican Americans were unable to rise from the lowest socioeconomic status, thus perpetuating their lack of power and influence. In western states, they may have been the largest minority, but their attempts to engage in politics and activism met with opposition from state and local governments. With the Anglo majority determined not to cede them any power, Mexican Americans felt invisible. Not surprisingly, they began to reject the society that seemed intent on blocking them from achieving the political representation they desired. For example, voters in Crystal City, Texas, elected an all Mexican-American city council in 1963, indicating that they would no longer tolerate being excluded.

b. Decades of disappointing attempts to gain political, economic, and social power for Mexican Americans culminated in the 1960s farm workers' movement known as *La Causa*. In the 1920s and 1930s, organizations for Mexican-American field and factory workers tried to improve their members' visibility and status in society, but Hispanics and Latinos remained an impoverished and poorly educated minority. Presidential candidate John F. Kennedy's "Viva Kennedy" movement vowed to focus more attention on Hispanic issues and inspired Mexican Americans to vote and form new organizations, but when Kennedy took office, he did not follow through on his promises. President Johnson won admiration for employing Mexican Americans in his administration and making sure that Hispanic communities were included in his antipoverty programs, but Mexican Americans in western states still felt marginalized. Consequently, many Mexican Americans concluded that they should stop waiting for Anglo governments to address Hispanic issues and form a grassroots movement to encourage Latino pride and activism. Their first triumph occurred in 1963, when the voters of Crystal City, Texas, replaced all of the Anglo city council members with Mexican Americans.

c. In the 1920s and 1930s, Mexican-American factory and field workers participated in efforts to advance their political power by joining organizations such as the League of Latin American Citizens and the American GI Forum. They continued to seek the government's involvement in Hispanic issues by participating in the "Viva Kennedy" movement and forming groups like the Political Association of Spanish-Speaking Organizations (PASO). Later, Mexican Americans supported President Johnson, who appointed their representatives to his administration and made sure that Hispanics benefited from his War on Poverty and Great Society programs. But they knew there was still much work to do, especially in the West and Southwest, where Mexican Americans were the largest minority but had not managed to amass much political power. That situation began to change when many Mexican Americans, including young adults who called themselves *Chicanos*, decided to begin a grassroots movement that aimed to use direct action to secure better political representation for the Hispanic population. In 1963, the voters of Crystal City, Texas, replaced all of the Anglos on the city council with Mexican Americans. They were subsequently accused of being Communists who wanted to recreate Cuba in the United States.

Test 5: Paraphrasing with Accuracy

DIRECTIONS Paraphrase each of the following statements.

Original 1. In Colonial America, reading was not regarded as an activity for the rich, and printed matter was spread among all kinds of people. (Adapted from Neil Postman, *Amusing Ourselves to Death.* New York: Penguin, 1985, p. 35.)

Paraphrase _____

_____

_____

Original 2. In the late 1950s, union leaders Walter Reuther and George Meany battled over how to define American labor's role in the world. The liberal Reuther wanted unions to think of themselves as part of an international labor movement. The more conservative Meany insisted that American union members should concentrate on their own interests and let workers in other countries take care of themselves.

Paraphrase _____

_____

_____

Original 3. Self-justification is not the same thing as lying or making excuses. . . . There is a big difference between what a guilty man says to the public to convince them of something he knows is untrue ("I did not have sexual relations with that woman"; "I am not a crook") and the process of persuading himself that he did a good thing. In the former situation, he is lying and knows he is lying to save his own skin. In the latter, he is lying to himself. (Tarvis and Aronson, *Mistakes Were Made*, p. 4.)

Paraphrase _____

_____

_____

Original 4. More than 7,000 Westerns have been made in the United States and shown to audiences around the world. Many foreigners' impressions of the American West were shaped by exposure to "cowboy and Indian" flicks. During the first fifty years of cinema, however, Native-American actors, directors, and screenwriters were almost entirely excluded from the more than 2,000 studio-made films dealing with Indian themes. Audiences were used to seeing white actors portraying Indians—so much so that in 1939, when Cherokee actor Victor Daniels was hired for the title role in *Geronimo*, he was required to wear heavy make-up so that he more closely resembled the white actors that usually played the Indian parts. (www.ecologycenter.org/tfs/lesson.php?id=13474.)

Paraphrase

_____

_____

_____

_____

_____

_____

C H A P T E R   2

Developing an Academic Vocabulary

This chapter tells you more about how to develop the kind of academic vocabulary that will help you read your textbook assignments. The chapter also introduces the topic of *allusions*—references to people, places, and events that writers make to explain their ideas. By the time you finish this chapter, you will have noticeably enlarged your vocabulary and taken a giant leap forward on the road to academic achievement.

Identify the Specialized Vocabulary of Each Course

Every textbook assignment is likely to introduce some of the words you need for your courses. However, it's still up to you to recognize and learn those words; so let's start with the first step: recognizing the words central to mastery of the subject matter.

 ## Learn the Words That Appear and Reappear

Read even a few pages of the sample chapter (pages 625–641) and you will see that words like *liberalism, resolution,* and *federal* appear repeatedly. The repetition of these words suggests that to understand the chapter, and probably later chapters as well, you must develop an *automatic,* or immediate, understanding of all three. These are not words you should have to ponder, or think about, before defining. The definitions should be firmly anchored in your memory just like the definitions of everyday words such as *house* or *dog.*

 ## Use Context to Build Detailed Definitions

In part at least, your understanding of new words will develop naturally as you see the same words in different contexts. Take, for instance, the words *liberal* and *liberalism,* which appear throughout the sample chapter. The first appearance of the word is in the heading (p. 626) "Liberal Forces at Work." Both the question that follows the heading—"In what ways did the Supreme Court work to expand and protect the rights of individuals during the 1960s?"—and the text—"The 1960s provided many groups in American society with hope, that they, together with the federal government, might successfully challenge inequities and expand their rights in American society."—suggest that *liberal* and *liberalism* have something to do with changing society and the role of government in bringing change about. Thus, only a page into the chapter, you are well on your way to defining both terms.

The next time a form of the word *liberal* appears, the context again suggests that the words *liberal* and *liberalism* are associated with change: "Until joined in the 1960s by the executive branch, the Supreme Court—the Warren Court—was at the forefront of liberalism, altering the obligations of the government and the rights of citizens." At this point, the most *approximate*, or closest, definition for *liberalism* would be "open to change." But as the passage continues and provides additional context, a more precise definition emerges:

> Also in the 1950s, the Court's *Yates v. United States* (1957) ruling began a reversal of earlier decisions about the rights of those accused of crimes and started to require many of the protections accorded individuals under the Bill of Rights. For the next decade and a half, the Court expanded freedom of expression, separated church and state, redrew voting districts, and increased protection to those accused of violating the law.

Now you have enough context to **infer**, or figure out on your own, a precise definition for *liberal*, which would be something like the following: "open to or supportive of social reform and change, often with the help of the government." That's a definition you could jot in the margins of your text (in pencil), on an index card, or in the pages of a notebook. That approximate definition is good enough to let you keep reading without checking the **glossary**—the end-of-book list of key definitions—or the dictionary.

Check the Glossary

Check the glossary or the dictionary when you finish your assignment. At that point, you can record the definition in pen and add both word and definition to the running list of vocabulary words you are building in order to master your textbooks.

Pay Attention to Words Followed by Definitions

Particularly in textbooks, authors are likely to define important words they think you might not know. To illustrate, here's another excerpt from the sample chapter. Note how the authors define the word *gerrymandering*: "The Court's rejection of statewide gerrymandering, or redrawing of voting districts, so as to favor one party, was less controversial but equally lasting in importance."

Not sure readers will know what gerrymandering is because it is generally restricted to political discussions, the authors make sure to provide a definition. Any time textbook authors take the trouble to define words by restating their meaning, make sure you add the words to your need to know vocabulary list.

Record All Words Set Off from the Text

Although history books, like the one from which the sample chapter is drawn, do not necessarily highlight the vocabulary essential to subject mastery, textbooks for other disciplines often do. Look, for example, at how a government textbook uses boldface type to set off the meaning of filibuster in the following excerpt:

A **filibuster** is a prolonged speech, or series of speeches, made to delay action in a legislative assembly. It had become a common— and unpopular—feature of Senate life by the end of the nineteenth century. It was used by liberals and conservatives alike for lofty as well as self-serving purposes. The first serious effort to restrict the filibuster came in 1917, after an important foreign policy measure submitted by President Wilson had been talked to death by, as Wilson put it, "eleven willful men." (Adapted from Wilson and DiIulio, *American Government*, p. 324.)

In addition to that paragraph devoted to defining the word *filibuster*, the authors also include what's called a **sidebar**, a short, often boxed additional piece of information that runs alongside the main text. Sidebars devoted to definitions are an important clue to a word's significance.

Here, to get you started developing your academic vocabulary, are two lists of words. The first list includes words often used in discussions of politics, government, and history; the second focuses on words essential to the study of psychology and sociology.

> **Filibuster** A filibuster is a last-ditch attempt to defeat a measure or bill by talking for so long that supporters give up on passing it because they want to get on with the Senate's business. The right to filibuster can be revoked by a vote of sixty senators who agree the filibuster must stop. The filibuster's first appearance seems to have been in 1854 when senators tried to stop the Kansas-Nebraska Act, which allowed the territories of Kansas and Nebraska to decide for themselves if they wanted slavery within their borders.

Words Common to Politics, Government, and History

1. **Legitimacy** being lawful or in accordance with accepted standards or laws.

   Sample sentence: Worried about rumors of a terrorist background, the United States has questioned the *legitimacy* of Iranian President Ahmadinejad.

2. **Partisan** devoted to or strongly in favor of a particular position, theory, cause or approach; also a dedicated supporter.

   Sample sentence: New legislation affecting the consumer's right to sue pharmaceutical companies for damages has been held up by *partisan* bickering.

3. **Commercial** related to commerce, or the buying and selling of goods, with profit as the chief aim.

   Sample sentence: After the Revolutionary War (1776– 1783), those in the *commercial* sector found their fortunes on the rise.

4. **Federal** related to a form of government in which individual states recognize a central authority. In the eighteenth and nineteenth centuries, a partisan of this approach was called a *Federalist*.

   Sample sentence: In the years following the Revolutionary War, *federalists* consistently clashed with partisans of states' rights, who argued that each state should maintain its independence on broad issues of governance.

5. **Ratify** to give formal approval.

   Sample sentence: Changes in the Articles of Confederation could only be made if the revision was *ratified* by all of the thirteen states.

6. **Constituents** members of a party or group, parts of a whole. (In addition to *constituents*, *constituency* can be considered the plural form.)

   Sample sentence: When Connecticut Senator Joe Lieberman lost touch with his Democratic *constituents*, they tried to vote him out of office, but after being defeated in the primary, Lieberman won his Senate seat as an independent.

7. **Elite** belonging to the upper class; wealthy; having special privileges or abilities. People who are part of the upper class are sometimes called *elites*, or *the elite*.

Sample sentence: Perhaps more than any statesman of the time, Alexander Hamilton made it clear that members of the *elite* were meant to govern, while ordinary people were meant to put their faith in their leaders.

8. **Embargo** a government order prohibiting the movement of ships or trade.

Sample sentence: The U.S. *embargo* on trade with Cuba is one of the most enduring *embargoes* in modern history.

9. **Amend** to modify, change, or fix, often involving a legal document. An *amendment* can refer to the process of revision or to the final product or statement produced.

Sample sentence: The singer demanded that the lawyer *amend* the contract while she waited in his office.

Sample sentence: Any *amendment* to the contract or to the final product will take time.

Sample sentence: The Nineteenth *Amendment* to the U.S. Constitution gave women the right to vote.

10. **Expenditures** outlays of money.

Sample sentence: Military *expenditures* for the Revolutionary War left the United States heavily in debt.

EXERCISE 1 **DIRECTIONS** Fill in the blanks with one of the words from the list below.

constituents	amendments
elites	partisan
commercial	expenditures
Federalist	legitimacy
ratified	embargo

1. Although America's _____ recovery was well underway by the 1780s, merchants were, nevertheless, hungry to develop new markets. (Adapted from Gillon and Matson, *The American Experiment*, p. 339.)

2. In 1790, the _____ of the new American government was still being questioned.

3. Founded in 1787, the _____ Party favored a strong central government and the establishment of a constitution.

4. Politicians pay too much attention to polls and not enough to the needs of their _____.

5. Prior to the revolution of 1776, many ordinary colonists, not just the _____, clung to the notion that evil British ministers rather than the king himself were forcing unfair measures upon them. (Adapted from Boyer, *Enduring Vision,* p. 153.)

6. President Thomas Jefferson's 1807 _____ on exports effectively ended what had been a boom time for merchants, but if those who sold goods legally suffered as a result, smugglers made a fortune.

7. The legislation was stalled in Congress due to _____ bickering and the refusal of both sides to compromise.

8. The consolidated Federal Funds Report covers government _____ for grants, salaries, wages, loans, and insurance.

9. Constitutional _____ one through ten make up the Bill of Rights.

10. The Equal Rights Amendment[†] has never been _____.

Words Common to Psychology and Sociology

1. Dynamics   the social, intellectual, or moral forces that produce an event, an effect, or a change.

Sample sentence: The underlying social *dynamics* of online relationships has not received the attention it deserves.

2. Norms   standards of behavior considered typical; unwritten but understood rules of society.

Sample sentence: As with so many aspects of group dynamics, the *norms* that develop in a group can play a

---

[†]Equal Rights Amendment: amendment to the Constitution that would have guaranteed equal rights for both sexes.

crucial role in its effectiveness. (Brehm and Kassin, *Social Psychology*, p. 289.)

3. **Assertive** willing to put forth one's opinions and wishes.

Sample sentence: Many people find it difficult to be *assertive* in social situations. (Brehm and Kassin, *Social Psychology*, p. 248.)

4. **Stimulus** motive or cause of action.

Sample sentence: The *stimulus* for the study was the appearance of an unusual virus that did not behave in typical fashion.

5. **Physiology** the branch of biology dealing with how physical organisms function.

Sample sentence: "She drew books from the Carnegie Library and studied *physiology* and hygiene, and learned a myriad* of things about herself and the ways of women's health." (Jack London, *The Valley of the Moon*.)

6. **Longitudinal** extending over a long period of time.

Sample sentence: To prove or disprove Erik Erikson's theory about developmental stages spanning a lifetime, researchers need to do *longitudinal* studies of large sample populations.

7. **Genetic** due to heredity; inheritable; transmissible.

Sample sentence: There may well be a *genetic* factor in the development of schizophrenia.

8. **Cognitive** related to thought rather than being a purely emotional response.

Sample sentence: His *cognitive* skills were way ahead of his age, but on an emotional level, he was more child than teenager.

9. **Therapeutic** having to do with the treatment of disease and producing a beneficial effect.

Sample sentence: The *therapeutic* effects of psychoanalysis have never been scientifically tested.

10. **Correlation** connection; relationship.

Sample sentence: There seems to be a high *correlation* between active learning and long-term remembering.

---

*myriad: great number.

EXERCISE 2 DIRECTIONS Fill in the blanks with one of the words in the list below.

norms	longitudinal
genetic	cognitive
dynamics	assertive
stimulus	therapeutic
physiology	correlation

1. *The War Hotel* is the title of a book written by Arlene Audergon; it deals with the psychological _____ underlying human conflict.

2. In a _____ setting, patients or clients should feel free to say things they are normally fearful of expressing.

3. Aware of the penalties they might pay, even the most independent and rebellious spirits have a difficult time ignoring society's

   _____ .

4. A 35-year-long study showed a high _____ between consistent physical exercise and a healthy old age.

5. An environmental _____ like the smell of cookies baking in the oven can trigger powerful memories.

6. The study of animal _____ has produced enormous health benefits for humans and sometimes for animals as well.

7. _____ studies strongly suggest that personality may be as much a product of the genes as the environment.

8. It's a mistake to assume that the words _____ and *aggressive* are synonyms: the first describes a person who is not shy about expressing an opinion, the second a person who insists on making his or her opinion everyone else's as well.

9. _____ therapies generally rely less on medication and more on changing thought patterns.

10. It was once believed that an extra *y* chromosome caused a

    _____ disposition to criminal behavior.

Use Context Clues for General Vocabulary

Textbook writers usually make it a point to explicitly define the specialized vocabulary of their academic disciplines, or subjects. Still, they can't define every potentially unfamiliar word in a textbook. Readers sometimes have to use the **context**, or setting, of the word to infer, or figure out, an **approximate meaning**, one that doesn't match the dictionary definition but is close enough to let readers continue without looking the word up. Based on the context, for example, what do you think *ideology* means in this excerpt?

In English-speaking countries the period from about 1850 to 1901 is known as the Victorian Age. The expression refers not only to the reign of England's Queen Victoria (1837–1901) but also to an *ideology* surrounding the family and governing the relations between men and women. For the Victorians, men were meant, by nature, to be strong and courageous, women to be nurturing and cautious. (Adapted from Bulliet et al., *The Earth and Its People,* p. 730.)

Because the passage provides an illustration of how Victorian ideology functioned—it governed relations between men and women—you might suspect that ideology is a "particular way of thinking." To read the rest of the chapter from which the above passage came, this approximate definition for *ideology* would be adequate even though the dictionary formally defines *ideology* as "the set of beliefs that forms the basis for political, economic, or social systems."

Turning to the dictionary every time you encounter an unfamiliar word can disrupt your concentration, so before looking a word up, see if context can help you develop an approximate definition. Four of the most common context clues are contrast clues, restatement clues, example clues, and general knowledge clues.

Contrast Clues

Sentences containing contrast clues tell you what an unfamiliar word does *not* mean, often in the form of **antonyms**, or words opposite in meaning. For instance, suppose you were asked what *ostentatious* means. You might not be able to define it. After all, the word doesn't turn up that often in everyday conversation. Now suppose as well that word had a context, or setting, like the following:

Contrary to what many of us assume, the very rich are seldom *ostentatious* in their dress; they do not need to wear showy clothes to impress others. Secure in their wealth, they can afford to look plain and unimpressive.

In this case, the context for the word *ostentatious* offers contrast clues to its meaning. The words *plain* and *unimpressive* are antonyms for *ostentatious*. Using the contrast clues, you could infer, or read between the lines and determine, that *ostentatious* means "being showy" or "trying to impress."

Restatement Clues

For clarity and emphasis, writers, particularly of textbooks, sometimes deliberately say the same thing two different ways. Look, for example, at this sentence:

In addition to being a member of humanity each of us also belongs to a particular social group, where we find our *peers*—like-minded people often close to us in age—with whom we can identify and relate.

Here the author tells us that in addition to being a member of the human race we all have other, more specific groups to which we belong. Among those groups are our *peers*, "like-minded people often close to us in age." Note how the author defines the word to make sure readers know what it means.

Example Clues

Be alert to passages in which the author supplies an example or illustration of an unfamiliar word. Examples of the behavior associated with a word can often give you enough information to determine an approximate definition.

Personification in writing is an effective device only if it is used sparingly. Unfortunately, if the tables are always groaning, the wind is always howling, and the lights are always winking, then the technique becomes tiresome.

You could correctly infer from the examples in this passage that *personification* means talking about things or events as if they were people.

General Knowledge Clues

Although contrast, restatement, and example are common context clues, not all context clues are so obvious. Sometimes you have to base your inference solely on your familiarity with the experience or situation described in the text, as in the following example:

> With only the most primitive equipment to guide their journey, the explorers ended up taking a very *circuitous* route to India.

This passage does not contain any contrasts, restatements, or examples. But you can still figure out that *circuitous* means "indirect or roundabout," given that people are inclined to get lost or take a long time if they are guided by primitive equipment.

Check Your Understanding

For each sentence, define the italicized word and identify the type of context clue being used.

1. General George Patton demanded that his soldiers remain *stalwart*, no matter what threats they faced; Patton is famous, notorious even, for slapping two soldiers he considered cowardly.

Context clue: _____

2. Many voters believe that a candidate's marital status is *relevant*, or related to, his or her political performance.

Context clue: _____

3. The scientist's long, *abstruse* explanation left her audience speechless with incomprehension.

Context clue: _____

_____

4. If you want to travel into the Grand Canyon, you have two choices of *conveyance*: your feet or a mule.

Context clue: _____

EXERCISE 3 DIRECTIONS Use context to identify an approximate definition for each italicized word.

1. By the seventeenth century, nutmeg was a favorite spice in Europe because of its flavor and *aroma.*

a. taste

b. appearance

c. smell

d. ingredient

2. *Proponents* of states' rights argued that letting the federal government interfere in state affairs was like asking for a return of the monarchy.

a. critics

b. supporters

c. creators

d. challengers

3. The music had a *cathartic* effect on the young man: Listening to the songs of his childhood, feelings long suppressed welled up to the surface and he started to weep.

a. emotional

b. angry

c. bland

d. comic

4. Angry at the *inequitable* distribution of luxuries so obvious in the city's commercial district, the teenagers robbed the well-heeled tourists and distributed the money to friends and family.

a. luxurious

b. usual

c. unequal

d. changing

5. Most scholars consider the *Oxford English Dictionary* to be the most comprehensive dictionary available, and they turn to it for definitions of brand new words as well as *obsolete* words or meanings no longer included in other dictionaries.

a. up-to-date

b. out-of-date

c. improperly used

d. grammatically correct

6. In the late nineteenth century, boxer John L. Sullivan *vanquished* all his opponents until "Gentleman Jim" Corbett demonstrated that speed and technique could subdue Sullivan's brute strength.

a. conquered

b. irritated

c. challenged

d. delayed

7. The story of the homeless woman's life did not make for a pleasing or happy *narrative.*

a. sound

b. joke

c. description

d. tale

8. "We seem to live in an era dominated by the personal, the small, and the *titillating.* The summer's big stories were Gary Condit and shark attacks. Before that there was Monica Lewinsky." (Samuelson, "Unwitting Accomplices," *Perspectives on Terrorism*, p. 17.)

a. personally disinterested

b. completely untrue

c. superficially stimulating

d. casually described

9. The American writer Gertrude Stein claimed that when she took a final exam with the philosopher William James, she wrote a note saying, "I am so sorry, but I really do not feel a bit like an examination paper in philosophy today." According to Stein, James replied, "I understand perfectly how you feel; I often feel like that myself" and gave her the highest grade in the class. Stein, however, was known to *embellish* reality for the sake of a good story.

a. enjoy

b. exaggerate

c. celebrate

d. emphasize

10. The rule of the generals was meant to be *provisional*, but they ended up staying in power for more than a decade.

a. rebellious

b. strong

c. failing

d. temporary

Learning Common Word Parts

Knowing something about the parts of words can help you remember their meanings. Trying, for instance, to learn the meaning of *primordial,* "existing first or very early in time," you could use the meaning of *prim* ("first") to learn the definition, telling yourself that something *primordial* was one of the *first* creatures or plants in history. Then during reviews, you could use the word part *prim* to jog your memory and recall the word's meaning. That means, however, that you need to have a working knowledge of common word parts and their definitions. This section will help you develop that knowledge. However, it will be up to you to do regular reviews of the word parts and meanings shown below.

Prefixes[†]

Prefix	Meaning	Examples
a, ab, de	away, away from	asexual, absent, dethrone
a, an	not	anonymous
in, im, il, ir, non	not	incorrect, immoral, illegal, irregular, nonstop
ad, as	to, toward	adhere, associate
ante	before	anteroom
anti	against	antidote
circum	around	circumference
com, con, syn	with, together	complete, construct, symphony
contra	against	contradict
de, dis	down from, away	decline
ex, e	out of	exclude, evade
in, im, il	into	incline, immerse, illuminate
inter	between	interstate

[†]prefixes: a letter or letters at the beginning of a word that modify or change the core meaning, e.g., *in*spect and *re*spect.

mono	one, alone	monarch
para	beside, beyond	paraphrase
phil	love	philanthropist
plut	wealth	plutocrat
poly	many	polygamy
post	after	postpone
pre, pro	before, forward, in place of	prepare, prophet pronoun
re	back	refer, retreat
sub, suc, suf, sup, sus	under	submerge, succumb, suffer, support, suspend
super	above, over	supervise
trans	across, beyond	transmit

Roots†

Root	Meaning	Examples
anthrop	man	anthropology, philanthropy
arch	chief	monarch, architect, archangel
bibl	book	bibliography, Bible
cap	head	capital, captain, decapitate
ced	move, yield	exceed, proceed, succeed
chron	time	chronology, chronicle
civ	city	civic, civilize
dic	speak	dictate, diction, Dictaphone
equ	equal	equalize

---

†roots: the parts of words that contain the central or core meaning, e.g., in*spect* and re*spect*.

fid	faith	confide
fin	end, finished	final
flor	flower	florist
flu, fluc, flux	flow	influence, fluctuate
gam	marriage	bigamist
graph, gram	write, written	grammar, graphic
hetero	different	heterosexual
homo	same	homosexual
lingua, lingu	tongue, language	bilingual
loc	place	location, local, allocate
log, ology	speech, study	dialogue, geology, biology
loqu	speech	loquacious
memor	memory	memorial, memorize
mit	send	admit, commit, permit
mo	set in motion	move, remove, mobile
ord	order	ordinary, ordain
path	feeling, suffering	pathetic, sympathy
phil, phile	love	philosopher
physic, physio	nature	physiology, physical
pon	place, put	postpone, opponent
popul	people	popular, population
port	carry	portable, porter, deportment
reg, rect	straighten, rule	regular, regal, rectangle
sequ, secu	follow	sequence, persecute
spec	look	specimen, spectacle, spectator
the	god	theology
ven	come	prevent
vid, vis	see	vision, visualize, video

For more about word parts, go to
www.wordinfo.info/words/index/info.

EXERCISE 4 **DIRECTIONS** Fill in the blanks left in each word with one of the word parts† listed in the following box.

circum	around
merit	deserve, achieve, earn
pend	hang
homo	same
plut	wealth
phil	love
super	above
loqu, locu	speech

1. Next time you visit the office of a doctor or a lawyer, look at the awards, diplomas, or trophies on the wall. They have been placed there intentionally to indicate that the person inhabiting the office has

   accomplished tasks that _____ approval or establish worth.

2. There are those who claim that what we have in the United States

   is not a democracy but a _____ocracy, or rule by the wealthy.

3. A _____atelist is someone who is passionate about stamp collecting.

4. Some philosophers have argued that we would all be better off if we

   were led by a _____ocracy.

5. The heavy, _____ulous leaves of the plant were covered in a dark, slimy mold.

6. The members of the group were extremely _____geneous, which may be why they all got along so well.

7. Because an important trial was _____ing, the district attorney had a hard time concentrating on the reorganization of her office.

8. The cafeteria col_____y between the student and her professor looked too intense to be interrupted.

9. The crown prince had a _____cilious manner that made it clear how important he thought himself.

10. Once he had measured the garden's _____ference, he had a better idea of how many trees he needed to go around the border.

_____

†Not all the word parts in the exercises appear on the list on pages 68–70.

EXERCISE 5 **DIRECTIONS** Use context and the list of word parts on pages 68–70 to create approximate meanings for the italicized words in the following sentences.

1. Although he was a brilliant man, his *linguistic* skills did not match his cognitive abilities and he had a hard time expressing himself.

   Linguistic means _____.

2. Although his days as a great athlete were long gone, he still liked to look at the *memorabilia* from his glory days.

   Memorabilia means _____.

3. The new city *ordinance* exacted huge fines from dog owners who let their dogs off the leash.

   Ordinance means _____.

4. Henry VIII used trumped-up charges of *infidelity* to win a divorce from his wife Ann Boleyn, whom he promptly had beheaded.

   Infidelity means _____.

5. If the bird flu virus becomes capable of human-to-human transmission, it will spread like a wildfire among the *populace*.

   Populace means _____.

6. Fearful of criticism, the new *regime* took power and immediately clamped down on freedom of the press.

   Regime means _____.

7. The man's *diction* suggested that he was British rather than American.

   Diction means _____.

8. In India, the yearly *per capita* income is rising as more and more technology companies are outsourcing to India instead of hiring workers at home.

   Per capita means _____.

9. The two government officials tried to appear friendly, but their *antipathy* was obvious.

   Antipathy means _____.

10. Bear and bare, mite and might, there and their, are all *homonyms*.

Homonyms means _____

_____.

 # Understanding the Author's Allusions

Allusions are references writers and speakers make to people, places, and events that are not directly related to the topic or issue under discussion, yet still contribute to the overall meaning conveyed. Take, for instance, the example below, in which the author discusses the Hubble telescope but includes an allusion to the Edsel, an extremely unsuccessful car model introduced by the Ford Motor Company in 1957. Launched with much fanfare, the Edsel was a bust and no one wanted to buy one. It was probably one of the biggest failures in automotive history. The question you have to answer is this: Why does the author of the following excerpt, Peter N. Spotts, allude to the Edsel in a discussion of the Hubble telescope?

> The latest findings cap "a spectacular year" for the repaired Hubble, and to think astronomers were once concerned that the instrument might become the orbiting *Edsel* of observatories.

Read the above without understanding the Edsel allusion, and you will only get part of the author's point: The Hubble had a good year. Without knowing what a flop the Edsel was, you won't get the rest of the point: Initially, astronomers were worried that the Hubble was going to be a huge failure like the Edsel.

Allusions and Common Knowledge

While some allusions come and go with current fashions or trends, others have made their way into the English language and are considered **common knowledge**. In other words, writers will use the allusions without explaining what the references mean. They just assume that the allusion is part of the reader's background. Edsel is one such allusion and the name Pavlov is another. Ivan Pavlov did a series of experiments with dogs in which he got the animals to associate food with the sound of a bell. After a while, whether or not food was present, the dogs would salivate if they heard a bell ring. Thus when someone is compared to Pavlov's dogs or considered to be showing a Pavlovian response, the implication is that he or she is responding in an automatic, or unthinking, way.

Note now how writer Colbert King alludes to Pavlov to describe the way he and his siblings responded at the sound of their father's whistle:

> The King kids, in a response that would have made Pavlov proud, could be seen abandoning marbles, cards, third base—everything—to make a beeline for home. (*Washington Post*, June 14, 1997.)

As you can see, the writer does not tell readers who Pavlov is or why his name appears in the sentence. The expectation is that readers will (1) recognize the name and (2) draw the appropriate inference, or conclusion, about what message the allusion conveys.

Learning Common Allusions

What follows are two lists of common allusions. The first explains terms related to World War II and its aftermath; the second, terms from the Bible. Use these lists to get started on increasing the number of common cultural allusions you automatically know. As you complete the following chapters in this textbook, note as well the boxes labeled **Allusion Alert**. They will introduce you to some common cultural references, which should be part of the background knowledge you bring to a text.

Allusions don't make their way into textbooks as frequently as, say, footnotes. However, they are extremely common in essays, magazines, journal articles, and news editorials. Thus, they are very much worth the time and effort it will take you to learn them.

World War II and Its Aftermath

World War II, like other momentous events, has left behind a number of references to people, places, and events that have become common knowledge. This list contains ten of the most frequently used. Put a slash through the box if you know the allusion. Put a check in it if you don't. Review the allusions you don't know until you feel that you have learned them.

☐ **1. Neville Chamberlain and the Policy of Appeasement.** Chamberlain was the British prime minister from 1937 to 1940. Desperate to avoid hostilities with German dictator Adolf Hitler, Chamberlain agreed in 1938 to surrender Czechoslovakia to Hitler in exchange for Hitler's empty promise to use peaceful means when resolving all future disputes. In other words, Chamberlain tried to *appease*, or soothe, Hitler in the hopes that the dictator would be satisfied. As a result, Chamberlain's name now suggests the blindness and futility of reasoning with, let alone trusting, a tyrant's word. His *policy of appeasement* is often cited by those who wish to warn against trying to placate, or satisfy, someone who is, in fact, implacable.

☐ **2. Rosie the Riveter.** The image of an overall-clad, smiling young woman called Rosie was created as part of a government propaganda campaign. The purpose of the campaign was to convince women that entering the work force was their patriotic duty. Women got the message and entered the workplace in droves. At least 6 million women took jobs in heavy industry to take up the slack for some of the 15 million men serving their country in wartime. Nowadays, allusions or references to Rosie can represent the positive power of propaganda: "Thanks to Rosie the Riveter, women did not feel guilty about walking away from the roles of housewife and stay-at-home mom." But it can also suggest the way women were somewhat abruptly shoved aside when men came home from the war: "After World War II ended, women disappeared from the factories almost as fast as Rosie the Riveter posters."

☐ **3. Pearl Harbor.** On December 7, 1941, the Japanese bombed Pearl Harbor in Hawaii in a surprise attack that, overnight, changed the American government's policy from isolation to intervention. Allusions to Pearl Harbor are used to suggest an event that causes fear and shock along with a need for retaliation. Interviewed after 9/11, Henry Kissinger said, "This is comparable to Pearl Harbor, and we must have the same response."

☐ **4. Final Solution.** At a meeting called "The Wannsee Conference," the Nazis came up with a plan for executing, as efficiently as possible, those millions of people they considered inferior—Jews, communists, gypsies, homosexuals, and just about anyone who wasn't a "pure German." But even they couldn't call their plan what it was, a system of mass murder. To disguise what they were doing, the Nazis used a euphemism—"The Final Solution." While the phrase is still used most often in association with the Nazis, it has also been linked to those who followed in their footsteps, like Pol Pot in Cambodia and Idi Amin in Uganda, heads of state who engaged in genocide, or the mass murder of a specific group with the conscious intention of removing it from the face of the earth.

☐ **5. Franklin Delano Roosevelt (F.D.R.) and the New Deal.** Franklin Delano Roosevelt was nominated as the presidential candidate of the Democratic Party in 1932, when the country was reeling from an economic depression that had begun in 1929. In his acceptance speech, Roosevelt said, "I pledge you, I pledge myself, to a new deal for the American people" to indicate that he had a plan for getting the country out of its economic slump. As soon as Roosevelt got into office, he began using the power of the federal government to pass legislation enacting emergency and work relief programs. He also gave aid to farmers, instituted Social Security, and developed protective legislation for unions and migrant workers. Thus, allusions to Franklin Delano Roosevelt, also known as F.D.R., and his New Deal usually suggest a politician or political party that believes in government intervention. "In his plan for the great society, Lyndon Baines Johnson was a throwback to F.D.R. and the New Deal."

☐ **6. Cold War.** During World War II, the United States and its allies were forced into a shotgun wedding with what was then the Soviet Union. But the union ended abruptly once the war was over. From roughly the late 1940s to the early 1990s, the Soviet Union and the United States did everything possible, short of all-out war, to undermine the other's power and influence. Although the term *Cold War* mainly refers to this particular period and these two countries, it can also refer to other similarly "cool" conflicts that don't end up in "hot" and open warfare. "When it came to the Chinese, the secretary of state had a Cold War mentality that was impervious to all contradictory evidence."

7. **Josef Stalin and the Gulags.** Dictator of the Soviet Union from 1928 to his death in 1953, Stalin used terror to repress and maintain control of those people and countries under his rule. Not surprisingly, the term *Stalinesque* has survived as a way of describing a powerful person or group who hands out harsh punishments for the slightest sign of disobedience. Among the punishments favored by Stalin was confinement to forced labor camps called *gulags*, where many died from cold, exhaustion, and starvation. While speakers and writers still talk about the original gulags that were filled to capacity under Stalin's rule, the term now general refers to places or situations where suffering and hardship prevail. "The Nigerian prison rivaled the worst of Stalin's gulags."

8. **Iron Curtain.** Although it is often ascribed to Winston Churchill, Britain's prime minister during World War II, no one knows for sure who invented the term *Iron Curtain*, which referred to the veil of secrecy that dropped down over the Soviet Union and the countries it controlled following World War II. Threatened by the success of the Marshall Plan* and consumed by personal paranoia, Stalin wanted to make sure that no information exchange could take place between capitalist and communist countries. While the phrase *Iron Curtain* still refers to the figurative barrier that existed between East and West after the war, it's also used to generally describe situations in which a barrier is erected to maintain strictest secrecy; for example, "The department has put up an Iron Curtain between us and the undercover cops on

*Marshall Plan: post–World War II efforts to help Europe recover from the war.

assignment" (actor Michael Chiklis on the TV drama *The Shield*).

☐ **9. Harry S. Truman.**[†] Like Stalin, but in a positive sense, the down-home personality of Harry Truman, the thirty-third president of the United States, lives on in the word **Trumanesque**, meaning plain-spoken and direct. Truman became famous for vivid one-liners like "The buck stops here" and "If you can't stand the heat, get out of the kitchen." Thus, allusions to Truman usually focus on his blunt and direct style; for example, "Reserved and intellectual, presidential candidate Adlai Stevenson was no Harry Truman and, although Americans seemed to admire Stevenson, they didn't quite trust him."

☐ **10. McCarthyism.** The allusion originates with Wisconsin Senator Joseph R. McCarthy. In the 1950s, in an attempt to increase his own political power, McCarthy aggressively accused, without a shred of evidence, hundreds of people of being communists or communist sympathizers. While McCarthy's initial attacks focused on members of the State Department, he met his match when he went after the Army, which launched its own investigation, ending in McCarthy being censured by the Senate. When not used in reference to McCarthy's actual attacks, *McCarthyism* is generally used to describe an atmosphere filled with unfounded accusations and suspicion; for example, "The new administration made it clear that McCarthyism, which had dominated the previous administration, was now a thing of the past."

[†]Because the human memory works best when it can make connections, learn as well the meaning of the phrase "**Truman Doctrine**," which was Truman's plan or policy to actively prohibit the spread of communism, particularly in areas where the United States was concerned about its own interests and influence.

EXERCISE 6 DIRECTIONS Fill in the blanks with the correct allusion.

Neville Chamberlain	McCarthyism
Cold War	Rosie the Riveter
Final Solution	Stalinesque
Pearl Harbor	Trumanesque
Iron Curtain	F.D.R.

1. By the fifties, women weren't supposed to model themselves after

_____; their ideal woman was supposed to be radio homemaker Betty Crocker.

2. To implement a national health care plan, the government needs a

president in the mold of _____.

3. When the Hutu president of Rwanda[†] claimed there was no official plan to wipe out every Tutsi man, woman, and child, government

officials all over the world chose to imitate _____ and believe the president, despite all evidence to the contrary.

4. _____ in his presidential style, Jimmy Carter was not given to pomp and show, but he, too, may turn out to be another underestimated president whose greatness will be recognized over time.

5. North Korean leader Kim Jong-il has maintained an

_____ between his country and the rest of the world. By keeping citizens isolated from western nations in particular, Kim Jong-il maintains strict control over the populace while keeping other nations guessing about his motives and his goals.

6. _____ in his demand for unquestioning obedience and his use of violence to obtain it, Iraqi dictator Saddam Hussein was as bloodthirsty and prone to paranoia as the long-dead Russian tyrant.

[†]Rwanda: In 1994, the Hutu tribal majority of Rwanda in Africa committed genocide against the Tutsi minority, while the rest of the world stood by and let it happen.

7. After the terrorist attacks of September 11, 2001, there were warnings against a return to _____ when the American government arrested and questioned possible terrorists at home and abroad. No one argued with the idea that rounding up the terrorists was a legitimate aim; but some wanted to make sure that there was sufficient evidence to take this step.

8. During the early years of the _____, some Americans built bomb shelters in their homes because they were convinced that a war was imminent.

9. In 2006, 120 survivors of genocide in Nazi Germany, Bosnia, Cambodia, and Rwanda wrote a letter urging the European Union to do more to stop the "ethnic cleansing" taking place in the Darfur region of Sudan. As one Holocaust survivor expressed it, he didn't survive a German concentration camp only to see Hitler's _____ repeated in another part of the world.

10. Lyndon Baines Johnson fabricated the Gulf of Tonkin attacks that launched the United States into war with Vietnam because he knew that the country would go into _____ mode and want some form of retaliation.

The Bible

The Bible is the source of many common allusions appearing in essays and editorials.

☐ **1. Lazarus.** Lazarus was dead and in his tomb four days when Jesus brought him back to life. The Gospel of John points to this miracle as the ultimate sign of Jesus' divinity. Today, someone who makes a comeback after hitting rock bottom physically, mentally, or financially is said to be a Lazarus or like Lazarus, rising from the dead. "After twenty years in prison, new DNA evidence proved Helen's innocence; like Lazarus, she got her life back and walked through the prison doors one last time."

☐ **2. Job.** In the Old Testament, God pointed to Job as an example of one of his most faithful followers. When

Satan scoffed, claiming that Job was a good and devout man only because he was wealthy with a big, happy family, God gave Satan permission to test Job's faith. Satan promptly destroyed all that Job owned, killed all ten of his children, and covered him with sores from head to toe. Despite his misery and suffering, however, Job refused to renounce his faith in God. To reward him, God healed Job and gave him "twice as much as he had before." Now, a person who has endured much suffering is said to have "the patience of Job." "When Senator Robert Dole returned from World War II, his suffering was written all over him, but like Job, he recovered and resumed his promising political career."

☐ **3. Prodigal Son.**[†] This figure from one of Jesus' parables[*] illustrates the idea that God forgives sinners who repent. The Prodigal Son is a young man who persuades his father to give him his inheritance. He then leaves home and squanders the money on "riotous living." (The word *prodigal* means "wastefully extravagant.") Broke, hungry, and ashamed of himself, the young man returns home, hoping only that his father will hire him as a servant. Instead, his father welcomes him back and celebrates his son's return with a huge feast. When an older brother complains that he stayed home and worked hard but was never treated to such a celebration, his father explains that it is right to rejoice when someone who "was lost . . . is found." Thus, a person who goes astray but comes to his senses and receives a hero's welcome is referred to as a "prodigal son"; for example, "Three months and hundreds of miles of occupied territory later, Kabila[‡] received a homecoming worthy of a prodigal son."

☐ **4. Good Samaritan.** In another of his parables, Jesus told the story of a man who had been robbed, beaten,

---

[†]The illustration of the allusion to the Prodigal Son comes from the *Dictionary of Allusions.*
[*]parables: stories with a moral.
[‡]Laurent Kabila: leader of rebel forces who fought to overthrow Mobutu Sese Seko in Zaire, Africa.

and left by the roadside to die. Although the man was clearly suffering, several people passed him and kept on going. Finally, a man from Samaria stopped to help. He gave the victim first aid, took him to an inn, gave the innkeeper money to cover some of the man's expenses, and promised to pay the rest on his return. Now, a "Good Samaritan" is a person who performs an act of kindness, especially for a stranger. "Trying to be a good Samaritan and help an old man being attacked by thugs, the boy was badly injured."

☐ 5. **Jonah and the Whale.** In the Old Testament, God commands Jonah to become one of his prophets, but Jonah refuses and heads off for a sea voyage instead. Enraged by Jonah's defiance, God whips up a huge storm, and Jonah admits to the frightened sailors on board that he is to blame for the tempest. The crew tosses him overboard, and the seas become calm again. But Jonah does not drown. Instead, he is swallowed by a "large fish," often interpreted to be a whale. Trapped inside the fish for three days and three nights, Jonah prays to God for forgiveness, claiming that he has learned his lesson, so God has the fish spit him out. A "Jonah" has come to mean a jinxed person who brings bad luck to an endeavor.

☐ 6. **Judgment of Solomon.** Solomon, a great king who ruled over Israel from about 970 to 928 BCE, was legendary for his wisdom. One tale in particular is often cited as evidence of his gift for governing. Two women came before him, each claiming to be the mother of an infant. Unable to tell which one was telling the truth, Solomon requested a sword, telling the women that the only fair thing to do was divide the child in half. The woman who falsely claimed the child as her own did not object. The real mother, however, begged Solomon not to harm the child, agreeing to give the baby to the other woman if he would spare the child's life. Solomon knew then that she was the child's real mother and handed her the infant. Thus, a "judgment of Solomon" suggests a decision needing an extraordinary degree of wisdom. "To keep peace among the members of the union, she needed the judgment of Solomon."

☐ 7. **Before the Flood.** The Old Testament reports that several generations after Adam and Eve were forced to leave the Garden of Eden, humankind had become corrupt and violent. Regretting his creation of these wicked people, God decided to cause the Great Flood that destroyed all living creatures except the people and animals in Noah's ark. This event happened early in the Bible's account of human history. Therefore, you'll see this expression used figuratively today to mean a very long time ago, as in "Politicians have been making empty promises since before the Flood."

☐ 8. **Sodom and Gomorrah.** In the Bible, these cities are destroyed by God with fire and brimstone because of the inhabitants' wickedness. An allusion to them now suggests a place devoted to vice and corruption. "Some of the tales coming out of Washington suggest Sodom and Gomorrah more than the seat of government."

☐ 9. **Tower of Babel.** After the flood, Noah's descendants wanted to build a tower as high as heaven in the land of Babylon. God was offended by the idea and prevented the tower from being completed by making people speak different languages so that they could no longer understand one another. Thus allusions to the Tower of Babel suggest a noisy scene of confusion. "You remember what happened when the government deregulated the airline industry and the nation's carriers reorganized themselves into flying cattle cars with a fare structure that seems to have been created during lunch hour at the Tower of Babel."[†]

☐ 10. **Cain and Abel.** Cain, the first child of Adam and Eve, murdered his brother Abel, becoming a fugitive and an exile as a result. In the Bible, when the Lord asks Cain what happened to his brother, Cain responds by saying, "I know not. Am I my brother's keeper?" The Lord then puts a mark on Cain so that everyone will know of his crime. This story has become the source of several allusions. Allusions to the brothers suggest destructive, even deadly, competition between former

---

[†]The Tower of Babel allusion comes from *Merriam-Webster's Dictionary of Allusions.*

friends or siblings. References to someone being (or not being) a brother's keeper indicate the person's willingness to take (or not take) responsibility for another while the mark of Cain suggests that a crime has been committed by the person bearing the mark. "Even if they are let out of prison, child molesters always bear the mark of Cain in the eyes of the public."

EXERCISE 7   **DIRECTIONS** Fill in the blanks with the correct allusion.

Lazarus	judgment of Solomon
Job	before the Flood
prodigal son	Sodom and Gomorrah
good Samaritans	Tower of Babel
Jonah	Cain and Abel

1. After campaigning against his former friends and political peers during the presidential election of 1800 and losing to Thomas Jefferson, Aaron Burr wanted to return to the fold like the

_____. However, Jefferson and his administration had no intention of welcoming Burr back and saw to it that he was prevented from serving any useful role.

2. The American Civil War split families apart; brothers joined opposing sides and suddenly looked at one another as if they were

_____.

3. Many people assume that Americans have paid income tax since

_____. On the contrary, it wasn't until 1913 that Congress authorized the income tax system we know today by ratifying the Sixteenth Amendment to the Constitution.

4. In some Christian communities of the fifteenth and sixteenth centuries, bad luck in the form of a failed crop, terrible weather, disease, or death would sometimes be blamed on a person thought to be a witch. Once accused of practicing the supernatural arts, this

man or woman was perceived as a _____, who would have to be burned at the stake or hanged to eliminate the source of the misfortune.

5. The writing in some academic journals reads as if it were written

not in an ivory tower but in the _____; that's how
incomprehensible it is.

6. Thousands of African Americans escaped slavery in the nineteenth-
century South thanks to the Underground Railroad, a network of
secret routes, transportation, and safe havens operated by

_____ whose antislavery convictions were so strong
that they were willing to risk their personal safety to help total
strangers gain their freedom.

7. When I left my rural hometown to go to school in New York City, my

parents acted as if I were departing for _____.

8. After Richard Nixon lost the 1960 presidential race to John F.
Kennedy, his political career seemed finished. He himself even bitterly told the media, "You won't have Nixon to kick around any-
more." But then, in one of the biggest comebacks since

_____, Nixon was elected America's thirty-seventh
president in 1908.

9. Knowing how to resolve the Arab-Israeli conflict requires the

_____.

10. General George Washington's army exhibited the patience of

_____ during the miserably cold winter of 1777–
1778 at Valley Forge, Pennsylvania. According to Washington, his
soldiers were inadequately clothed, starving, ill, and without fire-
wood or blankets or even shoes; nevertheless, they stayed at their
posts and didn't desert.

■ **DIGGING DEEPER**

LOOKING AHEAD As you read the following selection, pay close attention to the itali-cized words. When you finish, answer the questions about context clues and word parts.

MAD FOR WORDS

1 Prior to the completion of the *Oxford English Dictionary (OED)* in 1928, the most *acclaimed* dictionary in the English language was Samuel Johnson's *A Dictionary of the English Language*, published in 1755. Yet extraordinary as Johnson's achievement was, it paled by comparison to the multivolumed *OED*. Unlike the highly respected Dr. Johnson, who had included only the words he personally considered good, useful, or worthy, the makers of the *OED* made no such *distinctions* among words. Under the leadership of clergyman and scholar Richard Trench, *scores* of volunteers labored to include all of the words in the English language, along with sample sentences that illustrated changes in meaning over time.

2   Enthusiastic as Trench was, he didn't possess the organizational skills necessary to the *daunting* task at hand. It wasn't until the Scotsman and self-taught *linguist* James Murray signed on as editor, sometime in the mid-1870s, that the dreamed-of dictionary showed signs of becoming a reality. Murray created a *meticulous* system for the volunteers engaged on the project to follow. It was ordered right down to the way they should organize the slips of paper they sent on to his central office. Even then, of course, Murray discovered that some volunteers couldn't—or wouldn't—follow directions. Many entries were flat-out *illegible*, so hastily scribbled that neither Murray nor his staff could read them.

3   Fortunately for Murray, and above all for the project, there were a few volunteers who got everything right, creating entries that were well-organized, thorough, and completely legible. One volunteer in particular, William C. Minor, an American living in England, earned Murray's heartfelt admiration. Month after month, Minor showered the editor with neatly written scraps of paper, each one identifying a key meaning in the history of a specific word. Also included were a sample sentence and the date of the word's first appearance. Minor's contribution was so great that Murray set out to meet the man face to face, only to make an astonishing discovery: William Minor was an American physician

and convicted murderer, who was *incarcerated* in the Broadmoor Asylum for the criminally insane and condemned to stay there for the rest of his natural life.

4   Eight years before becoming Murray's favorite volunteer, Minor had murdered a man in cold blood, convinced that his victim— a complete stranger—intended to kill him. At the time of the murder, and indeed throughout his life, Minor was given to wild delusions about enemies sneaking into his room at night intent on doing him bodily harm. Work on the dictionary, however, seemed to quiet his *hallucinations.* It also helped relieve the misery and *tedium* of his day-to-day life.

5   Horrified by Minor's violent past and obvious madness, Murray was, nevertheless, drawn by the lonely man's passion for words. Minor, in turn, was wildly grateful that Murray respected his contribution, and he worked even more *diligently* in order to *retain* his new friend's admiration. That hard work did not go unrewarded. In 1899, Murray publicly announced his admiration for the man who was spending his life behind bars: "So enormous have been Dr. Minor's contributions during the past seventeen or eighteen years, that we could easily illustrate the last four centuries from his quotations alone."

6   But Murray's friendship and respect could not *stave off* the rising tide of madness that continued to *engulf* Minor during his thirty-year stay at Broadmoor. By 1902, even work on the dictionary could not calm Minor's mad fantasies. When Minor started to do himself physical harm, Murray helped get him returned to America, where the unfortunate man quickly declined into complete madness, giving up all work on the *OED.* Minor died in 1920, eight years before the *Oxford English Dictionary*—seventy years in the making—was published to great acclaim. What few knew, however, was the role a madman had played in its making.

Information for this reading drawn from
Simon Winchester, *The Professor and the Madman.*
New York: Harper Perennial, 1999.

Sharpening Your Skills

DIRECTIONS Answer the following questions by filling in the blanks.

1. What's a good approximate definition for *acclaimed* in paragraph 1?

_____

2. What's a good approximate definition for *distinctions* in paragraph 1?

_____

3. What's a good approximate definition for *scores* in paragraph 1?

_____

4. What's a good approximate definition for *daunting* in paragraph 2?

_____

5. *Lingua* is a Latin root meaning "language," and *ist* is a Greek suffix indicating "a person who performs a specific action." Put the two word parts together and you get the word *linguist* in paragraph 2. Based on context and word parts, what is a good approximate definition for *linguist?*

_____

6. What kind of context clue does the author provide for the word *meticulous* in paragraph 2? _____ What is a good approximate definition for *meticulous?* _____

7. In paragraph 2, what's a good approximate definition for *illegible?* _____ Based on that definition, what does the prefix *il* mean? _____

8. What word in paragraph 3 is an antonym for *illegible?*

_____

9. Paragraph 3 introduces the word *incarcerated*, which, in a slightly different form, was already introduced in Chapter 1; in this reading, it means _____. If you didn't know the word already, what kind of context clue does the author provide?

_____

10. What's a good approximate definition for *hallucinations* in paragraph 4?

_____

What word in paragraph 4 is a synonym for *hallucinations?*

_____

11. What's a good approximate definition for *tedium* in paragraph 4?

_____

12. What's a good approximate definition for *diligently* in paragraph 5?

_____

13. What's a good approximate definition for *retain* in paragraph 5?

_____ Which of the two meanings you learned for

the prefix *re* fits this definition? _____

14. What's a good approximate definition for *stave off* in paragraph 6?

_____

15. What's a good approximate definition for *engulf* in paragraph 6?

_____

Students who want to do a more in-depth review of context clues should use *Getting Focused*, the web-based reading program accompanying this text. The program is available at **college .cengage.com/devenglish/flemming/getting_focused/1e/ student_home.html**. Completing the introduction will provide a thorough and complete review of context clues.

For more work on words, go to **laflemm.com** and click on *Reading for Thinking*: "Online Practice." Complete the interactive exercises on context clues.

Test 1: Learning the Language of Government

DIRECTIONS Fill in the blanks with one of the following words.

amendment	commercial
ratify	elite
federal	embargo
constituents	legitimacy
expenditures	partisan

1. The U.S. Congress belongs to the legislative branch of the _____ government.

2. The nineteenth _____ to the Constitution, which guaranteed women the right to vote, was decided by a 24-year-old Tennessee legislator named Harry Burn, who switched from "no" to "yes" in response to a letter from his mother saying, "Hurrah, and vote for suffrage!" (Source of information: www.equalrightsamendment.org/era.htm.)

3. Russia's lower house of parliament has finally voted to _____ the international treaty on climate change.

4. The senator was in favor of sex education in the schools but fearful of how his _____ might react.

5. No _____ trade should be allowed in protected wilderness areas.

6. Claiming the vote had been rigged, the rebels immediately challenged the _____ of the newly elected government.

7. During the Revolutionary War, the Minutemen were a small but _____ force, which was highly mobile and quick to assemble.

8. As a _____ of no political party, the judge seemed a good choice for the Supreme Court.

9. The _____ Act of 1807 forbade all international trade to and from American ports.

10. In 2004, health _____ in the United States amounted to $1.9 trillion.

Test 2: Learning the Vocabulary of Psychology

DIRECTIONS Fill in the blanks with one of the following words.

dynamics	physiology
therapeutic	longitudinal
norms	genetic
assertiveness	cognitive
stimulus	correlation

1. For some people, society's _____ exist only to be ignored or challenged.

2. No one really understands the underlying _____ of physical attraction.

3. _____ therapy focuses on changing the patient's thought patterns.

4. _____ studies of twins over the course of their life-time suggest that, despite differences in environment, twins develop a similar behavior and temperament.

5. There is a positive _____ between smoking and lung cancer.

6. Trained to associate food with the sound of a bell, Pavlov's dogs responded to the _____ by salivating.

7. Oddly enough, when he took the antianxiety medication, his _____ increased, whereas he normally had difficulty expressing his opinions.

8. Research consistently shows a _____ component to both temperament and attitude.

9. The sports foundation was advertising for someone with a knowledge of anatomy and _____.

10. Studies have undermined the belief that the herb St. John's Wort has a _____ effect on depression.

Test 3: Using Context Clues

DIRECTIONS Use the sentences or passages to determine approximate definitions for the italicized words.

1. Currently, honeybees are disappearing and no one knows why. What scientists realize, however, is that the *ramifications* of the disappearance will be widespread. It won't just be harder to raise flowers, it will also be more difficult to produce a food supply rich in fruits and vegetables.

Ramifications means _____.

2. Most institutions function according to a *hierarchy* in which the people at the top get to make the most decisions and people at the bottom get to make few if any.

Hierarchy means _____.

3. When the author stood at the podium to speak, there were no signs of her previous *trepidation*. In contrast to her earlier mood, she was remarkably relaxed and calm. Her voice did not break; her hands did not shake, and she seemed totally in command of the situation.

Trepidation means _____.

4. That kind of *vituperation* has no place in a political campaign; he should be explaining his positions, not spewing insults.

Vituperation means _____.

5. When it comes to publicity, the *incumbent* president obviously has more access to the press than other candidates. As the person already holding the office, the president has automatic press coverage.

Incumbent means _____.

6. He had come from an extremely *affluent* home where money was no object. But he gave it all up to live a life of poverty and serve those needier than himself.

Affluent means _____.

7. Although she wanted to, there was no way to *mitigate* the harshness of her criticism.

Mitigate means _____.

8. The bulldog was remarkably *tenacious*. He wouldn't let go of the robber's leg even when the man rained blows down on his head. He let go only when his master yelled, "Stop!"

Tenacious means _____.

9. Books on time management are popular primarily because *procrastination* is so common. After all, how many of us can honestly say we have never put off or postponed something we didn't want to do—washing the dog, writing a paper, cleaning the house—until the very last possible minute?

Procrastination means _____.

10. After saving his mother from drowning, the twelve-year-old boy was *inundated* with letters praising him for his heroism.

Inundated means _____.

Test 4: Understanding Allusions

DIRECTIONS Fill in the blanks with one of the allusions listed below.

Cain and Abel	Lazarus
prodigal son	Tower of Babel
Job	good Samaritans
before the flood	judgment of Solomon
Jonah	Sodom and Gomorrah

1. After it was proven that Lieutenant Colonel Oliver North had secretly diverted millions of dollars to the Nicaraguan Contras[†] despite Ronald Reagan's pledge not to deal with terrorists, it

seemed that North's career was over. But _____-like, he has returned to prominence as the host of his own talk show on Fox News.

2. One minute everyone at the meeting was making sense, the next moment, he felt as if he was imprisoned in the _____.

3. Anyone who thinks brothers in the same business don't compete

needs to reread the story of _____.

4. Shock-jock Don Imus was fired for vile racial insults on the air, but once he repented, diehard fans were willing to welcome him back

into the fold like the _____.

5. Doctors are sometimes afraid to be _____ if they are involved in an accident. If they make a mistake in emergency treatment, victims or families might sue them for malpractice.

6. Parents dealing with teenagers need the patience of

_____.

7. To settle that dispute, the mediator will need the judgment of

_____ because both sides make a compelling case.

[†]Contras: name for anticommunist rebels, who tried to undermine Nicaragua's socialist government by terrorizing its supporters.

8. The generation gap has existed since _____.

9. The new player was considered a _____ because his last two teams had won only one game apiece; however, as soon as he was gone, both teams went on winning streaks.

10. To the other kids, attending the party was an ordinary event; but for the two freshmen raised as Mormons, it was _____ come to life.

Test 5: Interpreting Allusions

DIRECTIONS In the blanks following every passage, explain the meaning of each allusion.

1. Some people think that anyone sitting on the Supreme Court has the *judgment of Solomon*. They forget that Supreme Court justices are political appointees who may or may not make wise decisions.

   The allusion to the *judgment of Solomon* implies that _____

   _____.

2. Following the terrorist attacks of September 11, 2001, the FBI and Secret Service began questioning artists and antiwar activists; publishers began firing antiwar columnists and cartoonists, while university presidents began scolding faculty members who criticized the federal government. In response, American Civil Liberties Union president Nadine Strossen said, "The term *terrorism* is taking on the same kind of characteristics as the term *communism* in the 1950s." Her criticism was echoed by civil rights activists who began worrying about a possible return of *McCarthyism*.

   The allusion to *McCarthyism* implies that _____

   _____.

3. Cambodia was controlled from 1975 to 1979 by an extremist communist organization known as the Khmer Rouge. *Stalinesque* in its rule of helpless Cambodian civilians, this regime's motto was "To keep you is no benefit. To destroy you is no loss." The Khmer Rouge confiscated all private property and forced citizens to do backbreaking labor in the fields. Members of the Khmer Rouge also executed or starved to death at least a million people.

   The allusion to *Stalinesque* implies that _____

   _____.

4. Many people support using the military to eliminate terrorists just as soldiers crushed fascist dictatorships during World War II. They are contemptuous of diplomacy, which they liken to *Neville Chamberlain's policy of appeasement*.

The allusion to *Neville Chamberlain*'s policy of appeasement implies

that _____

_____.

5. Her husband disappeared for two years and then turned up one day expecting to be treated like the *prodigal son.*

The allusion to the *prodigal son* suggests that _____

_____.

6. When it comes to politics, Lyndon Johnson had a *Trumanesque* style that might have won him fans had he not been following in the footsteps of the glamorous and sophisticated John F. Kennedy.

The allusion to *Trumanesque* implies that _____

_____.

7. Sex offenders cannot erase their crimes by a jail sentence or good behavior. No matter what they do, they forever wear the *mark of Cain.*

The allusion to the *mark of Cain* implies that _____

_____.

8. When it comes to government spending on social programs, the candidate rivals *F.D.R.*

The allusion to *F.D.R.* implies that _____

_____.

9. To block damaging viruses and prevent hackers from gaining access to their files, computer users can load *Iron Curtain*–like software security programs on their systems.

The allusion to an *Iron Curtain* implies that _____

_____.

10. The Hundred Years' War between England and France began in 1337 and finally ended in 1453. Despite the conflict's name, however, fighting was not actually continuous for 116 years. Fighting was interspersed with extended periods of *Cold War* and even periods of peace.

The allusion to *Cold War* implies that _____

_____.

C H A P T E R 3

Reviewing the Essentials

> **In this chapter, you will learn**
>
> - **how to zero in on the essential elements of a paragraph: the topic, main idea, and supporting details.**
> - **how transitions help direct readers to topic sentences and supporting details.**
> - **how supporting details further explain or prove topic sentences.**

Overall, the explanations in *Reading for Thinking* assume you know how to *analyze*, or break down, a paragraph into its essential elements. Still it doesn't hurt to review the steps involved in pulling meaning from a paragraph. This chapter provides a brief review of how to make sure you and the author don't part company, with you assuming one meaning and the author intending another. It also tells you more about what introductory sentences and transitions add to paragraphs. Lastly, you'll get a chance to review and refine your ability to paraphrase and summarize.

Using Questions to Get to the Heart of a Paragraph

There are certainly going to be times when you read a paragraph, and the point of the paragraph seems to jump out at you. At moments like these, you know immediately what the author wanted to say to readers, and you don't have to consciously think about it. There will be other times, however, when the topic is so unfamiliar or the writer's style so complicated that you will have to think your way through the paragraph step by step. The explanation that follows is designed for precisely those moments.

Start with the Topic

To find the topic of a paragraph, ask yourself this question: "Which person, event, practice, theory, or idea is most frequently mentioned or referred to in the paragraph?" To illustrate, let's use the following:

> The use of animals in scientific research is a controversial subject that provokes strong emotions on both sides. Animal rights activists define animals as sentient* beings who can think, feel, and suffer. They insist, therefore, that the rights of animals be acknowledged and respected. The more conservative animal rights activists argue that the use of animals in research should be strictly monitored, while the more radical activists insist that research using animals should be banned altogether. In response to these objections, research scientists who experiment on animals have reorganized their research to take better care of the animals involved. They argue, however, that research on animals is ethical and necessary because it saves human lives and alleviates* human suffering.

What is the topic of this paragraph? Is it "animal rights activists" or the "use of animals in research"? If you said it was the "use of animals in research," you are right. That's the topic because it's the subject most frequently mentioned or referred to by the author. True, the phrase "animal rights activists" is mentioned or referred to several times but not as frequently as the phrase "use of animals in research."

---

*sentient: aware; possessed of consciousness.
*alleviates: relieves; eliminates.

Putting the Topic into Words

Notice the number of words needed to express the topic—five, to be exact. Occasionally, the topic of a paragraph can be expressed in a single word. However, you will frequently need a longer phrase to sum up the **precise topic**, i.e., the one that will lead you most directly to the author's **main idea**, or key point.

Look, for instance, at the following paragraph. What's the topic here?

Although the fighting took place far from the United States, the Vietnam War[†] deeply affected the way Americans lived their lives. Military service became an important, life-changing experience for more than two million Americans. In the typical tour of duty, soldiers encountered racial tensions, boredom, drugs, and a widespread brutality against the Vietnamese. Even those Americans who did not fight were changed by the war. Millions of young men spent a substantial part of their late adolescence or young adulthood wondering whether they would be drafted or seeking ways to avoid participation in the fighting. Far more men did not go to Vietnam than went, but the war created deep divisions among people of an entire generation. Those who fought in the war often resented those who did not. By the same token, some people who never went to Vietnam sometimes treated those who did with pity or condescension.[*] (Adapted from Schaller, Scharf, and Schulzinger, *Present Tense*, p. 301.)

Here again, no single word could effectively sum up the topic. The word *Americans* won't do. Nor will the phrase "Vietnam War." To express the thrust of the paragraph, we need phrases like "the effect of the Vietnam War on American life" or "the Vietnam War's effect on Americans." Note, too, that the words in these topics don't appear next to each other in the paragraph. Both topics were created by combining words from different parts of the paragraph and, in one case, adding the word *life*.

Keep in mind that the topic might well be expressly stated in the paragraph, but it doesn't have to be. Frequently, readers have to **synthesize**, or combine, different words in the paragraph to determine a topic that helps you unlock paragraph meaning. To be useful, the topic you select or create should be general enough to include everything discussed in the paragraph. At the same time, it should be specific enough to exclude what isn't.

[†]Vietnam War: a long civil war in Vietnam (1954–1975) that involved both France and the United States.
[*]condescension: behaving as if one were superior in some way.

EXERCISE 1 **DIRECTIONS** Read each paragraph. Then circle the letter of the correct topic.

1. According to the attachment theory of love, adults are characterized, in their romantic relationships, by one of three styles. *Secure lovers* are happy when others feel close to them. Mutual dependency in a relationship (each partner depends on the other) feels right to them. Secure lovers do not fear abandonment. In contrast, *avoidant lovers* are uncomfortable feeling close to another person or having that person feel close to them. It is difficult for avoidant lovers to trust or depend on a partner. The third type, *anxious-ambivalent lovers*, want desperately to get close to a partner but often find that the partner does not reciprocate the feeling, perhaps because anxious-ambivalent lovers scare away others. They are insecure in the relationship, worrying that the partner does not really love them. Research on the attachment theory shows that about 53 percent of adults are secure, 26 percent are avoidant, and 20 percent are anxious-ambivalent.

Topic a. mutual dependency in a relationship

b. attachment theory of love

c. secure lovers

2. Conjoined twins are usually classified into three basic categories, depending on where their bodies connect. Twins of the first type are conjoined in a way that never involves the heart or the midline of the body. For example, about 2 percent of all conjoined twins are attached at the head only. About 19 percent are joined at the buttocks. Twins of the second type are always joined in a way that involves the midline of the body. Many twins joined at the midline share a heart. Around 35 percent are fused together at the upper half of the trunk. Another 30 percent are joined at the lower half of their bodies. The third major type of conjoined twins includes very rare forms of physical connection. In this category are those in which one twin is smaller, less formed, and dependent on the other, as well as cases in which one twin is born completely within the body of his or her sibling.

Topic a. twins sharing a heart

b. twins

c. conjoined twins

3. Not too long ago, people made friends or started romances face-to-face. They met in school, at work, in bars, or through sports and mutual acquaintances. In 2002, though, an Internet social network service called Friendster was founded, and the process of developing relationships changed forever. Like the similar Facebook and MySpace sites that followed in its footsteps, Friendster gave each participant a free webpage on which to describe interests, opinions, and goals. Along with posting photographs or even video and audio files, it also allowed members to communicate with one another via e-mail or instant messaging. After the person in search of new friends first selected social search criteria such as age, hobbies, marital status, geographic location, or career field, the computer searched the profiles of the other members and provided a list of those with matching characteristics. The searcher could then browse these profiles and send messages to start a conversation with anyone who seemed interesting. Members loved this new way to expand their social networks, even if they never did meet some of their "friends" face to face. (Source of information: Simon Garfield, "How to Make 80 Million Friends and Influence People," *The Observer*, June 18, 2006, http://observer.guardian.co.uk/review/story/0,,1799881,00.html.)

Topic   a. friendship

b. dating rituals past and present

c. making friends in cyberspace

4. When her soldier-fiancé died in World War I, the British adventurer Gertrude Bell lost the chance of a husband. But as war often does with women, World War I gave Bell new ideas about how she wished to live her life. Extraordinarily independent even before the war, Bell, born to wealth, had done a good deal of amateur archaeology and traveled throughout the region the British then called Arabia (what we now call the Middle East). She took her first trip in 1900, and by 1912, she had returned six times. When the war came, she was an expert on all things related to the Arab people and their cultures. Few people, male or female, knew the land the way she did, and the British wanted maps for their attack on the city. (Because the British had changed from coal-burning to oil-burning battleship engines in 1911, the government needed to gain control of Baghdad's oil fields.) Thus the British government relied on Bell's expertise in its invasion of Baghdad. Bell's knowledge of the region proved invaluable, and after the invasion the government gave her an official position as a liaison between the Iraqi sheiks and the British government. While the British despised the Iraqis and spent the next forty years putting down rebellions, Bell never lost her admiration for the country or its people. She made Baghdad her home, organizing elections, writing a constitution, and founding the National Museum.

Topic a. women explorers in the British government

b. the British invasion of Baghdad

c. Gertrude Bell's knowledge of the Arab countries

 # Using the Topic to Discover the Main Idea

Once you know the topic of a paragraph, the next logical step is to determine the main idea. The main idea is the key point or central message of the paragraph. It's what unites, or ties together, all the sentences in the paragraph. Most paragraphs lacking a main idea end up being little more than collections of unrelated thoughts.[†]

To discover the main idea of a paragraph, you need to ask two more questions: (1) What does the author want to say *about* the topic? and (2) What one idea is developed throughout most of the paragraph?

Let's use the passage below as an example. The subject that recurs throughout the paragraph is "energy shortages." Now we just have to determine what the author is saying *about* that topic. Read the paragraph and see what you think.

> In the very near future, the world will face an energy shortage of extraordinary proportions. By the year 2040, the total population on Earth is expected to double to about 10 billion people. With the continued industrialization of Asia, Africa, and the Americas, world energy consumption is expected to triple. At that rate of consumption, the world's known oil supply will be depleted in about sixty years. The supply of gas will be depleted in about 100 years. If we are to maintain an acceptable quality of life, we must find new sources of energy that will make up for the shortages that are bound to occur in the coming decades.

If you go through the paragraph sentence by sentence, you'll see that each one further develops the point made in the first sentence: We're facing an energy shortage that's likely to arrive very soon.

[†]The exception would be scientific description paragraphs, which are meant to give readers the key characteristics of a theory, a thing, or an event.

This main idea is developed not just in the opening sentence but throughout the entire paragraph.

Check Your Understanding

Explain the difference between the topic and the main idea of a paragraph.

_____

_____

_____

EXERCISE 2 **DIRECTIONS** Read each paragraph. Then circle the letters that identify the topic and the main idea.

1. Impatient for victory as World War II dragged on, American leaders began to plan a fall invasion of the Japanese islands, an expedition that was sure to incur high casualties. But the successful development of an atomic bomb by American scientists provided another route to victory in World War II. The secret atomic program, known as the Manhattan Project, began in August 1942 and cost $2 billion. The first bomb was exploded in the desert near Alamogordo, New Mexico, on July 16, 1945. Only three weeks later, on August 6, the Japanese city of Hiroshima was destroyed by a bomb dropped from an American B-29 airplane called the *Enola Gay.* A flash of dazzling light shot across the sky; then, a huge purplish mushroom cloud boiled 40,000 feet into the atmosphere. Dense smoke, swirling fires, and suffocating dust soon engulfed the ground for miles. Much of the city was leveled almost instantly. Approximately 130,000 people were killed; tens of thousands more suffered severe burns and nuclear poisoning. On August 9, another atomic bomb flattened the city of Nagasaki, killing at least 60,000 people. Four days later, the Japanese, who had been sending out peace feelers since June, surrendered. Formal surrender ceremonies were held September 2 on the battleship *Missouri.* (Norton et al., *A People and a Nation*, p. 827.)

Topic a. the invasion of Japan

b. the atomic bomb

c. World War II

Main Idea a. Desperate for a victory, American leaders planned an invasion of the Japanese islands.

b. The atomic bomb gave the American forces another way to bring World War II to an end.

c. The question of whether the United States had to use the atomic bomb to end World War II is still the subject of debate.

d. Rather than dropping the atomic bomb, the United States should have invaded Japan.

 2. People have many different reasons for wanting children. Some really like children and want an opportunity to be involved with their care. Some women strongly desire the experience of pregnancy and childbirth. Many young adults see parenthood as a way to demonstrate their adult status. For people coming from happy families, having children is a means of reliving their earlier happiness. For those from unhappy families, it can be a means of doing better than their parents did. Some people have children simply because it's expected of them. Because society places so much emphasis on the fulfillment motherhood is supposed to bring, some women who are unsure of what they want to do with their lives use having a child as a way to create an identity. (Seifert et al., *Lifespan Development*, p. 484.)

Topic a. childhood

b. reasons for having children

c. parenting and past experience

Main Idea a. Some people have children to recreate the happiness they themselves experienced growing up.

b. There are several reasons why people have children.

c. Most people don't know why they have children; they just do what's expected of them.

d. Society places too much emphasis on the fulfillment motherhood is supposed to bring.

3. Most people know the name of César Chávez, the deservedly famous founder of the United Farm Workers (UFW)[†] union. Not so many people, however, know the name of Dolores Huerta (1930–), the woman who helped Chávez start the United Farm Workers union. Yet Huerta was a key figure in the UFW's early achievements,

---

[†]United Farm Workers: originally the National Farm Workers Association.

and both she and her role in the union are worthy of more recognition than they have so far received. Huerta's father had been a migrant worker, a union activist, and, ultimately a member of the New Mexico state legislature, so it's not surprising that his daughter would be drawn to union activity and political activism. By the time she had reached her twenties, Huerta was working with the Agricultural Worker's Organizing Committee, which is what brought her together with Chávez. Highly effective as an organizer, Huerta was Chávez's second-in-command, and she played a crucial role in the 1968–1969 grape boycott, which brought the once arrogant grape farm owners to their knees, establishing the UFW as a force to be reckoned with. Throughout the 1970s, Huerta was involved in the political arm of the UFW and played a critical role lobbying for farm worker legislative protections. She remained active in the cause of migrant workers throughout the 1980s and 1990s, despite being critically injured by police during a 1988 political demonstration.

Topic a. Dolores Huerta's relationship to her father

b. Dolores Huerta's relationship to César Chávez

c. Dolores Huerta's role in the UFW

Main Idea a. When it came to political activism, Dolores Huerta clearly followed in the footsteps of her extraordinary father.

b. Dolores Huerta continued her fight for social justice despite being badly hurt in a demonstration.

c. The contributions Dolores Huerta made to the cause of migrant workers and the founding of the UFW deserve to be remembered.

d. Although Dolores Huerta made significant contributions to the founding of the UFW, the media concentrated on Chávez as opposed to Huerta, making it seem as if Chávez founded the union all by himself.

4. The zoo industry insists that elephants in zoos throughout the country are well taken care of. Animal rights activists, however, challenge the zoo industry's claims, and there is an angry debate brewing about the health of elephants confined in zoos, with the federal government deciding to review the animals' situation in confinement. According to Elliot Katz, a veterinarian and president of the California-based organization In Defense of Animals, "the state of elephant health in the U.S. is appallingly poor." Katz claims that experts in the field believe elephants should not be walking back and forth on concrete floors. Their feet are designed to walk for miles on soil, not back and forth on cold concrete. Katz would seem to know whereof he speaks because in 2006 a number of zoo-held elephants died from complications brought on by sore feet. Members of the zoo industry, however, consider the deaths exceptions. Willie Theisscon, head elephant keeper at the Pittsburgh Zoo, argues that elephants dying of foot complications are probably older animals—elephants can live into their sixties—and probably came from facilities where their feet were injured. But he insists that almost all such facilities have been upgraded so that the problem no longer exists. (Source of information: www.idausa.org/.)

Topic a. the treatment of animals by zoos

  b. elephants in the wild versus elephants in zoos

  c. zoo industry's treatment of elephants

Main Idea a. The zoo industry has been viciously attacked by animal rights activists who claim zoos are killing the elephants they are supposed to protect.

  b. No matter what the conditions, elephants are animals that cannot accustom themselves to life in a zoo.

  c. Animal rights activists and the zoo industry are in a heated debate about whether elephants in zoos are dying because the zoos do not take proper care of the animals.

  d. Animal rights activists have correctly identified a serious danger to elephants in zoos—the miles they walk on concrete floors are harmful to their feet.

 # Look for Topic Sentences

Topic sentences are general sentences that sum up main ideas in paragraphs. While not all paragraphs contain topic sentences, many do. This is particularly true of textbooks, where authors want to make sure readers understand the point of each paragraph. Because topic sentences are so common in textbooks, it's in your interest to know what kinds of sentences fit that label.

As their name implies, topic sentences make a comment or point about the topic of the paragraph. They tell readers what the author wants to say *about* the topic. For instance, the topic of paragraph 2 on page 101 was "conjoined twins." The topic sentence, in turn, made a claim about twins who are born with their bodies joined together: "Conjoined twins are usually classified into three basic categories, depending on where their bodies connect." Similarly, on page 101, the topic of paragraph 1 was "the attachment theory of love," while the topic sentence offered this comment: "According to the attachment theory of love, adults are characterized, in their romantic relationships, by one of three styles."

In searching for the topic sentence, always look for a general sentence that is developed in more specific detail by the remaining sentences in the paragraph. Take, for instance, the following paragraph. Does the author use the second sentence to further explain the first, or does he switch to a different point altogether?

[1]Many people think that talking about *lifestyles*—tastes, preferences, and ways of living—is a trivial pursuit at best. [2]However, studying lifestyle differences reveals a lot about the differences in social classes. [3]Upper- and middle-class people think it important to be active outside their homes—in parent-teacher associations, charitable organizations, and any number of community activities. [4]They are also likely to make friends with colleagues and business associates, inviting them into their homes. [5]Usually, their spouses help cultivate these relationships. [6]In contrast, members of the working class are less likely to be involved in organizations not directly related to their family. [7]They are also less inclined to entertain their coworkers at home, although outings after work for drinks or dinner are common. (Source of information: Thio, *Society: Myths and Realities,* p. 211.)

In this example, the author begins by telling readers that many people don't think lifestyles are an important topic of discussion. But, as you can see, he does not continue that train of thought in the second sentence. Instead, he moves in the opposite direction to develop a different idea altogether: Lifestyles can say a lot about social class. The other sentences then pick up on this point and illustrate it.

Anytime you see this pattern, with the second sentence *not* following up on the first, you can be sure that the topic sentence is *not* the first sentence in the paragraph. A topic sentence, by definition, raises questions in the minds of readers. The remaining sentences then have to further explain it in order to lay those questions to rest. If the second sentence doesn't further develop the first, then the first sentence is not the topic sentence.

The last key characteristic of a topic sentence is this: The topic sentence is the only sentence that can function as a one-sentence summary of the paragraph. The topic sentence is the sentence that can, in brief, answer the question, "What's this paragraph about?"

For instance, consider the paragraph on lifestyles and social class. If you asked the question, "What's this paragraph about?" and answered with sentence 3, "Upper- and middle-class people think it important to be active outside their homes—in parent-teacher associations, charitable organizations, and any number of community activities," you would be misleading the person asking the question. The focus of the paragraph is not just on the middle class. The focus is more general than that, making sentence 2 the only sentence general enough to sum up the paragraph.

Understand the Role of Introductory Sentences

Given the paragraph on class and lifestyle (p. 108), you might now be asking, "When the second sentence is the topic sentence, what role does the first sentence play?" For an answer to that question, read on.

Although the writers of textbooks and reference works usually don't spend much time building up to the main idea, they do sometimes need to pave the way for the topic sentence. When authors feel that a little explanation is necessary before introducing the main idea, they use introductory sentences.

Introductory sentences are general sentences that prepare readers for the topic sentence by doing one or more of the following: (1) providing background information, (2) presenting a traditional point of view that will be challenged in the topic sentence, (3) defining a term central to the topic sentence, (4) offering a brief note about the history behind a person or an issue mentioned in the topic sentence, and (5) catching the reader's interest with a personal anecdote* or joke.

Introductory Sentences and Reversal Transitions

 Here now is another paragraph that opens with an introductory sentence followed by the author's topic sentence.

Introductory Sentence
Topic Sentence
If you miss a few hours of sleep, you may feel a little groggy for the next day but still believe that you can muddle through without difficulty. Yet, perhaps not surprisingly, sleep deprivation is

*anecdote: personal story, which is often humorous.

among the most common causes of motor vehicle accidents. Such accidents are most likely to occur in the early morning hours when drivers are typically at their sleepiest. This makes sense because sleep deprivation slows reaction times and impairs concentration, memory, and problem-solving ability. Thus the effects of sleep deprivation make it more difficult to be a careful driver. (Adapted from Nevid, *Essentials of Psychology*, p. 135.)

If you look at the previous example of a topic sentence in second position (p. 108) and then at this paragraph on sleep deprivation, you will notice that both open with what we can call reversal transitions (*although, yet*). Like all transitions, a **reversal transition** clarifies the relationship between sentences and paragraphs, signaling to the reader what direction the author's train of thought is about to take. Reversal transitions tell readers, "There's a shift coming up. The next sentence you read is going to challenge, modify, or offer a contrast to what you just learned from the previous sentence."

As you may have guessed, reversal transitions frequently appear when the author opens a paragraph with an introductory sentence. In the above paragraph on sleep deprivation, for instance, the author tells readers what people generally think about lost sleep. Then he uses the word *yet* to signal to readers, "What we think about losing sleep is not altogether correct." A reversal transition opening the second sentence of a paragraph is a strong clue that the topic sentence is coming right up.

Reversal Transitions

Actually	Nonetheless
Although	On the contrary
But	On the other hand
Contrary to	Still
Conversely	Unfortunately
Despite the fact	While this might
Even so	seem true [sensible,
However	correct, right, etc.]
In contradiction	Yet
In opposition	Yet in fact
Ironically	Yet, in point of fact,
Just the opposite	Yet in reality

Check Your Understanding

Identify the main characteristics of a topic sentence.

1. _____

2. _____

3. _____

4. _____

5. _____

The next section of this chapter will show you more topic sentence locations. For now, though, here is an exercise in which the topic sentence is in the first or second position. Restricting the topic sentence locations in this way allows you to clearly see the difference between introductory and topic sentences.

EXERCISE 3 **DIRECTIONS** Read each paragraph. Then circle *a* or *b* to identify the topic sentence.

1. On May 22, 1964, President Lyndon Johnson announced to the American public his determination to create a "Great Society" that would forever eliminate poverty and injustice. In pursuit of his Great Society, President Johnson decided to implement two new programs (Medicare and Medicaid), which would guarantee basic health insurance to all older adult and low-income Americans. Initially, Johnson's proposal met with opposition from interest groups like the American Medical Association. Thus Congress was nervous about approving funding for the programs and angering special-interest groups. But Johnson, whose powers of political persuasion were legendary on Capitol Hill, persuaded Congress to pass the necessary legislation. Medicare was authorized by the Social Security Act of 1965. Medicaid came into being through Title XIX of the Social Security Act. Both programs are still in existence today and, for many, they are the only sources of basic health care coverage.

   a. The first sentence is the topic sentence.

   b. The second sentence is the topic sentence.

2. The letters and journals of America's early Pilgrims are filled with complaints about food or, more precisely, about the lack of it. The first settlers, so adventurous when it came to travel, were amazingly

slow to recognize that seventeenth-century America offered almost every kind of food imaginable; it just wasn't the same food they were used to eating at home. No, there wasn't much mutton, or lamb, to be had, but there were lobsters in abundance, along with oysters, duck, salmon, scallops, clams, and mussels. There were also sweet and white potatoes, peanuts, squash, green beans, strawberries, and tomatoes. Luckily for the settlers, the Indians in the New World grew and relished all of these foods and taught the Pilgrims to do the same. Still it took a while for the Pilgrims to develop a taste for the new fare. During their first years in New England, for instance, the English settlers refused to eat clams or mussels. Because they hadn't eaten them in the Old World, in the new one they fed them to the pigs. No wonder their Native-American neighbors often looked on in amazement or maybe it was amusement.

a. The first sentence is the topic sentence.

b. The second sentence is the topic sentence.

3. Much evidence in the English language implies that weddings are more important to women than to men. A woman cherishes the wedding and is considered a bride for a whole year, but a man is referred to as a groom only on the day of the wedding. The word *bride* appears in *bridal attendant, bridal gown, bridesmaid, bridal shower,* and even *bridegroom. Groom* comes from the Middle English *grom,* meaning "man," but that meaning of the word is seldom used outside the context of the wedding. With most pairs of male/female words, people habitually put the masculine word first—*Mr. and Mrs., his and hers, boys and girls, men and women, kings and queens, brothers and sisters, guys and dolls,* and *host and hostess*—but it is the *bride and groom* who are talked about, not the *groom and bride.* (Adapted from Nilsen, *About Language,* p. 251.)

a. The first sentence is the topic sentence.

b. The second sentence is the topic sentence.

4. Obesity is viewed as a serious health problem for a number of different reasons. For one thing, researchers have discovered that body fat produces proteins that trigger inflammation, thus contributing to the development of heart disease, stroke, and diabetes. In fact, gaining just 10 pounds increases one's risk of heart disease and stroke considerably. And gaining 11 to 18 pounds actually doubles an individual's risk of developing diabetes. Also, fat cells secrete estrogen, a hormone that contributes to the development of breast cancer. Research has shown that women who gain more than 20 pounds double their risk of getting breast cancer. Weight gain also increases the risk of developing colon, kidney, and gall-bladder cancer. Clearly, fat does not just lie harmlessly inert* in the body. On the contrary, fat cells pump out substances that alter the body's chemistry, affect major organs, and contribute to disease. (Source of information: Nancy Shute, "Why That Beer Belly Is a Killer," *U.S. News & World Report,* February 9, 2004, p. 55.)

a. The first sentence is the topic sentence.

b. The second sentence is the topic sentence.

5. Desperately in need of more soldiers in 1863, two years before the Civil War ended, the Union government issued a new and stricter draft law. However, although Union officials knew that the new law would cause grumbling among the country's male citizens, they never expected New York City, a center of abolitionist* support, to explode in five days of rioting, now known as the Civil War Draft Riots. According to the new law, all white American males between ages 20 and 35 were eligible for the draft; so too were all unmarried men between 35 and 45. The catch was that those who could afford it could buy their way out of the draft. Anyone who could come up with three hundred dollars—for the time, an enormous sum—could escape the draft's clutches. For members of the poor and working classes, this was another way of saying that poor men would be drafted while rich ones would remain safely at home. Those who couldn't afford to buy their way out of the draft had their names entered into a lottery. If their names were selected, they would be marched off to battle, no excuses accepted. On July 11, 1863, the first draft lottery took place in New York City, and for twenty-four hours the city remained quiet. Then suddenly on Monday, July 13, the poorer neighborhoods exploded. In the first day of rioting, urban mobs targeted only government buildings considered to be symbols of the draft law's injustice. But as the mobs grew bigger and more furious, they harassed, beat, and, in some cases, lynched any black male who crossed their path. They also attacked those white men and women known to support the abolitionist cause. Abby Hopper Gibbons, the daughter of abolitionist Isaac Hopper, had her house torched.

a. The first sentence is the topic sentence.

b. The second sentence is the topic sentence.

---

*inert: without moving; lifeless.
*abolitionist: refers to those men and women who challenged the institution of slavery.

More About Topic Sentence Locations

Some authors postpone introducing the topic sentence until the second or third sentence in a paragraph. Sometimes they hold off introducing the topic sentence until they are in the middle of the paragraph, as in this next example:

¹In general, bats have a varied diet. ²Flowers, insects, and fish are among their favorite foods. ³Some bats, however, really are like the bats in horror movies. ⁴They do, indeed dine on blood. ⁵<u>Contrary to their onscreen image, however, these so-called vampire bats don't attack and kill humans.</u> ⁶They get their dinner from sleeping livestock. ⁷Under the cover of darkness, they make small, pinprick incisions with their razor-sharp teeth. ⁸Then they drink their fill from their sleeping prey. ⁹Vampire bats are so skillful at getting their dinner, they usually don't even wake the sleeping animals.

In this paragraph, the author uses several sentences to introduce the topic—vampire bats—leaving the topic sentence to appear in sentence 5, the middle of the paragraph.

Topic Sentences at the End

Sometimes authors wait until the last sentence to introduce the main idea. Instead of starting with the topic sentence, they build up to it with a series of specific examples, as shown in the following paragraph:

¹In China, blogger Shi Tao was sentenced to ten years in prison after his blog sent out details of how the government planned to handle the fifteenth anniversary of the Tiananmen Square massacre,* during which protestors were killed or imprisoned because of their public demands for a more democratic government. ²According to Reporters Without Borders, Yahoo!, the Internet service provider for Shi's e-mail, helped the government link Shi's account to the offending messages. ³In Iran, Kianoosh Sanjar was arrested for using his blog to provide details about the arrest of dissidents* by the Iranian government. ⁴Amnesty International claims that Sanjar is being held incommunicado* and is at risk of being tortured. ⁵In Tunisia, after Mohammad Abbou posted a series of articles denouncing the government's torture of political prisoners, he was arrested and sentenced to four years in prison.

---

*massacre: slaughter of many innocent people.
*dissidents: people who protest or disagree.
*incommunicado: incapable of being found; unavailable.

Topic Sentence

[6]Similar incidents have taken place in Vietnam. [7]When Nguyen Vu Binh wrote a series of articles demanding more political and economic freedom for Vietnamese citizens, he found himself sentenced to seven years in prison. [8]<u>In the United States, bloggers are sometimes harshly criticized for their frequently outspoken, even impolite expressions of opinion concerning political figures and government policies; however, countries that don't cherish freedom of expression go a lot further in their determination to make bloggers toe the line.</u> (Source of information: www.independent .co.uk/world/science_technology/article1932749.ece.)

Question-and-Answer Topic Sentences

Particularly in textbooks, authors are fond of posing questions at the start of a paragraph. If the answer follows the question, it is usually the topic sentence.

Topic Sentence

What is genetics? <u>In its simplest form, genetics is the study of heredity, and it explains how certain characteristics are passed on from parents to children.</u> Much of what we know about genetics was discovered by the monk Gregor Mendel in the nineteenth century. Since then, the field of genetics has vastly expanded. As scientists study the workings of genetics, they've developed new ways of manipulating genes. For example, scientists have isolated the gene that makes insulin, a human hormone, and now use bacteria to make quantities of it. (Magliore, *Cracking the AP Biology Exam,* p. 105.)

Check Your Understanding
1. To find the topic, ask:
2. To discover the main idea, ask:
3. To check that you have correctly identified the topic sentence, ask:

EXERCISE 4 **DIRECTIONS** Read each paragraph and then write the number of the topic sentence in the blank. Circle any reversal transitions introducing the topic sentences.

1. [1]Compared with a corporate executive or a military officer, a teacher may not appear to have a great deal of power. [2]But teachers have a special type of power. [3]Henry Adams[†] caught the sense of the teacher's *long-term* power in the words "A teacher affects eternity: No one can tell where his influence stops." [4]The teacher's powerful influence arises from the fact that he or she has an impact on people when they are still at a very impressionable stage. [5]Teachers take "a piece of living clay and gently form it, day by day." [6]Many careers are open to you, but few offer such truly inspiring power. (Adapted from Ryan and Cooper, *Those Who Can, Teach*, p. 148.)

Topic Sentence _____

2. [1]Before the collapse of the Communist party in Eastern Europe, the East German secret police, the *Staatsicherheit* (or Stasi), was an enormous bureaucracy that reached its tentacles into every part of society. [2]It had 85,000 full-time employees, including 6,000 people whose sole task was to listen in on telephone conversations. [3]Another 2,000 steamed open mail, read it, resealed the letters, and sent them on to the intended recipients. [4]The Stasi also employed 150,000 active informers and hundreds of thousands of part-time snitches. [5]Files were kept on an estimated 4 to 5 million people in a country that had a total population, including children, of just 17 million. [6]Although East Germany had a large standing army, the Stasi kept its own arsenal of 250,000 weapons. (Adapted from Janda et al., *The Challenge of Democracy*, p. 452.)

Topic Sentence _____

3. [1]What causes plants to bloom? [2]Although you may think that plants flower based on the amount of sunlight they receive, they actually bloom according to the amount of uninterrupted darkness; this principle of plant bloom is called *photoperiodism*. [3]Plants that bloom in late summer and fall, like asters and sedum, are called short-day plants. [4]They require long periods of darkness and only short periods of light. [5]Plants that flower in late spring and early

---

[†]Henry Adams: American historian (1838–1918).

summer, such as daisies and poppies, are called long-day plants. [6]They need only short periods of darkness to blossom.

Topic Sentence _____

4. [1]On May 28, 1934, Elzire Dionne gave birth to five daughters who became famous as the Dionne Quintuplets. [2]Their birth made immediate headlines and was celebrated as a medical miracle. [3]Unfortunately, the little girls' fame was their downfall; almost from the moment of birth, they were exploited by everyone around them. [4]The parents of the quintuplets were poor and didn't know how to support their family, which already included six children. [5]Confused and desperate, they agreed to put their five daughters on display at the Chicago World's Fair. [6]For a brief moment, it seemed as if the girls were saved from a miserable fate when the family physician, Dr. Allan Roy Dafoe, stepped in and insisted the girls were too frail to be on exhibit. [7]But after Dafoe took control of the girls' lives, he made himself rich by displaying the quintuplets to tourists and collecting fees for product endorsements.

Topic Sentence _____

5. [1]George W. Bush is only the second man after John Quincy Adams to follow in the footsteps of his father and serve as president of the United States. [2]John Quincy Adams, America's sixth president, was the son of second president John Adams. [3]As a matter of fact, the elder George Bush calls his son "Quincy." [4]George W. Bush and John Quincy Adams share other similarities, too. [5]Both men are their fathers' oldest sons. [6]Both men held public office before being elected president. [7]Adams was a U.S. senator and served as secretary of state, while Bush was governor of Texas. [8]Both men were in their fifties when they successfully ran for president. [9]Both men also achieved the presidency in a contested election because neither of them had won the popular vote.

Topic Sentence _____

6. [1]On the surface, effective listening might seem to require little more than an acute sense of hearing. [2]But, in fact, there's a big difference between hearing and listening. [3]*Hearing* occurs when sound waves travel through the air, enter your ears, and are transmitted by the auditory nerve to your brain. [4]As long as neither your brain nor your ears are impaired, hearing is involuntary. [5]It occurs spontaneously with little conscious effort on your part. [6]*Listening*, in contrast, is a voluntary act that includes attending to, understanding,

and evaluating the words or sounds you hear. [7]If you sit through a lecture without making an effort to listen, there's a good chance that the speaker's words will become just so much background noise. (Flemming and Leet, *Becoming a Successful Student*, p. 93.)

Topic Sentence _____

7. [1]When we are extremely fearful or angry, our heartbeat speeds up, our pulse races, and our breathing rate tends to increase. [2]The body's metabolism accelerates, burning up sugar in the bloodstream and fats in the tissues at a faster rate. [3]The salivary glands become less active, making the mouth feel dry. [4]The sweat glands may overreact, producing a dripping forehead, clammy hands, and "cold sweat." [5]Finally, the pupils may enlarge, producing the wide-eyed look that is characteristic of both terror and rage. [6]In effect, strong emotions are not without consequences; they bring about powerful changes in our bodies. (Rubin et al., *Psychology*, p. 370.)

Topic Sentence _____

8. [1]Scientists believe that the probable maximum human life span is about 150 years; the record of the oldest person to date is Shigechiyo Izumi (1865–1986) of Japan, who lived to be 120 years and 237 days. [2]There are two theories as to why all living things grow old and die. [3]The *free-radical theory* states that free radicals, certain chemicals produced as a by-product of biological activity, are particularly harmful to healthy cells. [4]As a person ages, free radicals gradually destroy cells until they can no longer function properly, causing the entire body (especially whole organ systems such as the kidneys or heart) to break down and die. [5]The *programmed senescence theory* suggests that the rate at which we age is predetermined, and that our genetic makeup controls the aging and death of the cells. [6]After enough of the cells die, the organs cease to function and death occurs. (Barnes-Svarney, ed., "Theories on Aging," *New York Public Library Science Desk Reference*, p. 161.)

Topic Sentence _____

9. [1]In 1919, President Woodrow Wilson was serving his second term in office. [2]Suddenly, without warning, in September of that year, he suffered a near-fatal stroke, which left him partially paralyzed and nearly blind. [3]When the president's doctors told Edith Wilson that her husband would recover faster if he stayed in office rather than resigning, she made a decision. [4]For more than six months, Edith Wilson concealed the seriousness of her husband's condition by running the country for him, thereby earning her nickname as "the secret president." [5]Edith read all of the documents sent to her husband for his signature and made the decision about which ones would be brought to his attention and which not. [6]When the president seemed too ill to concentrate, she took charge and made decisions for him, communicating those decisions to his staff. [7]Wilson never fully recovered and, in 1921, at the end of his presidential term, Woodrow and Edith retired. [8]In 1924, after living three more years in virtual seclusion, President Woodrow Wilson died. [9]Edith lived to be eighty-nine years old and died in 1961.

Topic Sentence _____

10. [1]Recalling his first visit to Miami in 1948, author Isaac Bashevis Singer wrote, "Miami Beach resembled a small Israel. . . . Yiddish resounded around us in accents as thick as those you would hear in Tel Aviv.[†]" [2]Today's Miami, however, is more Havana than Tel Aviv. [3]In 2000, 57 percent of the 2.3 million residents of Miami–Dade County were Hispanic, most of them Cuban Americans who had fled their island country en masse after Fidel Castro seized power in 1959. [4]By 1973, three hundred thousand had settled in Greater Miami. [5]Thousands more, who left Cuba with Castro's approval, arrived in 1980. [6]Far from being a struggling minority, Miami's Cuban Americans have created a confident, fully developed ethnic community, which influences not only the city's cultural atmosphere but also its political and economic agenda. (Adapted from Boyer, *Enduring Vision*, p. 984.)

Topic Sentence _____

Check Your Understanding
Define the following five terms.
Topic: _____
_____
Main idea: _____
_____

[†]Tel Aviv is the capital of Israel.

Topic sentence:_____

_____

Introductory sentence:_____

_____

Reversal transition: _____

_____

 For more on main ideas and topic sentences, go to **laflemm.com**. Click on *Reading for Thinking*: *Key Concepts*.

 ## Paraphrasing Topic Sentences

When it comes to taking notes or remembering what you read, the ability to paraphrase topic sentences is crucial. Accurately paraphrasing the topic sentence is proof you have understood the general meaning of the passage, so what better place to review paraphrasing than here. The first exercise asks you to choose the best paraphrase; the second to create your own.

EXERCISE 5   DIRECTIONS   Read the paragraph and look closely at the underlined topic sentence. Then circle the letter of the best paraphrase of the topic sentence. *Note*: The paraphrases in this exercise are more complete than the ones introduced in Chapter 1. They are closer to the kinds of paraphrases you might do for a paper.

1. ¹When the Revolutionary War ended in 1783, the thirteen states then in existence established a permanent government. ²That first post–Revolutionary War government took the form of a confederation—a loosely united organization of the thirteen states—which allowed Congress to do two things without the approval of the states: conduct foreign affairs and establish weights and measurements. ³While the early confederation protected the monarchy-weary states against any oppression by a centralized power, the looseness and

lack of a central governing authority had some serious consequences. [4]Each state had its own taxes and currencies, making it
all but impossible to conduct interstate commerce. [5]There was also
no central body capable of collecting money through taxes. [6]Nor
was there a central authority with the power to form a militia if the
country were under threat unless, of course, all members of the
confederation agreed to one. [7]Not surprisingly, finding a point of
complete agreement among the thirteen members of the confederation was no easy task. (Source of information: www.salemwitchtrials
.com/history/1783-1800.)

Paraphrase a. The Articles of Confederation gave America's early government
what little organization the individual states would submit to.

b. From the very beginning, the United States has been torn
between the need for a central government and the desire of the
individual states to maintain their autonomy.

c. Lacking any real power, Congress in the early years of the U.S.
government accomplished nothing of any importance.

d. Although America's early confederation form of government protected the states from the tyranny of an oppressive government,
it also created a number of difficulties.

2. [1]If you have ever lived in the country, you are probably familiar with
the croaking sound frogs make in the night. [2]For many country
dwellers, it's a comforting sound, a sign that the city has been left far
behind. [3]But unless strong action is taken immediately, the croaking
of frogs might not be a sound anyone hears ten years from now. [4]All
the evidence suggests that frogs and others in the class known as
amphibia—for example, salamanders and toads—are threatened by
extinction. [5]There are already reports that two-thirds of several
amphibian species in Central and South America have vanished. [6]The
twin causes of the amphibians' demise are pollution and humans
invading their natural habitats. [7]Among the amphibians, though,
frogs—the most populous group in the class—are under special
attack. [8]For years now, the chytrid fungus has been spreading
around the world leaving dead frogs in its path. [9]The fungus coats the
frogs' skin, closing off their pores. [10]As a result, the frogs have trouble breathing and absorbing water. [11]Ultimately, they die of dehydra-
tion and suffocation. [12]In an effort to save frogs and other
amphibians, conservationists have founded Amphibian Ark, a project
that contacts zoos around the globe and asks them to adopt and care
for at least 500 members of the amphibian class. (Source of information: http://science.howstuffworks.com/bye-bye-kermie.htm.)

Paraphrase a. The comforting sound of frogs croaking in the night is a familiar sound to anyone who has lived in the country.

b. The class of animals known as *amphibia* are under the threat of extinction.

c. The class of animals known as *amphibia* includes salamanders.

d. Many different species are currently under threat of extinction.

EXERCISE 6 **DIRECTIONS** Read each paragraph and underline the topic sentence. Then paraphrase it in the blanks that follow. *Note*: For the purposes of this exercise, paraphrase in complete sentences as if you were paraphrasing for a term paper.

EXAMPLE <u>¹In an attempt to solve the problem of bullying in the schools, a number of elementary and middle schools around the country are making a serious effort to find a solution.</u> ²At the administrative level, supervisors and principals are sending out questionnaires, asking students if they have ever been bullied. ³The goal of the questionnaire is to determine the incidence of bullying behavior in a particular school. ⁴Administrators are also increasing student supervision in places like the playground and the cafeteria, where trouble is likely to arise. ⁵They are also asking teachers to actively patrol the halls and be alert to signs of bullying. ⁶In the classroom, teachers are discussing the subject with students and asking them to write about what causes some students to bully others.

Paraphrase *Nationwide, elementary and middle school administrators are introducing strong measures to combat bullying among students.*

EXPLANATION Every sentence following the first one refers to the "effort" schools are making to stop bullying. Each sentence offers more specific information about what that means in practical terms. Thus sentence 1 is the topic sentence. Like the topic sentence, the paraphrase must indicate the two kinds of schools and the action they are taking against bullying.

1. ¹For many decades, Congress made frequent use of the legislative veto to control presidential actions. ²A legislative veto requires that an executive decision lie before Congress for a specified period (usually thirty or ninety days) before it takes effect. ³Congress could then veto the decision if a resolution of disapproval was passed by either house (a one-house veto) or both houses (a two-house veto). ⁴Unlike laws, such resolutions do not need to be signed by the president. ⁵Between 1932 and 1980 about two hundred laws were

passed providing for a legislative veto, many of them involving presidential proposals to sell arms abroad. (Wilson and Dilulio, *American Government*, p. 429.)

Paraphrase _____

_____

2. [1]Between January and May 2007, beekeepers lost one-quarter of their colonies, which is a lot of bees. [2]Anyone inclined to ho-hum at this information should think again because honeybees are not just important to gardeners, who need bees to pollinate* their flowers; on the contrary, the disappearance of honeybees could cause a food crisis. [3]Honeybees pollinate nuts, avocados, apples, celery, squash, cucumbers, cherries, and blueberries. [4]And that's not even a complete list. [5]Experts estimate that about a third of the human diet is insect-pollinated, and 80 percent of the time, the honeybee is the pollinator of choice. [6]Honeybees are also part of the cycle that brings meat to the table. [7]Cattle feed on alfalfa, and alfalfa crops need bees as pollinators. [8]If scientists can't figure out why honeybees are disappearing, meat eaters might be forced to turn vegetarian at precisely the time when even vegetables are in short supply.

Paraphrase _____

_____

 # The Function of Supporting Details

In addition to main ideas, paragraphs also include major and minor supporting details. **Major supporting details** are the examples, reasons, studies, statistics, facts, and figures that explain, develop, or prove an author's main idea. **Minor supporting details** further explain major details. They supply an interesting fact, tell a story, or add repetition for emphasis.

Because topic sentences are general sentences that sum up or interpret a variety of events, facts, examples, or experiences, they are subject to misunderstanding. Writers, therefore, use supporting details to avoid being misinterpreted or misunderstood. Supporting details are the author's way of saying to readers, "I mean this, not that."

---

*pollinate: fertilize.

For an illustration of supporting details at work, look at the following sentence: "Most people who have survived near-fatal automobile accidents tend to behave in the same fashion." Given only this one sentence, could you be sure you understood the author's message? After all, that sentence could mean different things to different people. Perhaps survivors have nightmares or fears about their health. But then again maybe they just become very slow and careful drivers.

Look now at the following paragraph. Note how the supporting details clarify the author's meaning.

> Most people who have survived near-fatal automobile accidents tend to behave in the same fashion. They are fearful about driving even a mile or two over the speed limit and flatly refuse to go faster than the law allows. If they are not at the wheel, their terror increases. As passengers, they are inclined to be anxious and are prone to offering advice about how to take a curve or when to stop for a light.

In this instance, the supporting details illustrate the three types of behavior that the author has in mind. Those illustrations are the author's way of answering questions such as "What does 'behave in the same fashion' mean?"

Types of Supporting Details

Supporting details can range from reasons and examples to statistics and definitions. The form they take depends on the main idea they serve. Look, for example, at the following paragraph. Here the writer wants to convince readers that a book defending the right to be fat is very much worth reading.

> [1]Marilyn Wann's book *Fat! So?* deserves a large and appreciative audience, one that does not consist solely of those who are overweight. [2]For starters, Wann is refreshingly unembarrassed about being fat (she tips the scales at 270), and that takes courage in a culture as obsessed as ours is with being thin. [3]If anything, the author encourages her readers—in the chapter titled "You, Too, Can Be Flabulous"—to embrace the word *fat* and use it in favorable contexts, such as "You're getting fat; you look great." [4]Yet, despite her lively, and often humorous, style, Wann is good at describing the real misery society inflicts on fat people. [5]Her chapters on the suffering endured by overweight teenagers are particularly moving; and they make a strong case for the need to attack, and attack hard, the tendency to treat the overweight as second-

class citizens. [6]The book is also filled with sound advice about healthy eating habits. [7]Clearly, the author is not encouraging her readers to go out and gorge themselves on pizza and beer. [8]What she is suggesting is that they eat right to get fit, rather than thin. [9]Insisting that some people can, because of heredity, never be anything but overweight, Wann argues that they should not suffer for the genetic hand they've been dealt. [10]On the contrary, they should learn how to flaunt* their excess poundage and make society accept them just as they are.

In this paragraph, the major details all give reasons why Marilyn Wann's book deserves a wide audience. The minor details, in turn, flesh out and emphasize the major ones. Note, too, that at least two of the minor details are as important as the major detail they develop. In sentence 6, the author suggests that Wann's book is good because it offers sound advice about healthy eating. But without the presence of the minor details that follow, it would be hard to understand how a book celebrating fat could also provide tips on healthy eating. Minor details in 7 and 8 help explain this seeming contradiction: Wann's advice focuses on eating to be fit rather than thin.

Minor Details Can Be Meaningful

Readers shouldn't be fooled by the labels *major* and *minor*. Sometimes minor details can be as meaningful as major ones. Therefore, you need to judge them in terms of what they contribute to the major details they modify. If a minor detail simply adds a personal note or provides emphasis, you don't need to think about it much. Above all you certainly don't need to include it in your notes. But if a major detail doesn't make much sense without the minor one that follows, then both details are equally important.

EXERCISE 7 **DIRECTIONS** Read each paragraph and write the number or numbers of the topic sentence in the first blank. Then answer the questions that follow by circling the correct response or filling in the blanks.

EXAMPLE [1]What makes an effective leader? [2]To be sure, no one characteristic or trait defines an effective leader. [3]It is true, however, that effective leaders get the most out of employees or group members by holding them to very high standards or expectations. [4]Setting high standards increases productivity because people tend to live up to the expectations set for them by superiors. [5]This is an

*flaunt: to show off.

example of the *Pygmalion*† effect, which works in a subtle, almost unconscious way. ⁶When a managerial leader believes that a group member will succeed, the manager communicates this belief without realizing that he or she is doing so. ⁷Conversely, when a leader expects a group member to fail, that person will not usually disappoint the manager. ⁸The manager's expectation of success or failure becomes a self-fulfilling prophecy. ⁹Thus it pays for a manager to expect the best from employees. (Adapted from DuBrin, *Leadership*, p. 85.)

a. Topic sentence: ___3___

b. The major details help answer what question or questions about the topic sentence? *Why do effective leaders set such high standards?*

c. *True* or (*False.*) Sentence 5 is a major supporting detail. Explain your answer. *This supporting detail further explains the previous one, making it a minor but far from unimportant detail.*

d. *True* or (*False.*) Sentence 6 is also a major supporting detail. Explain your answer. *The point made in sentence 6 clarifies how the Pygmalion effect functions in a "subtle, almost unconscious way."*

EXPLANATION Sentence 3 answers the opening question and most effectively sums up the paragraph. Explanations for the *true* and *false* answers already appear in the blanks above.

1. ¹Despite its rapid spread, Islam is not a religion for those who are casual about regulations; on the contrary, adhering to its rules takes effort and discipline. ²One must rise before dawn to observe the first of five prayers required daily, none of which can take place without first ritually cleansing oneself. ³Sleep, work, and recre-

---

†Pygmalion: According to myth, Pygmalion, the king of Cyprus, carved and then fell in love with the statue of a woman who was transformed into a human being. The phrase *Pygmalion effect* reflects the myth's suggestion that wishing or believing something can make it happen.

ational activities take second place to prayer. ⁴Fasting for the month of Ramadan,* undertaking the pilgrimage to Mecca at least once in a lifetime, paying tax for relief of the Muslim poor, and accepting Islam's creed require a serious and energetic commitment. ⁵On the whole, the vast majority of Muslims worldwide do observe those tenets.* (Adapted from Goodwin, *Price of Honor,* p. 29.)

a. Topic sentence: _____

b. The major details help answer what question or questions about

the topic sentence? _____

_____

_____

c. *True* or *False.* Sentence 3 is a major supporting detail.

Explain your answer. _____

_____

_____

d. *True* or *False.* Sentence 4 is also a major supporting detail.

Explain your answer. _____

_____

_____

2. ¹The orchestra conductor Arturo Toscanini was born with a phenomenal memory that served him well throughout his career. ²For example, Toscanini could remember every single note of every musical score he had ever studied. ³Once, when he couldn't find a musical score for a performance, he simply wrote it down from memory. ⁴When the score was finally found, it was clear that Toscanini had not made one single error. ⁵When his eyesight failed him late in life, Toscanini conducted all of his concerts from memory. ⁶Audiences agreed that his lack of sight did not in any way hinder the conductor's performance.

a. Topic sentence: _____

_____

*Ramadan: Muslim holy month.
*tenets: rules; principles.

b. The major details help answer what question or questions about

the topic sentence? _____

_____

_____

c. *True* or *False*. Sentence 3 is a major detail.

Explain your answer. _____

_____

_____

d. *True* or *False*. Sentence 6 is a minor detail.

Explain your answer. _____

_____

_____

3. ¹Those cuddly toys known as teddy bears seem to have been around
forever. ²But actually the first teddy bears came into being when President Theodore "Teddy" Roosevelt showed himself too much of a
sportsman to shoot a staked bear cub. ³In 1902, Roosevelt visited Mississippi to settle a border dispute, and his hosts organized a hunting
expedition. ⁴To make sure that the president would remain in a good
mood, they staked a bear cub to the ground so that Roosevelt couldn't
miss. ⁵To his credit, Roosevelt declined the offer to shoot the bear.
⁶When the incident was publicized, largely through political cartoons,
a Russian candy store owner named Morris Mitchom made up a toy
bear out of soft, fuzzy cloth and placed it in his shop window with a
sign reading "Teddy's Bear." ⁷The bear was a hit with passersby, and
teddy-bear mania spread rapidly throughout the country.

a. Topic sentence: _____

b. The major details help answer what questions or questions

about the topic sentence? _____

_____

_____

c. *True* or *False.* Sentence 4 is a minor detail.

Explain your answer. _____

_____

_____

d. *True* or *False.* Sentence 6 is a major detail.

Explain your answer. _____

_____

_____

4. [1]Many people don't know the difference between a patent and a trademark; however, there is a difference. [2]Usually granted for seventeen years, a patent protects both the name of a product and its method of manufacture. [3]In 1928, for example, Jacob Schick invented and then patented the electric razor in an effort to have complete control over his creation. [4]Similarly, between 1895 and 1912, no one but the Shredded Wheat company could make shredded wheat because the company had the patent. [5]A trademark is a name, symbol, or other device that identifies a product and makes it memorable in the minds of consumers. [6]*Kleenex, Jell-O,* and *Sanka* are all examples of trademarks. [7]Aware of the power that trademarks possess, companies fight to protect them and do not allow anyone else to use one without permission. [8]Occasionally, however, a company gets careless and loses control of a trademark. [9]*Aspirin,* for example, is no longer considered a trademark, and any company can call a pain-reducing tablet an aspirin.

a. Topic sentence: _____

b. The major details help answer what question or questions about

the topic sentence? _____

_____

_____

c. *True* or *False.* Sentence 3 is a minor detail.

Explain your answer. _____

_____

_____

d. *True* or *False.* Sentence 5 is a major detail.

Explain your answer. _____

_____

_____

Key Words and Supporting Details

When you are trying to differentiate between major and minor details to decide what to remember or what to include in your notes, check the topic sentence for words like *studies*, *groups*, *causes*, *reasons*, *characteristics*, and *tenets*. Topic sentences containing these broad, general category words are almost always followed by major supporting details that identify the individual *studies*, *groups*, *causes*, *theories*, and so on.

In the following paragraph, the topic sentence tells readers that in 1950 U.S. agriculture underwent some "profound changes." But unless you know what those changes were, the sentence doesn't tell you much. It's up to the major details to identify which changes the author had in mind.

Read the paragraph to identify those sentences that introduce specific examples of changes. When you finish, write the number of major details on the blank at the end of the paragraph.

[1]Around 1950, agriculture in the United States underwent a number of profound changes. [2]For one thing, agriculture became energy intensive. [3]In 1950, an amount of energy equal to less than half a barrel of oil was used to produce a ton of grain. [4]By 1985, the amount of energy needed to produce a ton of grain had more than doubled. [5]Searching for ways to increase the yield of the lands already in use, farmers also began to rely heavily on inputs of water, chemical fertilizers and pesticides (many of which are petroleum-derived products), and high-yield strains of crops. [6]In some areas, especially the drier regions of the Southwest, irrigation projects allowed dry lands to be cultivated. [7]In contrast to past agricultural practices, farmers also began to concentrate on producing only one or two profitable crops as opposed to a variety of crops. (Adapted from Kaufman and Franz, *Biosphere 2000*, p. 182.)

_____

If you wrote a *3* in the blank, then you effectively used the key phrase "profound changes" to identify major details. Although the paragraph has a total of seven sentences, only sentences 2, 5, and 7 introduce one of the profound changes mentioned in the topic sentence.

Transitional Clues to Major Details

You already know about reversal transitions. However, it's time to talk more about addition or continuation transitions, two examples of which (*for one thing* and *also*) appear in sentences 2, 5,and 7 in the previous example paragraph. **Addition transitions** at the beginning or in the middle of sentences tell you that the author is continuing to develop an idea already introduced. They also tell you that the upcoming sentences won't contradict what's come before. Instead, the sentences will continue the same train of thought with *new* content. Addition transitions are the author's way of saying, "Here is more new information or evidence supporting the main idea I've introduced."

Here's an example of a paragraph that contains two clues to major details: (1) a topic sentence with a general word that can be more specifically individualized, and (2) addition transitions that signal more support for an idea already introduced. The key phrase in the topic sentence and the addition transitions are italicized.

[1]Emotional intelligence is a difficult term to define precisely; however, the term can be generally described using *five main characteristics.* [2]*The first key characteristic* of emotional intelligence is self-awareness, or knowing one's own feelings. [3]This characteristic may, in fact, be the most important component of emotional intelligence. [4]*Another key characteristic* is the ability to manage one's emotions. [5]Emotionally intelligent people can soothe themselves in difficult times and bounce back quickly from disappointments. [6]People with high levels of emotional intelligence can *also* use their emotions in service of their goals. [7]Faced with a challenge, they can summon up the enthusiasm and confidence necessary to pursue their desires. [8]*In addition to these three characteristics,* emotionally intelligent people are *also* likely to have empathy. [9]They are, that is, able to recognize and identify the feelings of others. [10]They possess what are commonly called "people skills." [11]*The fifth and final characteristic* of emotional intelligence is the ability to help others deal with their feelings. [12]This characteristic is an important factor in maintaining meaningful relationships. (Adapted from Bernstein and Nash, *Essentials of Psychology,* p. 288.)

In this paragraph, the author uses the major details to nail down that opening phrase "five main characteristics." Each time he introduces a new characteristic—as opposed to further describing one already mentioned—he uses a transitional device that signals to the reader, "Here's another characteristic of those five I previously mentioned."

Expanding the Definition of Transitions

What follows is a list of addition transitions. It is important to note, however, that experienced readers recognize that such lists have limitations. Writers know how important transitional devices are to readers, and the good ones try hard to provide them. But they don't limit themselves solely to transitional words or phrases. They also use repetition of a key word (*characteristics* in the sample paragraph) or a reference to the previous sentence to help readers move smoothly from thought to thought. That's why, for example, the entire phrase "The fifth and final characteristic" is italicized in the passage above, rather than just the word "final," which appears on the list below. In addition to being the subject of the entire sentence, that phrase is also a transitional device designed to tell readers, "Here's the last of those five characteristics I mentioned in the opening of the paragraph and have been describing up to this point."

Addition or Continuation Transitions

Along the same lines	In other words
Also	In the same vein
An additional	More precisely
Even better	Moreover
Even more	More to the point
Even worse	One; two; three
Final; finally	Then, too
First; second; third	Too
In addition	Yet another
In more specific terms	

Check Your Understanding

Explain the difference between major and minor details.

_____

_____

_____

_____

EXERCISE 8   DIRECTIONS   Identify major and minor details by writing the appropriate sentence numbers in the boxes of the accompanying diagram.

EXAMPLE   [1]Twins can be either identical or fraternal. [2]Identical twins are formed from one fertilized egg that splits in two, resulting in two children of the same sex who look very much alike. [3]One-third of all twins born are identical. [4]Fraternal twins are formed from two different fertilized eggs; these twins can be of different sexes and look quite different from one another. [5]Two-thirds of all twins are fraternal.

Main Idea

There are two kinds of twins: fraternal and identical.

Major Detail

2

Major Detail

4

Minor Detail

3

Minor Detail

5

EXPLANATION In this example, each major detail fleshes out the two terms introduced in the topic sentence, *identical* and *fraternal*. Both details are followed by minor ones that give readers additional information about the different kinds of twins. *Note*: Although this paragraph neatly balances major and minor details, this is not the case in every paragraph and major details may or may not be followed by minor ones. It's also possible for one major detail to be followed by two minor ones.

1. [1]Nightclub acts that use lions and tigers may be entertaining, but they are, for a number of reasons, bad for both the animals and their trainers. [2]Making these animals learn tricks forces them to ignore their natural instincts. [3]Even worse, using lions and tigers for entertainment means that these proud creatures spend most of their lives in cages rather than roaming free in their natural habitat. [4]Club performances that feature lions and tigers are also bad because they are unsafe for both handlers and spectators. [5]These powerful beasts are fundamentally wild, and no amount of training can guarantee they will not, without warning, turn and attack. [6]The horrific attack that took place on trainer Roy Horn of the famed duo Siegfried and Roy is a tragic illustration of that fact. [7]Horn had thirty years of training performing tigers behind him, but all that experience did not prevent him from being attacked and severely injured by a tiger.

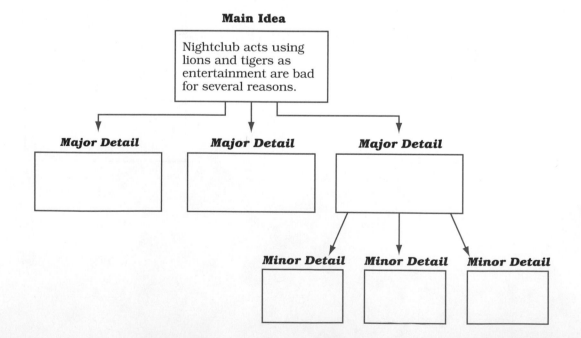

Main Idea

Nightclub acts using lions and tigers as entertainment are bad for several reasons.

Major Detail

Major Detail

Major Detail

Minor Detail

Minor Detail

Minor Detail

2. [1]Students who complete their first two years of higher education at community colleges reap definite benefits. [2]Community colleges are less expensive. [3]Courses usually cost only a fraction of what they do at four-year universities, allowing students and their parents to save thousands of dollars. [4]A second benefit of community colleges is their location. [5]They are generally close to students' homes, so they are not only convenient but also allow students to live at home instead of moving to a dorm or an off-campus apartment. [6]Yet another benefit is the more personalized instruction offered by community colleges. [7]Classes tend to be smaller than those at universities, so students can get more attention and more help from their instructors.

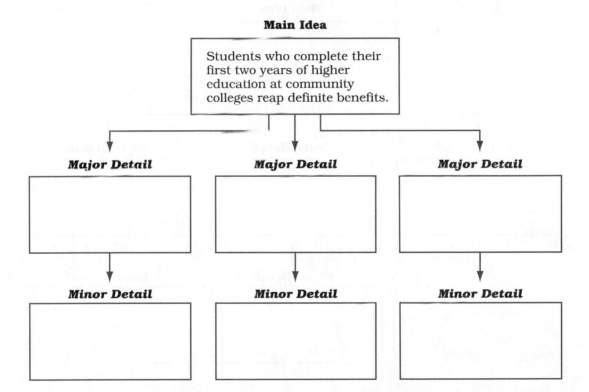

Main Idea

Students who complete their first two years of higher education at community colleges reap definite benefits.

Major Detail

Major Detail

Major Detail

Minor Detail

Minor Detail

Minor Detail

3. [1]According to the National Association for the Education of Young Children, media violence is having profound effects on our kids. [2]Long-term viewing of media violence appears to desensitize children to the pain and suffering of others. [3]It also seems to make children more aggressive. [4]After they watch violent television programs, children often replicate the actions they have just seen on TV. [5]Finally, media violence often makes young children more fearful of the world around them. [6]They cannot distinguish between fantasy and reality, so watching violent TV shows makes them believe that the world is a scary place. (Source of information: Adults and Children Together Against Violence, www.actagainstviolence.org/.)

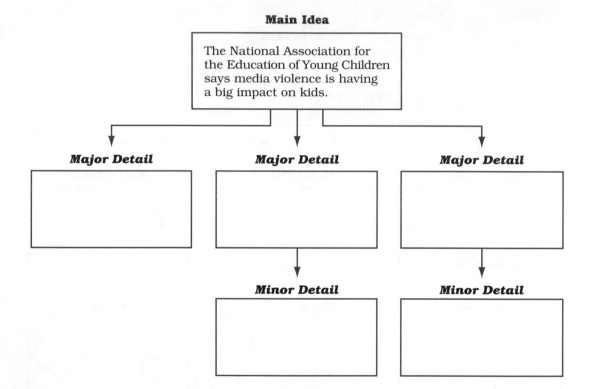

Main Idea

The National Association for the Education of Young Children says media violence is having a big impact on kids.

Major Detail

Major Detail

Major Detail

Minor Detail

Minor Detail

4. ¹Volcanic eruptions and their aftereffects are among the Earth's most destructive natural events. ²But whether a volcano poses an imminent threat to human life and property depends on its status as an *active*, a *dormant*, or an *extinct* volcano. ³An active volcano is one that is currently erupting or has erupted recently. ⁴Certain active volcanoes, such as Kilauea on Hawaii or Stromboli in the eastern Mediterranean, erupt almost continuously. ⁵Active volcanoes can be found on all continents except Australia and on the floors of all major ocean basins. ⁶Indonesia, Japan, and the United States are the world's most volcanically active nations. ⁷A dormant volcano is one that has not erupted recently but is considered likely to do so in the future. ⁸The presence of relatively fresh volcanic rocks in a volcano's vicinity is an indication that it is still capable of erupting. ⁹The presence of hot water springs or small earthquakes occurring near a volcano may also indicate that the volcano is stirring to wakefulness. ¹⁰A volcano is considered extinct if it has not erupted for a very long time (perhaps tens of thousands of years) and is considered unlikely to do so in the future. ¹¹A truly extinct volcano is no longer fueled by a magma source and, thus, no longer capable of erupting. ¹²Volcanoes, however, can surprise us. ¹³Residents of the Icelandic island of Heimaey believed that their volcano Helgafjell was extinct, until it erupted in 1973. (Adapted from Chernicoff and Fox, *Essentials of Geology*, p. 73.)

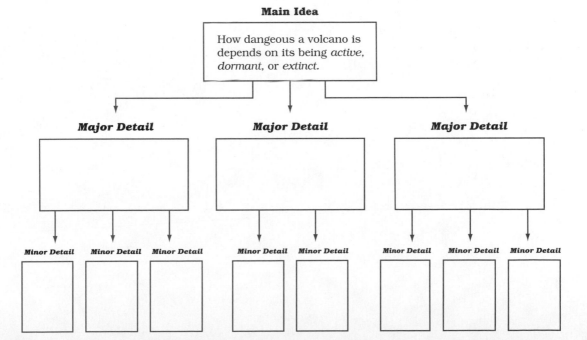

**Allusion
Alert**

The paragraph on pages 125–126 introduced you to the Greek myth of Pygmalion, the sculptor who created the ideal woman and thereby offended the goddess Aphrodite. As his punishment, Aphrodite made him fall in love with his own creation.

Allusions to Pygmalion now suggest attempts to transform someone or something into a finer version of what they were originally. The famous musical *My Fair Lady*, for instance, tells the story of a poor flower girl who is transformed into an elegant lady. It's based on a play appropriately titled *Pygmalion* by George Bernard Shaw. How then would you paraphrase the following sentence, which uses an allusion to the myth of Pygmalion?

The play and the movie *Dreamgirls* tells the story of how Motown mogul Berry Gordy played Pygmalion to a very young and supremely talented Diana Ross.

Paraphrase _____

_____

_____

_____

■ **DIGGING DEEPER**

LOOKING AHEAD Perhaps no other figure in the United States is more closely associated with the animal rights movement (p. 99) than philosopher Peter Singer. Currently a professor at Princeton, Singer's positions on the equality of human and animal concerns made him a controversial figure, as Ronald Bailey, the author of the following reading, points out.

PETER SINGER AND ANIMAL RIGHTS

1 The *New Yorker* calls him "the most influential living philosopher." His critics call him "the most dangerous man in the world." Peter Singer, the Ira W. DeCamp Professor of Bioethics at Princeton University's Center for Human Values, is most widely and controversially known for his view that animals have the same moral status as humans. He is the author of many books, including *Practical Ethics* (1979), *Rethinking Life and Death* (1995), and *Animal Liberation* (1975), which has sold more than 450,000 copies. In 2007, he published *Writings on an Ethical Life* (Ecco Press) and *A Darwinian Left: Politics, Evolution, and Cooperation* (Yale University Press), which argues that the left must replace Marx with Darwin if it is to remain a viable force.

2   Singer is perhaps the most thoroughgoing philosophical utilitarian[†] since Jeremy Bentham.[‡] As such, he believes animals have rights because the relevant moral consideration is not whether a being can reason or talk but whether it can suffer. Jettisoning the traditional distinction between humans and nonhumans, Singer distinguishes instead between persons and nonpersons. Persons are beings that feel, reason, have self-awareness, and look forward to a future. Thus, fetuses and some very impaired human beings are not persons in his view and have a lesser moral status than, say, adult gorillas and chimpanzees.

3   Given such views, it was no surprise that anti-abortion activists and disability rights advocates loudly decried the Australian-born Singer's appointment at Princeton last year. Indeed, his language regarding the treatment of disabled human beings is at times

---

[†]utilitarian: A utilitarian believes society should be organized to maximize happiness for the greatest number of beings.

[‡]Jeremy Bentham: Bentham was the first philosopher to develop the theory of utilitarianism. He argued that "nature . . . put man under the governance of two sovereign masters, pleasure and pain." Bentham eventually abandoned the principle of avoiding pain to focus on the idea that what is *good* is that which brings the greatest happiness to the greatest number of people.

appallingly similar to the eugenic arguments[†] used by Nazi theorists concerning "life unworthy of life." Singer, however, believes that only parents, not the state, should have the power to make decisions about the fates of disabled infants.

4   Singer has made similarly controversial plunges into social policy. In a recent *New York Times Magazine* essay, he argued that the affluent in developed countries are killing people by not giving away to the poor all of their wealth in excess of their needs. How did he come to this conclusion? "If . . . allowing someone to die is not intrinsically different from killing someone, it would seem that we are all murderers," he explains in *Practical Ethics.* He calculates that the average American household needs $30,000 per year; to avoid murder, anything over that should be given away to the poor. "So a household making $100,000 could cut a yearly check for $70,000," he wrote in the *Times.*

5   Rigorous adherence to a single principle has a way of hoisting one by one's own petard.[‡] Singer's mother suffers from severe Alzheimer's disease, and so she no longer qualifies as a person by his own standards, yet he spends considerable sums on her care. This apparent contradiction of his principles has not gone unnoticed by the media. When I asked him about it during our interview at his Manhattan apartment in late July, he sighed and explained that he is not the only person who is involved in making decisions about his mother (he has a sister). He did say that if he were solely responsible, his mother might not be alive today.

6   Singer's proclamation* about income has also come back to haunt him. To all appearances, he lives on far more than $30,000 a year. Aside from the Manhattan apartment—he asked me not to give the address or describe it as a condition of granting an interview—he and his wife Renata, to whom he has been married for some three decades, have a house in Princeton. The average salary of a full professor at Princeton runs around $100,000 per year; Singer also draws income from a trust fund that his father set up and from the sales of his books. He says he gives away 20 percent of his income to famine relief organizations, but he is certainly living on a sum far beyond $30,000. When asked about

---

[†]eugenic arguments: The theory of eugenics emerged in the late nineteenth century to argue that the human race needed to be protected from the reproduction of those considered unfit or impaired. The Nazis embraced eugenic arguments with a vengeance. While some utilitarians would say "the greatest number of *people*," utilitarians like Singer would say, "the greatest number of sentient, or conscious, beings."

[‡]hoisted by one's own petard: to find one's self injured by the device that you intended to use on others. The phrase comes from Shakespeare's play *Hamlet.*

*proclamation: announcement.

this, he forthrightly admitted that he was not living up to his own standards. He insisted that he was doing far more than most and hinted that he would increase his giving when everybody else started contributing similar amounts of their incomes.

7   There is some question as to how seriously one should take the dictates of a person who himself cannot live up to them. If he finds it impossible to follow his own rules, perhaps that means that he should reconsider his conclusions. Singer would no doubt respond that his personal failings hardly invalidate his ideas.

8   In his mid-50s, Singer is a rail-thin, quietly genial man who seems very comfortable with himself. At one point, I asked him, "If it resulted in an overall increase in the happiness of morally significant beings, whoever they may be, would you favor the slow, painful torture of professional philosophers, including ethicists?" His reply was good-natured: "I find it fortunately hard to imagine the circumstances in which that would occur, but if I were absolutely persuaded that this was the only way to do it, I guess I would have to."

Sharpening Your Skills

DIRECTIONS Answer the following questions by circling the letter of the correct response or filling in the blanks.

1. In paragraph 3, the author writes that Singer's "language regarding the treatment of disabled human beings is at times *appallingly* similar to the eugenics arguments used by Nazi theorists concerning 'life unworthy of life.'" Based on the context, what is a good approximate definition for appallingly?

   a. charmingly

   b. wittingly

   c. carefully

   d. horrifyingly

2. In paragraph 7, the author writes, "Singer would no doubt respond that his personal failings hardly *invalidate* his ideas." Based on the context, what's a good approximate definition for *invalidate?*

   a. challenge

   b. improve

   c. disprove

   d. enhance

3. Which sentence best expresses the main idea of paragraph 3?

    a. Singer's views have evoked support from animal rights activists all over the world.

    b. Singer's views have outraged those who don't believe abortion should be legal as well as those concerned about the rights of the disabled.

    c. Singer's views express an obvious disrespect for people with disabilities, a fact that has provoked outrage among disability rights activists and their supporters.

4. In paragraph 4, the topic sentence is

    a. sentence 1.

    b. sentence 2.

    c. sentence 3.

5. Which sentence best expresses the main idea of paragraph 6?

    a. Peter Singer is fearful of being attacked were his address to become known.

    b. Peter Singer can't escape the fact that he doesn't appear to practice what he preaches.

    c. Peter Singer has a huge fortune, which makes it easy for him to give money away.

6. In paragraph 6, the addition transition is _____; the reversal transition is _____.

7. In paragraph 4, the figures $30,000, $100,000, and $70,000 are used to make what point?

_____

_____

8. The writer mentions Singer's mother in paragraph 5 as a way of illustrating

    a. how Singer seems to contradict his own principles.

    b. Singer's adherence to a single principle.

    c. why Singer is so disliked.

9. Why does it make sense for the author to allude to Jeremy Bentham in this reading?

_____

_____

_____

10. In paragraph 5, the author writes, "Rigorous adherence to a single principle has a way of hoisting one by one's own petard." How is Singer, at least in the author's eyes, being hoisted by his own petard?

   a. He is showing that he himself cannot adhere to his own principles, thereby weakening his argument.

   b. His care of his mother reveals that Singer is a nicer person than many people think.

   c. Singer is revealing that his vast wealth is not being spent in service to others.

Students who want to do a more in-depth review of paragraph essentials should use *Getting Focused*, the web-based reading program accompanying this text. The program is available at **college.cengage.com/devenglish/flemming/getting_focused/ 1e/student_home.html**. Completing questions 2, 3, and 5 will provide a very thorough and complete review.

To get more practice analyzing paragraphs, go to **laflemm.com** and click on *Reading for Thinking*: "Online Practice." Complete the interactive exercises on identifying paragraph elements.

Test 1: Recognizing Topics and Topic Sentences

DIRECTIONS Read each paragraph and circle the letter of the correct topic. Then write the number of the topic sentence in the blank.

1. ¹Throughout the 1950s, repeated attempts were made to unionize migrant farm workers. ²But because workers had to follow the crops they picked, they were never in one place for very long and were hard to organize. ³However, in the 1960s, a Mexican-American farm worker named César Chávez succeeded against all odds at unionizing agricultural workers. ⁴Using the donations he had gathered from friends and supporters, Chávez traveled from farm to farm speaking to California's migrant workers, most of whom were Mexican Americans like himself. ⁵Used to union activists who came to their fields and talked down to them, the farm workers knew immediately that Chávez understood and respected them in a way other union organizers had not. ⁶One by one, they joined his organization, the National Farm Workers Association. ⁷In 1965, Chávez and fellow union organizer Dolores Huerta persuaded union members to take part in a strike initiated by Filipino grape pickers. ⁸Then, while Huerta continued organizing, Chávez took the grape pickers' case to the media, arguing that no one should eat grapes because the people who picked them were denied the right to basic necessities like toilet facilities. ⁹To the grape growers' misfortune, millions of Americans agreed and stopped eating grapes. ¹⁰Costing the growers millions, the boycott lasted until 1970. ¹¹When it was over, the National Farm Workers Association had become a force to be reckoned with. ¹²Farm owners had to recognize the union, which was renamed the United Farm Workers.

Topic a. the life of César Chávez

b. the organizing of farm workers by César Chávez

c. the grape boycott of 1970

d. unsuccessful efforts to organize migrant workers

Topic Sentence _____

2. ¹The sinking of the luxury liner *Lusitania* by a German submarine helped propel the United States into World War I. ²Although initially it was claimed that the *Lusitania* had been torpedoed for no reason except German viciousness, later evidence contradicted that story. ³In fact, the *Lusitania*'s cargo was almost completely contraband.*

---

*contraband: goods prohibited by law or treaty from being imported.

[4]It was carrying fifty-one tons of shrapnel shells and five thousand boxes of bullets. [5]Within eighteen minutes of being hit at 2:10 p.m. on the afternoon of May 6, 1915, the *Lusitania* sank beneath three hundred feet of water. [6]Because there weren't enough crew members to man the forty-eight lifeboats, panic reigned and hundreds of people died—1,195 to be exact. [7]Furious at what was perceived to be German treachery, the American public began to support the idea of going to war against Germany.

Topic a. the sinking of the *Lusitania*

b. German aggression in World War I

c. propaganda lies in World War I

d. submarine warfare

Topic Sentence ____

3. [1]In 1987, Brazilian labor leader and environmentalist Francisco "Chico" Mendes was awarded the United Nations Global 500 Prize, along with a medal from the Society for a Better World. [2]Sadly, medals couldn't save Chico Mendes's life when he took on a group of cattle ranchers in Acre, Brazil. [3]Determined to drive out rubber workers like the ones Mendes represented, the ranchers openly used threats and violence to do it. [4]Mendes, who had both a reputation and the respect of his fellow workers, was a special thorn in the ranchers' side, and they threatened his life. [5]Mendes took their death threats seriously but refused to abandon his labor activities. [6]On December 15, 1988, he told a friend, "I don't think I'm going to live." [7]One week later, Mendes was shot in the chest as he stepped out of his house.

Topic a. famous labor leaders

b. the murder of Chico Mendes

c. labor conditions in Brazil

d. honors given to Chico Mendes

Topic Sentence ____

4. [1]The Underground Railroad was an informal network of routes traveled by a few thousand American slaves escaping to freedom between 1840 and 1860. [2]These routes included paths through woods and fields; transportation such as boats, trains, and wagons; and homes where runaways hid from slave owners and law-enforcement officials. [3]In keeping with the idea of a railroad, slaves were referred to as "passengers," while homes that gave them shelter were "stations." [4]The people who assisted them were known as "conductors." [5]These conductors were abolitionists and included both free blacks and many sympathetic whites, particularly those who were Quakers. [6]Abolitionists defied fugitive slave laws to shelter and feed runaways and to guide them along the safest routes out of the South to free states in the North. [7]Harriet Tubman, for example, liberated at least 300 slaves after she herself had used the Underground Railroad to escape.

Topic a. Harriet Tubman

b. the Underground Railroad

c. role of Quakers in the abolitionist movement

d. rules of the Underground Railroad

Topic Sentence _____

5. [1]For decades, pawnshops have had a sleazy reputation. [2]They were the place to go for people who were completely broke or selling stolen goods. [3]Pawnshops, however, are sprucing up their reputation. [4]One reason pawnshops are trying to look more respectable is the rise of legislation limiting their existence. [5]The legislation has come from communities that consider the pawnshops signs of urban decay and don't like the fact that their numbers are increasing. [6]Anxious to contain the effects of pawnshops on their communities, some city councils and zoning committees have capped the number of licenses available. [7]Pawnshop owners have responded to this implicit threat by changing their image. [8]Dave Beck, who owns a pawnshop in North Carolina, calls pawnshops the "Wal-Marts of pre-owned merchandise." [9]Other pawnshop owners have bought local commercial time to advertise their new look, complete with bright lights and employees dressed in suits and ties. (Source of information: Charisse Jones, "Pawnshop Trying to Cash In on New Image," *USA Today*, May 25, 2007, p. 3A.)

Topic a. selling stolen goods

b. the new look of pawnshops

c. pawnshop signs

d. pawnshop owners

Topic Sentence _____

Test 2: Recognizing Topic Sentences and Accurate Paraphrases

DIRECTIONS Read each paragraph and write the number of the topic sentence in the blank. Then circle the letter of the statement that best paraphrases the topic sentence.

1. [1]In the past, young adults who went off to college would earn their degrees, get jobs, and move out into their own homes or apartments. [2]Today, however, twenty-something college graduates are more likely to return home for an extended period of time. [3]In fact, one informal poll of college seniors revealed that 63 percent of them planned to move back home after graduation. [4]This nationwide "back-to-the-nest" trend is the result of several factors. [5]Because of the unstable economy, jobs are more scarce, so recent graduates are often unemployed. [6]Even those lucky enough to find jobs are concerned about keeping them. [7]Plus, young people with entry-level salaries are finding it difficult to afford their own place to live. [8]In high-cost-of-living cities, such as New York, Boston, and San Francisco in particular, recent college graduates often do not make enough money to pay the exorbitant rents. [9]Even in lower-rent areas, young people in their twenties who have student loans to repay or who plan to attend graduate school cannot afford to pay their bills and live on their own. (Source of information: "Back to the Nest: Welcome Home," *Newsday*, May 23, 2002, www.twentysomething.com/newsday.htm.)

Topic Sentence _____

Paraphrase a. An unstable economy is changing U.S. society in a number of ways.

b. Many twenty-somethings are moving back home because they cannot handle financial responsibility.

c. Today's young people know far more about handling money than their counterparts in a previous generation did.

d. For several reasons, many college graduates are going back to their parents' home to live.

2. [1]What is the difference between a computer virus and a computer worm? [2]Both can infect and damage computer systems. [3]However, computer viruses and computer worms differ in the way they reproduce and spread. [4]A *virus*, which is short for "vital information resources under siege," is a program or code that secretly enters a computer by piggybacking on e-mail messages, files, or programs shared between two different computer systems. [5]Then the virus infects its new host by attaching itself to the files within that computer and deleting or changing them or even overwriting entire programs. [6]Just like a biological virus in the human body, a computer virus replicates itself so that it will continue to be contagious when data is shared with another computer system. [7]In 2000, for example, the famous "Love Bug" virus, which traveled via e-mail messages, destroyed files in computers all over the world. [8]*Worms,* too, are malicious programs that reproduce and spread. [9]But unlike viruses, they do not need to attach themselves to other files. [10]They are programs that run independently and spread on their own through computer networks. [11]Thus they do not require human intervention to make their way from one computer to another. [12]The famous Internet worm of 1988, for example, copied itself across the Internet, destroying many computer systems as it went. [13]Currently, computer analysts are worried about the Sasser worm, which disabled computers in Britain, South Africa, and Taiwan.

Topic Sentence _____

Paraphrase a. Both computer viruses and computer worms are programs that damage computer systems.

b. Although computer viruses and computer worms can both do significant damage to computers, they replicate and spread in different ways.

c. Computer worms are far worse than computer viruses because they do not require human participation to spread.

d. Computer viruses must reproduce themselves to be a significant threat.

3. [1]In 1949, President Harry S. Truman decided to use Cape Canaveral in Florida as a testing site for missiles. [2]The Cape Canaveral location was so perfectly adapted to the job of missile launching that it became the site of the Kennedy Space Center, where not just missiles but also rockets and space shuttles are launched. [3]The site worked because Cape Canaveral is a rather remote area that is nevertheless accessible by roads and highways. [4]Thus it could be used as a place to build and launch missiles without endangering people living in the area. [5]Although over the years the Kennedy Space Center has expanded to cover 140,000 acres, it is still remote enough to ensure the safety of nearby communities.

(Sources of information: Kennedy Space Center, "The Kennedy Space Center Story" [1991 edition], October 22, 2002, www .ksc.nasa.gov/kscpao/kscstory/ch1/ch1.htm; Cliff Lethbridge, "The History of Cape Canaveral," Spaceline.org, 2000, http://spaceline .org/capehistory.html.)

Topic Sentence _____

Paraphrase a. Cape Canaveral became the site of the Kennedy Space Center because it turned out to be the perfect place for testing and launching missiles, rockets, and space shuttles.

b. Cape Canaveral was the only site in the United States where missiles, rockets, and space shuttles could be launched.

c. Cape Canaveral's remoteness led to its selection as America's missile and rocket launch site.

d. Harry S. Truman chose Cape Canaveral as the site of the Kennedy Space Center.

4. [1]Members of living history clubs are deeply passionate about history, so much so that they are not content to simply read about a particular era. [2]Instead, members of living history clubs seek to re-create life as it was lived in their favorite time period. [3]The 24,000 members of the Society for Creative Anachronism,[†] for example, study the European Middle Ages and Renaissance by re-creating the arts and skills of those eras. [4]Each participant makes and wears clothing from the period and creates a "persona," a person whom he or she would have liked to have been. [5]When the club's members gather at meetings, which may take the form of feasts or tournaments, they reenact the behaviors of those who lived during that era. [6]They might, for instance, practice sword fighting or learn a craft like brewing, weaving, or candle making. [7]Similarly, hundreds of Civil War buffs frequently dress as soldiers and reenact whole battles, often while a crowd of spectators looks on. [8]The reenactors spend weekends camping in canvas tents, eating foods that were available to their historical counterparts, and trying to capture what it was like to have lived during the nineteenth century. [9]Other living history groups around the country focus on re-creating the Roman Empire, the pirate era, or the Wild West. (Sources of information: Society for Creative Anachronism, www.ansteorra.org/

[†]anachronism: something that is out of its proper or appropriate order in time. For example, a play about ancient Rome would never have an actor looking at a watch because the watch is an *anachronism*.

regnum/hospitaler/articles/fip.htm; Living History Society, www
.livinghistorysociety.org.)

Topic Sentence _____

Paraphrase a. Many people are fascinated by a certain period of history.

b. The Society for Creative Anachronism is a group that reenacts the Middle Ages and Renaissance.

c. Historical reenactments of important events are often marred by clothing, furniture, or speech that does not fit the time period.

d. Members of living history clubs enjoy re-creating a particular historical era.

Test 3: Recognizing and Paraphrasing Topic Sentences

DIRECTIONS Read each paragraph and write the number of the topic sentence in the blank. Then paraphrase the topic sentence on the lines that follow. *Note*: These paraphrases can be similar to those you might take for marginal reading notes.

 1. [1]The largest demographic* group in the United States, called "baby boomers," consists of those born between 1946 and 1964. [2]Because baby boomers are presently the segment with the greatest economic impact, they are the target for numerous products and services. [3]This includes cars, housing, foreign travel, and recreational equipment. [4]Boomers are also heavy consumers of banking and investment services. [5]They are the heaviest users of frozen dinners and are a growing market for movies, especially highly original ones with adult themes. [6]They are also the target of marketing efforts for children's products and services. (Hoyer and MacInnis, *Consumer Behavior*, p. 357.)

Topic Sentence _____

Paraphrase _____

_____

2. [1]In 1976 in an effort to combat the possible widespread outbreak of swine flu, President Gerald Ford directed the Centers for Disease Control (CDC) to launch a project called the National Influenza Immunization Program (NIIP). [2]In response four manufacturers set out to make 200 million doses of the drug because the CDC wanted every person in the United States to be vaccinated against the disease. [3]The CDC also developed a plan to take jet immunization guns into schools, factories, shopping centers, nursing homes, and health departments. [4]However, complications soon began to arise. [5]The vaccine, for instance, could not be produced as fast as initially planned. [6]This setback, along with legal issues, drastically disrupted the production timetable and delayed the beginning of the program by three months. [7]At the same time, the whole NIIP was suffering from public relations problems. [8]Although the program received widespread support at first, the media began to criticize it when no new cases of swine flu occurred. [9]Then when three elderly

*demographic: related to the characteristics of a population.

people died after being vaccinated, the press connected their deaths to the swine flu immunizations, despite a lack of evidence. [10]However, in time, a connection *was* established between the swine flu vaccination and a nervous system disease called Guillain-Barré syndrome (GBS). [11]The vaccine was thought to have caused 500 people to develop this complication, resulting in death for 25 of the victims and paralysis for many others. [12]When the NIIP was finally cancelled on December 16, 1976, only 24 percent of the population had been vaccinated, and the immunizations had killed more people than swine flu had. [13]When it was finally over, the 1976 National Influenza Immunization Program turned out to have been one of the greatest public health fiascos of all times. (Source of information: Joel Warner, "The Sky Is Falling: An Analysis of the Swine Flu Affair of 1976," Haverford College, March 9, 1999, www.haverford .edu/biology/edwards/disease/viral_essays/warnervirus.htm.)

Topic Sentence _____

Paraphrase _____

_____

3. [1]Coral reefs are extremely important to the environment, performing many useful functions; above all, they provide a habitat for organisms that cannot survive elsewhere. [2]Yet coral reefs all over the world are being threatened by human activities. [3]Logging near the waters of Bascuit Bay in the Philippines has destroyed 5 percent of the coral reefs in the bay. [4]Dynamite fishing around the world has not only killed large numbers of fish, it has also blown apart a significant number of coral reefs in Kenya, Tanzania, and Mauritania. [5]Coral reefs have also fallen victim to the tourist industry. [6]Coral and shells are hot tourist commodities, and they have been collected in large quantities for sale to souvenir-hungry tourists. [7]Undoubtedly, the most violent assault on the reefs has come from nuclear testing. [8]France, for example, has detonated* more than 100 nuclear devices in Polynesian waters once rich with coral reefs that are rapidly disappearing.

Topic Sentence _____

Paraphrase _____

_____

_____

*detonated: set off; caused to explode.

4. [1]Officials in countries such as Egypt, Afghanistan, and Greece are pressing European and American museums to return ancient art objects illegally taken from them long ago. [2]However, the museums that display these antiquities argue that they have good reasons for not returning them to their original owners. [3]Museums fear, for instance, that returning treasures to their place of origin would result in the dismantling of their collections and loss of revenue from museum visitors. [4]Museum officials also insist that many of the antiquities are too fragile to move. [5]London's British Museum, for example, says that sculptures sawed off the Parthenon in 1801 are too delicate to transport from England to Greece. [6]Museum officials argue, too, that they are better equipped to preserve such priceless treasures and accuse some countries of not taking proper care of precious artifacts. [7]Those on the side of the museums point out that in unstable or war-torn countries like Afghanistan, where the looting and destruction of museums is still a very real possibility, antiquities are at great risk. [8]Plus, returning works of art to their place of origin often significantly reduces public access to them. [9]Russia's Hermitage Museum, for example, reluctantly returned a rare copper bowl to Kazakhstan, and now the bowl is kept in a mosque where few visitors are allowed to go. (Source of information: Betsy Carpenter with Gillian Sandford, "Who Owns the Past?" *U.S. News & World Report*, December 15, 2003, pp. 58–60.)

Topic Sentence _____

Paraphrase _____

_____

5. [1]Americans have a worldwide reputation as couch potatoes, and recent events in Las Vegas suggest that it is well-deserved. [2]Given that the casinos alone are the size of football fields, Las Vegas is no longer an easily walkable city, and four miles is proving way too much for many tourists, even the young and healthy. [3]Thus motor scooters for the ailing and elderly are in big demand in Las Vegas, and those who rent them are doing a booming business. [4]The new twist is that many of those doing the renting are neither ailing nor old. [5]They are perfectly fit tourists, such as twenty-seven-year-old Simon Lezama, who says that renting a scooter allows him to "drink and drive, be responsible, and save my feet." [6]While some find the notion of using scooters designed for those with disabilities unethical, many others echo Lezama, who happily followed what seems to be a growing trend: "I saw everybody was getting them. I figured

I might as well, too." (Source of information: Kathleen Hennessey, "Vegas Visitors Are Indulging in Exercise Avoidance," *USA Today,* May 25, 2007, p. 2A.)

Topic Sentence _____

Paraphrase _____

_____

Test 4: Taking Stock

DIRECTIONS Read each paragraph. Then answer the questions by circling the correct letter or response and filling in the blanks.

1. Although there is no equivalent English word for it, *schadenfreude* is the German term for the feeling of pleasure one gets when hearing of another's misfortune. The word comes from *schaden*, meaning "damage," and *freude*, meaning "joy." Psychologists say that we are expressing schadenfreude, for example, when we feel spiteful delight in watching celebrities fail. We're interested in court trials of the rich and famous because we are secretly—sometimes even openly—glad that the high-and-mighty have been brought down to a less-exalted position. Schadenfreude is the glee we experience when the pretty homecoming queen trips on her dress. And it's the satisfaction we get from watching rivals and enemies flounder. Historian Peter Gay, for instance, admitted to feeling schadenfreude when, as a Jewish child during the Nazi era, he watched German athletes lose competitions in the 1936 Olympic games. Some psychologists insist that it's perfectly normal to occasionally feel schadenfreude even toward people we love, like friends and family members, if they have achieved successes in the past that we wished for ourselves but did not achieve. Feelings of schadenfreude are considered abnormal only when they are constant or if they lead to attempts to make others fail so that we can feel better about ourselves. (Sources of information: Kathleen McGowan, "Seven Deadly Sentiments," *Psychology Today,* January/ February 2004, pp. 46–48; "Word of the Day: Schadenfreude," Dictionary.com, May 10, 2000, http://dictionary.reference.com/ wordoftheday/archive/2000/05/10.html.)

   1. Based on the context, what is the meaning of *glee* in the following sentence: "Schadenfreude is the glee we experience when the pretty homecoming queen trips on her dress."

   _____

   2. What is the topic?
      a. German words used in English
      b. psychology
      c. the meaning of the term *schadenfreude*
      d. schadenfreude and celebrities

3. Which sentence is the topic sentence?

a. Although there is no equivalent English word for it, *schadenfreude* is the German term for the feeling of pleasure one gets when hearing of another's misfortune.

b. Psychologists say that we are expressing schadenfreude, for example, when we feel spiteful delight in watching celebrities fail.

c. We're interested in court trials of the rich and famous because we are secretly—sometimes even openly—glad that the high-and-mighty have been brought down to a less exalted position.

d. Feelings of *schadenfreude* are considered abnormal only when they are constant or if they lead to attempts to make others fail so that we can feel better about ourselves.

4. How would you paraphrase the topic sentence?

_____

_____

_____

5. a. *True* or *False*. The following sentence is a major detail: "Psychologists say that we are expressing schadenfreude, for example, when we feel spiteful delight in watching celebrities fail."

b. *True* or *False*. The following sentence is a major detail: "Schadenfreude is the glee we experience when the pretty homecoming queen trips on her dress."

2. According to neuropsychologist Prathiba Shammi, the human brain has to complete a two-step process to comprehend humor. In the first step, the brain has to realize that something surprising or unexpected has occurred. For example, consider a sign in a Hong Kong tailor's shop that reads "Please have a fit upstairs." If we are going to find this sign amusing, then our brain has to recognize that the tailor seems to be inviting us to come upstairs to display some kind of emotional outburst. That thought still won't seem funny, though, until our brain completes the second step and searches our working memory for a meaning that makes sense. In this case, our mind realizes that tailors "fit" clothes on people; that particular sense of *fit* was what the sign intended. After we complete both mental steps, we can see the humor. This same process occurs when we hear the punch line of some jokes. First, we feel surprise because for a split second the joke doesn't make any sense. Next, though, our mind searches for a meaning that *does* make sense and then we mentally put the two together to see why the joke is funny. (Source of information: Lee Dye, "Humor on the Brain," ABCNews.com, http://abcnews.go.com/sections/science/DyeHard/dye990414.html.)

1. What is the topic?

    a. the brain

    b. humor

    c. comprehending humor

    d. the elements of a funny joke

2. Which sentence is the topic sentence?

    a. According to neuropsychologist Prathiba Shammi, the human brain has to complete a two-step process to comprehend humor.

    b. First, we have to realize that something surprising or unexpected has occurred.

    c. That thought still won't seem funny, though, until our brain completes the second step and searches our working memory for a meaning that makes sense.

    d. This same process occurs when we hear the punch line of some jokes.

3. How would you paraphrase the topic sentence?

_____

_____

_____

4. The transitions identifying the major details are _____

_____

5. a. *True* or *False*. The following sentence is a minor detail: "For example, consider a sign in a Hong Kong tailor's shop that reads, 'Please have a fit upstairs.'"

    b. *True* or *False*. The following sentence is a major detail: "This same process occurs when we hear the punch line of some jokes."

3. Do you want to own more stuff? Do you crave more clothes, jewelry, stereos, a big-screen TV, new appliances, a better computer, recreation and fitness equipment, a more expensive car, and a big house to put it all in? If so, like many Americans, you may be caught up in a cycle of acquisition, which begins with a desire to have more possessions. This desire causes us to buy all of the latest high-tech devices, gadgets, fashions, and so on. As the pile of new stuff grows, we realize that we need more space to put it all in, so we buy bigger and more expensive houses. The size of an average U.S. house, which in 2003 was 2,200 square feet, increased 24 percent from 1985. Of course, a larger house means a larger mortgage payment. Thus, after we move all of our stuff into our bigger homes, we have to spend more time and energy making money to pay for it all. Consequently, we work more and more to be able not only to pay for what we already have but also to buy even more. In the end, we spend less and less time in the big houses that contain the stuff we already have because we have to go to work to earn the money to pay for all of it. And the cycle begins again. (Source of information: S. E. Gloger, "Home Sweet Cocoon: Heartland Economics," *Future Magazine*, Winter 2003, www.futuremagonline.com/archive/2003/winter/2.html.)

1. Based on the context, what is the meaning of *acquisition* in the following sentence: "If so, like many Americans, you may be caught up in a cycle of *acquisition*, which begins with a desire to have more possessions."

---

2. What is the topic?

   a. personal possessions

   b. big houses

   c. the cycle of acquisition

   d. making money in America

3. Which sentence is the topic sentence?

   a. Do you want to own more stuff?

   b. If so, like many Americans, you may be caught up in a cycle of acquisition, which begins with a desire to have more possessions.

   c. As the pile of new stuff grows, we realize that we need more space to put it all in, so we buy bigger and more expensive houses.

d. Consequently, we work more and more to be able not only to pay for what we already have but also to buy even more.

4. How would you paraphrase the topic sentence?

_____

_____

_____

5. a. *True* or *False.* The following sentence is a minor detail: "The size of an average U.S. house, which in 2003 was 2,200 square feet, has increased 24 percent from 1985."

  b. *True* or *False.* The following sentence is a major detail: "In the end, we spend less and less time in the big houses that contain the stuff we already have because we have to go to work to earn the money to pay for all of it."

4. A 2003 Allstate Insurance survey revealed that there are five different types of American driving personalities. The company labeled the first type "Auto-Bahners." This group, which includes 17 percent of all drivers, contains those who describe themselves as "fast" and "aggressive" but also "good" drivers. These drivers consider driving exciting and often speed; most have driven more than twenty miles over the speed limit at least once. Many have been pulled over by the police, some even ticketed, within the last five years. The second group, the "Auto-Nomous," accounts for 21 percent of drivers. They, too, describe themselves as "good" drivers, but they tend to find driving more relaxing than exciting. These people, two-thirds of whom are male, describe themselves and their cars as "rugged" and "powerful." Not surprisingly, six in ten of them drive either a pickup truck or a sport utility vehicle. Another 23 percent of drivers are the "Auto-Matics." These people do not enjoy driving; almost two-thirds say that they dislike it or are indifferent to it. Of all drivers, Auto-Matics tend to be the least confident about their driving skills; nonetheless, they tend to like owning "trendy" and "attention-getting" vehicles. A fourth category of drivers are the "Auto-Pragmatics." Members of this group, 15 percent of all drivers, use words and phrases like "cautious," "economically conscious," and "environmentally friendly" to describe themselves and their vehicles. Predominantly female, these drivers are the most safety-conscious of all motorists. The majority of the last category, the "Auto-Pilots," is female. This group, another 15 percent of all drivers, includes many people who have children under eighteen living at home. Like the Auto-Pragmatics, they consider themselves to be safe drivers, but the type of vehicle they drive is not important to them. Of all drivers, Auto-Pilots are the most likely to drive a minivan. (Source of information: "What's Your Driving Personality?" *Road & Travel*, August 8–23, 2003, Survey, www.roadandtravel.com/newsworthy/newsandviews03/allstatesurvey2.htm.)

1. What is the topic?

   a. Allstate Insurance

   b. driving in America

   c. types of Americans

   d. types of driver personalities

2. Which sentence is the topic sentence?

   a. A 2003 Allstate Insurance survey revealed that there are five different types of American driving personalities.

   b. The company labeled the first type "Auto-Bahners."

   c. This group, which includes 17 percent of all drivers, contains those who describe themselves as "fast" and "aggressive" but also "good" drivers.

   d. Of all drivers, Auto-Pilots are the most likely to drive a minivan.

3. How would you paraphrase the topic sentence?

_____

_____

_____

4. a. *True* or *False.* The following sentence is a major detail: "The second group, the 'Auto-Nomous,' accounts for 21 percent of drivers."

   b. *True* or *False.* The following sentence is a major detail: "The majority of the last category, 'Auto-Pilots,' is female."

5. What word or phrase in the topic sentence provides a clue to the major details?

_____

5. In general, the term *noise pollution* refers to any form of unwelcome or annoying sound, from the barking of a neighbor's dog to the rattling of a construction-site jackhammer. However, the term noise pollution has long been difficult to accurately define because noise differs from other forms of pollution in several respects. For one thing, noise can completely disappear. Unlike chemicals and other kinds of pollutants, which remain in the air, water, or soil even after polluting stops, noise does not remain in the environment after its source ceases to generate it. Second, noise pollution cannot be measured as easily as can other forms of pollution. Scientists can analyze soil, water, and air samples to determine how many pollutants they contain and then decide if the amounts are unhealthy. However, it is more difficult to determine how much exposure to noise causes damage. Finally, the definition of the word *noise* is subject to individual opinion. To some people, the sound of loud music or the roar of a motorcycle engine may be pleasant or exhilarating while to others those same sounds seem grating and stressful. (Source of information: The Right to Quiet Society, Frequently Asked Questions, www.quiet.org/faq.htm.)

1. What is the topic?

    a. noise

    b. pollution

    c. noise pollution

    d. sound

2. Which sentence is the topic sentence?

    a. In general, the term *noise pollution* refers to any form of unwelcome or annoying sound, from the barking of a neighbor's dog to the rattling of a construction-site jackhammer.

    b. However, the term noise pollution has long been difficult to accurately define because noise differs from other forms of pollution in several respects.

    c. For one thing, noise can completely disappear.

    d. To some people, the sound of loud music or the roar of a motorcycle engine may be pleasant or exhilarating while to others those same sounds seem grating and stressful.

3. How would you paraphrase the topic sentence?

_____

_____

_____

4. *a.* *True* or *False*. The following sentence is a major detail: "Finally, the definition of the word *noise* is subject to individual opinion."

b. *True* or *False*. The following sentence is a minor detail: "To some people, the sound of loud music or the roar of a motorcycle engine may be pleasant or exhilarating while to others those same sounds seem grating or stressful."

5. Identify, according to the order in which they occur, the transitions introducing major details.

_____

C H A P T E R   4

Recognizing Patterns of Organization

In this chapter, you will learn

- **how to identify the most common patterns of organization in paragraphs.**

- **how recognizing the patterns can focus your attention while reading and help improve remembering.**

Although no single rule exists for organizing information in writing, there are several organizational patterns that make frequent appearances, especially in textbooks. This chapter introduces seven of those patterns and offers some tips on how to recognize the primary, or most important, pattern in a paragraph.

Pattern 1: Definition

Leaf through any textbook and, more often than not, you'll notice numerous definitions. In fact, textbook authors frequently devote whole paragraphs to defining terms essential to their subject matter.

The definition pattern usually opens with the word or term being explained. The word is frequently highlighted in some way, through boldface, colored type, or italics. The meaning then follows right on the heels of the highlighted word, while the remainder of the paragraph expands on the definition in one or more of the following ways: (1) gives an example of the word in context, (2) describes problems associated with the definition, (3) traces the history of the word, or (4) compares it to a word with a similar meaning.

Here to illustrate is a paragraph organized by the definition pattern. Note how the paragraph has been underlined and annotated to highlight both word and meaning.

Free association:
client says anything, no matter how unimportant

Form of therapy first used by Freud.

Free Association. In **free association** , the client is instructed to say anything that crosses his or her mind, no matter how trivial or irrelevant it may seem. The father of psychoanalysis, Sigmund Freud, who first used free association as therapy, believed these free associations would eventually work their way toward uncovering deep-seated wishes and desires that reflect underlying conflicts. In classical psychoanalysis, the client lies on a couch with the analyst sitting off to the side, out of the client's direct view and saying little. By remaining detached, the analyst hopes to create an atmosphere that encourages the client to free associate. (Nevid, *Psychology Concepts and Applications,* p. 357.)

In this case, the author wants readers to understand the meaning of the phrase "free association." To that end, he gives the phrase special emphasis. First, the phrase gets a paragraph and an italicized title all to itself. Next the author uses boldface to highlight the term yet again, right before defining it. Thanks to all these clues, the reader knows that the phrase is important and is on the alert for its meaning.

As is typical for the definition pattern, the author follows the word and meaning with a description of the context in which the word is used—a therapeutic setting. He also tells readers a little bit about the history: Sigmund Freud was the first to use free association in a therapeutic setting.

Typical Topic Sentences

Sentences like the following are all strong contenders for a definition pattern of development.

1. **Minerals** are naturally occurring in organic solids consisting of one or more chemical elements in specific proportions (Chernicoff and Fox, *Essentials of Geology*, p. 25).

2. Over the past forty years, journalists and advocacy organizations have persuaded many states to pass **sunshine laws**—regulations that ensure government meetings and reports are made available to the press (Turow, *Media Today*, p. 44).

3. A file-management utility lets you view, rename, copy, move, and delete files and folders (Beckman and Quinn, *Computer Confluence*, p. 163).

4. The name "Vienna Secession" refers to a group of Viennese artists living in Austria at the turn of the century.

5. The phrase "identification with the aggressor" refers to the tendency of victims to become dependent on those who hurt or oppress them.

Pattern Pointer

▶▶▶▶

To fully understand and remember a key definition, consider making a concept map like the one shown here.

client says anything that comes to mind

Free Association

first used by Freud

no censorship allowed

Multiple-Definition Paragraphs

Multiple-definition paragraphs are also common in textbooks. Because paragraphs do not usually extend beyond ten or twelve sentences, space is limited, and this version of the definition pattern usually includes little more than the words or terms followed by a definition. Textbook authors often use the multiple-definition pattern when they are dealing with related terms. Here's an example:

There are many different kinds of personality disorders. People with a **narcissistic personality disorder** have an inflated or grandiose sense of themselves, while those suffering from a **paranoid personality disorder** show a high degree of suspiciousness or mistrust. Those with a **schizoid personality disorder** have little if any interest in social relationships, display a limited range of emotional expression, and are perceived as distant and aloof. Those with a **borderline personality disorder** tend to have stormy relationships with others, dramatic mood swings, and an unstable self-image. In total, the *Diagnostic and Statistical Manual of Mental Disorders*, a handbook for mental-health professionals, identifies ten different personality disorders. The most widely studied of these is the **antisocial personality disorder (APD)**. This disorder is characterized by a complete disregard for all social conventions or rules. In the United States, personality disorders affect 10 to 15 percent of the population.

Tables

Keep in mind, too, that multiple-definition paragraphs are often accompanied by tables such as the one below. When it comes time for exam review, these tables come in handy. That's because they neatly itemize individual terms, names, or events on the left and give the meaning on the right. A table is a ready-made study aid, which you can use to review what you've learned from your textbook assignment.

Schizoid personality disorder	Aloof and distant from others, with shallow or blunted emotions
Antisocial personality disorder	A pattern of antisocial and irresponsible behavior, callous treatment of others, and lack of remorse for wrongdoing
Borderline personality disorder	A failure to develop a stable self-image, together with a pattern of tumultuous moods and stormy relationships with others and lack of impulse control
Paranoid personality disorder	Persistent belief that other people are planning injury or harm
Avoidant personality disorder	Pattern of avoiding social relationships out of fear of relationships

Pattern Pointer

When you are dealing with multiple definitions, consider making your own visual aids. If the author doesn't include a table like the one on page 166, drawing your own table is a great way to make your mind process not just the meanings of the different terms but also their relationship to one another.

EXERCISE 1 **DIRECTIONS** Read each passage and identify the term being defined. Paraphrase the definition. Then identify the method or methods the author uses to define the key term.

EXAMPLE **Corporate crime** is defined as a criminal act committed by one or more employees of a corporation while being attributed to the organization itself. Between 1984 and 1990, 2,000 corporations were convicted in federal courts for offenses ranging from tax-law violations to environmental crimes. One problem with the term *corporate crime* is definitional. In 1989, the supertanker *Exxon Valdez* ran aground in Prince William Sound, Alaska, spilling 11 million gallons of crude oil. The spill became North America's largest ecological disaster. Prosecutors were interested in determining the guilt or innocence of the captain, his officers, and his crew. But there were additional and far-reaching questions. Did the Exxon Corporation sacrifice the environment by putting profit above safety? If so, was this a corporate crime? (Adapted from Adler, Mueller, and Laufer, *Criminology*, p. 38.)

The paragraph defines the following term or terms: *corporate crime*

Restate the definition or definitions in your own words.

Corporate crime refers to a criminal action taken by a corporate employee but blamed on the corporation itself.

Which of the following methods does the author use to help define the key term or terms?

    ✓   The author gives an example of behavior or events that fit the definition.

        The author supplies a history of the word's development.

_____ ✓ _____ The author describes a problem associated with applying the definition.

_____ The author compares the word defined to a word similar in meaning.

EXPLANATION The author defines the term *corporate crime* and gives an example of behavior associated with it; for example, tax violations and environmental crimes. The author also shows that it's not always easy to know what instances, experiences, or events fit the definition.

1. **Branding**, the creation of a specific name to advertise a product, such as Quaker Oats for oatmeal, started to grow in importance in the late nineteenth century. Prior to that time, manufacturers of flour and other basic products like candy, sugar, and beans sold the merchandise in sacks without any name. But eventually manufacturers tried to distinguish their products from others. Henry Parson Cromwell, for example, created the name *Quaker Oats* and launched an advertising campaign to extol the virtues of his product. *Quaker Oats* was followed by a host of products with specific brand names, such as *Heinz ketchup, Borden's milk,* and *Pillsbury flour.* (Adapted from Harper, *The New Mass Media,* p. 231.)

The paragraph defines the following term or terms: _____

Restate the definition or definitions in your own words.

_____

_____

Which of the following methods does the author use to help define the key term or terms?

_____ The author gives an example of behavior or events that fit the definition.

_____ The author supplies a history of the word's development.

_____ The author describes a problem associated with applying the definition.

_____ The author compares the word defined to a word similar in meaning.

2. Created by the Constitution, the **Supreme Court** is the highest court in the land. Although the original Supreme Court consisted of a chief justice and five associates, nine judges currently sit on the Supreme Court, and its decisions, once made, are irrevocable, or irreversible. However, defendants displeased with a decision made by a lower court can appeal that ruling to the Supreme Court in the hopes of having it overturned. In 2006, for instance, the Circuit Court of Appeals of New York found in favor of Evelyn Coke, a seventy-three-year-old employee in the home-care industry, who sued her employers for back payment of overtime compensation, which had been denied her based on a 1930s Department of Labor regulation created when home-care for the elderly did not yet exist. The court ruled that Coke deserved to be appropriately compensated for her overtime hours. Coke's employers, Long Island Care at Home, appealed the decision to the Supreme Court in the hopes of having it reversed. In 2007, the Supreme Court overruled the lower court's decision. (Sources of information: http://www.msnbc.msn .com/id/19173596; http://usgovinfo.about.com/library/weekly/ aa081400a.htm.)

The paragraph defines the following term or terms. _____

Restate the definition or definitions in your own words.

_____

_____

_____

Which of the following methods does the author use to help define the key term or terms?

_____ The author gives an example of behavior or events that fit the definition.

_____ The author supplies a history of the word's development.

_____ The author describes a problem associated with applying the definition.

_____ The author compares the word defined to a word similar in meaning.

Pattern 2: Process

The process pattern orders events according to when they occurred in real time and identifies the steps or stages necessary to explaining how something functions or works. Here to illustrate is a paragraph describing the digestion process. Once again, the passage is marked to highlight both the steps in the process and the kind of test question such material might generate.

Digestive system prepares food to be turned into energy.

TG: Explain the process of digestion.

In the human body, the ⎡digestive system⎤ breaks down food so that it can be used for energy. As ①food enters the mouth, chewing, along with enzymes in the saliva, break it down into small pieces. ②Next the esophagus contracts and pushes the food into the stomach, where muscles, enzymes, and digestive acids turn the food into a thick liquid. That ③liquid is emptied into the small intestine, where most of its nutrients are absorbed. ④What remains travels to the large intestine, where water is removed from digested food and turned into waste. (Adapted from Barnes-Svarney, *The New York Public Library Science Desk Reference*, p. 166.)

Verbal Clues to the Pattern

Words such as *steps*, *stages*, *phases*, *procedures*, and *process* are all signs that you are dealing with a process pattern. So too are the transitions in the following list.

Transitions Identifying a Sequence of Steps	
Afterward	In the final stage
At this point	In this stage
By the time	Next
Finally	Then
First; second; third	Toward the end

Typical Topic Sentences

Sentences like the ones shown below are typical of the process pattern:

1. Soil erosion often proceeds at a rapid pace.
2. The bestowing of sainthood is an extremely complex process.
3. The steam engine relies on the conversion of energy from one form to another.
4. Storing information in long-term memory requires several steps.
5. The weathering of rocks takes place over an extended period of time.

Flow Charts

Paragraphs organized according to the process pattern are often accompanied by flow charts. These are diagrams that use boxes or circles connected by arrows to map a sequence of steps, stages, or operations. For an example, read the following paragraph. Then look over the flow chart that accompanies it.

Most salespeople follow a six-step procedure when making a sale (see illustration below). The first step is to research potential buyers and choose the most likely customers, or prospects. The next step involves approaching the prospective clients or customers. At this stage, first impressions are crucial, and salespeople who understand each customer's particular situation are likely to make a good first impression—and make the sale. The third step revolves around actual delivery of the sales presentation, which in many cases means demonstrating the product while pointing out its advantages over competitors. Following the presentation, the prospect might have questions or objections, which the salesperson has to answer. To close the sale, the salesperson asks the prospect to buy the product, often by posing questions that assume the sale has been completed; for example, "When would you want delivery?" If the salesperson is correct in assuming the sale has been made, the final step is the follow-up call after delivery. During the follow-up stage, the salesperson should make it clear that he or she is available for future advice and help. (Adapted from Pride, Hughes, and Kapoor, *Business*, p. 480.)

The Six Steps of the Personal-Selling Process

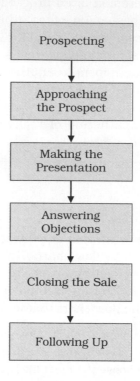

Prospecting

↓

Approaching
the Prospect

↓

Making the
Presentation

↓

Answering
Objections

↓

Closing the Sale

↓

Following Up

**Pattern
Pointers**

1. Never get so caught up in the individual steps or stages that you lose sight of the larger process or sequence they describe. Keep thinking what each step contributes to the larger whole.

2. If the process pattern seems hard to grasp, draw your own diagram or make a flow chart like the one shown with the sample paragraph.

3. During exam review, see if you can summarize, from memory, all the steps in a process, without missing a single one.

EXERCISE 2   **DIRECTIONS** Read the paragraph on the Heimlich maneuver (p. 173). Then decide which summary more effectively summarizes the paragraph.

EXAMPLE Tune in to television shows like the popular *CSI*, and you'll see plenty of crime-solving tools that are nothing but products of the writers' imaginations. Luminol, however, isn't one of them. In fact, forensics specialists regularly use this very real chemical to detect invisible bloodstains at crime scenes. First, they close the curtains and turn out the lights. Then they spray Luminol onto carpets, floors, walls, or furniture. Because the chemicals react with a protein in blood, bloodstains glow greenish-blue. Even trace amounts of blood will light up, for tiny blood cells are left clinging even to surfaces that have been washed with heavy-duty cleaning chemicals. Investigators photograph or videotape the glowing patches, recording any sign of a pattern. Finally, they collect samples and run additional tests to be completely sure that the substance causing the glow was indeed blood. (Source of information: Tom Harris, "How Luminol Works," http://science.howstuffworks.com/luminol.htm.)

Summary a. Forensic specialists use Luminol to identify bloodstains. Closing off as much light as possible, they spray Luminol everywhere. Blue-green stains indicate where blood spattered. Investigators then photograph the stains in the hopes of finding a pattern. Finally, they run tests to be completely sure that the Luminol-induced stains were actually blood.

(b.) Forensic specialists use a chemical called Luminol to identify invisible bloodstains. Making the room as dark as possible, they spray all surfaces. Because Luminol reacts with a protein in blood, even stains that have been washed out will glow a greenish-blue. Investigators then photograph the stains in search of a pattern. To rule out any error, they also run tests on the stained surfaces to make double sure it's blood.

EXPLANATION Summary *a* leaves out a pertinent detail: Luminol isn't used to identify all bloodstains. It's used to identify invisible ones.

The Heimlich Maneuver

You can save the life of a choking victim by performing the Heimlich maneuver. If a person suddenly cannot breathe, cough, or speak, the person's airway is probably blocked by something that needs to be removed. To perform the Heimlich maneuver, stand behind the victim and make a fist with one hand. Then reach your arms around the person from behind. Place your fist against the person's belly just above the bellybutton and below the rib cage. Next, cover your fist with your other hand and press into the belly with a quick, upward thrust. If the object in the person's throat doesn't come flying out, perform another thrust. Repeat thrusts over and over until you dislodge the object. At the same time, yell for help and tell someone to call 911.

Summary a. Stand behind the victim, making a fist with one hand. Next, reach your arms around the person from behind, and place your fist against the victim's abdomen, right below the ribs. Cover your fist with your other hand and press into the belly with a quick, upward thrust, which should dislodge the object. If it does not, repeat the thrust movement until it does.

b. If someone seems to be choking, it's time to perform the Heimlich maneuver. Standing behind the person, make a fist. Then reach your arms around the person, placing your fist against the person's belly right below the rib cage. Cover your fist with the other hand and make a quick, upward thrust to dislodge whatever is in the person's throat.

EXERCISE 3 **DIRECTIONS** Read each paragraph. Then in the blank at the end, identify the pattern of organization with *P* for process or *D* for definition.

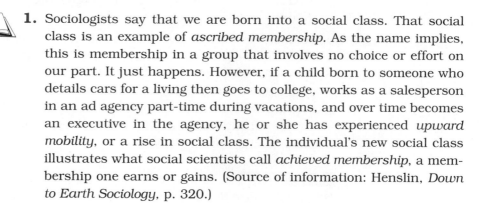

1. Sociologists say that we are born into a social class. That social class is an example of *ascribed membership*. As the name implies, this is membership in a group that involves no choice or effort on our part. It just happens. However, if a child born to someone who details cars for a living then goes to college, works as a salesperson in an ad agency part-time during vacations, and over time becomes an executive in the agency, he or she has experienced *upward mobility*, or a rise in social class. The individual's new social class illustrates what social scientists call *achieved membership*, a membership one earns or gains. (Source of information: Henslin, *Down to Earth Sociology*, p. 320.)

———

2. When learning a new skill, **distributed practice** has been shown to be the more effective method of learning. This is learning or training that is divided into segments, usually with rest periods in between so a number of learning sessions are spread out over time. Despite the findings of learning researchers, though, many college students are inclined to rely on **massed practice**. This is learning that takes place all at one time without breaks or interruptions. In the context of college, the nickname for this term would be *cramming*.

———

3. Cloud seeding is a process state governments and private businesses use to increase the amount of snow or rain falling in a particular area. The process begins with meteorologists who use radar, satellites, and weather stations to track storm fronts. Next, they measure storm clouds for temperature, wind, and composition. When the meteorologists determine that cloud conditions are right, pilots "seed" the clouds with dry ice (frozen carbon dioxide). Seeding involves an aircraft flying above the clouds and dropping dry-ice pellets directly into them. Almost immediately, the dry ice begins attracting the clouds' moisture, which freezes to the dry ice's crystalline structure. Finally, precipitation drops from the clouds to the earth in the form of rain or snow. (Source of information: North Dakota State Water Commission Atmospheric Resources, "Cloud Modification Project," 1997; www.swc.state.nd.us/arb/graphics/cloudmod.pdf.)

———

4. When you have a problem, try this six-step strategy to find a solution. In the first stage, identify exactly what the problem is. To do this, you must specifically describe your current state and then decide how that state differs from what you want to achieve. For example, let's say that you are part of a study group that wastes time chatting instead of going over course material. To make the group stay focused on studying so that your time together is more productive, you might say, "Our problem is that we're not covering all the material we need to study because we spend so much time talking." Once you know the problem, the next step is to analyze it. For instance, at your next study session, record the exact amount of time the group spends studying and the exact amount of time it spends chatting. Then consider all of the possible causes of the problem. Perhaps it's the group's lack of clear goals or the tendency of one or two members to tempt the others to gossip. After analyzing the problem, go on to the third step: generating possible solutions by brainstorming as many alternatives as possible. For example, you might consider beginning each session ten minutes earlier to allow everyone a chance to visit before getting started. You might also think about beginning each session by listing goals to accomplish, setting times for short chat breaks, or by appointing someone whose official job is to speak up when digressions occur. Then, go on to the fourth step of the process and select one or more of the solutions you thought up in step three. Choose a solution that seems the most practical. Your solution should also have the fewest drawbacks and the greatest potential for success. In the fifth step, implement the solution. Complete the six-step strategy by evaluating the solution and making adjustments as needed. If the problem persists, be willing to go back to steps one or two. If necessary, begin the whole process again. (Source of information: Gershenfeld, *Groups: Theory and Experience*, pp. 305–309.)

Pattern 3: Sequence of Dates and Events

Authors who write about history and government frequently use a sequence of dates and events to explain or argue their claims. That means the supporting details present a series of dates and events listed according to the order in which they occurred in real time. Here's an example.

TG: What are the dates of the Mexican-American War?

TG: What event helped encourage a war with Mexico?

TG: What was the name of the treaty that ended the Mexican-American War?

The Democrat James Polk became president of the United States in 1844. From the very beginning of his presidency, Polk made it clear that he intended to expand the boundaries of the United States. In 1846, he ordered General Zachary Taylor to take troops into Mexican territory. On April 24 of the same year, the Mexican military fired on Taylor's troops and war between the United States and Mexico began, even though Congress had not yet officially declared it so. By 1847, U.S. troops had arrived in Mexico City and were claiming victory. (The opening phrase in the Marines' anthem—"From the Halls of Montezuma"—is a reference to the arrival of those troops in Mexico's capital.) In 1848, Mexico and the United States signed the Treaty of Guadalupe Hidalgo, which ceded a portion of Mexican land that today includes Arizona, Utah, Nevada, and New Mexico to the United States. Polk had his wish: He had expanded and redefined U.S. borders. But in an effort to assuage* the war's critics—and there were many who considered the war with Mexico unjust—the U.S. government paid the Mexican government $15 million.

Notice how many of the sentences in this paragraph open with dates. That's a sure sign that the author is using the sequence of dates and events pattern to organize information.

Transition Clues

Sequence of dates and events paragraphs are likely to use time-order transitions like those listed in the following box.

---

*assuage: calm; soothe.

Time-Order Transitions	
After	In the years that followed
During the period	Between† _____ and _____
between	On _____ of that year
By the end of	_____ year(s) later
At the end of	When _____ ended

Typical Topic Sentences

Along with numerous dates and events, the time-order transitions listed above are clues to this pattern. So, too, are topic sentences like those you see here.

1. From 1753 to 1815, Native Americans cooperated and fought with or tried to avoid the Spanish, French, British, and Anglo-Americans who had intruded on their homelands. (Boyer et al., *The Enduring Vision*, p. 168.)

2. British children's writer Frances Hodgson Burnett started her career in 1853 at the age of four by telling stories to her siblings; by the time she died in 1924, she had written fifty-two books and thirteen plays.

3. For twenty years, between 1776 and 1796, the Anglo-American revolutionary Thomas Paine was intensely productive as both writer and theorist.

4. Throughout the sixteenth and seventeenth centuries, Calvinist Protestants† tried to purify English religion and society.

5. The young Latina singer Selena had a brief but enormously influential career.

---

†Blanks indicate where dates, years, or numbers would go.
†Calvinist Protestants believe that humanity is burdened by sin, and only those who God elects to save can escape a fiery damnation.

**Pattern
Pointers**

1. Never lose sight of the overall main idea or key point the dates and events are there to explain. Use the main idea to determine if all the dates and events are equal in importance.

2. If you think the paragraph is hard to understand and the sequence of dates and events difficult to follow, try making a timeline like the one shown here.

1844	Polk becomes president
	Wants to expand U.S. borders
1846	Orders Taylor into Mexican territory
April 24	Mexican troops fire on Taylor's troops
	War unofficially began
1847	U.S. troops in Mexico City claiming
	victory
1848	Mexico and U.S. sign Treaty of Guadalupe
	Hidalgo, ceding huge portion of
	Mexican land to U.S.

■ **EXERCISE 4** **DIRECTIONS** Read each paragraph. Underline the topic sentence. Then paraphrase it and list the supporting details, making sure to use chronological order for the crucial dates and events. Abbreviate and paraphrase as much as possible without losing the original meaning. *Note*: Your paraphrasing here should be informal as it would be for your reading notes.

EXAMPLE Close to forty years after its birth, break dancing has lost some of its popularity, but after hitting the street in the late 1960s, it is still a well-known dance style. Break dancing officially began in 1969 with singer James Brown's performance of the song "Get on the Good Foot," which encouraged wildly energetic and athletic dance moves. Throughout the 1970s, the new style continued to develop as African-American and Latino young people incorporated movements from the martial arts, gymnastics, and acrobatics into their dancing. At the end of the 1970s, break dancing became a feature of urban block parties in the Bronx in New York. During this time, a group of talented young performers known as Rock Steady Crew added amazingly difficult moves, including the "windmill" from the Chinese martial arts and the "flare" from men's gymnastics. In the 1980s, films like *Beat Street*, *Breakin'*, and *Flashdance* led to break dancing's entry into mainstream popular culture. The media lost interest in the craze by the late 1980s. As a result during the 1990s, much of America assumed that it was a fad of the past. In the late twentieth and early twenty-first centuries, though, break dancers doing moves even more powerful and complex than before began to reappear in television commercials as well as in music videos and competitions. Now a new generation of young break dancers is spinning, kicking, and back flipping to the beat. The annual Battle of the Year international break dancing competition is still held and still attracts thousands of young fans. (Source of information: Tonya Jameson, "Breaking Out," *Charlotte Observer*, July 27, 2003, pp. 1H, 8H.)

Main Idea   *Break dancing is still popular after close to forty years.*

Supporting Details   *1. 1969: James Brown's song "Get on the Good Foot" encourages wild dance moves.*

2. 1970s: African Americans and Latinos incorporate moves from different sources, e.g., martial arts, gymnastics.

3. End of 70s: Rock Steady Crew adds difficult dance moves and block parties help make break dancing even more popular.

4. 1980s: Movies like Beat Street *popularize break dancing.*

5. Late 80s and 90s: Break dancing seems to fade but made a comeback and now there's a new generation.

EXPLANATION As they should, the notes paraphrase the topic sentence and include the dates and events needed to illustrate break dancing's long and continued popularity.

1. Watergate,[†] the scandal that rocked the nation, began on June 17, 1972, when five men were caught trying to burglarize the offices of the Democratic National Committee. The arrest of the five led to an investigation that uncovered a White House plan of systematic espionage* against political opponents. Deeply involved in that plan were the two top aides to President Richard Nixon, John Ehrlichman and H. R. Haldeman. On May 19, 1973, Attorney General Elliot Richardson appointed a special prosecutor, Harvard Law School professor Archibald Cox, to conduct a full-scale investigation of the break-in at the Watergate Hotel. On May 17, 1973, the Senate Committee on Presidential Activities had opened hearings, and on July 13 White House aide Alexander Butterfield told the committee that President Nixon had taped all of the conversations that occurred in his office. However, Nixon refused to turn the tapes over to the investigating committee, and, on October 20, he ordered the dismissal of prosecutor Cox. After the resulting storm of public protest, Nixon agreed to turn over the tapes in June 1974. Once members of the committee had examined the tapes, they discovered that eighteen-and-one-half minutes had been mysteriously erased. By July 30, the House Judiciary Committee had approved three articles of impeachment. Rather than face almost certain disgrace, Richard Milhous Nixon resigned on August 9, 1974.

Main Idea _____

_____

Supporting Details _____

_____

_____

_____

_____

_____

_____

[†]The Watergate, the origin of the scandal's name, is a hotel-apartment-office complex in Washington, D.C., where the Democratic National Committee's offices were located.
*espionage: spying.

_____

_____

_____

_____

_____

_____

2. In 1578, Queen Elizabeth granted her friend and political supporter Sir Humphrey Gilbert permission to found a colony in America. Five years later, Gilbert and two hundred colonists set sail only to dis appear. At that point, Gilbert's half-brother, Sir Walter Raleigh, petitioned the queen to take over the colonizing of the New World. In 1584, an English fort and settlement with more than one hundred men was established on an island off the coast of present-day North Carolina. The British settlers named the island Roanoke and described it as an American Eden. However, they abandoned it within a year because of bad relations with the Native Americans already living there. In 1587, another group of British colonists arrived on the island and within a month, one of the women on the island gave birth to the first child born in the New World, naming her Virginia Dare. Only a week after the birth, the baby's grandfather, Captain John White, had to return to England because the group was already running out of supplies. Due to conflicts with Spain, White did not return to Roanoke until 1590. But to his horror and shock, there was nothing left of the former colony. The only signs of human presence were the letters "CRO" and "CROATAN" carved on two trees. Everything and everyone else had mysteriously vanished. To this day, no one knows what happened to the colonists White left behind on Roanoke Island.

Main Idea _____

_____

Supporting Details _____

_____

_____

_____

_____
_____
_____
_____
_____
_____
_____

 ## Pattern 4. Simple Listing

In passages using the process or sequence of dates and events patterns, the order of events and steps is extremely important. The writer who describes a process is not about to put the last step first or vice versa. The same is true for the sequence of dates and events pattern. No writer of a history text tracing the events in the Civil War is going to describe the battle of Antietam (1862) after the Battle of Gettysburg (1863).

In the simple listing pattern, however, all the major details are equally important and can be switched around to suit the writer's purpose. A writer who uses the simple listing pattern mainly wants to identify certain skills, factors, studies, reasons, and so on, related to a particular topic or issue—making the order in which they appear irrelevant. Look, for example, at the two paragraphs that follow. The content of each is the same. The order is not.

Paragraph 1

Victims of eating disorders display several distinct symptoms. They are preoccupied with their weight or their physical appearance and often exhibit signs of low self-esteem. They are inclined to suffer from anxiety, moodiness, or depression and may also diet obsessively or avoid eating altogether. Or just the opposite, they may overeat, purge, and then start eating again. In either case, the victims exhibit rapid weight loss or pronounced weight changes. Those suffering from eating disorders may also exhibit compulsive* behaviors such as hoarding food or eating specific

_____

*compulsive: uncontrollable.

foods only on certain days. They are likely to wear baggy clothes to hide their bodies and withdraw from others, avoiding social situations that include food. Some victims even isolate themselves completely. Those in the grip of an eating disorder are likely to experience faintness, dizziness, and an inability to concentrate. Problems such as constipation or diarrhea are also common. (Source of information: Robert Segal et al., "Eating Disorders: Types, Warning Signs, and Treatments," Helpguide.org, May 24, 2006, www.helpguide.org/mental/eating_disorder_treatment.htm.)

In Paragraph 1, the author announces that eating disorders have several symptoms. Knowing full well that most readers are going to ask, "What are they?" the author describes each symptom. Nothing in the paragraph, however, suggests that any one symptom is more important than the others or precedes the others in time. Thus, the author is free to list them in any way she thinks appropriate. Note how easily the order can be changed without changing the paragraph's meaning.

Paragraph 2

Victims of eating disorders are likely to experience faintness, dizziness, concentration difficulties, and bowel problems like constipation or diarrhea. They are likely to wear baggy clothes to hide their bodies and withdraw from others, avoiding in particular any social situation involving food. Some completely isolate themselves and may exhibit obsessive behaviors such as hoarding food or eating specific foods only on certain days. They may diet obsessively and avoid eating, or just the opposite, they may overeat and purge; in either case, they exhibit rapid weight loss or pronounced weight changes. Often suffering from anxiety, moodiness, or depression, they are preoccupied with their weight and physical appearance and are likely to exhibit signs of low self-esteem. Although there are other less common symptoms, the ones listed here are the typical signs of an eating disorder.

As you can see, unlike any of the patterns you've studied so far, simple listing has a loose and readily reorganized structure.

Typical Topic Sentences

Topic sentences typical of the simple listing pattern *almost* always (note the qualifier *almost* and see, for instance, sentence 4) contain some general words like those listed on the next page.

cases	efforts	parts	roles
changes	examples	policies	studies
characteristics	illustrations	principles	symptoms
decisions	inventions	qualities	traits

As you know from Chapter 3, when these words appear in a topic sentence, they also help identify major details.

The following topic sentences are all typical of those likely to appear in the simple listing pattern.

1. Between 1793 and 1831, the Supreme Court decided several cases in favor of the federal government and against states' rights.

2. These are just a few of the numerous inventions that Dean Kamen has patented in the last two decades. (Note the wording, which is typical of simple listing topic sentences appearing at the very end of a paragraph.)

3. Before global warming, several characteristics helped polar bears survive and even thrive in the Arctic.

4. Many people believe that Hillary Clinton can become the first woman president of the United States.

5. In places like China, Vietnam, Egypt, and Algeria, efforts are being made to censor, even silence, bloggers who speak out against repressive governments.

Topic sentences like ones shown above are most likely to be at the very beginning of a simple listing paragraph—first to third sentence—although they can also appear at the very end.

Pattern Pointers

1. If the topic sentence contains a general word that needs to be specifically itemized—for example, *statistics*, *studies*, *reasons*, use that word as a guide to selecting the major details. Any sentence that introduces a new case, characteristic, etc., is worth remembering and/or recording in your notes. Any sentence that doesn't is probably not especially significant.

2. If all the vocabulary in the paragraph is familiar, the simple listing pattern gives up its meaning fairly quickly. Unfortunately, the information the simple listing pattern conveys is

often so loosely connected, it can be hard to remember. Thus you should think about adding a visual aid to your notes, perhaps making a concept map like the one shown below.

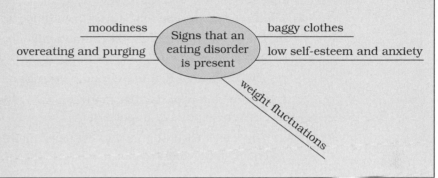

EXERCISE 5 **DIRECTIONS** Read each paragraph. Then identify the topic sentence and the best paraphrase of that sentence by circling the appropriate letters. Write the crucial word or phrase from the topic sentence in the blanks and list the qualities, traits, etc., that clarify it.

1. [1]Although the 1964 Civil Rights Act has eleven titles or divisions, six are of special significance. [2]According to Title I of the Civil Rights Act, it's illegal to apply different voter registration requirements to people of different races. [3]Title II states that "all persons shall be entitled to the full and equal enjoyment of the goods, services, facilities, and privileges, advantages, and accommodations of any place of public accommodation." [4]Thus it outlaws discrimination in places like hotels, motels, restaurants, theaters, and sports arenas. [5]Titles III and IV mandate the desegregation of public schools and other public facilities and give the U.S. Attorney General the authority to file suits to force schools to achieve racial balance. [6]Title VI states that "no person in the United States shall, on the ground of race, color, or national origin, be excluded from participation in, be denied the benefits of, or be subjected to discrimination under any program or activity receiving Federal financial assistance." [7]According to this section, a federally funded agency found guilty of discrimination could lose its funding. [8]Title VII of the Act prohibits employment discrimination in any business on the basis of race, color, religion, sex, or national origin. [9]It authorizes the Equal Opportunity Employment Commission and individuals to bring lawsuits against employers who violate this law. (Source of information: Civil Rights Act of 1964, http://usinfo.state.gov/usa/infousa/laws/majorlaw/civilr19.htm.)

1. The topic sentence is

  a. sentence 1.

  b. sentence 2.

  c. sentence 3.

2. The best paraphrase of that topic sentence is

  a. The 1964 Civil Rights Act dramatically changed U.S. society, particularly when it came to voter registration.

  b. The 1964 Civil Rights Act had eleven significant parts.

  c. Of the eleven parts that made up the 1964 Civil Rights Act, six were especially important.

  d. The 1964 Civil Rights Act focuses mainly on obstacles to equal employment.

3. The crucial word or phrase in the topic sentence is —————

_____.

4. The following supporting details clarify and explain that word or phrase.

_____

_____

_____

_____

_____

_____

_____

_____

2. [1]Art museums all over the world have begun, somewhat grudgingly, to return works of art stolen in World War II by the Nazis, who routinely forced Jewish art dealers and collectors to sell their belongings for prices that amounted to theft. [2]The Israel Museum of Jerusalem transferred the title of one of its most prized paintings, *Boulevard Montmartre: Spring* by Camille Pissarro to the family of Max Silberberg, a collector who died in a concentration camp and whose paintings had been sold in one of the Nazis' notorious "Jewish auctions." [3]A similar decision to transfer ownership was made by the North Carolina Museum of Art in Raleigh, which conceded that a sixteenth-century painting by Lucas Cranach belonged to the family of Dr. Philipp von Gomperz. [4]A recent ruling by the Dutch government removed close to 200 pieces of art from the walls of Holland's museums so that the artworks could be returned to the family of Jacques Goudstikker, who had been forced to sell the Nazis his art collection for a fraction of its worth. [5]Even Austria, which at first had flatly ignored claims that several works by famed Viennese artist Gustav Klimt really belonged to victims of Nazi persecution, has relented and returned several Klimt paintings to the original owner's family.

1. The topic sentence is

   a. sentence 1.

   b. sentence 2.

   c. sentence 3.

2. The best paraphrase of that topic sentence is

   a. The families of Holocaust victims have just begun to receive reparations for what relatives suffered during World War II.

   b. Art museums have fought hard to retain ownership of artwork confiscated from victims of Nazi persecution.

   c. Museums all over the world are returning to the families of the original owners artwork that was confiscated by the Nazis.

   d. Museums are embarrassed by revelations that they benefited from the Holocaust.

3. The crucial word or phrase in the topic sentence is _____

_____.

4. The following supporting details clarify and explain that word or phrase.

_____

_____

_____

_____

_____

_____

_____

EXERCISE 6 **DIRECTIONS** Circle the appropriate letter to identify the primary pattern used in each paragraph.

1. In December 2006, legendary blues and rock singer James Brown died of pneumonia at the age of seventy-three. At the time of his death, Brown was considered by many to have been the most influential force in popular music for over fifty years. Born in Barnwell, South Carolina, in 1933, Brown was abandoned by his mother at the age of four and grew up on the streets of Augusta, Georgia. Homeless, he survived mainly by petty crime, and by 1949 he had spent more than three years in reform school for attempted car theft. Reform school, however, brought Brown together with gospel singer Bobby Byrd. Byrd took Brown into his family and into his singing group, the *Gospel Starlighters,* which eventually became the *Famous Flames.* By January 1956, the "Flames" had a record deal and a rhythm and blues (R & B) top ten hit, "Please, Please, Please." Brown eventually went solo, dominating music throughout the 1960s with a string of hits, including "Out of Sight," "I Got You," and "Papa's Got a Brand New Bag," which won him a Grammy in 1966. By 1968, his song "Say It Loud—I'm Black and I'm Proud" had become an anthem of racial pride. In 1986, Brown was inducted into the Rock and Roll Hall of Fame. In 1987, he won the best R & B vocal performance award for his hit "Living in America." Performers as diverse as rocker Mick Jagger and rapper Chuck D credited Brown with influencing their music and their performance style. As journalist Greg Bluestein expressed it, "Brown was to rhythm and dance music what [Bob] Dylan was to lyrics"—the unchallenged popular innovator and, above all, the 'Godfather of Soul!'"

   a. definition

   b. process

   c. sequence of dates and events

   d. simple listing

2. The term *modern art* is a broad, general term that covers any number of different styles. Surrealism, for example, would fall under the category of modern art. Founded by the artist André Breton in the twenties, the goal of the surrealists was to create art that mirrored the workings of the unconscious mind, where logic did not apply. Thus the surrealists featured familiar objects in unlikely contexts or combinations. In a surrealist painting, a headless statue, for instance, might stand beside a stack of bananas. Although Salvador Dalí is probably the best known of the group, the truly great surrealists were artists like Max Ernst, Joan Miró, and

René Magritte. Cubism would also qualify as modern art, and it appeared even before surrealism. Cubism began with the work of Pablo Picasso and Georges Braque, both of whom followed the advice of the painter Paul Cézanne. In 1904, Cézanne argued that artists should treat nature in terms of "the sphere, the cylinder, and the cone." Picasso's 1907 "The Vase, Bowl, and Lemon" is a classic example of cubist style, which reduced reality to underlying geometric forms. For many Americans, however, modern art will always refer to the abstract expressionists, the painters who came to fame in the 1950s and replaced recognizable subjects with lines, colors, and forms. Because most of the abstract expressionists who became internationally famous started out in New York City, they were also known as "The New York School." The three most famous artists in this group were Jackson Pollock, Willem de Kooning, and Mark Rothko.

a. definition

b. process

c. sequence of dates and events

d. simple listing

3. Historians have rightly called the era spanning the early fifteenth century to the early sixteenth century the "Age of Discovery" or the "Age of Exploration." In 1419, Portugal's Prince Henry the Navigator[†] began funding the efforts of mapmakers, shipbuilders, and instrument makers, and, by the mid-1400s, Portuguese sailors were traveling down the West African coast. In the 1490s, explorer Vasco da Gama[‡] sailed around Africa's Cape of Good Hope and as far as the Indian Ocean. For the next twenty-five years, Portugal sent thousands of sailors to sea in an effort to establish trading outposts from West Africa to China. By 1500, the Portuguese had become the first Europeans to reach Brazil. Around the same time, inspired by Portugal's success, Spain began aggressively exploring new lands with the express purpose of conquest and colonization. Between 1492 and 1504, Christopher Columbus, financed by the Spanish King Ferdinand and Queen Isabella, became the first European to reach the Bahamas as well as several other Caribbean islands and Central America. In 1519, Ferdinand Magellan left Spain to claim undiscovered lands for the Spanish crown. During his travels, he sailed around the tip of South America to the Pacific Ocean. Although Magellan was killed in the Philippines in 1521, in the following year his

[†]Prince Henry the Navigator (1394–1460): A nobleman of English, French, and Spanish ancestry, Prince Henry sponsored voyages of exploration in an effort to serve his king.
[‡]Vasco da Gama (1460–1524): Portuguese explorer who found a route from Portugal to the East.

ship became the first to circumnavigate the globe. From 1519 to 1531, Spaniards Hernando Cortés and Francesco Pizarro explored Central and South America, conquering the Aztec and Incan civilizations to claim the lands as Spain's. (Source of information: Steven Kries, "Lecture 2: The Age of Discovery," *The History Guide,* April 15, 2003, www.historyguide.org/ earlymod/lecture2c.html.)

a. definition

b. process

c. sequence of dates and events

d. simple listing

4. During the process of labor, the mother's uterus contracts rhythmically and automatically to force the baby downward through the vaginal canal. The contractions occur in relatively predictable stages. The **first stage of labor** usually begins with fairly mild and irregular contractions of the uterus. As contractions become stronger and more frequent, the *cervix* (the opening of the uterus) dilates, or widens, enough for the baby's head to fit through. Toward the end of this stage, which may take from eight to twenty-four hours for a first-time mother, a period of **transition** begins. The cervix nears full dilation, contractions become more rapid, and the baby's head begins to move into the birth canal. Although this period generally lasts for only a few minutes, it can be extremely painful because of the increasing pressure of the contractions. The **second stage of labor** includes complete dilation of the cervix to the actual birth. It usually lasts between one and one-and-one-half hours. During the **third stage of labor**, which lasts only a few minutes, the afterbirth (the placenta and umbilical cord) is expelled. (Adapted from Seifert and Hoffnung, *Child and Adolescent Development,* pp. 131–132.)

a. definition

b. process

c. sequence of dates and events

d. simple listing

 # Pattern 5: Classification

In the classification pattern, too, the order in which information is presented is unimportant. The significant difference between simple listing and classification is that paragraphs using the classification pattern always make the same point: They tell readers how some larger group can be broken down into smaller subgroups, or classes, each with its own set of specific characteristics. Here's an illustration.

Hippocrates classified people according to the four fluids in their body.

TQ: Explain Hippocrates' system of classification.

Like his contemporaries,* the Greek physician Hippocrates believed that the human body consisted of four *humours*, or fluids: black bile, yellow bile, blood, and phlegm. Hippocrates' contribution was to classify human beings according to the predominant fluid in their bodies. Persons with an excess of black bile were labeled ① *melancholic* and were presumed to be depressed and pessimistic. The ② *choleric*, possessing excess yellow bile, were considered quick-tempered and irritable. Persons with a predominance of blood were classified as ③ *sanguine*. They were expected to be cheerful and optimistic. The ④ *phlegmatic*, possessing excess phlegm, were thought to be unemotional and uninvolved with the world at large. While the theory of the four humours has long since been discarded, the terms used to describe personality persist.

Although most classification paragraphs have a topic sentence that names the number of categories, this is not always the case. Sometimes the author just describes the subgroups of a larger category and leaves it to readers to total up the number of categories.

In addition to bills, members of Congress also pass resolutions. A *simple resolution* is used for matters such as establishing the rules under which the Senate or the House will operate. A *concurrent resolution* settles housekeeping and procedural matters that affect both the House and the Senate. Simple and concurrent resolutions are not signed by the president and do not have the force of law. A *joint resolution* requires the approval of both houses. It also requires the signature of the president and is the same as law. A joint resolution is necessary to propose a constitutional amendment and, in this case, the resolution must be approved by a two-thirds vote of both houses. (Adapted from Wilson and Dilulio, *American Government*, p. 351.)

In this paragraph, the main idea is suggested or implied: Congress passes three kinds of resolutions.

Typical Topic Sentences

Topic sentences like those that follow are clues to the classification pattern. Note the presence of verb phrases such as "are classified"

*contemporaries: people born during the same period.

and "can be divided," which are typical of this pattern. Note as well that some topic sentences label the categories, while others identify only the number of groups to be described.

---

1. Burns are classified into three different types based on degree of severity.

2. Geologists have divided the earth into three layers, each with its own composition and temperature.

3. Beginning in the nineteenth century, three distinct Jewish communities developed—Orthodox, Reform, and Conservative—each with a different view on the importance of tradition.

4. There are five different kinds of listening.

Pattern Pointers

1. Classification patterns can be quite lengthy. Don't, however, let the length intimidate you. Just look for the larger group being divided and the number and names of categories along with their key characteristics (*Note*: Categories don't always get names.) If the author explains how the categories are created—for example, "Burns are classified into three different types based on degree of severity"—make sure you remember and/or record the method of classification as well as the categories that are the end result.

2. If you are having a difficult time sorting out the categories in a classification chart, try making a chart like this:

Three different kinds of burns based on degree of severity		
First degree burns 1. Burns are red and sensitive. 2. Burns affect the outer layer of skin and cause pain and swelling. 3. The skin may peel or appear whitish; it can also become clammy, as in sunburn.	Second degree burns 1. Burns affect the epidermis and underlying dermis. 2. Burns cause redness, swelling, and blisters. 3. Burns often affect sweat glands and hair follicles.	Third degree burns 1. Burns affect the epidermis, dermis, and hypodermis. 2. Visible burn areas may be numb, but the victim may still complain of pain. 3. Healing is slow and scarring present.

<table>
<tr><td colspan="1">Check Your Understanding</td></tr>
<tr><td>

Explain how the simple listing and the classification pattern are both similar and different.

_____

_____

_____

_____

_____

</td></tr>
</table>

EXERCISE 7 **DIRECTIONS** Read each paragraph. Then fill in the blanks and list the subgroups along with brief descriptions of each one. Paraphrase as much as possible.

1. [1]According to one theory, there are nine different personality types that describe human behavior. [2]The *reformer* likes to create order and believes that he or she knows the right way of doing things. [3]For the *reformer*, the world is an imperfect place desperately in need of fixing. [4]The *helper* feels a strong sense of personal responsibility for others and is fulfilled when lending a hand to those in need. [5]The *motivator* places the highest value on the kind of success that can be recognized and acknowledged by others in the world. [6]The *romantic* sees him- or herself as different from the rest of society and longs to be recognized as unique. [7]The *thinker* could not care less about being recognized. [8]What matters is being alone to think deep thoughts. [9]The *skeptic* questions authority even when it gets him or her into trouble, and it usually does. [10]The *enthusiast* considers the world a constant source of wonder and looks for pleasure in life. [11]The *leader* is convinced the world is in serious trouble and in need of guidance. [12]Fortunately, the leader is available to provide the appropriate guidance. [13]The *peacemaker* believes passionately in harmony and is committed to resolving conflict; even when involved with people who enjoy a good fight, the peacemaker looks for a compromise. (Source of information: www.9types.com.)

    1. _____ is the larger group being subdivided into

    _____ smaller subgroups.

2. Does the author explain the basis for the classification? _____

If so, what is the basis for the classification? _____

3. List and describe the subgroups in your own words.

_____

_____

_____

_____

_____

_____

_____

_____

2. [1]Fish are vertebrates* that live in water and breathe with gills. [2]Based on their skeletons, the 25,000 species of fish can be broken down into three main groups. [3]The *agnatha* class are the most "primitive." [4]They lack both a jaw and a bony skeleton. [5]Examples would be lamprey eels and hagfish. [6]Lacking true bones, fish in this group are extraordinarily flexible. [7]The hagfish, for instance, can tie itself into a knot. [8]Although their ancestors had real bones, the *chondrichthyes* have a skeleton made out of cartilage. [9]These fish— sharks, skates, rays, and ratfish—have loosely attached lower jaws with big and very noticeable teeth. [10]The *osteichthyes* are called bony fish because their skeletons are made of calcium. [11]Catfish and trout belong to this group. [12]Like all bony fish, they are fast-moving and able to maneuver with ease. [13]Highly adaptable creatures, they often have very specialized mouths, which help them to explore underwater resources with great efficiency.

1. _____ is the larger group being subdivided into

_____ smaller subgroups.

2. Does the author explain the basis for the classification? _____ If

so, what is the basis for the classification? _____

---

*vertebrates: creatures with a backbone.

3. List and describe the subgroups in your own words.

_____

_____

_____

_____

_____

_____

_____

_____

_____

─■ **EXERCISE 8** DIRECTIONS Circle the appropriate letter to identify the primary pattern organizing each paragraph

1. No matter what it looks like on television crime shows, posting bail after an arrest is no simple matter. When a suspect is arrested, he or she is first taken to a police station to be booked, or processed. The police officer in charge then records the suspect's personal information (name, address, birthday, appearance) along with information about the alleged crime. Next, the officer conducts a criminal background check, takes the suspect's fingerprints and mug shots, confiscates any personal property (to be returned later), and places the suspect in a jail cell. For less serious crimes, suspects may be allowed to post bail immediately after being booked. For more serious crimes, suspects have to wait, sometimes as long as two days, for a bail hearing, at which point a judge will determine if the accused is eligible for bail and at what cost. The amount of bail depends on the severity of the crime. However, it is also at the judge's discretion.* Some jurisdictions* have bail schedules that recommend a standard amount. For example, in Los Angeles, the bail schedule recommends $25,000 for perjury or sexual assault, $100,000 for manslaughter, and $1,000,000 for kidnapping with intent to rape. (Source of information: http://people.howstuffworks.com/bail1.htm.)

---

*discretion: thoughtful judgment.
*jurisdictions: areas of control or authority.

a. definition

b. process

c. sequence of dates and events

d. simple listing

e. classification

2. Most people need an **incentive** to join big organizations like the Sierra Club, People for the Ethical Treatment of Animals, or the National Rifle Association. But not all incentives are the same. In fact, there are three different kinds. *Solidarity incentives* are the feelings of pleasure, status, or companionship that arise out of meeting face to face. To offer this incentive, large organizations usually need to organize themselves as coalitions of small local units. It's the local units that provide the most occasions for face-to-face meetings. *Material incentives*—things valued in monetary terms—are also important to potential members of large organizations. The Illinois Farm Bureau, for instance, offers its members a chance to buy farm supplies at reduced prices. The *purpose incentive*—the appeal of shared goals—is perhaps the most difficult of the three incentives for organizations to provide. Finding some goal or objective that appeals to large numbers of people and working toward it in a way that appeals to everyone involved is a formidable task. (Source of information: Wilson and Dilulio, *American Government*, pp. 270–271.)

a. definition

b. process

c. sequence of dates and events

d. simple listing

e. classification

3. A **tsunami** is a series of ocean waves generated by a sudden displacement of the sea floor. The term is derived from a Japanese word meaning "harbor wave." Tsunamis are sometimes referred to as **seismic sea waves** because submarine and near-coast earthquakes are their primary cause. They are also popularly called "tidal waves," but this is a misnomer;* tsunamis have nothing to do with tides. Tsunamis can occur with little or no warning, bringing death and massive destruction to coastal communities. (Murck et al., *Environmental Geology*, p. 131.)

---

*misnomer: inappropriate name.

a. definition

b. process

c. sequence of dates and events

d. simple listing

e. classification

4. Heart attacks are commonly associated with a gut-wrenching pain in the chest. However, in addition to severe chest pain, a host of other symptoms signals the onset of a heart attack. Some victims of a heart attack notice a numbing or tingling of the left arm. Nausea or shortness of breath are also significant symptoms, as is the sudden onset of dizziness. A sense of pressure and squeezing in the chest is an additional symptom, as is pain in the shoulder and neck. Sweating, if combined with nausea and a feeling of faintness, is a symptom as well.

a. definition

b. process

c. sequence of dates and events

d. simple listing

e. classification

5. Louis Braille (1809–1852) invented the system of reading and writing that people who are blind or visually impaired still use today. A bright young boy who was legally blind by the age of four, Braille knew all too well what blindness meant. In 1812, three-year-old Braille was playing in his father's leather-working shop when he injured his eye with a sharp tool. The eye became infected and the infection spread. One year later, the boy was completely blind. In 1819, Braille's parents sent their child to the Royal Institution for Blind Youth in Paris, where the boy quickly became frustrated with the slow system of running his fingers over the huge, raised letters in the few books available to blind children. In the 1820s, Braille heard about a code devised by a French army captain who wanted his soldiers to be able to read messages at night. The teenager began to think about how he could adapt this code for blind people. By 1829, Braille had come up with a system that uses different combinations of raised dots to represent each letter of the alphabet, and he published the first book using the Braille system. However, in 1852 Braille died. At the time of his death, Braille's method of reading and writing for the blind was still not widespread. Then, in 1868, sixteen years after Braille's death, Dr. Thomas Rhodes Armitage, whose sight was failing him, founded the Royal National

Institute for the Blind in Britain and began promoting Braille's system. It caught on and eventually came to be used in almost every country in the world. Thus Braille's system has been adapted to many different languages.

a. definition

b. process

c. sequence of dates and events

d. simple listing

e. classification

Pattern 6: Comparison and Contrast

In all kinds of textbooks, authors are likely to compare (discuss similarities) and/or contrast (cite differences). Sometimes, in fact, writers devote an entire chapter section to pointing out the similarities and differences between two topics, but more often the comparison and contrast pattern is confined to organizing a single paragraph. Here is an example.

TQ: Explain the difference between assertive and aggressive behavior. Give examples for each type.

My Uncle Ralph always keeps cool.

My ex-wife is a good example.

Examples.

⬚ Assertive behavior ⬚ involves <u>standing up for your rights</u> and expressing your thoughts and feelings <u>in a direct, appropriate way</u> that <u>does not violate the rights of others</u>. It is a matter of getting the other person to understand your viewpoint. People who exhibit assertive behavior skills <u>are able to handle conflict</u> situations <u>with ease and assurance</u> while maintaining good interpersonal relations. In contrast, ⬚ aggressive behavior ⬚ involves <u>expressing</u> your <u>thoughts and feelings</u> and defending your rights <u>in a way that openly violates the rights of others</u>. Those exhibiting aggressive behavior seem to believe that the rights of others must be subservient to theirs. Thus they <u>have a difficult time maintaining good interpersonal relations</u>. They are likely to <u>interrupt, talk fast, ignore others</u>, and <u>use sarcasm</u> or other forms of verbal abuse to maintain control. (Adapted from Reece and Brandt, *Effective Human Relations in Organizations*, pp. 350–353.)

A paragraph like this one with its two topics—assertive and aggressive behavior—and its emphasis on the difference between them has comparison and contrast written all over it. It just about cries out for you to predict a test question that asks for a description of how the two topics are similar and/or different.

Typical Topic Sentences

Sentences like the ones that follow are also clues to the comparison and contrast pattern. Note the consistent presence of two topics (see underscores).

1. Viewed with <u>contempt while he was in office,</u> Abraham Lincoln became a <u>hero only long after his death</u>.

2. In the Wild West, the life of a <u>cowboy</u> was not all that different from that of a <u>cowgirl</u>, as the life of Calamity Jane well illustrates.

3. Although <u>Carl Jung</u> began as a disciple of <u>Sigmund Freud</u>, the two men eventually diverged in their thinking.

4. Like his Persian predecessor, philosopher and physician <u>Ibn Sina</u> (980–1037), the Spanish-Arab philosopher <u>Ibn Rushd</u> (1126–1198) believed that the universe is eternal and the individual mortal.

5. Unlike former <u>Secretary of State Henry Kissinger</u> (1973–1977), former <u>Secretary of State Colin Powell</u> (2001–2005) did not have much influence over the president.

Transitions

In addition to topic sentences like those above, the following transitions are also clues to the comparison and contrast pattern.

Transitions That Introduce Similarity

Along the same lines	Just as
By the same token	Just like
In like manner	Likewise
In much the same vein	Similarly
In the same manner	

Transitions That Signal a Difference

And yet	In opposition	On the one hand
But	In reality	On the other hand
Conversely	Nevertheless	Still
Despite that fact	Nonetheless	Unfortunately
However	On the contrary	Whereas
In contrast		

Pattern Pointers

1. The presence of two topics, each described in some detail, is the major clue to recognizing the comparison and contrast pattern. However, the trick to reading the pattern is to stay focused on this question: What point do these similarities and differences illustrate or prove?

2. If you are struggling to understand a particularly difficult comparison and contrast paragraph or reading, try a split diagram like this one:

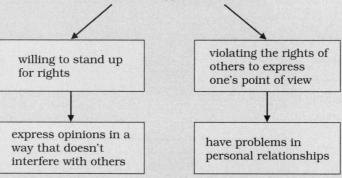

Assertive and Aggressive Behavior

willing to stand up for rights → express opinions in a way that doesn't interfere with others

violating the rights of others to express one's point of view → have problems in personal relationships

Check Your Understanding

Write a comparison and contrast paragraph on any one of the following:

1. the comedy of Bill Murray and Dane Cook
2. the talents of Beyonce and Britney Spears
3. the music of Nellie Furtado and Kelly Clarkson
4. using text messaging versus e-mail
5. E-books and print books
6. Hip-hop and country-western music

EXERCISE 9   **DIRECTIONS** Read each paragraph. Identify the two topics. Then paraphrase the topic sentence along with the similarities and/or differences between the topics.

1. Social drinking differs significantly from alcoholism. Social drinkers usually drink in moderation and limit the amount of alcohol they consume. Alcoholics, in contrast, drink in ever-increasing amounts. Often they do not stop drinking until they pass out. Social drinkers sip, while alcoholics gulp. Social drinkers drink to have more fun at social gatherings, while alcoholics drink alone, often to relieve stress or avoid facing problems. Social drinkers don't usually think or talk about drinking; alcoholics are preoccupied with how and when they will drink again. Finally, social drinkers do not experience physical, psychological, or job-related problems caused by their drinking. Alcoholics, however, often let drinking damage their health, harm their relationships with others, and destroy their careers. (Source of information: Bernstein et al., *Psychology*, p. 597.)

Topic 1 _____

Topic 2 _____

Main Idea _____

_____

Similarities _____

_____

_____

_____

Differences _____

_____

_____

_____

_____

2. Although chimpanzees can't talk, they are still remarkably similar to humans. For example, the physical proportions for the body parts of both humans and chimpanzees are relatively close. Both species also have similar hands, feet, legs, and facial features. In fact, the DNA of humans and chimpanzees is 98.4 percent identical. In addition to these physical similarities, chimpanzee societies parallel human ones in a variety of ways. Human beings establish political systems and fight wars. Likewise, groups of chimpanzees form hierarchies with high-ranking and low-ranking chimps, and they too engage in warfare against other groups. Moreover, observation of chimps in the wild has confirmed that chimpanzees display emotions that are similar to what humans experience. Humans grieve for lost loved ones, and chimps appear to do the same. In one case, a healthy young chimp seemed to fall into a severe depression after his mother's death. He eventually stopped eating and died. Research on the brain suggests that emotions like grief arise from ancient parts of the brain found in both species. (Source of information: "Are Chimpanzees Capable of Understanding and Recognizing Emotions?" www.whozoo.org/AnlifeSS2001/serishoo/Are%20Chimpanzees %20Capable%20of.htm.)

Topic 1 _____

Topic 2 _____

Main Idea _____

_____

Similarities _____

_____

_____

_____

Differences _____

_____

_____

_____

EXERCISE 10 **DIRECTIONS** Circle the appropriate letter to identify the primary pattern used in each paragraph.

1. Alfred Binet (1857–1911) is considered the father of the IQ test. Binet first attempted to create an intelligence test in 1904. The French Ministry of Public Instruction had commissioned him to develop a technique or method that would identify children who needed educational assistance. In 1905, Binet fulfilled the request by creating the Binet-Simon Scale. Considered the first intelligence test, the Binet-Simon Scale consisted of thirty separate tasks, such as naming parts of the body, counting coins, defining words, and filling in blanks left in sentences. All the tasks on the test were arranged in order of increasing complexity and were designed to establish the test-taker's mental age. In 1908, Henry Herbert Goddard translated the test into English and brought it to the United States, where it became the model for future intelligence tests.

   a. definition

   b. process

   c. sequence of dates and events

   d. simple listing

   e. classification

   f. comparison and contrast

2. The most widely used classification of temperaments is based on a study of middle-class and upper-middle-class infants from the New York City area—the New York Longitudinal Study (NYLS). Investigators involved in the study identified three general temperament types that could be used to classify most children in the group. "Easy children" are playful and respond positively to new situations. They adapt readily to change, are inclined to be happy, and are quick to develop regular feeding and sleeping schedules. About 40 percent of the NYLS children fell in this category. "Difficult children" react negatively to new situations or people. They have irritable dispositions and difficulty establishing regular sleeping and feeding schedules. About 10 percent of the group were in this category. "Inhibited children" have low activity levels and avoid new situations. They also have difficulty adjusting to unfamiliar situations. Faced with the unfamiliar, they are likely to become withdrawn, subdued, or mildly distressed. This category described about 15 percent of the entire group. (Adapted from Nevid, *Essentials of Psychology,* p. 306.)

a. definition

b. process

c. sequence of dates and events

d. simple listing

e. classification

f. comparison and contrast

3. A new study suggests that chimpanzees, just like human beings, are inclined to help strangers experiencing difficulty or distress. Felix Warneken of the Max Planck Institute for Evolutionary Anthropology in Leipzig, Germany, conducted three experiments with adult chimps living on an island sanctuary in Uganda and two experiments with three-year-old children living in Germany. In the first of the three chimp experiments, one of the researchers struggled to reach a stick on the other side of a barred enclosure. Watching his struggles were thirty-six chimpanzees, one of whom could hand him the stick. In most instances, one of the chimpanzees did precisely that. It reached out and handed the researcher the stick he was struggling to grasp. A similar trial with thirty-six human youngsters showed the same results. In another one of the experiments, chimpanzees climbed platforms and navigated hurdles in order to offer aid to a researcher. The children involved in a similar experiment did the same. (Source of information: B. Bower, "Ape Aid," *Science News*, June 30, 2007, p. 406.)

a. definition

b. process

c. sequence of dates and events

d. simple listing

e. classification

f. comparison and contrast

4. In an amazing about-face, numerous industries and industry trade groups have begun to push for more federal regulation. The Flavor and Extract Manufacturers Association of the United States, for instance, is working with unions to limit workplace exposure to diacetyl, a chemical used to artificially flavor popcorn and known to cause lung damage. Along with environmental groups, Philips Lighting and General Electric are promoting bans on conventional lightbulbs, which consume large amounts of energy and need to be replaced every few months. The goal is to replace the conventional bulbs with more energy-efficient ones. The makers of fireworks are asking for mandatory testing to avoid the possibility that fireworks might explode in an unexpected way. Even more astonishing, the owners of Philip Morris cigarettes are asking the Food and Drug Administration to regulate the manufacture and marketing of tobacco products.

a. definition

b. process

c. sequence of dates and events

d. simple listing

e. classification

f. comparison and contrast

 # Pattern 7: Cause and Effect

Because connecting cause to effect is so basic to our thinking, you'll find cause and effect paragraphs in every type of textbook. No matter what the subject matter, at some point authors need to explain how one event (the cause) produces another event (the effect).

Ultraviolet radiation is harmful

TQ: What are some of the effects of ultraviolet radiation?

Effects

The ultraviolet (UV) radiation from the sun that reaches the Earth's surface is a health threat. At the very least, exposure to the sun's rays causes ①aging and wrinkling of the skin. At the very worst, it is responsible for, ②cataracts, ③sunburn, ④snowblindness, and ⑤skin cancer, which claims around 15,000 lives each year in the United States alone. Exposure to UV radiation also ⑥suppresses the immune system, enabling cancers to become established and grow. In addition, ⑦radiation slows plant growth, ⑧delays seed germination, and ⑨interferes with photosynthesis.* (Adapted from Kaufman and Franz, *Biosphere 2000,* p. 266.)

Cause and effect paragraphs are a likely source of test questions. When you encounter them in your reading, make sure you can (1) clearly identify both cause (or causes) and effect (or effects) and (2) explain how one led to or produced the other. Not surprisingly, cause and effect passages are a common source of exam questions like the one that appears in the margin next to the paragraph on ultraviolet radiation.

---

*photosynthesis: process by which plants use sunlight to create food.

Typical Topic Sentences

Topic sentences like those listed here are typical of the cause and effect pattern.

---

1. Thanks to the newly invented telescope, Galileo Galilei (1564–1642) was able to detect lunar mountains.

2. Teacher and writer Paulo Friere (1921–1997) knew that poverty can create a "culture of silence"—a sense that talking about one's misery is useless.

3. Liberation theology has spread beyond Latin America and inspired other social-change movements throughout the world.

4. The social and political program known as *perestroika* stemmed from Mikhail Gorbachev's recognition that socialism in the former Soviet Union had been an economic and political disaster.

5. The "great man" theory of history resulted from historians' attempt to explain the French Revolution and the rise of Napoleon Bonaparte.

Common Transitions and Verbs

Along with topic sentences like those listed above, the transitions and verbs listed below are likely to make their way into paragraphs organized by cause and effect.

Transitions That Signal Cause and Effect

As a result	In reaction
Consequently	In response
Hence	Therefore
In the aftermath	Thus

Verbs That Connect Cause and Effect

brings about	initiates
causes	leads to
creates	produces
engenders	results in; results from
evokes	sets off
fosters	stems
generates	stimulates
induces	triggers

Common Conjunctions

Conjunctions are linking words that tie parts of sentences together. The words *and*, *but*, *or*, and *so* are all examples of conjunctions. In paragraphs dealing with cause and effect, you are likely to see conjunctions such as *because*, *as*, and *since* used to introduce a cause (or causes). The conjunction *so* introduces an effect (or effects).

Chain of Cause and Effect

Be alert to cause and effect paragraphs involving *chains of causes and effects* in which the effect of one event becomes the cause of another. Note in the following paragraph how the introduction of rabbits, the effect of one situation, becomes the cause of another.

Thomas Austin was a dedicated British sportsman who had been an avid rabbit hunter while living in Britain. After moving to Australia, Austin was disappointed to learn that there were no wild rabbits to hunt. Determined to pursue his hobby, he ordered from England 24 rabbits to release in the wild and become prey for him and his hunter friends. The rabbits, however, had no natural predators and a phenomenal ability to reproduce. Not surprisingly, the wild rabbit population exploded, leaving Austin with more rabbits than he had bargained for. In 1867, Austin said he had killed almost 15,000 rabbits on his property alone. Vast tracts of land had also been devastated by rabbits with Australia losing not just vegetation but entire species to millions of rabbits living off the land.

Diagrammed, the cause and effect relationship in this passage would look something like this:

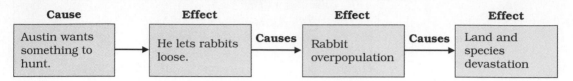

Cause	Effect		Effect		Effect
Austin wants something to hunt.	He lets rabbits loose.	**Causes**	Rabbit overpopulation	**Causes**	Land and species devastation

In this case, effects turn into causes of other effects, which is exactly what happens in chains of causes and effect.

Pattern Pointer

If you feel that the cause and effect relationship under discussion is not completely clear, draw a diagram that highlights the relationship between cause and effect.

EXERCISE 11 **DIRECTIONS** Read each paragraph. Then fill in the blanks and circle the letter of the statement that best describes the role of the supporting details.

1. Instinctive behavior is caused by specific signals from the environment called *releasers*. For example, stalking behavior in cats may be "released" by the sight of prey. Among male ring doves, the sight of an adult female triggers, or releases, the bowing associated with courtship. Similarly, fighting behavior in territorial male European robins can be released not only by the sight of another male within their territories but also by the sight of a tuft of red feathers at a certain height. This response occurs because red feathers at a certain height are normally on the breast of a competitor. Thus the red feathers signal that a rival is nearby. (Adapted from Wallace, *Biology*, p. 450.)

1. In this paragraph, the author describes how _____

cause(s) or lead(s) to _____ .

2. The supporting details

a. focus on the cause or causes.

b. focus on the effect or effects.

c. focus on both cause and effect.

2. During the Civil War, the South had fewer men than the North to send to war. Thus a larger proportion of southern families were left to the care of women. Some women worked farms and herded livestock to support their families. Others found themselves worse off: They and their families were left in poverty as the war turned the countryside black and dry. Because of their dire straits, some women tried to persuade their husbands to desert. However, the vast majority of women on the domestic front fully supported the war despite the misery it caused them. (Adapted from Berkin et al., *Making America,* p. 102.)

1. In this paragraph, the author describes how ———————

————————— cause(s) or lead(s) to ——————— ———————.

2. The supporting details

a. focus on the cause or causes.

b. focus on the effect or effects.

c. focus on both cause and effect.

EXERCISE 12 **DIRECTIONS** Circle the appropriate letter to identify the primary pattern of the paragraph.

1. Between 1970 and 1990, the number of cross-cultural marriages steadily increased. But that trend changed starting in late 1990 when the share of Hispanics and Asians married to whites began to decline. What's the cause of that drop? Researchers believe that the sheer number of immigrants arriving in the last decade makes it more likely for them to marry among themselves. Zhenchao Qion, professor of sociology at Ohio State University, believes the decline is likely to continue because immigrants are still arriving in large numbers, making it more likely that they will marry someone of the same heritage. (Source of information: Haya El Nasser, "Cross-Cultural Marriage Rates Falling," www.usatoday.com/news/nation/2007-02-15-cross-cultural-marriages_x.htm?csp=1.)

a. definition

b. process

c. sequence of dates and events

d. simple listing

e. classification

f. comparison and contrast

g. cause and effect

2. All of the gasoline now pumped into automobile and airplane tanks began as crude oil formed millions of years ago beneath ocean floors. In ancient seas, when tiny aquatic plants and animals died, they sank to the bottom. Sand and mud settled over them. This process was repeated over and over again, each time burying large quantities of organic material and pushing it deeper and deeper into the earth as new layers accumulated on top. The heavy weight of the sediment created pressure and temperatures above 150° Fahrenheit, and the subterranean* organic matter began to "cook." Over time, the heat transformed it into a liquid hydrogen and carbon substance. This crude oil, lighter than both water and rock, drifted upward through microscopic spaces in the rock until it was stopped by a layer of dense, impermeable rock and forced to collect. Today, oil companies drill down into these reservoirs to extract this energy-rich petroleum; send it to oil refineries, and convert it into fuel for vehicles.

a. definition

b. process

c. sequence of dates and events

d. simple listing

e. classification

f. comparison and contrast

g. cause and effect

3. American house forms have changed over time as new building materials became available and living styles changed, but in the early days of America's history, there were essentially three types of houses. The Cape Cod was among the most common and earliest house types. The typical Cape was two rooms deep with a huge central chimney and a roof that started just above the windows. Because it had low ceilings and few rooms, a Cape was one of the easier houses to heat, a big advantage when a fireplace was the main source of warmth. The Classic Cottage had a slightly higher front wall than the Cape and allowed for a second tier of windows. In the Classic Cottage, the chimney could be in the middle of the house or at the end. The big advantage of the cottage style was the increased amount of space it offered. The Colonial house was a one-and-one-half to two-story rectangle, built with a front door dividing up nine symmetrically* placed windows, sometimes referred to as "five-over-four and a door." Colonial houses were typically made out of wood

---

*subterranean: beneath the earth.
*symmetrically: evenly.

or brick and had columns or pediments at the front door entry. The Colonial style house was associated with people of some wealth, who could afford to consider comfort as well as shelter.

a. definition

b. process

c. sequence of dates and events

d. simple listing

e. classification

f. comparison and contrast

g. cause and effect

4. Because students don't all learn in the exact same way, it's hard to define what makes a good, never mind a great, teacher. There are, however, several traits that good teachers, overall, do seem to share. Good teachers generally have a gift for explaining things. They know how to vary or modify an explanation based on student response. Good teachers also know how to keep their cool. Even when students are acting out, successful teachers don't get angry or sarcastic. Instead they find other ways to control the situation and get students back on track. Research has also shown that good teachers have a lively sense of humor. They know that mixing a joke into a discussion is an excellent way to hold students' interest. Good teachers also have a thorough command of their subject. Elementary school teachers, for instance, have a wide general knowledge of many different fields, and enough depth in each area to provide clear explanations and effectively answer questions. For their part, high school teachers have an in-depth command of one or two specific content areas. (Source of information: R. J. Kizlik, "Tips on Becoming a Teacher," www.adprima.com/tipson.htm.)

a. definition

b. process

c. sequence of dates and events

d. simple listing

e. classification

f. comparison and contrast

g. cause and effect

5. The legal term *due process* identifies an established course of action that must be followed during judicial* proceedings. The basis for due process can be found in the Fifth Amendment of the Constitution,

---

*judicial: related to the courts.

which says: "No person shall be deprived of life, liberty, or property without due process of law." Due process reflects the Constitution's guarantee that criminal legal proceedings will be fair. Because the courts must abide by due process, every individual tried by a court has to be notified that the proceedings are taking place. Every person called to court for the prosecution of a crime must have an opportunity to defend himself or herself prior to any punishment which might involve the taking of life, liberty, or property. In addition to the Fifth Amendment, the Fourteenth Amendment requires that the states, as opposed to the federal government, honor an individual's right to due process.

a. definition

b. process

c. sequence of dates and events

d. simple listing

e. classification

f. comparison and contrast

g. cause and effect

6. Dogs have been companions to humans for some 14,000 years, and the relationship probably began because dogs could be trained to help in the humans' hunt for food. Cats, in contrast, have been companions to humans for only one-third of that time. Once cats teamed up with humans, they played a role very different from that of dogs. In the past, and until fairly recently, dogs were usually considered the servants of humans. They performed as guards, guides, and protectors in activities ranging from hunting to farming. Cats, however, couldn't be trained to do anything they didn't want to do, which is perhaps why they were worshipped as gods in some societies. The cat was held in such high esteem by the Egyptians, for instance, that there were laws protecting them from injury or death. While many early cultures treated dogs with affection—the greyhound, for instance, appears in many Egyptian tomb carvings—there is little evidence that they ever achieved the status of a deity.

a. definition

b. process

c. sequence of dates and events

d. simple listing

e. classification

f. comparison and contrast

g. cause and effect

7. Espionage is a dangerous and frequently short-lived profession. But thanks, in large degree, to his talent for duplicity and subterfuge,* double-agent and traitor Harold Adrian Russell "Kim" Philby (1912–1988) managed to avoid detection for over thirty years. From 1929 to 1933, while attending Cambridge University, Philby developed what became a lifelong admiration of communism and—while still a student—was recruited to work for the former Soviet Union's feared intelligence agency, the KGB.† Throughout the 1930s, under cover as a journalist, Philby continued to serve as a Soviet spy. His journalist activities attracted the attention of officials in the British Secret Intelligence Service (SIS), who were unaware of his loyalty to the KGB, and, in 1940, Philby was offered a position as a British intelligence officer. He seized this opportunity as a way of gaining access to information about British and American military strategy and, most important, atomic bomb production. Yet even as he betrayed his native country by passing those details on to his Soviet colleagues, Philby performed his SIS duties so well that he rose rapidly to become first the head of the counterespionage division in 1944 and then, in 1949, the Washington, D.C.–based liaison* between the British Embassy and the U.S. Central Intelligence Agency. In 1945, he was awarded the Order of the British Empire as a reward for his work during World War II. However, in 1951, his double life came close to unraveling when he alerted two fellow KGB agents that they were under SIS surveillance, giving them time to avoid arrest and escape to Moscow. Philby's British colleagues rightly suspected him of tipping off those two spies and asked him to resign from the SIS. But in 1955, after Philby had endured years of SIS interrogation without cracking and admitting his true allegiance, he was reemployed as an SIS officer. It wasn't until 1962 that Philby's house of cards finally collapsed. Testimony from a Soviet defector exposed him once and for all to be a KGB agent, and Philby fled to the Soviet Union. (Source of information: "Harold 'Kim' Philby and the Cambridge Three," PBS, January 2002, www.pbs.org/wgbh/nova/venona/dece_philby.html.)

a. definition

b. process

c. sequence of dates and events

d. simple listing

e. classification

f. comparison and contrast

g. cause and effect

---

*subterfuge: trickery.
†KGB: the Russian initials for what was, in fact, an agency of espionage and repression, the Committee for State Security.
*liaison: go-between.

8. *Habeas corpus petitions* are frequently filed by individuals serving prison sentences. The petitions are usually written to show that the court ordering the imprisonment made an error of some sort, making the imprisonment illegal. Habeas corpus petitions are also filed in family court by parents who have been denied custody of a child. In *Brown v. Vasquez*, the Supreme Court ruled that "the writ of habeas corpus is the fundamental instrument for safeguarding individual freedom against arbitrary* and lawless state action." In Latin, *habeas corpus* means "you have the body." (Source of information: www.lectlaw.com/def/h001.htm.)

   a. definition

   b. process

   c. sequence of dates and events

   d. simple listing

   e. classification

   f. comparison and contrast

   g. cause and effect

9. There are four major kinds of exercise, and each one offers different benefits to the body. The first type of exercise includes those that are *aerobic*. Aerobic means "with oxygen"; this kind of exercise—activities like jogging, walking, bicycling, and swimming—requires the lungs and heart to provide a steady supply of oxygen. As a result, these exercises strengthen the cardiovascular system, which in turn lowers the risk of heart disease. Aerobic exercise also helps reduce body fat and can relieve stress and feelings of depression. The second type of exercise is *anaerobic,* meaning "without oxygen." The exercises in this group draw on energy already stored in the body's muscles, so engaging in them does not require additional oxygen. Anaerobic activities, such as sprinting and lifting heavy weights, require short bursts of power that improve speed and muscle strength, so they tend to boost athletic performance. Lifting or resisting the force of lighter weights falls into the third category of exercise, *strength training.* Exercises in this category include working out on weight machines or performing calisthenics, such as push-ups and sit-ups, to tone and strengthen muscles. The final type, *flexibility exercise,* lengthens the muscles and increases the range of motion. This category includes exercises like yoga and Pilates, both of which improve posture, maintain mobility, prevent injury, and encourage mental and physical relaxation.

---

*arbitrary: based on a whim.

(Source of information: Aetna InteliHealth, "Types of Exercise," www.intelihealth.com/IH/ihtlH/WSIHW000325/8914/36127.html.)

a. definition

b. process

c. sequence of dates and events

d. simple listing

e. classification

f. comparison and contrast

g. cause and effect

10. The story of a Canadian boy named David Reimer has been one of the unintentional experiments that shed light on the nature and nurture of human sexuality. During a routine circumcision in 1965, the boy's genitals were damaged to such an extent that doctors, including the renowned psychologist and sexual identity expert John Money, thought the boy should be raised as a girl. Bruce was then named Brenda and started life as a female. Although in 1972 Money reported that the boy was developing as a female in a perfectly normal way, independent follow-ups of the case provided a much different view. By 1979, at the age of fourteen, Bruce had had two years of estrogen therapy and was still dreaming of being a boy rather than a girl. Plagued by these dreams, he refused to continue his life as a female. It was at this point that his parents informed Bruce of his medical history. Brenda, renamed Bruce, lived as a man, married, and adopted his wife's children, but was plagued by feelings of depression and rage. In May 2004, he took his own life. (Adapted from Freberg, *Discovering Biological Psychology*, p. 284.)

a. definition

b. process

c. sequence of dates and events

d. simple listing

e. classification

f. comparison and contrast

g. cause and effect

Primary Versus Mixed Patterns

In a good many paragraphs, there may be more than one organizational pattern, but it's still clear that one pattern is primary, or the one most essential to developing the main idea. However, there will be times when the patterns seem equally mixed and it may be difficult to tell which one predominates. For an illustration, see the following paragraph.

TG: Define the term "*scientific method.*"

TG: Explain each step in the scientific method.

Examples of research questions

Example of hypothesis

All <u>research studies</u> of human development <u>follow some form of</u> **scientific method,** or <u>set of procedures</u> designed to <u>ensure objective observations</u> and <u>interpretations</u> of observations. Even though it is not always possible to follow these procedures perfectly, they form an ideal to which psychological research tends to aspire (Cherry, 1995; Levine & Parkinson, 1994). The procedures or steps in the scientific method are as follows: [1]*Formulating research questions*. Sometimes these questions refer to previous studies, such as when a developmental psychologist asks, "Are Professor Deepthought's studies of thinking consistent with studies from less developed countries?" Other times they refer to issues important to society, such as "Does preschool education make children more socially skilled later in childhood?" [2]*Stating questions as hypotheses*. A **hypothesis** is a <u>statement that expresses a research question</u> precisely. In making a hypothesis out of the preschool education question above, a psychologist would further define the terms *preschool education* and *socially skilled:* "Do children in day care learn to share toys with other children at an earlier age than children cared for at home?" [3]*Testing the hypothesis*. Having phrased a research question as a hypothesis, researchers can conduct an actual study of it. The choice of study method usually depends on convenience, ethics, and scientific appropriateness. (Seifert and Hoffnung, *Child and Adolescent Development,* pp. 16–17.)

In this paragraph, the authors combine two patterns—definition and process—to make their point. Both are equally important to the paragraph's meaning, so readers would jot down both the definitions *and* the sequence of steps in the scientific method.

Common Combinations

It is not unusual for writers to combine definition and process patterns. These two patterns often work together because writers need to define the key terms essential to understanding the steps in a process or sequence. Some of the other patterns likely to be combined are process with cause and effect, classification with comparison and contrast, and definition with classification. The regularity with which these patterns combine suggests the following tip: If you recognize one member of a common combination, check first for its most likely companion.

Common Combinations

Process with Cause and Effect and/or Definition

Classification with Comparison and Contrast

Sequence of Dates and Events with Cause and Effect

EXERCISE 13 **DIRECTIONS** Circle the appropriate letter or letters to identify the organizational pattern or patterns used in each paragraph.

1. Although the Indian caste* system was officially outlawed in 1949 by the Indian Constitution, it persists to this day in one form or another and remains a source of political discontent. India's caste system divides the population into four basic groups. The *Brahmin* class includes priests and scholars. Members of this class are not characterized by wealth or possessions, but its members are the object of regard and respect because of their spiritual or intellectual gifts. Next come the *Kshatriyas,* whose members are rulers, warriors, and large property owners. This class is likely to be characterized by the possession of great wealth. Next in the hierarchy is the *Vaishyas* caste, which includes merchants and traders. Those in this group may or may not have great wealth, but they are all engaged in some form of commercial transaction. The *Shudra* caste includes those who wait on and serve members of the other three classes. Members of this group are servants and chauffeurs. Outside of the caste system entirely are the *harijans,* once known as the "untouchables." These people perform the jobs no one else wants to do, such as garbage collecting and leather dying. Although the caste system has weakened with the passage of time, it still exists, albeit* more in the country than in the city. In some Indian locales, the caste system is mainly a state of mind, with some individuals believing themselves worthy of being treated as Brahmins while others feel as if the name "untouchable" still applied. (Sources of information: "Are Hindu Attitudes Towards Race Skin Deep?" www.beliefnet.com/story/145/story_14568_2.html; www.csuchico .edu/~cheinz/ sllabi/asst001/spring98/india.htm.)

---

*caste: related to social class.
*albeit: admittedly, even though.

a. definition

b. process

c. sequence of dates and events

d. simple listing

e. classification

f. comparison and contrast

g. cause and effect

2. Although everyone thinks it won't happen to them, house fires are one of the most common causes of deadly accidents, and no one is immune to the threat of a house fire. Still, there are several precautions people can take to make sure they survive a house fire. The most obvious is to install smoke detectors. If you are renting, make sure the landlord installs smoke detectors, and be sure to check the batteries. Get a fire extinguisher and have someone from the local fire station show you how to use it. Keep an evacuation kit on hand. The evacuation kit should include copies of identification; insurance cards or tags, including those for pets; and any essential medical supplies, such as insulin or blood pressure medication. Have an escape route and know where you plan to exit the house or apartment in case of a fire. If you are living in a multi-story apartment building with a fire escape, make sure it is usable. If it isn't, tell the landlord and make sure that he or she makes the proper repairs. Know where the doors to the stairs are and take the stairs every once in a while to make sure you can negotiate them without difficulty.

a. definition

b. process

c. sequence of dates and events

d. simple listing

e. classification

f. comparison and contrast

g. cause and effect

3. On April 26, 1986, the worst accident in the history of nuclear power took place at the Chernobyl plant about 110 km north of Kiev in Ukraine. At the Chernobyl plant, the uranium was contained in fuel rods surrounded by graphite bricks, which served to moderate the nuclear reaction. (In the United States, commercial generating plants do not use graphite, and they have a containment dome.) The accident occurred when engineers turned off most of the reactor's automatic safety and warning systems to keep them from interfering with an unauthorized safety experiment. At this point, cooling water was one of the safety systems turned off. Unfortunately, the remaining water in the reactor then turned to steam, and the steam reacted with the nuclear fuel and the graphite bricks. An explosive mixture of gases formed and ignited. The reactor was destroyed, the roof blew off the building, and the graphite bricks caught fire. Officials in the former Soviet Union claimed the fire was extinguished on April 29. According to Soviet reports, 500 people were hospitalized and the acknowledged death count stood at 31. The incidence of thyroid cancer, leukemia, and other radiation-related illnesses is high among people who were living near the power plant. More ominously, the radioactive particles produced by the explosion were dispersed all over the planet by the natural circulation of air. It will be years before all of the effects of the Chernobyl disaster can be assessed. (Adapted from Sherman et al., *Basic Concepts of Chemistry*, p. 484.)

a. definition

b. process

c. sequence of dates and events

d. simple listing

e. classification

f. comparison and contrast

g. cause and effect

4. Two small lakes in a remote part of Cameroon, a small country in central Africa, made international news in the mid-1980s when deadly clouds of carbon dioxide (CO_2) gas from deep beneath the surface of the lakes escaped into the surrounding atmosphere, killing animal and human populations far downwind. The first gas discharge, which occurred at Lake Monoun in 1984, asphyxiated* thirty-seven people. The second, which occurred at Lake Nyos in 1986, released a highly concentrated cloud of CO_2 that killed more than 1,700 people. The two events had similarities other than location: Both occurred at night during the rainy season, both involved volcanic crater lakes, and both are likely to recur unless there is some type of technologic intervention.*

---

*asphyxiated: killed by loss of air.
*intervention: interference.

a. definition

b. process

c. sequence of dates and events

d. simple listing

e. classification

f. comparison and contrast

g. cause and effect

5. In 1862, Congress passed the **Homestead Act**. This measure offered 160 acres of land free to any American citizen who was a family head and over twenty-one years old. The only conditions were that the settler live on the land for five years and make improvements to it. In the well-watered East, 160 acres was a sizable farm. Yet in the semi-arid West, it was barely enough to support a family. To prosper, a farmer needed at least twice that amount. Despite these risks, the Homestead Act produced an explosion of settlement. Within a half century after passage of the Homestead Act, all western territories had gained enough settlers— at least 60,000—to become states. As a result of the Homestead Act, most western areas experienced enormous population growth. (DiBacco et al., *History of the United States*, p. 315.)

a. definition

b. process

c. sequence of dates and events

d. simple listing

e. classification

f. comparison and contrast

g. cause and effect

6. When you are searching for a job, your résumé is an important first step that can pave the way for a successful interview; it will, at least, if you avoid making any of the following mistakes. Don't ever lie about your level of education or past work experience. If you are found out, it's not just the job that you will lose. You'll also lose your chance of getting a good reference for your next position. Make sure, too, that you proofread both your cover letter and résumé in order to avoid all typos or misspellings. Don't rely on your computer for this crucial task because your computer won't know if you confused *you're* and *your* or *unions* with *onions*. Proofread your résumé yourself. Then ask someone whose grammar and spelling you trust to go over it a second time. It's easy for you to miss a typo because you know what you intended to write and that's the word you are likely to see, even if you left out a key letter. Stay away from "cute" layouts or stationery. It's a common misconception that job candidates need to make their letter or résumé stand out by making one or both unconventional. While this might work if you are applying for a job as a graphic artist, it has its drawbacks for résumés or inquiry letters. Your idea of what's clever may not be shared by the person reading requests for interviews. Then, too, some companies scan résumés into computer files and, if you have been too inventive with your style, your résumé may not scan correctly. Lastly, keep it short. Don't spend a lot of time telling the prospective interviewer how terrific you are because if the letter or the résumé gets too long, the interviewer might not read it. (Source of information: http://comcast.careerbuilder.com/JobSeeker/careerbytes.)

a. definition

b. process

c. sequence of dates and events

d. simple listing

e. classification

f. comparison and contrast

g. cause and effect

7. The German psychoanalyst Erich Fromm argued that there were five character types typical of Western society. Those Fromm called *receptive* feel the source of all good things is somewhere outside themselves. In relationships, they tend to be passive and wait to be approached or sought out. *Exploitative* character types also believe that the source of everything good is external. However, they don't wait for other people to give them what they want. They use cunning and manipulation to take what they think they deserve. In contrast, *hoarding* character types don't believe that the external world has much to offer. For that reason, they hoard or save whatever they already possess and are miserly about giving away money, affection, or attention. According to Fromm's framework, *marketing* personalities see themselves as products. They value themselves only so far as others place a high value on what they have to offer. Marketing personalities also change rapidly to suit the social and economic marketplace. For Fromm, the *productive* character type was the healthiest of the five. These personality types see themselves and the external world as twin sources of goodness. Finding a balance between giving and taking from the world around them while, at the same time, maintaining their own sense of a personal identity is the goal they try to achieve.

a. definition

b. process

c. sequence of dates and events

d. simple listing

e. classification

f. comparison and contrast

g. cause and effect

8. Life in the big city has always had its drawbacks. Compared to small towns and rural communities, huge metropolitan areas like Los Angeles and New York are typically plagued by higher crime rates, more pollution, and high costs of living. But another major problem—traffic-choked highways—is quickly rising to the top of the list for many major cities. With drivers in some large cities now spending the equivalent of more than two workweeks per year stuck in traffic, gridlock is starting to stunt economic growth as businesses and young professionals choose not to move to metropolitan areas with chronically congested roads. To combat this problem, many political and business leaders are advocating the widening of existing highways into "superhighways" of nine or more lanes in each direction. Phoenix, Arizona, for example, plans to expand a 12-mile stretch of Interstate 10 from 14 lanes to an average of 22 lanes. Atlanta, Georgia, may widen a stretch of Interstate 75 to 23 lanes. Both Houston, Texas, and Washington, D.C., also hope to bring segments of their highways up to 18 lanes or more. Building bigger roads, they hope, will end bottlenecks, allowing the ever-growing number of vehicles to move freely and keeping the area economically competitive. (Source of information: Larry Copeland, "Cities Afraid of Death by Congestion," *USA Today*, March 1, 2007.)

a. definition

b. process

c. sequence of dates and events

d. simple listing

e. classification

f. comparison and contrast

g. cause and effect

9. According to experts, if you want to gauge how healthy the economy is, check the sales of lipstick because lipstick sales seems to go up when the economy is bad and down when the economy is good.

Why is that? When the economy is good and women feel confident, they purchase more expensive items, such as shoes and spa treatments. When the economy is poor, they treat themselves with less expensive perks, such as a new shade of lipstick. In 2000, for example, when the economy was still booming, lipstick sales totaled $600 million. During 2001, while the economy grew steadily worse, lipstick sales rose 7.5 percent, to $647 million. At the beginning of 2002, sales peaked at about $700 million. Throughout 2003, as the economy improved, lipstick sales dropped by 3 percent. Although this news was not good for cosmetic companies, it indicated that female consumers were feeling better about spending their money on more expensive items. (Source of information: Paul J. Lim, "Here's How to Read the Tea Leaves Like Alan Greenspan," *U.S. News & World Report,* January 12, 2004, p. 34.)

a. definition

b. process

c. sequence of dates and events

d. simple listing

e. classification

f. comparison and contrast

g. cause and effect

10. The U.S. Food and Drug Administration (FDA) allows this country's food industry to put a number of surprisingly disturbing ingredients into the products consumers buy and eat. For example, baked goods such as bread, bagels, doughnuts, cookies, and pizza crusts contain an extract made from human hair. Some of this extract, which improves dough's stretchiness and allows it to be more easily processed by machines, is synthetic, but its natural form often comes from Chinese women who sell their hair to chemical processing plants to support their families. Another unpleasant ingredient in many foods is an extract from the anal glands of beavers, which is used to enhance the flavor of raspberry fillings, jams, and jellies. Still another cringe-worthy food additive is a coloring made from the crushed-up dead carcasses, eggs, and larvae of insects brushed off of cacti in Peru and the Canary Islands, among other places. This bug extract gives the red, pink, or purple color to foods like yogurt and ice cream. In fact, bugs are present in many foods, colorful or not. The FDA allows a jar of peanut butter to contain more than 100 insect parts. A can of tomatoes can contain one maggot or as many as nine fly eggs. Processed foods are also permitted to include, in restricted amounts, rodent hairs, mold, and mammal excrement. (Source of information: David Stipp, "Food for Thought," *Fortune*, July 7, 2003, www.fortune.com.)

a. definition

b. process

c. sequence of dates and events

d. simple listing

e. classification

f. comparison and contrast

g. cause and effect

Allusion Alert

Watergate (introduced on page 180) has become an automatic reference to political scandal, as it is in the following sentence: "Although the press tried desperately to make Bill Clinton's affair with a White House intern have a Watergate-like significance, the public, while generally viewing it with contempt, never felt the same kind of outrage that Watergate had induced."

Now that you are familiar with what an allusion to Watergate suggests, how would you paraphrase the following sentence? "To television evangelists,* the imprisonment of Jim Bakker for embezzlement was as devastating as Watergate was to the Republicans."

---

*evangelists: enthusiastic preachers of the Christian gospel.

■ DIGGING DEEPER

LOOKING AHEAD On page 169 of this chapter, you read a paragraph describing the Supreme Court. In this reading, you'll learn more about one of the best known and most esteemed members of that court, Oliver Wendell Holmes, whose judicial decisions helped strengthen the Constitutional protections for freedom of speech.

OLIVER WENDELL HOLMES AND FREEDOM OF SPEECH

1 Until 1919, the notion of freedom of speech was honored more in theory than in practice. True, free speech was guaranteed by the Bill of Rights and the First Amendment. But that didn't mean free speech couldn't land a person in jail. In fact, in 1918, Socialist leader Eugene V. Debs was sentenced to ten years for an anti-war speech given before only 1,200 people. In the early part of the twentieth century, the First Amendment guaranteed little more than what Supreme Court Justice Oliver Wendell Holmes called the right to "say what you choose if you don't shock me."

2 Like Debs before him, jail time was what Jacob Schenck got in 1919 for preaching draft resistance. When Schenck's case came before the Supreme Court, the justices, Holmes included, unanimously upheld his conviction. Yet writing the opinion on the case, Holmes seemed determined to distinguish between unpopular speech and harmful speech. In the mind of Holmes, the circumstances or context of the words mattered and they mattered a lot: "The question in every case is whether the words are used in such circumstances and are of such a nature as to create a clear and present danger that they will bring about the substantive evils that the United States Congress has a right to prevent." In an effort to further clarify the circumstances he had in mind, Holmes used a practical example that was to make legal history: "After all, the most stringent protection of free speech would not protect a man falsely shouting fire in a theater and causing panic."

3 Holmes was taken by surprise when the Court's decision and his role in it caused a storm of criticism. He was particularly stung by the comment from Professor Ernst Freund at the University of Chicago, who argued that "tolerance of opinion is not a matter of generosity but of political prudence.*" A man of great ego and even greater integrity, Holmes needed to understand the furious

---

*prudence: wisdom.

objections of his peers. For that reason, he agreed to talk to legal expert and free speech advocate Zechariah Chaffee from Harvard Law School. Chaffee convinced Holmes that free speech served the public good and set the stage for the dissenting opinion that Holmes was to write in the case known as *Abrams v. United States.*

4   Jakob Abrams and several others had been convicted of distributing pamphlets criticizing President Woodrow Wilson for sending troops to Russia to defend the Czar in the summer of 1918. Found guilty of hindering the war effort, Abrams and his cohorts appealed the guilty verdict all the way to the Supreme Court. The Court, however, was taken with Holmes's "clear and present danger" test and used it to sustain Abrams's conviction. The justices must have been surprised when Holmes, who seems to have disserved his nickname "The Great Dissenter," did not agree with their decision. Instead, he joined with Supreme Court Justice Louis Brandeis to write yet another opinion that profoundly influenced all future discussions of freedom of expression.

5   Calling the defendants in the case "puny anonymities," Holmes insisted that their pamphlets might well express sentiments that were loathsome but that didn't make their words a serious threat. Clearly, Holmes had had a change of heart between the *Schenck* and *Abrams* cases because the opinion he wrote on *Abrams* returns again and again to the notion of immediacy, suggesting that if the court couldn't see an *imminent* emergency, it had no business tampering with the First Amendment: "Only the emergency that makes it immediately dangerous to leave the correction of evil counsels to time warrants making any exception to the sweeping command, 'Congress shall make no law . . . abridging the freedom of speech.'" With that dissent, Holmes laid the groundwork for the legal system's current interpretation of free speech and its willingness to allow, in Holmes's words "the expressions of opinions we loathe," as long as they do not offer an immediate threat to the well-being of others.

Sharpening Your Skills

DIRECTIONS Answer the following questions by circling the letter of the correct response or filling in the blanks.

1. Based on the context, how would you define *stringent* in paragraph 2?

   a. careless

   b. open

   c. strict

   d. colorful

2. Based on context, how would you define *cohorts* in paragraph 4?

_____

3. What's the overall main idea of the entire reading?

    a. Oliver Wendell Holmes tended to confuse and annoy his colleagues on the Supreme Court because they were never sure which side he would take on freedom of speech.

    b. Oliver Wendell Holmes was instrumental in developing the legal standards for judging freedom of speech.

    c. Oliver Wendell Holmes was the greatest justice in the history of the Supreme Court.

    d. Oliver Wendell Holmes was inclined to be contradictory.

4. Which sentence correctly paraphrases the first sentence of this reading?

    a. Before 1919, there was no legal protection for freedom of speech.

    b. Before 1919, freedom of speech was not strongly protected despite the guarantee in the Bill of Rights.

    c. After 1919, freedom of speech was valued in theory but not in reality.

5. The Schenck case is mentioned to

    a. illustrate Holmes's readiness to disagree with his colleagues.

    b. illustrate how Holmes's attitude toward free speech evolved.

    c. illustrate how much anti-war sentiment existed at the time.

6. Why does Holmes claim that the right of freedom of speech does not protect someone shouting "fire" in a theater?

_____

_____

7. On what basis did Holmes dissent in the *Abrams* case?

_____

_____

8. What two reversal transitions appear in paragraph 4?

_____

9. Why is it significant in Holmes's eyes that the defendants in the *Abrams* case are "puny anonymities" (paragraph 5)?

_____

_____

10. Based on what you know about Oliver Wendell Holmes, which quote do you think is his and why?

a. The character of every act depends upon the circumstances in which it is done.

b. Do not go where the path may lead, go instead where there is no path and leave a trail.

Please explain what in the reading led you to this conclusion:

_____

_____

_____

_____

Students who want to do a more in-depth review of patterns should use *Getting Focused*, the web-based reading program accompanying this text. The program is available at **college.cengage.com/ devenglish/flemming/getting_focused/1e/student_home .html**. Completing questions 6 and 7 will provide a very thorough and complete review.

To get more practice analyzing paragraphs, go to **laflemm.com** and click on *Reading for Thinking*: "Online Practice." Complete the interactive exercises on recognizing patterns.

Test 1: Recognizing Typical Topic Sentences

DIRECTIONS Each of the following statements suggests an organizational pattern. Read the sentence. Then circle the appropriate letter to indicate the pattern it suggests.

1. For all his aristocratic tastes and tendencies, Thomas Jefferson was able to convince the general public that he was a man of the people, whereas Alexander Hamilton, who shared Jefferson's taste for life's luxuries, never bothered to conceal his affinity for the wealthy.

   a. sequence of dates and events

   b. cause and effect

   c. comparison and contrast

   d. simple listing

2. In the human body, the three types of muscle tissue are *smooth*, *skeletal*, and *cardiac*.

   a. comparison and contrast

   b. classification

   c. process

   d. definition

3. Clinical research has proven that laughter not only improves people's moods but also stimulates the body's natural painkillers, improves the immune system, and speeds the healing process.

   a. cause and effect

   b. sequence of dates and events

   c. definition

   d. comparison and contrast

4. Although same-sex friendships are important to both men and women, research indicates that men's friendships are based on mutually shared activities, such as playing or watching sports, whereas women's friendships are based more on intimate conversation and the expression of feelings.

   a. comparison and contrast

   b. simple listing

   c. process

   d. classification

5. In his adventurous forty-four years of life, Benjamin Franklin Ficklin (1827–1871) fought in the Mexican-American War; founded the Pony Express mail service; fought in the Civil War; and served as blockade runner and spy.

a. cause and effect

b. definition

c. comparison and contrast

d. sequence of dates and events

6. Research results can be evaluated by several different criteria.

a. cause and effect

b. classification

c. definition

d. simple listing

7. *Diplomacy* is the practice of conducting negotiations between two groups or nations.

a. process

b. cause and effect

c. definition

d. comparison and contrast

8. Tropical hurricanes and cyclones destroy lives and property, but they also bring critical precipitation to crops and drinking water supplies and maintain global heat balance by moving warm air away from the tropics to middle and upper latitudes.

a. comparison and contrast

b. cause and effect

c. process

d. sequence of dates and events

9. A number of different methods are available to explore the origins of abnormal behavior.

a. simple listing

b. process

c. cause and effect

d. comparison and contrast

10. The Bessemer process of making steel begins with the melting of cast iron.

a. simple listing

b. process

c. classification

d. comparison and contrast

Test 2: Recognizing Organizational Patterns

DIRECTIONS Circle the letter or letters that identify the organizational pattern or patterns used in each paragraph.

1. A **cartel** is an organization of independent firms whose purpose is to control and limit production and maintain or increase prices and profits. A cartel can result from either formal or informal agreement among members. Like collusion,* cartels are illegal in the United States but occur in other countries. The cartel most people are familiar with is the Organization of Petroleum Exporting Countries (OPEC), a group of nations rather than a group of independent firms. During the 1970s, OPEC was able to coordinate oil production in such a way that it drove the market price of crude oil from $1.10 to $32.00 a barrel. For nearly eight years, each member of OPEC agreed to produce a certain limited amount of crude oil as designated by the OPEC production committee. Then in the early 1980s, the cartel began to fall apart as individual members began to cheat on the agreement. Members began to produce more than their allocation in an attempt to increase profits. As each member of the cartel did this, the price of oil fell, reaching $12 per barrel in 1988. Oil prices rose again in 1990 when Iraq invaded Kuwait, causing widespread damage to Kuwait's oil fields. But as repairs have been made to Kuwait's oil wells, Kuwait has increased production and oil prices have dropped. (Boyes and Melvin, *Fundamentals of Economics,* p. 109.)

   a. definition

   b. classification

   c. simple listing

   d. process

   e. sequence of dates and events

   f. comparison and contrast

   g. cause and effect

2. The Bermuda Triangle is, without a doubt, a strange and mysterious area of the Atlantic Ocean. During the last century, more than one hundred ships, boats, and airplanes have disappeared in this area. For example, the USS *Cyclops*, a Navy ship with 306 people aboard, disappeared there in 1918. Also lost without a trace was an entire squadron of five Navy torpedo bombers that took off from Fort

---

*collusion: a secret agreement between parties for the purpose of illegal activities.

Lauderdale, Florida, in 1945. In 1947, a United States C-54 bomber disappeared near Bermuda and was never seen again. One year later, the same thing happened to the British airliner *Star Tiger*. And in 1968, the *Scorpion*, a nuclear submarine, vanished only to be found after a long search. It was finally located in the waters on the fringes of the Triangle, but none of its crew members were on board.

a. definition

b. classification

c. simple listing

d. process

e. sequence of dates and events

f. comparison and contrast

g. cause and effect

3. Eighteenth-century assemblies bore little resemblance to twentieth-century state legislatures. Much of assembly business would today be termed administrative; only on rare occasions did assemblies formulate new policies or pass laws of real importance. Members of the assemblies also saw their roles differently from that of modern legislators. Instead of believing that they should act positively to improve the lives of their constituents, eighteenth-century assemblymen saw themselves as acting defensively to prevent encroachments on the people's rights. In their minds, their primary function was, for example, to stop the governors or councils from enacting oppressive taxes, rather than to pass laws that would actively benefit their constituents. (Adapted from Norton et al., *A People and a Nation*, p. 111.)

a. definition

b. classification

c. simple listing

d. process

e. sequence of dates and events

f. comparison and contrast

g. cause and effect

4. Numerous studies suggest that people who consider themselves happy have four key traits in common. For instance, happy people generally have high self-esteem. They have a good self-image and believe that they are intelligent, healthy, ethical, and personable. A second trait common to happy people is a sense of personal control. People who describe themselves as happy believe that they can make decisions which affect the course of their lives. Another characteristic of happy people is an optimistic outlook; in other words, they are inclined to focus on the positive rather than the negative. The fourth trait of happy people is an outgoing personality. Most happy people are extroverted and have a solid circle of friends. (Source of information: David G. Meyers and Ed Diener, "The Pursuit of Happiness," *Scientific American*, 1997 Special Issue: The Mind, pp. 44–47.)

a. definition

b. classification

c. simple listing

d. process

e. sequence of dates and events

f. comparison and contrast

g. cause and effect

5. In the second century BC, the Chinese developed a method of converting cast iron into steel by melting the iron and then blowing air on it, thereby reducing the carbon content. But it wasn't until 1845 that American inventor William Kelly brought four Chinese steel experts to Kentucky; mastered the Chinese process; refined it, and then took out a patent. Kelly, however, went bankrupt in the financial panic that gripped the country in 1857 and had to sign ownership over to Henry Bessemer, who had been working on a similar process of steel production. By 1858, Bessemer had developed the first method of mass-producing steel. He then set up the first steelworks in Sheffield, England. Three years after Bessemer's triumph, the German-born inventors William and Frederick Siemens introduced the Open-Hearth furnace, capable of sustaining the high temperatures needed to make "Bessemer's process" work efficiently. Once the Siemens's furnace was improved on by Pierre Émile Martin of France, the stage was set for a revolutionary change in industrial production of all kinds. (Source of information: www.lycos.com/into/bessemer-process-steel.html.)

a. definition

b. classification

c. simple listing

d. process

e. sequence of dates and events

f. comparison and contrast

g. cause and effect

Test 3: Recognizing Organizational Patterns

DIRECTIONS Circle the letter or letters that identify the organizational pattern or patterns used in each paragraph.

1. In general, people use three different methods of learning, and most rely more heavily on one method than another. **Visual learners** absorb new information best when they can see it. Thus they like to learn through reading and are likely to take detailed notes with many diagrams and symbols. If visual learners have a choice between learning from a book or learning from a lecture, they are inclined to choose the book. **Auditory learners** rely most on their sense of hearing to learn new material, preferring to learn from lectures, discussions, and tours. At museums, they are the first ones to sign up for guided tours or make use of guides on tape by purchasing headphones. **Kinesthetic learners** are at their best when they are physically active. Thus they are likely to gesture while reviewing new information, and they like to use learning techniques that require movement. For example, kinesthetic learners might jot notes on sticky pads and attach the notes to the pages of a textbook because this method allows for maximum physical involvement. In the same vein, they are also likely to build models and take things apart to see how they work. (Source of information: "Three Different Learning Styles," University of South Dakota, www.usd.edu/trio/tut/ts/styleres.html.)

   a. definition

   b. classification

   c. simple listing

   d. process

   e. sequence of dates and events

   f. comparison and contrast

   g. cause and effect

2. Magazines and journals are both print publications; however, they differ in a number of ways. One major difference is purpose. The primary purpose of magazines is to entertain readers, promote particular viewpoints, and sell products. The main purpose of journals, however, is to report on new research in a specific field. For example, a professional journal, such as the *Journal of the American Medical Association*, contains information about recent medical research. The two types of publication differ, too, in terms of article length, authors, and audience. Magazine articles, which are generally short, are written by staff or freelance writers who use

lay terms to appeal to a wide audience. Journal articles, however, are longer and generally written by experts who use specialized jargon that will be understood only by those with education or training in a particular field. Magazine articles usually do not provide much, if any, information about sources, but journal articles always include footnotes or endnotes, along with bibliographic information. Finally, the two publications differ in terms of their publishers and frequency of publication. The issues of a magazine, published by general or commercial presses, appear either weekly or monthly. Journals, though, are generally published by universities, professional societies, or scholarly presses, and many of them appear just quarterly or annually. (Source of information: Denise Woetzel, "What's the Difference Between Journals and Magazines?" Guilford Technical Community College, December 9, 2001, http://webster.gtcc.cc.nc.us/library/jourmag.html.)

a. definition

b. classification

c. simple listing

d. process

e. sequence of dates and events

f. comparison and contrast

g. cause and effect

3. Bats and dolphins gather information about their surroundings by bouncing sound waves off objects in a three-step process. First, both animals send sound waves into the atmosphere. Bats make high-pitched sounds by moving air past their vocal chords, and dolphins transmit clicking sounds from nasal sacs in their foreheads. Next, these sounds hit an object in the animal's vicinity, bounce off the object, and return in the form of echoes. In the third step, the animal hears and interprets the echoes. Its brain processes the information, assessing the object's size and shape to form a mental image of it. It is even possible for bats and dolphins to determine how far away the object is based on how long it takes the echo to return.

a. definition

b. classification

c. simple listing

d. process

e. sequence of dates and events

f. comparison and contrast

g. cause and effect

4. Dean Kamen is a self-taught physicist and highly successful inventor-entrepreneur with numerous inventions to his credit. Kamen invented the first portable infusion pump capable of delivering drugs like insulin to patients who otherwise would have spent their time in hospitals rather than at home. Kamen also invented the first book-sized dialysis machine, allowing patients with kidney failure to receive treatment at home instead of in a hospital. Then, after watching a man trying to negotiate a curb in his wheelchair, Kamen created the Ibot Transporter, a six-wheeled chair that can climb stairs and rocky terrain. Moving away from the medical field, Kamen is currently at work on a machine that would generate power for industry and home use while simultaneously serving as a water purification system.

   a. definition

   b. classification

   c. simple listing

   d. process

   e. sequence of dates and events

   f. comparison and contrast

   g. cause and effect

5. In February and March 2007, thousands of pets, mostly cats, died as a result of eating food contaminated by melamine, a chemical used in making plastics. While the outrage and grief over the loss of so many pets has fueled investigation into the safety of pet food, it needs to have an even more wide-ranging effect. Consumers need to be aware that globalization, with its opening up of foreign markets, may have endangered the food supply for humans as well. Currently, not enough inspectors are available to see that all the food coming into the United States is safe. General inspectors examine mainly "at-risk" foods, those foods, such as meat, that are subject to contamination. Fruits and vegetables arrive in the market with hardly any inspection at all. This situation needs to be changed, and the pet food recall of 2007 is an alarm that we need to heed.

   a. definition

   b. classification

   c. simple listing

   d. process

   e. sequence of dates and events

   f. comparison and contrast

   g. cause and effect

Test 4: Taking Stock

DIRECTIONS Read each paragraph. Then answer the following questions by circling the letter of the correct response or filling in the blanks.

1. [1]Global positioning system (GPS) technology has been around since 1978 and put to a number of good uses, from tracing tanks on the battlefield to finding hikers lost in a snowstorm. [2]Now, however, parents of teenagers have discovered a brand new use for GPS technology: helping them keep in touch with their kids so that they know, for instance, exactly where their children are and how fast they are driving. [3]Not surprisingly, this use of GPS technology has sparked an intense debate with the parents expressing the pros in the argument while teenagers just as intensely point to the cons. [4]Advocates of using the GPS devices in this way say they help reduce risky behavior and may even save lives. [5]More specifically, they argue that teenagers won't speed if they know their parents will be alerted—some GPS systems send an e-mail to parents if kids go over the speed limit—and that teenagers driving at or below the speed limit might help reduce the number of kids who die in car crashes. [6]According to the National Highway Traffic Safety Administration, motor vehicle crashes are the leading cause of death among 15- to 20-year-olds. [7]Jack Church, spokesman for Teen Arrive Alive, a Florida company that offers GPS-enabled cell phones, made exactly this point in a 2006 *San Francisco Gate* article: "This is about parents being given tools to better protect their kids. That's not Big Brother. That's parenting." [8]Teenagers, however, don't view this use of GPS devices as better parenting. [9]They see it as snooping and argue that it's an invasion of privacy. [10]Interviewed on the subject, 17-year-old Katt Hemman from Kansas told the *Southeast Missourian* in 2006 that parents' arguments in favor of using the tracking technology are pure hypocrisy. [11]From her point of view, many parents would not sanction warrantless wiretapping; therefore, they should not feel they have a right to invade their teenagers' privacy without permission. [12]"A marginal increase in safety isn't worth forfeiting our civil rights, and adults who balk at being spied on and then turn around and spy themselves are hypocrites," she said. (Source of information: www.pbs.org/newshour/extra/features/jan-june07/gps_2-19.html.)

   1. What is the topic? _____

   2. The topic sentence is sentence _____.

3. How would you paraphrase the topic sentence?

_____

_____

4. The supporting details develop what word or phrase in the topic sentence?

_____

5. Which pattern or patterns do you see at work in the paragraph?

a. definition

b. process

c. sequence of dates and events

d. classification

e. simple listing

f. comparison and contrast

g. cause and effect

2. [1]The National Security Act of 1947 was signed into law by Harry S. Truman on July 20, 1947. [2]Its purpose was to realign and reorganize the country's military forces—ground, sea, and air—all of which had operated autonomously during World War II. [3]The National Security Act also called for a Secretary of Defense, whose job it would be to unify the military's training procedures and goals. [4]James V. Forrestal got the job because he had served as Secretary of the Navy for almost three years. [5]On the face of it, Forrestal, bright, ambitious, and knowledgeable, seemed a perfect choice; however, he would be gone in less than two years and would leave the government under tragic circumstances. [6]A staunch cold warrior, Forrestal was, from the beginning of his tenure, inclined to see communist threats everywhere. [7]In fact, he coined the term "semi-war" to defend his belief that the country needed to remain permanently on high alert. [8]In addition to feeling constantly under siege, Forrestal was deeply wounded when, in 1948, columnists Drew Pearson and Walter Winchell accused him of everything from tax evasion to collaborating with the Nazis. [9]Things only got worse for Forrestal when he learned that Truman was ready to fire him because he was not fully supportive of the new plan for founding the country of Israel. [10]Rather than be publicly dismissed, Forrestal resigned on March 28, 1949. [11]Upon leaving office, Forrestal seemed so distraught, he was sent to Florida for a rest, but when his behavior became increasingly erratic, he was rushed to a military hospital in Bethesda, Maryland. [12]On May 22, 1949, Forrestal jumped out a sixteenth-story window, the sash of his bathrobe wrapped tightly around his neck. [13]To this day, exactly what propelled him out that window is still unknown. [14]Yet, whatever the circumstances of his death, Forrestal's burial in Arlington cemetery on May 25, 1949, drew huge numbers of mourners, who wanted to pay their respects to the man later biographers would later call a "driven patriot.[†]" (Sources of information: www.arlingtoncemetery.net/jvforres.htm; www.spartacus.schoolnet.co.uk/USAforrestal.htm.)

1. What is the topic? _____

2. The topic sentence is sentence _____.

3. How would you paraphrase the topic sentence?

_____

_____

4. The supporting details develop what word or phrase in the topic sentence?

_____

5. Which pattern or patterns do you see at work in the paragraph?

   a. definition

   b. process

   c. sequence of dates and events

   d. classification

   e. simple listing

   f. comparison and contrast

   g. cause and effect

[†]This is an allusion to a biography about Forrestal titled *Driven Patriot.*

CHAPTER 5

Understanding, Outlining, and Synthesizing Longer Readings

In this chapter, you will learn

- **how to adapt what you know about paragraphs to longer, multiparagraph readings.**

- **how to recognize the thesis statements that put main ideas into words.**

- **how to locate major and minor supporting details.**

- **how to create informal outlines.**

- **how to write thesis statements that synthesize two or more ideas from different sources.**

In this chapter, you'll use some of the same skills you polished in Chapters 3 and 4. However, you'll apply

241

those skills, with some modification, to readings a good deal longer than a paragraph. In addition, you'll learn how to read, outline, and synthesize different sources on the same subject.

Understanding Longer Readings

To thoroughly understand a paragraph, you need to answer three questions:

1. What's the topic?

2. What's the main idea?

3. Which supporting details are essential to understanding that main idea?

Fortunately, the same questions also apply to readings longer than a single paragraph. Still, that's not to say there are no differences between reading a single paragraph and reading longer selections. There are, in fact, six crucial differences you need to take into account.

The Main Idea Controls More Than a Paragraph

In longer readings, one main idea unifies not just a single paragraph but all or most of the paragraphs in the selection. Because it controls the content of the other paragraphs, you can think of this main idea as the "controlling main idea." The controlling main idea gives all the other paragraphs a purpose. They exist to explain, clarify, and argue its meaning.

Several Sentences May Be Needed to Express the Main Idea

The main idea of an entire reading can often be summed up in a single sentence. But sometimes it requires several sentences, maybe even a paragraph. For that reason, many composition textbooks use the term **thesis statement** to talk about the stated main idea of a research paper or an essay. Following that tradition, we'll use the same term here to emphasize that the main idea of a reading cannot always be summed up in one single sentence.

Introductions Are Likely to Be Longer

In paragraphs, introductions are usually limited to only a sentence or two. However, in longer readings, introducing the main idea may require several paragraphs. While it's true that textbook authors are likely to present readers with the main idea in the first or second paragraph, don't assume that's the case with magazine or journal articles and essays. In these materials, writers sometimes include lengthy introductions to provide background or to stimulate reader interest.

Thesis Statements Don't Wander Quite So Much

Topic sentences can appear anywhere in a paragraph—at the beginning, middle, or end. Thesis statements, in contrast, are more fixed in their location. Yes, an author occasionally builds up to the main idea and puts the thesis statement at the very end of a reading. But that's not typical. Far more likely is the appearance of the thesis statement at the beginning of a reading. Thus the opening paragraphs in an essay, an article, or a chapter section deserve particularly close attention.

Major Supporting Details Can Take Up More Space

In longer readings, one supporting detail essential to the main idea can take up an entire paragraph. Thus longer readings require you to do a good deal more sifting and sorting of information as you decide which individual statements are essential to your understanding of a major detail.

Minor Details Can Occupy an Entire Paragraph

As they do in paragraphs, minor details in longer readings further explain major ones. They add colorful facts or supply repetition for emphasis. Like major details, minor details can also take up an entire paragraph. And just as in paragraphs, minor details may or may not be important.

Sometimes minor supporting details supply the more specific examples or explanations necessary for a clear understanding of a major detail. When this is the case, the minor details should be considered essential. But if they simply offer a colorful or humorous anecdote or just provide repetition for emphasis, you need not store them away in your long-term memory. Nor should you make an effort to include them in your notes.

Now that you know how reading a paragraph is different from reading a more extended piece of writing, it's time to put what you have learned into practice. Read the following selection.

Research on Leadership

1   In business, managers have to be leaders. Thus it comes as no surprise that researchers have been studying the nature of leadership in business. <u>At the University of Michigan, researchers have</u> *Thesis* <u>found that leadership behavior among managers can be divided</u> *Statement* <u>into two categories—job-centered and employee-centered.</u>

Topic Sentence 2   <u>Job-centered leaders closely supervise their employees in an effort to monitor and control their performance.</u> They are primarily concerned with getting a job done and less concerned with the feelings or attitudes of their employees—unless those attitudes and feelings affect the task at hand. In general, they don't encourage employees to express their opinions on how best to accomplish a task.

Topic Sentence 3   <u>In contrast, employee-centered leaders focus on reaching goals by building a sense of team spirit.</u> An employee-centered leader is concerned with subordinates' job satisfaction and group unity. Employee-centered leaders are also more willing to let employees have a voice in how they do their jobs.

Topic Sentence 4   <u>The Michigan researchers also investigated which kind of leadership is more effective.</u> They concluded that managers whose leadership was employee-centered were generally more effective than managers who were primarily job-centered. That is, their employees performed at higher levels and were more satisfied. (Adapted from Van Fleet and Peterson, *Contemporary Management*, p. 332.)

Having read "Research on Leadership," look closely at the thesis statement. Now look at the topic sentences of the remaining paragraphs. Can you see how those topic sentences clarify the thesis statement? This reading illustrates how thesis statements and topic sentences work together. The thesis statement introduces the author's general point. Then the topic sentences of each paragraph expand and clarify that point. Within each paragraph, the major details should always clarify the topic sentence; however, they may or may not directly support the thesis statement.

The following diagram expresses the relationship between the thesis statement and the topic sentences within a reading or an essay.

Thesis Statement

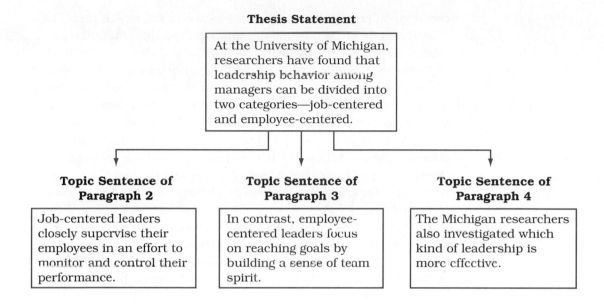

At the University of Michigan, researchers have found that leadership behavior among managers can be divided into two categories—job-centered and employee-centered.

Topic Sentence of Paragraph 2

Job-centered leaders closely supervise their employees in an effort to monitor and control their performance.

Topic Sentence of Paragraph 3

In contrast, employee-centered leaders focus on reaching goals by building a sense of team spirit.

Topic Sentence of Paragraph 4

The Michigan researchers also investigated which kind of leadership is more effective.

Before going on to Exercise 1, read the following selection and underline the thesis statement. Remember, the thesis statement shouldn't unify just one paragraph. It should unify the entire reading.

The Death Penalty Through the Ages

1 In the United States today, the federal government and 38 states—including Florida, Texas, New York, and North Carolina—have statutes allowing the death penalty for certain crimes. Still, capital punishment is now reserved almost exclusively for murderers, and nationwide, fewer than 100 criminals are executed every year.

2 In times past, though, the death penalty was imposed not only more often but also for more offenses, some rather trivial by modern standards. In ancient Babylon, for example, the Code of King Hammurabi allowed the death penalty for 25 different crimes that did not involve the taking of a life. Around 1500 BCE, the Egyptians imposed the death penalty for killing a cat, an animal they considered sacred. In the seventh century BCE, the Draconian[†] Code of Athens actually prescribed capital punishment for *every* crime committed. In the fifth century BCE, the Romans punished with death anyone who sang insulting songs, burned a stack of corn too close to a house,

---

†Draconian: Draco was a Greek leader whose laws were considered extremely harsh. Thus his name has become an adjective meaning "harsh and severe."

committed perjury, or disturbed the peace in the city at night. In 438, the Code of Theodosius designated more than 80 different crimes as punishable by death.

3   During the Middle Ages, the death penalty was used for a number of major as well as minor crimes. In Britain, for example, people were put to death for everything from stealing a loaf of bread to sacrilege* or treason. From 1509 to 1547, during the reign of Henry VIII, as many as 72,000 people were executed for various offenses. By the 1700s, the list of crimes punishable by death increased to 220 offenses. These offenses included stealing, cutting down trees, sending threatening letters, and producing counterfeit money.

4   English settlers in America initially brought with them to the New World the idea of severe punishments for crimes both large and small. In addition to executing murderers, the Capital Laws of New England, in effect from 1636 to 1647, punished with death anyone convicted of witchcraft, adultery, assault, blasphemy,* idolatry,* and perjury. In 1665, the New York colony imposed capital punishment on anyone found guilty of challenging the king's rights or striking a parent. Although these laws were relaxed for fear of discouraging new colonists, by 1780 the Commonwealth of Massachusetts was still executing those convicted of crimes such as burglary, homosexuality, and arson. As late as 1837, North Carolina required death for the crimes of assisting with arson, engaging in bigamy, encouraging slaves to riot, and hiding slaves with the intention of freeing them. (Sources of information: U.S. Department of Justice, Office of Justice Programs, Bureau of Justice Statistics, "Capital Punishment Statistics," www.ojp .usdoj.gov/bjs/cp.htm; Michael H. Reggio, "History of the Death Penalty," *PBS Frontline*, 1999, www.pbs.org/wgbh/pages/frontline/ shows/execution/readings/history.html.)

Tempting as it might be to assume that the first paragraph of this reading contains the thesis statement, that assumption would lead you astray. Neither of the sentences in paragraph 1 is developed beyond the first paragraph. Therefore, the first paragraph cannot possibly contain the thesis statement.

Look now at paragraph 2. The first sentence is the topic sentence. All of the sentences after the first one serve to illustrate the "rather trivial" offenses that once warranted the death sentence.

---

*sacrilege: treating religious beliefs or objects with disrespect.
*blasphemy: using profane language, swearing.
*idolatry: excessive devotion to images of worship or false gods.

However, the topic sentence of paragraph 2 also expresses the main idea of the entire reading: In other words, it is also the thesis statement of the entire reading. Both paragraphs 3 and 4—like the individual sentences in paragraph 2—identify some of the "trivial" offenses referred to in paragraph 2.

Check Your Understanding

Without looking back at the text, describe how longer readings differ from single paragraphs. When you finish, compare your list to the original explanation.

1. _____

_____

2. _____

_____

3. _____

_____

4. _____

_____

5. _____

_____

6. _____

_____

EXERCISE 1   **DIRECTIONS** Underline the thesis statement in each reading.

EXAMPLE

Is Your Home Clean?

1 Surveys show that, overall, Americans scrub and wipe down their homes fairly often. A Bounty Home Care Council survey, for example, revealed that bathrooms are cleaned an average of five times a month, and that 42 percent of people clean their bathrooms twice a week or more. However, environmental microbiologist Dr. Charles

Gerba of the University of Arizona has shown that many clean homes just *look* clean. In reality, they are often breeding grounds for bacteria. <u>Indeed, the homes that seem the cleanest are often the ones teeming with the most disease-causing germs. This happens because cleaning tools and techniques not only don't kill the pathogens, they also spread the germs all over the place.</u>

Thesis
Statement

2   Dr. Gerba's research has shown that a clean bathroom is often smeared with millions of harmful microorganisms. This is because about half the population uses sponges and rags to clean. Yet only 24 percent of Americans disinfect them after each use, about 40 percent rinse them only with water, and 16 percent just put the sponges and rags away after using them. Consequently, bathroom sponges and rags are filled with germs; the more they are used, the more microorganisms get spread around on surfaces.

3   Clean kitchens, too, often harbor more dangerous bacteria than messy kitchens. As a matter of fact, research has shown that even in the most spotless of homes, bacteria associated with fecal matter, such as *E. coli,* are regularly found in the sink and on countertops. These germs are spread by unwashed hands; raw meat; and the sponges, dishrags, and dish towels used to clean up. For example, a kitchen sponge that has been used for only two or three days is filled with millions of bacteria, so the more it's used to wipe surfaces, the more it spreads germs around.

4   Dr. Gerba's research has also shown that freshly laundered clothes are not truly clean either. In one study, he swabbed the inside of 100 household washing machines in Florida and Arizona and found that more than 60 percent tested positive for coliform bacteria, which comes from fecal matter, and 20 percent tested positive for *staphylococcus,* a major cause of food-borne illness. Swabs of dryers showed that even high-heat settings don't kill salmonella and another bacteria (*mycobacterium fortuitium*) that causes skin infections. Thus every time a new load of clothes or towels goes into either the washer or the dryer, these harmful germs get into the fabrics.

5   However, Dr. Gerba and other experts say that changing to different tools and techniques will help kill and stop the spread of germs. They recommend cleaning with sturdy paper towels and then throwing them away. They also suggest using bleach on surfaces and in the laundry, as well as putting rags, towels, and sponges in the microwave for at least one minute after each use. (Sources of information: Amanda Hesser, "Squeaky Clean? Not Even Close," *New York Times*, January 28, 2004, p. F1; "Paper Towels Help Wipe Out Harmful Bathroom Germs," *PR Newswire*, November 2, 2000; Jo Werne, "Clean Kitchen Can Be a Hotbed of

Germs," *Knight Ridder/Tribune News Services*, October 12, 1995; "Germs in the Laundry," Clorox Company, *PR Newswire,* June 4, 1999.)

EXPLANATION In this reading, the thesis statement consists of two sentences rather than one. The thesis statement tells readers that the author intends to explore two related points: (1) Clean homes are often not really clean at all, and (2) this is because improper cleaning tools and techniques can spread germs. Paragraphs 2, 3, and 4 then provide the supporting details that clarify both parts of this thesis statement.

1. Gender and Listening

1   Men and women learn different styles of listening just as they learn different styles for using verbal and nonverbal messages. Not surprisingly, these different styles can create major difficulties in opposite-sex interpersonal communication. According to Deborah Tannen in her best-selling *You Just Don't Understand: Women and Men in Conversation,* women seek to build rapport and establish a closer relationship and use listening to achieve these ends. Men, on the other hand, will play up their expertise, emphasize it, and use it in dominating the interaction. Women play down their expertise and are more interested in communicating supportiveness. Tannen argues that the goal of a man in conversation is to be given respect, so he seeks to show his knowledge and expertise. A woman, on the other hand, seeks to be liked, so she expresses agreement.

2   Men and women also show that they're listening in different ways. In conversation, a woman is more apt to give lots of listening cues such as interjecting "Yeah" or "Uh-uh," nodding in agreement, and smiling. A man is more likely to listen quietly, without giving lots of listening cues as feedback. Subsequent research seems to confirm Tannen's position. For example, an analysis of calls to a crisis center in Finland revealed that calls received by a female counselor were significantly longer for both men and women callers (Salminen and Glad, 1992). It's likely that the greater number of listening cues given by the women encouraged the callers to keep talking. This same study also found that male callers were helped by "just listening," whereas women callers were helped by "empathic understanding."

3   Tannen argues, however, that men listen less to women than women listen to men. The reason, says Tannen, is that listening places the person in an inferior position, whereas speaking

places the person in a superior position. Men may seem to assume a more argumentative posture while listening, as if getting ready to argue. They may also appear to ask questions that are more argumentative or that seek to puncture holes in your position as a way to play up their own expertise. Women are more likely to ask supportive questions and perhaps offer criticism that is more positive than men. Women let the speaker see that they're listening. Men, on the other hand, use fewer listening cues in conversation. Men and women act this way to both men and women; their customary ways of talking don't seem to change depending on whether the listener is male or female.

4   There is no evidence to show that these differences represent any negative motives on the part of men to prove themselves superior or of women to ingratiate themselves. Rather, these differences in listening seem largely the result of the way in which men and women have been socialized. (DeVito, *The Interpersonal Communication Book*, p. 122.)

2. **Our Oldest Enemy: The Locust**

1   In 2001, America, Russia, and China were invaded by vast armies bent on nothing less than total destruction. In early June of that year, the enemy entered these countries on foot, creeping along at just a mile an hour at first. But two weeks later, they had begun to take to the air, swooping in from the skies to plunder the land and covering hundreds of miles a day, obliterating everything in their path.

2   Specialized emergency teams went into action. Aircraft roared into the skies, flying only sixty-five feet above the ground in a skillful counterattack. The initial battle raged for a week; sporadic fighting continued until July, when the three countries finally declared themselves victorious. At war's end, the enemy dead numbered in the *billions*.

3   It had been no human invasion but a far more fearsome and rapacious* threat: locusts. Using chemicals sprayed from aircraft or importing hundreds of thousands of locust-eating ducks, humans wreaked havoc on these prodigiously* destructive pests. Nevertheless, throughout most of history, the reverse has been true. When a plague of locusts arrives, it has been people who have suffered more than the insects.

---

*rapacious: greedy.
*prodigiously: enormously.

4   The earliest written record of a locust plague is probably in the Book of Exodus, which describes an attack that took place in Egypt in about 3500 BCE: "They covered the face of the whole land, so that the land was darkened . . . ; not a green thing remained, neither tree nor plant of the field, through all the land of Egypt" (Exodus 10:12–15). Another biblical account, in the Book of Job, describes trees "made white" as locusts stripped even the bark from the branches.

5   Locusts have always spelled disaster. In a single day, a typical large swarm (about 40 million insects) can eat 80,000 tons of corn, devouring a city's food supply for an entire year in just hours. In 125 BCE, locusts destroyed the grain crop in northern Africa; 80,000 people died of starvation. In 591 AD, a plague of locusts in Italy caused the death of more than a million people and animals. In 1613, disaster struck the French region of La Camargue when locusts ate enough grass in a single day to feed 4,000 cattle for a year. Between 1873 and 1877, locusts blackened the skies of the American West from California to Missouri, causing $200 million in crop damage. At the time, in fact, the U.S. government pronounced the locust to be "the most serious impediment to the settlement of the West." The Nile Valley suffered in 1889 when locusts so thoroughly destroyed crops over an estimated 2,000-square-mile area that even the mice starved in their wake. Between 1949 and 1963, locust swarms in Africa caused an estimated $100 million worth of damage annually. In 1988, the Ethiopian cereal crop was laid waste, leaving a million people without food. The 2001 invasion of America destroyed more than 12 million acres of farmland, forcing some areas, such as the state of Utah, to declare an agricultural emergency. (Sources of information: Adams and Riley, eds., "The Ravenous Millions," *Facts and Fallacies,* p. 50; June Southworth, "Day of the Locusts," *The Daily Mail* (London), June 20, 2001; Frithjof Voss, "Simply the Pest," *Geographical,* March 1, 2000, pp. 98–99.)

3. Killer Bees

1   Although their name makes them sound like something out of a horror film, killer bees really do exist. And while they are not quite so terrifying as their name implies, they are definitely not an insect—like the ladybug—that one should invite into the garden. On the contrary, both animals and humans would do well to avoid these sometimes ferociously angry bees.

2   Killer bees (officially called Africanized honeybees) originated in Brazil in 1956 as an experiment in mating the African honeybee

with local bees. The breeders were hoping to get bees that would produce more honey. Instead, they produced extremely aggressive bees that have attacked—and in some cases killed—both people and animals. Each year the bees move about 350 miles (563 kilometers) north; in 1990, they crossed the U.S. border into Hidalgo, Texas.

3   Similar to the rumors that surround sharks, myths about African bees abound.* For example, it's not true that they fly faster than domestic honeybees. On the contrary, both types of bees average between 12 and 15 miles per hour. Also, the sting of the African bee actually has less, not more, venom than that of domestic honeybees. African bees are also a good deal smaller than domestic ones, not gigantic as has been rumored.

4   Still, African bees do have some features that make them an insect to avoid. When an African bee's body is crushed—from a swat, for example—it releases an odor that incites nearby bees to attack. Also, African bees vigorously and aggressively protect their hives. About ten times as many African bees as European bees will sting when their colonies are invaded. The good news is that scientists believe the African bees' aggressiveness will eventually diminish as they interbreed with the more peaceful European bees to the north.

4. The Moon Landing and the Conspiracy Theorists

1 Despite all the evidence to the contrary, many people seriously believe that NASA's* Apollo space program never really landed men on the moon. On the contrary, they claim that the moon landings were nothing more than a huge conspiracy, perpetrated by a government desperately in competition with the Russians and fearful of losing face. According to the theory, the U.S. government knew it couldn't compete with Russia in the race to space, so it was forced to fake a series of successful moon landings. As the 2001 television program "Conspiracy Theory: Did We Land on the Moon?" revealed, conspiracy theorists believe they have several pieces of evidence proving unquestionably that there was a cover-up. They claim, for instance, that astronauts could never have safely passed through the Van Allen belt, a region of radiation trapped in Earth's magnetic field. If the astronauts had really gone through that belt, they would have died, say those crying fraud. Scientists, however, have a twofold response to this argu-

_____
*abound: exist in great number.
*NASA: National Aeronautics and Space Administration.

ment. They point out that the metal hulls of the spaceship were designed to block radiation and that the spacecrafts passed so quickly through the belt that there wasn't time for the astronauts to be affected. Conspiracy theorists, however, are not impressed by this argument, preferring to believe their own version of events.

2   Conspiracy theorists also argue that the lander should have blasted a crater in the moon's surface when it descended. Photographs of the lunar surface, however, reveal no such craters. For some, this is clear proof of NASA's deception. They discount NASA's claims that the lander was purposely designed to land gently in order to disturb the moon's surface as little as possible.

3   Other photographs supposedly support the theory of a faked moon landing. These photographs do not show any stars. Supporters of a conspiracy insist, therefore, that the photos are fake. They refuse to acknowledge NASA's argument that the cameras were set to photograph bright objects like the astronauts' white suits. The faint light of the stars was not strong enough to register on the film.

4   Proponents of a conspiracy also want to know why the U.S. flag planted on the moon is rippling when it should be still because there is no air on the moon. They don't seem to grasp scientists' explanation that a flag can ripple in the vacuum of space. They also flatly don't believe the more commonsense explanation: The cloth of the flag rippled because the astronaut in the photograph was adjusting the rod that held it. They seem to consider this explanation just too simple to be true.

In other words, despite all proof to the contrary, conspiracy theorists are determined to believe that a hoax has been perpetrated on the American public. From their point of view, only a few wise souls like themselves have been smart enough to spot it. If the rest of us would only open our eyes to their "evidence," perhaps we would see the error of our ways. Yes, and if we would only let the scales drop from our eyes, we might also recognize the existence of the tooth fairy!

 ## Major and Minor Details

Major details in longer readings directly explain the thesis statement. They answer potential questions readers might raise; further define any general words or terms; and, when necessary, offer proof of an author's claim. While major details in a paragraph consist of single sentences, in longer readings you may find that an entire paragraph is devoted to explaining one major detail. When this happens, you'll have to decide how much of the paragraph is essential to your understanding of that one detail.

As they do in paragraphs, minor details in longer readings further explain or flesh out major details; they also provide color or emphasis. But here again, you can't assume that minor details are automatically not essential to your understanding of the thesis statement. It all depends on what they contribute to your understanding of the major details they modify.

Read the following selection. As you do, think about which supporting details are essential to your understanding of the underlined thesis statement.

Defining Love

Thesis Statement

1 What is love? No one knows for sure. However, researcher R. J. Sternberg has a theory. <u>According to Sternberg, love consists of three separate ingredients, and each one is crucial either to falling in love or to staying in love.</u>

2   Passion is a feeling of heightened sexual arousal, and it's usually accompanied by a strong, romantic attraction. In the throes* of passion, each lover feels that life is barely worth living unless the other is present. Unfortunately, passionate feelings almost always diminish over time, although they are still essential to a loving relationship. Luckily, if there's a strong sense of intimacy between the partners, the loss or decrease of passion can be accepted and the love maintained.

3   Intimacy—feelings of closeness, sharing, and affection—is essential to staying in love. Both partners need to feel that they view the world in similar ways and can turn to one another in times of great sadness or joy. If the one you love is not the one you feel particularly close to, over time you may find that love doesn't last. Typically in a relationship, intimacy grows steadily at first and then levels off.

4   Commitment refers to a conscious decision to stay with a person both in good times and in bad. Like intimacy, a sense of commitment is essential to staying in love as time passes. But unlike intimacy, commitment frequently requires some hard work and determination. It seldom comes without effort.

While reading the thesis statement in this selection, you probably wondered what three ingredients the author had in mind. Anticipat-

---

*throes: pangs; spasms.

ing that question, the author defines all three. Those definitions are the major details that refer directly to the thesis statement. However, the minor details that expand on those major details cannot simply be ignored—not if you want to understand Sternberg's theory. Minor detail or not, it is important to remember that if intimacy is lacking, love doesn't last—at least that is R. J. Sternberg's point of view.

Thesis Statements and Major Details

In trying to differentiate between major and minor details, it's important to use any and all clues provided by the thesis statement. For example, the thesis statement in the reading about love pointed out that love consists of "three separate ingredients." This phrase is a tip-off to the major details. It practically guarantees that each major detail will describe one of the three ingredients.

Key Words in Thesis Statements

Any time a thesis statement focuses on general words, such as *reasons, studies, groups, causes,* and *theories,* those words need to be further explained to be meaningful to readers. After all, if you know that there are three reasons for increased violence in the schools, this information doesn't help you much until you know what the reasons are. When you see words such as *reasons, causes,* and so on in what you think is the thesis statement, check to see if the paragraphs that follow further explain those reasons or causes. If they do, you have gained on two fronts: (1) You have confirmed your guess about the thesis statement and (2) you have discovered a key to the major details.

Look now at the opening paragraph of a reading from a psychology text. Read it through and see if you can find a word or phrase that points the way to the major details.

In everyday life, requests for compliance are common. A stranger asks you to yield a phone booth so that she can make a call. A salesperson suggests you buy a more expensive watch than the one you first asked to see. Or a coworker asks to borrow a dollar in order to buy a danish during coffee break. Have you ever wondered what determines whether or not you say yes? Although many different factors come into play when we agree to a request, there are three essential strategies for inducing compliance.

Based on that paragraph, do you have the strong sense that the major details will describe the three strategies that encourage compliance? If you do, you are right. That is precisely the function of the major details that follow the opening paragraph. See for yourself:

1 One way of encouraging compliance is to use the *foot-in-the-door strategy.* The name comes from a technique long used in the days when salespeople went door to door to sell their wares. As the saying went at the time, "If you can get your foot in the door, the sale is almost a sure thing." In psychological terms, the foot-in-the-door strategy means that if someone can get you to comply with some small request, you are very likely to comply with a much larger demand. For example, if the committee to re-elect your local mayor wants you to put a huge sign in your front window promoting her candidacy, members of the committee might first ask you to display a bumper sticker. Once you agree to display the bumper sticker, they might ask you to wear a button. Once you've agreed to those two smaller requests, you would more than likely be ready to put that sign in your window.

2 Psychologists suspect that the foot-in-the-door strategy works because we observe our own behavior. Recognizing that we have agreed to a small request, we convince ourselves that the next, larger demand isn't all that different. Thus we're ready to comply.

3 The *door-in-the-face strategy*—the name was coined by psychologist Robert Cialdini—is a variation on foot-in-the-door, and it works like this: If you have flatly said no to a large and inconvenient request ("slammed the door in someone's face"), you're more likely to agree to a smaller bid for help. Say, for example, your neighbor comes by and asks you to pick up his daughter at school for the next week while he is working overtime. Chances are you will say no because it requires too big a chunk of your time. But if he comes back the next day and says he got a friend to handle Monday, Wednesday, and Friday, you are likely to agree to take over on Tuesday and Thursday.

4 This strategy works because it seems as if the person making the request is being reasonable and making a concession. For that reason, the person doing the favor feels that it is only fair to comply with the smaller request.

5 If you or someone you know has ever purchased a car, you will recognize the *low-ball* technique of encouraging compliance. In the context of car buying, the salesperson offers a "low-ball" price that is significantly less than that of the competition. Once the customer seems interested, the salesperson begins to bump up the

price. In other words, the low-ball technique gets you to comply with a request that seems to cost little or nothing. Once you say yes, the person starts tacking on additional items. For example, your roommate asks for a ride to the local ticket office, where she hopes to get tickets to a hot concert. Because the ticket office is only five minutes away by car, you say, "Sure, no problem." It's at that point that your roommate tells you she has to be there by 5:00 in the morning because that's when the line starts forming. If you agree, you've just succumbed to the low-ball technique. (Source of information: Coon, *Essentials of Psychology*, p. 625.)

Particularly in textbooks, thesis statements frequently offer clues to major details in the form of phrases such as "three common factors," "four major reasons," or "five different categories." In general, every one of the factors, reasons, or categories is likely to be a major detail. Keep that in mind while you are completing your textbook assignments or doing research.

EXERCISE 2 ▐DIRECTIONS▐ Read each selection and look carefully at the underlined thesis statement. Then answer the questions by filling in the blanks or circling the letter of the correct response.

▐EXAMPLE▐

The Ancient Roman Circus

Thesis
Statement

1   Although nowadays we think of the circus as an amusing entertainment for kids, originally it was not quite such a harmless event. To be sure, the first circus, like its modern counterpart, included death-defying events. But there was one big difference. In the early Roman circus, death was a very real possibility, and circus spectators were accustomed to—and expected—bloodshed.

2   The Roman Circus Maximus began under the rule of Julius Caesar, and it specialized in two big events—brutal fights between gladiators (or between gladiators and animals) and equally bloody chariot races. In most cases, both events ended in the death of either a person or an animal. If nobody died, the audience was likely to be disappointed. Even worse, the emperor would be displeased.

3   Not surprisingly, the circus event that was in fashion usually reflected the taste of the man in power. Julius Caesar, for example, favored aggressive chariot races. Because the charioteers were usually slaves racing to win their freedom, they drove their horses unmercifully, and serious accidents were an exciting possibility. In

the hope of surviving, the charioteers wore helmets and wrapped the chariot reins around their bodies. They also carried knives to cut themselves free if necessary. Spills occurred more often than not, and the charioteers would be thrown from the chariot and dragged repeatedly around the ring by runaway horses. Knives and helmets notwithstanding, most did not survive, not that the screaming crowd cared.

4   During the reign of Augustus, from 27 BC to 14 AD, a fight to the death between man and beast was the most popular circus event, and more than 3,500 lions and tigers perished in the circus arena, taking hundreds of gladiators with them. Under the half-mad Emperor Nero, who ruled during the first century AD, the most popular circus spectacle was lion versus Christian, with the Christians the guaranteed losers. Fortunately for both Christians and the slaves who followed in their wake, this savage circus practice was outlawed in 326 AD by the Emperor Constantine.

5   Although the pitting of Christians against lions was staged in a special arena, most of the circus events that took place in Rome were staged in the largest arena of them all—the Colosseum. The capacity of this great stadium, completed in 79 AD, was enormous. It seated close to 50,000 people. In one Colosseum season alone, 2,000 gladiators went to their deaths, all in the name of circus fun.[†]

1. How would you paraphrase the thesis statement?

Unlike the modern circus, the ancient Roman circus was a good deal more deadly.

2. Which question about the thesis statement do the major supporting details help to answer?

a. What are the similarities between ancient and modern circuses?

(b.) How did early circus events all but guarantee death?

EXPLANATION As it should, the paraphrase restates the point of the thesis statement but alters the words. The most likely question raised by the thesis statement is _b_. The main idea of the entire reading is that ancient circuses were often deadly, and the reader needs to know why this was so.

[†]Charles Panati, _Browser's Book of Beginnings_, Boston: Houghton Mifflin, 1984, pp. 262–264.

1. The Five Languages of Love

1 According to relationship expert Dr. Gary Chapman, author of *The Five Love Languages,* people not only have very different personalities, they also express love in different ways. <u>Chapman believes that every individual best expresses love—and prefers to receive love—through one of five different communication styles.</u> He calls these styles "love languages."

Thesis Statement

2   Some people feel that love is best expressed through **quality time** spent as a couple. Quality time, according to Dr. Chapman, does not mean simply being in the same room together; instead, it involves doing things as a couple and devoting attention to one another. People who prefer quality time as their love language feel loved when they are taken out on dates or when their partners set aside time for them, even if it's just to chat for a few moments.

3   Other people, however, prefer **words of affirmation** as a way of giving or receiving love. These individuals like to be told that they are loved. They expect to hear "I love you" or "I appreciate you" often, and they like compliments, encouragement, and praise. They like to hear things such as "That dress looks great on you" or "You have a wonderful smile."

4   **Gifts** are yet another love language. People who use this language see presents as much more than material objects. For them gifts are symbols of love and signs of affection.

5   People who express love through **acts of service**, however, aren't impressed by gifts. They believe that helping others is the best expression of love. Voluntary acts of service are what makes them happy. Cooking, doing chores, changing the baby's diaper, and walking the dog are ways to make members of this group feel cared for and supported.

6   According to Chapman, **physical touch** is the fifth kind of love expression. People using this form of communication prefer to communicate their feelings for their partners by holding hands, kissing, hugging, or having sex. They feel secure and loved when they can touch and be touched in return.

7   Chapman believes that problems arise when two people involved in a romantic relationship have different styles of expression. If each person expresses him- or herself in a language the other doesn't really understand or recognize, then expressions of affection may go unnoticed and undermine the relationship. For example, people who prefer expressing love through sharing quality time may doubt their partner's affection if the partner doesn't want to do lots of things as a couple. Similarly, people who need

to hear words of affirmation will feel rejected if their partners don't tell them how much they care. But while it's true that speaking different love languages can lead to misunderstanding, there is still hope. If couples become aware of the different love languages and learn to give and receive affection in a partner's preferred style, they can enhance, even revitalize, a romantic relationship. (Sources of information: www.fivelovelanguages.com/thefivelovelanguages/index.html; Family First, "The Five Love Languages," www.familyfirst.net/marriage/fivelovelang.html.)

1. How would you paraphrase the thesis statement?

_____

_____

2. Which question about the thesis statement do the major supporting details help to answer?

    a. What makes some love languages more effective than others?

    b. What are the five love languages?

    c. How can couples learn to use the same love language?

2. Taking Spam Off the Menu

Thesis Statement   1   Most computer users who have e-mail addresses are familiar with spam—unwanted e-mail messages advertising a product or service. Spam includes offers for everything from weight-loss aids to get-rich-quick schemes. It's the electronic version of the "junk mail" delivered to mailboxes or the online equivalent of a telemarketing phone call. Experts estimate that one in every ten e-mail messages sent today is spam. The average Internet user receives almost 1,500 junk messages each year.

  2   Spam is a cheap form of advertising. That's why it's attractive to marketers. A business can buy a list of consumers' e-mail addresses from another company or compile its own list by performing a sweep of the World Wide Web. Once the list is composed, e-mail messages can be sent out instantly to thousands of possible customers. Sending ten messages or ten million messages costs about the same.

  3   Consumers, however, find spam extremely annoying. Determining which messages are spam and then deleting them is irritating and time-consuming. Unwanted e-mail is one of the major complaints of subscribers to Internet service providers.

4   Employers dislike spam too. On the job, when workers spend even a few minutes a day dealing with spam, the labor costs can add up quickly. As a result, many companies are spending additional money on filters to screen out spam altogether. These filters sometimes cause problems because they can block important, necessary messages from getting through.

5   Companies that choose to filter messages often purchase anti-spam software or hire a firm that specializes in blocking unwanted spam. Symantec's Brightmail is one successful anti-spam program. It maintains thousands of e-mail accounts that collect and identify sources of spam. Then it installs software on its clients' e-mail gateways, including those of many of the largest Internet service providers. When a known spam message tries to get through the gateway, the software blocks it.

1. How would you paraphrase the thesis statement?

_____

_____

2. Which question about the thesis statement do the major supporting details help answer?

a. Why is spam unwanted?

b. How does spam compare to junk mail?

c. Which software does the best job of blocking spam?

Outlining Longer Readings

For reading assignments that cover fairly familiar or uncomplicated material, you can probably prepare for class discussions or exams simply by reviewing your underlining and your annotations. However, if the material is at all complicated, you may want to take notes using an informal outline.

Like a formal outline, an **informal outline** signals relationships by aligning or indenting sentences, words, or phrases. With informal outlines, however, you needn't worry about using *all* sentences or *all* phrases, and you don't have to fuss over capital or lowercase letters. You can use whatever symbols seem appropriate to the material and combine letters, numbers, abbreviations, dashes, and so on, as you need them. In other words, informal outlines are not governed by a fixed set of rules. The main thing to keep in mind is the goal of your informal outline: to develop a clear blueprint of the author's ideas and their relationship to one another.

Here are some pointers for creating clear, concise, and complete informal outlines.

Start with the Title

The title of an essay, an article, or a chapter section usually identifies the topic being discussed. Sometimes it will identify the main idea of the entire reading. Thus your outline should usually open with the title.

Follow with the Thesis Statement

After the title comes the paraphrase of the thesis statement. Because indenting to show relationships is crucial to outlining, put your paraphrase at the left-most margin of your notepaper.

List the Major Details

Now's the time to read over the supporting paragraphs and sift out the major details. At this point, keep in mind that the major details you select have to be carefully evaluated in relation to the thesis statement, and minor details in a paragraph should be included only if they are essential to the major ones. Outlining, like underlining, requires conscious and consistent selectivity. Here's an outline of the reading from pages 257–258.

The Ancient Roman Circus

The first circus began in ancient Rome, but it was much bloodier than the circus we know today.

1. The first circus, Circus Maximus, originated under Julius Caesar.
2. Ancient circuses specialized in bloody events; emperor and spectators were upset if no one died.

3. Which event was featured depended on the emperor in power.

    a. Julius Caesar liked chariot races: slaves raced for freedom and risked their lives, often dying in the process.

    —dragged around the ring when they couldn't cut themselves free

    b. During reign of Augustus, hundreds of gladiators died, taking with them more than 3,500 lions and tigers.

    c. Under Nero, Christians were thrown to the lions.

4. Colosseum in Rome staged biggest circuses.

    a. It held 50,000 people.

    b. In one season, 2,000 gladiators went to their deaths.

Always Indent

As the sample outline illustrates, an outline is not a list. When you make an outline, you have to indent to indicate whether different ideas carry equal weight. Major details, for example, should all be aligned under one another to indicate that they are equal in importance. Similarly, if you are summarizing several different chapter sections, then the main ideas of each section should be aligned one underneath the other.

Be Consistent

Letters, numbers, dashes (—), stars (☆☆☆), or asterisks (**) can help you separate major and minor details. Whichever symbols you use, be sure to use them consistently within the outline. Don't switch back and forth, sometimes using numbers for major details and sometimes using letters. In the long run, this kind of inconsistency will only confuse you.

Be Selective

When you outline, reduce the content of the original text as much as possible. Try to retain essential details and eliminate nonessential ones. When adding supporting details to your outline, always decide what you need to include and what you can safely leave out.

EXERCISE 3 | DIRECTIONS | Read the following selections. Underline and anno-
tate them. Then make a concise and complete outline for each.

| EXAMPLE |

World War II: Interning Japanese Americans

1 Compared with previous wars, the nation's wartime civil liberties
record during World War II showed some improvement, particularly where African Americans and women were concerned. But
there was one enormous exception: the treatment of 120,000
Japanese Americans. The internment* of Japanese Americans
was based not on suspicion or evidence of treason; their
crime was solely their race—the fact that they were of Japanese
descent.

Stereotypes and
revenge cause
internment policy

2 Popular racial stereotypes used to fuel the war effort held that
Japanese people abroad and at home were sneaky and evil, and
the American people generally regarded Japan as the chief enemy
of the United States. Moreover, the feeling was widespread that
the Japanese had to be repaid for the bombing of Pearl Harbor.
Thus, with a few notable exceptions, there was no public outcry
over the relocation and internment of Japanese Americans.

3 Yet there were two obvious reasons why internment was
completely unnecessary. First and foremost, there was absolutely
no evidence of any attempt by Japanese Americans to hinder the
American war effort. The government's own studies proved that
fact beyond question. Thus, it's not surprising that in places
where racism was not a factor, in Hawaii for example, the public
outcry for internment was much more muted.

4 Second, Japanese American soldiers fought valiantly for the
United States. The all Japanese-American 442nd Regimental
Combat Team—heavily recruited from young men in internment
camps—was the most decorated unit of its size in the armed
forces. Suffering heavy casualties in Italy and France, members of
the 442nd were awarded a Congressional Medal of Honor, several
Distinguished Service Crosses, 350 Silver Stars, and more than
3,600 Purple Hearts. (Adapted from Norton et al., *A People and a
Nation*, p. 795.)

Example of
Japanese-
American bravery

Title *World War II: Interning Japanese Americans*

Main Idea *In World War II, the imprisonment of Japanese Americans spoiled
an otherwise creditable civil rights record.*

*internment: imprisonment.

Supporting Details

1. Racial stereotypes used to power the war effort encouraged

people to see Japanese Americans as the enemy.

2. General belief that the Japanese had to be paid back for

bombing Pearl Harbor.

3. Two reasons why internment unnecessary

    1) No evidence of wrongdoing, a fact proven by government

    studies

    2) Japanese-American soldiers fought bravely to defend the U.S.

    —An all Japanese-American combat team was

    recruited largely from internment camps, and it was

    the most decorated of its size.

EXPLANATION Your outline of this reading might have used letters instead of numbers and left out dashes altogether. Still, the content would have been similar. Given the thesis statement in paragraph 1, you need to include the causes of internment as well as the reasons why the authors consider it an "enormous exception" to an otherwise creditable record on civil rights.

1. The Gains and Losses of Beauty

1 No doubt about it, extremely good-looking people have a significant social edge. They are less lonely; less socially anxious (especially about interactions with the opposite sex); more popular; more sexually experienced; and . . . more socially skilled (Feingold, 1992b). The social rewards for physical attractiveness appear to get off to an early start. Mothers of highly attractive newborns engage in more affectionate interactions with their babies than do mothers of less attractive infants (Langlois et al., 1995). Given such benefits, one would expect that the beautiful would also have a significant psychological advantage. But they don't. Physical attractiveness (as rated by judges) has little if any association with self-esteem, mental health, personality traits, or intelligence (Feingold, 1992b).

2   One possible reason why beauty doesn't affect psychological well-being is that *actual* physical attractiveness, as evaluated by others, may have less impact than *self-perceived* physical attractiveness. People who view themselves as physically attractive do

report higher self-esteem and better mental health than those who believe they are unattractive (Feingold, 1992b). But judges' ratings of physical attractiveness are only modestly correlated* with self-perceived attractiveness. When real beauties do not see themselves as beautiful, their appearance may not be psychologically valuable.

3   Physically attractive individuals may also fail to benefit from the social bias for beauty because of pressures they experience to maintain their appearance. In contemporary American society, such pressures are particularly strong in regard to the body. Although both facial and bodily appearance contribute to perceived attractiveness, an unattractive body appears to be a greater liability than an unattractive face (Alicke et al., 1986). Such a "body bias" can produce a healthy emphasis on nutrition and exercise. But it can sometimes lead to distinctly unhealthy consequences. For example, men may pop steroids in order to build up impressive muscles. Among women, the desire for a beautiful body often takes a different form.

4   Women are more likely than men to suffer from what Janet Polivy and her colleagues (1986) call the "modern mania for slenderness." This zeal* for thinness is promoted by the mass media. Popular female characters in TV shows are more likely than popular male characters to be exceedingly thin; women's magazines stress the need to maintain a slender body more than do men's magazines (Silverstein et al., 1986b). (Brehm and Kassim, *Social Psychology*, p. 180.)

Title _____

Main Idea _____

_____

Supporting Details _____

_____

_____

_____

_____

_____

---

*correlated; related to.
*zeal: strong desire.

_____

_____

_____

_____

_____

_____

2. But If It's Natural, It Must Be Good for You

1 Depending on who's doing the estimating, Americans spend between $5 and $10 billion per year on herbal supplements with funny-sounding names like *echinacea*, *ginseng*, and *golden seal*. The production, marketing, and selling of herbal supplements is a serious and profitable business with countless people consuming a variety of herbal medicines in an effort to cure both minor and major health problems. Yet herbal medicines are not regulated by the Food and Drug Administration. In fact, few scientific studies are available to prove their curative powers. There are even fewer to detect the possibility that some herbal medications might cause harm.

2 Amazingly, American consumers don't seem to care that there is so little science backing up claims for herbal medicines. Generally, consumers don't even seem worried about the ill effects of ingesting herbs. The reigning assumption is that herbs are natural and anything natural can't hurt you. However, that assumption is misguided, even dangerous—just try ingesting a leaf of "natural" poison ivy. If they really want to take care of their health, consumers should demand more proof that herbal supplements can do what their makers claim. More to the point, consumers should wonder about the side effects of taking supplements that have not undergone much, if any, rigorous testing.

3 The herb widely known as *comfrey*, for example, is sold as a gel or an ointment for treating minor cuts and burns. And comfrey does contain allantoin, a chemical that aids in skin repair. But comfrey is also sold as a treatment for ulcers and stomach upsets, even though there is no compelling evidence that it can help either condition. On the contrary, some evidence shows that it can destroy liver cells, so ingesting it might be extremely dangerous. Still, you are unlikely to find any warning label on a bottle

of comfrey tablets, and the herb is a popular item in natural food stores.

4   It's been widely claimed that another herbal supplement, *ginseng,* can improve memory and mood while also boosting energy. In Germany, where there is a formal body that regulates the sale of herbal medicine, ginseng has undergone repeated testing, and the herb seems to live up to claims about its benefits. The problem with ginseng is less that the claims are exaggerated and more that authentic ginseng is hard to find and extremely expensive. Thus a bottle of tablets or powder labeled as ginseng may have very little of the herb but quite a few additives or fillers, and some of those additives might not be altogether harmless.

5   Additives were the problem with an herbal mixture called *Zhong gan ling.* Used for centuries in China as a cold medication, it has never been proven effective against the common cold. In fact, one California woman ended up being treated for a condition that resembled leukemia. Test results showed that her body was responding to a veterinary painkiller that had been added to the herbal medicine she was taking, which just happened to be Zhong gan ling. Although the FDA immediately banned the particular mixture the woman had ingested, other forms of Zhong gan ling can still be found on the shelves of natural food stores.

6   Anyone who thinks of herbs as "all natural" and therefore harmless should also recall what happened several years ago to some people who took an alleged weight-loss herb known as *ephedra* or *ma hung.* Ephedra contains ephedrine, a substance that acts as a stimulant to the body and seems to encourage weight loss. But the amount of ephedrine in each plant varies according to the conditions under which the herb was grown. If a particular batch of the herb contains extremely high levels of ephedrine, then ingesting the herb can cause both blood pressure and heart rate to soar. No wonder then that ephedra caused at least 800 people to have problems such as fluctuating blood pressure, dizziness, and heart palpitations. When ephedra was being marketed as one of the components of "herbal phen-fen," an allegedly miraculous, "all natural" diet drug, scores of people who used it suffered permanent heart valve damage. At least a dozen people died as a result of taking the dietary supplement, which is more proof that "all natural" is not synonymous with being safe for human consumption. (Source of information: Christian Millman, "Remedies: Natural Disasters," *Men's Health,* Vol. 14, April 1, 1999, pp. 90, 92, 94.)

Title _____

Main Idea _____

_____

_____

Supporting Details _____

_____

_____

_____

_____

_____

_____

_____

_____

_____

_____

_____

Check Your Understanding

Describe the main goal of an informal outline.

_____

_____

Synthesizing Sources

Imagine you are assigned to read an account of President John Adams's[†] tenure in the White House and that the reading emphasizes Adams's praiseworthy efforts to stop the country's undeclared war with the French. Now imagine as well that you are assigned an outside reading, which harshly criticizes Adams's role in bringing about passage of the Alien and Sedition Acts.[‡] Having read about two different sides of the same subject, John Adams, how do you think you should proceed? Should you take notes on each reading separately? Or should you try to **synthesize**, or combine and connect, the two different positions into one unified or connected whole?

If you opted for the second choice, it may be because you already know the basic rule of remembering: The human mind has an easier time storing connected pieces of information than unrelated ideas, theories, or facts. Thus whenever you read different authors who talk about the same subject, at some point it pays to see if you can synthesize the different ideas.

Consider the two readings just mentioned. Each one focuses on a different aspect, or side, of Adams's career. One reading notes a positive accomplishment, the other focuses on a more negative achievement. A statement like the following synthesizes the two readings and could help you remember the ideas expressed in both: "Fans of John Adams like to point to his abilities as a peacemaker during the conflict with the French, but his critics can't forget that the Alien and Sedition Acts came into being during his presidency." Using that sentence as your thesis statement, you can then add supporting details from both readings as a way of reviewing for exams.

Taking the time to synthesize two or even three different sources of information into one statement does more than encourage remembering. It also deepens your understanding of individual viewpoints. To synthesize different sources, you have to think about each of them and figure out how the headings connect or relate to one another. This kind of prolonged processing of information not only improves both comprehension and remembering, it also provides you with ideas for term papers.

[†]John Adams: (1735–1826) the second president of the United States (1797–1801).
[‡]Alien and Sedition Acts: acts that discriminated against the foreign born and blurred the distinction between political dissension and attempts to overthrow the government.

Synthesizing for Term Papers

Synthesizing is particularly important when you write research papers. For example, imagine that you were assigned a paper on the Patriot Act, which came into being in response to the terrorist attacks on September 11, 2001. From your research, you might discover that there is a good deal of disagreement on the effectiveness of the Patriot Act. Some writers say it is essential to protecting the country, others argue that it is ineffective. You yourself may feel it is unnecessarily intrusive. Thus your final paper might synthesize your point of view with the ideas of others into a thesis statement like the following: "While portions of the Patriot Act were certainly necessary given the fear that gripped the country following September 11, 2001, in calmer times, some elements of the Act need to be modified because they do more to undermine civil rights than they do to eliminate terrorism." Then again, you might argue the opposite: "While it is easy to understand the widespread criticism of the Patriot Act because it does, in fact, intrude on civil rights, it's also clear that in times like the current ones, even the portions of the Act that intrude on civil liberties are absolutely necessary."

Step-by-Step Synthesizing

Synthesizing two or more sources into one statement requires these steps:

1. Identify and paraphrase the main idea of each reading.

2. Determine the relationships among the readings, figuring out where they are similar or dissimilar (see the chart on page 272).

3. Write a sentence that, in general terms, identifies the connection or connections among the different sources; for example, "For Sigmund Freud, unacknowledged sexual desires were the main source of neurotic behavior in adults, but Freud's followers Carl Jung and Alfred Adler chose not to follow in his footsteps. While Jung emphasized the power of historical patterns to control behavior, Adler focused on the way in which a sense of inferiority could motivate both positive and negative reactions to the world."

4. Include the names of the people taking each position if those names are (1) central to the opinion being expressed (e.g., almost no one else holds the opinion), or (2) the instructor wants the names included in the assignment.

If you are synthesizing for a term paper, you need a fifth step: Indicate whether you (1) agree with the sources you've looked at, (2) disagree wholly or in part, or (3) hold a completely different point of view.

Ten Questions for Synthesizing Sources

Sometimes the connections among sources are obvious, particularly when writers all agree or disagree. But for those times when the connections are not so obvious, the questions that follow will prove useful.

1. Do the authors generally agree but offer different examples or reasons to prove the same point?

2. Does one author offer an interpretation that is challenged by the other?

3. Do the authors express a similar point of view only in different forms, say poem and essay, fiction and nonfiction?

4. Do the authors completely disagree or only partially disagree?

5. Do the readings address the same topic or issue but from different time frames—for example, past and present—or from the point of view of different groups—for example, the elderly and the young or the working person versus a corporation?

6. Does one author focus on the cause or causes of a problem while the other looks more closely at a solution?

7. Does one author zero in on the causes of an event while the other concentrates on the aftermath of that event?

8. Do the authors come from different schools of thought? Does one author, for example, concentrate on the psychological roots of an event while the other views it from an economic perspective?

9. Did the ideas of one author influence the work of another?

10. Does one author offer a personal account of events that the other describes in more impersonal or objective terms?

EXERCISE 4 **DIRECTIONS** Read each group of passages. Then circle the number of the statement that most effectively synthesizes or connects all three. *Note*: Keep in mind that an effective synthesis statement should not try in any way to contradict the passages it combines.

EXAMPLE

a. John Steinbeck's *The Grapes of Wrath* movingly conveys the misery facing the migrant workers who, throughout the Depression, traveled Route 66 across the country searching for work. Steinbeck writes, "Route 66 is the path of a people in flight, refugees from dust and shrinking land, from the thunder of tractors and shrinking ownership, from the twisting winds that howl up out of Texas, from the floods that bring no richness to the land and steal what little richness is there."

b. Statistics suggest the magnitude of the Great Depression's effect on the business world. The stock market crash in October 1929 shocked investors and caused a financial panic. Between 1929 and 1933, 100,000 businesses failed; corporate profits fell from $10 billion to $1 billion; and the gross national product was cut in half. Banks failed by the thousands. (Adapted from Norton et al., *A People and a Nation*, p. 754.)

c. As unemployment soared during the Great Depression, both men and women suffered homelessness. In 1932, a squad of New York City police officers arrested twenty-five in "Hoover Valley," a village of tents and crates constructed in Central Park. All over the country, people were so poor they were forced to live in miserable little camps called "Hoovervilles," named in sarcastic honor of President Herbert Hoover, whose policy on the Depression was to pretend it didn't exist.

Synthesis Statement
1. During the Great Depression, no one suffered more than the men and women who earned their living as migrant workers.

(2.) Whether we look to the world of fiction or fact, it's clear that the Great Depression took a terrible toll on people from all walks of life, from bankers to migrant workers.

3. John Steinbeck's description of the hardships people faced during the Great Depression is enormously moving to this day, and Steinbeck's novel is more real than any statistic.

EXPLANATION Passages *a*, *b*, and *c* all describe specific groups that suffered as a result of the Great Depression. Statement 1 is not a good synthesis statement because it puts the suffering of migrant workers above the suffering of the other groups, and none of the passages makes that point. Sentence 2 is a more effective synthesis statement because it combines the ideas in all three passages without adding any ideas that weren't there in the first place. Statement 3 is incorrect because it focuses solely on Steinbeck's novel and ignores the other sources.

1. a. When World War II broke out in Europe on September 1, 1939, the United States was the only world power without a propaganda agency. Since World War I, Americans had been suspicious of the claim that propaganda could be used to good effect. Many believed that British propaganda had helped maneuver the United States into World War I. They also had not forgotten the bloody anti-German riots touched off by movies like America's own *Beast of Berlin* (1919). To most Americans, *propaganda* was simply a dirty word, no matter what its purpose.

b. In 1939, as the world began to career into World War II, the president of the United States, Franklin Delano Roosevelt, applied pressure on Hollywood to make feature films that were little more than propaganda vehicles, but Hollywood producers were not so ready to give in. Committed to the doctrine of pure entertainment, pure profit, and, above all, the need for America to stay out of the war, most balked at making films that reflected the horror engulfing Europe.

c. The Japanese bombed Pearl Harbor on December 7, 1941. Astonished and outraged, the United States entered World War II. On December 17 of the same year, President Roosevelt appointed Lowell Mellett as head of the Hollywood propaganda office. Mellett's job was to make sure that Hollywood films aided the war effort, and, for the most part, Hollywood was happy to cooperate by making films that celebrated the war effort and castigated* America's enemies.

Synthesis Statement 1. Until the bombing of Pearl Harbor, the United States did not have an official propaganda office, a terrible mistake that produced unexpected and horrifying consequences.

2. Before the bombing of Pearl Harbor, Hollywood, like most of America, mistrusted propaganda. But after the bombing, propaganda became an acceptable part of the war effort and Hollywood embraced it.

---

*castigated: harshly criticized or punished.

2. a. The Egyptians revered Maat as the goddess of justice who weighed the hearts of the dead on a scale. The right balance guaranteed a happy afterlife; the wrong one promised torment.

   b. The ancient Greeks worshipped Dike as the goddess of justice. When the Romans inherited her, they renamed her Justitia and represented her with a blindfold around her eyes to symbolize her lack of bias.*

   c. With the arrival of Christianity and the rejection of the ancient gods, the goddess of justice was demoted to a saint and people apparently became suspicious of her ability to fairly deal out justice. Santa Justitia was often depicted holding an unevenly balanced scale. The implication was that the rich got different justice than the poor.

Synthesis 1. While the ancient Greeks and Romans held the goddess of jus-
Statement tice in great respect, the early Christians seem to have been a bit more suspicious of how justice was meted* out.

   2. The Christians refused to accept all of the ancient gods and goddesses, including Justitia, the goddess of justice.

3. a. In the 1992 election, political action committees (PACs) contributed more than $50 million to the various campaigns. The 1996, 2000, and 2004 elections saw even greater amounts of PAC money pour into campaign coffers. This sort of funding of the presidency puts a price tag on democracy: Whoever contributes the most money has the most access to the president.

   b. In the name of campaign reform, some people would increasingly restrict the contributions of political action committees (PACs). Yet these contributions, no matter how high the sums, are nothing more than a legitimate form of free speech. Any group who wants to contribute to a political campaign as a show of support should have the right to do so.

   c. Given the millions of dollars contributed to the last four presidential campaign funds, it's not hard to understand why enthusiasm for campaign reform has never been higher. Yet while outlawing all contributions by political action committees (PACs) seems extreme, it's clear that they have to be more closely monitored and accounted for.

---

*bias: prejudice in favor of one side or another. (For more on this subject, see Chapter 9.)
*meted: distributed.

Synthesis Statement 1. When it comes to the campaign contributions of political action committees, or PACs, there's a good deal of disagreement. But on one point, no one disagrees: PACs have contributed huge sums to the presidential campaigns.

2. Political action committees (PACs) and their contributions to political campaigns may be controversial, but there is no proof of the claim that has so often been made—that they weaken the democratic process.

4. a. In 2003, many people objected to President Bush's decision to wage war on Iraq, and they used the Internet to organize huge demonstrations against the war.

b. In the campaign for the elimination of land mines* around the world, computers played a key role. Those who supported the elimination of the mines kept in touch and up to date via e-mail.

c. In 1998, activists fighting to make insurers extend hospital stays for breast cancer patients used the Internet to publicize their fight and collect signatures for petitions.

Synthesis Statement 1. Because of the Internet, people who never found the time to write letters are managing to stay in touch.

2. Thanks to the Internet, it's become easier for political activists around the world to stay in touch.

5. a. With its brilliant and innovative techniques, D. W. Griffith's *The Birth of a Nation* dramatically changed the face of American movies forever. Before Griffith, movies contained neither close-ups nor fade-outs. It was Griffith who brought those two techniques to the screen. With the exception of Orson Welles and the film *Citizen Kane*, no other director and no other film have been as influential as Griffith and *The Birth of a Nation*.

 b. By 1910, motion pictures had become an art form, thanks to creative directors like D. W. Griffith. Griffith's most famous work, *The Birth of a Nation* (1915), an epic film about the Civil War and Reconstruction, used innovative techniques—close-ups, fade-outs, and battle scenes—that gave viewers heightened drama and excitement. Unfortunately, the film fanned racial prejudice by depicting African Americans as a threat to

---

*land mines: explosive devices, usually laid below the surface of the ground, that explode if stepped on.

white moral values. An organized black protest against it was led by the infant National Association for the Advancement of Colored People (NAACP). (Norton et al., *A People and a Nation*, p. 583.)

c. Despite the film's famed innovations, it's nearly impossible for moviegoers to take pleasure in D. W. Griffith's *The Birth of a Nation*. Powered by racism, the film enrages more than it entertains, and it's no wonder that the NAACP picketed the film when it first appeared. Members of the group correctly feared that Griffith's film would revitalize the Ku Klux Klan.

Synthesis 1. D. W. Griffith was a famous film director who profoundly influ-
Statement enced the American film industry; in fact, Griffith changed the face of American film.

2. Although no one can deny the contribution that D. W. Griffith's *The Birth of a Nation* made to film history, many find it hard to overlook the racism that runs through the film.

EXERCISE 5 **DIRECTIONS** Read each set of statements. Then write a synthesis statement that links them together.

EXAMPLE

a. Even before the war, Nazi officials had targeted Jews throughout Europe for extermination. By war's end, about six million Jews had been forced into concentration camps and had been systematically killed by firing squads, unspeakable tortures, and gas chambers. (Norton et al., *A People and a Nation*, p. 843.)

b. To protest Hitler's treatment of the Jews during World War II, the philosopher Simone Weil went on a prolonged hunger strike. In the end, Weil starved to death rather than take food while the prisoners of concentration camps were being reduced to walking skeletons.

c. Born to a wealthy Swedish family, Raoul Wallenberg could easily have ignored the horror Adolf Hitler unleashed on the world. But he chose not to. Using his considerable daring, charm, and brains, Wallenberg saved the lives of thousands of Jewish refugees who would have died a horrible death without his help.

Synthesis
Statement

During World War II, the tragic plight of the Jews stirred people like Simone Weil and Raoul Wallenberg to extraordinary acts of heroism.

> **EXPLANATION** All three passages focus on the plight of the Jews during World War II, and two of the passages describe how two people tried to stop or hinder what was happening. As you can see, the synthesis statement weaves together those two threads of thought.

1. a. Having studied the meditative states of monks and yogis,* researcher Elmer Green advocates and practices meditation. For him, it is a way of making the mind enter a deeper state of consciousness and tap into the creative imagination.

b. In the 1960s and 1970s, the Essalen Institute at Big Sur was the center of what was then called the "human potential movement." At the heart of Essalen and the movement in general was Michael Murphy, who had cofounded the institute with his former classmate Richard Price. Although Murphy eventually moved away from the anti-intellectualism of Essalen's teachers, he remains committed to the daily practice of meditation. For him, the meditative state is a way to unlock human creativity.

c. Although many exaggerated claims have been made for the benefits of meditation, research supporting those claims has not always been forthcoming. Much of the existing research consists of personal anecdotes, or stories, and many of the studies designed to test the effects of meditation have been poorly designed.

Synthesis
Statement

_____

_____

_____

2. a. Every society is concerned with the socialization of its children—that is, with making sure that children learn early on what is considered socially correct and morally ethical behavior.

b. In Asian societies, the family is considered the most important agent of socialization.

---

*yogis: people versed in meditation and focused more on the spirit than on the body.

c. In the last decade, a number of studies have suggested that in the United States, a child's peer group may be overtaking the family as the most powerful agent of socialization.

Synthesis
Statement _____

_____

_____

 # Synthesizing Longer Readings

The following readings are a good deal longer than any you have worked with so far, but the same principles apply. The first step in synthesizing sources is to identify the overall main idea of each one. The examples shown here and on the following pages are no exception. Read this selection on Harry Truman and, when you finish, write what you believe is the main idea in the blanks.

Reexamining Truman's Motives

1   What motivated President Harry Truman to order the dropping of the atomic bomb? Truman explained that he did it for only one reason: to end the war as soon as possible and thus prevent the loss of one million American casualties in an invasion of Japan. An earlier generation of historians, writing in the aftermath of the war, echoed President Truman's explanation. But more recently historians have revised this interpretation: They argue that Japan might have surrendered even if the atomic bombs had not been dropped, and they dispute Truman's high estimate of casualties as being pure fiction and several times the likely figure. These revisionists* have studied the Potsdam Conference of July 1945 attended by Truman, Joseph Stalin, and Winston Churchill. In their research, they have demonstrated the value of diaries as historical evidence by consulting those kept by certain participants, notably Secretary of War Henry Stimson and Truman himself.

2   Scholars cite Stimson's diary as evidence that Truman's chief motivations included not only ending the war but also impressing the Russians with America's military might and minimizing the USSR's* military participation in the final defeat and postwar

---

*revisionists: people who challenge a long-standing view or theory.
*USSR: Union of Soviet Socialist Republics.

occupation of Japan. On July 21 Stimson reported to Truman that the army had successfully tested an atomic device in New Mexico. Clearly emboldened by the news, Truman said that possession of the bomb "gave him an entirely new feeling of confidence. . . ." The next day, Stimson discussed the news with British prime minister Churchill. "Now I know what happened to Truman," Churchill responded. "When he got to the meeting after having read this report he was a changed man. He told the Russians just where they got off and generally bossed the whole meeting."

3   A few historians contend that the decision to drop the atomic bomb was partly racist. As evidence, they point to Truman's handwritten diary entry in which he discussed using the bomb against "the Japs," whom he denounced as "savages, ruthless, merciless and fanatic." Others cite these words to claim that Truman desired to avenge the Japanese attack at Pearl Harbor. It is clear that while personal diaries can help to settle some historical disagreements, they can also generate new interpretive disputes.

4   The deeply emotional question about the necessity for dropping the atomic bomb has stirred debates among the public as well as among historians. In 1995, for example, the Smithsonian Institution provoked a furor with its plan for an exhibit prompted by the fiftieth anniversary of the decision to drop the bomb. Rather than incur the wrath of politicians, veterans' groups, and other Americans outraged by what they perceived to be an anti-American interpretation of events, the Smithsonian shelved most of the exhibit. (Norton et al., *A People and a Nation*, p. 766.)

Main Idea _____

_____

In this reading, the authors open with a question: What motivated Truman to drop the atomic bomb? But the first answer—he wanted to end the war with Japan as soon as possible—is *not* the answer the authors want to develop. The answer they are really interested in exploring doesn't come until the fourth sentence: More modern historians have revised their opinion about Truman's motivation. The rest of the reading then explains why some historians have changed their minds.

Here now is the second excerpt, taken from a textbook published in 1965. As you read it, consider how this author's perspective compares with the one expressed in the first reading.

Truman's Choice

1   Although many Americans have expressed contrition over exploding the first atomic bombs, it is difficult to see how the Pacific war could otherwise have been concluded, except by a long and bitter invasion of Japan. . . . The explosion over Hiroshima caused fewer civilian casualties than the repeated B-29 bombings of Tokyo, and those big bombers would have had to wipe out one city after another if the war had not ended in August. Japan had enough military capability—more than 5,000 planes with kamikaze*-trained pilots and at least two million ground troops—to have made our planned invasion of the Japanese home islands in the fall of 1945 an exceedingly bloody affair for both sides. And that would have been followed by a series of bitterly protracted battles on Japanese soil, the effects of which even time could hardly have healed. Moreover, as Russia would have been a full partner in these campaigns, the end result would have been partition of Japan, as happened in Germany.

2   Even after the two atomic bombs had been dropped, and the Potsdam declaration* had been clarified to assure Japan that she could keep her emperor and surrender was a very near thing, Hirohito* had to override his two chief military advisers and take the responsibility of accepting the Potsdam terms. That he did on 14 August, but even after that, a military coup d'état* to sequester* the emperor, kill his cabinet, and continue the war was narrowly averted. (Morrison, *The Oxford History of the American People*, pp. 1044–1045.)

Main Idea _____

_____

In this case, everything in the passage points to the first sentence being the one that expresses the overall main idea. The supporting details all stress that Truman had no other choice but to drop the atomic bomb on Hiroshima and Nagasaki.

Look now at reading number 3 from writer Harold Evans, author of *American Century* who claims that the truth about Hiroshima is known and ignored.

---

*kamikaze: suicidal air attack.
*Potsdam declaration: the result of the meeting in which Truman, Stalin, and Churchill decided how to administer defeated Germany.
*Hirohito: the emperor of Japan.
*coup d'état: the sudden overthrow of government by a small group of persons previously in positions of authority.
*sequester: isolate.

The Myth of the Atomic Bomb

1   Research over five decades has confirmed that Truman and his civilian advisers knew enough early enough to appreciate that a siege strategy of sea blockade and non-atomic bombing had a prospect, though not a certainty, of ending the war before the November date set for Operation Olympic, the invasion of Kyushu.[†]

2   The state of knowledge was summarized in a historiographical review in *Diplomatic History* (Spring 1995) by J. Samuel Walker: "The consensus among scholars is that the bomb was not needed to avoid an invasion of Japan and to end the war within a relatively short time. It is clear that alternatives to the bomb existed and that Truman and his advisers knew it." It is clear, too, that this last fact is the one there has been the most effort to fudge. The myth of Hiroshima the unavoidable seems to have embedded itself in the American psyche in a remarkable manner. It has survived for five decades in high school and college textbooks and in popular journalism. In the publications and television programs on the fiftieth anniversary of Hiroshima and Nagasaki there was an emotional aversion to acknowledging the summation of research. Critical historians were denounced as "diabolical revisionists," as if history were not a continual process of discovery and revision.

3   The most dramatic manifestation of the attitude was the response to an exhibition planned for the Smithsonian National Air and Space Museum in Washington, [D.C.,] in 1995. The exhibit, focused on the *Enola Gay* B-29, intended to highlight all aspects of the bombing, including pictures of the victims. It was canceled because of a hue and cry, led by the American Legion[‡] and then taken up by sections of Congress, that to discuss the bombing was unpatriotic, pro-Japanese and a dishonor to American servicemen. This is curious. It is not as if the servicemen had anything to do with the decision to drop the bombs. The Smithsonian's mistake may have been to confuse a simple commemoration of the sacrifices made by American servicemen with an attempt at dramatizing a complex history, to offer a seminar instead of a salute. But what was striking about the responses was the eruption of hostility to presenting any fact—anywhere at any time—that does not conform with the official version of the events of 1945. (Harold Evans, *American Century*, p. 324.)

[†]Operation Olympic and the invasion of Kyushu: Both refer to a planned invasion of Japan.
[‡]American Legion: An organization for war veterans founded in 1919.

If the authors of the first reading suggested that Truman's explanation might not be fully backed by evidence, the author of the third reading takes an even stronger stance: He bluntly insists that earlier explanations about Hiroshima are, in his words, a "myth." After opening with some of the evidence supporting his position, the author comes right to his point: Despite evidence to the contrary, Americans are unwilling to acknowledge the "fact" that Truman had other alternatives besides dropping the atomic bomb.

Now that we have all three main ideas identified and paraphrased, we need to synthesize them into a statement that sums up their relationship to one another. To that end, here's a list of the main ideas from each of the readings. Look them over to see how they might be synthesized, or combined, into a statement that accurately reflects all three viewpoints:

---

1. Although earlier historians accepted the idea that President Truman had no choice but to drop the atomic bomb on Hiroshima, later ones have challenged that idea based on the evidence of personal documents.

2. Truman had no choice but to drop the bomb on Hiroshima.

3. The notion that Harry Truman had to drop the atomic bomb on Hiroshima is a myth, and the evidence shows he had alternatives.

The first connection to be made is that two of the readings are generally in agreement; the third is completely opposed. The second thing uniting readings 1 and 3 is that both authors cite "new" evidence in support of their claims. Also, readings 1 and 3 both come from a later time frame, while the second belongs to a much earlier era.

Because the first and third readings are quite similar, they have to be considered in light of this question: Are there any differences between the two? The answer is yes. Reading 1 is much more tentative than reading 3, which insists that the traditional explanation of why Truman authorized the bombing is a myth, or worthless.

On the following page are four statements, all of which illustrate different ways to synthesize the information.

1. While an earlier generation of historians accepted the idea that the bombing of Hiroshima was a necessity to end the war, current historians show different degrees of skepticism.

2. Until the 1960s, many writers perpetuated the notion that the bombing of Hiroshima was a necessity to end the war, which is what the Truman administration had claimed. By the 1990s, however, a note of doubt had crept into the discussion. In fact, some, like Harold Evans, the author of *American Century*, bluntly called Truman's explanation a "myth."

3. In the 1960 textbook *The Oxford History of the American People*, Henry Morrison insisted that Harry Truman had no other choice but to bomb Hiroshima. However, four decades later, the authors of the textbook *A People and a Nation* were not sure that Truman's explanation held up in light of new evidence, while Harold Evans, the author of *American Century*, insisted that, for him at least, there was no doubt: All the evidence indicated that Truman's explanation was false.

4. In the time that has passed since Truman dropped the atomic bomb on Hiroshima and Nagasaki, new evidence has emerged contradicting Truman's claim that he had no choice but to drop the bomb on the two cities. As a result, some historians have begun to doubt that what Truman claimed was true, while others have openly labeled his original explanation false.

Note the differences in emphasis in these four statements. Statement 1 emphasizes how time has affected historians' point of view. Statement 2 also notes how time has affected the evaluation of Truman's actions, but the focus of that statement is on Harold Evans. Statement 3 briefly describes each point of view, while statement 4 focuses on present-day evaluations of Truman's decision.

EXERCISE 6 **DIRECTIONS** Read the selections that follow. Then choose a synthesis statement that best expresses the relationship among the three.

1. Reading 1: Sports and Drugs

1 Very little is done about the most common form of cheating in pro sports: drug use. "The current drug tests we have—only careless and stupid people flunk them," says Charles Yesalis, a leading authority on drugs in sports who teaches epidemiology* at Penn State. "It's done for public relations, directed at naïve journalists and naïve fans." This means there is no realistic way to sanction players who are violating the rules on performance-enhancing drugs, except if those athletes voluntarily turn themselves in. To toughen things up would mean taking on the unions that represent players and also drawing attention to the problems of drugs in sports.

2 Nobody has an interest in doing this. The public certainly isn't clamoring for a crackdown—in one 2003 poll, for instance, only 16 percent of Americans said they thought drugs in baseball were a problem (compared to 40 percent concerned about pay gaps among players). The teams and the leagues also aren't anxious to take action. "Unless the drugs hit the bottom line, unless it impacts them financially, nothing will ever be done," says Yesalis. "Many of these drugs work and it is the bigger-than-life athlete doing the bigger-than-life feat that has made sports the multibillion-dollar industry it is. The entertainment value is so great, the money is so great, and the fans don't care. That's why it will continue." (Callahan, *The Cheating Culture*, pp. 236–237.)

Reading 2: Cyclists Losing Their Wheels and Their Fans

1 Ever since Floyd Landis tested positive for synthetic testosterone after winning the Tour de France in 2006, cycling as a sport has taken a terrible hit. Races have been cancelled and teams have lost sponsors. In 2007, the Belgian bicycle race, Tour de Flanders, faced a 77 percent decline in its live audience while television networks in the United States and Europe cut back heavily on their coverage. The century-old Championship of Zurich, which had endured for almost a century, was cancelled because Swiss organizers were

---

*epidemiology: study of how diseases are caused, spread, and controlled.

fearful of new doping scandals. As Henri van der Aat, the managing director of a sports consulting agency, told the *International Herald Tribune*, "In every boardroom, if you talk about sponsorship for any big cycling race, they all discuss the doping problems."

2   Fearful that cycling as a moneymaking sport will become a thing of the past if something doesn't change, new rules have been instituted. The blood of the top 600 riders will be profiled so that authorities have a baseline figure to work with when evaluating test results. There will also be a noticeable increase in random, out-of-competition testing. Riders must even sign agreements that they will provide DNA samples in case doping disputes arise. During competition, testing will be done on a daily basis, with blood and urine samples being taken from each winner. As cycling legend Greg LeMond pointed out in response to these changes, the time had come for the sport to clean up its act. Unfortunately, in LeMond's words, "The sport was almost killed in the process." (Source of information: Juliet Macur, "When the Wheels Come Off a Sport," www.nytimes.com, May 13, 2007.)

Reading 3: Breaking Records by Any Means

1 Charles Yesalis is a Penn State professor of health policies. He is also the co-author of the book *The Steroids Game*. Something of an expert on the subject, Yesalis is not optimistic that performance-enhancing drugs will disappear from baseball any time soon. From Yesalis's perspective, players don't have any incentive to clean up their sport. Players lack an incentive, Yesalis says, because the public doesn't seem to care if athletes do or do not rely on drugs to break or make records. Although a 2004 poll by *USA Today* found that 91 percent of those polled support testing for steroids—suggesting that most of those participating in the poll disapprove of steroid use—those negative feelings haven't made themselves felt at ticket turnstiles.

2   After all, Yesalis points out, 2004 was rife with rumors about drug use among baseball players, yet it was also a banner year for the sport. In fact, major league baseball set an attendance record. Yesalis claims that it is mainly his generation (sixty plus) that really cares about drug use, because they grew up watching baseball heroes like Ted Williams, Willie Mays, and Mickey Mantle, players who did not rely on steroids to set world records. He believes that younger fans see sports as pure entertainment, and sports only becomes more entertaining when players break records. In the eyes of younger fans, how records are broken is irrelevant to the entertainment value.

3   David Wallechinsky, the author of *The Complete Book of the Summer Olympics*, generally agrees with Yesalis. He says that fans want to hold onto sports heroes so badly, they are willing to ignore drug scandals. Hall of Fame pitcher Jim Palmer adds that owners and managers are also part of the problem. Like the fans, they don't want to know why someone who normally hits forty-five home runs a season is suddenly hitting sixty-five. All they know is that every seat in the stadium is filled and scalpers are getting hundreds of dollars per ticket. Baseball historian Bill James points out another negative consequence of looking the other way when athletes use drugs to break existing records: The new records won't mean much. According to James, because so many records were broken by wide margins, they probably will just be regarded as "funny numbers." (Source of information: Tom Weir, "Drug free Sports: Do the Fans Care?" www.usatoday.com/sports/2004-12-07-drug-free-sports_x.htm.)

Synthesis Statement

a. Charles Yesalis and David Wallechinsky both agree that the problem of baseball players using performance-enhancing drugs will not disappear any time soon because the public doesn't care if athletes use drugs to break records. As long as the public doesn't care, neither will the athletes.

b. Several experts on the use of performance-enhancing drugs in sports agree that there are several reasons why the problem is not likely to disappear.

c. For a while now, those knowledgeable about the use of performance-enhancing drugs in sports have argued that the problem will not disappear any time soon because no one seems to care about it. The current response to doping among world-class cyclists, however, strongly suggests the experts may be wrong.

2. Reading 1: Tragedy on Campus

1 At 7:15 a.m. on Monday, April 16, 2007, police were called to the West Ambler Johnston Residence Hall at Virginia Tech University, where they found two students—one male and one female—shot to death. After interviewing witnesses, officers concluded that the double homicide was the result of a domestic dispute. The gunman, they believed, had fled the campus. However, they couldn't have been more wrong. The killer, 23-year-old Virginia Tech student Seung-Hui Cho, had just begun. He had paused only to return to his dormitory, collect a package, take it to the post office, and mail it to NBC News. While he ran this errand, word of the murders began to spread via cell phones and instant messaging, but students, unaware of the danger, continued

making their way to their first classes of the day. At 9:26 a.m., Virginia Tech officials sent out a campuswide e-mail to confirm that a shooting incident had occurred and to urge students to remain cautious. Meanwhile, Cho was heading for a classroom building. At 9:45 a.m., campus police responded to a 911 call from Norris Hall, where they heard the sound of rapid gunfire coming from the second floor. Cho had chained the front doors shut from the inside and was moving from room to room, randomly shooting students and professors as they tried to bar the door or jump from the windows to safety. By the time officers broke in and ran upstairs, Cho had committed suicide, after killing 32 people in the deadliest shooting rampage in American history.

2   News reports of the tragedy immediately provoked a worldwide outpouring of emotion. Within hours, tens of thousands of people were logging on to online forums and social network sites like FaceBook and MySpace to express their sorrow, offer sympathy, and vent their rage. A new website called VTtragedy.com was so overwhelmed with visitors that it crashed. On Virginia Tech's media-swarmed campus, shocked and distraught students clung to each other and deposited notes, candles, flowers, and other mementos at a memorial wall for the victims. The day after the massacre, thousands attended a tearful assembly in the university's coliseum, where U.S. President George W. Bush acknowledged the nation's sorrow and grief. All over the country, mourners wore the university's orange and maroon school colors and held candlelight vigils to honor the victims and show support for Virginia Tech's students. Flags on public buildings everywhere, including the White House, were lowered to half-mast. The U.S. Senate and House of Representatives observed a moment of silence in remembrance of the victims, and the U.S. State Department received condolences from many international heads of state, including kings, queens, presidents, prime ministers, and the pope. (Sources of information: "Timeline: How the Virginia Tech Shootings Unfolded," NPR, April 17, 2007, www.npr.org/templates/story/story.php?storyId=9636137; David Miller, "An Outpouring of Online Grief," CBS News, April 17, 2007, www.cbsnews.com/stories/2007/04/17/tech/main2695882.shtlm.)

Reading 2: Was NBC Wrong?

1 On April 16, 2007, Virginia Tech University student Seung-Hui Cho armed himself with two guns and extra ammunition. Then he marched to a campus dormitory and classroom building, and opened fire on fellow students and professors. By the time Cho ended his shooting spree by putting a bullet through his head, he

and thirty-two innocent people were dead. Inevitably, as details of the story unfolded, people wanted to know why. What caused a 23-year-old to snap and commit the worst mass-murder shooting by a lone gunman in U.S. history? Two days later, NBC News thought it had some answers. After receiving a videotape, photographs, and writings Cho had mailed during the two hours separating his first two killings from the second part of his rampage, the network decided to broadcast excerpts. These materials would, NBC announced, provide everyone with some insight into the killer's motives.

2   However, as clips from the gunman's angry ramblings and pictures of the gun-wielding Cho were splashed across television screens and newspaper pages, many were outraged by the network's decision to air the "multimedia manifesto" of a cold-blooded killer. They argued that Cho's incoherent, paranoid explanations revealed only that he was mentally ill. Therefore, they could never help anyone understand why he committed his crimes. What's more, they said, the NBC broadcasts had had profoundly negative consequences, like additional distress for those whose loved ones had been killed. Choosing to show the videotape and photos just two days after the murders was, believed many, unforgivably insensitive to the victims' grieving families and friends.

3   NBC's decision was also a bad one, said critics, because airing Cho's pictures and ramblings gave him the publicity and attention he had craved. By refusing to air the materials, the network could have rightly denied the killer his wish for immortality. Instead, NBC gave Cho exactly what he wanted by forever planting his image into the minds of millions of viewers. But perhaps the worst effect of all was the broadcast's potential to inspire other troubled minds. By airing Cho's demented ramblings, said NBC's critics, the network elevated the potential for copycat violence and jeopardized public safety. (Sources of information: Bronwen Maddox, "Why NBC Was Right to Show Those Demented Ramblings," *The Times*, April 20, 2007, www.timesoline.co.uk/tol/news/world/us_and_americas/article1680113.ece.)

Reading 3: NBC's Side of the Story

1   Should NBC News have broadcast the videotaped tirade mailed in a package by mass murderer Seung-Hui Cho, the Virginia Tech University student who shot and killed 32 people and then himself on April 16, 2007? Many said absolutely not and strongly criticized NBC for its decision. There are, however, arguments that can be made in support of NBC's choice.

2   Those who opposed the decision to air a homicidal maniac's disturbed and often incoherent ramblings accused the network of using sensational journalism to boost its ratings and profits, thereby damaging its reputation as a respected news source. Yet NBC may well have been right to share the package's contents with the public. For two days a shocked and grieving nation had wanted to know why Cho went on such a deadly rampage. Letting Cho himself reveal to the world his disturbed state of mind certainly didn't answer that question. But the broadcast did reveal the massacre to be the work of just one very sick young man. Thus, to some degree, it allayed the nation's fear of terrorist and conspiratorial plots and served a useful purpose.

3   It's also possible to challenge the notion that airing the video is likely to spur incidents of copycat violence. In nearly every case of school violence similar to the one at Virginia Tech, watching a video is not what triggered a physical assault. Instead, the violence was triggered either by mental illness or by a history of school bullying.

4   A news organization's obligation is to report the news, even if it is gruesome. Thus, NBC professionally and responsibly fulfilled its mission to keep the public informed about a major development in the story. (Sources of information: Bronwen Maddox, "Why NBC Was Right to Show Those Demented Ramblings," *The Times*, April 20, 2007, www.timesonline.co.uk/tol/news/world/us_and_americas/article1680113.ece; Earl Ofari Hutchinson, "Copycatting Cho," *The Huffington Post*, April 21, 2007, www.huffingtonpost.com/earl-ofari-hutchinson/copycatting-cho_b_46479.html.)

Synthesis   a. After NBC aired the videotaped tirade of Seung-Hui Cho, who
Statement   shot and killed thirty-two Virginia Tech students and then himself, the public expressed its outrage at the network's attempts to earn ratings from such a tragedy.

b. When the disturbed student from Virginia Tech, Seung-Hui Cho, murdered thirty-two innocent people and then killed himself, the outpouring of sympathy for the victims and their families was immediate. Just as immediate was the angry controversy that erupted over NBC's decision to air the killer's videotaped explanations of his crime.

c. When NBC decided to air the videotaped ramblings of Seung-Hui Cho, the student who murdered thirty-two students before killing himself, it underestimated the outrage the broadcast would provoke. The network found itself at the center of a controversy that earned the network a good deal of news coverage, most of it critical or furious.

Allusion Alert

Page 257 introduced a reading on ancient Roman circuses. With the discussion of the Roman circus still fresh in your mind, it's a good time to introduce the allusion to "bread and circuses," which originates with the Roman writer Juvenal, who wrote, "Two things only the people anxiously desire—bread and circuses." Juvenal was making the point that every time the people of Rome were discontented about something, it was easy to distract them with free food and mindless entertainment.

Juvenal's comment has survived in the form of an allusion, which implies that when problems seem large, difficult, or unpleasant, we—or those in power—opt for distractions rather than a solution, "Evita Perón knew how to distract the people of Argentina from her extravagant spending habits: If complaints about her free-spending way began to surface, the people could always count on Evita for a rich diet of bread and circuses." In this case, the writer uses the allusion to bread and circuses to suggest that Evita Perón did not try to change if complaints about her spending increased. Instead, she would resort to diverting the people of Argentina from whatever anger they were feeling.

Now it's your turn to interpret this allusion. Read and paraphrase the following sentence: "When the candidate arrived, there was a large and expectant crowd, but halfway through her speech, members of the audience began to leave, obviously disgusted by a campaign platform that relied heavily on bread and circuses."

Paraphrase _____

_____

_____

■ **DIGGING DEEPER**

LOOKING AHEAD The explanation of synthesizing mentioned how in-depth processing of new information acts as a memory aid. The following reading will tell you more about the human memory and how it functions.

CAN WE TRUST OUR MEMORIES?

1 Although we'd like to think that our memories accurately reflect events we've witnessed or experienced, our recollections may not be as reliable as we believe them to be. Contemporary memory researchers reject the view that long-term memory works like a video camera that records exact copies of experience. Their view, generally called **constructionist theory**, holds that memory is a reconstructive process. What we recall from memory is not a replica of the past, but a representation, or *reconstruction*, of the past. We stitch together bits and pieces of information stored in long-term memory to form a coherent* explanation or account of past experiences and events. Reconstruction, however, can lead to distorted memories of events and experiences.

2 According to constructionist theory, memories are not carbon copies of reality. From this vantage point, it is not surprising that people who witness the same event or read the same material may have very different memories of the event or of the passage they read. Nor would it be surprising if recollections of your childhood are not verbatim records of what actually occurred but rather reconstructions based on pieces of information from many sources—from old photographs, from what your mother told you about the time you fell from the tree when you were ten, and so on.

3 Constructionist theory leads us to expect that memories may be distorted. These distortions can range from simplifications, to omissions of details, to outright fabrications (Koriat & Goldsmith, 1996). Even so, we shouldn't presume that all memories are distorted. Some may be more or less accurate reflections of events. Others, perhaps most, can be likened more to impressionist paintings than to mental snapshots of experiences.

4 **Recovery of Repressed Memories** Controversy has swirled around the issue of whether long-repressed memories of childhood experiences that suddenly surface in adulthood are credible. In most cases, such memories come to light during

---

*coherent: connected, orderly.

hypnosis or psychotherapy. On the basis of recovered memories of sexual trauma* in childhood, authorities have brought charges of sexual abuse against hundreds of people. A number of these cases have resulted in convictions and long jail sentences, even in the absence of corroborating evidence. But should recovered memories be taken at face value?

5   A total lack of memory of traumatic childhood events is rare, although it is possible that such memories may be lost in some cases (Bradley & Follingstad, 2001; Wakefield & Underwager, 1996). We also know that false memories can be induced in many subjects in experimental studies (Loftus, 1997; Zoellner, Foa, Brigidi, & Przeworski, 2000). Entire events that never happened can enter a subject's memory and seem just as real and accurate as memories of events that really did occur. However, evidence of false memory creation in experimental studies does not prove that recovered memories in actual cases are, in fact, false.

6   In sum, many investigators believe that some recovered memories may be genuine and that others are undoubtedly false (L. S. Brown, 1997; L. J. Rubin, 1996; Scheflin & Brown, 1996). The problem is that in the absence of corroborating evidence, we simply lack the tools to differentiate between true memories and false ones (American Psychological Association, 1995; Loftus, 1993a; Loftus & Ketcham, 1994).

7   From a constructionist standpoint, we should not be surprised that memories may be distorted, even when the person believes them to be true. The use of suggestive interviewing or therapeutic techniques or hypnosis can heighten suggestibility to false memories. Psychologists and other mental health professionals need to be cautious about assuming the veracity of recovered memories and vigilant about monitoring their own roles so that they don't contribute to the construction of false memories. (Nevid, *Psychology*, pp. 229–233.)

Sharpening Your Skills

DIRECTIONS Answer the following questions by circling the letter of the correct response or filling in the blanks.

1. Based on the context, how would you define the word *replica* in the following sentence? "What we recall from memory is not a *replica* of the past, but a representation, or reconstruction, of the past."

---

*trauma: serious injury or shock to the body.

a. copy

b. remainder

c. memory

d. thought

2. In paragraph 2, which two phrases restate the word *replica* in paragraph 1?

_____

3. Based on the context, how would you define the word *corroborating* in the following sentence? "The problem is that in the absence of *corroborating* evidence, we simply lack the tools to differentiate between true memories and false ones."

a. irrelevant

b. challenging

c. convincing

d. distracting

4. What is the topic of the reading? _____

5. Which of the following sentences best expresses the main idea of the entire reading?

a. Memory researchers believe that with enough effort, we can avoid distorting our memories of past events; however, to avoid distortion we have to give conscious attention to what happens in the present.

b. Recovered memories, despite the controversy surrounding them, are authentic.

c. Memory researchers now believe that when we remember, we combine bits of information stored in long-term memory in order to recreate some version of past experience that makes sense.

d. In contrast to the constructionist theory of memory, new research suggests that we store exact copies of our experiences in long-term memory.

6. Which paragraph introduces the thesis statement?

a. paragraph 1

b. paragraph 2

c. paragraph 3

7. What two reversal or contrast transitions appear in paragraph 1?

_____

8. Which is the primary pattern of organization in paragraph 1?

    a. simple listing

    b. definition

    c. comparison and contrast

    d. classification

9. In the reading as a whole, what pattern is primary?

_____

10. What is the author's answer to the question posed in the title? _____

    Please explain: _____

_____

_____

Test 1: Identifying Main Ideas

DIRECTIONS Circle the appropriate letter to identify the main idea of each selection.

 ### 1. Marital Satisfaction in New Families

1 Almost all studies that measure marital satisfaction before and after the birth of the first child have found that the birth of a child is a mixed marital blessing (Cowan & Cowan, 1988). Jay Belsky and Michael Rovine (1990) found that couples who were least satisfied with their marriages before the birth were most likely to report a decline in satisfaction after. Problems that existed before were likely to have been magnified by the additional stresses brought on by the birth.

2   Babies, however, do not appear to create severe marital distress where none existed before; nor do they bring couples with distressed marriages closer together. Rather, the early postpartum* months bring on a period of disorganization and change. The leading conflict in these first months of parenthood is division of labor in the family. Couples may regain their sense of equilibrium in marriage by successfully negotiating how they will divide the new responsibilities. Husbands' participation in child and home care seems to be positively related to marital satisfaction after the birth. One study found that the more the men shared in doing family tasks, the more satisfied were the wives at six and eighteen months postpartum and the husbands at eighteen months postpartum (Cowan & Cowan, 1988).

3   While many couples experience a difficult transition to parenthood, they also find it rewarding. Children affect parents in ways that lead to personal growth; enable reworking of childhood conflicts; build flexibility and empathy; and provide intimate, loving human connections. They also give a lot of pleasure. In follow-up interviews of new parents when their children were eighteen months old, Philip Cowan and Carolyn Cowan (1988) found that almost every man and woman spoke of the delight they felt from knowing their child and watching the child develop. They reported feeling pride for and closeness to their spouses, more adult with their own parents, and a renewed sense of purpose at work. (Adapted from Seifert et al., *Lifespan Development*, p. 488.)

---

*postpartum: following a birth.

a. Studies of marital happiness suggest that children are the key to a happy marriage.

b. While the birth of a first child is a plus for a marriage, more than one child can be a strain.

c. Studies of marital happiness suggest that a baby can unite an unhappy couple.

d. Studies of marital satisfaction suggest that the birth of a first child has both positive and negative effects.

2. The "Revolving Door"

Every year, hundreds of people leave important jobs in the federal government to take more lucrative positions in private industry. Some go to work as lobbyists, others as consultants to business, still others as key executives in corporations, foundations, and universities. Many people worry that this "revolving door" may give private interests a way of improperly influencing government decisions. If a federal official uses his or her government position to do something for a corporation in exchange for a cushy job after leaving government or if a person who has left government uses his or her personal contacts in Washington to get favors for private parties, then the public interest may suffer.

From time to time there are incidents that seem to confirm these fears. Michael K. Deaver, once the deputy chief of staff in the Reagan White House, was convicted of perjury in connection with a grand jury investigation of his having used his former government contacts to help the clients of his public relations firm. Lyn Nofziger, a former Reagan White House aide, was convicted of violating the Ethics in Government Act by lobbying the White House, soon after he left it, on behalf of various businesses and labor unions.

In 1988, federal investigators revealed evidence of corrupt dealings between some Department of Defense officials and industry executives. Contractors and their consultants, many of whom were former Pentagon personnel, obtained favors from procurement officials, gaining an edge on their competitors. How systematic is this pattern of abuse? We don't know. Studies of the revolving door in federal regulatory agencies have found no clear pattern of officials' tilting their decisions in hope of landing a lucrative business job.

Agencies differ in their vulnerability* to outside influences. If the Food and Drug Administration is not vigilant*, people in that agency who help decide whether a new drug should be placed on the market may have their judgment affected somewhat by the possibility that, if they approve the drug, the pharmaceutical company that makes it will later offer them a lucrative position. On the other hand, lawyers in the Federal Trade Commission who prosecute businesses that violate the antitrust laws may decide that their chances for getting a good job with a private law firm later on will increase if they are particularly vigorous and effective prosecutors. (Wilson and Dilulio, *American Government*, pp. 284–285.)

a. People leave jobs in the government all the time to take jobs in private industry; there is no shame in that.

b. A number of people worry that the revolving door shared by government and industry could inappropriately affect government policy and decision making.

c. The public interest is bound to suffer if people with jobs in the Food and Drug Administration go to work for the pharmaceutical companies.

d. Because of the revolving door that shuttles government officials into cushy corporate jobs as soon as they leave office, government decision making is hopelessly skewed in favor of big corporations.

---

*vulnerability: sensitivity or openness.
*vigilant: watchful.

Test 2: Recognizing Thesis Statements and Supporting Details

DIRECTIONS Underline the thesis statement. Then answer the questions by filling in the blanks or circling the letter of the correct response. *Note*: To decide if a detail is major or minor, you will probably need to look at the sentences in the context of the paragraphs where they appear. The numbers in parentheses identify the paragraph where the detail appears.

1. Feminist Objections to Pornography

1 Beginning around 1978, some—though not all—feminists became very critical of pornography (e.g., Griffin, 1981; Lederer, 1980; Morgan, 1978). Why are feminists opposed to pornography? In general, there are three basic reasons for their objections.

2   First, they argue that pornography debases women. The milder, softcore versions portray women as sex objects whose breasts, legs, and buttocks can be purchased and then ogled.* This scarcely represents a respectful attitude toward women. Second, pornography associates sex with violence toward women. As such, it contributes to rape and other forms of violence against women and girls. Robin Morgan put it bluntly: "Pornography is the theory and rape is the practice" (1980, p. 139). Third, pornography shows, indeed glamorizes, unequal power relationships between women and men. A common theme in pornography is that of men forcing women to have sex, and so the power of men and subordination of women is emphasized. Consistent with this point, feminists do not object to sexual materials that portray women and men in equal, humanized relationships—what we would term *erotica*.

3   Feminists also note the intimate relationship between pornography and traditional gender roles. They argue that pornography may serve to perpetuate traditional gender roles. By seeing or reading about dominant males and submissive,* dehumanized females, each new generation of adolescent boys is socialized to accept these roles. (Adapted from Shibley Hyde, *Understanding Human Sexuality*, p. 524.)

1. Based on the title, what question should you use to guide your reading?

_____

*ogled; stared at.
*submissive: obedient.

2. In your own words, what is the main idea of the reading?

_____

_____

3. Based on the thesis statement, how many major details should you be looking for?

_____

4. Which of the following is *not* a major detail?

a. Pornography associates sex with violence toward women. (2)

b. Robin Morgan put it bluntly: "Pornography is the theory and rape is the practice." (2)

5. Which of the following is a minor detail?

a. Feminists argue that pornography debases women. (2)

b. Pornography glamorizes unequal power relationships. (2)

c. A common theme in pornography is that of men forcing women to have sex. (2)

2. The Meaning of Touch

1   Touching and being touched is an essential part of being human. However, the amount and meaning of touch change with age, purpose, and location. Infants and their parents, for example, engage in extensive touching behavior, but this decreases during adolescence. The amount of touching behavior increases after adolescence as young people begin to establish romantic relationships. No matter how much we are touched, however, most of us want to be touched more than we are (Mosby, 1978).

2   In general, the meaning of touch varies with the situation, and there are five basic categories of meaning. *Positive affective touches* transmit messages of support, appreciation, affection, or sexual intent. *Playful touches* lighten our interactions with others. *Control touches* are used to get other people's attention and to gain their compliance. *Ritualistic touches* are those we use during communication rituals such as greeting others and saying good-bye. *Task-related touches* are those that are necessary for us to complete tasks on which we are working. Touches also can fit into more than one category at a time. We can, for example, touch others as part of a ritual to express positive affection.

3   Age, sex, and region of the country also influence the amount people touch. To illustrate, people between eighteen and twenty-five and between thirty and forty report the most touching, while old people report the least (Mosby, 1978). Women find touching

more pleasant than men do, as long as the other person is not a stranger (Heslin, 1978). Finally, people who live in the South touch more than people who live in the North (Howard, 1985).

4   The United States is generally a noncontact culture. People do not engage in a great deal of touching. There are, however, situations in which people are likely to touch (Henley, 1977). People are more likely to touch, for example, when giving information or advice than when receiving information or advice. People are more likely to touch others when giving orders than when receiving orders, when asking for a favor than when granting a favor, or when trying to persuade others than when being persuaded. (Adapted from Gudykunst et al., *Building Bridges*, pp. 319–320.)

1. Based on the title, what question would you use to guide your reading?

_____

2. In your own words, what is the main idea of the reading?

_____

_____

3. Which of the following is a major detail?

   a. People who live in the South touch more than do people who live in the North. (3)

   b. Age, sex, and region influence the amount people touch. (3)

   c. People are more likely to touch, for example, when giving information or advice. (4)

4. Which of the following is a major detail?

   a. In general, the meaning of touch varies with the situation and there are five basic categories of meaning (2).

   b. We can, for example, touch others as part of a ritual to express positive affection (2).

   c. People between eighteen and twenty-five and between thirty and forty report the most touching (3).

5. Which of the following is a minor detail?

   a. Women find touching more pleasant than men do, as long as the other person is not a stranger (3).

   b. The amount and meaning of touch change with age, purpose, and location (1).

   c. Age, sex, and region of the country also influence the amount people touch (3).

Test 3: Outlining Longer Readings

DIRECTIONS Read each selection. Then use the blanks to make an informal outline.

1. Phobias

1 **Phobias** are intense and irrational fears of everything from spiders to open spaces. Some of the more common phobias are fear of heights, blood, flying, dogs, and enclosed spaces. The key element that distinguishes a phobia from a normal fear is that a phobia is irrational, or not based on reason. For instance, someone who is phobic about spiders would be just as terrified by a harmless Daddy Long Legs as he or she would be by a deadly tarantula. In the United States, phobias are the most prevalent of the anxiety disorders. They affect 7 to 10 percent of adults and children (Kessler et al., 1994; Robins et al., 1984; U.S. Surgeon General, 1999).

2 Perhaps the most disabling phobia is **agoraphobia**. Agoraphobia is an intense fear of being away from a safe place like one's home; of being away from a familiar person, such as a spouse or close friend; or of being in a place from which departure might be difficult or help unavailable. For those who suffer from agoraphobia, attempts to leave home cause extreme anxiety. Thus agoraphobics are often severely housebound. For them, theaters, shopping malls, public transportation, and other potentially crowded places are particularly threatening. Most individuals who suffer from agoraphobia also have a history of panic attacks. In fact, their intense fear of public places starts partly because they don't want to go where they feel panicking would be dangerous or embarrassing.

3 **Social phobias** revolve around the fear of being negatively evaluated by others or acting in a way that is embarrassing or humiliating. This anxiety is so intense and persistent that it impairs the person's normal functioning. *Common social phobias* are fear of public speaking or performance ("stage fright"), fear of eating in front of others, and fear of using public restrooms (Kleinknecht, 2000). A *generalized social phobia* is a more severe form in that victims experience fear in virtually all social situations (Mannuzzi et al., 1995). Sociocultural factors can alter the form of social phobias. For example, in Japan, where cultural training emphasizes group-oriented values and goals, a common social phobia is *taijin kyofu sho*—fear of embarrassing those around you (Kleinknecht, 1994). (Adapted from Bernstein et al., *Psychology*, 6th ed., pp. 566–567.)

Main Idea _____

_____

Supporting Details _____

_____

_____

_____

_____

_____

_____

_____

_____

_____

_____

_____

_____

_____

_____

_____

_____

2. Taking a Conversational Turn

1 Have you ever conversed with another person who wouldn't stop talking? If so, you may have wondered whether that person was clueless, obnoxious, or just playing by a different set of cultural rules. Whatever the reason for such behavior, lopsided conversations usually remind us that turn taking is a fundamental part of the give and take we expect from others in our everyday interactions.

Because most people don't verbalize intentions to speak or listen, learning to navigate conversational twists and turns can be a real challenge. The signals we use to regulate the flow of speech consist largely of verbal cues and gestures.

2   When we are speaking and want to continue speaking, we use signals that communicate our intention to listeners. It's a way of preventing unwanted interruptions. Such signals include raising the volume of our voice, uttering *um*'s and *ah*'s, continuing to gesture, gazing away from the listener, and so on.

3   However, if we don't want to continue speaking, we can relinquish our turn by dropping the volume and pitch of our voice, slowing the tempo of our speech, pausing, not gesturing, making eye contact with a listener, or raising our eyebrows. These are **turn-yielding signals**. Some research shows that conversants are more inclined to take turns when speakers use these signals. (Duncan, 1972).

4   As listeners, we also employ turn-taking signals. To express a desire to speak, we employ various **turn-requesting signals**. These signals include an open mouth, audible inhalations, a raised index finger or hand, forward body lean, eye contact, quickened or exaggerated head nods, and simultaneous speech (i.e., listener's speech overlaps the speaker's). (Adapted from Remland, *Nonverbal Communication in Everyday Life*, pp. 255–256.)

Main Idea _____

_____

Supporting Details _____

_____

_____

_____

_____

_____

_____

_____

_____

_____

_____

_____

_____

_____

_____

_____

_____

_____

_____

_____

Test 4: Recognizing Effective Synthesis Statements

DIRECTIONS Read each set of passages. Then identify the synthesis statement that effectively combines them.

1. a. Eleanor Roosevelt (1884–1962) shattered the traditional, ceremonial role of the first lady and used her position and talents to make her own positive contributions to American society. She assisted her husband, Franklin D. Roosevelt, by traveling all over the country to gather information about the American people and their needs. However, she also took up her own causes. Eleanor worked hard to promote civil rights for African Americans, and it was she who convinced her husband to sign a series of executive orders that prevented discrimination in the administration of his New Deal projects. She also devoted her considerable energies to many different organizations dedicated to social reforms. In particular, she argued for equal rights and equal opportunities for women. She advocated women's right to work outside their homes and secured government funds to build childcare centers. She also used her gifts for public speaking, writing, and organizing to work toward the elimination of child labor. Throughout her years as first lady, Eleanor managed to transcend society's stereotypical views of presidential wives to effect, in her own right, many significant improvements in social justice and equality.

b. As first lady, Hillary Rodham Clinton (1947–) used her intelligence and talents to improve the lives of people across the United States and all over the world. Before becoming first lady, she worked on issues affecting children and families. While in the White House, she published a book, *It Takes a Village,* in which she argued that all areas of society must work together to improve the lives of American children. Also during the two-term presidency of her husband, Bill Clinton, she headed a task force devoted to improving the health care system. In this position, she traveled all over the country, talking to health care professionals and American citizens about how the government could provide access to high-quality, affordable medical care. In addition, she visited many countries, serving as a goodwill ambassador for the United States and supporting human rights, women's rights, and health care reform. At the end of her term as first lady, she managed to do what none of her predecessors had done before: She established an independent political organization and successfully ran for the U.S. Senate. By 2007, to no one's surprise, she was running for president.

c. On April 12, 1945, after serving a mere eighty-two days as vice president, Harry Truman became the president of the United States and his wife Bess became the first lady. It wasn't long before Bess Truman became known as one of the busiest and most hard-working hostesses in Washington. What she wasn't known for, though, was holding press conferences. She abolished the custom—established by her predecessor Eleanor Roosevelt—of holding regular meetings with reporters. Unused to being in the spotlight, Bess Truman was more interested in public service. She served as honorary president of the Girl Scouts and the Washington Animal Rescue League. She also held honorary memberships in the Daughters of the Colonial Wars and the Women's National Farm and Garden Association. Known for her ability to remember the names of everyone she met at state affairs, Bess also made it a habit to personally answer the letters she received as the president's wife. Like her husband, Bess Truman was considered extremely down-to-earth, and she was proud of her frugal ways, which did not change with her status. During her time in the White House, she never spent more than three dollars on a manicure and, instead of having an in-house hairdresser, she made it a point to have her hair styled off the premises.

Synthesis a. As first ladies go, Bess Truman was probably the nicest and
Statement most frugal woman to ever live in the White House.

b. In their political ambitions, Eleanor Roosevelt and Hillary Clinton were very similar first ladies.

c. As first ladies, Eleanor Roosevelt and Hillary Clinton were very active politically; Bess Truman, however, kept her distance from politics.

d. Bess Truman carefully dismantled the political organization Eleanor Roosevelt had established while her husband was in office, and it wasn't until Hillary Clinton's term as first lady that a president's wife, once again, displayed a desire for political power.

2. a. The Warren Report

1 When President John F. Kennedy was assassinated in Dallas, Texas, on November 22, 1963, a traumatized American public wanted to know who was responsible. Police promptly captured

ex-Marine Lee Harvey Oswald and charged him with the murder, but when he too was gunned down by local nightclub owner Jack Ruby in the police department's basement, new questions immediately arose. Had Oswald acted alone, or had he and Ruby been involved in a conspiracy to murder America's leader? Had Ruby been sent to silence Oswald and prevent him from exposing his co-conspirators?

2   In an attempt to answer these and other questions, Kennedy's successor, President Lyndon Johnson, quickly appointed a group that included two senators, two members of Congress, and two attorneys. It was headed by Supreme Court Justice Earl Warren. Known as the Warren Commission, this group was instructed to "evaluate all the facts and circumstances surrounding [the] assassination, including the subsequent violent death of the man charged with the assassination." Over the next ten months, the commission attempted to reconstruct the sequence of events surrounding Kennedy's and Oswald's murders by reviewing the investigative reports of the Dallas police department, the Federal Bureau of Investigation, the Secret Service, the Central Intelligence Agency, and other federal agencies. Members of the commission heard the testimony of 552 witnesses and visited Dallas to see the crime scene.

3   The culmination of this investigation was an 888-page final report presented to President Johnson on September 24, 1964. In this document, the Warren Commission concluded that Oswald was a psychologically disturbed person. The commission also concluded that he acted alone to kill President Kennedy and wound Texas Governor John Connally. In addition, the commission endorsed the theory that one bullet had missed while the other two bullets had caused all of the injuries. The first of those two bullets had struck President Kennedy in the upper back, passed through him, and then hit Governor Connally, who had been sitting directly in front of the president in an open limousine. The second of those two bullets had hit Kennedy in the head, fatally wounding him.

4   Although the Warren Commission did not completely rule out the possibility of a domestic or foreign plot to kill the president, it stated that it had been unable to find any evidence of one. Unable to uncover any connection between Oswald and Ruby, the commission found Ruby innocent of conspiracy, concluding that he was motivated by rage. Ruby had simply decided to appoint himself Oswald's judge and executioner.

5   To most Americans, these conclusions seem perfectly sound. The Warren Commission, they believe, fulfilled its mission by

thoroughly investigating the matter, finding the truth, and providing much-needed reassurance during a time of national crisis. (Sources of information: "Warren Commission," *U.S. History Encyclopedia*, www.answers.com/warren%20commission; "Warren Commission," *Columbia Encyclopedia*, www.answers.com/warren%20commission.)

b. Doubts About the Warren Commission

1 In the wake of President John F. Kennedy's murder in Dallas, Texas, on November 22, 1963, a seven-member panel headed by Supreme Court Chief Justice Earl Warren undertook the task of investigating the assassination and determining whether the alleged assassin Lee Harvey Oswald had acted alone. After examining all of the evidence related to the events, the Warren Commission published a report concluding that neither Lee Harvey Oswald nor Jack Ruby, the man who shot and killed Oswald the day after he was arrested, had been involved in any type of conspiracy to murder Kennedy. Instead, the commission stated, both men had been mentally unstable, lone gunmen.

2 But almost before the ink on the Warren Commission's report was dry, people began to criticize its findings. Books such as the influential *Inquest* by Edward Jay Epstein and *Rush to Judgment* by Mark Lane, both published in 1966, argued that the commission's investigation had not been thorough enough to be conclusive. Others attacked the commission's conclusions as a "whitewash" and criticized its methods while pointing out errors and the omission of important information. Although two more U.S. government investigations—in 1968 and 1975—agreed with the Warren Commission's conclusions, President Johnson himself and even four of the seven members of the commission were said to have privately expressed doubts about the group's findings. In 1967, New Orleans District Attorney Jim Garrison fueled suspicions about the existence of a conspiracy by trying businessman Clay Shaw for participating in a plot to kill the president, but Shaw was acquitted because of lack of evidence. In 1978–1979, a special committee of the House of Representatives reexamined all of the evidence and declared that Oswald had indeed fired the fatal shots but had probably been part of a conspiracy. This conclusion was based on evidence that a fourth bullet, which missed, had been fired by a second assassin on the ground. So far, no one has been able to disprove the Warren Commission's conclusions. Still, the facts about the Kennedy assassination remain the subject of ongoing debate. (Sources of information: Gerald A. Danzer

et al., *The Americans*, Boston: McDougal Littell, 2007, p. 889;
"Warren Commission," *U.S. History Encyclopedia*, www.answers
.com/warren%20commission; "Warren Commission," *Columbia
Encyclopedia*, www.answers.com/warren%20commission;
"Warren Commission," *Law Encyclopedia*, www.answers.com/
warren%20commission.)

c. A New Theory About Kennedy's Death

1 By conducting a new bullet analysis, a research team has further
undermined the theory that a lone gunman assassinated
President John F. Kennedy in 1963. The team, which included a
top former FBI laboratory expert and two Texas A&M University
scientists, obtained boxes from two of the four total lots of
Mannlicher-Carcano bullets manufactured in 1954. From one of
those lots came the ammunition used by assassin Lee Harvey
Oswald to kill the president. Selecting 30 bullets, ten from each of
three different boxes, and using new techniques not available in
the 1960s, the researchers then analyzed the bullets' chemical
composition. They found that many bullets within the same box
have a similar composition; therefore, fired bullet fragments that
have the same chemical makeup do not necessarily come from the
same bullet. Researchers were also able to match the chemical
composition of fragments from one of their test bullets, which was
not even in the same box of ammunition used by Oswald, to one
of the five bullet fragments found at the assassination scene.

2 These findings are significant because they call into question
the number of bullets that were fired at President Kennedy.
Scientists who first analyzed the lead in the bullet fragments
found at the scene of the crime had asserted that each of the
bullets in a box of ammunition was so unique that the recovered
fragments had to have come from just two bullets traced to the
batch in Oswald's possession. This conclusion supports the
theory that Oswald was the lone assassin. But only two of
Oswald's bullets struck President Kennedy. Therefore, if the
fragments actually came from *three or more* bullets, then at least
one other bullet could have been fired by a second shooter.
Although the researchers did not go so far as to say that their
study supports theories that Oswald was involved in a conspiracy,
they did point out that previous analysis of the ammunition does
not conclusively rule out the possibility of a second assassin, and
they urged authorities to reexamine the five bullet fragments
recovered after the assassination. (Sources of information: John
Solomon, "Scientists Cast Doubt on Kennedy Bullet Analysis,"

Washington Post, May 17, 2007, p. A03, www.washingtonpost.com; "Bullet Evidence Challenges Findings in JFK Assassination," *Science Daily*, May 17, 2007, www.sciencedaily.com/releases/2007/05/070517142528.htm.)

Synthesis a. While some have always accepted the Warren Commission
Statement   report as accurate, the controversy about its findings continues
              to the present day.

b. New research has now conclusively proven what was once considered a ridiculous and unfounded rumor—that Lee Harvey Oswald did not assassinate John F. Kennedy.

c. Current research supports the findings of the 1964 Warren Report.

d. Despite all evidence to the contrary, conspiracy theorists refuse to believe that the assassination of John F. Kennedy was the act of one lone gunman.

Test 5: Taking Stock

DIRECTIONS   Read the following selections. Then answer the questions by circling the letter(s) of the correct response(s).

1. The Benefits of Sleep

1   In our modern society, it's difficult to get enough sleep. We lead busy, overworked lives and often have to forgo sleep to get everything done. Round-the-clock television shows tempt us to stay up late. And if we do manage to get a full night's sleep or grab a nap, we run the risk of being labeled "unmotivated" or "lazy" by the go-getters around us. Yet research suggests that those who insist on getting their rest are the wisest of all. Studies indicate that sufficient sleep is as important to health as regular exercise and a nutritious diet. It may even make us smarter.

2   First, adequate sleep is essential to warding off disease. Research has shown that when the body is sleep-deprived, the immune system does not fight infection as effectively. One University of Chicago study, for example, focused on volunteers who slept only four hours a night for six days in a row. The participants' metabolism and hormone production were not functioning efficiently after the six days, leading researchers to conclude that a chronic lack of sleep leaves the body vulnerable to serious diseases, from high blood pressure to obesity. Another study indicated that lack of sleep actually increases the risk of heart attack.

3   Getting sufficient sleep also seems good for our brains. Studies show that during sleep, the brain develops, checks, and expands its nerve connections. Thus sleep gives the brain a chance to strengthen itself, leading to clearer thinking when we're awake. This explains why babies and children sleep so much: Their brains are still developing, so they need a lot of sleep to improve their networks of brain cells. Sleep may also be necessary to purge the brain of sensation overload. During the day, our minds are bombarded with stimulation in the form of sensory experiences, thoughts, and feelings. Sleep gives the brain time to sift through all of this information and either store it or delete it. Without time to evaluate and reorganize, the brain could become overwhelmed and unable to remember anything.

4   Indeed, numerous studies reveal that sleep has a significant effect on memory. When people are deprived of sleep, they don't learn as well as when they have enough sleep. In one study, two groups of students listened to a story. That night, one group was deprived of sleep and the other was allowed to sleep normally. The

next day, each group was asked to recall some details about the story. The sleep-deprived group exhibited much poorer recall of the story than the group that had slept. Researchers therefore conclude that sleep deprivation reduces the ability to retain information.

5   Other studies support this conclusion. At Harvard University, for example, researchers found that people can improve their scores on memory tests simply by sleeping soundly for a minimum of six hours the first night after learning new information. In another study, Canadian researchers taught research subjects a game in the afternoon and then served some of them liquor before bedtime. The alcohol interfered with sleep, and the participants did not get adequate rest. The next day the sleep-deprived participants performed 40 percent worse than those who remained sober and got enough sleep. Additional studies at the University of California have shown that sleep-deprived people also have trouble learning new skills.

6   Clearly, we need to stop viewing a good night's rest as an unnecessary luxury. Sleep is crucial to good health and mental functioning. Instead of skimping on sleep, we should be finding ways to get more of it. (Source of information: Robert A. Stickgold et al., "You Will Start to Feel Very Sleepy . . . ," *Newsweek*, January 19, 2004, pp. 58–60.)

1. Which statement best paraphrases the thesis statement?
   a. Sleep has come to be stigmatized in modern society.
   b. Adequate sleep is crucial to good health.
   c. Getting enough sleep contributes to good health and facilitates learning.
   d. Many researchers are studying why we sleep.

2. Which statement best paraphrases the topic sentence of paragraph 3?
   a. The brain adjusts its network of nerve cells while we sleep.
   b. Babies and children need more sleep than adults do.
   c. Sleep prevents the brain from becoming overloaded by too much information.
   d. Sleep has positive effects on the brain.

3. Within the paragraph, is this sentence in paragraph 3 a major or minor detail? "During the day, our minds are bombarded with stimulation in the form of sensory experiences, thoughts, and feelings."

    a. major detail

    b. minor detail

4. What pattern or patterns do you see at work in the reading?
    a. definition

    b. cause and effect

    c. comparison and contrast

    d. simple listing

5. Which of the following paragraphs best summarizes the reading?

    a. According to the latest research, sleep benefits us both physically and mentally. Recent studies indicate that adequate sleep enhances the functioning of the immune system, helping the body fight off major diseases and even heart attacks. In addition, sleep helps the brain function more effectively. Getting sufficient sleep gives the brain time to improve nerve connections and sort through all the thoughts and sensations it must handle during the day. Studies also indicate that sleep is important to building memory and aiding the learning process.

    b. The latest scientific research indicates that a lot of sleep is good for us. People may criticize those who take naps or insist on getting eight or nine hours of sleep every night, for those who like to relax are considered to be less driven or ambitious. Those who love to sleep can now assure critics that the more we rest, the better off we are. For example, studies have shown that you learn better when you get plenty of sleep. Numerous experiments indicate that information-recall suffers when people do not get sufficient sleep while trying to learn new information or a new skill. So sleep is an essential component of clear thinking.

    c. Studies are proving that sleep is essential to good health. Adequate sleep boosts the immune system, helping the body protect itself from all kinds of serious illnesses. It also protects us against heart disease. Research at Harvard University indicates that sleep helps us remember things better, too. Clearly, we have to stop working so much and watching so many late-night TV programs because these activities are interfering with our ability to get the rest we need.

2. Low-Fat versus Low-Carb Diets

1 Millions of Americans want to lose weight, and they know that to get rid of unwanted pounds, they'll have to change their eat-

ing habits. The two most popular options today are a diet that's low in fat or a diet that's low in carbohydrates. But is one more effective than the other? Advocates for each diet continue to debate which method is better. Thus when choosing between the two, most people evaluate the differences in food choices and short-term and long-term effectiveness, along with the health risks and benefits.

2   Both diets forbid the consumption of sugar and junk foods like potato chips; however, the allowed foods on each differ significantly. A low-fat diet includes high-carbohydrate foods like bread, pasta, fruit, and potatoes and shuns high-fat foods like bacon and mayonnaise. A low-carb diet is the complete opposite; it emphasizes protein, so dieters can eat as much meat and cheese as they want. However, avoiding bread, cereal, and other high-carbohydrate foods is a must. Dieters need to decide whether they'd rather go for long periods of time without bread or without meat. Depending on one's tastes and preferences, one diet may be more appropriate than the other. Meat lovers, for example, may find the low-carb diet more appealing.

3   Many dieters are willing to ignore their preferences, though, in exchange for short-term effectiveness; in this respect, the low-carb diet is clearly the better of the two. Several studies have shown that, over a six-month period, those who adhere to a low-carb diet tend to lose twice the weight as those who follow a low-fat diet. Plus, low-carb dieters can eat more calories than low-fat dieters and still lose weight. Consequently, those who are looking for quick results are more apt to choose the low-carb approach.

4   Yet research indicates that the low-fat diet may offer more long-term success. Although the low-carb diet results in faster initial weight loss, studies show that a year after dieting those who followed a low-carb plan had regained much more weight than those who chose a low-fat diet. Therefore, people who are determined to lose weight and keep it off may do better on a low-fat plan.

5   Those who are still undecided after considering the types of food and the effectiveness of each diet might want to consider one last point of comparison: the health benefits and risks. Although some studies conclude that high-fat, low-carb diets do not raise artery-clogging cholesterol levels as was expected, many health professionals do not recommend a low-carb diet because its long-term health risks are still unknown. A low-fat diet, however, is thought to be nutritionally more sound because it permits one to consume a variety of essential nutrients.

1. Which statement best paraphrases the thesis statement?
   a. Millions of Americans need to lose weight.

   b. Low-fat and low-carb diets differ in essential ways, which makes it hard to decide which one is better.

   c. Because it keeps the weight off, a low-fat diet is better than a low-carb diet.

   d. A low-carb diet is healthier and more effective than a low-fat diet.

2. Which statement best paraphrases the topic sentence of paragraph 5?
   a. When choosing a diet plan, people should consider the potential risks.

   b. The health benefits are the most important factor in selecting the right diet option.

   c. People who are undecided might consider choosing one diet over the other based on each one's effects on health.

   d. Low-carb diets are not as unhealthy as people suspected they might be.

3. Within the paragraph, is this sentence in paragraph 3 a major or minor detail? "Several studies have shown that, over a six-month period, those who adhere to a low-carb diet tend to lose twice the weight as those who follow a low-fat diet."
   a. major detail

   b. minor detail

4. What pattern or patterns do you see at work in the reading?
   a. simple listing

   b. cause and effect

   c. comparison and contrast

   d. classification

5. Which of the following paragraphs best summarizes the reading?
   a. America has become a nation of overweight and obese people; at any given time, millions of people are trying to follow either a low-fat or a low-carb diet. Unfortunately, though, both diets have major drawbacks. For example, both prohibit the consumption of certain kinds of popular foods. Thus people who choose the low-fat approach have to give up foods like cheese and mayonnaise, while those who try the low-carb approach can't eat even one slice of bread. The low-fat approach doesn't work very quickly, and the low-carb approach usually results

in only temporary weight loss. In addition, the low-carb plan may increase long-term health problems; no one really knows for sure. Clearly, there's no one perfect diet.

b. When choosing between a low-fat or a low-carb diet, most people usually examine four points of comparison. First, they consider the foods they could eat as part of each diet, for one emphasizes carbohydrates and the other emphasizes protein. A second point of comparison is short-term effectiveness; those who want to shed pounds quickly often select the low-carb method. A third important difference is long-term effectiveness, so those who desire permanent weight loss may get better results with a low-fat diet. Finally, dieters compare the two diets' potential impact on health.

c. It's obvious that a low-fat diet is better than a low-carb diet. Sure, you get to indulge in juicy meats swimming in rich cheese sauces if you choose the low-carb approach, but you might be sacrificing your long-term health while you do so. And you may shed a few pounds fast by not eating bread for a few months, but you'll probably gain all the weight back within a year. If you choose the low-fat approach, though, you'll be healthier and slimmer for life.

C H A P T E R   6

The Role of Inferences in Comprehension and Critical Reading

In this chapter, you will learn

- **how inferences are essential to helping readers identify the words central to the author's discussion.**

- **how to infer main ideas that are implied but not stated in paragraphs.**

- **how to infer the connections between supporting details.**

- **how to draw logical conclusions that might not have been intended by the author but are still clearly suggested by the text.**

This chapter shows you how to put into words what the author suggests but doesn't say outright. In short, it teaches you the art of drawing inferences. And it's no accident that this

318

chapter bridges the gap between the comprehension and critical reading parts of this textbook. Essential to understanding
an author's meaning, drawing appropriate inferences also lies
at the heart of critical reading.

Drawing Inferences to Help Create Connections

Later in this chapter, we'll talk about paragraphs in which the
reader has to infer the overall main idea implied by all (or most) of
the sentences in the passage. Drawing inferences, however, is
already crucial at the level of individual sentences. As the following
section will demonstrate, writers rely on readers to draw inferences
that create connections between sentences and give the passage an
overall feeling of coherence, or connectedness.

As you know from identifying topics, one of the ways writers create connection is by making certain people, places, events, and
ideas reappear in a passage through a chain of references. The
reader, in turn, must identify and follow that chain of references to
make the same chain of connections the writer intended. This is
where drawing inferences becomes critical.

Identifying Chains of Reference

Writers use a number of different devices to make sure that readers make the right connections between sentences. Here are some
common methods writers use, along with a description of how readers respond.

Nouns and Pronouns

One way writers create a chain of references is to introduce a noun[†]
and then refer to it with pronouns, leaving it up to readers to connect the pronouns and **antecedents**, the nouns to which pronouns
refer. Here's a fairly straightforward illustration:

[†]The grammatical term *noun* identifies people, places, ideas, and things—e.g.,
Ludacris, Iraq, capitalism, and houses.

Edward Thorndike (1874–1949) is a famous figure in learning theory. *He* conducted several experiments in order to gain further understanding of the learning process. He also formulated many important laws of learning. (Engler, *Personality Theories*, p. 209.)

The pronoun *he* in the second sentence is the author's way of saying, "I am still talking about Edward Thorndike, but I can't always call him by name so I'm using the pronoun 'he.'" Notice, though, that the author expects readers to keep track of the topic, in this case Edward Thorndike, by inferring the relationship between pronoun and antecedent.

Tricky Pronouns and Antecedents

The example about Edward Thorndike might make it seem as if inferring relationships between pronouns and antecedents is so easy the subject is not worth mentioning. But connecting the two can get tricky, particularly if there is more than one pronoun and antecedent relationship or if the noun is followed by a pronoun clause† rather than a single word.

Staying on the trail of pronouns and their antecedents can also become more difficult when the nouns to which the pronouns refer are quite a distance away. In the following passage, the pronouns are italicized. When you finish reading the excerpt, fill in the blanks in parentheses following the pronouns with the nouns they represent, or stand in for.

¹One problem with court-assigned counsel for the poor concerns degree of effort. ²Although most attorneys assigned by the court

to defend *those who cannot afford counsel* (_____)

probably take *their* (_____) job seriously, some feel

only a loose commitment to *their* (_____) clients. ³Paying

clients, in *their* (_____) eyes, deserve better service and

are apt to get *it* (_____). (Schmalleger, *Criminal Justice Today*, p. 41.)

In this case, the first pronoun starts off representing, or standing in for, the clients who cannot afford to pay. The next string of pronouns represents the attorneys, with the last pronoun *it* referring not to a person but to a good defense.

---

†Pronoun clauses would consist of the pronoun and verb—e.g., "The man *who would be king* must have a strong stomach for criticism."

In every instance, it's up to readers to infer the relationship between pronoun and antecedent based on clues in the text and the reader's knowledge of English. Readers generally know, for instance, that the pronoun *it* would not refer to a person but to an object, event, or idea.

Taking a Closer Look at *This, That,* and *Which*

Writers sometimes use *this, that,* or *which* to refer to an entire idea rather than a single noun. Look, for example, at the following pair of sentences:

[1]No public figure wants to be crucified for having concealed warnings of terrorist attacks if the attacks actually occur because the warnings would almost certainly be revealed. [2]On the simplest level, *this* is why we've had two warnings from the Bush adminis tration against unspecified terrorist threats. (Adapted from Robert J. Samuelson, "Unwitting Accomplice," *Perspectives on Terrorism,* p. 19.)

In this case, "this" doesn't refer to a single word. It refers to an entire thought: Public officials are afraid that if they get a warning of a terrorist attack but don't reveal it and the warning becomes a reality, they will be harshly criticized by the public and the media. That entire thought is packed into the pronoun *this.* As you can see, it is the reader's job to unpack the pronoun by drawing the right inference.

In the next example, you need to connect two *that* pronouns to their antecedents. Read the passage and fill in the two blanks that follow.

[1]Scholars who comment on the history of mass communication research are carrying out important work. [2]Their intent is to explore the concerns and beliefs *that* have guided professors of media journalism over the decades, as well as the assumptions about individuals and society *that* are reflected in their conclusions. (Turow, *Media Today,* p. 128.)

The first pronoun *that* in sentence 2 refers to _____.

The second pronoun *that* in sentence 2 refers to _____

_____.

The first *that* refers to the "concerns and beliefs." These two nouns have to be the antecedent. "Scholars" couldn't be the antecedent because the scholars are the ones studying the professors' work.

The second *that* follows right after the phrase "assumptions about individuals and society." Thus, you would be correct to infer first that "assumptions about individuals and society" is the antecedent for the pronoun. Happily, your first guess would be correct. But if the noun closest to the pronoun doesn't make sense to you as an antecedent, make sure you always look farther back in the passage until you find a noun that does fit.

It's worth noting, too, that the pronoun *their* at the end of sentence 2 refers to professors of journalism, not to the scholars described in sentence 1. Read the second sentence again, and you'll see that the scholars are exploring the concerns and beliefs of journalism professors as well as, or in addition to, "the assumptions" reflected in the professors' conclusions.[†]

Like *this* and *that*, the pronoun *which* can also refer to a thought larger than a single word or phrase. For example,

> Power is an ingredient in almost every relationship, but the role of power, or who has more of *it*, is seldom discussed, *which* may be the reason why relationships can be hard to maintain.

In this excerpt, the first pronoun, *it*, refers to, or stands in for, one single word, "power." But the second pronoun, *which*, represents a whole string of words: "the role of power, or who has more of it, is seldom discussed." Here then is another illustration why pronouns like *this*, *that*, and *which* bear watching. Pass them over too quickly, and you might connect them to a single word, rather than to the larger idea they really represent.

Anytime a passage is hard to understand, take a moment to make sure you understand the relationship between the pronouns and the antecedents. Making clear connections between the two can often help you clarify sentence meaning.

General Category Substitutes

Instead of a pronoun, writers can also use a more general term that can include and, therefore, refer to the person, event, or idea they want to focus on throughout the passage. For instance, in the excerpt that follows, the word *document* is a more general stand-in for "the Constitution."

[†]For confirmation of how important it is for readers to connect pronouns and antecedents, see Eileen Simmons, "The Grammar of Reading," *English Journal* 95 (May 2006): 48–52.

[1]Once the states received copies of the *Constitution*, Americans began an intense discussion about whether to ratify the regular changes *it* proposed. [2]They expressed a great spectrum of opinions about different provisions within the *document*, and they used the press, the pulpit, and public podiums to spread their views on *it* to every layer of society. (Gillon and Matson, *The American Experiment*, p. 266.)

In this example, the author uses *document*, a general word stand-in, as well as the pronoun *it* to keep readers' attention focused on the Constitution, which is the topic of the discussion.

Substitute by Association

Writers sometimes build a chain of references by using words associated with the key word already introduced. In the following passage, for instance, the author starts out using pronouns to refer to the dogs in the bomb squad, "*their* behavior." But by the end of the second sentence, she uses a phrase associated with dogs to refer to her central topic.

[1]The dogs in the bomb squad had been carefully trained to stay at attention until the whistle blew. [2]But once it did, *their* behavior changed dramatically, and there was much wild yipping and tail wagging.

In this example, the author uses the phrase "yipping and tail wagging" as a signal that tells readers, "I'm still talking about those dogs."

EXERCISE 1 **DIRECTIONS** Read each passage. Then answer the questions by filling in the blanks.

EXAMPLE [1]Early in the twentieth century, U.S. engineer Frederick Taylor (1911) published the first systematic presentation of what was soon called scientific management. [2]Taylor assumed that the primary goal of an organization is to maximize efficiency. [3]For a manufacturing company, *this* means getting maximum productivity. (Thio, *Society: Myths and Realities*, p. 145.)

In sentence 3, the author uses the pronoun *this* to refer to *maximizing efficiency*.

EXPLANATION Here the author uses the pronoun *this* rather than saying that "maximizing efficiency means getting maximum productivity." The pronoun *this* tells the reader that the author is continuing the train of thought from the previous sentence, where he discusses the primary goal of an organization, to "maximize efficiency." Sentence 3 illustrates what the term means when it's applied to a manufacturing company.

1. [1]It is possible to speak of social *character types or qualities* that are frequently shared by the people of a particular culture. [2]The psychologist Eric Fromm identified five character orientations that are common in Western societies. (Engler, *Personality Theories*, p. 138.)

   In sentence 2, the author uses _____ to refer to *character types or qualities* introduced in sentence 1.

2. [1]When Julieta Venegas released her much-anticipated third *album* in November 2003, her fans were understandably shocked. [2]Titled *Si,* the collection found the formerly introspective chanteuse* from Tijuana singing about being happily in love. (Lechner, *Rock en Espanol*, p. 110.)

   In sentence 2, the author used _____ to refer to the word *album* introduced in sentence 1.

3. [1]Sir Isaac Newton's *book Mathematical Principles of Natural Philosophy* was published in Latin in 1687, when he was forty-five. [2]*It* is considered by many to be the most important publication in the history of physics.

   In sentence 2, the author uses the pronoun *it* and

   _____ to refer to the word *book* introduced in sentence 1.

4. [1]With his election to the presidency, *Harry Truman* inherited the government's plan to build an atomic bomb. [2]Like his predecessor, Franklin Delano Roosevelt, the new president readily assumed the bomb should and would be used and never questioned that long-standing assumption. (Adapted from McMahon and Paterson, *The Origins of the Cold War*, p. 98.)

   In sentence 2, the author uses _____ to refer to *Harry Truman* introduced in sentence 1.

5. [1]Publishers are well aware that not every *book* will top the best-seller list. [2]In fact, most books sell no more than a few thousand copies, leading wary publishers to carefully weed through submitted manuscripts looking for appealing titles.

   In sentence 2, the author uses _____ and _____ to refer to the word *book* introduced in sentence 1.

   _____
   *chanteuse: singer.

6. [1]The colonists who chose to protest taxation by the British govern-ment in 1765 and 1767 did not think of themselves as rebels or rev-olutionaries. [2]Indeed, most of *them* would have been shocked at the suggestion that *they* were no longer British patriots.

In sentence 2, the author uses *them* and *they* to refer to the word

_____ introduced in sentence 1.

7. [1]In the late 1960s, many celebrities, including the Beatles and the Beach Boys, followed the Indian guru* *Maharishi Mahesh Yogi.* [2]But when the Beatles went to India to spend three months studying under the *Maharishi,* Ringo Starr returned home with his wife Mau-reen. [3]The couple was apparently unhappy with the great sage's accommodations. (Adapted from Kurlansky, *1968,* p. 130.)

In sentence 3, the author uses _____ to refer to the *Maharishi Mahesh Yogi* introduced in sentences 1 and 2.

8. [1]Robert Kennedy loved children. [2]Where other politicians would smile with babies or strike an instructive pose with children, Bobby always looked as though he wanted to run off and play with them. [3]Children could sense *this* and were happy and uninhibited around him. (Kurlansky, *1968,* p. 138.)

In sentence 3, the pronoun *this* refers to _____

_____.

9. Instead of sending his children away to school, Karl Wittgenstein, the father of the philosopher Ludwig Wittgenstein, had his children educated at home by tutors, *which* made it possible for Ludwig to develop his intellectual powers at his own pace. (Adapted from Janik and Toulmin, *Wittgenstein's Vienna,* p. 175.)

In this sentence, the pronoun *which* refers to _____

_____.

10. [1]*Dr. Andrew Ellicott Douglass and his assistants,* who had turned up in virtually all the pueblos of the Southwest with their drills, had aroused the suspicion of the Indians. [2]The scientists tried to win them over by living with them for a time. [3]They made efforts to learn the Indians' language and complicated code of courtesy. (Cream, *The First Americans,* p. 168.)

*guru: wise person.

In sentences 2 and 3, the author uses _____

and _____ to refer to *Dr. Andrew Ellicott Douglass and his assistants* introduced in sentence 1.

Inferring Main Ideas

Now that we've looked at some of the inferences needed to create coherence or unity in writing, it's time to look at how sentences sometimes combine to suggest an overall main idea that is strongly suggested but never stated in a topic sentence. Here's the first example in which the author doesn't include a topic sentence yet still manages to suggest a main idea that ties all the sentences together.

> The philosopher Arthur Schopenhauer lived most of his life completely alone. Separated from his family and distrustful of women, he had neither wife nor children. Irrationally afraid of thieves, he kept his belongings carefully locked away and was said to keep loaded pistols near him while he slept. His sole companion was a poodle named *Atma* (a word that means "world soul"). However, even Atma occasionally disturbed his peace of mind. Whenever she was bothersome or barked too much, her master would grow irritated and call her *mensch*, which is German for "human being."

In this paragraph the author offers a number of specific statements about Schopenhauer's character and behavior: (1) he lived most of his life alone, (2) he distrusted women, (3) he always thought he was going to be robbed, (4) his only companion was a dog, and (5) he would call his dog a "human being" if she irritated him. However, none of those statements sums up the point of the paragraph.

This is a case where the author leaves it to the reader to come up with the implied main idea that can sum up all the specific details in the same way a topic sentence could. In this instance, a main idea like the following would fit the bill: Schopenhauer had little use for his fellow human beings. That's the general main idea that logically follows from the details presented in the paragraph.

The Difference Between Logical and Illogical Inferences

Experienced readers know that writers sometimes suggest rather than state the main idea. Thus if they can't find a general sentence to sum up the paragraph, they infer one that flows naturally or logically from the paragraph. However, they are always careful to draw a **logical inference**, one solidly based on the author's actual statements.

To recognize the difference between a logical and an illogical inference, imagine that we had come up with this implied main idea from the paragraph about Schopenhauer: "Schopenhauer's miserable childhood made it impossible for him to have healthy relationships with other people." Although the paragraph offers plenty of evidence that Schopenhauer did not have healthy relationships with people, it doesn't discuss his childhood. While common sense suggests that an adult who doesn't like people may have had a troubled childhood, readers cannot rely solely on common sense to draw inferences about implied main ideas. To be effective, *inferences must rely heavily on what the author explicitly, or directly, says.* Inferences based more on the reader's experience than the author's actual statements can cause a communication breakdown between reader and writer.

Evaluating Inferences

To evaluate your ability to distinguish, or see the difference, between logical and illogical inferences, read the next paragraph. When you finish, look at the two implied main ideas that follow and decide which one fits the paragraph and which one does not.

> In the West, the Middle Eastern country of Kuwait has a reputation for being more liberal than other Middle Eastern countries, at least where women's rights are concerned. Yet the majority of female students are not permitted to study abroad, no matter how good their grades. Similarly, female students almost never receive funding for international athletic competitions. Although the Kuwaiti government promised to give women the right to vote once the Persian Gulf War of 1990–1991 was over, the women of Kuwait are still not allowed to participate in elections. Kuwaiti feminists, however, remain hopeful that the government will one day keep its promise.

Based on this paragraph, which implied main idea makes more sense?

1. It's clear that the government of Kuwait will never honor its promise to let women vote.

2. Despite Kuwait's liberal reputation, women are not treated as the equals of men in many key areas.

If you chose the second implied main idea, you've grasped the difference between logical and illogical inferences. This implied main idea is solidly backed by what the author actually says. The specific details supplied by the author support the idea that Kuwaiti women lack equality in key areas. The second implied main idea is also not contradicted by anything said in the paragraph. That's important. If you infer a main idea that is undermined or contradicted by any of the author's statements, you need to draw a different inference.

Unlike implied main idea 2, the first implied main idea is contradicted by the paragraph's last sentence. If Kuwaiti feminists still have hope, there's no reason to infer that the Kuwaiti government will *never* honor its promise to give women the right to vote. Another problem with the first implied main idea is that the paragraph does not focus solely on voting rights. It also addresses funding for female athletes and travel privileges for female students. None of the statements addressing these issues can be used as the basis for implied main idea 1, making it clear that this inference is illogical.

Logical Inferences

1. are solidly grounded, or based on, specific statements in the passage.

2. are not contradicted by any statements made in the passage.

3. rely more heavily on the author's words than on the reader's background knowledge or common sense.

Illogical Inferences

1. do not follow from the author's actual statements.

2. are contradicted by the author.

3. rely too heavily on the reader's personal experience or general knowledge rather than on the author's words.

EXERCISE 2 **DIRECTIONS** Read each passage. Then circle the letter of the implied main idea.

EXAMPLE Over the years, countless numbers of men and women have paid large sums of money for a treatment commonly known as *cell therapy*. Their reason was simple: They believed lamb cell injections could help them maintain their youth. These people either did not know or did not choose to believe that animal cells, when injected into the human body, are destroyed by the immune system. Others in pursuit of youth have tried *chelation therapy,* which is supposed to pull heavy metals like lead and mercury from the body. Proponents claim that the treatments improve cell function, inhibit the aging process, and prevent heart disease, all by eliminating toxicity from the body, yet researchers have never proved these effects. In fact, critics say that patients are not even "toxic" to begin with, so the therapy has nothing to treat. Other seekers of the fountain of youth have tried oral sprays of Human Growth Hormone. The sprays can supposedly accomplish everything from eliminating wrinkles to improving memory and concentration. However, not only have such treatments never been shown to work, but they also may produce side effects such as increased risk of cancer and cardiovascular disease.

Implied Main Idea (a.) Therapies designed to keep people young generally do not work.

    b. Therapies for staying younger should be available for everyone, not just for those rich enough to afford them.

    c. Treatments designed to help people maintain youth invariably do more harm than good.

> **EXPLANATION** Nothing in the paragraph suggests that therapies to maintain youth should be made available to everyone nor does the paragraph suggest that all the treatments could cause harm. Most of the statements suggest that these therapies are useless against aging, making inference *a* the best choice for an implied main idea.

1. In all fifty states, the law protects the confidentiality of Catholics' confessions to priests. Even when a person reveals during confession that he or she has physically harmed another, priests are required to observe canon law* and withhold the information from law enforcement authorities. South Carolina and Oregon, for example, both protect the priest-penitent* privilege even when a confession reveals sexual abuse of children. However, other states—including New Hampshire and Kentucky—do not permit priests to offer confidentiality to child-abuse suspects, even when those suspects are in the darkness of the confessional. Other states distinguish between conversations inside and outside the confession box. While many states, such as New Jersey, still grant confidentiality to all priest-penitent conferences regardless of their setting, others are ruling that conversations outside the confession box may not always qualify as

---

*canon law: a code of laws established by a church council.
*penitent: person confessing his or her sins.

privileged communications. In Idaho, for example, a court ruled that an abusive father's confession to a hospital chaplain was not protected by canon law.

Implied Main Idea a. Some states are limiting priest-penitent confidentiality in the interest of protecting the welfare of those who may be in danger.

b. All laws protecting the confidentiality of Catholic confessions should be stricken from the books.

c. The states should not tamper with laws protecting the confidentiality of confession.

2. The founding fathers based the Constitution of the United States on republican rather than democratic principles. In other words, laws were to be made by the representatives of citizens, not by the citizens directly. Yet whatever the intentions of the founding fathers may have been, eighteen U.S. states provide for legislation by *initiative*. In other words, voters can place legislative measures (and sometimes constitutional amendments) directly on the ballot as long as they get the required number of signatures on a petition. Forty-nine states allow *referendums*, a procedure that lets voters reject a measure adopted by the state legislature. Fifteen states permit *recalls*. If enough signatures can be collected, an elected official has to go before the voters, who may well vote him or her out of office. This is precisely what happened to Governor Gray Davis of California in 2003—a recall election propelled him out of office.

Implied Main Idea a. Whatever the founding fathers had in mind, there are still a number of ways in which the United States is governed by democratic rather than republican principles.

b. The founding fathers did not want a democracy in which the majority ruled.

c. Over the years, U.S. citizens have consistently challenged the legality of the Constitution through initiatives, recalls, and referendums.

 3. On the one hand (if you can forgive the pun*), left-handers have often demonstrated special talents. Left-handers have been great painters (Leonardo da Vinci, Picasso), outstanding performers (Marilyn Monroe, Jimi Hendrix), and even presidents (Ronald Reagan, George H. W. Bush). (As these examples suggest, left-handedness is considerably more common among males than among females.) And

---

*pun: a play on words.

left-handedness has been reported to be twice as common among children who are mathematical prodigies as it is in the overall population (Benbow, 1988). On the other hand, left-handers have often been viewed as clumsy and accident-prone. They "flounder about like seals out of water," wrote one British psychologist (Burt, 1937, p. 287). The very word for "left-handed" in French—*gauche*—also means "clumsy." Because of such negative attitudes toward left-handedness, in previous decades parents and teachers often encouraged children who showed signs of being left-handed to write with their right hands. (Rubin et al., *Psychology*, p. 59.)

Implied Main Idea a. Left-handed people tend to be more creative than right-handed people; nevertheless, the world has been organized to suit right-handers rather than left-handers.

b. Although some very gifted people have been left-handers, left-handed people have a reputation for being clumsy or awkward.

c. Very few great athletes have been left-handers.

4. The topaz, a yellow gemstone, is the birthstone of those born in November. It is said to be under the influence of the planets Saturn and Mars. In the twelfth century, the stone was used as a charm against evil spirits, and it was claimed that a person could drive off evil powers by hanging a topaz over his or her left arm. According to Hindu tradition, the stone is bitter and cold. If worn above the heart, it is said to keep away thirst. Christian tradition viewed the topaz as a symbol of honor, while fifteenth-century Romans thought the stone could calm the winds and destroy evil spirits.

Implied Main Idea a. It was once thought that the topaz could ward off evil spirits.

b. The superstitions surrounding the topaz are yet another example of human ignorance.

c. There are many superstitions associated with the topaz.

EXERCISE 3 DIRECTIONS Read each passage. Then circle the letter of the implied main idea.

1. The widely acclaimed singer and guitarist Buddy Holly died in a 1959 plane crash at age 22. Famed singer Otis Redding was only 26 when he was killed in a plane crash in 1967. At age 27, legendary rock guitarist Jimi Hendrix died from suffocation in 1970 after swallowing a mix of liquor and pills. Jim Morrison, lead singer of the popular rock band The Doors, was also only 27 when he died of mysterious causes in 1971. Just two weeks after

Hendrix's death, rock-and-roll idol Janis Joplin died of a heroin overdose, also at the age of 27. In 1978, Sid Vicious, the 21-year-old bass player of the influential Sex Pistols punk-rock band, took his own life. In 1994, Kurt Cobain, world-renowned lead singer for the band Nirvana, committed suicide; he was also only 27 years old. Rapper Tupac Shakur was only 26 years old when he was shot four times after watching Mike Tyson fight in Las Vegas. The rapper died of his wounds six days later. Christopher George Wallace, popularly known as Biggie Smalls, or the notorious BIG, was only 24 when he was killed in a drive-by shooting in Los Angeles on March 9, 1997.

Implied Main Idea

a. Plane crashes have taken the lives of many of rock's biggest stars.

b. Many celebrities have died when they were at the peak of their fame.

c. Many of rock and hip-hop's biggest stars died young.

d. Like hip-hop, the world of rock music was plagued by violence.

2. A Harris poll indicated that Americans, on average, believe that there is a 50 percent chance that they will be seriously hurt in a car accident. In reality, the chance of this is about 5 percent. The average woman believes that she has a 40 percent chance of getting breast cancer. However, the chance of this happening is actually only one in ten, or 10 percent. Women also believe that they have a 50 percent chance of having a heart attack, but the actual risk is just one in ten. The average man believes that he has about a 40 percent chance of getting prostate cancer, yet in reality the risk is also only one in ten. Although most people estimate their chance of getting HIV/AIDS to be about one in ten, the risk is actually about one in twenty, or 5 percent. (Source of information: Humphrey Taylor, "The Harris Poll #7: Perceptions of Risks," HarrisInteractive, January 27, 1999, www.harrisinteractive.com/harris_poll/index.asp?PID=44.)

Implied Main Idea

a. Most people underestimate their chances of developing many diseases or being hurt in an accident.

b. In general, people are inclined to worry about things that never happen.

c. Most people accurately estimate their chances of developing many diseases or being hurt in an accident.

d. Most people overestimate their chances of developing deadly diseases or getting in an accident.

3. Cleveland child psychologist Sylvia Rimm interviewed 5,400 children in eighteen states about their worries, fears, relationships, and confidence. She also talked with another 300 children in focus groups. She discovered that overweight children feel less intelligent and less confident than their normal-weight peers. Overweight children also worry more than their slimmer peers. Rimm discovered as well that heavier children are lonelier and sadder than other kids, describing family relationships more negatively than average-weight children describe theirs. Unfortunately, most overweight kids are forced to endure their peers' hurtful taunts and ridicule much more frequently than normal-weight kids do. (Source of information: Nanci Hellmich, "Heavy Kids Battle Sadness Along with Weight," *USA Today*, March 29, 2004, p. 8D.)

Implied Main Idea   a. According to Sylvia Rimm, average-weight children are very cruel to overweight children.

b. Sylvia Rimm's research indicates that negative emotions and problems lead children to overeat and become overweight.

c. Sylvia Rimm's survey indicates that overweight children suffer more than their average-weight peers do.

d. Childhood obesity is a growing problem in the United States.

4. In June 1840, Lucretia Mott and Elizabeth Cady Stanton attended the World Anti-Slavery Convention in London. Although both were activists in the cause of abolition, Mott was an actual delegate to the convention as were several other American women. Mott, however, never formally took her convention seat. It was denied her after several male delegates, among them Stanton's husband, vehemently expressed their disapproval of women abolitionists participating in the convention on an equal footing with men. Although there were strong protests to the exclusion of women from the proceedings, those opposed to the female delegates carried the day, and all the women attending were restricted to sitting in the balcony of the meeting hall and assuming the role of onlookers rather than participants. Still, it was in the balcony that Mott struck up a friendship with Elizabeth Cady Stanton. The two women bonded because of their mutual anger at being excluded from influencing a cause they had both supported for years. As a result of their exclusion, the two women vowed to found their own movement and hold their own convention. Mott and Stanton were true to their word. Eight years later, in 1848, the first women's rights convention took place in Seneca Falls, New York. The Seneca Falls Convention is now considered the official starting point of a feminist movement that would forever change the social role of women in the United States and eventually give them the right to vote in 1918.

Implied Main Idea
a. The 1848 Seneca Falls Convention forever changed the role of women in the United States.

b. Thanks to Lucretia Mott, Elizabeth Cady Stanton was inspired to become a feminist, and she became the voice for an entire generation of women.

c. Had Mott and Stanton not been excluded from the World Anti-Slavery Convention, the Seneca Falls Convention might never have taken place.

d. Lucretia Mott profoundly influenced the life of Elizabeth Cady Stanton, who went on to become a leader of the nineteenth-century feminist revolution.

EXERCISE 4 **DIRECTIONS** Read each passage. Then circle the letter of the implied main idea.

1. For many years, studies have suggested that being married is beneficial to a woman's health because married women tend to have lower rates of heart disease and stroke than unmarried women. However, researchers wanted to find out whether this is true for both happily and *un*happily married women. In one study, psychologists followed 422 upper-middle-class women for twelve years, from their forties into their fifties. They checked the women's blood pressure, blood fats, glucose levels, and abdominal fat because all these factors indicate the risk for heart disease and stroke. They discovered that women who were either unhappily married or divorced by age fifty were twice as likely as single women or women who were happily married in their forties to be at risk for heart attacks and strokes. Other studies, too, are producing similar results. (Source of information: Marilyn Elias, "Marriage Taken to Heart," *USA Today,* March 5, 2004, p. 8D.)

Implied Main Idea
a. Research has shown that married women are healthier than unmarried women.

b. Studies suggest that while a happy marriage may be good for a woman's health, an unhappy marriage does not produce the same benefit.

c. According to recent studies, single women are actually healthier than married women.

d. Studies indicate that women who marry in their forties tend to be healthier than women who marry in their twenties.

2. After Reverend Martin Luther King Jr. and Robert F. Kennedy were assassinated in 1968, Congress banned mentally ill people from buying or owning guns. Today, however, anyone who does not reveal a *record* of mental illness when buying a gun will probably not get caught. Why? The answer is simple: Thirty-one states do not have access to the records of those committed to mental institutions. Only a handful of states provide mental-health information to the national database used to screen gun buyers. In fact, two-thirds of all states don't even compile such information. Furthermore, according to Americans for Gun Safety, fourteen states cannot search the records for people who have been convicted of domestic violence misdemeanors. Thus they cannot identify a would-be gun buyer with a history of domestic violence. Seven states cannot stop individuals who have been served with restraining orders from purchasing a gun. Fully one-fourth of all computerized records on convicted felons are inaccessible to those performing background checks of gun buyers. (Sources of information: "History of Mental Illness Doesn't Prevent Gun Buys," *USA Today*, March 24, 2004, p. 12A; "Checks Are Spotty," *USA Today*, March 24, 2004, p. 12A.)

Implied Main Idea a. Mentally ill people can easily buy guns.

b. Background checks on gun buyers are a waste of time; they do nothing to decrease the crime rate.

c. The failure of states to share background information diminishes the effectiveness of background checks for gun purchases.

d. If all guns were banned, there would be no need for background checks.

3. In our busy society, many people *multitask*, or do several things at the same time. For example, they talk on cell phones while driving, cook dinner while cleaning, and surf the Internet while sending instant messages to friends. Are people who multitask more productive than people who do just one thing at a time? Researchers conducted four experiments in which young adults were asked to switch between different tasks like solving math problems or sorting objects. As subjects worked, researchers measured the speed at which they completed their tasks. The measurements indicated that subjects lost time whenever they had to shift their thinking to move from one task to another. The more complex or unfamiliar the tasks, the more time was lost as subjects shifted their attention and concentration. Even if each mental shift took only half a second, the time added up throughout the course of the experiment. (Source of information: Porter Anderson, "Study: Multitasking Is Counterproductive,"

CNN.com, August 5, 2001, www.cnn.com/2001/CAREER/trends/08/05/multitasking.study.)

Implied Main Idea
a. Multitaskers are more productive than people who do one thing at a time.

b. Multitaskers are not more productive than people who do one thing at a time.

c. Multitasking is effective at work but nowhere else.

d. Multitasking benefits employers but takes a negative toll on employees.

4. At this point, a convincing body of evidence suggests that the Wild West was never as wild as it is imagined by most Americans. Books like Richard Slotkin's immensely readable *Gunfighter Nation* have convincingly argued that while violence and lawlessness were present in the early days of the western states, there were actually many more attempts to cooperate and build primitive codes of law than there were gunfights. In fact, as Terry L. Anderson and Peter J. Hill, the authors of *The Not So Wild, Wild West: Property Rights on the Frontier*, point out, probably no more than a dozen bank robberies occurred in the heyday of the so-called Wild West, the years between 1869 and 1900. Yet Americans don't seem to care much about the evidence in those scholarly books. Tourists still line up in droves to re-enact, for just one example, the gunfight at the O.K. Corral between Wyatt Earp and the Clanton boys. Those same tourists keep dude ranches and fake ghost towns booming. They are also the main reason why groups like the "Cheyenne Gunslingers Association," "Gunfighters for Hire," and "Cowboys of the Old West" continue to multiply no matter what the historians say.

Implied Main Idea
a. Writers of history textbooks are completely out of touch with the interests of the American people.

b. Americans' fascination with the Wild West continues despite convincing evidence that the West was not nearly as wild as people imagine.

c. The people who travel west to re-enact the adventures that supposedly took place in the heyday of the Wild West (1869–1900) are just wasting their money.

d. If historians didn't write just dry, dusty prose, perhaps more people would pay attention to books claiming to dispel the myth of the Wild West.

5. The general tendency is to consider tabloids like the *National Enquirer* and *The Sun*† of little importance. They are small, trashy newspapers that people read as a guilty pleasure rather than to understand current events. Yet to consider tabloids as lacking in any serious influence is to ignore the long career of Alfred C. W. Harmsworth (1865–1922). A British pioneer of tabloid journalism, Harmsworth made a fortune buying respectable but unprofitable newspapers and turning them into highly profitable tabloids. More than once, Harmsworth used his newspapers to sway political events. In 1915, for instance, having heard a rumor that the lack of artillery shells had lost Britain an early battle in World War I, Harmsworth's paper *The Times* promoted the story with such zeal, it brought about the resignation of the British prime minister. What became known as "The Shell Crisis" eventually forced a change in government. It was also commonly joked that next to the German kaiser,* Harmsworth was the second most important cause of World War I, so passionate was the newspaper mogul* in his determination to make war on Germany. Similarly passionate in the cause of war was tabloid owner William Randolph Hearst. In 1898, Hearst, owner of the *New York Journal*, rightly assumed that a war with Spain over Cuban independence would sell a lot of papers. Hearst sent reporters to Cuba to write stories that would tug at American heartstrings. The reporters did their job and sent back dispatches about the torture of female prisoners and the execution of Cuban rebels. However, it was the sinking of the American battleship *Maine* in Havana Harbor that gave Hearst an even bigger scoop. After the *Maine* sunk, the Hearst newspapers, based on no evidence, put the blame on Spain, and the headline read in big letters: "CRISIS AT HAND: SPANISH TREACHERY."

Implied Main Idea a. Because tabloids peddle sensationalism, their owners and editors are always enthusiastic about war.

b. Harmsworth and Hearst proved that garbage and gossip sell newspapers.

c. Tabloid owner Alfred Harmsworth was feared by politicians, both liberal and conservative, and he was responsible for ruining the careers of several government officials.

d. The political influence of men like Harmsworth and Hearst suggests that tabloids are not so trivial as some think.

---

†*The Sun* is a British tabloid.
*kaiser: German for emperor.
*mogul: wealthy and influential owner of a company.

EXERCISE 5 **DIRECTIONS** Read the paragraph. Then write a sentence that expresses the implied main idea.

EXAMPLE The plant known as kudzu was introduced to the South in the 1920s. At the time, it promised to be a boon* to farmers who needed a cheap and abundant food crop for pigs, goats, and cattle. However, within half a century, kudzu had overrun seven million acres of land, and many patches of the plant had developed root systems weighing up to three hundred pounds. Currently, no one really knows how to keep kudzu under control, and it's creating problems for everyone from boaters to farmers.

Implied Main Idea *Intended to help farmers, kudzu has proven to be more harmful than beneficial.*

EXPLANATION At the beginning of the paragraph, the author tells readers that in the 1920s kudzu was viewed as a benefit for farmers. However, by the end of the paragraph, the author tells us what a pest the plant has become. It makes sense to infer a main idea that unites these two different perspectives.

1. For football and baseball players, the mid-twenties are usually the years of peak performance. Professional bowlers, however, are in their prime in their mid-thirties. Writers tend to do their best work in their forties and fifties, while philosophers, architects, and politicians seem to reach their peak even later, after their early sixties. (Adapted from Coon, *Essentials of Psychology*, p. 139.)

Implied Main Idea _____

_____

2. The webs of some spiders contain drops of glue that hold their prey fast. Other webs contain a kind of natural Velcro that tangles and grabs the legs of insects. Then, too, spider webs don't always function simply as traps. Some webs also act as lures. Garden spiders use a special silk that makes their intricate decorations stand out, and experiments have shown that the decorated parts attract more insects. Other kinds of spiders, like the spitting spider, use webs as weapons. The web is pulled taut to snap shut when a fly enters.

---

*boon: benefit; favor.

Implied Main Idea _____

_____

3. The day you learned of your acceptance to college was probably filled with great excitement. No doubt you shared the good news and your future plans with family and friends. Your thoughts may have turned to being on your own, making new friends, and developing new skills. Indeed, most people view college as a major pathway to fulfilling their highest aspirations. However, getting accepted may have caused you to wonder: What will I study? How will I decide on a major? Will I do the amount of studying that college requires? Will I be able to earn acceptable grades? (Adapted from Williams and Long, *Manage Your Life*, p. 157.)

Implied Main Idea _____

_____

4. Every year the scene is so unchanging I could act it out in my sleep. In front of the Hayden Planetarium on a muggy Saturday morning, several dozen parents gather to wave goodbye to their boys as the bus ferries them off for eight weeks of camp. First-time campers are clutchy. Old-timers are cocky. My own sons fret at length about carsickness. Then the parents give the kids a final hug and shuffle sullenly back to their depopulated urban nests. But not this year. When the bus pulled out of the planetarium's circular driveway four Saturdays ago, at last removing the waving boys at the tinted windows completely from our view, one parent interrupted the usual hush by very tentatively* starting to clap. Then other parents joined in, first clapping and finally laughing uproariously. (Frank Rich, "Back to Camp," *New York Times*, July 22, 1995, p. 19.)

Implied Main Idea _____

_____

5. In the nineteenth century, when white settlers moved into territory inhabited by Navajo and other tribal peoples, the settlers took much more than they needed simply to survive. They cut open the earth to remove tons of minerals, cut down forests for lumber to build homes, dammed the rivers, and plowed the soil to grow crops to sell at distant markets. The Navajo did not understand why white

---

*tentatively: hesitantly; shyly.

people urged them to adopt these practices and improve their lives by creating material wealth. When told he must grow crops for profit, a member of the Comanche tribe (who, like the Navajo, believed in the order of the natural environment) replied, "The Earth is my mother. Do you give me an iron plow to wound my mother's breast? Shall I take a scythe* and cut my mother's hair?" (Norton et al., *A People and a Nation*, p. 499.)

Implied Main Idea _____

_____

Check Your Understanding
Explain the difference between logical and illogical inferences.

Allusion Alert

The paragraph on page 337 discussed *tabloids*, newspapers like the *National Enquirer* that are inclined to sensationalize current events. A term related to, and sometimes synonymous with, tabloids is *yellow journalism*. The term refers specifically to a kind of journalism—sensationalistic, irresponsible, and, kindly put, inventive—that came into vogue in the late nineteenth century. However, it's also generally used as an allusion to suggest that a newspaper, magazine, or journalist is sinking to new lows in reporting.

For instance, when the deputy director of the Environmental Protection Agency was angered by an article that appeared in the magazine *Mother Jones*, he wrote: "The *Mother Jones* article on the East Liverpool incinerator adds heat, not light, to an already heated situation. Your study in black-and-white is, in the end, merely *yellow journalism*." The allusion to yellow journalism is a thinly veiled insult, which says by implication, "What you wrote is utterly worthless."

_____

*scythe: a sharp, curved knife used to cut wheat.

The term originated with a comic strip in the newspaper *New York World* owned by Joseph Pulitzer. The strip featured a yellow-shirted character called "the yellow kid." William Randolph Hearst, the owner of the *New York Journal*, a rival newspaper, copied the comic strip and copied as well Pulitzer's reliance on journalism that was sensational, melodramatic,* and hyperbolic.* Because both newspapers featured a similar reporting style and a similar comic character clad in yellow, the color got linked to that type of journalism. Thus the term *yellow journalism* was born. Now that you understand the origins and implications of allusions to yellow journalism, how would you paraphrase the following sentence?

Original After the coalition forces invaded Iraq, reporter Judith Miller's accounts of Iraq's weapons of mass destruction and plans to use them were proven to be so inaccurate and exaggerated that some critics accused Miller of yellow journalism.

Paraphrase _____

_____

_____

_____

Drawing Inferences About Supporting Details

Even when the topic sentence is present in a paragraph, readers still need to draw **bridging inferences**. These are inferences readers draw in order to understand how supporting details relate to one another and contribute to the main idea. Bridging inferences answer questions like: What is the function of this sentence? Does it further explain the previous sentence, or does it refer to or revise a point made earlier in the paragraph?

---

*melodramatic: emotionally extreme.
*hyperbolic: exaggerated.

Although bridging inferences are not essential to every supporting detail in a paragraph, they are necessary for a good many. Without them, it would be difficult for readers to follow the writer's train of thought. Here's an example:

[1]In the nineteenth century, questions about natural resources caught Americans between the desire for progress and the fear of spoiling the land. [2]By the late 1870s and early 1880s, people eager to protect the natural landscape began to coalesce* into a conservation* movement. [3]Prominent* among them was Western naturalist John Muir, who helped establish Yosemite National Park in 1890. [4]The next year, under pressure from Muir and others, Congress authorized President Benjamin Harrison to create forest reserves—public land protected from cutting by private interests. [5]Such policies met with strong objections. [6]Lumber companies, lumber dealers, and railroads were joined in their opposition by householders accustomed to cutting timber freely for fuel and building materials. [7]Public opinion on conservation also split along sectional lines. [8]Most supporters of regulation came from the eastern states. [9]In the East, resources had already become less plentiful. [10]Opposition was loudest in the West, where people were still eager to take advantage of nature's bounty.* (Norton et al., *A People and a Nation*, p. 509.)

In this paragraph, the topic sentence is the first sentence. It tells us that by the nineteenth century Americans were caught between a simultaneous desire for progress and a fear of ruining the land in pursuit of that progress. The paragraph then gives an account of both sides, describing the first conservationists as well as those who opposed the policies proposed by conservationists. But if you look closely at sentences 1 and 2, you'll see that it's up to the reader to make the connection that binds the sentences together, to make them cohere, or connect. To correctly understand just those two sentences, readers need to add the following information:

1. The people mentioned in sentence 2 are no longer trapped between the desire for progress and the desire to protect the land; they have opted for protecting the land and its natural resources.

2. The people eager to protect the natural landscape in sentence 2 are also Americans like those referred to in sentence 1.

---

*coalesce: combine, unite.
*conservation: related to protecting and preserving the environment.
*prominent: famous, well-known.
*bounty: gifts.

Now look at sentence 3, which reads, "Prominent among them was Western naturalist John Muir, who helped establish Yosemite National Park in 1890." Here again, it's up to readers to infer why the author follows sentence 2 with sentence 3. Readers are the ones who supply the following information:

1. The antecedent for them is "people eager to protect the natural landscape" and coalescing "into a conservation movement."
2. John Muir agrees with the conservationists that the land's natural resources cannot be sacrificed to progress.
3. Establishing a park is one method conservationists use to protect the land.

Sentence 4 continues with another example of the actions conservationists took to protect the landscape—pressuring the government for forest reserves. But at no point do the authors say, "*Another action that conservationists took to protect the land* was pressuring the government." It's readers who have to supply the chain of reasoning behind the sentence.

The same thing is true for sentence 5, "Such policies met with strong objections." The authors don't say, "such policies *designed to protect the land*." They rely on readers to infer and add that detail.

The need for reader-supplied inferences persists throughout the passage. Look closely, for instance, at sentences 8 and 9: "Most supporters of regulation came from the eastern states. In the East, resources had already become less plentiful." The connection between these two sentences is implicit rather than explicit, and the reader is the one who supplies the cause and effect relationship that connects the two. Because the eastern states were beginning to notice that resources were less plentiful, they were more inclined to be supporters of regulation.

 # Writers and Readers Collaborate

You may be used to thinking that writers supply all of the text you read. But, in fact, the writer does only part of the job. Writers try to put enough information on the page to explain or prove their point. But if they put every word necessary to creating the meaning, the end result would be so repetitive and long, no one would read it. Thus they are forced to rely on readers to supply some of the information necessary to their intended meaning. No matter what you may have thought in the past, you need to think of reading as an act of collaboration in which you help create the text you read. If you don't make an effort to collaborate with the author, the text's meaning may well elude you.

EXERCISE 6 DIRECTIONS Read each passage. Then circle the letter of the correct answer or fill in the blanks.

EXAMPLE [1]In the 1820s American politics was not just a matter of voting in periodic elections. [2]On the contrary, vast numbers of Americans participated directly in politics. [3]One gauge of this was the huge number of public meetings involving large audiences that attended for the purpose of discussing current political issues. [4]On occasion, audiences were so large that members of the elite even grew fearful that the meetings would get out of hand and democracy would take the form of "mobocracy." [5]The organizers, however, were overjoyed that the meetings included not only a cross section of the electorate but many others who lent valuable collective support, even though they could not vote. (Adapted from Gillon and Matson, *American Experiment,* p. 379.)

1. What is the stated or implied main idea of this passage?

  a. In the early days of American independence, the wealthy were worried about democracy turning into mob rule.

  b. In the 1820s, organizers of large public meetings worked hard to make large numbers of people attend.

  (c.) In the 1820s, Americans made it a point to be actively involved in politics.

2. In sentence 3, the pronoun *this* refers to *Americans' participation in politics; Americans' direct political participation* .

3. What inference do readers need to make to understand the function of sentence 3 in the paragraph?

  a. Sentence 3 reverses the train of thought introduced in sentence 2.

  (b.) Sentence 3 offers proof of the claim made in sentence 2.

  c. Sentence 3 repeats for emphasis the point of sentence 2.

4. What inference do readers need to make to understand the function of sentence 4 in the paragraph?

  a. Sentence 4 offers proof of the claim made in sentence 3.

  (b.) Sentence 4 describes a consequence of the events mentioned in sentence 3.

  c. Sentence 4 repeats for emphasis the point made in sentence 3.

5. What inference do readers need to make to understand the function of sentence 5 in the paragraph?

    a. Sentence 5 describes a criticism of events mentioned in sentence 4.

    (b.) Sentence 5 offers a contrasting opinion to the one expressed in sentence 4.

    c. Sentence 5 offers proof of the claim made in sentence 4.

EXPLANATION In this passage, the authors return in every sentence to the same point: In the early days of the nineteenth century, Americans took an active role in politics. Then, sentence by sentence, the authors offer evidence for this point of view; discuss the anxiety direct participation in politics evoked in some, and describe the pride the organizers of such mass meetings took in their success.

1. [1]There is no denying the importance of the future. [2]In the words of the scientist Charles F. Kettering, "We should be concerned about the future because we will have to spend the rest of our lives there." [3]However, important or not, the future isn't easy to predict. [4]In 1877, when Thomas Edison invented the phonograph, he thought of it as an office dictating machine and lost interest in it; recorded music did not become popular until twenty-one years later. [5]When the Wright brothers offered their invention to the U.S. government and the British Royal Navy, they were told airplanes had no future in the military. [6]A 1900 Mercedes-Benz study estimated that worldwide demand for cars would not exceed 1 million, primarily because of the limited number of available chauffeurs. [7]In 1899, Charles H. Duell, the Commissioner of the U.S. Patent Office, said, "Everything that can be invented has been invented." (Beekman and Quinn, *Computer Confluence*, p. 62.)

1. What is the stated or implied main idea of this passage?

    a. People who predict the future are frequently mistaken.

    b. Although it's not easy, correctly predicting the future of technology can be done.

    c. "Expert" opinion about the future of new technology has almost always been wrong.

2. What inference do readers need to make to understand the function of sentence 3 in the paragraph?

    a. Sentence 3 modifies and revises the point made in sentence 1.

    b. Sentence 3 repeats the point made in sentence 1.

    c. Sentence 3 illustrates the point made in sentence 1.

3. What inference do readers need to make to understand the function of sentence 4 in the paragraph?

   a. Sentence 4 offers a criticism of the point made in sentence 3.

   b. Sentence 4 further illustrates the point made in sentence 1.

   c. Sentence 4 illustrates the point made in sentence 3.

4. What inference do readers need to make to understand the function of sentence 5 in the paragraph?

   a. Sentence 5 offers a contrasting opinion to the point made in sentence 4.

   b. Sentence 5 illustrates the point made in sentence 4.

   c. Sentence 5 offers another illustration of the point made in sentence 3.

5. What inference do readers need to make to understand the function of sentence 6 in the paragraph?

   a. Sentence 6 illustrates the point made in sentence 5.

   b. Sentence 6 challenges the point made in sentence 5.

   c. Sentence 6 offers another illustration of the point made in sentence 3.

6. What inference do readers need to make to understand the function of sentence 7 in the paragraph?

   a. Sentence 7 continues a sequence of dates and events begun in sentence 4.

   b. Sentence 7 illustrates the point made in sentence 6.

   c. Sentence 7 further illustrates the point made in sentence 3.

2. [1]In October 2006, Iceland resumed the practice of commercial whaling, granting the fishing industry the right to harvest annually thirty minke whales and nine fin whales. [2]The Icelandic government made the decision despite a twenty-one-year international moratorium on the practice. [3]Government officials argue that whales are a sustainable resource and that whales taken in the amounts specified by the new rules will not endanger the mammals' overall existence. [4]In response to the new rule, the International Fund for Animal Welfare began gathering letters of protest. [5]But for the people of Iceland, where tourism is a major source of revenue, those letters may not be as disturbing as the effects felt by the tourism industry. [6]According to Clive Stacey, managing director of *Discover the World*, a British company that sends on average 7,000 tourists a year to Iceland, every day brings new cancellations of planned trips to Iceland, so much so that the company has put up a website, where visitors can express themselves on the controversy surrounding the resumption of whaling. [7]Many of the responses posted on the website have been less than supportive of the government's decision: "We had told all our friends to go and visit Iceland to see the whales, as well as the wonderful scenery, but how can we do that now?" (Source of information: Jennifer Conlin, "In Transit: The Resumption of Whaling Hurts Iceland Tourism," *New York Times*, November 12, 2006, p. 2.)

1. What is the stated or implied main idea of this passage?

   a. Iceland's government is going to regret the resumption of whaling once tourists stop visiting the country as a way of protesting the killing of whales.

   b. Tourists and animal rights activists have reacted negatively to Iceland's decision to resume whaling.

   c. Iceland's resumption of whaling is a regrettable decision on the part of the Icelandic government.

2. What word or phrase in sentence 2 refers to the action described in sentence 1? _____

3. What inference do readers need to make to understand the function of sentence 3 in the paragraph?

   a. Sentence 3 illustrates the point made in sentence 1.

   b. Sentence 3 explains why the action described in sentence 1 took place.

   c. In different words, sentence 3 repeats the point made in sentence 2.

4. Which phrase in sentence 4 refers to or stands in for the information presented in sentences 1 through 3?

   a. the new rule

   b. the International Fund for Animal Welfare

   c. gathering letters of protest

5. What inference do readers need to make to understand the function of sentence 5 in the paragraph?

   a. Sentence 5 illustrates sentence 4.

   b. Sentence 5 describes the cause of an event mentioned in sentence 3.

   c. Sentence 5 describes an effect of events mentioned in sentences 1 through 4.

6. What inference do readers need to make to understand the function of sentence 6 in the paragraph?

    a. Sentence 6 explains the causes of the "effects" mentioned in sentence 5.

    b. Sentence 6 further illustrates the "effects" mentioned in sentence 5.

    c. Sentence 6 contradicts the point made in sentence 5.

7. What's the implied reason for the cancelled trips mentioned in sentence 6? _____

8. What inference do readers need to make to understand the function of sentence 7 in the paragraph?

    a. Sentence 7 describes the effects of the website mentioned in sentence 6.

    b. Sentence 7 describes the criticism leveled at the website mentioned in sentence 6.

    c. Sentence 7 challenges the ideas put forth in sentences 4 through 6.

9. What phrase in sentence 7 refers to the resumption of whaling mentioned in sentences 1 through 3? _____

3. [1]Every year about 28 million Americans go to tanning salons, where exposure to ultraviolet (UV) radiation stimulates the skin to tan just as if it had been exposed to the sun. [2]According to the indoor tanning industry, those who use tanning salons are reaping a dual benefit. [3]Industry representatives claim that by using UV light to tan in small increments, without reddening, prevents sunburn, and sunburn is a major cause of the skin cancer melanoma. [4]They also argue that exposure to UV light in tanning salons stimulates the body's production of vitamin D, believed to be helpful in preventing a variety of cancers. [5]While these arguments make spending money at a tanning booth seem like a good investment, medical experts might well disagree. [6]In 1994, a Swedish study found that 18- to 30-year-old women who went to tanning salons ten times or more a year were seven times more likely to develop melanoma than women who did not use tanning salons. [7]A 2002 study at Dartmouth Medical School found that people who used tanning beds had two-and-a-half times the risk of developing a type of skin cancer called squamous cell carcinoma. [8]They also had a greater chance of developing basal cell carcinoma, another kind of skin cancer. [9]As for the second indoor tanning benefit—an increased supply of vitamin D—nutritionists insist that the proper diet provides adequate amounts of the vitamin without the accompanying skin cancer risks.

1. What's the stated or implied main idea of this passage?

   a. Medical research does not support claims made by the tanning industry concerning the benefits of indoor tanning.

   b. The tanning industry argues that there are two basic benefits from tanning indoors, but there is research indicating that at least one of these claims is false.

   c. Indoor tanning might be bad for people but tanning outdoors is even more dangerous.

2. What inference do readers need to make to understand the function of sentence 3 in the paragraph?

   a. Sentence 3 offers evidence for the point made in sentence 2.

   b. Sentence 3 illustrates part of the point made in sentence 2.

   c. Sentence 3 reverses the train of thought begun in sentence 2.

3. What inference do readers need to make to understand the function of sentence 4 in the paragraph?

   a. Sentence 4 further describes the benefit mentioned in sentence 3.

   b. Sentence 4 challenges a point made in sentence 2.

   c. Sentence 4 further explains a point made in sentence 2.

4. In sentence 4, the pronoun *they* refers to _____

   _____.

5. What inference do readers need to draw to understand the function of sentence 5?

   a. Sentence 5 further clarifies a point made in sentence 2.

   b. Sentence 5 challenges the claims made in sentences 2 through 4.

   c. Sentence 5 provides another illustration of the point made in sentence 4.

6. In sentence 5, the phrase "these arguments" refers to _____

   _____.

7. What inference do readers need to draw to understand sentence 6?

   a. Sentence 6 identifies the first date and event in the sequence of dates and events introduced in sentence 5.

   b. Sentence 6 describes a study that further explains the point made in sentence 5.

   c. Sentence 6 offers further proof for the claim made in sentence 4.

8. What inference do readers need to draw to understand sentence 7?

   a. Sentence 7 further develops the sequence of dates and events begun in sentence 6.

   b. Sentence 7 compares a study at Dartmouth Medical School with the Swedish study mentioned in sentence 6.

   c. Sentence 7 introduces a study that further supports the point of sentence 5.

9. What is the antecedent for the pronoun *they* opening sentence 8?

   _____

10. What inference do readers need to draw to understand sentence 9?

   a. Sentence 9 further supports the point of sentence 5.

   b. Sentence 9 further explains the point made in sentence 8.

   c. Sentence 9 repeats the idea introduced in sentence 1.

 # Implied Main Ideas in Longer Readings

Longer readings, particularly those in textbooks, generally include thesis statements expressing the main idea of the entire reading. However, even writers of textbooks occasionally imply a main idea instead of explicitly stating it. When this happens, you need to respond much as you did to paragraphs lacking topic sentences. Look at what the author explicitly says and ask what inference can be drawn from those statements. That inference is your *implied main idea*.

To illustrate, here's a reading that lacks a thesis statement, yet still suggests a main idea.

J. Edgar Hoover and the FBI

1 Established in 1908, the Federal Bureau of Investigation (FBI) was initially quite restricted in its ability to fight crime. It could investigate only a few offenses, such as bankruptcy fraud and antitrust violations, and it could not cross state lines in pursuit of felons. It was the passage of the Mann Act in 1910 that began the FBI's rise to real power. According to the Act, the FBI could now cross state lines in pursuit of women being used for "immoral purposes," such as prostitution. Prior to the Mann Act, the FBI had been powerless once a felon crossed a state line; now at least the FBI could pursue those engaged in immoral acts.

2   It was, however, the appointment of J. Edgar Hoover in 1924 that truly transformed the FBI. Hoover insisted that all FBI agents had to have college degrees and undergo intensive training at a special school for FBI agents. He also lobbied* long and hard for legislation that would allow the FBI to cross state lines in pursuit of all criminals. He got his wish in 1934 with the Fugitive Felon Act, which made it illegal for a felon to escape by crossing state lines. Thanks to Hoover's intensive efforts, the way was now open for the FBI to become a crack crime-fighting force with real power.

3   And fight crime the agency did. Its agents played key roles in the investigation and capture of notorious criminals in the 1930s, among them John Dillinger, Clyde Barrow, Bonnie Parker, Baby Face Nelson, Pretty Boy Floyd, and the boss of all bosses—Al Capone.

4   In 1939, impressed by the FBI's performance under Hoover, President Franklin D. Roosevelt assigned the FBI full responsibility for investigating matters related to the possibility of espionage by the German government. In effect, Roosevelt gave Hoover a mandate* to investigate any groups he considered suspicious. This new responsibility led to the investigation and arrest of several spies. Unfortunately, J. Edgar Hoover did not limit himself to wartime spying activities. Instead, he continued his investigations long after World War II had ended and Germany had been defeated.

5   Suspicious by nature, Hoover saw enemies of the United States everywhere, and his investigations cast a wide net. In secret, the agency went after the leaders of student and civil rights groups. Even esteemed civil rights leader Martin Luther King Jr. was under constant surveillance by the FBI. Investigation techniques during this period included forging documents, burglarizing offices, opening private mail, conducting illegal wiretaps, and spreading false rumors about sexual or political misconduct. It wasn't until Hoover's death in 1972 that the FBI's secret files on America's supposed "enemies" were made public and these investigations shut down. (Source of information: Adler, *Criminal Justice*, pp. 146–147.)

If you look for a sentence or group of sentences that sum up this reading, you're not going to find it. There is no thesis statement that sums up the positive *and* negative effects of J. Edgar Hoover on the FBI. It's up to the reader to infer a main idea like the following:

---

*lobbied: worked to influence government officials.
*mandate: legal right.

"J. Edgar Hoover was a powerful influence on the FBI. Although he did some good, he also tarnished the agency's reputation and image."

This implied thesis statement neatly fits the contents of the reading without relying on any information not supplied by the author. It is also not contradicted by anything said in the reading itself. In short, it meets the criteria of a logical inference.

EXERCISE 7   **DIRECTIONS** Read each selection. Circle the letter of the statement that most effectively sums up the implied main idea of the entire reading.

The Hermits of Harlem

1   On March 21, 1947, a man called the 122nd Street police station in New York City and claimed that there was a dead body at 2078 Fifth Avenue. The police were familiar with the house, a decaying three-story brownstone in a rundown part of Harlem. It was the home of Langley and Homer Collyer, two lonely recluses* famous in the neighborhood for their odd but seemingly harmless ways.

2   Homer was blind and crippled by rheumatism. Distrustful of doctors, he wouldn't let anybody but Langley come near him. Using his dead father's medical books, Langley devised a number of odd cures for his brother's ailments, including massive doses of orange juice and peanut butter. When he wasn't dabbling in medicine, Langley liked to invent things, like machines to clean the inside of pianos or intricately wired burglar alarms.

3   When the police responded to the call by breaking into the Collyers' home, they were astonished and horrified. The room was filled from floor to ceiling with objects of every shape, size, and kind. It took them several hours to cross the few feet to where the dead body of Homer lay, shrouded in an ancient checkered bathrobe. There was no sign of Langley, so authorities began to search for him.

4   When they found him, he was wearing a strange collection of clothes that included an old jacket, a red flannel bathrobe, several pairs of trousers, and blue overalls. An onion sack was tied around his neck; another was draped over his shoulders. Langley had died some time *before* his brother. He had suffocated under a huge pile of garbage that had cascaded down upon him.

---

*recluses: people who live alone, cut off from others.

5   On several occasions, thieves had tried to break in to steal the fortune that was rumored to be kept in the house. Langley had responded by building booby traps, intricate systems of trip wires and ropes that would bring tons of rubbish crashing down on any unwary intruder. But in the dim light of his junk-filled home, he had sprung one of his own traps and died some days before his brother. Homer, blind, paralyzed, and totally dependent on Langley, had starved to death.[†]

Implied Main Idea   (a.) In the end, the Collyer brothers' eccentric and reclusive ways led to their deaths.

    b. The Collyer brothers' deaths were probably suicides.

    c. The Collyer brothers have become more famous in death than they ever were in life.

    EXPLANATION In this case, *a* is the most appropriate inference because statements in the reading suggest that the brothers' eccentricity contributed to their deaths. It was, for example, a trap of Langley's own devising that killed him. However, there is no evidence that either of the brothers chose to die and the only reference to the brothers' fame is to how well known they were in the neighborhood.

1. Frustration

1 **External frustrations** are based on conditions outside of the individual that impede progress toward a goal. All the following are external frustrations: getting stuck with a flat tire, having a marriage proposal rejected, finding the cupboard bare when you go to get your poor dog a bone, finding the refrigerator bare when you go to get your poor tummy a T-bone, finding the refrigerator gone when you return home, being chased out of the house by your starving dog. In other words, external frustrations are based on *delay, failure, rejection, loss,* or another direct blocking of motives.

2 **Personal frustrations** are based on personal characteristics. If you are four feet tall and aspire to be a professional basketball player, you very likely will be frustrated. If you want to go to medical school, but can earn only D grades, you will likewise be frustrated. In both examples, frustration is actually based on personal limitations. Yet failure may be *perceived* as externally caused.

[†]Adams and Riley, "Hermits of Harlem," *Facts and Fallacies*, p. 226.

3   Whatever the type of frustration, if it persists over time, it's likely to lead to aggression. The frustration–aggression link is so common, in fact, that experiments are hardly necessary to show it. A glance at almost any newspaper will provide examples such as the following:

Justifiable Autocide

BURIEN, Washington (AP)—Barbara Smith committed the assault, but police aren't likely to press charges. Her victim was a 1964 Oldsmobile that failed to start once too often.

When Officer Jim Fuda arrived at the scene, he found one beat-up car, a broken baseball bat, and a satisfied 23-year-old Seattle woman.

"I feel good," Ms. Smith reportedly told the officer. "That car's been giving me misery for years and I killed it."

(As quoted in Coon, *Essentials of Psychology*, p. 419.)

Implied Main Idea a. External frustration is the more painful type of frustration, and it frequently leads to aggressive feelings and actions.

b. Although there are two different types of frustration, both can, if they persist, lead to aggressive behavior.

c. Experiencing personal frustration is more psychologically wounding than the effects of external frustration.

2. When Diets Don't Work, Some Turn to Surgery

1   Although she had tried all her life to lose weight, by the time she was thirty-one, five-foot-four-inch pop singer Carnie Wilson weighed 300 pounds. She was so overweight that she had little energy to pursue her career. She also suffered from a dangerous condition called sleep apnea. "I would wake myself up choking about fifteen times a night, gasping for air, my heart racing. I wasn't breathing. It was the fat choking my airway. I was tired all the time, and I was borderline diabetic. I had hypertension, my triglycerides were really high, and my cholesterol was like 270 or 280. Oh, God, and the joint pain—it was impossible. I was having trouble walking. I was short of breath all the time. I could not support the weight any more. My body was giving out. I was thirty-one, and the doctors told me I could have a heart attack at any time."

2   But then former television actress Roseanne told Carnie about the weight-loss surgery that had helped her trim down. Carnie researched her options, consulted doctors, and chose to undergo a gastric bypass. This operation reduces the stomach to little more than a small pouch, and the small intestine is rerouted to limit the absorption of nutrients. Following her 1999 surgery, Carnie was able to eat only a few bites of food at a time. A year and a half later, she was down to 150 pounds. Today, she pro-

motes weight-loss surgery in advertisements. She says that without her surgery, she would have swelled to 400 or 500 pounds, and she doesn't think she would have lived another ten years. Now, though, she says, "I feel alive. I feel healthy and inspired and attractive and light on my feet. I don't feel weighted down or sick or unhealthy or abnormal . . . or gross."

3   Not only has Carnie's progress been the topic of many a newspaper and magazine article, but she also allowed the operation to be televised over the Internet, where about 2.5 million people watched. Since then, Randy Jackson, a judge on *American Idol,* says of his weight-loss surgery: "I've tried a lot of diets, almost all of them, and this is the only thing that's been good for me." Viewers of the *Today* show watched weatherman Al Roker, who weighed 320 pounds before his 2002 gastric bypass operation, shrink in size before their eyes. Other celebrities, too, including actor Michael Genadry of the TV series *Ed,* vampire novelist Anne Rice, and blues singer Etta James, have told the world about their weight-loss success following the procedure.

4   Not surprisingly, ordinary overweight Americans have been listening to the celebrity endorsements, and some, the ones who are desperate and financially able, have chosen to have their stomachs stapled. But their decision may not be wise, no matter what the celebrities say. After all, one in every 200 people dies from this operation. Many others develop hernias, blood clots, and infections. While it's true that losing weight reduces some health problems, it may actually trade one set of complications for others just as serious.

5   Those who survive gastric bypass surgery still face a sometimes grueling, physical battle. They can no longer eat fatty or fried foods. Nor can they eat sugar and refined foods. Because the top portion of the small intestine has been bypassed and the body can no longer easily digest these kinds of foods, ingesting them leads to "dumping," which takes the form of violent vomiting, dizziness, cramps, or diarrhea. Carnie Wilson, who dumped hard five times following her surgery, said, "It's the most horrible feeling I can imagine. . . . You feel like you're dying."

6   Because the operation makes it more difficult for the body to absorb calcium, those who have had a gastric bypass must take calcium supplements for the rest of their lives to avoid developing osteoporosis. Iron absorption, too, is reduced, so patients have to take iron supplements to ward off anemia. Many need to have their blood drawn and analyzed every six months to watch for potential problems. Doctors are concerned that the risk for adolescents is even greater because their bodies are not fully developed.

7 But health risks aren't the only dangers that come with stomach stapling. Psychologists point out that such surgery does nothing to cure people of their emotional issues, and this is particularly true for teenagers. Dr. Jenn Berman, a California psychotherapist, says, "When a teen is overweight or obese, many times it's because [he or she] never learned emotional coping skills and turned to food [as comfort] instead. When you take that one coping skill away, it can be dangerous because the tendency is to look for another one. As harmful as overeating can be, it's way down the list compared to drugs, alcohol, and acting out sexually. Kids aren't prepared to deal with such an extremely drastic change." Plus, adults and teens often have a tough time adjusting to their new bodies, even if they now possess the bodies they've always wanted. Carnie Wilson says, "Your body changes from week to week. Your body gets way ahead of your mind. You look in the mirror, and you think: Who am I? It brings up a lot of issues." (Sources of information: Stephanie Booth, "Teenage Waist-land," *Salon*, March 4, 2004, www.salon.com/mwt/feature/2004/03/16/gastric_bypass/index_np.html; Douglas Kalajian, "The Downsizing of Carnie Wilson," *The Palm Beach Post*, June 11, 2002, p. 1D; Tanya Barrientos, "Popular Weight-Loss Surgery on Rise Despite Risks," *Philadelphia Inquirer*, February 20, 2004.)

Implied Main Idea a. Celebrities willing to share their personal stories of weight loss have helped many obese teenagers.

b. Despite the celebrity endorsements, gastric bypass surgery for the obese is not without its drawbacks.

c. To spend large sums of money on gastric bypass surgery, instead of dieting, is disgraceful.

d. Gastric bypass surgery is a solution to obesity that only the rich can afford.

EXERCISE 8 **DIRECTIONS** Read each selection. Then write the implied main idea in the blanks that follow.

1. Defining the Government's Role in Health Care

1 The process of defining Washington's role in the U.S. health care system began after the Civil War, when Congress authorized a network of hospitals for disabled Union veterans. The system of

federally funded medical facilities steadily expanded in the twentieth century to serve veterans of World War I, World War II, and later conflicts.

2   Efforts to extend the government's health care role even further met bitter opposition from the medical profession. The Sheppard-Towner Act of 1921 appropriated $1.2 million for rural prenatal and infant-care centers run by public health nurses. However, the male-dominated American Medical Association (AMA) objected to this infringement on its monopoly, and Congress killed the program in 1929. Efforts to include health insurance in the Social Security Act of 1935 failed in the face of opposition from the AMA and private insurers. President Truman proposed a comprehensive medical insurance plan to Congress in 1945, but the AMA again fought back, stigmatizing* the plan as an encroaching wedge of "socialized medicine."

3   Medicare and Medicaid (1965), which provide health insurance for the elderly, the disabled, and the poor, broke this logjam. Nevertheless, lobbyists for the AMA, hospitals, and private insurance companies succeeded in limiting Washington's function to that of bill payer, with no role in shaping the health care system or, most important, in containing costs. The new programs assured millions of Americans better health care, but proved very expensive. From 1970 to 1990, Medicare costs ballooned from $7.6 billion to $111 billion and Medicaid from $6.3 billion to $79 billion. As the population aged, long-term care for older adults became an especially pricey component.

4   Rising costs made up only part of a larger tangle of problems. While the United States boasted the world's best health care, its benefits were unevenly distributed. Inner-city minorities and rural communities often lacked adequate care. Life expectancy, infant mortality, and other health indexes varied significantly along racial, regional, and income lines. Although many workers belonged to prepaid health systems, millions of Americans lacked health insurance. (Adapted from Boyer, *Promise to Keep*, p. 206.)

Implied Main Idea _____

_____

_____
*stigmatizing: branding as disgraceful.

2. Will African Penguins Go the Way of the Passenger Pigeon?

1 One hundred years ago, a million and a half African penguins waddled and swam along the coasts of South Africa and Namibia. Today, only about 120,000 African penguins remain, and they are confined to a few small islands off the coast of South Africa. Fortunately for the penguins' future, they are adorable. Only two feet tall with big eyes and a black stripe around their bellies, the birds attract human visitors in droves. If they are lucky, their popularity with humans will keep them alive.

2 African penguins feed on anchovies and sardines, which until recently could readily be found in nearby waters. But around 1997, the sardines began to disappear from waters near the penguins' habitat. Some of the fish were relocating because global warming had increased water temperature and sent the fish in pursuit of cooler temperatures. However, tons of sardines and anchovies were also swept up in the nets of commercial fishermen, who have been depleting the fish population along the coast of Africa. The disappearance of their usual food supply has left the penguins stranded and starving.

3 The islands where the penguins live are also home to feral, or wild, cats who have made a meal out of penguin chicks whenever they could find them. In addition to the cats, penguin parents have had to protect their chicks from the aggressive kelp gull, a tough predator that searches out unprotected nests in order to swoop down and devour vulnerable chicks. The penguins used to be able to dig their nests so deep they could escape the threat of gulls, but settlers have dug out so much penguin guano to use as fertilizer, the ground is not as soft as it used to be, and it is harder for the birds to dig deep nests. As if threats by land and air weren't enough, in 2000 an oil spill made the waters even more dangerous than the beach. A huge bird-rescue operation saved almost forty thousand penguins, but thousands more did not survive.

4 Environmentalists are currently mounting a campaign to save the African penguin. While relocating the birds would be difficult, supporters of the campaign are raising money to build igloos, where the birds can be protected from the sun's heat and gulls' attacks. Environmentalists are also overseeing the removal of feral cats from the island in the hopes of increasing the penguins' slim chances for survival. (Source of information: Michael Vines, "Dinner Disappears, and African Penguins Pay The Price." www.nytimes.com/2007/06/04/world/africa/04robben.html.)

Implied Main Idea _____

_____

 ## Making Connections Between Paragraphs

Inferring the connections that link paragraphs is essential to understanding multiparagraph readings. Look, for example, at these two paragraphs from a reading discussing the reality and the myth of frontiersman Davy Crockett.

> The Walt Disney version of Davy Crockett, *Davy Crockett, Indian Fighter*, became a runaway hit in 1954 when an unknown actor named Fess Parker donned Crockett's trademark coonskin cap and played him on television. The show spawned several movies—and millions of coonskin caps—among them the 1960 epic *The Alamo*, starring Richard Nixon supporter John Wayne. Wayne even helped pay for a movie ad that showed Crockett at the Alamo. The caption for the ad—"There were no ghostwriters at the Alamo, only Men"—openly alluded to rumors that John F. Kennedy, Nixon's opponent in the presidential race, had a ghostwriter for his Pulitzer Prize–winning book, *Profiles in Courage*.
>
> But Wayne, who died of lung cancer in 1979, must have spun in his grave when Paul Andrew Hutton's 1989 essay, "Davy Crockett: An Exposition of Hero Worship," was published. Hutton argued that young men volunteering for the Vietnam War had been inspired by their twin heroes, John F. Kennedy and Davy Crockett. According to Hutton, when Kennedy "issued a clarion* call to fight for freedom in a distant land," young men answered the call because "they knew full well what he was talking about, for they had been brought up on those same *liberal* values by Disney's Davy Crockett." (Source of information: Allen Barra, "American Idols," Salon.com, April 10, 2004.)

To move smoothly between these two paragraphs, readers are expected to infer a cause and effect relationship: John Wayne, a staunch supporter of Republican Richard Nixon, would have spun in his grave *because* he would have hated the idea of Crockett being linked to Kennedy, the man who challenged and beat his political favorite. But here again, the author does not include that information in the supporting details. Readers have to draw the right inference. In other words, bridging inferences are essential not just to connecting sentences but to connecting paragraphs as well.

_____

*clarion: loud and clear.

EXERCISE 9 DIRECTIONS Read the following selection. Then circle the appropriate letters to identify the implied main idea and the connections between paragraphs that readers need to infer.

A Boy Soldier's Story

1   When Ishmael Beah was interviewed on Jon Stewart's *The Daily Show*, the normally wise-cracking Stewart showed a serious side. Even he, whose gift for on-the-spot quips seems genetically inspired, couldn't find anything amusing to say about Beah's book, *A Long Way Gone: Memoirs of a Boy Soldier*. Beah, who now lives in Brooklyn, New York, grew up in Sierra Leone, Africa, and writes about being a twelve-year-old soldier in the civil war that tore his country apart throughout the 1990s until an uneasy peace was achieved in 2002. The book does not make for good bedtime reading, unless, of course, the reader is looking for nightmares.

2   Beah's journey into hell began when members of the rebel army, the Revolutionary United Front (RUF) led by Foday Sankoh, entered his village, intent on slaughtering everyone in it. Along with several other young boys, Beah ran away, only to end up moving from village to village, desperately trying to find shelter and food. When he did finally find a safe haven, it was on a government military base.

3   But the boy's new-found safety came at a price. He was given a choice: Become a soldier or leave the base and face the rebel army, notorious for amputating the arms of its victims. Since this was no choice at all, Beah accepted the AK-47 handed to him and became one of the government's child soldiers. Fueled by the mix of cocaine and gunpowder all the boys were given to keep them as mindless and conscience-free as possible, Beah and his cohorts were willing to do anything asked of them no matter how bloody or horrible. As Beah writes of one incident, "We walked around the village and killed everyone who came out of the houses and huts."

4   Jon Stewart was right to skip the jokes during his interview with Beah. There are few bright moments in his largely tragic story, unless one counts the time where Beah escaped the anger of rebel supporters by having some rap cassettes with him when he was captured. Miming the lyrics and dancing to the sounds of *LL Cool J* and *Naughty by Nature* among others, Beah entertained the villagers intent on maiming or killing him. In exchange, they offered him his release.

5   Yet what is probably most astonishing about *A Long Way Gone* is the fact that its author seems to have survived "childhood" with his humanity intact. When his commander volunteers Beah and a

few other very young boys for rehabilitation, it seems to prove the truth of his father's motto, "If you are alive, there is hope for a better day." Although he and the other boys initially fought all attempts to make them stop being bloodthirsty child soldiers, their resistance finally gave way, and they begin to act like what they were, children.

6   After leaving the rehabilitation center, Beah lived for a while with his uncle because the rebels who had driven him from his village had kept their word: They had destroyed the village and slaughtered Beah's parents, along with the rest of the inhabitants. At fifteen, Beah had no home to go to, so his relatives took him in. While living with his uncle, Beah was selected to speak at the United Nations because the international delegates wanted to better understand the fate of child soldiers. The UN appearance led to Beah's coming to the United States, where he graduated from high school and Oberlin College with a degree in political science.

7   Beah, now in his twenties, has grown up, but he hasn't forgotten his nightmarish past. Instead, through his memoir, he uses it to make a point: "I believe children have the resilience to outlive their sufferings if given a chance." His memoir is a testament to those words. (Sources of information: www.comedycentral.com/motherload/ml_video=82274; www.npr.org/templates/story/storyid=7519542.)

1. What is the implied main idea of the reading?

   a. The civil war in Sierra Leone destroyed the lives of countless children.

   b. Ishmael Beah's life story illustrates how tragic war is, especially for children, who seldom recover from the psychological wounds of war even if they do get over the physical wounds.

   c. Tragic as Ishmael Beah's early years were, his story still suggests that his father was right: "If you are alive, there is hope for a better day."

   d. Although Ishmael Beah's horrifying time as a child soldier is over, he is still haunted by the experience.

2. To understand why paragraph 2 follows paragraph 1, the reader has to infer which connection?

   a. Paragraph 2 illustrates why the peace mentioned in paragraph 1 is considered "uneasy."

   b. Paragraph 2 explains why Beah decided to write his memoirs.

   c. Paragraph 2 illustrates why the book can cause the "nightmares" mentioned in paragraph 1.

3. To understand why paragraph 3 follows paragraph 2, the reader must infer which connection?

    a. Paragraph 3 further explains why the book can cause nightmares.

    b. Paragraph 3 offers an exception to the book's description of a tragic time in Ishmael Beah's life.

    c. Paragraph 3 explains why Beah had to run when the rebels arrived in his village.

4. To understand why paragraph 4 follows paragraph 3, the reader must infer which connection?

    a. Paragraph 4 further explains why the book can cause nightmares.

    b. Paragraph 4 offers an exception to the book's description of a tragic time in Ishmael Beah's life.

    c. Paragraph 4 illustrates how Beah and his cohorts were "willing to do anything asked of them, no matter how bloody or horrible."

5. To understand why paragraphs 5, 6, and 7 follow paragraph 4, the reader has to infer which connection?

    a. Paragraphs 5, 6, and 7 continue the description of Beah's tragic childhood.

    b. Paragraphs 5, 6, and 7 move away from the boy's nightmarish childhood to say something positive related to his experience.

    c. Paragraphs 5, 6, and 7 describe the chain of events that led Beah to the UN.

 Drawing Logical Conclusions

It's time to point out that readers truly intent on mastering an author's message don't limit themselves to drawing just the inferences intended by the author. To deepen their understanding, readers frequently elaborate on an author's ideas by drawing conclusions that follow from the reading but were not necessarily intended by the author. This next passage and the two conclusions that follow provide an example.

Exit exams are tests that high school students in some states must take to successfully pass a course or earn a diploma. Although exit exams have numerous supporters, they have come under persistent fire where diplomas are concerned. In Massachusetts, for instance, state officials had to quell a rebellion of school superintendents who wanted to award diplomas to 4,800 students who had failed the exam. In Florida, protesters demanded that the governor give diplomas to 14,000 seniors who had failed the exit exam. Given all this controversy, the question that has to be answered is, "What's wrong with exit exams?" After all, high school exit exams ensure that a diploma accurately indicates how much information students have actually absorbed from their courses. This is important because it's widely assumed that grade inflation is rampant in some schools. Thus the passing grades that allow students to get a diploma are not necessarily proof that they have mastered the course material. However, when that diploma is backed up by an exit exam, we can be sure students have mastered the courses identified on their transcripts. By the same token, exit exams should help reassure prospective employers who have begun to lose faith in the diploma as proof of achievement. In short, the presence of an exit exam grade on a student's transcript will add value to the diploma.

In this case, the implied main idea is something like this: "Exit exams are a good idea and school administrators should not cave in to the pressure to abandon them." The author does not say this explicitly. Instead, she implies her main idea by offering reasons why exit exams are valuable for documenting achievement.

However, based on what the author says, you can also draw two conclusions that she does not address: (1) the author would probably agree with legislation that made high school exit exams mandatory throughout the nation, and (2) the author would probably be unwilling to sign a petition demanding that students who failed their exit exams be allowed to receive diplomas anyway. Based on what the author actually says, these are legitimate or logical conclusions. Both follow from what the author says about exit exams even though nothing in the paragraph explicitly addresses either conclusion.

Far less logical would be the following conclusion: "The author believes that the school superintendents should have been allowed to give diplomas to the 14,000 students who failed in Florida." Under some special conditions, the author might well agree, but given the usual circumstances, she would probably be against such petitions because she argues so forcefully in favor of exit exams.

Check Your Understanding

How do the inferences in this section differ from those described in the preceding section?

_____

_____

_____

EXERCISE 10 **DIRECTIONS** Read each passage. Circle the letter of the conclusion that can be drawn from the passage.

EXAMPLE Some 6,000 languages are spoken in the world today, but about 2,400 of them are dying out because the number of speakers is rapidly declining. About 500 of these languages are already spoken by fewer than 100 people. Experts estimate that over the next 100 years, fully 90 percent of all current languages will be either totally or virtually extinct, replaced by "mega-languages" such as English, Spanish, French, or Arabic. Just as we become alarmed when a species of plant or animal nears the brink of extinction, we should be equally concerned about languages that might become extinct. In the same way that we lose something when a particular plant or animal dies out, we lose an entire system of knowledge when a language dies. All kinds of information not fully translatable into other tongues die with it. In addition, the loss of a language can rob individuals of their culture and, consequently, their very identities. Anthropologist Wade Davis has said, "When you strip away language and the culture it embodies, what you have left is alienation,* despair, and tremendous levels of anger." The plight of many Native Americans, who were forced by the U.S. government to speak English, is a good example of how individuals suffer when their language is taken away from them. (Sources of information: Thomas Hayden, "Losing Our Voices," *U.S. News & World Report*, May 26, 2003, p. 42, www.usnews.com/usnews/issue/030526/misc/26tongue .htm; Margit Waas, "Taking Note of Language Extinction," originally published in *Applied Linguistics* 18(1):101–103, 1997, www.colorado .edu/iec/alis/articles/langext.htm.)

---

*alienation: the condition of being withdrawn or unresponsive.

Which conclusion follows from the reading?

a. The author probably speaks several different languages.

b. The author probably opposes teaching English to citizens of other countries.

c. The author would probably support efforts to create text and audio computer files of endangered languages.

EXPLANATION Answer *a* won't do because there is nothing in the passage to indicate how many languages the author does or does not speak. Answer *b* has to be eliminated because the author does not indicate that English shouldn't be taught to citizens of other countries. On the contrary, since language is said to carry with it an entire culture, she suggests that preserving English, and any other language, by keeping it alive is a good thing. Thus answer *c* is the only conclusion that follows logically from the paragraph. A writer worried about what's being lost when a language dies out is very likely to conclude that preserving text on computer files is a good thing to do.

1. In his book *After Virtue*, philosopher Alasdair MacIntyre argues that virtue is the product of social training. From MacIntyre's point of view, virtue can be acquired only in a community where the young are consciously initiated into the reigning social values, including what it means to be a good person. MacIntyre interprets the word *community* in its broadest sense, making it refer to families, schools, religious institutions, political groups, and even avenues of entertainment. From his perspective, it's important that these aspects of the community be respected because it is their authority that persuades the child to accept their teachings and pursue the path of virtue. Far from simplistic in his thinking, MacIntyre recognizes that communities are historical entities that can change over time. It follows, then, that the virtuous life can also be redefined as the character of the community undergoes historical change.

Which conclusion follows from the reading?

a. MacIntyre is probably a modern-day disciple of Plato, who believed that virtue was inborn in special people who had a natural knowledge of perfection.

b. MacIntyre is following in the footsteps of St. Augustine, who believed that virtue is a gift of God.

c. MacIntyre would probably take the side of Aristotle, who believed that virtuous behavior is not inborn but can be learned.

2. Periodically, the price of gasoline soars and infuriated Americans blame Congress, the White House, and the Organization of the Petroleum Exporting Countries (OPEC). According to an editorial in the *Miami Herald*, however, if Americans want to know who is really responsible for high gas prices, they should look in the mirror. "The real cause of gas-pump sticker shock," says the *Herald*, "is American consumers' addiction to the automobile and the lifestyle it allows." The editorialist goes on to point out that far too many Americans act as if they are entitled to own big, gas-guzzling cars and oversized pickup trucks, which together accounted for *half* of all vehicles sold in this country in 2003. The result? America has an insatiable* appetite for oil, and OPEC simply takes advantage of our dependence on its product. Rather than demanding lower gas prices, says the *Herald*, Americans should be driving as little as possible and insisting that their leaders do more to make mass transportation available, reliable, and affordable. (Source of information: "Gas-Guzzling Americans Drive Oil Prices Higher," *Charlotte Observer*, April 4, 2004, p. 5E.)

Which conclusion follows from the reading?

a. The *Miami Herald* editorialist quoted in the passage would heartily agree with those who advocate drilling in the Arctic National Wildlife Refuge as a way of solving the oil shortage.

b. The *Miami Herald* editorialist is likely to endorse policies designed to force OPEC to lower its prices so that gas and oil will be available at cheaper prices.

c. The *Miami Herald* editorialist is likely to be strongly in favor of legislation that improves the quality of mass transportation across the country.

3. America lost three million private-sector jobs between 2000 and 2004, and experts estimate that about one million of these jobs were outsourced, or transferred, to workers in countries like China and India, where labor costs for even highly skilled positions are much lower than labor costs in the United States. According to AFL-CIO president John J. Sweeney, this practice of shipping jobs overseas is the reason why out-of-work Americans are having a hard time finding employment. The loss of good manufacturing jobs, in particular, has ripped apart communities and permanently lowered U.S. living standards. Laid-off workers often have no choice but to take low-wage jobs that bring many families down to the poverty line. Not surprisingly, many workers believe it is unethical

---

*insatiable: never satisfied.

for companies to rob people of jobs, exploit foreign labor, and then sell the goods produced abroad back to Americans. Companies like Boeing, however, argue that they have no choice but to send work to other parts of the globe. Boeing's executives say that the company has had to move jobs to places like South Africa, China, and Russia to keep production costs low, remain competitive, and increase profits. Like Boeing, at least 40 percent of *Fortune* 1000 companies have either moved U.S. jobs overseas or are planning to do so. Some point out that Americans have been buying products labeled "Made in Taiwan" or "Made in China" for decades. (Sources of information: John J. Sweeney, "Outsourcing Robs U.S. Jobs," *USA Today*, March 31, 2004, p. 22A; Paul J. Lim, "Lost in the Outsourcing Debate," *U.S. News & World Report*, March 30, 2004; John Cook and Paul Nyhan, "Outsourcing's Long-Term Effects on U.S. Jobs at Issue," *Seattle Post-Intelligencer*, March 10, 2004.)

Which conclusion follows from the reading?

a. John J. Sweeney probably agrees with those who advocate tax breaks for companies with overseas manufacturing plants.

b. John J. Sweeney would be likely to support a bill that limits tax breaks for companies that rely heavily on outsourcing rather than employing a largely American work force.

c. John J. Sweeney would probably agree with those who argue that the sluggish growth in new jobs is due to American workers' increased productivity.

4. Almost all college and professional sports organizations prohibit athletes from using certain performance-enhancing drugs. The National Football League (NFL), for example, forbids players from taking at least seventy different substances, including steroids, and imposes stiff penalties for using drugs. Because of stiff penalties like the ones the NFL imposes, most athletes choose not to take illegal performance-enhancing drugs. However, many athletes are still using *legal* performance-enhancing substances to get an edge on their competitors. Some, for instance, take creatine, a natural substance that increases the production of energy in the muscles. Others take androstenedione, a drug that works like a steroid to increase performance. St. Louis Cardinals baseball player Mark McGuire was using it in 1998 when he broke the home-run record.

Players use supplements, of course, for their own personal benefit. They want to get as far as they can by winning places on professional teams with lucrative contracts and then breaking records. But athletes also argue that pressure from coaches, fans, and the media to deliver thrilling performances encourages them to do whatever they can to improve their game. "The drug use," says William Kraemer, a professor of exercise physiology at the University of Connecticut, "is a reflection of what the consumer wants. Put it this way: Would people come to see the Indianapolis 500 if the cars only went 55 miles per hour?" But others argue that any use of performance-enhancing substances, legal or illegal, is unethical. Critics of supplements say that even the legal ones give the athletes who take them an unfair advantage and force *all* athletes to take them just to keep up. Critics also point out that drug use in professional and collegiate sports has led adolescents to believe that they should use supplements. Despite warnings from the medical community, up to 11 percent of high school boys have taken performance enhancers. This statistic has led many people—including President George W. Bush, who called on major league sports to implement harsh drug policies in his 2004 State of the Union address—to conclude that adult players, who serve as role models to young athletes, behave immorally when they take supplements of any kind. (Sources of information: David Schrag, "Supplements Create Risks to Users," *University Wire*, January 20, 2004; Mark Emmons, "Why They Choose to Use: Steroids Speak to Athletes' Fears and Greed," *Mercury News–San Jose*, November 11, 2003, www.mercurynews.com/mld/mercurynews/sports/7233767.htm.)

Which conclusion follows from the reading?

a. George W. Bush would probably agree that a baseball player who used steroids yet broke the record for the most home runs in one season should still be elected to baseball's Hall of Fame because it's performance, not character, that counts.

b. George W. Bush would most likely say that USA Track and Field officials, who want to place a lifetime ban and a fine of up to $100,000 on any athlete who tests positive for steroids, are being too harsh.

c. George W. Bush would probably support legislation that made steroids illegal under the federal Controlled Substances Act.

■ **DIGGING DEEPER**

LOOKING AHEAD The passage on page 324 described how Harry Truman inherited the plan to build the atomic bomb. The reading that follows tells you more about the man who made the plan a reality.

J. ROBERT OPPENHEIMER AND THE MANHATTAN PROJECT

1 [1]J. Robert Oppenheimer (1902–1967) was a man who, initially at least, seemed destined to lead a charmed life. [2]Handsome, brilliant, and charismatic,* Oppenheimer had been born into a well-to-do family that readily indulged his varied interests in everything from writing poetry to collecting and analyzing minerals. [3]As a young man, he had whizzed through Harvard and earned his doctorate in physics by the age of twenty-three.

2 [1]Oppenheimer was just thirty-eight when what seemed to be the biggest plum of all fell in his lap. [2]In 1942, the Army engineer General Leslie Groves was looking for someone to head up "The Manhattan Project."[†] [3]The project's top-secret goal was to develop an atomic bomb that would turn the United States into a military superpower. [4]Its success would require the work of many gifted scientists, ranging from chemists to mathematicians.

3 [1]While Groves was no scientist, he was also no fool. [2]He knew that geniuses often have egos that match their intellect. [3]Thus someone had to be found who could understand the complicated work of those participating in the project and simultaneously play peacemaker during those unavoidable moments when egos might collide and the project be endangered. [4]Groves found the man he wanted in J. Robert Oppenheimer.

4 [1]Oppenheimer gathered together the cream of the scientific world and persuaded the group to live in almost total isolation, for some twenty-plus months, hidden away in New Mexico, with little or no contact to the outside world. [2]On December 2, 1942, the Italian physicist Enrico Fermi, one of the men working at Los Alamos, created the first self-sustaining, nuclear chain reaction, on Stagg Field at the University of Chicago Football Stadium. [3]At that point, the energy was available for the explosion of an atomic bomb, and on July 16, 1945, in Alamogordo, New Mexico, Groves

---

*charismatic: having a powerful and attractive personality.
†The project got its name from the fact that much of the money raised to get it underway came from Columbia University in Manhattan.

and Oppenheimer watched as an enormous ball of fire followed by a mushroom cloud rose in the skies over the flat, dry desert.

5   [1]Oppenheimer, who until that moment, had been hell-bent on building an atomic bomb, is said to have quoted a sentence from Hindu scripture at the moment the bomb exploded: "I am become death, the shatterer of worlds." [2]The physicist's sense of doubt was apparently not momentary. [3]Shortly after, Oppenheimer wrote to his former high school teacher expressing doubts about the "accomplishments" of The Manhattan Project: "You will believe that this undertaking has not been without its misgivings; they are heavy on us today, when the future which has so many elements of high promise, is yet only a stone's throw away from despair." [4]The bombing of Nagasaki and Hiroshima in August 1945 only intensified Oppenheimer's change in feeling from exhilaration to shame.

6   [1]Hiroshima's streets were teeming with people when the first atomic bomb, nicknamed "Little Boy," struck, killing 100,000 people (by 1950, radiation deaths would swell the number to 200,000). [2]Nagasaki was hit three days later with an atomic bomb called "Fat Man." [3]The bomb obliterated 44 percent of the city and 54 percent of the people.

7   [1]Oppenheimer was devastated by his role in the destruction and never really accepted the government's explanation—that dropping the atomic bomb forced the Japanese to surrender and avoided even greater bloodshed. [2]He informed government officials that he and most other scientists involved in creating the atomic bomb would not continue working on the project, particularly if the government wished to pursue the even bigger and potentially deadlier hydrogen bomb. [3]Oppenheimer also made it a point to express his guilt to Harry Truman, the president who had made the decision to drop the bombs on Hiroshima and Nagasaki. [4]Oppenheimer told Truman at a meeting, "I feel we have blood on our hands." [5]Truman was not especially sympathetic. [6]He responded by telling Oppenheimer the blood on his hands would "come out in the wash."

8   [1]If Truman was unsympathetic, Oppenheimer's fellow scientist Edward Teller was furious. [2]Teller wanted Oppenheimer's help convincing government officials that they needed to build a fusion, or hydrogen, bomb, and he was convinced that Oppenheimer's public reluctance was seriously undermining support for what many called the super bomb, or simply "The Super." [3]Once the Soviets had detonated an atomic bomb of their own in 1949, Teller was even more obsessed by the need to build The Super, but Oppenheimer was still, as were many other scientists, dead set against it.

9 [1]When the time came and he had his chance, Teller made sure that Oppenheimer suffered for what Teller considered a personal betrayal. [2]In 1954, the country was at the height of its hysteria over communists in the U.S. government, and Oppenheimer was called to Washington for a security clearance review. [3]Most of those called to testify gave Oppenheimer unqualified praise and approval. [4]Teller, however, said that he had serious doubts about Oppenheimer's being given a security clearance that would allow him access to government secrets: "I would feel personally more secure if public matters would rest in other hands." [5]Because Lewis Strauss, the head of the Atomic Energy Commission, already detested Oppenheimer for what he considered the man's arrogance, Oppenheimer was denied security clearance. [6]From that point on, he would never again play a role in how the government used the destructive weapons he, perhaps more than anyone else, had made possible.

10 [1]Oppenheimer continued to work as the director for the Institute of Advanced Study in Princeton, New Jersey, but he was never the same. [2]The review of his security clearance and its subsequent withdrawal had been a public humiliation for his proud, even vain spirit. [3]Oppenheimer's security clearance was reinstated in 1963 by Lyndon Baines Johnson, but it made little difference. [4]Four years later, J. Robert Oppenheimer was dead of throat cancer. (Sources consulted: Harold Evans, *The American Century*. New York: Knopf, 1998, pp. 323–327, 376, 448–449; David Halberstam, *The Fifties*. New York: Random House, 1993, pp. 24–40.)

Sharpening Your Skills

DIRECTIONS Answer the following questions by circling the letter of the correct response or filling in the blanks.

1. Which of the following best expresses the implied main idea of the reading?

a. The personal animosity Edward Teller felt for J. Robert Oppenheimer destroyed Oppenheimer's career, and Oppenheimer never forgave Teller for his betrayal.

b. The Manhattan Project, which was initially considered a feather in Oppenheimer's cap, was the cause of his personal and professional downfall.

c. J. Robert Oppenheimer's guilt over the success of The Manhattan Project is understandable and appropriate, given what he let loose on the world.

d. Harry Truman and J. Robert Oppenheimer were of very different minds when it came to evaluating the success of The Manhattan Project.

2. What is a likely inference a reader might draw from the phrase "initially at least" in paragraph 1?

a. Oppenheimer's life always remained as charmed as it seemed in his early years.

b. Oppenheimer never really had a charmed life, even from the very beginning.

c. Oppenheimer's life did not turn out to be so charmed as it had seemed at first.

3. The pronoun *its* opening sentence 4 in paragraph 2 refers to

_____.

4. In sentence 2 of paragraph 3, the pronoun *their* refers to

_____.

5. In sentence 3 of paragraph 3, the word *egos* is a stand-in, or substitute, for _____.

6. To understand sentences 1 and 2 in paragraph 7, readers need to make what connection?

a. Oppenheimer refused to do any more work on the atomic bomb because he didn't want to work alone.

b. Oppenheimer refused to do any more work on the atomic bomb because the Japanese had surrendered, and there was no longer any reason for the bomb to be used.

c. Oppenheimer refused to do any more work on the atomic bomb because he was horrified by the bombing of Hiroshima and Nagasaki and his role in the destruction.

d. Oppenheimer refused to continue working on the atomic bomb because he hated Edward Teller.

7. To connect paragraphs 4 and 5, which inference does the reader need to draw?

a. The reality of the explosion made Oppenheimer think about how destructive the bomb could be.

b. Oppenheimer was the kind of man inclined to quote poetry at every opportunity.

    c. Oppenheimer felt proud because he had helped create such a destructive weapon.

    d. Oppenheimer was a Buddhist and building the atomic bomb contradicted his beliefs.

8. To connect paragraphs 5 and 6, which inference do readers need to draw?

    a. The U.S. government had purposely picked a time when many civilians would be on the street.

    b. The numbers of deaths estimated from the bombing of Hiroshima and Nagasaki rose with time.

    c. The number of civilians killed in the bombing was a major reason for the change in Oppenheimer's feelings.

9. To connect paragraphs 7 and 8, which inference does the reader need to draw?

    a. Teller believed that Oppenheimer worked to get all the credit for the hydrogen bomb.

    b. Teller was convinced that Oppenheimer hindered work on the hydrogen bomb because Oppenheimer personally disliked Teller himself.

    c. Teller believed that Oppenheimer didn't want the hydrogen bomb developed because that would make the atomic bomb less important.

    d. Teller felt none of Oppenheimer's guilt about the detonation of the atomic bomb.

10. Based on the reading, what conclusion seems more likely?

    a. Harry Truman abandoned all work on the hydrogen bomb.

    b. Harry Truman eventually went along with Teller and gave the go-ahead for a project devoted to The Super.

Please explain.

_____

_____

_____

Students who want to do a more in-depth review of patterns should use *Getting Focused*, the web-based reading program accompanying this text. The program is available at **college .cengage.com/devenglish/flemming/getting_focused/1e/ student_home.html**. Completing question 4 will provide a very thorough and complete review.

To get more practice drawing inferences and conclusions, go to **laflemm.com** and click on *Reading for Thinking*: "Online Practice." Complete the interactive exercises for inferences and drawing conclusions.

Test 1: Drawing Inferences About Pronouns and Other Noun Substitutes

DIRECTIONS Answer the following questions by circling the letter of the correct response or filling in the blanks.

1. ¹In the early 1800s, leading Republicans had hoped to end the nation's political factionalism.* ²*They* sought compromise among sectional interests and welcomed the remaining Federalists into their fold. ³*They* praised the one-party system. (Gillon and Matson, *The American Experiment*, p. 379.)

In sentences 2 and 3, to what does the pronoun *they* refer?

a. American citizens

b. political factions

c. leading Republicans

d. early 1800s

2. ¹As film-industry attorney Schuyler Moore has written, "The saving grace in the film industry is that when the rare blockbuster occurs, *it* can make up for the losses of a lot of other films." ²Moore compares movies to wildcat oil drilling—a lot of capital is required to make enough films to produce a rare blockbuster. ³This system naturally favors the big studios that take care of their own distribution. ⁴Independent filmmakers farm their distribution out to third parties, a costly but necessary operation. (De Fleur and Dennis, *Understanding Mass Communication*, p. 144.)

In sentence 1, to what does the pronoun *it* refer?

a. the film industry

b. the losses

c. the blockbuster

d. the saving grace

In sentence 3, to what does the phrase "this system" refer?

a. the saving grace

b. blockbusters making up for losses

c. the movie industry

d. big studios underselling little ones

---

*factionalism: tendency to disagree.

3. [1]Before the bombing of Hiroshima and Nagasaki in 1945, the use of the atomic bomb did not raise profound moral issues for policymakers. [2]The weapon was conceived in a race with Germany, and *it* undoubtedly would have been used against Germany had the bomb been ready much sooner. (Adapted from McMahon and Paterson, *The Origins of the Cold War*, p. 96.)

In sentence 2, what word first refers to the atomic bomb? _____

In sentence 2, what does *it* refer to? _____

4. [1]After his father retired as the head of IBM, Thomas Watson Jr. took over and led IBM into the computer field with a vengeance, dwarfing all competitors in the decades to come. [2]After establishing its first microcomputer as the de facto* business computing standard in 1981, the conservative giant was slow to adjust to the rapid-fire changes of the 1980s and 1990s, *which* made it possible for more nimble companies to seize emerging markets. (Adapted from Beekman and Quinn, *Computer Confluence*, p. 72.)

What word or phrase in sentence 2 is used as a stand-in, or substitute, for *IBM*? _____

In sentence 2, to what does the pronoun *which* refer?

a. IBM's establishing of the first microcomputer

b. becoming the de facto business standard

c. IBM's slowness to adjust to rapid-fire changes

d. Thomas Watson's taking over for his father as head of the company

5. [1]In the late 1920s and early 1930s, the United States renounced its unpopular policy of military intervention and shifted to a new method to maintain its influence in Latin America, including support for strong local leaders, the training of national guards, economic and cultural penetration, export-import bank loans, financial supervision, and political subversion.* [2]Although this *general approach* predated his presidency, Franklin Roosevelt gave *it* a name in 1933, the "Good Neighbor Policy," which means that the United States would be less blatant* in its domination—less willing to defend exploitative business practices, less eager to launch military expeditions, and less reluctant to consult with Latin American officials.

---

*de facto: in reality; for all practical purposes.
*subversion: undermining from within.
*blatant: obvious.

What does the phrase *general approach* refer to in sentence 2?

a. support for strong local leaders

b. training of national guards

c. economic and cultural penetration

d. a new method to maintain its influence

What does the pronoun *it* in sentence 2 refer to?

a. presidency

b. general approach

c. Roosevelt's presidency

d. financial supervision

What does the pronoun *which* refer to in sentence 2?

_____

Test 2: Recognizing the Implied Main Idea

DIRECTIONS Read each paragraph. Then circle the letter of the implied main idea.

1. Every year desperate, distraught cancer victims travel to the Philippines in the hopes of being cured by people who call themselves "psychic surgeons." These so-called surgeons claim to heal the sick without the use of a knife or anesthesia, and many victims of serious illness look to them for a cure. But curing the sick is not what these surgeons are about. When they operate, they palm* bits of chicken and goat hearts; then they pretend to pull a piece of disease-ridden tissue out of the patient's body. If a crowd is present, and it usually is, the surgeons briefly display the lump of animal tissue and pronounce the poor patient cured. Not surprisingly, psychic surgeons cannot point to many real cures; nevertheless, the desperate and dying still seek them out.

Implied Main Idea a. More people than ever before are flocking to psychic surgeons.

b. Psychic surgeons are complete frauds.

c. When people are desperate, they are inclined to abandon their skepticism.

2. Do you like to watch colorful birds? Then keep your eyes peeled for the gorgeous indigo bunting, with its marbled mix of green, yellow, and blue feathers. Well, at least the male is a fabulous creature; the female is a rather drab brown. If your tastes run to splashes of pure brilliant color, then scan the woods for the scarlet tanager, whose fire-engine-red color is interrupted only by pure black wings. Unless, of course, you're looking at a female, who's a bit on the dowdy side. If you prefer your birds even more flamboyant,* then keep your eyes peeled for the Halloween-colored Baltimore oriole, who likes to hang out around swampy areas. The female is a bit bolder and more inclined to appear at bird feeders. Unfortunately, she's—you guessed it—a drab brown.

Implied Main Idea a. Bird watching has become a more popular hobby than ever before, but unfortunately, it still has a nerdy image.

b. Although female birds are likely to be less colorful than males, they are a good deal more aggressive.

c. Among certain birds, only the males are colorful.

*palm: conceal in one's hand.
*flamboyant: showy; outrageous.

3. For a long time, scientists have speculated that birds might actually be descended from dinosaurs; but they haven't had any proof, at least not until recently. In 1998, diggers in China's fossil-rich earth found dinosaur bones bearing what appeared to be feather-like markings. According to paleontologist Philip Currie, the fossils are the evidence needed to prove the dinosaur–bird connection. However, Larry Martin, a paleontologist at the University of Kansas, is less convinced that the impressions on the bones came from feathers. Still, he, like almost everyone else who tries to reconstruct the past, is anxious to see the new fossils when they go on display. From his point of view, seeing just may be believing.

Implied Main Idea a. Although not everyone is convinced, there is now some real evidence suggesting that birds descended from dinosaurs.

b. Thanks to the discovery of dinosaur bones in China, it's now definite that birds descended from dinosaurs.

c. The fossil record suggests that dinosaurs were the descendants of birds.

4. Writer and feminist Gloria Steinem became a Playboy Bunny to give readers an inside look at what female employees of the Playboy Clubs had to go through to please the boss as well as the customers. The journalist Carol Lynn Mithers posed as a man to get a job on a sports magazine and published the results in a *Village Voice* article called "My Life as a Man." Anchorman Walter Cronkite voted under false names twice in the same election to expose election fraud. *Miami Herald* reporters went undercover to expose housing discrimination. CBS's *60 Minutes* set up a bar called the Mirage, staffed it with undercover journalists, and watched as various city officials demanded bribes for their services. The *Chicago Sun-Times* sent female journalists into downtown Chicago clinics that performed costly abortions on women who were not pregnant. In 1992, ABC News's *Prime Time Live* used undercover reporters and hidden cameras to document charges that some Food Lion grocery stores sold tainted meat and spoiled fish. In 1999, another *Prime Time Live* reporter posed as a telephone psychic to expose the fraudulent practices of the psychic hotline industry. (Source of information: Joe Saltzman, "A Chill Settles Over Investigative Journalism," *USA Today*, July 1997, p. 29.)

Implied Main Idea   a. Investigative journalists of the past have used deception to expose corruption.

b. No ethical journalist would use deception to get a story.

c. Since Food Lion sued and won its case against the journalists who exposed some unsafe practices in Food Lion stores, investigative journalism has been on the decline.

5. Social scientists have been studying the phenomena of both speed and online dating for a while now, with some interesting results. At the University of Pennsylvania, Robert Kurzban and Jaspon Weed studied more than 10,000 clients of HurryDate—a company that gathers men and women together for a round robin of speed dates lasting about three minutes each. At the end of the "dates," those attending find out who was interested in dating whom. Kurzban and Weed found that the women attending the group dating sessions were much pickier than the men. Women usually got a "yes, I'd like to see her again" from about half the men they chatted with. Men who participated got that response from only about one-third of the women they talked to. A similar German study found that the female subjects—attractive women in particular—were very choosy about whom they would see again. The men, in contrast, indicated that they wanted to get acquainted with most of the women they had encountered during the speed dating sessions. In another study of more than 20,000 online daters, the results indicated that women were interested in more than looks. They wanted to know about the men's level of education and their profession. Although education didn't rate high with men, a woman's having blond hair appeared to be an advantage.

Implied Main Idea   a. Studies of speed and online dating indicate that men are much pickier than women about whom they will date.

b. Studies of speed and online dating indicate that women care more about a man's education and profession than they do about his looks.

c. Studies of speed and online dating suggest that women tend to be more selective than men.

Test 3: Recognizing the Implied Main Idea

DIRECTIONS Read each paragraph. Then circle the letter of the implied main idea.

1. In one 1970s experiment conducted by psychologist Leonard Bickman, a male who wore a suit and tie, a milk company uniform, or what appeared to be a security guard's uniform approached pedestrians on a Brooklyn street and asked them to pick up some litter, give some change to a man who needed it for a parking meter, or move to a different location. When the man was wearing a guard's uniform, 36 percent of the people approached did as they were asked. When the man was wearing a suit and tie, 20 percent complied. But when he was wearing the milk company uniform, only 14 percent complied with the request. Similarly, in a 1988 study, a female dressed in a dark blue uniform; a business suit; or stained T-shirt, pants, and tennis shoes approached pedestrians in a St. Louis shopping center. The woman would point at her accomplice and say, "This fellow is overparked at the meter and doesn't have any change. Give him a nickel." When the woman was wearing a uniform, 72 percent of those asked complied with her request. When she was wearing the business suit, 48 percent of people did as they were asked. But when she was wearing the T-shirt and pants, only 52 percent complied. In 1993, when communication researcher Chris Segrin analyzed nineteen similar experiments, he found that all had yielded similar results. (Adapted from Remland, *Nonverbal Communication in Everyday Life*, pp. 266–267.)

Implied Main Idea a. The results of several studies suggest that people like, trust, and respect individuals who wear uniforms.

b. The results of several studies suggest that we are more likely to comply with the requests of people in official uniforms or business attire.

c. Several studies suggest that we respond positively to those who dress the way we do.

d. New studies about the effect of clothing on behavior suggest that most people are naturally compliant, no matter what the person giving the orders is wearing.

2. Some people choose to handle conflict by engaging in **avoidance**, or not confronting the conflict at all. They simply put up with the situation, no matter how unpleasant it may be. While seemingly unproductive, avoidance may actually be useful if the situation is short-term or of minor importance. If, however, the problem is really bothering you or is persistent, then it should be dealt with. Avoiding the issue often uses up a great deal of energy without resolving the aggravating situation. Very seldom do avoiders feel that they have been in a win-win situation. Avoiders usually lose a chunk of their self-respect since they so clearly downplay their own concerns in favor of the other person's. (Berko et al., *Communicating*, p. 248.)

Implied Main Idea a. Meeting problems head-on is the only way to solve them.

b. Most people handle conflict by engaging in avoidance; unfortunately, it's a strategy that never works.

c. Although avoiding conflict can be effective in some situations, it's an ineffective strategy when the problem is persistent.

d. People who use the strategy of avoidance to manage conflict always end up with low self-esteem.

3. For generations, Smokey Bear has warned Americans that forest fires are tragic and should be prevented, and it's true that fires often destroy large areas of natural vegetation. However, fires also produce new growth. The ash that results from a fire enriches the soil. Fire also stimulates the release of new seeds. Lodgepole pine cones, for instance, release new seeds only when temperatures greater than 113°F melt the waxy coating that encases them. Fire also burns away trees' leaves and branches, allowing sunlight, which is necessary for seed growth, to reach the forest floor. In addition, wildfires strengthen existing growth. They eliminate dead material that accumulates around live growth. Wildfires also help weed out smaller plants. This removal of both live and dead vegetation reduces the remaining plants' competition for water, sunlight, nutrients, and space, allowing them to grow stronger.

Implied Main Idea a. Odd as it may seem, fire is an effective fertilizer.

b. Wildfires are certainly hazardous, but they are also beneficial.

c. The National Park Service should do more to promote fires in our national forests.

d. Smokey Bear has been an invaluable public relations tool in the ongoing battle against practices that cause forest fires.

4. According to the National Alliance for Youth, 15 percent of youth sports events involve some kind of verbal or physical abuse from competitive parents or coaches. To combat increasing instances of "sideline rage," some youth sports leagues require parents to attend classes or workshops on appropriate fan behavior. Some leagues even insist that parents sign a pledge of good conduct. If parents fail to attend the workshop or sign the pledge, their children cannot play on the team. The Positive Coaching Alliance holds similar workshops all over the country to teach coaches how to handle players' parents or referees. Other youth sports leagues are simply creating new rules that prohibit spectators from yelling from the stands at participants. Some of these leagues even fine anyone who shouts out criticism of coaches, players, or referees. In addition, many state legislatures have recently passed or are now considering bills that impose more severe punishments on anyone who attacks a referee at a sporting event. The Illinois legislature, for example, mandated a minimum $1,000 fine for battery* of a sports official.

Implied Main Idea   a. Parents who live through their children are likely to interfere if their children are not on the winning side in competitive games.

b. A number of measures are now being aimed at curbing the parental "sideline rage" that has become a serious problem at sports events for kids.

c. When it comes to "sideline rage," the parents are much worse than the coaches.

d. Several state legislatures are enacting laws designed to curb bad behavior on the part of coaches and parents.

*battery: physical abuse.

▶◉ Test 4: Drawing an Effective Inference

DIRECTIONS Write a sentence that expresses the implied main idea of the passage.

1. When the Barbie doll first appeared in prefeminist 1959, she had large breasts, a tiny waist, rounded hips, shapely legs, and her little feet were shod in high-heeled shoes. Barbie wore heavy make-up, and her gaze was shy and downcast. She was available in only two career options: airline stewardess or nurse. In the 1960s era of feminism, though, Barbie had her own car and house. A "Barbie Goes to College" play set was also available. In 1967, Barbie's face was updated to sport a more youthful, model-like appearance with a direct and fearless gaze. By the 1970s, Barbie's career options had expanded to include doctor and Olympic medalist. She also got another facelift that left her with a softer, friendlier look. She now had a wide smile and bright eyes. During the 1980s and 1990s, when girls were encouraged to grow up to be independent wage earners, Barbie's options increased even more to include professions such as business executive, aerobics instructor, and firefighter. Today, Barbie has a thicker waist, slimmer hips, and smaller breasts, and she comes in black, Asian, and Latina versions.

Implied Main Idea _____

_____

2. In 1984, Congress passed a law prohibiting anyone from selling one of his or her organs to a person in need of a transplant. Since then, however, the number of people on waiting lists to receive an organ has risen steadily, and now about 6,000 individuals die every year because the need for organs greatly exceeds the number donated. As a possible solution, the American Medical Association has begun encouraging transplant centers and organ procurement organizations to study whether more people would donate organs if they or their loved ones received a small financial reward for doing so. The question is: Is this practice ethical? Dr. Gregory W. Rutecki of the Center for Bioethics and Human Dignity believes that it is not. According to Dr. Rutecki, "Introducing money into an enterprise that has until now been solely characterized by acts of selfless goodwill is crass and . . . can lead to abuse." Dr. Rutecki argues that even modest financial incentives would quickly deteriorate into an organ black market, where human body parts are sold to the highest bidder. He is also concerned that the introduction of money could compromise the ethics of "informed consent," a decision to donate that is made with an understanding of all the risks involved. Poor people, in particular, would be likely to feel coerced into donating organs. Then there is the possibility of severe abuse within a system that permits financial compensation. Ruthless people might actually begin stealing body parts from living individuals to sell. According to Dr. Rutecki, motivating potential donors with money could lead to nightmarish consequences, so it is *not* the solution to the organ shortage problem.

Implied Main Idea _____

_____

3. Over billions of years, the human body has evolved to function and to thrive in a gravitational environment. When astronauts spend extended periods of time in outer space, where there is no gravity, they lose muscle mass. That's because weightlessness allows many muscles in the body to go unused. Without the constant pull of gravity to work against, the muscles become very weak. Astronauts who spend months aboard a space station can barely stand when they return to Earth. Their heart muscles deteriorate, too. They also lose bone mass, so their skeletal system is weakened. The redistribution of fluids in a zero-gravity environment also results in fluid loss. In addition, the immune system does not function as effectively.

Implied Main Idea _____

_____

4. Yoga, a series of deep-breathing and stretching movements, relaxes the body by slowing heart rate and respiration, and by lowering blood pressure. Yoga also massages the lymph system. This stimulates the elimination of waste products from the body. Yoga seems to improve cardiovascular circulation in cardiac patients, too. It relieves the insomnia and mood swings of menopausal women and often reduces the pain of many people who suffer from backaches. In addition, the stretches and poses of yoga improve balance, flexibility, strength, and endurance. As a result, more and more athletes and exercise buffs are adding yoga to their fitness routines.

Implied Main Idea _____

_____

5. Most scientists would agree that animals experience fear. Many mammals, for example, exhibit the "fight or flight" response when confronted by a predator. More and more scientists are also now claiming that many mammals feel grief as well. Elephants, for instance, seem to mourn over dead or dying family members for days. Chimpanzees who lose a relative sometimes exhibit signs of depression and even refuse to eat. Scientists have also found evidence that animals might be capable of love and affection. Two whales that mate, for example, stroke each other with their flippers and swim slowly side by side. In addition, many creatures are clearly capable of feeling playful happiness. Mammals such as dolphins frolic and chase each other, especially when they're young. Scientists claim that young dolphins are not just developing adult skills. They are displaying feelings of joy in the fun they're having.

Implied Main Idea _____

_____

Test 5: Inferring Supporting Details

DIRECTIONS Read each paragraph. Then answer the questions about supporting details by filling in the blanks.

1. Next time you hear complaints about how long it takes the Food and Drug Administration to approve a new drug, you might want to remind that person about the 1950s thalidomide scandal. The drug known as thalidomide was produced by a small German pharmaceutical firm called Chemie Grünenthal, and it appeared on the market around 1957. Sold as a tranquilizer and a treatment for morning sickness, thalidomide was inadequately tested. Yet assured by the drug's makers that it was safe, doctors prescribed it and thousands of patients, most of them pregnant women, dutifully ingested it. Then in the early 1960s, hospitals in Germany, the United States, Canada, Great Britain, and the Scandinavian countries began to report the birth of babies with horrifying deformities. The infants had hands but no arms, feet but no legs. However, it wasn't until Dr. William McBride, a physician in Australia, made the connection between thalidomide and the babies' deformities that the drug was finally removed from the market. But that was in 1961. By that time, twelve thousand deformed infants had already been born. Astonishing as it might seem in light of its tragic past, thalidomide actually made a comeback in the 1990s when it was discovered that the drug might be useful in the treatment of leprosy and AIDS.

Implied Supporting Detail The author does not say what caused twelve thousand deformed infants to be born. Instead she expects readers to infer that _____

_____

_____.

2. In 1963, Martin Luther King Jr. sought to increase the support of the movement for civil rights. In May, he helped organize demonstrations for the end of segregation in Birmingham, Alabama. The protesters found the perfect enemy in Birmingham's police commissioner, Eugene "Bull" Connor, whose beefy features and snarling demeanor made him a living symbol of everything evil. Connor's police used clubs, dogs, and fire hoses to chase and arrest the demonstrators. President John F. Kennedy watched the police dogs in action on television with the rest of the country and confessed that the brutality made him sick. He later observed that "the civil rights movement should thank God for Bull Connor. He's helped it as much as Abraham Lincoln." As a result of the demonstrations, the president sent the head of the Justice Department's civil rights division to Birmingham to try to work out an arrangement that would permit desegregation of lunch counters, drinking fountains, and bathrooms. The president also made several calls to business leaders himself, and they finally agreed to his terms. (Schaller et al., *Present Tense*, p. 235.)

Implied Supporting Detail The authors never explain why President Kennedy thought Bull Connor actually helped the civil rights movement. Instead, they ex-

pect you to infer that Connor helped the movement by _____

_____

_____.

 3. During a national address focusing on civil rights, President John F. Kennedy acknowledged that the nation faced a moral crisis. He rejected the notion that the United States could be the land of the free "except for the Negroes." Reversing his earlier reluctance to request civil rights legislation, he announced that he would send Congress a major civil rights bill. The law would guarantee service to all Americans regardless of race in public accommodations— hotels, restaurants, theaters, retail stores, and similar establishments. Moreover, it would grant the federal government greater authority to pursue lawsuits against segregation in public education and increase the Justice Department's powers to protect the voting rights of racial minorities. (Schaller et al., *Present Tense*, p. 236.)

Implied Supporting Detail The authors do not specifically define the moral crisis facing the

nation. Instead they expect readers to infer that _____

_____

_____

was the cause of a moral crisis in America.

 4. On Christmas Day 1859, the ship HMS *Lightning* arrived at Melbourne, Australia, with about a dozen wild European rabbits bound for an estate in western Victoria. Within three years, the rabbits had started to spread beyond western Victoria, after a bushfire destroyed the fences enclosing one colony. From a slow start, the spread of the rabbits picked up speed during the 1870s, and by 1900 the rabbit was the most serious agricultural pest ever known in Australia. Rabbits eat grass, the same grass used by sheep and cattle, and so quickly the cry went up: "Get rid of the rabbit!" The subsequent history of control attempts in Australia is a sad tale of ecological ignorance. Millions of rabbits were poisoned and shot at great expense with absolutely no effect on their numbers. Nowhere else has the introduction of an exotic species had such an enormous impact and spotlighted the folly of such introduction experiments. (Adapted from Krebs, *The Message of Ecology*, p. 8.)

Implied Although the author does not specifically say how the rabbits got

Supporting Detail off the estate, he expects readers to infer that they _____

_____

_____ .

Test 6: Drawing Your Own Conclusions

Answer the following questions by circling the letter of the correct response.

1. Research has shown that people are more likely to help others when they're in a good mood. Psychologists have named this tendency the *good mood effect.* In one experiment conducted over the course of a year, pedestrians in Minneapolis were stopped and asked to participate in a survey. When researchers examined the responses in the light of the weather conditions, they found that people answered more questions on sunny days than on cloudy ones. In another experiment, researchers found that the more the sun was shining, the larger the tips left by restaurant customers. Yet another experiment focused on pedestrians at a shopping mall, who were asked to change a dollar. Researchers discovered that when the request occurred outside a bakery or coffee shop, where strong, pleasant odors like freshly baked chocolate chip cookies or freshly brewed French roast coffee were in the air, people were more likely to help than they were if the request was made in a place with no pleasant smells emerging from it. (Source of information: Brehm and Kassim, *Social Psychology,* pp. 367–368.)

Which conclusion follows from the passage?

a. If you're trying to raise money for your favorite charity, you would be better off stationing yourself outside a doughnut shop than in front of your neighborhood cleaners.

b. Someone who tries to raise money for charity by standing in front of the local police station in hopes of donations will never collect a dime.

c. If you want to raise money for your local basketball team, you should probably go door to door accompanied by two of the team members.

2. Several states in America are converting one lane of some of our nation's busiest highways into a toll lane. These pay-as-you-go routes allow drivers to buy their way out of traffic jams and sail past nonpaying motorists stuck in congestion. Some states are allowing private companies to build the new toll lanes in exchange for the revenue generated from them. Other states are simply designating existing lanes as toll lanes. However, many people consider this trend unfair. Several driver advocacy groups claim that tolls amount to yet another tax on people who have no choice but to drive. As AAA spokesperson Mantill Williams put it, "Our overall

philosophy is tolls are a regressive* tax on motorists." Others have dubbed the new routes "Lexus Lanes"† and criticize them as a luxury for only those who can afford to pay. Advocates of toll lanes, however, say that they are just like any other convenience that some people choose to pay for and some people don't. "It offers a model of personal choice for drivers," says John Horsley of the American Association of State Highway and Transportation Officials. "If you're willing to pay a bit more, you can get there faster." (Source of information: Fred Bayles, "Toll Lanes: A Freer Ride for a Price," *USA Today*, April 8, 2004, p. A3.)

Which conclusion follows from the passage?

a. John Horsley would probably support a transportation bill before Congress that allows states to add toll lanes with special privileges to portions of interstate highways.

b. Mantill Williams is likely to agree with those who think toll lanes are a great way of giving more flexibility and more options to state governments.

c. The author of this passage is firmly opposed to adding toll lanes to our nation's busy highways.

3. Is it ethical to keep animals in zoos? Some animal rights groups say no. They believe that animals have a right to be free and conclude, therefore, that *all* zoos are wrong because they deprive creatures of their freedom. Those in favor of zoos, however, argue that the need for species conservation outweighs the cost to individual animals. They justify the existence of zoos because of the role they play in the preservation of animal populations, particularly through captive breeding programs. Furthermore, they maintain that the alternative to zoos— letting species simply dwindle or perish altogether in the wild—is the less ethical choice. However, Dr. Michael Hutchins of the Department of Conservation and Science for the American Zoo and Aquarium Association believes that even zoos that focus on conservation may not be doing enough to justify keeping animals in captivity. According to Dr. Hutchins, "A strong commitment to individual animal welfare is equally important." Many agree with Dr. Hutchins that zoos behave ethically *only* if they work toward the dual goals of conserving species while providing high-quality care in as natural an environment as possible. (Source of information: Bridget M. Kuehn, "Is It Ethical to Keep Animals in Zoos?" *Journal of the American Veterinary Medical*

_____

*regressive: decreasing proportionately as the amount taxed increases.
†The Lexus is an expensive car; thus, the implication of the allusion is that the new routes help those rich enough to buy expensive cars.

Association, December 1, 2002, www.avma.org/onlnews/javma/dec02/ 021201d.asp.)

Which conclusion follows from the passage?

a. Dr. Michael Hutchins probably agrees that it is perfectly acceptable for traveling circuses to include animals in their acts.

b. Dr. Michael Hutchins would be likely to defend researchers who keep animals in laboratories to conduct experiments on them.

c. In all likelihood, Dr. Michael Hutchins would be willing to donate or raise funds for zoo renovation projects devoted to recreating an animal's natural habitat in the wild.

4. Controversial Dutch author and filmmaker Ayaan Hirsi Ali may have been named one of *Time* magazine's most influential people in 2005, but reactions to the story of how she came to reject Islam and advocate an end to what she calls its persecution of women have been mixed. Born in Somalia in 1969, she and her family eventually moved to Kenya, where she was raised in the religion of Islam. In 1992, according to her biography, Hirsi Ali balked at the idea of an arranged marriage to a distant cousin in Canada. To avoid the marriage, Hirsi Ali fled to the home of a female relative in the Netherlands. While living there, she earned a degree in political science and worked as a Somali-Dutch translator, often translating for battered Muslim women who sought refuge from abusive male relatives. Although she did not renounce her religion until 2002, it was at this point that Hirsi Ali's quarrels with Islam truly began. According to Hirsi Ali, the September 11, 2001, terrorist attacks on the United States led her to conclude that she could no longer believe in the God worshiped by the nineteen Muslim terrorists. Thus, in 2002, Hirsi Ali not only became an atheist, she also began to argue against what she called a "politically correct" approach to religious communities whose cultural values violated fundamental human rights along with the law. She was particularly outspoken about the role of women in the Muslim world, insisting that "the position of women is, in my view, nowhere as bad as it is in the Muslim world." While Hirsi Ali has won the admiration of many, she has her share of critics. Her challengers insist that she stereotypes all Muslim women as victims and fails to make distinctions between distortions of Islamic thought and authentic Islamic beliefs. Critics also say she persistently misrepresents her former faith, particularly in her reading of the Koran, which, they insist, does not justify the mistreatment of women as Ali claims. (Source of information: Andrew Anthony, "Taking the Fight to Islam," *The Observer,* February 4, 2007,

http://observer.guardian.co.uk/review/story/0.200525800.html;
Hirsi Ali, *The Caged Virgin*, p. 18.)

Which conclusion follows from the passage?

a. Critics are correct to claim that Hirsi Ali's view of Islam stems from her own unhappy experience, not from her knowledge of Islamic thought and practice.

b. Despite her ideas about Islam, Hirsi Ali would probably agree that *madrasahs*, schools that include education in the religion of Islam, deserve public support.

c. Hirsi Ali would probably not send a child of hers to a school that included Islamic religious training in the curriculum.

Test 7: Recognizing Implied Main Ideas in Longer Readings

DIRECTIONS Circle the letter of the statement that best expresses the implied main idea.

 1. Explaining the Growth of the Bureaucracy*

1 What accounts for the growth of bureaucracies and bureaucrats since the late 1800s? Was all this growth the result of bureaucratic incompetence and unresponsiveness? Many observers believe that the growth can be attributed directly to the expansion of the nation itself. There are a great many more of us—more than 248 million in 1990, compared with fewer than 5 million in the 1790s—and we are living closer together. Not only do the residents of cities and suburbs require many more services than did the predominantly rural dwellers of the early 1800s, but the challenges of urban and industrial life have intensified and outstripped the capacity of families or local and state governments to cope with them. Thus the American people have increasingly turned to their national government for help.

2 There is considerable evidence that the growth of bureaucracies is "of our own making." Public opinion polls indicate widespread public support for expanding federal involvement in a variety of areas. Even when public support for new programs is low, pollsters find Americans unwilling to eliminate or reduce existing programs. Furthermore, the public's expectations about the quality of service it should receive are constantly rising. The public wants government to be more responsive, responsible, and compassionate in administering public programs. Officials have reacted to these pressures by establishing new programs and maintaining and improving existing ones.

3 The federal bureaucracy has also expanded in response to sudden changes in economic, social, cultural, and political conditions. During the Great Depression and World War II, for example, the federal bureaucracy grew to meet the challenges these situations created. Washington became more and more involved in programs providing financial aid and employment to the poor. It increased its regulation of important industries and during the war imposed controls over much of the American economy. As part of the general war effort, the federal government also built

---

*bureaucracy: management of a government through bureaus or departments staffed by nonelected officials.

roads and hospitals and mobilized the entire population. When these crises ended, the public was reluctant to give up many of the federal welfare and economic programs implemented during the time of emergency. (Gitelson et al., *American Government*, p. 358.)

Implied Main Idea a. Bureaucracies are simply a fact of modern life, and there is no escaping them.

b. At least three different factors account for the growth of bureaucracies.

c. The expansion of government programs has encouraged the growth of bureaucracies and tripled the number of bureaucrats.

2. Holiday Cheer

1 The observance of public school holidays began at the end of the nineteenth century. The goal of school holidays, at that time at least, was to bring people together. Holiday celebrations in the schools—particularly Christmas—were meant to unite a nation of immigrants. But as Bob Dylan would say, "The Times They Are A-Changin'."

2 In Chicago, the principal of the Walt Disney Magnet School saw his attempt at holiday harmony backfire. This elementary school has a mix of students, including African American, Asian, Muslim, Hispanic, Yugoslavian, Romanian, and Jewish children, so the principal tried to tone down Christmas by issuing a ban on Santa Claus and any other symbols or activities associated with "a specific religious tradition." Teachers protested—one gave the principal a copy of *How the Grinch Stole Christmas*—and the head of the school board overturned the ban. With Christmas parties, decorations, and carols in full swing throughout the school, Essam Ammar, a Muslim parent, asked, "How am I going to raise my children as proud Muslims with all this going on?"

3 As passions intensify over how to celebrate the holiday season, some parents are demanding that a wide variety of other religious and ethnic holidays, including the Hindu Diwali festival, Hanukkah, and Kwanzaa, get equal time with Christmas. Others protest any diminution* of Christmas traditions, such as bans on trees and Santa Claus, in some communities. At the moment, there seems to be no resolution in sight.

---

*diminution: act of decreasing.

Implied Main Idea a. Celebrating the holiday season in public schools began as an effort to bring together people who might otherwise stay separated.

b. School is no place to celebrate holidays if those holidays cause conflict.

c. Observing the holidays in public schools has become far more complicated than it once was as different ethnic groups compete to celebrate their particular holidays.

Test 8: Inferring Implied Main Ideas in Longer Readings

DIRECTIONS Read the selection and then write the implied main idea in the blanks.

1. Improving Your Memory

1 Do you, like just about everyone else, want to improve your memory? Well, the good news is that you can. All you have to do is put the following advice into practice, and you'll see immediate results.

2 For example, remembering when Christopher Columbus discovered America is easy enough if you use visualization. You could, for example, imagine Columbus standing on the beach with his ships in the harbor in the background. Fortunately, unrealistic images work just as well or better, and you could imagine Columbus's boat having the large numerals *1492* printed on its side, or Columbus reviewing his account books after the trip and seeing in dismay that the trip cost him $1,492. You could even envisage something still more fanciful. Because 1492 sounds like the phrase "for tea, nightie two," you might imagine Columbus serving tea in his nightie to two Indians on the beach. A weird image like this is often easier to remember than a realistic one because its silliness makes it more distinct (Levin, 1985).

3 Visual imagery also works well for remembering single terms, such as unfamiliar words in a foreign language. The French word for snail, *l'escargot,* can be remembered easily if you form an image of what the word sounds like in English—"less cargo"—and picture an event related to this English equivalent, such as workers dumping snails overboard to achieve "less cargo" on a boat. The biological term *mitosis* (which refers to cell division) sounds like the phrase "my toes itch," so it is easier to remember if you picture a single cell dividing while scratching its imaginary toes.

4 Another device for memory improvement is called the method of loci, or locations. With this method, you purposely associate objects or terms with a highly familiar place or building. Suppose you have to remember the names of all the instruments in a standard symphony orchestra. Using the method of loci, choose a familiar place, such as the neighborhood in which you live, and imagine leaving one of the instruments at the doorstep of each house or business in the neighborhood. To remember the instruments, simply take an imaginary walk through the neighborhood, mentally picking up each instrument as you come to it.

5   Research on loci has found the method effective for remembering a wide variety of information (Christen and Bjork, 1976). The same loci, or locations, can work repeatedly on many sets of terms or objects without one set interfering with another. After memorizing the musical instruments in the previous example, you could still use your neighborhood to remember the names of exotic fruit, without fear of accidentally "seeing" a musical instrument by mistake. Loci can also help in recalling terms that are not physical objects, such as scientific concepts. Simply imagine the terms in some visual form, such as written on cards, or, better yet, visualize concrete objects that rhyme with each term and leave these around the mental neighborhood.

6   Imagery and visual loci work for two reasons (Pressley and McDaniel, 1988). First, they force you to organize new information, even if the organization is self-imposed. Second, they encourage you to elaborate mentally on new information. In "placing" musical instruments around the neighborhood, you have to think about what each instrument looks like and how it relates to the others in a symphony. These mental processes are essential for moving information into long-term memory. (Adapted from Seifert, *Educational Psychology*, pp. 199–201.)

Implied Main Idea   _____

_____

2. Remembrance of Things Past

1   A whiff of perfume, the top of a baby's head, freshly cut grass, a locker room, the musty odor of a basement, the floury aroma of a bakery, the smell of mothballs in the attic, and the leathery scent of a new car—each may trigger what Diane Ackerman (1990) has called "aromatic memories." Frank Schab (1990) tested this theory in a series of experiments. In one, subjects were given a list of adjectives and instructed to write an antonym, or word opposite in meaning, for each adjective. In half of the sessions, the sweet smell of chocolate was blown into the room. The next day, subjects were asked to list as many of the antonyms as they could— again, in the presence or absence of the chocolate aroma. As it turned out, the most words were recalled when the smell of chocolate was present at both the learning and the recall sessions. The reason? The smell was stored in the memory right along with the words, so it later served as a retrieval cue.

2   The retrieval of memories is influenced by factors other than smell. In an unusual study, Duncan Godden and Alan Baddeley

(1975) presented deep-sea divers with a list of words in one of two settings: fifteen feet underwater or on the beach. Then they tested the divers' recall in the same or another setting. Illustrating what is called *context-dependent memory*, the divers recalled 40 percent more words when the material was learned and retrieved in the same context. The practical implications are intriguing. For example, recall may be improved if material is retrieved in the same room in which it was initially learned (Smith, 1979).

3   Indeed, context seems to activate memory even in three-month-old infants. In a series of studies, Carolyn Rovee-Collier and her colleagues (1992) trained infants to shake an overhead mobile equipped with colorful blocks and bells by kicking a leg that was attached to the mobile by a ribbon. The infants were later more likely to recall what they learned (in other words, to kick) when tested in the same crib and looking at the same visual cues than when there were differences. Apparently, it is possible to jog one's memory by reinstating the initial context of an experience. This explains why I will often march into my secretary's office for something, go blank, forget why I was there, return in defeat to my office, look around, and ZAP!, suddenly recall what it was I needed.

4   Studies also reveal that it is often easier to recall something when our state of mind is the same at testing as it was while we were learning. If information is acquired when you are happy, sad, drunk, sober, calm, or aroused, that information is more likely to be retrieved under the same conditions (Bower, 1981; Eich, 1980; Eich et al., 1994). The one key complicating factor is that the mood we're in leads us to evoke memories that fit our current mood. When we are happy, the good times are most easy to recall; but when we feel depressed or anxious, our minds become flooded with negative events of the past (Blaney, 1986; Ucros, 1989). (Adapted from Brehm and Kassim, *Social Psychology*, p. 231.)

Implied Main Idea   _____

_____

Test 9: Taking Stock

DIRECTIONS Read each passage. Then answer the questions by filling in the blanks or circling the letter of the correct response.

1. [1]After a 1997 study published by the *New England Journal of Medicine* revealed that drivers are four times more likely to be involved in accidents while talking on cell phones, states such as New York decided to ban handheld cell phones and permit motorists to use only hands-free models. [2]Do hands-free phones solve the problem of driver distraction? [3]Over the last several years, psychologist David Strayer and his colleagues at the University of Utah have conducted several experiments to study the consequences of talking on cell phones while driving. [4]In 2001, they found that people who were talking on both handheld and hands-free cell phones while reacting to traffic signals were likely to react slower than people who were not on the phone. [5]In another study, published in 2003 in the *Journal of Experimental Psychology: Applied*, researchers placed 110 volunteers in a driver training situation that mimicked the inside of a car and was enclosed by screens that displayed realistic-looking surroundings. [6]Some of the participants talked on hands-free cell phones to other students while they simulated driving on a highway and in a city in heavy traffic. [7]These participants exhibited a slower reaction time than students who did not talk on cell phones. [8]They took longer to brake and longer to accelerate, moved their eyes less, and paid less attention to their environment. [9]They did not remember elements of their surroundings as accurately as participants without cell phones. [10]Three of the cell phone users even rear-ended a simulated car in front of them. (Sources of information: Ellen Goodman, "The $64,000 Question: Just How Dangerous Is Car-Phoning?" *Boston Globe*, July 10, 2001, p. A9; University of Utah News and Public Relations, "Cell Phone Users Drive 'Blind,'" January 27, 2003, www.utah.edu/unews/releases/03/jan/cellphone.html.)

   1. What is the implied main idea?

   _____

   _____

   2. What kind of transition opens sentence 3?

   _____

   3. How would you define the word *simulated* in sentence 6?

   _____

4. The author expects the reader to infer that New York's decision to ban handheld cell phones was

   a. pure coincidence and not related to the 1997 study mentioned in the first sentence.

   b. a result of the 1997 study mentioned in the first sentence.

   c. a plan that had been in the making long before the 1997 study mentioned in the first sentence.

5. How might David Strayer respond to claims that the New York legislation had solved the problem of cell phones being a distraction while driving?

   _____

   _____

2. [1]In the Middle Ages some time around 1347, a disastrous plague known as the Black Death swept through western Europe. [2]Estimates suggest that the plague killed close to one-third of the population by the time it passed out of Europe. [3]In France, the death rate was so high that Cardinal Clement VI had to consecrate the Rhone River so that corpses could be allowed to sink into its waters and disappear. [4]France had neither time nor room to provide a proper burial. [5]In the seventeenth century, a smallpox epidemic decimated the Native-American tribes in the New World. [6]The first major outbreak of the disease struck the Northeast Atlantic coast between 1616 and 1619, leaving the Massachusetts and Algonquin tribes reduced from 30,000 people to 300. [7]In 1918, a deadly flu epidemic roamed around the world, taking a terrifying toll wherever it appeared. [8]In a single year, it killed more Americans than died in battle in World Wars I and II, the Korean war, and the Vietnam War. [9]Although official estimates suggest that twenty million people died as a result, the true number can never be known because medical facilities were in such chaos that it was difficult to keep accurate records. (Sources of information: James Surowiecki, "The High Cost of Illness," *New Yorker*, May 12, 2003; Gina Kolata, *Flu.* New York: Farrar, Straus and Giroux, 1999; boisestate.edu/westernciv/plague; www.thefurtrapper.com.)

1. What is the implied main idea?

   _____

   _____

2. How would you define *decimated* in sentence 5?

_____

3. Sentences 5, 7, and 8 open with what kind of transition?

_____

4. To make sense out of sentence 4, readers have to infer what answer to this question: Why did France lack time and room?

_____

_____

5. In her book *Flu*, which describes the effects of the 1918 flu epidemic mentioned in the passage, author Gina Kolata uses the word "obsessed" to describe researchers determined to track down the virus that caused that flu. Based on the passage, what do you think is the motive for their obsession?

_____

_____

C H A P T E R 7

Defining the Terms *Fact* and *Opinion*

In this chapter, you will learn

- **how to tell the difference between *fact* and *opinion*.**

- **how to recognize statements that mix opinion with fact.**

- **how to distinguish between *informed* and *uninformed* opinions.**

- **how to recognize *irrelevant facts* and *reasons*.**

- **how textbooks often include opinions as well as facts.**

The goal of this chapter is to ensure that you fully understand the terms *fact* and *opinion*. After you know exactly what the two terms mean, you'll be in a good position to evaluate how well or how poorly writers use facts to buttress, or support, opinions they want readers to share.

Facts Versus Opinions

Statements of **fact** provide information about people, places, events, and ideas that can be **verified**, or checked, for accuracy. Facts do not reveal the author's personal perspective, or point of view. The following are all statements of fact:

- American Samoa consists of seven islands in the South Pacific.
- The Treaty of Versailles ended World War I.
- For his work on atomic structure, scientist Niels Bohr was awarded the 1922 Nobel Prize in physics.
- John Wilkes Booth assassinated Abraham Lincoln on April 14, 1865.
- In February 1903 more than 1,200 Mexican and Japanese farm workers organized the Japanese-Mexican Labor Association.

These facts can be checked in encyclopedias or in other reference books in libraries anywhere in the world, and they will always be the same. Facts do not vary with place or person. Whether you live in Dayton, Ohio, or Fairbanks, Alaska, if you look up Martin Luther King Jr.'s date of birth, it will always be the same: January 15, 1929.

Troubling Facts

Because facts can be checked, they are generally not subject to question or argument. However, statements of fact can be questioned if they are not widely known. For example, it's a fact that Muhammad, the Arab prophet who founded Islam, preached several sermons that focused on the rights of women. But since that fact is not widely known, it's likely to be questioned.

Then, too, facts can and do change over time as new discoveries come to light or methods of research improve. This is especially true in fields like science, history, and medicine, where information is considered factual only insofar as it is based on existing knowledge. As scientists and historians gain more precise knowledge of the world, the facts on which they base their theories sometimes undergo dramatic change.

For example, it was once considered a fact that the Sun revolved around the Earth. But in the sixteenth century, a Polish astronomer named Nicolaus Copernicus used the laws of planetary motion to challenge that "fact." Copernicus proved that, *in fact*, the Earth revolves around the Sun.

Generally, however, facts are fixed pieces of information. They often consist of dates, names, and numbers that cannot be affected by the writer's background or training. Facts can be verified, or checked, and *proved* accurate or inaccurate, true or false, to the satisfaction of most people. Thus, unless they are newly discovered, facts are not often the subject of disagreement.

Statements of Fact

- can be checked for accuracy or correctness.
- can be proven true or false.
- are not affected by the writer's background or training
- rely heavily on names, dates, and numbers.
- are not usually the subject of disagreement unless they are not widely known.

Calling It a Fact Doesn't Necessarily Make It One

Because people tend to accept facts without giving them too much thought, some writers and speakers preface opinions with the phrase "the fact is," as in the following sentence: "*The fact is* that Richard Nixon, had he not resigned, would have been impeached." Despite the opening phrase, this statement really is an opinion, and not everyone would agree with it. In effect, what the author tries to do is bully readers into agreeing that the statement is an indisputable, or unquestionable, fact when it's anything but. Similarly, beware of expressions like "it's a well known fact that . . . ," "in point of fact," and "without a doubt." Writers sometimes use this kind of confident language to discourage readers from evaluating opinions disguised as facts.

Finding Facts on the World Wide Web

If you are using a search engine like Google to locate facts via the World Wide Web, always double-check the results of your search. This advice is doubly important if the website addresses you explore don't end in the letters *edu*, *gov*, or *org*, endings that indicate large (and generally reliable) institutions.

One of the wonderful things about the Internet is that it allows ordinary people to share their knowledge or expertise with others. However, many of these amateur experts, while knowledgeable, don't necessarily have a team of editors to verify their information. Thus they unwittingly can and occasionally do misinform.

One recent Web search, performed by the author of this text, revealed—to the author's amazement—that Frances Hodgson Burnett, the creator of a famous children's book, *The Secret Garden*, had an amazingly long life. According to one website, Burnett was born in 1849 and died in 1974, making her 125 years old at the time of death. Now this "fact" is impressive. Unfortunately, it's also incorrect. Burnett was born in 1849, but she actually died in 1924, a fact confirmed by a quick search of *several sites* related to Burnett's life and work. Someone managing the website had missed the error. Where the Web is concerned, this kind of error is not all that unusual. Books, particularly reference books, have usually been double-checked by teams of people. Websites, however, are sometimes the product of one or two overworked souls, who can and sometimes do make mistakes. Unfortunately, they don't have a copyeditor and proofreader waiting in the wings to spot the errors. Thus the error remains until some sharp-eyed researcher or reader spots it and notifies the appropriate website manager.

As you know from Chapter 1, the World Wide Web is a wonderful source for researching all kinds of things, including factual information. But you should always confirm the accuracy of your facts by checking to see if two or more websites agree on the same facts.

Opinions

Statements of **opinion** reflect the writer's perspective on the subject being discussed. Shaped by an author's personal experience, training, and background, opinions about the same subject can vary from person to person, group to group, and place to place. For an illustration, ask a group of teenagers how they feel about high school dress codes. Then ask their parents. Don't be surprised if you uncover a marked difference of opinion.

Unlike facts, opinions cannot be verified by using outside sources. They are too **subjective**—too personal—to be checked in reference books or historical records. The following are all statements of opinion:

- Jennifer Lopez is an artist of extraordinary talent.
- Thanks to cellist Yo-Yo Ma, the glorious music of Argentinian Astor Piazzolla is now more widely known.
- Pet owners deserve legal punishment if their animals do someone harm.
- This country needs stricter gun-control laws.
- Young women under the age of thirty are not generally inclined to call themselves feminists.

Because opinions are so heavily influenced by one's training, knowledge, and experience, it's impossible to talk about them as accurate or inaccurate, right or wrong. For example, if you own a dog and firmly believe that dogs make more desirable pets than cats, no cat lover can *prove* you wrong because you're expressing an opinion, not stating a fact.

Evaluating Opinions

Saying that everyone has the right to an opinion doesn't mean that opinions can't be judged or evaluated. They most certainly can. Critical readers want and need to distinguish between informed and uninformed opinions. **Informed opinions** are well argued. They are backed by reasons and/or evidence. **Uninformed opinions**, in contrast, are unsupported by evidence or backed by inappropriate reasons. Once you can distinguish between the two, you'll be surprised at how often writers give their opinions without bothering to support them. So, yes, the old saying is true: Everyone has the right to an opinion. But it's also true that every opinion does not deserve the same consideration or respect. (For more on informed and uninformed opinions, see pages 413–414.)

Opinions on the Web

As you know from pages 405–406, you should double-check any facts you locate on the Web. For different reasons, the same is true for opinions. After all, anyone can put an opinion on the Web. Just think of the many *Web logs*, or *blogs*, personal websites where people express their opinions on any range of topics from politics to movies.

Opinions on the Web aren't necessarily evaluated by anyone except the person holding them. This means that those opinions don't have to be informed by logic or research. On the Web, you will find people willing to express an opinion without even pretending to cite evidence or outline their logic. They feel they don't have to. Convinced of their own rightness, they often don't even acknowledge that someone else might hold a different opinion.

The following chapters discuss more fully how to evaluate persuasive writing that puts forth an opinion. The advice in those chapters applies as much or more to the Web as it does to books, magazines, and newspapers. Any opinion on the Web needs to be very carefully evaluated before you decide to make it your own.

Statements of Opinion

- can be evaluated but cannot be verified for accuracy or correctness.

- cannot be proven true or false, right or wrong (although they can be termed ethical or unethical, moral or immoral).

- are shaped by the writer's knowledge, background, or training.

- often communicate value judgments, indicating that the author thinks something is right or wrong, good or bad.

In addition to the characteristics listed in the preceding box, the language a writer uses is another important clue to the presence of opinions.

The Language of Opinions

- Statements of opinion often include verbs or adverbs such as *suggests, appears, seems, might, could* or *should be, possibly, probably, likely, apparently, presumably, arguably, allegedly, supposedly.*

- Statements of opinion often make comparisons using words such as *more, most, better, best, greatest, finest.*

- Statements of opinion sometimes include words that make value judgments: *beautiful, perfect, significant, interesting, critical, key,* and *crucial.*

- Opinions are frequently prefaced, or introduced, with phrases such as *one interpretation of, another possibility is, this study suggests, in all likelihood, it would seem, arguably, supposedly.*

Check Your Understanding

What's the essential difference between facts and opinions?

_____

_____

_____

EXERCISE 1   **DIRECTIONS** Label each statement *F* for fact or *O* for opinion.

_____ **1.** All this uproar about animal rights is nonsense. Animals don't have rights.

_____ **2.** In 1909, Ernest Rutherford showed that atoms were mostly space.

_____ **3.** When it was under Spanish control, the city of Los Angeles was called *El Pueblo de Nuestra Señora la Reina de los Angeles del Río de Porciúncula*, which means "The Town of Our Lady the Queen of the Angels by the Little Portion River."[†]

_____ **4.** For a brief time, 2004 presidential candidate Howard Dean of Vermont seemed to breathe new life into the Democratic party.

_____ **5.** Martin Luther King Jr.'s "Letter from Birmingham Jail" was published in 1963 by the American Friends Service Committee, a Quaker organization.

_____ **6.** Teenagers today are obsessed with money and success. They don't care about making the world a better place.

_____ **7.** The atomic weight of carbon is closer to 12 than to 14.

_____ **8.** Although the singer Selena has been given the credit, it was the band La Mafia that made *tejano* music popular in the United States.

_____ **9.** Dionysus was the Greek god of wine and fertile crops.

_____ **10.** Queen Victoria of England died on January 22, 1901; at her death, she had been queen for almost sixty-four years.

Blending Fact and Opinion

Reading critically would probably be a good deal easier if authors kept statements of fact and opinion neatly divided. But they don't. Whether consciously or unconsciously, writers of all kinds—and textbook

---

[†]Bill Bryson, *Made in America*, New York: Morrow, 1994, p. 106.

authors are no exception—can't always avoid coloring a fact with an opinion. Your job as a critical reader is to make sure you recognize when and where fact and opinion blend together. Then you won't mistakenly accept as fact an opinion you haven't consciously thought through or considered. Take, for example, the following sentence:

> At least thirty-eight states have sensibly decided to give terminally ill patients the right to refuse medical treatment.

At a quick glance, this sentence might appear to be a statement of fact. After all, it's easy enough to verify how many states have given terminally ill patients the right to reject medical treatment. But think again about the author's use of the word *sensibly*. This is a word with positive **connotations**, or associations. Use it to describe someone, and chances are he or she would be pleased. What the author has done in the above sentence is to include her opinion of the action taken by those thirty-eight states. That makes the statement a blend of both fact and opinion.

Now what about the next sentence? How would you label it—fact, opinion, or a blend of both?

> In 1944, Russian troops entered eastern Czechoslovakia, and the nightmare of life under Communist rule began.

The first part of this sentence is a fairly obvious statement of fact. Any encyclopedia can tell you when Russian troops entered Czechoslovakia. But what about the phrase *nightmare of life under Communist rule?* Do you detect any trace of opinion in those words? If you said yes, you're well on your way to being a critical reader. People who took part in or supported the Communist regime in Czechoslovakia would probably not agree that life under Communist rule was a nightmare. What we have here, then, is another example of a statement blending fact and opinion.

 ## Connotative Language Is a Clue

To discover when writers have mixed a pinch of opinion in with their facts, you'll need to be alert to **charged**, or **connotative**, **language**—language that carries with it strong positive or negative associations. Writers dealing in pure fact tend to rely heavily on **denotative language**. They use words that suggest little more than their **denotation**, or dictionary definitions. Words like *table, chair,* and *rock,* for example, carry little or no emotional impact. Thus they are considered far more denotative than connotative.

> ### Check Your Understanding
>
> Explain how an author can mix an opinion in with a fact.
>
> _____
>
> _____
>
> _____

Changing the Connotation with the Context

Change the **context**, or setting, of a word, and it can become more connotative than denotative. For example, the word *stories* in the following sentence evokes little more than its denotation.

> *Aesop's Fables* is a collection of *stories* written by a Greek story-teller.

However, look what happens when the context of the word *stories* changes:

> In an effort to deny Jean a promotion, a jealous coworker spread *stories* about her character.

With this change in context, the word *stories* no longer refers to "an account of events"; instead, it becomes a synonym for *lies* and takes on a negative connotation. This example illustrates a key point about labeling language connotative or denotative: *Context is crucial.* Don't assume that a word that is denotative in one sentence is always lacking an emotional charge. A word can be connotative or denotative, depending on the setting in which it appears.

EXERCISE 2 **DIRECTIONS** Read each sentence and look carefully at the italicized word or words. Then label each statement *F* for fact, *O* for opinion, or *B* for a blend of both.

F **EXAMPLE** *Twentieth-century author* Gertrude Stein spent most of her life in France.

EXPLANATION The phrase *twentieth-century author* does not carry with it any positive or negative associations. It simply identifies the time in which Stein lived. The amount of time Stein actually spent in France can also be verified.

_____ **1.** Displaying his usual blend of *stamina, strength,* and *determination,* Lance Armstrong won his seventh consecutive Tour de France bicycle race in 2005.

_____ **2.** "Zulu" is a *general name* for some 2.5 million Bantu-speaking peoples who live in South Africa.

_____ **3.** The Amazon River is the *second longest river* after the Nile.

_____ **4.** Nuclear weapons are the *major plague of this century.*

_____ **5.** In the nineteenth century, Marshal James "Wild Bill" Hickok was *fearless* in his pursuit of outlaws.

_____ **6.** *Famed revolutionary hero* Emiliano Zapata was *beloved* by the poor of Mexico.

_____ **7.** Gospel music is the kind of *intense joyful music* that *makes the spirit sing.*

_____ **8.** Francisco Goya was a Spanish painter of the *late eighteenth and early nineteenth centuries.*

_____ **9.** John James Audubon was a nineteenth-century *painter and naturalist.**

_____ **10.** John D. Rockefeller, founder of the Standard Oil Company, was famous for his charity work, but he was also known as a *robber baron* whose business methods were brutally *ruthless.*

EXERCISE 3   **DIRECTIONS** Some of the following statements are purely factual. Others blend fact and opinion. Label the statements that are pure fact with an *F*. Label the statements that blend fact and opinion with a *B*. For those sentences you mark with a *B*, underline the word or words that led you to your conclusion.

B   **EXAMPLE** Singer Ednita Nazario's <u>splendid</u> album "Corazón" was produced by Dolores del Infante, an alias for Latin singer Robi Rosa.

EXPLANATION In this statement, the author provides factual information about the album, but the word "splendid" announces the author's opinion of the music.

_____ **1.** According to the Television Advertising Bureau, an extraordinary 98.2 percent of all American households have a television set.

_____ **2.** Psychiatrist Bruno Bettelheim spent decades studying fairy tales and their effect on children.

---

*naturalist: person who studies nature.

_____ **3.** An astounding number of people have tattoos covering 98 percent of their body.

_____ **4.** Amazingly, Diane Nash was only twenty-two years old when she led the campaign to desegregate the lunch counters in Nashville, Tennessee.

_____ **5.** Jerry Garcia, the long-time lead singer for the Grateful Dead, died on August 9, 1995.

_____ **6.** Juan Rodríguez Cabrillo explored the coast of California in 1542.

_____ **7.** At the end of World War I, victorious Britain and France greedily divided up the Turkish Empire.

_____ **8.** Highly acclaimed for her book about the Vietnam war, *Fire in the Lake*, writer Frances FitzGerald returned to the subject of Vietnam in *Vietnam: Spirits of the Earth*, published in 2002.

_____ **9.** After World War II, Great Britain turned Palestine over to the United Nations, which in November 1947 voted to create the State of Israel.

_____ **10.** In 1908, the phenomenal Jack Johnson became the first African American to win the world heavyweight championship.

▰▰◖ **Informed Versus Uninformed Opinions**

While everybody has a right to an opinion, it doesn't follow that every opinion deserves the same degree of attention or respect. Imagine, for example, that a friend saw you taking an aspirin for a headache and told you that chewing a clove of garlic was a far better remedy. When you asked why, he shrugged and said: "I don't know. I heard it someplace." Given this lack of explanation, argument, or evidence, it's unlikely that you would start chewing garlic cloves to cure a headache. Uninformed opinions—opinions lacking sufficient reasons or evidence—usually do fail to persuade.

More likely to convince are informed opinions backed by logic or evidence. For an example, look at this paragraph, which opens by expressing an opinion about the Internet's darker side.

Although the Internet provides us with a convenient way to conduct research and to shop, it also has a darker side. Every day, hundreds of people report that they are victims of online stalking. In 2000, police arrested John Edward Robinson, the first Internet serial killer, who murdered at least five women he met and corresponded with online. In 1999, the FBI investigated 1,500 online child solicitation* cases, a number more than double that of the previous year. Criminals are also using the Internet to steal credit card numbers, thereby costing cardholders and issuers hundreds of millions of dollars per year. Still other criminals are using the Internet for adoption fraud. For example, Internet adoption broker Tina Johnson caused much heartache and created an international dispute in 2001 when she took money from two couples in two different countries for the adoption of the same infant twin girls. More recent Internet crimes have involved the distribution of illegal drugs such as anabolic steroids. In September 2007, the FBI made a number of arrests involving men distributing steroids through MySpace.com profiles. (Source of information: www .cybercrime.gov/porterindict.htm.)

In this example, the author opens with an opinion—that the Internet, whatever its advantages, also has a "darker side." Aware, however, that not everyone might agree, she adds a significant number of facts and reasons designed to make her opinion convincing. Among other things, we learn that on a daily basis hundreds of people report they are the victims of online stalkers. We also hear about an Internet serial killer and about criminals' use of the Internet to steal credit cards and market illegal drugs. All these supporting details are factual. One way or another, they can be verified. By the end of the passage, it's clear that we are dealing with an informed opinion, one worthy of serious consideration.

Checking for Relevance

In judging or evaluating opinions, critical readers are careful to check for **relevance**. They check to be sure that facts or reasons cited in support of an opinion are relevant, or clearly connected, to the opinion expressed. Consider, for example, the following passage. Would you say the facts are relevant?

The Italian government takes excellent care of Italy's mothers. Pregnant women in Italy are guaranteed paid leaves, combined with free medical care. According to a 1971 law, pregnant women must be allowed to stay at home during the last two months of pregnancy, and new mothers can stay at home for the first three months following their babies' birth. During this five-month period, the government guarantees women who worked before their pregnancy 80 percent of their former salaries.

---

*solicitation: approaching someone for sexual purposes.

Here the author claims that the Italian government takes excellent care of mothers. Thus the facts listed need to illustrate that "excellent care," and indeed they do. The facts describe the financial and medical aid offered to mothers by the Italian government. They are all relevant to the author's claim because they certainly suggest that the government's benefits make life easier for mothers.

Relevant and Irrelevant Facts

Identifying the facts an author uses to support an opinion is only the first step. The next step is to see how well the facts connect or relate to the opinion expressed. Now let's take a look at another paragraph. Are these facts also relevant?

> Health care workers must all be tested for the virus that causes AIDS. To date, more than 100,000 people have died from AIDS-related illnesses. In addition, current figures from the national Centers for Disease Control and Prevention show that thousands more are already infected with HIV, the virus that causes AIDS, and will probably develop full-blown AIDS.

To make her opinion about AIDS testing convincing, the author needs factual statements that support a cause and effect connection between infected health care workers and the spread of the virus that causes AIDS. Such facts would be relevant and would help justify her opinion.

But those are not the kind of facts the author supplies. Instead, she offers two facts proving that AIDS is a serious epidemic. Unfortunately, these facts are not especially relevant to her opinion about testing of health care workers. Critical readers would not be convinced.

Check Your Understanding
Explain the difference between relevant and irrelevant facts.
_____
_____
_____

Relevant and Irrelevant Reasons

As you undoubtedly realize, it's not just facts that have to be relevant to the opinion expressed. The reasons offered in support also have to be relevant. For instance, how would you rate the reasons in the following paragraph? Are they all relevant?

> In 2007, when radio personality Don Imus made cruel and stupid racist jokes at the expense of the Rutgers women's basketball team, he was fired, despite his making an apology. While no sane person questions that Imus should have been penalized in some way for his despicable comments, his termination by MSNBC was a mistake. As Imus himself pointed out, he is a good person, who has donated large sums of money to organizations for disabled children. He has also made cruel and racist jokes before without being penalized in any way. What made this time any different? What's shocking about Imus's fall from grace is that none of the famous politicians who have been on his show over the years stood up for him and protested his dismissal. People like John Kerry and Lowell Weicker were noticeably silent on the subject of Imus's comments and their drastic consequences, which says a lot about the content of their character.[†]

Actually, none of the reasons given here is especially relevant to the opinion expressed: MSNBC made a mistake in terminating Don Imus for his racist comments. The first reason offered in support of this position is that Imus is a good person, who has shown his goodness by giving money to a good cause. That Imus has given large sums of money to good causes is true, but that fact doesn't come close to explaining why firing Imus is a mistake. The author may mean that it's a mistake to fire a person who is decent at heart, which is an attractive idea. It would be nice if bad things didn't happen to decent people. Still, that logic, appealing or not, doesn't address the issue of why firing Imus for his comments was a "mistake" on MSNBC's part.

The next reason offered also does not address the stated opinion. In this case, the author tells us that Imus has said things like this before and gotten away with it. Once again, the reason isn't related to the issue. It does not address MSNBC's alleged mistake. After all, maybe MSNBC fired him because these latest comments suggested Imus would never learn, and managers gave up on him.

The last reason—Imus has interviewed famous politicians over the years and none of them stood by him—is completely off the mark. Who Imus interviewed in the past tells us nothing about why firing him was an error, and that's what the reasons in the passage need to do to be relevant.

[†]Under new management, Imus returned to radio in December of 2007.

Compare now the following paragraph to the previous one:

In 2007, when radio personality Don Imus made cruel and stupid racist jokes at the expense of the Rutgers women's basketball team, he was fired, despite his making an apology. While no sane person questions that Imus should have been penalized in some way for his despicable comments, his termination by MSNBC was a mistake. When MSNBC fired Don Imus, they cut off any chance for a discussion this country needs to have about a central question: How do we respect free speech and at the same time discourage people from thinking that racist, ethnic, and sexist jokes are amusing? Censoring cruel and disrespectful jokes or wisecracks doesn't make the feelings that generate them go away, and it's those feelings that we need to talk about. It would have been a valuable lesson for Imus's fans if, after making his despicable comments, no one of any reputation ever booked his show again. The lesson then would have been clear: People who make comments like these rightfully lose the respect and support of their fellow citizens, who are ashamed and disgusted by such offensive speech and the prejudiced attitude it suggests. In the end, Imus would have been fired by the low ratings he so justly deserves. Thanks to MSNBC, Imus is not a pathetic loser. In the eyes of some of his fans, he's a martyr to freedom of speech.

Although you still might be shaking your head at the very idea that firing Don Imus was a mistake, you should also recognize that the reasons given here are relevant to the claim that firing him was a mistake. The logic in this passage goes something like this: Firing Don Imus was a mistake because (1) it cut off a discussion about free speech that the country needs to have; (2) it eliminated the possibility that celebrities who otherwise might have appeared on Imus's show could have taken a stand and publicly showed what they now thought of him; and (3) it made Imus a martyr when, over time, he might have been shown up as a biased, racist fool. All of these reasons go back to the question raised by the opinion expressed: Why was it a mistake to fire Imus? That makes them relevant whereas any reason that doesn't address that issue is irrelevant.

Check Your Understanding

Write a passage in which you support the firing of Imus (if you didn't think it was the right thing to do, pretend that you agree). Be prepared to explain in class why your facts and reasons are related.

EXERCISE 4 | DIRECTIONS | Read each passage. Then write *R* or *I* in the blank at the end. *R* indicates that all the facts and reasons are relevant. *I* indicates that you spotted one or more irrelevant facts or reasons.

1. Every American should seriously consider buying one of the new hybrid gasoline-electric cars. Thousands of people have already bought a Honda Insight or a Toyota Prius, both of which cost just over $20,000. The demand for these cars, which combine a small gasoline engine with an electric motor, already exceeds production. Within the next two years, various auto manufacturers plan to introduce a hybrid sport utility vehicle, a hybrid minivan, and a hybrid truck. It's clear that hybrid vehicles are a growing trend, and one day in the near future, there should be one in every American garage. Fortunately, there are signs that hybrid autos are catching on and becoming trendy among celebrities. Anxious to imitate their idols, ordinary Americans will probably follow suit.

———

2. The career of legendary queen of salsa Celia Cruz (1924–2003) was both long and influential. During her half-century career, Cruz recorded more than seventy albums and traveled all over the world, entertaining four generations of fans with her extraordinary voice and flamboyant performances. More than anything else, she helped define salsa, an Afro-Cuban musical style characterized by Latin rhythms. Cruz also received numerous awards and honors— including the prestigious National Medal of Arts, a Grammy Award, and an honorary doctorate degree from Yale University—all in recognition of her contributions. Perhaps most important, Cruz is credited with breaking down racial and cultural barriers by winning a mainstream audience over to Latin music. Twenty of her albums went gold, selling more than 500,000 copies each. Because her music appeals to a wide range of people and because she took such pride and joy in her Cuban heritage, she served as a passionate ambassador of Hispanic culture. Proud of her accomplishments, Cruz always credited them to her father, saying, "In a sense, I have fulfilled my father's wish to be a teacher as through my music, I teach generations of people about my culture."

———

3. Although the so-called Mozart effect has been widely accepted by many educators, parents, legislators, and music marketers, new evidence indicates that it may not exist. In 1993, researchers at the University of Wisconsin claimed that college students who lis-

tened to ten minutes of a Mozart sonata prior to taking a spatial-reasoning test significantly improved their ability to perform tasks such as cutting and folding paper. This study gave birth to the belief that listening to Mozart's music helps increase intelligence. However, researchers have not been able to duplicate the results of this first experiment. As a matter of fact, a Harvard University graduate analyzed the conclusions of sixteen similar studies and found no scientific proof that music increased IQ or improved academic performance. Researchers at Appalachian State University and two Canadian universities have come to the same conclusion.

_____

4. When the threat of bioterrorism became very real in the fall of 2001, some companies began to market home-testing kits for the detection of substances tainted by anthrax, a deadly respiratory disease spread by bacteria. Costing from twenty to twenty-five dollars, the kits were available primarily over the Internet. Alarmed by the public's positive response to the kits, members of several different consumer groups issued warnings against their purchase, and for good reason. Testing for anthrax should not be done by individuals. Even when the government tested buildings for the presence of anthrax, the results of those tests were not always accurate. In the case of a test performed at one site, for example, the results were initially negative. But later tests showed that there were actually anthrax spores present. The government has the capability to test and retest, using a variety of different and more refined methods, to double- and even triple-check for accuracy. Average homeowners, however, do not have such resources at their disposal. Ordinary people are likely to perform the test and take the results as accurate. Yet there is always the possibility of a false positive that indicates anthrax is present when it isn't; or, even worse, a false negative, suggesting the house is safe from disease when it's not. Performing the same test two or three different times is probably not the solution either. Often what's needed is a more sophisticated screening device, precisely the kind available in laboratories but not available to the ordinary consumer.

_____

5. Furious at acts of violence perpetrated by some animal rights activists, critics have bitterly criticized the leading philosopher of the animal rights movement, Peter Singer. Yet linking Singer to acts of violence is a mistake for a number of reasons. In a 2006 BBC documentary, Singer noticeably softens his position on the use of animals in research. The documentary, *Monkeys, Rats and Me*, shows Singer in a conversation with Tipu Aziz, a scientist conducting experiments on monkeys in order to find a cure for Parkinson's disease. Aziz implicitly challenges Singer's position against using animals for research by telling the philosopher that the experiment has used only one hundred monkeys; yet it has led to positive treatment for 40,000 patients. Singer does not mount any protest in reply. Instead, he maintains that he has never said "no animal research could be justified." When questioned later about his shift in position, Singer insists there was no shift: "Since I judge actions by their consequences, I have never said that no experiment on an animal can ever be justified." This is a distinctly utilitarian* position, which rules out the use of violence in pursuit of a goal.

 # Fact and Opinion in Textbooks

Many students assume that textbook writers restrict themselves to facts and avoid presenting opinions. Although that may be true for some science texts, it's not true for textbooks in general, particularly in the areas of psychology, history, and government. Look, for example, at the following passage. Do you detect the presence of an opinion?

 Presidents are not just celebrities, they are the American version of royalty. Lacking a royal family, Americans look to the president to symbolize the uniqueness of their government. (Gitelson et al., *American Government*, p. 311.)

If you said the entire passage was an opinion, you'd be right. There's no way to verify how *all* Americans feel about the role of the president. And a good many may have no interest in royalty, so why would they look for a substitute?

As the excerpt illustrates, textbooks do, indeed, offer opinions. However, that's not a failing as long as the authors offer support for the opinions expressed in their writing.

Here, for example, is another textbook excerpt. The authors open with an opinion about the American military's attempt to manage news during the Gulf War. Note, however, that the opinion is not left unsupported. On the contrary, a specific example follows right on its heels.

---

*utilitarian: related to the idea that actions can be labeled good or bad, depending on the number of people (or creatures) who benefit.

Opinion   Part of the strategy [during the first Gulf War] was to "spin" the news so that U.S. successes were emphasized and losses minimized.

Example
offered as
support   When announcing that eleven marines had been killed in action, for example, the military first showed twenty minutes of footage on Iraqi bridges and buildings being blown up, and the American deaths were treated virtually as an afterthought. The strategy, which worked, was to force nightly news programs to divide their attention between the bad news—eleven killed at the outset of a potentially difficult ground war—and the good news—visually spectacular footage of a truck traveling across a bridge seconds before the bridge blew up. (Johnson et al., *American Government*, p. 354.)

The two excerpts on these pages should make it clear that opinions are not limited to the editorial pages of newspapers. They also turn up in textbooks, which means you need to be alert to the ways in which an author can mix a personal point of view in with what seem to be pure facts.

◼ **EXERCISE 5**   **DIRECTIONS** Read each textbook passage. Fill in the blank at the end with an *F* to indicate that the passage is purely factual or a *B* to indicate that opinions are blended in with the facts.

1. While well over 80 percent of the people vote in many European elections, only about half of the people vote in American presidential elections (and a much smaller percentage vote in congressional elections). Many observers blame this low turnout on voter apathy* and urge the government and private groups to mount campaigns to get out the vote.

But . . . voting is only one way of participating in politics. It is important (we could hardly call ourselves a democracy if nobody voted), but it is not all-important. Joining civic associations, supporting social movements, writing to legislators, fighting city hall—all of these and other activities are ways of participating in politics. It is possible that, by these measures, Americans participate in politics *more* than most Europeans—or anybody else for that matter. Moreover, it is possible that low rates of registration indicate that people are reasonably well satisfied with how the country is governed. If 100 percent of all adult Americans registered and voted, . . . it could mean that people are deeply upset about how things are run. (Wilson and Dilulio, *American Government*, pp. 145–146.)

_____

_____
*apathy: lack of interest or feeling.

2. Methaqualone was first synthesized in 1951 in India, where it was introduced as an antimalarial drug but found to be ineffective. At the same time, its sedating effects resulted in its introduction in Great Britain as a safe, nonbarbiturate sleeping pill. The substance subsequently found its way into street abuse; a similar sequence of events occurred in Germany and Japan. In 1965, methaqualone was introduced into the United States as the prescription drugs Sopors and Quaalude. It was not listed as a scheduled (controlled) drug. By the early 1970s, "ludes" and "sopors" were part of the drug culture. Physicians overprescribed the drug for anxiety and insomnia, believing that it was safer than barbiturates. Thus the supplies for street sales came primarily from legitimate sources. (Adapted from Abadinksy, *Organized Crime*, p. 383.)

_____

3. Author and pastor Charles Swindoll is credited with saying, "The longer I live, the more I realize the impact of attitude on life." Swindoll is convinced that attitude is more important than appearance, giftedness, or skill. For example, people who go through life with a positive mental attitude see daily obstacles as opportunities rather than roadblocks and are therefore more likely to achieve their personal and professional goals. People who filter daily experiences through a negative attitude tend to focus on what is going wrong and find it difficult to achieve contentment or satisfaction in any aspect of their lives. It makes no difference how attractive, intelligent, or skilled they are; their attitude holds them back. (Reece and Brandt, *Effective Human Relations in Organizations*, p. 149.)

_____

4. Filipinos began settling in the Yakima Valley around 1918–1920. The majority of those who settled there became agricultural laborers. By the late 1920s, there were many who worked on truck farms, in orchards, and in packinghouses. Some leased plots for independent farming. . . . If Filipinos were going to settle in the Yakima Valley, they had to secure work within agriculture; Yakima was a single-economy region.

By 1927 Filipinos had engendered the resentment of many whites who viewed them as competitive sources of labor. So deep was the anti-Filipino animosity that mob attacks took place the same year. Filipinos were attacked wherever vigilante groups encountered them. Some Filipinos were even assaulted in their homes, while others were forcibly rounded up and placed on outbound trains. (Chan et al., *Peoples of Color in the American West*, p. 243.)

_____

Allusion Alert

On page 409, you learned that Dionysus was the Greek god of wine and fertile crops. But there's something else you need to know about Dionysus. When the Greeks worshiped him at festivals celebrating the return of spring, rituals performed in his honor were often marked by drunken displays of sexually uninhibited behavior. Thus, allusions to Dionysus suggest behavior that is wild, uninhibited, and sexually provocative; for example, "Every era seems to get its own particular stereotype; if the fifties were considered staid* and repressed, the sixties were supposedly given over to Dionysian revels, while the seventies were said to be ruled by disco." In this case, the reference to Dionysus suggests the sixties were a time when people threw off their inhibitions, as opposed to the fifties when people were allegedly bound by convention.*

Now that you know what allusions to Dionysus suggest, how would you paraphrase the following sentence: "In the eyes of most parents, it's other people's children—never their own—who attend frat parties that are indistinguishable from the Greek revels of Dionysus."

Paraphrase _____

_____

---

*staid: dull.
*convention: tradition, social rules.

■ DIGGING DEEPER

LOOKING AHEAD If it surprised you to discover that textbooks are richer in opinions than you once thought, you may be equally surprised to learn that some textbooks are subjected to censorship by competing groups, each of whom believes that certain images, words, or ideas must be eliminated from all reading materials lest they do significant harm to the students exposed to them.

POLICING THE LANGUAGE

1 For her 2003 book, *The Language Police: How Pressure Groups Restrict What Students Learn*, writer and educational consultant Diane Ravitch created what she called "A Glossary of Banned Words" and "Stereotyped Images to Avoid." A little more than thirty pages, the list actually would have been a good deal longer had Ravitch been able to obtain bias guidelines from every publisher, state testing agency, and professional association. But she was not. Although such guidelines are widely used by the publishers of elementary and high school textbooks and tests, they are a closely guarded secret because, as the author points out, the word *censorship* has negative connotations. No one wants to admit engaging in it. Thus most of the written guidelines Ravitch was able to gather have euphemistic titles like "Principles for Bias, Sensitivity, and Language Simplification." Such titles imply—as they were meant to—that nothing is being censored. Instead, the publisher or professional association involved is simply being "sensitive" to the harm that might be inflicted if kids were allowed to encounter such words or images in textbooks. In reality, though, such groups are afraid of coming under attack from religious groups, feminists, advocates for the disabled, educational reformers, and multiculturalists among others, who have managed to exert a powerful influence on elementary and high school publishing.

2 What are some of these distressing words that made the banned list? Anyone imagining a host of obscenities and racial epithets obviously hasn't the faintest idea of how easily ordinary— and seemingly unobjectionable—language can damage youthful minds. The apparently harmless word *bookworm*, for example, made Ravitch's list. It's objectionable because it could discourage students from becoming avid readers. The terms *boyish figure* and *boys' night out* are also banned for being sexist. *Yacht* and *polo*

need to be eliminated because they are elitist and refer to activities most people aren't rich enough to pursue. Like words, some topics breed trouble, and the following all appear on Ravitch's list of likely suspects: *evolution, bodily functions, situation ethics, suicide, divorce,* and *crimes that have gone unpunished.*

3   In California, the decades-old children's story "The Little Engine That Could" was rejected because the little engine was openly identified as male and thus could be considered a symbol of sexism. On a standardized test, the New York State Education Department omitted references to *Jews* in Isaac Bashevis Singer's story about growing up in pre–World War II Poland, presumably because references to a person's ethnic background are considered insulting. It didn't seem to matter to those censoring the test that Singer is famous for his stories, not just of life in general, but of Jewish life in particular. Similarly, a passage in which Annie Dillard wrote about being a white child going to an all-black library was revised to eliminate all references to race, even though Dillard's purpose was to highlight her childhood feelings about race.

4   According to Ravitch, her awakening to the excessive control exerted over elementary and high school textbooks and tests came when she was involved in a national testing project. When test makers attempted to include a short informational passage about peanuts in a proposed national test of fourth graders, it was rejected by the "bias and sensitivity review panel" because the peanuts were described as "nutritious" and the passage failed to take into account that for people who are allergic to peanuts, the nuts are deadly. Another passage on quilting in the nineteenth century got eliminated because it showed women in what was considered a stereotypical context—involved in sewing. To those "sensitive" to the stereotype, it apparently did not matter that such a situation was completely realistic and appropriate for nineteenth-century women. From Ravitch's perspective, one of the "stranger recommendations of the bias and sensitivity panel working on the national tests involved the rejection of a passage about a blind hiker who scaled Mount McKinley, the highest peak in North America." This passage did not make the grade for two reasons: (1) Its emphasis on hiking and climbing suggested a regional bias; and (2) it suggested that, in the context of hiking, blind people are at a disadvantage because they cannot see the terrain. For bias hunters, these two reasons made the passage unacceptable.

5   But Ravitch does not include all these examples simply to draw attention to them. On the contrary, she is on a mission. She openly calls the presence of such censorship in schools a "huge scandal in American education" and insists that "no one asked the rest of us whether we want to live in a society in which everything objectionable to every contending party has been expunged from our reading materials."

6   Ravitch and her many supporters, who also want to end the reign of the language police, are not making a case for textbooks and tests that approve of ethnic slurs or sexist insults. Instead, they argue that religiously removing all controversial topics or language from high school textbooks and tests has several consequences, all of them bad. (1) Often an author's work is gutted of meaning. Leave out, for instance, Singer's reference to Jews and you lose his reason for writing. (2) History and science are misrepresented. If we eliminate references to women doing women's work in the nineteenth century, we lose sight of a crucial aspect of that era. It was a world divided into two spheres of influence: The domestic sphere belonged to women; all the rest belonged to men. By the same token, eliminate references to the theory of evolution and we disregard the assumptions shared by most members of the current scientific community. (3) The text becomes devoid of reality and forfeits both the interest and the respect of student readers. If the books they read purify the reality they know, high school students are unlikely to take their textbooks seriously. Thus a history book that refuses to acknowledge the horrors of past wars or the tragedies that have resulted from racial or religious hatred is likely to make students think that history has nothing to do with the real world and is, therefore, not worthy of serious attention.

7   To quote Diane Ravitch, "How boring for students to be restricted only to stories that shatter their self-esteem or that purge complexity and unpleasant reality from history and current events. How weird for them to see television programs and movies that present life and all its confusing and sometimes unpleasant fullness, then to read textbooks in which language, ideas, and behavior have been scrubbed of anything that might give offense." How weird indeed! (Sources of information: Ravitch, *The Language Police*; Diane Ravitch, "You Can't Say That," *Wall Street Journal*, February 13, 2004, Editorial Page.

Sharpening Your Skills

DIRECTIONS Answer the following questions by filling in the blanks or circling the letter of the correct response.

1. What question or questions based on the title would you use to guide your reading?

   _____

   _____

2. In your own words, what is the main idea of this reading?

   _____

   _____

3. In paragraph 2, what is the function of the third sentence?

   a. It's a topic sentence.

   b. It's a major detail.

   c. It's a minor detail.

   d. It's a transitional sentence.

4. Does paragraph 3 open with a fact or an opinion?

   _____

5. What's the implied main idea of paragraph 3?

   _____

   _____

6. In paragraph 4, the references to peanuts, quilting, and mountain climbing are supporting details that help make what point?

   _____

   _____

7. The two transitions in paragraph 5 tell readers to expect

   a. more of the same.

   b. a contrasting position.

   c. a sequence of events.

   d. the effects of the event described.

8. In paragraph 6, what transition reverses the opening point of view expressed in the opening sentence?

_____

9. Circle the letter of the conclusion that follows from this reading.

a. Although Diane Ravitch is personally upset by censorship from pressure groups, she would not encourage parents to write letters of complaint.

b. Diane Ravitch hopes her book will get the public's attention and force publishers of elementary and high school texts to stop caving in to pressure groups.

c. Diane Ravitch is probably an atheist.

d. Diane Ravitch is a supporter of home schooling.

10. Based on the reading, what conclusion would you draw about the author's position on textbook censorship?

a. The author seems to agree with Ravitch.

b. The author seems to disagree with Ravitch.

c. The author doesn't reveal her personal point of view.

How did you arrive at your conclusion?

_____

_____

Students who want to do a more in-depth review of patterns should use *Getting Focused*, the web-based reading program accompanying this text. The program is available at **college .cengage.com/devenglish/flemming/getting_focused/1e/ student_home.html**. Completing question 8 will provide a very thorough and complete review.

To get more practice differentiating between fact and opinion, go to **laflemm.com** and click on *Reading for Thinking*: "Online Practice." Complete the interactive tutorial on fact and opinion.

Test 1: Distinguishing Between Fact and Opinion

DIRECTIONS Label each of the following statements *F* for fact, *O* for opinion, or *D* for a blend of both.

_____ **1.** As George Orwell so correctly said, "The great enemy of clear language is insincerity."

_____ **2.** Among people suffering from depression, one portion of the brain is significantly smaller than the other.

_____ **3.** The planet Neptune was discovered in 1846 by the German astronomer Johann G. Galle.

_____ **4.** The assassination in Dallas, Texas, of John Fitzgerald Kennedy, the thirty-fifth president of the United States, was among the most tragic acts of the twentieth century.

_____ **5.** The Mexican revolutionary Emiliano Zapata (1879–1919) had a profound influence on modern Mexico.

_____ **6.** Louise Brown, the world's first test-tube baby, was born on July 25, 1978.

_____ **7.** We should return to the days when films were made in black and white rather than color.

_____ **8.** Iraq has the world's second largest reserves of crude oil.

_____ **9.** People who walk along the street with cell phones pressed to their ears are just trying to prove they have friends who want to talk to them.

_____ **10.** According to the Centers for Disease Control and Prevention in Atlanta, Georgia, food-borne diseases cause approximately 325,000 hospitalizations and 5,000 deaths per year.

Test 2: Checking for Relevance

Read each passage. Write *R* or *I* in the blank at the end. *R* indicates that all the facts and reasons are relevant. *I* indicates that you spotted one or more irrelevant facts or reasons.

1. On March 12, 2003, death row inmate Delma Banks Jr.[†] had eaten his last meal and was ten minutes away from being executed when the U.S. Supreme Court spared him by agreeing to review his case. The Court's decision suggests that, in Banks's case at least, justice has been served, and Banks will get a chance to prove his innocence. There is very little evidence that Banks, who was convicted for killing a sixteen-year-old boy in 1980, actually committed the crime. Physical evidence is lacking, and the key witnesses in his trial were two drug addicts, who testified against Banks in exchange for having charges against themselves dropped. During his trial, Banks's defense attorney did an ineffective job. For example, he made no objection to the racist tactics prosecutors used to select the all-white jury that decided the fate of his black client. Banks had no prior criminal record and always insisted that he was innocent. According to the three former federal judges who urged the Supreme Court to intervene, Banks's case puts into question the very "integrity of the administration of the death penalty in this country." (Source of information: Bob Herbert, "Pull the Plug," *New York Times,* April 24, 2003, www.nytimes.com/2003/04/24/opinion/24HERB.html.)

_____

2. Even though Elvis Presley died on August 16, 1977, he is certainly not forgotten. On the contrary, the legend of Elvis lives on. To honor the twentieth anniversary of his death, RCA released a four-volume CD set, *Elvis Presley Platinum: A Life in Music.* It was so popular that record stores couldn't keep it on the shelves. In honor of that same anniversary, more than fifty thousand fans descended on Graceland, Elvis's Tennessee home. In 1997 and 1998, the San José Ballet toured the country performing a ballet in the singer's honor, calling it *Blue Suede Shoes* after one of Presley's earliest and biggest hits. Sightings of Elvis, real and bogus, continue to be reported to this day; in fact, an up-to-date list can be found at www.elvissightingbulletinboard.com. Anyone who needs further proof that for many "The King" lives on in memory need only type his

_____

[†]On February 24, 2004, the U.S. Supreme Court threw out the death sentence of Texas inmate Delma Banks Jr. and granted him the right to further appeal his conviction.

name into a search engine and sit back to watch the results pile up to somewhere well over a million.

———

3. The label *organic* doesn't necessarily mean that food has been grown or raised without pesticides and human-made fertilizers. Currently, what's considered organic in one state may not be in another. Some states' certification programs allow organic produce to be grown with certain fertilizers and insecticides that other states specifically prohibit. Moreover, twenty states have no rules whatsoever governing organic food. "As it now stands, in an unregulated state there's nothing to stop some farmers from just sticking an organic label on their tomatoes, say, and putting them out for sale without ever having followed any organic principles," observes Katherine DiMatteo, executive director of the national Organic Trade Association. (Adapted from Jennifer Reid Holman, "Can You Trust Organic?" *Self,* November 1997, p. 163.)

———

4. Like Susan B. Anthony, Lucretia Mott, and Elizabeth Cady Stanton, Ernestine Rose was one of the founding members of American feminism; yet her name has barely made it into the history books. One reason for this omission may be that Rose was an outsider who fit none of the nineteenth-century patterns of American womanhood. Like Stanton, Rose was an eloquent speaker, whose gift for words drew praise even from those who disagreed with her. After listening to Rose speak, the editor of the *Albany Express* in 1854 wrote, "Though we dissented much—very much—from what she said, yet we did admire her eloquence, her pathos,* her elocution. She spoke wonderfully well." Fellow abolitionists William Lloyd Garrison and Lucretia Mott admired her as well and paid no attention to the many attacks on her character made by those who despised her political beliefs. In an 1869 volume titled *Eminent Women of the Age*, no mention of Rose appears. (Source of information: Jacoby, *Freethinkers*, p. 102.)

———

5. Autism is a brain disorder that is generally diagnosed when a child is between the ages of one and three. As the disease takes its toll, victims of the disease have difficulties with speech, imaginative play, and interaction with others. Despite claims to the contrary,

———

*pathos: sad or tragic feeling.

the disease has become an epidemic. In a landmark 2007 case, some 4,800 petitioners sued the federal government, claiming that ordinary vaccinations against childhood diseases had caused their children to develop autism. As Roy Richard Grinker points out in his book, *Unstrange Minds: Remapping the World of Autism*, psychiatrists have broadened the definition of autism so that the term now applies to more people. Because more people have been included in the definition of the disease, it is also more widely known, making more child psychiatrists prepared to diagnose it. A 2004 study by the Institute of Medicine found no compelling evidence linking autism to childhood vaccines, but there are undoubtedly other environmental factors contributing to the epidemic that is claiming more and more victims. (Source of information: Richard Monastersky, "Making Autism Familiar," *Chronicle of Higher Education*, May 11, 2007, pp. A-24–27.)

————

Test 3: Checking for Relevance

DIRECTIONS Read each passage. Write *R* or *I* in the blank at the end. *R* indicates that all the facts and reasons are relevant. *I* indicates that you spotted one or more irrelevant facts or reasons.

1. The penny still plays several necessary roles, so Americans should not eliminate this coin. First, rendering the penny obsolete would hurt the poor. Because merchants usually round up to the nearest nickel on cash purchases, lower-income Americans, who conduct most of their business using cash, would wind up paying more. The nonprofit organization Americans for Common Cents claims that rounding will cost consumers an additional $600 million a year. Those who advocate keeping the penny also say that eliminating it would hurt charities because they collect millions of dollars in donated pennies. Finally, the penny should remain in circulation because Americans are fond of it. According to Americans for Common Cents, polls consistently show that up to 65 percent of Americans oppose getting rid of this coin.

   _____

2. Local, state, and federal governments violate citizens' right to privacy when they post public records on the Internet. Easy access to the personal information contained in voter registration records, property-tax rolls, and court records should alarm every American. Putting such data online simply makes public records *too* public and makes it much too easy to obtain personal information that should be kept private. Websites that post such information do a disservice to the people of the United States. That's why local and state governments should not improve the public's access to sensitive records by putting them online.

   _____

3. In the United States, the ability to speak Spanish can be an advantage personally and professionally. The Hispanic population is growing rapidly. Currently, 3.5 million Hispanics reside in this country. In many communities, their numbers have doubled in the last decade, and in many cities and counties, even in states like Kansas, Hispanics now account for almost half of the population. Thirty-two percent of all California residents are now Hispanic. With this many Spanish-speaking neighbors, English-speaking citizens will see the Spanish language entering more and more into

pop culture like television commercials and music. Speaking Spanish will also be a tremendous asset in the workplace as increasing numbers of businesses seek to hire bilingual employees who can communicate with Hispanic customers. In particular, professionals who interact with the public on a daily basis—such as law-enforcement officers and nurses—will benefit from knowing Spanish.

———

4. The laws that prohibit convicted felons who have served out their sentences from voting are both inconsistent and unfair. As the *New York Times* has pointed out, the laws vary significantly from state to state. In some states, for instance, felons on parole can't vote, but those on probation can. In other states, felons can apply to have their voting rights restored. However, local governments can, without giving a reason, deny the application. Unfortunately, the states that do restore felons' voting rights once their time has been served are not always efficient when it comes to notifying the men and women leaving prison about their rights. Some supporters of Al Gore insist that the removal of suspected felons from the voter rolls in Florida tipped the 2000 election scales in the direction of George W. Bush. Recently, too, different courts of appeals ruled that taking away voting rights from those who have served time for a felony may well violate the Voting Rights Act of 1965.[†] The courts of appeals are correct. Released prisoners have served their time. They have paid their debt to society. Disenfranchising them is not only undemocratic, it also completely undermines the notion that people who have committed a serious crime can be rehabilitated. In effect, the refusal to return the vote to those who have committed yet paid for a crime suggests that there is no such thing as an ex-felon. On the contrary, it suggests the opposite: Once a felon, always a felon. This is hardly the message we should be sending to those men and women struggling to once again become productive citizens.

———

5. Video bloggers, or vloggers, regularly record video diaries of their most intimate thoughts and feelings and put them on the Internet so they can share them with the world. This is just one more example of what Professor Jean Twenge of San Diego State University

---

[†]On August 6, 1965, President Lyndon Johnson signed into law legislation designed to protect voters from discrimination by state governments that placed restrictions, conditions, or limitations on voting rights.

has suggested in her study of today's college students: They belong to the most narcissistic generation in all of academic history. While college students of a decade ago were obsessing about whether all the good jobs were disappearing, these kids are obsessing about how many hits their video got on YouTube, the highly popular video-sharing site. Michael L. Wesch, an assistant professor of cultural anthropology at Kansas State University, has written a paper about social networking on the Web and, to test some of his ideas, he made a video and put it on YouTube. Within a few weeks, Wesch's video had had more than two million hits and was a testament to the way the Internet is changing how we communicate. Unfortunately, the Internet seems to be changing our notion of privacy as well, and more and more people are using it to discuss their childhood traumas along with their sexual triumphs and inadequacies. (Source of information about the anthropological study: Jeffrey R. Young, "An Anthropologist Explores the Culture of Video Blogging," *Chronicle of Higher Education*, May 11, 2007, p. A42.)

Test 4: Taking Stock

DIRECTIONS Read the passage. Then answer the questions by filling in the blanks or circling the letter of the correct response.

Saving the Manatees

1   Since 1967, the manatee, a gentle marine mammal that lives in Florida waters, has been on the federal government's endangered species list. Yet between 1974 and 2002, biologists still counted as many as 4,673 manatee deaths. During that time, predictions that the manatee would soon become extinct prompted animal advocates, like members of the Save the Manatee Club and the Sierra Club, to insist on greater protections. Beginning in 1978, the Florida legislature responded by passing laws establishing areas where boating is banned or restricted, lowering boat speed limits in areas populated by manatees, and limiting permits for waterfront development. While these laws seem to have helped the manatees, they have also created conflict between environmentalists and Florida residents who feel that their lifestyles and livelihoods have been adversely affected.

2   Laws designed to protect manatees seem to have reduced the number of deaths. Manatees swim from the ocean into warmer rivers during the winter months; therefore, many of them are injured or killed in collisions with boats. Limiting boaters' speeds and prohibiting them from entering areas where manatees tend to congregate have lowered the mortality rate. In 1972, the first aerial population survey indicated that there might be only 600 to 800 manatees; several censuses in the 1990s, though, indicated that their numbers were somewhere between 1,500 and 2,500. In January 2001, a survey conducted by the Florida Fish and Wildlife Conservation Commission (FWCC) counted 3,300 manatees, far more than expected. In 2004, the FWCC counted 2,505 manatees and in 2006, 3,111 were counted.[†]

3   These statistics have served as ammunition for those who advocate removing the manatee from the endangered species list and reevaluating manatee protections. Thus in 2006, the State Wildlife Commission voted to downgrade manatees from *endangered* to *threatened.* Many Floridians oppose the current restrictions because of the personal and economic effects they have had on the state's

---

[†]The FWCC does not claim that the surveys provide an accurate picture of the manatee population or its chances of survival.

human residents. Not only do the laws restrict boaters and those who fish, but they also prevent property owners and developers from using their lands as they see fit. Thus, all these groups have argued against manatee protection measures, seeing them as a hindrance to personal freedom. (Sources of information: Craig Pittman, "Fury Over a Gentle Giant," *Smithsonian*, February 2004, pp. 54–60; "Synoptic Surveys: 1991–2004," Save the Manatee Club, www .savethemanatee.org/population4a.htm.)

1. What question or questions based on the title could help you focus your reading?

   _____

   _____

2. In your own words, what is the main idea of the entire reading?

   _____

   _____

3. Based on the context, the word *hindrance* in paragraph 3 means
   a. help.
   b. obstacle.
   c. guarantee.
   d. erase.

4. Which pattern(s) organize the details in paragraph 1?
   a. definition
   b. sequence of dates and events
   c. comparison and contrast
   d. simple listing
   e. cause and effect

5. Which pattern(s) organize the details in paragraph 2?
   a. definition
   b. sequence of dates and events
   c. comparison and contrast
   d. cause and effect
   e. classification

6. The first sentence in paragraph 1 is

    a. a fact.

    b. an opinion.

    c. a blend of fact and opinion.

7. The last sentence in paragraph 1 is

    a. a fact.

    b. an opinion.

    c. a blend of fact and opinion.

8. In the first sentence of paragraph 2, the word *seem* suggests

    a. a fact.

    b. an opinion.

9. The word *ammunition* in paragraph 3 suggests that the controversy over protecting the manatees

    a. is not emotionally charged.

    b. involves people who are generally friends with one another.

    c. has a degree of hostility.

10. In paragraph 3, the author expects readers to draw which inference from sentence 1?

    a. Advocates of removing the manatee from the endangered species list don't consider the statistics accurate.

    b. Advocates of removing the manatee from the endangered species list argue that the statistics prove the manatees are no longer in danger of extinction.

    c. Advocates of removing the manatee from the endangered species list believe those statistics favor the cause of the manatees' protectors.

CHAPTER 8

Identifying Purpose and Tone

In this chapter, you will learn

- how *informative* writing and *persuasive* writing differ.

- why discovering the author's purpose is essential to critical reading.

- how the title and the source of a reading help you predict the writer's purpose.

- how thesis statements help you confirm or revise your prediction.

- how tone relates to purpose.

- how to recognize an ironic tone.

Most writing falls into three categories: (1) writing meant to inform, (2) writing designed to persuade, and (3) writing intended purely to entertain. Because we're focusing on critical reading issues, such as evaluating evidence and separating fact from opinion, this chapter is solely concerned with writing meant to inform or to persuade.

439

Determining whether a writer intends to inform or to persuade can sometimes be difficult whereas writing bent on entertaining is pretty easy to recognize. The only possible complication or difficulty might be that you don't share the author's sense of humor.

 # Understanding the Difference Between Informative Writing and Persuasive Writing

To be a good critical reader, you need a clear understanding of how informative writing and persuasive writing differ.

Informative Writing

The goal of **informative writing** is to make the audience more knowledgeable about a particular subject. Informative writing usually leans heavily on factual information and doesn't promote any one opinion. If anything, informative writing is likely to offer competing opinions on the same subject while the author remains objective, or impartial, refusing to champion one opinion over another.

Here's a good example of writing meant primarily to inform.

 Two factors in the development of obesity in children are beyond human control. These two factors are heredity and age. Like it or not, thinness and fatness do run in families. Overweight children tend to have overweight parents, and underweight children tend to have underweight parents (LeBow, 1984). In addition, most people inevitably put on fat more during certain periods of life than during others. Late childhood and early puberty form one of these periods; at this time, most children gain fat tissue out of proportion to increases in other tissues, such as muscle and bone. (Adapted from Seifert and Hoffnung, *Child and Adolescent Development*, p. 390.)

In this example, the topic is obesity in children, and the authors briefly describe two of its causes: heredity and age. Notice, however, that they do not express a point of view about the subject. Nor do the authors suggest that readers should adopt a particular point of view. Their primary purpose is to dispense information, not to persuade.

Persuasive Writing

Persuasive writing promotes a particular point of view; its goal is to make readers share the author's position or perspective. While writers intent on persuasion often pair their opinions with facts, the facts are carefully chosen. They are there to convince readers that the author is right. Although authors writing to persuade sometimes present opposing points of view, they do so to discredit the opposition and show readers why these contradictory opinions contain flaws of some sort and aren't worthy of serious consideration. Unlike those with an informative purpose, authors of persuasive writing don't present themselves as objective. Although the best of them try to keep an open mind and treat opposing positions fairly, they are still committed to their own views and write in the hope that you will share them. Here, to illustrate, is a passage written with a persuasive intent.

Four women widowed by the September 11 terrorist attacks—Kristen Breitweiser, Patty Casazza, Lorie Van Auken, and Mindy Kleinberg—have demonstrated the power of ordinary citizens to influence a huge bureaucracy—the federal government. By tirelessly organizing protests and rallies, lobbying members of Congress, meeting with White House officials, gathering documents, and just plain refusing to give up, they have shown Americans the power of determined political activism. By demanding that agencies like the FBI and CIA explain how terrorists could have found the country so unprepared, these four widows have reminded the government of its responsibilities to its citizens. The four women have also modeled the kind of vigilance that citizens of a democracy should exercise. Kristen Breitweiser has admitted that, prior to September 11, she never read newspaper articles about the Middle East, Osama bin Laden, or Al-Qaeda. Now she realizes that she—and her fellow citizens—should have been keeping themselves informed about world affairs. Perhaps the most important thing that these women have done, though, is to lay the groundwork for a safer future. Through the commission they helped bring into being, all Americans have learned what needs to be done to make sure a tragedy like September 11 never happens again. (Source of information: Sheryl Gay Stolberg, "9/11 Widows Skillfully Applied the Power of a Question: Why?" *New York Times*, April 1, 2004, p. A1, www.nytimes.com/2004/04/01/national/01FAMI.html.)

The author of this passage has a strong conviction. He believes that the four widows who prodded Congress into forming a commission to investigate 9/11 did the country a great service. In an effort to persuade readers to share his point of view, he offers several reasons designed to convince.

Check Your Understanding

Sum up the essential difference between informative writing and persuasive writing.

_____

_____

_____

_____

 ## The Importance of Purpose

Identifying the primary **purpose**, or reason, for writing is important because the author's purpose determines how critically you need to read. After all, your time is limited. You can't possibly check every source or ponder everything you read. With purely informational writing, you can relax a bit and read to understand the author's message. Just make sure that the writer is objectively describing events or ideas without using charged language to tell you how to interpret or view them. In fact, a writer whose primary purpose is to inform is very likely to give you different explanations of the same events so that you can develop your own opinions.

However, the more an author leans toward persuasion, the more consistently you must *evaluate* what you read, considering the amount and kind of evidence offered. Because persuasive writing tries to affect how you think, feel, and behave, you need to look for reasons, check facts, and consider the effect of word choice before you let yourself be influenced.

In a very real way, the author's purpose shapes or determines your reading response. The clearer it becomes that an author is intent on persuasion, the more willing you must be to do a close and critical reading in an effort to determine the author's **bias**, or personal leaning.

Determining the Primary Purpose

To be sure, a good deal of writing blends information and persuasion. For example, a writer who wants to inform her readers about changes that have taken place in Berlin, Germany, since the Berlin Wall† came down also needs to persuade readers that her account is accurate and trustworthy. Similarly, an author may wish to convince his readers that they should give more money to AIDS research. But to make that position persuasive, the author will probably inform them about current funding.

As a critical reader, you should always try to determine an author's **primary**, or major, purpose. Be aware, however, that it's not always possible to be absolutely certain whether a writer meant to inform *or* to persuade. Some writers inform and persuade in equal measure.

Check Your Understanding
In your own words, why is knowing the author's purpose important?
_____
_____
_____
_____

◢◣◯ Predicting Purpose

The only way to truly identify an author's purpose is to read what he or she has to say. However, even before you begin reading, you can use two very important clues to predict the author's purpose—the source of the reading and the author's background.

---

†Berlin Wall: the wall that divided East and West Berlin. It was erected by the Communist government to keep East Germans from fleeing to democratic West Germany.

Use the Source as a Clue to Purpose

The source, or location, of a reading is often a solid clue to purpose. Technical manuals, guidebooks, science texts and journals, reference books, dictionaries, reports of scientific experiments, and newspaper accounts of current events are usually written primarily to inform. Writing drawn from these sources usually does not promote any one particular point of view, but instead offers an *objective*, or impersonal, account of both people and events.

Unlike the preceding sources, editorials; opinion pieces; letters to the editor; and book, movie, and theater reviews in both newspapers and magazines are all likely to promote one particular point of view over other, competing points of view. The same applies to pamphlets published by political parties or special-interest groups, books and articles challenging or revising commonly held beliefs or theories, biographies of famous people, and journals promoting particular causes. All these sources are likely to feature persuasive writing.

Check the Author's Background

Information about the author's background is not always available to you. But when it is, it can be a useful clue to purpose. For example, a government official who represents the U.S. Department of Health and Human Services and reports on the use of antibiotics in poultry raising is less likely to have a persuasive intent than the president of the New England Poultry Association. If a writer represents a group that could benefit from what he or she claims, then you should suspect a persuasive purpose. You might be wrong, but the chances are good that you will be right.

EXERCISE 1 **DIRECTIONS** What follows is a list of possible sources for written material. Next to each item on the list is a blank. Put a *P* in the blank if you think the source is likely to contain persuasive writing. Put an *I* in the blank if you think it's likely to contain informative writing.

EXAMPLE

   P   A letter to the editor of the *Pittsburgh Post Gazette* responding to news that researchers had unveiled genetically engineered mice able to run faster and longer than naturally bred mice.

   I   A front-page article about the attempts of several states to eliminate, revise, or maintain bilingual education programs.

EXPLANATION Like editorials, letters to the editor express an opinion, often one that is passionately held by a writer who would like to sway the minds of others. Front-page articles, in contrast, are supposed to report on, rather than judge, the events described.

_____ **1.** An article about Cuban leader Fidel Castro appearing in the *Encyclopaedia Britannica*

_____ **2.** An article about Fidel Castro appearing on the front page of the *New York Times*

_____ **3.** A biography of Fidel Castro titled *The Man Who Destroyed Cuba*

_____ **4.** A book titled *An Encyclopedia of American Architecture*

_____ **5.** A government pamphlet titled *Historic Buildings in the Southern States*

_____ **6.** A book review of a work titled *The Triumph of American Architecture*

_____ **7.** A government report on global warming

_____ **8.** A letter about global warming written to the editor of the *Atlanta Times*

_____ **9.** A book titled *The Field Guide to North American Birds*

_____**10.** An article about the disappearance of songbirds appearing in a journal titled *Save the Earth Now*

Titles Also Provide Clues

Another clue to purpose is the title of a reading. Titles that simply describe a state of affairs—"Teamwork Used to Teach Math"—usually signal that the writer just wants to inform readers without necessarily persuading them. Titles that express an opinion are quite a different matter. A title like "Teamwork and Mathematics Don't Mix" should immediately suggest to you that the author's primary purpose is persuasion.

Sometimes, of course, the title is no help whatsoever in determining the author's purpose. For example, titles like "A Look at the Nation" or "Family Affairs" don't reveal the author's purpose.

EXERCISE 2 DIRECTIONS Read each pair of titles. If the title suggests the writer wants mainly to inform, put an *I* in the blank. If it suggests that the author wants mainly to persuade, put a *P* in the blank.

EXAMPLE

a. Bilingual Education Is on the Rise ___I___

b. Congress Should Pass "English Only" Legislation ___P___

EXPLANATION The first title simply describes a state of affairs without passing any judgment. The second title takes a definite stand, indicating that the writer wants readers to be persuaded.

1. a. Against Assisted Death _____

b. Assisted Death in the Netherlands _____

2. a. Support for Same-Sex Schools Is Increasing _____

b. It Will Take More Than Same-Sex Schools to Get Rid of Gender Bias _____

3. a. Women Don't Belong in the Military _____

b. Women in the Military _____

4. a. Astrology: The Science of Crackpots* _____

b. Understanding Astrology _____

5. a. The Science of Cloning _____

b. Let's Be Cautious About Cloning _____

EXERCISE 3 **DIRECTIONS** Try creating titles that express your intent. Make title *a* a statement that suggests your purpose is to inform. Make title *b* a statement that reveals your intention to persuade. The topic is provided for you.

EXAMPLE

Topic Animal Rights

a. *The History of the Animal Rights Movement in America*

b. *Animals Don't Have Rights; People Do*

---

*crackpots: persons with odd ideas.

EXPLANATION Title *a* suggests that the writer is intent on descri ing the animal rights movement, whereas title *b* suggests that the author wants to discourage support for the movement.

1. **Topic** The Super Bowl

   a. _____

   b. _____

2. **Topic** School Prayer

   a. _____

   b. _____

3. **Topic** Online Courtships

   a. _____

   b. _____

4. **Topic** Divorce

   a. _____

   b. _____

5. **Topic** Cloning

   a. _____

   b. _____

The Main Idea Is the Clincher

The title, source, and any available information about the author's background can frequently suggest his or her purpose. But it's the author's stated or implied main idea that is the clincher, or deciding factor. It will tell you whether your initial prediction about purpose is accurate or in need of revision.

Main Ideas in Informative Writing

In writing meant to inform, authors describe, but they do not judge or evaluate, events, people, or ideas. Here, for example, the writer describes an author's beliefs about Greek culture.

> In *Black Athena*, Martin Bernal argues that the Greeks were deeply indebted to the Egyptians for almost every aspect of their culture.

Based on this thesis statement, which does not in any way evaluate Bernal's work, experienced critical readers would assume the author intends to describe Martin Bernal's book without making any claims about its value. While the remainder of the reading could prove them wrong—critical readers continuously test and revise their expectations—it's more than likely that their first response will prove correct.

Main Ideas in Persuasive Writing

Writers intent on persuasion will usually state or imply a main idea that identifies some action that needs to be taken, some belief that should be held, or some value judgment that should be shared. Here is an example.

> Martin Bernal has expended enormous energy on *Black Athena,* but he is absolutely wrong to assert, as he does, that he has rewritten the history of the eastern Mediterranean. (Emily Vermeule, "The World Turned Upside Down," *New York Review of Books*, March 26, 1992, p. 43.)

Faced with this thesis statement, most critical readers would correctly assume that the author wants readers to share her opinion of *Black Athena.*

Look now at the next two thesis statements. Which one do you think suggests that the author's goal is to persuade? Put a *P* in the blank next to that statement.

_____ **1.** A number of factors cause children to become obese, or seriously overweight.

_____ **2.** Because obesity is a serious health problem, parents need to pay close attention to what their children eat.

If you filled in the blank next to statement 2, you correctly recognized that the first statement did not encourage readers to pass any judgment or take any action. Statement 2, in contrast, strongly suggests that readers should share the author's feelings about the obesity of children—it's a serious health problem. It also encourages parents to act on those feelings by keeping a close watch on their children's diet. This is the kind of thesis statement that tells readers to look for and evaluate the author's evidence for such a claim.

EXERCISE 4 DIRECTIONS Read each pair of thesis statements. Write an *I* in the blank if the writer intends mainly to inform. Write a *P* if the statement encourages readers to share the writer's point of view.

EXAMPLE

a. In the 1990s, lawsuits involving bias in the workplace tripled after the government enacted new antidiscrimination legislation.

   I

b. In the United States, lawsuits have begun to replace logic and common sense; it's time to put an end to frivolous litigation.

   P

EXPLANATION Statement *a* simply identifies an existing state of affairs, while statement *b* calls readers to action.

1. a. In 1996, Buck and Luther, two Atlantic bottlenose dolphins, were retired from Navy service with full honors. To prepare them for a return to the sea, the Navy sent them to a retraining center in Florida. But some person or group set the dolphins free before retraining was completed, and the two dolphins barely survived their punishing first few weeks at sea.

   _____

b. It's sad but true that we humans often hurt wild animals in our attempts to help them. When two Atlantic bottlenose dolphins, Buck and Luther, were retired from Navy service, they were sent to a retraining center in preparation for their return to the ocean and life on their own. Unfortunately, some misguided animal lovers decided to speed up the process and liberated the dolphins before they were ready. As a result, Buck and Luther barely survived their newfound freedom.

   _____

2. a. The Tuskegee Study of Untreated Syphilis in the Negro Male was begun in 1932, when the U.S. Public Health Service began tracking 399 black men with syphilis. The study's stated purpose was to chart the natural history of the disease without recourse to any treatment, but the men recruited for the study were never told its true purpose.

   _____

b. In May of 1997, President Clinton apologized on behalf of the nation to the survivors of the Tuskegee Study of Untreated Syphilis in the Negro Male. But his apology can never erase the horrible stain that experiment left on America's history.

_____

3. a. The study of working-class women by sociologists Elaine Wethington and Ronald Kessler has been widely discussed and highly publicized. However, when closely examined, it's clear that their work brings little or nothing new to the debate about women and work.

_____

b. Sociologists Elaine Wethington of Cornell University and Ronald Kessler of the University of Michigan found that women who worked at low-wage, part-time jobs were more stressed than women who worked full time.

_____

4. a. Radon, particularly combined with smoking, poses an important public health risk and it should be recognized as such.

_____

b. According to the Environmental Protection Agency, radon, a naturally occurring radioactive gas, which collects in many homes, is linked to more than 20,000 deaths annually from lung cancer.

_____

5. a. Now that scientists have found the hormone that triggers hunger, they should take the next step and discover how this hormone can be controlled. Such a discovery would be an enormous advance in the war against obesity.

_____

b. Based on research at the University of Texas Southwestern Medical Center, scientists believe they have found the hormone that triggers feelings of hunger.

_____

The Effect of Purpose on Tone

Tone in writing is much like tone of voice in speech. It's the emotion or attitude created by the writer's choice of words, content, and style. Good writers know how to create and vary tone. Good readers recognize how tone can help identify purpose.

Tone in Informative Writing

Critical readers know that informative writing is likely to have a cool, objective, or neutral tone, the kind of tone that relies heavily on denotative language and doesn't try to affect readers' emotions. In informative writing, the tone is unlikely to reveal the author's personal feelings about the topic discussed.

Look, for example, at the following passage from page 440, written solely to inform. Notice the absence of charged language. Note, too, that the authors' personal feelings are not revealed.

 Two factors in the development of obesity in children are beyond human control. These two factors are heredity and age. Like it or not, thinness and fatness do run in families. Overweight children tend to have overweight parents, and underweight children tend to have underweight parents (LeBow, 1984). In addition, most people inevitably put on fat more during certain periods of life than during others. Late childhood and early puberty form one of these periods; at this time, most children gain fat tissue out of proportion to increases in other tissues, such as muscle and bone. (Seifert and Hoffnung, *Child and Adolescent Development*, p. 390.)

In this passage, the authors simply want to tell readers about the two factors in obesity that are beyond human control, and their tone matches their purpose. It's objective and to the point.

Tone in Persuasive Writing

In persuasive writing, tone can vary enormously. Although it can be cool and reserved, it's more likely to express some emotion. Tone in persuasive writing can be coaxing, admiring, enthusiastic, rude, even sarcastic. How, for example, would you describe the tone of the following passage?

I have been fat all my life and I am thoroughly sick of apologizing for it. This is my declaration of independence from all you skinny people out there who have insisted how much better off I would be if I lost a few pounds. Tragically, we live in a culture that celebrates the thin and denigrates* the fat. This state of affairs leads to the kind of desperate and dangerous dieting I have engaged in for most of my adult life. And I am not alone in this obsession with losing weight. At some time in their lives, at least 80 percent of the American population has dieted to lose weight, even though studies show the majority of diets fail (Fett and Dick, 91). We would probably all be a lot better off if we spent time improving our souls instead of our bodies. No matter what we do, our bodies will decay; our souls will not.

At the beginning of the paragraph, judging by the words alone, it appears that the author wants only to inform readers about his own miserable dieting experience. He seems to focus solely on himself. He doesn't express any wish to affect other people's lives. But the passionate and angry tone is a dead giveaway to the author's real purpose, which is more persuasive than informative. By the end of the passage, it's clear the author wants us to believe that we should stop thinking so much about dieting and instead spend more time concentrating on our spiritual well-being.

Checking the match between tone and purpose is important. Informative writing that suddenly becomes angry and emotional in tone may be more persuasive in intent than you initially realized. Or, it may be that the writer honestly intends to inform, but his or her bias interferes with the writer's ability to stay fair and balanced. Whatever you do, *don't think of tone as verbal decoration.* For writers, it's a tool to create meaning. For readers, it's a crucial clue to the author's primary purpose. Tone also tells you how willing the author might be to at least acknowledge another point of view.

Words Useful for Describing Tone	
admiring	appalled
amused	astonished
annoyed	awed (filled with wonder)
angry	bullying
anxious	cautious

---

*denigrates: criticizes; demeans.

confident	mistrustful
contemptuous	nostalgic (looking fondly
critical	toward the past)
cynical	outraged
disgusted	passionate
disrespectful	playful
dumbfounded (very surprised)	puzzled
embarrassed	regretful
engaged (deeply involved)	sad
enthusiastic	sarcastic
horrified	shocked
humorous	solemn
insulted	soothing
insulting	sorrowful
ironic (saying the opposite of	sure
what is intended)	surprised
joyful	trusting

EXERCISE 5 **DIRECTIONS** After reading each selection, identify the author's purpose. Then circle the letter of the word or phrase that best fits the author's tone.

EXAMPLE Jazz singer Ella Fitzgerald was a quiet and humble woman who experienced little of the love she sang about so exquisitely for more than fifty years. Her voice, even in later years when she suffered from crippling arthritis, was always filled with a clear, light energy that could set the toes of even the stodgiest* listeners tapping. Although Fitzgerald, an African American, came of age in an era when racism was rampant, whatever bitterness she felt never spilled over into her music. She sang the lyrics of a white Cole Porter or a black Duke Ellington with the same impossible-to-imitate ease and grace, earning every one of the awards heaped on her in her later years. When she performed with Duke Ellington at Carnegie Hall in 1958, critics called Fitzgerald "The First Lady of Song." Although she died in 1996, no one has come along to challenge her title, and Ella Fitzgerald is still jazz's first lady.

Purpose a. to inform

b. to persuade

---

*stodgiest: lacking in life; without energy.

Tone a. coolly annoyed

(b.) enthusiastic and admiring

c. emotionally neutral

EXPLANATION Throughout the passage, the author describes Ella Fitzgerald in strong, positively charged language, creating an enthusiastic and admiring tone that encourages readers to share the admiration. The purpose, therefore, is persuasive.

1. As a mail carrier for more than twenty years, I can tell you firsthand that we are much maligned members of the population. Customers see only the flaws in mail delivery. They never appreciate the huge effort that makes service both speedy and efficient. For an absurdly small price, you can send mail anywhere in the country, from Hawaii to Alaska. You'd think this would impress most people, but no. Instead of thanking us for services rendered, they whine and complain about the few times mail gets lost. And just because a few members of the postal service have engaged in violent behavior, people now use the insulting expression *going postal* to refer to unexpected outbreaks of violence brought on by stress. This phrase unfairly insults the rest of us hardworking employees who do our jobs without complaint day in and day out.

Purpose a. to inform

b. to persuade

Tone a. comical

b. insulted

c. emotionally neutral

2. In his book *An Anthropologist on Mars*, the renowned neurologist* Dr. Oliver Sacks gives readers an important and insightful perspective on injuries and disorders of the brain. According to Dr. Sacks, some injuries and disorders result in greater creativity and achievement. With compassionate insight, Dr. Sacks describes, for example, a painter who becomes colorblind through a car accident. Initially in despair, the painter eventually started painting stunning black-and-white canvases that won him more critical acclaim than he had received before his mishap.

  As in his previous works, Dr. Sacks gives readers an unexpected perspective on disease and injury. In *An Anthropologist on Mars*, he

_____

*neurologist: a doctor who specializes in the workings and diseases of the nervous system.

once again makes us rethink and reconsider our most cherished beliefs about health and illness. His book should be required reading for anyone interested in the power of human beings to adapt to and ultimately overcome loss.

Purpose a. to inform

b. to persuade

Tone a. admiring

b. cautious

c. emotionally neutral

3. Deep processing, which is effective for many kinds of learning, involves analyzing information in terms of its meaning. If, for instance, you want to learn a new word, it frequently helps to break the word down into meaningful parts. For example, to remember the meaning of *taciturn* ("inclined to silence; not liking to speak"), you might think about it as being partially made up of the more common word *tacit*, meaning "unspoken." Or, perhaps you've never quite managed to remember the difference between *libel* and *slander*. If you think about the fact that *libel* appears to contain the same word-root found in *library*, that will make it easier to remember that *libel* means "making false statements harmful to a person's reputation" *in writing* [think how libraries are filled with writing] while *slander* refers to making those kinds of statements *orally*. (Adapted from Gamon and Bragdon, *Learn Faster & Remember More*, p. 159.)

Purpose a. to inform

b. to persuade

Tone a. outraged

b. relaxed and friendly

c. emotionally neutral

4. Between 1860 and 1920, mechanization and assembly-line production gradually cut the work week from sixty-six hours in 1860 to forty-seven in 1920. As a result, from mid-century on, working-class Americans began thinking about what they might do with their time off from their jobs. For men, at least, the answer was clear: They could play, watch, or read about baseball. Baseball had been around since 1845, and during the second half of the century, the sport's popularity really began to swell. The National League, established in 1876, and the American League, formed in 1901, played their first World Series in 1903. The Boston Americans beat the Pittsburgh Pirates in that first series, and from that point on, baseball generally went unchallenged as the national pastime of American men. Women, however, were more interested in playing croquet and riding a bicycle in their spare time.

Purpose a. to inform

b. to persuade

Tone a. sarcastic

b. comical

c. emotionally neutral

5. Owners of sport utility vehicles (SUVs) should show their patriotism by getting rid of their gas-guzzling cars. SUV ownership contributes to this country's unhealthy dependence on foreign oil. Just look at the Ford Excursion, a nine-foot-long, four-ton monster that gobbles up an entire gallon of gas to travel a mere twelve miles. SUV owners use more than their fair share of oil and keep America beholden to the Middle East for fuel. SUVs also contribute to the destruction of our planet's environment. Over its lifetime, the Ford Excursion spews seventy tons of carbon dioxide—the main cause of global warming—into the atmosphere. As a result, environmental groups like the Sierra Club have nicknamed the Excursion the "Ford Valdez" after the *Exxon Valdez*, an oil tanker that dumped 11 million gallons of oil into the ocean.

Purpose a. to inform

b. to persuade

Tone a. irritated

b. casual

c. emotionally neutral

Check Your Understanding

Explain the relationship between tone and purpose.

_____

_____

_____

_____

Learning to Recognize Irony

No discussion of tone would be complete without some mention of **irony**—the practice of saying one thing while implying exactly the opposite. This might sound confusing at first, but, like most of us, you've probably used irony more than once in your life. Haven't you ever had a really horrible day and said to someone, "Boy, what a great day this was!" Or, seeing a friend wearing a sad expression, maybe you said, "Gee, you look happy."

If either of these examples sounds familiar, then you know more about irony than you think, and you're prepared for writers who assume an ironic tone like the one used in the following passage.

> The school board has decided to reduce the school budget once again. But why take half measures? Why not eliminate the budget altogether and close our schools? After all, a little learning is a dangerous thing. Better to keep our children totally ignorant and out of harm's way.

The author of this paragraph doesn't want his readers to take what he says *literally,* or at face value. After all, who would seriously suggest that keeping children ignorant is a good idea? The author's point is just the opposite of what he actually says. He doesn't want the school budget further reduced. But instead of saying that directly, he makes an outrageous suggestion that draws attention to where the cuts could lead.

When writers present what seems to be an outrageous or impossible opinion as if it were obvious common sense, critical readers assume the writer is being ironic, and they respond by inferring a message directly opposed to the author's actual words. As you might expect, *an ironic tone is a good indicator of a persuasive purpose.*

Check Your Understanding
What is irony?
_____
_____
_____

EXERCISE 6 **DIRECTIONS** Read each passage and circle the letter that best identifies the author's tone.

1. According to the American Association of Furriers, wearing fur coats is once again back in fashion. Now that's good news for the thousands of mink, rabbits, foxes, and raccoons that are brutally slaughtered so that fashionable men and women can sport a trendy fur coat or hat. No doubt these animals are honored to suffer and die for the sake of human vanity.

   Tone a. anxious

   b. comical

   c. emotionally neutral

   d. ironic

2. When the voters of Michigan sent Charles Diggs Jr. to the United States House of Representatives in 1954, he became the first black congressman in the state's history. He was not, however, the first black congressman in the United States. During the period of Reconstruction, from 1865 to 1877, the U.S. government tried to rebuild the South after the political and economic devastation of the Civil War. Black citizens held prominent government positions throughout the nation, including the posts of mayor, governor, lieutenant governor, state supreme court justice, U.S. senator, and U.S. congressman. (Juan Williams, *Eyes on the Prize.* New York: Penguin, 1987, p. 49.)

   Tone a. outraged

   b. lighthearted

   c. emotionally neutral

   d. ironic

3. It is refreshing to note that many right-thinking citizens are calling for a ban on the celebration of Halloween because the holiday encourages devil worship. Hallelujah? It doesn't take the intellect of a TV evangelist to see that the wearing of "Casper the Friendly Ghost" costumes leads children to the wanton embrace of Beelzebub.* And it is a known fact that candy corn is the first step toward addiction. Only the devil (or an underemployed dentist) would knowingly offer popcorn balls to innocent children. But why stop at Halloween? Many other holidays conceal wickedness behind a vicious veil of greeting

   ───────────
   *Beelzebub: another name for the devil.

cards and Bob Hope TV specials. (Steve Ruebal, "Toss Out Halloween? Let's Not Stop There," *USA Today*, October 29, 1991, p. 11A.)

Tone a. confident

b. ironic

c. emotionally neutral

d. friendly

4. According to one of your readers, insufficient attention has been paid to the possibility that men are also victims of domestic violence. It is his opinion that men are, in fact, just as likely to be victimized by women as women are by men. The difference is that men, for fear of looking unmasculine, fail to report it. Well, I'm just all broken up at the thought of this new social problem. I can imagine how horrible it is for a 220-pound male to be terrorized by a 120-pound female. The poor thing must live in terror at the thought of her menacing approach. A man like that is certainly as much in need of our sympathy as are the women who end up hospitalized or worse in the wake of a domestic dispute.

Tone a. ironic

b. friendly

c. emotionally neutral

d. sympathetic

5. On December 1, 1955, Rosa Parks left the Montgomery Fair department store late in the afternoon for her regular bus ride home. All thirty-six seats of the bus she boarded were soon filled, with twenty-two Negroes seated from the rear and fourteen whites from the front. Driver J. P. Blake, seeing a white man standing in the front of the bus, called out for the four passengers on the row just behind the whites to stand up and move to the back. Nothing happened. Blake finally had to get out of the driver's seat to speak more firmly to the four Negroes. "You better make it light on yourselves and let me have those seats," he said. At this, three of the Negroes moved to stand in the back of the bus, but Parks responded that she was not in the white section and didn't think she ought to move. She was in no-man's-land. Blake said that the white section was where he said it was, and he was telling Parks that she was in it. As he saw the law, the whole idea of no-man's-land was to give the driver some discretion* to keep the races out of each other's way. He was doing just that. When Parks refused again,

---

*discretion: ability or power to decide.

he advised her that the same city law that allowed him to regulate no-man's-land also gave him emergency police power to enforce the seg-regation codes. He would arrest Parks himself if he had to. Parks replied that he should do what he had to do; she was not moving. She spoke so softly that Blake would not have been able to hear her above the drone of normal bus noise. But the bus was silent. Blake notified Parks that she was officially under arrest. (Taylor Branch, *Parting the Waters.* New York: Simon & Schuster, 1988, p. 128.)

Tone a. ironic

  b. admiring

  c. emotionally neutral

  d. irritable

Clues to Purpose

Informative Writing

- is found in textbooks, newspapers, lab reports, research find-ings, case studies, and reference works.
- uses a title that simply names or describes a topic.
- includes a main idea that describes a situation, event, per-son, concept, or experience without making a judgment or offering an evaluation.
- relies more on denotative than connotative language.
- relies mainly on facts and gives opinions largely to illustrate what others think.
- takes an emotionally neutral tone.
- remains objective and reveals little or nothing about the author's personal feelings.
- includes pros and cons of the same issue.

Persuasive Writing

- is found in newspaper editorials, political pamphlets, opin-ion pieces, and articles or books written to explain the au-thor's position on current or past events.
- uses a title that suggests a point of view.
- states or suggests a main idea identifying an action that needs to be taken or a belief that should be held—or at the very least considered.

- often relies heavily on connotative language.

- relies a good deal on opinion and uses facts mainly to serve opinions.

- often expresses a strong emotional tone that reveals the author's personal feelings.

- includes only the reasons for taking an action or explains why arguments against it are not sound.

- often employs irony.

- Uses rhetorical questions,[†] which expect no answers because the answer is obvious.

Allusion Alert

Throughout the period of Reconstruction,* "carpetbagger" was the negative term applied to some Northerners who went south after the Civil War to exploit the unstable financial situation for personal gain. The name came from the satchel-like bags they carried, which were made out of leather and two pieces of carpet. To mistrusting southerners, the bags suggested the outsiders were staying only long enough to make a killing and leave. Now when we refer to a carpetbagger or call someone a carpetbagger, we are suggesting or saying that the person is an opportunist making a move purely to suit his or her own interests—for example, "Like all carpetbaggers, Mr. Allen underestimates those he has come to fleece."

Now that you understand the original meaning of the word *carpetbagger*, how would you paraphrase this sentence? "Although she won the election, critics attacked Hillary Clinton as a 'carpetbagger' when she moved to New York in 2000 to run for the Senate."

Paraphrase _____

_____

_____

_____

_____

[†]For example, What kind of person would harm an innocent child? For an explanation of rhetorical questions, see pages 481–482.
*Reconstruction: The period (1865–1877) after the Civil War when the Southern states were controlled by the federal government.

■ DIGGING DEEPER

LOOKING AHEAD The reading on pages 455–456 described how baseball became a national pastime in the second half of the nineteenth century. Here now is a description of how Americans took baseball to Japan, expecting to spread American values along with an American game. However, that's not exactly how things turned out.

BASEBALL INVADES JAPAN

1   Baseball, the "American pastime," was one of the new leisure-time pursuits that Americans took with them into different parts of the world. The Shanghai Base Ball Club was founded by Americans in China in 1863, but few Chinese paid much attention to the sport, largely because the Imperial Court renounced the game as spiritually corrupting. However, when Horace Wilson, an American teacher, taught the rules of baseball to his Japanese students some time around 1870, the game received enthusiastic welcome as a reinforcement of traditional virtues. In fact baseball quickly became so much a part of Japanese culture that one Japanese writer commented, "Baseball is perfect for us. If the Americans hadn't invented it, we probably would have."

2   During the 1870s, Japanese high schools and colleges organized baseball games, and in 1883 Hiroshi Hiraoka, a railroad engineer who had studied in Boston, founded the first official local team, the Shimbashi Athletic Club Athletics. Fans displayed wild devotion to this and similar teams as they developed over the next several years.

3   Before Americans introduced baseball to Japan, the Japanese had no team sports and no concept of recreational athletics. When they learned about baseball, they found that the idea of a team sport fit into their culture very well. But the Japanese had difficulty applying the American concept of leisure to the game. For them, baseball was serious business, involving hard and often brutal training. Practices at Ichiko, one of Japan's two great high school baseball teams in the late nineteenth century, were dubbed "Bloody Urine" because many players passed blood after a day of drilling. There was a spiritual quality as well, linked to Buddhist values. According to one Japanese coach, "The purpose of [baseball] training is not health but the forging of the soul, and a strong soul is only born from strong practice. . . . Student baseball must be the baseball of self-discipline, or trying to attain the truth, just as in Zen Buddhism." This attitude prompted

Japanese to consider baseball as a new method to pursue the spirit of Bushido, the way of the samurai.*

4   When Americans played baseball in Japan, the Japanese thought them to be strong and talented but lacking in discipline and respect. Americans insulted the Japanese by refusing to remove their hats and bow when they stepped up to bat. An international dispute occurred in 1891 when William Imbrie, an American professor at Meijo University in Tokyo, arrived late for a local game. Finding the gate locked, he climbed over the fence in order to watch the game. The fence, however, had sacred meaning and some Japanese fans attacked Imbrie for his sacrilege. Imbrie suffered facial injuries, prompting the American embassy to lodge a formal complaint. Americans assumed that their game would encourage Japanese to become like westerners to some extent, but the Japanese transformed the American pastime into an expression of team spirit, discipline, and nationalism that was uniquely Japanese. (Norton et al., *A People and a Nation*, p. 535.)

Replete with bats, gloves, and uniforms, this Japanese baseball team of 1890 very much resembles its American counterpart of that era. The Japanese adopted baseball soon after Americans became involved in their country, but also added their cultural qualities to the game.
© Albert Harlingue/Roger-Viollet/The Image Works.

---

*samurai: professional warrior.

Sharpening Your Skills

DIRECTIONS Answer the following questions by circling the letter of the correct response or filling in the blanks.

1. In paragraph 1, what two more general words do the authors use to refer to *baseball* in order not to repeat the word over and over?

   _____

2. In paragraph 3, what is the antecedent for *they* in the second sentence?

   _____

3. Read this pair of sentences from paragraph 3. Then circle the letter of the relationship readers have to infer in order to understand why the authors followed one with the other: "For them, baseball was serious business, involving hard and often brutal training. Practices at Ichiko, one of Japan's two great high school baseball teams in the late nineteenth century, were dubbed 'Bloody Urine' because many players passed blood after a day of drilling."

   a. The second sentence challenges the idea that baseball was a serious business.

   b. The second sentence explains what made the Japanese serious about baseball.

   c. The second sentence illustrates just how serious baseball was for the Japanese.

4. Which statement best expresses the main idea of the entire reading?

   a. Although Japan enthusiastically embraced American baseball, the Japanese were never able to rival the speed and skill of American players.

   b. Given their long tradition of team sports, the Japanese quickly embraced baseball and ended up being better at the game than the Americans.

   c. American baseball fit perfectly into Japan's worldview, and it became, for the Japanese, more a national symbol than a leisure-time sport.

   d. Baseball was a popular sport in Japan long before it became the national pastime in the United States.

5. What definition do the authors provide for the word *Bushido*, introduced in paragraph 3?

_____

6. The phrase "Bloody Urine" appears in the reading to make what point?

    a. Before the Americans introduced baseball, the Japanese had no concept of recreational sports.

    b. American baseball was a perfect match for Japan's culture.

    c. The Japanese made baseball a scrious and strenuous endeavor.

7. The topic sentence of paragraph 4 is

    a. the first.

    b. the second.

    c. the third.

    d. the fourth.

8. Overall, which three patterns organize this reading?

    a. comparison and contrast; cause and effect; sequence of dates and events

    b. definition; process; classification

    c. sequence of dates and events; definition; simple listing

    d. simple listing; definition; classification

9. What is the authors' purpose?

    a. The authors want to tell readers how the Japanese modified American baseball to suit their culture.

    b. The authors want to persuade readers that it's not healthy to play baseball the way the Japanese did in the nineteenth century.

What word would you use to describe the tone?

_____

10. Based on paragraph 4, what conclusion could you draw?

    a. The Americans purposely tried to insult the Japanese because they disliked the changes made to what they thought of as "their game."

    b. The Japanese expected the Americans to know and follow their traditions when playing baseball in Japan.

    c. Like soccer audiences today, Japanese baseball fans in the nineteenth century were always spoiling for a fight.

Students who want to do a more in-depth review of tone and purpose should use *Getting Focused*, the web-based reading program accompanying this text. The program is available at **college .cengage.com/devenglish/flemming/getting_focused/1e/ student_home.html**. Completing questions 9 and 10 will provide a very thorough and complete review.

To get more practice with tone and purpose, go to **laflemm.com** and click on *Reading for Thinking*: "Online Practice." Complete the interactive exercise on identifying tone and purpose.

Test 1: Identifying Purpose and Tone

DIRECTIONS Circle the appropriate letters to identify the author's purpose and tone.

1. In areas with a large Mexican population, politicians running for office are likely to talk about amnesty for the millions of illegal immigrants currently living in the United States. However, it's time that they did more than talk, because the number of Mexican men and women living here illegally is growing at a rapid rate. The majority are productive, law-abiding people, who simply want to earn a better standard of living for themselves and their families. In many cases, they have already endured great hardship just to get to this country. Once here, they are often forced by unscrupulous employers to accept low wages and poor working conditions because they fear being deported. Granting them amnesty would give illegal immigrants the right to complain and the right to demand fair working conditions. It is the compassionate and humane thing to do. The idea should not be abandoned once the campaign speeches are over and the votes have been counted.

   The author's primary purpose is

   a. to inform.

   b. to persuade.

   The author's tone is

   a. emotionally neutral.

   b. casual.

   c. arrogant.

   d. sympathetic.

 2. From 1972 through 1996, the South was more Republican than the nation as a whole. The proportion of white southerners describing themselves to pollsters as "strongly Democratic" fell from more than one-third in 1952 to about one-seventh in 1984. There has been a corresponding increase in "independents." As it turns out, southern white independents have voted overwhelmingly Republican in recent presidential elections. If you lump independents together with the parties for which they actually vote, the party alignment among white southerners has gone from six-to-one Democratic in 1952 to about fifty-fifty Democrats and Republicans. If this continues, it will constitute a major realignment in a region of the country that is rapidly growing in population and political clout. (Wilson and Dilulio, *American Government*, p. 161.)

The author's primary purpose is

a. to inform.

b. to persuade.

The author's tone is

a. emotionally neutral.

b. critical.

c. solemn.

d. surprised.

3. Oregon and Washington have proven that voting by mail is superior to the old method of voting in a polling place. First, surveys clearly show that voting by mail is an option people want. Seventy percent of Oregonians and 65 percent of Washingtonians prefer voting by mail. They like the convenience of a mail-in ballot that allows them to integrate voting more easily into their busy lives. Furthermore, voters feel that voting by mail allows them to make more informed choices. For example, one Washington survey revealed that residents believe they make better decisions because they can take more time with their ballot at home rather than rushing to complete it in a voting booth. Not surprisingly, the benefits of voting by mail have produced a dramatic increase in voter turnout during elections. For instance, almost 80 percent of registered voters in Oregon submitted a ballot in the 2000 presidential election, compared to a nationwide average of 51 percent voter turnout. Other states should follow the example set by Washington and Oregon.

The author's primary purpose is

a. to inform.

b. to persuade.

The author's tone is

a. anxious.

b. emotionally neutral.

c. confident.

d. sarcastic.

4. For more than four decades, ecologists and environmentalists have revered Rachel Carson, author of the 1962 book *Silent Spring*, for alerting the world to the dangers of chemical pesticides. Arguing that pesticides such as DDT upset the balance of nature, kill wildlife, and cause cancer in humans, Carson created widespread "chemophobia" that culminated in a ban on DDT's use. Unfortunately, though, Carson's impassioned and vividly written plea for protecting nature and human health has left generations of readers with a skewed view of pesticides. According to Dr. I. L. Baldwin, a professor who reviewed *Silent Spring* in a 1962 issue of the journal *Science*, Carson greatly exaggerated the risks. Using questionable statistics and anecdotes, such as the doubtful tale of a woman who immediately developed cancer after spraying her basement with DDT, Carson pronounced this pesticide to be a human carcinogen* even though most scientists disagreed. Carson was also irresponsible in her refusal to acknowledge the pesticides' benefits, which far outweighed their potential for harm. As Dr. Baldwin pointed out, pesticides have dramatically improved human health and welfare by getting rid of insects and parasites that destroy crops and transmit deadly diseases. Today, mosquito-borne malaria is still a leading cause of death and illness worldwide because Carson's devotees won't allow DDT to be restored as a weapon in the battle against this disease. (Source of information: John Tierney, "Fateful Voice of a Generation Still Drowns Out Real Science," *New York Times*, June 5, 2007, www.nytimes.com/2007/06/05/science/earth/05tier.html.)

The author's primary purpose is

a. to inform.

b. to persuade.

The author's tone is

a. amused.

b. objective.

c. sad.

d. critical.

5. The Apollo Space Program of the 1960s and 1970s was responsible for a series of moon landings. In 1967, the project got off to a tragic start when fire killed three astronauts during a preflight test on the launch pad. The tragedy, however, did not put an end to the space program. In 1968 and 1969 a series of successful missions took astronauts into space for six to ten days at a time. Apollo missions 7, 8, 9, and 10 tested the equipment and operations necessary for placing men on the moon's surface. On July 20, 1969, the *Apollo 11* mission fulfilled its purpose when astronauts Neil Armstrong and Buzz Aldrin did what had once seemed impossible: They

---

*carcinogen: cause of cancer.

walked on the moon while people all over the world stayed glued to their television sets and watched in awe. A second lunar landing occurred that same year as part of the *Apollo 12* mission. In 1970, *Apollo 13* was supposed to result in a third landing. However, damage to the spacecraft caused the mission to be aborted, and the astronauts barely made it safely back to Earth. Near tragedy, however, did not prove a permanent obstacle. In 1971 and 1972, four more Apollo flights produced four more lunar landings. *Apollo 14, 15, 16,* and *17* astronauts walked on the moon, performed scientific experiments, collected samples of moon rocks, and took photographs.

The author's primary purpose is

a. to inform.

b. to persuade.

The author's tone is

a. emotionally neutral.

b. skeptical.

c. critical.

d. admiring.

Test 2: Taking Stock

DIRECTIONS Read each passage. Then answer the questions by circling the letter of the correct response(s) or filling in the blanks.

1. Fix Roads Now

1   [1]Far too many of America's roads and highways are a mess. [2]They are crumbling and marred by potholes, and many are simply inadequate for the huge number of vehicles that travel them every day. [3]As a result, unsafe driving conditions and congestion are costing lives. [4]Already, nearly 43,000 deaths occur on our roads every year. [5]If improvements aren't made quickly, that number is expected to rise to almost 52,000 per year by 2009.

2   [1]Poor road conditions and congestion are also costing Americans money. [2]Highway deaths and injuries waste about $230 billion a year in medical expenses, lost wages, and travel delays. [3]Highway accidents are also a major source of legal and insurance expenses. [4]Traffic jams slow the delivery of goods and services and often prevent people from getting to work on time. [5]It's been estimated that bad roads rob the U.S. economy of $70 billion per year.

3   [1]Unsafe roads also reduce our quality of life. [2]Accidents cause pain, suffering, and long-term disability. [3]Congested highways increase commute times and shorten time spent with our families. [4]Bumper-to-bumper traffic slows us down and increases our anxiety, contributing to tension and stress-related diseases. [5]And one thing Americans do not need is more stress. (Source of information: Kit Bond, "Roads Are a Good Investment," *USA Today,* February 18, 2004, p. A10.)

1. Which statement best sums up the main idea?

   a. America's roads and highways are ancient.

   b. America's highways are the cause of countless accidents and injuries.

   c. America's roadways need to be improved and repaired as quickly as possible.

   d. America's roads and highways are worse than those in other countries.

2. To understand the relationship between sentences 2 and 3 in paragraph 2, readers have to infer that sentence 3

a. offers an exception to the point made in sentence 2.

b. introduces an additional illustration of sentence 1.

c. reverses the point introduced in sentence 1.

3. The author's primary purpose is

a. to inform.

b. to persuade.

4. Which type of transition opens sentence 3 in paragraph 1?

a. time order

b. cause and effect

c. comparison

d. contrast

5. How would you paraphrase the topic sentence in paragraph 2?

_____

_____

6. Which of the following sentences is a major detail?

a. And one thing Americans do not need is more stress.

b. Highway deaths and injuries waste about $230 billion a year in medical expenses, lost work, and travel delays.

7. Paraphrase the cycle of causes and effects the author expects you to infer from the following sentence: "Bumper-to-bumper traffic slows us down and increases our anxiety, contributing to tension and stress-related diseases."

_____

_____

_____

8. Which pattern or patterns organize this reading?

a. definition

b. simple listing

c. comparison and contrast

d. cause and effect

e. classification

9. How would you describe the author's tone?

   a. humorous

   b. sad

   c. worried

   d. objective

10. Which of these conclusions follows from the reading?

   a. The author would applaud a federal program dedicated to highway repair.

   b. The author believes that America's highways were poorly constructed when first built.

   c. The author believes that America's highways cannot be repaired; they must be replaced.

   d. The author would not support any federally funded program, even if it was devoted to improving the roadways.

2. And the Winner Is Google

1   ¹When searching the World Wide Web, computer users can choose from a number of different search engines, or tools for finding and compiling a list of relevant websites. ²A few of the most popular search engines are Yahoo!, Dogpile, AltaVista, and Google. ³The most successful of these is Google, which now handles more queries than its rivals do—and for good reason. ⁴Google has become the dominant search engine because it is more effective and efficient than any of the others.

2   ¹True, Google and the other search engines function in much the same way. ²They all send "spiders" or "robots" out to crawl through cyberspace from link to link. ³At each website, they gather information about what's there by indexing all the words. ⁴Then when someone requests information on a topic by typing in keywords, search engines assemble a list based on the index they have created. ⁵Google, however, is different from the others in one aspect. ⁶As it assesses each website, it notes how many other Web pages provide links to those pages. ⁷Then when it provides search results, Google presents them in rank order, with the most-linked-to ones at the top.

3   ¹Because of this special ranking feature, Google's results are more accurate and of higher quality than those of other search engines. ²Search engines often return hundreds of thousands of responses for just one keyword or phrase. ³Most search engines make no attempt, though, to sift through the results to identify

what might be useless. [4]Unlike its rivals, Google is based on the democratic idea that the best sites are the ones linked to the most, which is generally correct. [5]Therefore, inherent* in what Google presents in response to a query is a consensus about which sites are truly worthwhile. [6]In Google's search results, "junk" is usually sifted to the bottom, leaving the most valuable sites at the top of the list.

4   [1]In addition to being more relevant and more useful, Google's results are also more comprehensive and arrive faster. [2]The size of its database,* unlike some compiled by other search engines, continues to expand. [3]In 2002, for example, it indexed the information of more than 3 billion Web pages, far more than any other search engine. [4]Studies show that Google consistently produces more search results than its competitors and also finds more unique hits—results found by it and it alone—than any of the others. [5]Plus, it's known for being lightning fast; searches typically take under 20 seconds to complete.

5   [1]For all these reasons, the amazing Google has rightly become the leader of the pack. [2]Its method is so superior that around 2001, the verb *to google* entered the English language. [3]Clearly, no matter what information researchers seek, Google can help them find it. (Source of information: Joel Achenbach, "Search for Tomorrow," *Washington Post*, February 15, 2004, p. D01.)

   1. Which statement best sums up the main idea?

      a. Currently, Google is considered the best search engine on the Web.

      b. Among search engines, Google is highly favored by those who use the Web for serious research.

      c. When you need to search the Web for information, you can use different search engines.

      d. The World Wide Web offers a wealth of information for researchers.

   2. To understand the relationship between sentences 1 and 2 in paragraph 2, readers have to infer that sentence 2

      a. offers a specific illustration of sentence 1.

      b. reverses the opening point and introduces the main idea.

      c. identifies the effect of the cause introduced in sentence 1.

*inherent: natural to.
*database: pool of information.

3. The author's primary purpose is

    a. to inform.

    b. to persuade.

4. In sentence 1 of paragraph 3, the phrase "this special ranking feature" is a substitute, or stand-in, for what phrase in paragraph 2?

_____

5. Which pattern or patterns organize this reading?

    a. definition

    b. time order

    c. comparison and contrast

    d. cause and effect

    e. classification

6. Which statement most effectively sums up the implied main idea of paragraph 2?

    a. Like other search engines, Google sends out "spiders" that crawl from site to site.

    b. Web search engines all work in a similar way.

    c. While it's true that search engines all work in pretty much the same way, Google has a key feature that the others do not.

    d. Unlike other search engines, Google uses "spiders" to crawl through cyberspace link by link; then it makes a list of the most popular sites.

7. Which statement most effectively paraphrases the topic sentence in paragraph 3?

    a. Like other search engines, Google uses just one or two keywords to return hundreds of thousands of responses.

    b. With a Google search, the best sites appear at the top of the list, whereas the least useful sites appear at the bottom.

    c. The ability to rank results makes Google a more effective search engine.

8. In paragraph 2, which type of transition opens sentence 5?

    a. cause and effect

    b. comparison

    c. reversal

    d. addition

9. How would you describe the author's tone?

    a. sarcastic

    b. admiring

    c. angry

    d. shocked

10. From this reading, you could correctly draw which conclusion?

    a. People who use the Web for research want to get a list that includes as many different sites as possible.

    b. People who use the Web for research do not want to sift through ten useless sites in an effort to find two good ones.

    c. People who use the Web for research do not particularly care if a search engine is slow as long as it gives them good results.

    d. None of the other search engines will ever be able to overtake Google in popularity.

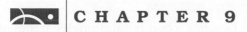

CHAPTER 9

Recognizing and Evaluating Bias

In this chapter, you will learn

- **how to spot bias in informative writing.**
- **how to determine the degree of bias in persuasive writing.**
- **how to evaluate bias in persuasive writing.**

Chapter 9 focuses on the subject of *bias*. You'll learn how a writer's personal feelings can find their way into informative writing despite his or her best efforts to remain emotionally uninvolved or objective. You'll also learn how to recognize when bias is clouding a writer's judgment or ability to be fair. When that happens, critical readers take note and reserve judgment until they can become better informed.

Bias and Context

The word *bias* has a bad reputation. We frequently use it to suggest that someone has a closed mind and cannot or will not listen to opposing points of view. But *bias* merely refers to a point of view or personal leaning. In other words, expressing a bias isn't necessarily bad.

Because of our background, experience, and training, most of us have personal opinions that influence how we see and interpret the world around us. Thus how critical readers respond to bias depends a good deal on context, on where that bias appears. It also depends on how strongly the bias is expressed.

For example, unless they are writing for the editorial page, newspaper reporters are expected to describe events as objectively as possible. If reporters describe events in highly connotative or emotionally charged language that reveals a personal point of view, they are doing readers a disservice. Their biases are inappropriate in that context.

In contrast, newspaper editorials are supposed to express a personal bias. That's one of the reasons we read them. We want, for example, to get columnists Maureen Dowd's and Bob Herbert's perspectives on some current issue or event. However, even writers determined to persuade should offer readers a fair and reasonable argument. If a writer is so committed to one point of view that he or she cannot be logical or fair, then the degree of bias is excessive, and we need to be wary of accepting that writer's point of view without casting around for other opinions.

In sum, then, all writers have biases, and there's nothing wrong with revealing them in the appropriate context. What's important is that writers not let bias interfere with their ability to be logical and fair.

 # Recognizing Bias in Informative Writing

Writers whose primary goal is to inform rather than to persuade usually work hard to keep their biases to themselves. For example, the author of a modern American history textbook might be a long-time Republican who considers Democrat Lyndon Baines Johnson one of history's worst presidents. Yet in writing a chapter about Johnson's presidency, the author should control his or her inclination to criticize Johnson's record. Like writers of reference works, authors of textbooks are expected to provide an impersonal and objective account of events and allow students to form their own opinions.

Pure Information Is Hard to Find

Writers are only human. Try as they might, they can't always eliminate every shred of personal bias from their writing. Although the overall tone of a passage may be emotionally neutral, the connotations of individual words or phrases can still suggest a personal bias or leaning. Note, for example, the italicized words in the following paragraph. These words have negative connotations and suggest that the authors do not admire the way former president Harry Truman handled foreign policy.

President Truman . . . had a personality that tended to increase international tensions. Whereas Roosevelt had been ingratiating,* patient, and evasive, Truman was *brash,* impatient,* and direct. *He seldom displayed the appreciation of subtleties so essential to successful diplomacy.* In his first meeting with V. M. Molotov, the Soviet commissar of foreign affairs, Truman sharply *berated** the Soviet Union* for violating the Yalta accords,* a charge Molotov denied. When Truman *shot back* that the Soviets should honor their agreements, Molotov stormed out of the room. The president was pleased with his "tough method." "I gave it to him straight 'one-two to the jaw.'" This *simplistic display of toughness* became a trademark of American Cold War* diplomacy.* (Norton et al., *A People and a Nation,* p. 488.)

The authors of this textbook passage don't seem to be fans of Harry Truman. After all, would a fan refer to Truman's "simplistic display of toughness"? But what about the next passage? Do you think the writer is also a critic of Harry Truman? Or is he a fan?

---

*ingratiating: eager to please.
*brash: hasty and unthinking.
*berated: criticized harshly at length.
*Soviet Union: the name of fifteen separate republics formerly governed by the Communist party, also called "Soviet Russia."
*Yalta accords: agreements made at the end of World War II in the city of Yalta, located near the Black Sea.
*Cold War: a period of hostile rivalry between the United States and Communist Russia.
*diplomacy: the conduct of relations between nations by government officials.

On his first day in office, Harry Truman remarked to a newspaperman, "Did you ever have a bull or a load of hay fall on you? If you ever did, you know how I felt last night." Yet President Truman's *native intelligence enabled him to grasp quickly the situation into which he was so suddenly thrown*, and on which he had not been briefed by Roosevelt. He had to have a few boon* companions from Missouri around the White House for relaxation, but *he won the friendship and respect of gentlemen in politics* such as Dean Acheson, soldiers such as General Marshall, and foreign statesmen such as Clement Attlee. He made good cabinet, judicial, and ambassadorial appointments; *he kept a firm hand* on the new Department of Defense and the foreign service; and, *with more fateful decisions than almost any president in our time, he made the fewest mistakes.* Truman was always folksy, always the politician, *but nobody can reasonably deny that he attained the stature of a statesman.* (Morison, *The Oxford History of the American People*, p. 1051.)

Unlike the authors of the first passage, the author of this paragraph admires Harry Truman and his record as president. As you can see, his choice of words encourages readers to do the same.

When they recognize bias in writing meant to inform, critical readers don't throw up their hands in horror and refuse to read further. Instead, they identify the author's particular leaning and make sure that they don't absorb it right along with the author's description of events or ideas.

What's Left Out *Is* Significant

Sometimes the intrusion of bias in informative writing is obvious in the author's choice of words. But bias can also be more subtle. Sometimes writers reveal bias not by what they say but by what they leave out. For instance, a history writer who records only the successful or praiseworthy actions of President Franklin Delano Roosevelt but leaves out Roosevelt's order to intern, or imprison, Japanese-Americans during World War II reveals a bias in favor of Roosevelt. Anytime an author describes a person or position where opposing points of view are possible without mentioning—or just barely acknowledging—the opposition, your critical antennae should go up. The writer's purpose may be informative, but you, the reader, are still not getting the whole story.

*boon: in this context, good-natured or jolly.

Check Your Understanding
Explain why context is important to evaluating bias.

Rhetorical Questions Can Reveal a Hidden Bias

As you may know from composition class, rhetoric is the art of using language to persuade. Thus it probably comes as no surprise that **rhetorical questions**—questions that do not require or call for a reply—are a signal of both persuasive intent and personal bias. You can certainly expect rhetorical questions to turn up in persuasive writing, but they can also appear in writing that is meant to inform. They are a tip-off to the unexpected presence of bias. Here's an example.

> Given that more teenagers than ever before are grappling with problems such as depression, alcoholism, and drug abuse, desperate parents are looking for help. Many are turning to wilderness programs, which promise to change the attitude and behavior of the young people by exposing them to and training them for life in the outdoors. Most of these programs are in western states such as Idaho and Utah. Some are on farms or in deserts. Almost all share the same premise: Sustained exposure to a natural world where kids have to fend for themselves can provide troubled young boys and girls with new skills and increased self-confidence. Yet promising as these programs may sound, they raise a crucial question: Is the wilderness—with its inherent, overwhelming, and often uncontrollable dangers—really the place to heal the psyches of troubled children?

Until the last sentence, this passage is mainly informative. The author describes the purpose, location, and theory behind wilderness programs. But in the final sentence, she uses a rhetorical question that reveals her bias. The question, with its emphasis on nature's dangers, is phrased in a way that ensures only one answer—a definite no. Because it doesn't really expect any answer except the one suggested, the rhetorical question reveals a persuasive purpose and personal bias not apparent in the other sentences.

When authors ask questions that don't require an answer, those questions are rhetorical, and you need to be aware of the bias such questions reveal.

Informative Writing Lacking in Bias

- uses an emotionally neutral tone throughout.
- describes both sides of an issue equally without evaluating or judging either side.
- includes no personal opinions or value judgments from the author.
- includes little or no connotative language.

Informative Writing That Reflects a Bias

- may use charged language that interrupts or replaces an emotionally neutral tone.
- reveals an author's personal opinion.
- emphasizes either positive or negative views of a subject but doesn't give equal space to both sides.
- uses rhetorical questions.

EXERCISE 1　**DIRECTIONS** Each of the following passages comes from a source where one would expect the author to eliminate any evidence of bias. Read each one. Then circle the appropriate letter to indicate whether the author or authors have eliminated all evidence of bias.

EXAMPLE

Trial Elements

1 A trial is often compared to a boxing match. Both are contests between *adversaries*, persons who oppose or fight one another. In a trial, the adversaries are called **litigants** and, rather than hitting each other, they challenge each other's evidence and testimony. For this reason, an American trial is often labeled an **adversary proceeding**. The judge acts as a referee and interprets the rules of the "match."

2   The person who files suit in a civil case is called a **plaintiff**. In a criminal trial, the prosecution brings the charges. The U.S. attorney is the prosecutor in federal cases. In state trials, the prosecutor may be known as the state's attorney, county prosecutor, or district attorney. The person being sued or charged with the crime is the **defendant**.

3   Every trial has two purposes: to establish the facts of the case and to find the law that applies. The role of the jury is to decide questions of fact. (Adapted from Hardy, *Government in America*, p. 502.)

Presence of Bias   a. The author is describing the elements of a trial and clearly favors our legal system.

b. The author is describing the elements of a trial and is clearly critical of our system.

c. It's impossible to determine the author's personal feelings.

EXPLANATION   Drawn from a textbook, this selection does not reveal any bias for or against the U.S. legal system. The language remains almost completely denotative, and there is no evidence of the author's personal opinion.

1. The Presidency of John F. Kennedy

1   John F. Kennedy's ambitious social program, the New Frontier, promised more than Kennedy could deliver: an end to racial discrimination, federal aid to education, medical care for the elderly, and government action to halt the recession* the country was suffering. Only eight months into his first year, it was evident that Kennedy lacked the ability to move Congress, which was dominated by conservative Republicans and southern Democrats. Long-time members of Congress saw him and his administration as publicity hungry. Some feared the president would seek federal aid to parochial schools. The result was the defeat of federal aid to education and of a Kennedy-sponsored boost in the minimum wage.

2   Still struggling to appease conservative members of Congress, the new president pursued civil rights with a notable lack of vigor. Kennedy did establish the President's Committee on Equal Employment Opportunity to eliminate racial discrimination in government hiring. But he waited until late 1962 before honoring a

*recession: economic downturn.

1960 campaign pledge to issue an executive order forbidding segregation in federally subsidized housing. Meanwhile, he appointed
five die-hard segregationists to the federal bench in the Deep
South. The struggle for racial equality was the most important
domestic issue of the time, and Kennedy's performance disheartened* civil rights advocates. (Adapted from Norton et al., *A People
and a Nation,* p. 991.)

Presence of Bias   a. The authors are admirers of John F. Kennedy.

b. The authors are critical of John F. Kennedy.

c. It's impossible to determine the authors' personal feelings.

2. The Civil Rights Act of 1964

1   In 1961, a new administration, headed by President John F.
Kennedy, came to power. At first Kennedy did not seem to be
committed to civil rights. His stance changed as the movement
gained momentum and as more and more whites became aware
of the abuse being heaped on sit-in demonstrators, freedom riders
(who tested unlawful segregation on interstate bus routes), and
those who were trying to help blacks register to vote in southern
states. Volunteers were being jailed, beaten, and killed for advocating activities among blacks that whites took for granted.

2   In late 1962, President Kennedy ordered federal troops to
ensure the safety of James Meredith, the first black to attend the
University of Mississippi. In early 1963, Kennedy enforced the
desegregation of the University of Alabama. In April 1963, television viewers were shocked to see civil rights marchers in Birmingham, Alabama, attacked with dogs, fire hoses, and cattle prods.
(The idea of the Birmingham march was to provoke confrontations
with white officials in an effort to compel the national government
to intervene on behalf of blacks.) Finally, in June 1963, Kennedy
asked Congress for legislation that would outlaw segregation in
public accommodations.

3   Two months later, Martin Luther King Jr. joined in a march on
Washington, D.C. The organizers called the protest a "March for
Jobs and Freedom," signaling the economic goals of black America. More than 250,000 people, black and white, gathered peace-
ably at the Lincoln Memorial to hear King speak. "I have a dream,"
the great preacher extemporized,* "that my four little children will

---

*disheartened: disappointed.
*extemporized: spoke without practice or preparation.

one day live in a nation where they will not be judged by the color of their skin but by the content of their character."

4　　Congress had not yet enacted Kennedy's public accommodations bill when he was assassinated on November 22, 1963. His successor, Lyndon B. Johnson, considered civil rights his top legislative priority. Within months, Congress enacted the Civil Rights Act of 1964, which included a vital provision barring segregation in most public accommodations. This congressional action was, in part, a reaction to Kennedy's death. But it was also almost certainly a response to the brutal treatment of blacks throughout the South. (Janda et al., *The Challenge of Democracy*, pp. 549–550.)

Presence of Bias　a. The authors are admirers of John F. Kennedy.

b. The authors are critical of John F. Kennedy.

c. It's impossible to determine the authors' personal feelings.

3. **Lowell, Robert** (1917–1977)

American poet from a famous aristocratic American family; regarded by most critics as the best English language poet of his generation and by certain readers as beyond criticism altogether. For better or for worse, Lowell was the modern poet-as-film-star: his private affairs were apparently carried out mainly in public (this is miscalled "confessionalism"): his themes included the personalities and behavior of his relatives, his various marriages and liaisons,* the (presumably) affective disorder* which landed him in the hospital many times, and so on. Lowell was extremely gifted, but the conventional view of his development—even where it judges the most recent poems as failures—is not quite correct, for it mistakes potential for achievement, and overrates him. (Adapted from Martin Seymour-Smith, *Who's Who in Twentieth-Century Literature.* New York: McGraw-Hill, 1976, p. 216.)

Presence of Bias　a. The author admires Robert Lowell.

b. The author is critical of Robert Lowell.

c. It's impossible to determine the author's personal feelings.

---

*liaisons: love affairs.
*affective disorder: a disorder that involves extreme shifts in emotion; in Lowell's case, from great enthusiasm to deep depression.

4. The Animal Rights Movement

1 Opposition to animal research has a long history, going back at least as far as the antivivisectionist* movement of the nineteenth century. In recent years the growth of the animal rights movement was spurred by a book called *Animal Liberation* (1975), by Australian philosopher Peter Singer. Singer argued that many uses of animals by humans—for food, for clothing, and as captive research subjects—reflected "speciesism": the exploitation of certain species (nonhuman animals) for the benefit of another (humans). Because animals, like humans, can feel pain, Singer argued, they are entitled to just as much consideration as humans are.

2 In Singer's view, speciesism is a form of discrimination that is just as evil as racism and sexism. "Would the experimenter be prepared to perform his experiment on a human infant?" Singer asks. "If not, then his readiness to use nonhumans is simple discrimination" (Singer, 1976, p. 156).

3 Many animal rights supporters have advanced their views in books and articles and have worked for laws and regulations that would ensure the humane treatment of animals. Others have resorted to acts of terrorism in the name of animal rights (Jasper & Nelkin, 1992). Some activists have invaded animal laboratories, destroyed equipment, stolen data, and let the animals out of their cages. Animal rights activists have also staged dramatic demonstrations . . . in an attempt to convince the public of what they see as the cruelty of animal research.

4 The animal rights movement has been accused by researchers of painting a distorted picture of animal research. In fact, most animal research is neither cruel nor painful, and the large majority of animal researchers are concerned about animal welfare (Novak, 1991). When researchers employ surgical procedures with animals, they almost always use anesthesia to eliminate pain. Many animal rights supporters acknowledge such humane practices but believe that animal research remains unnecessarily intrusive. But the moral fervor of other animal rights advocates has led them to engage in misleading portrayals of scientists as sadists and laboratories as torture chambers. (Rubin et al., *Psychology,* pp. 68–69.)

---

*antivivisectionist: person opposed to the cutting of living animals for scientific purposes.

Presence of Bias   a. The authors support the animal rights movement.

b. The authors are critical of the animal rights movement.

c. It's impossible to determine the authors' personal feelings.

5. Frida Kahlo

1 The Mexican artist Frida Kahlo (1907–1954) was born Magdalena Carmen Frida Kahlo y Calderon in Coyoacán, Mexico. Although she began her education intending to be a physician, she was forced to change her mind when she suffered a terrible accident at the age of eighteen. The accident left her so debilitated that a life devoted to medicine would have been far too strenuous for her to pursue.

2 While she was recovering from the accident, Kahlo began painting. In 1928, she approached famed muralist Diego Rivera (1886–1957) and asked for his opinion of her work. Rivera thought she had talent and encouraged her. One year later, the two were married. Their relationship, however, was stormy, and they were divorced in 1939, only to remarry the following year.

3 Kahlo's first public exhibition took place in 1938. In 1939, her work was exhibited in a Paris exhibition called "Mexique." As a result of the exhibition, one of her works, a self-portrait, was purchased for the famed French museum the Louvre. Although her problems with Rivera and her constant physical pain—her body had never completely recovered from the accident—encouraged Kahlo's growing dependency on alcohol, Kahlo continued to paint, further developing her brand of colorful, personalized surrealism.* However, she did not have a major exhibition in her own country until 1953, one year before her death. Overshadowed in her lifetime by her famous husband, Kahlo overtook him in death, so much so that her name has become better known than his. Yet in comparing the works of the two artists, a key question emerges. Does Kahlo's fame rest on the quality of her work or on the current tendency to celebrate women artists whatever their degree of talent? (Christopher Fresa, *Modern Painters.* Cleveland: Bogus Publications, 1999, p. 200.)

Presence of Bias   a. The author admires Kahlo's work.

b. The author is critical of Kahlo's work.

c. It's impossible to determine the author's personal feelings.

---

*surrealism: a movement in art and literature emphasizing the expression of the imagination as it might appear in dreams, with the emphasis on free association rather than logic and reason.

Responding to Bias in Persuasive Writing

We don't expect to find bias in informative writing, and encountering it usually comes as a surprise. Persuasive writing, in contrast, raises different expectations. We expect writers to be personally engaged—to tell us about the personal reasons, experiences, or feelings that led them to their points of view. In short, we expect persuasive writing to reveal a bias. What we don't expect, even in persuasive writing, is that writers are imprisoned or blinded by their biases. Despite their personal feelings, we expect them to acknowledge opposing points of view and to treat those points of view fairly. A writer who fails to acknowledge opposing points of view or, even worse, ridicules or insults them should not be completely trusted. Yes, the writer may sound confident and convincing, but critical readers are not impressed. They don't assume that a confident tone is always based on solid evidence, and they demand to know a bit more before deciding to support or share the writer's point of view.

Acceptable Versus Unacceptable Bias

To understand the difference between acceptable and excessive or unacceptable bias in persuasive writing, compare the following two passages.

> After reading about courses teaching television literacy,* I must say I am appalled by the sheer idiocy that abounds on so many college campuses today. What should instructors do if they discover that students have trouble reading their textbooks because they have spent too much time watching television? What else? Give those same students more television to watch. That way, teachers can avoid making demands on students *and* avoid doing their job. All they need to do is flip on the television set and call themselves "media specialists."

The author of this passage expresses a strong bias against courses in television literacy. But the problem with the passage is not the author's bias. The problem is that the author doesn't explain or defend those feelings. Instead, in a tone of outraged irony, he

---

*television literacy: the condition of being educated or knowledgeable on the subject of television.

ridicules the opposing point of view. In this case, the author's bias interferes with his ability to treat fairly those who hold an opposing point of view. This degree of bias is unacceptable. It is so excessive it interferes with the writer's ability to persuade.

To see how an author can express a bias and still be persuasive, read the following passage. Although the author freely admits her bias, she still keeps an open mind and points out not just what's wrong about opposing points of view, but what's right as well.

> I must admit to being troubled by courses that make commercials and soap operas the focus of study. Although I agree that TV programming plays a powerful role in most people's lives and that its influence over our minds and imaginations should be critically examined, I'm not sure courses in television literacy are the answer. A better alternative would be to make television viewing a small portion of a course on critical reading and thinking. Then students could apply their critical skills to both television scripts and images. This approach would eliminate what seems to be a legitimate objection to courses in television literacy—that they encourage students to do more of what they already do: Watch too much TV.

In this passage, the author expresses a definite bias: She is not in favor of courses "that make commercials and soap operas the focus of study." Still, that bias does not prevent her from giving the opposing point of view its due. She admits that the influence of television "should be critically examined," and she suggests an alternative to courses in television literacy: critical thinking or reading courses that would allot a small portion of time to analyzing scripts and images.

To evaluate bias in persuasive writing, review the following list. Anytime you encounter a writer intent on persuasion, make sure you can say no to these four questions.

Questions to Help Evaluate Bias in Persuasive Writing

---

1. Does the author use a tone that drips with sarcasm or seethes with anger?

2. Does the author insist that an opposing point of view is not possible for sane people? (For *sane*, you can also substitute words like *patriotic*, *honest*, and *ethical*.)

3. Does the author rely more on insulting the opposition than on explaining the merits of his or her point of view?

4. Does the author insist that opposing points of view have no value or merit without explaining why those opposing views are mistaken or inaccurate?

If you answer yes to even one of the four questions, you need to find a more balanced discussion of the issue before taking sides.

Check Your Understanding

Define acceptable bias.

_____

_____

_____

_____

EXERCISE 2   **DIRECTIONS**   Each of the two selections expresses a bias, but only one expresses such a strong bias that critical readers might be suspicious of the author's ability to fairly evaluate opposing points of view. Circle the appropriate letter to correctly identify the author's degree of bias.

1. Jefferson's Bible

1 While serving as third president of the United States, Thomas Jefferson began a project to revise the Bible. Jefferson studied the Scriptures every day and selected what he considered to be the Bible's best and most authentic material. Concentrating on the New Testament—specifically the Gospels of Matthew, Mark, and Luke—Jefferson literally cut out his favorite passages (which he said were like "diamonds in a dunghill") with a razor and pasted them together to create his own version. In doing so, he censored any mention of Jesus as God or the Son of God. He also eliminated all miracles and supernatural events.

2   For example, his version does not include any reference to the immaculate conception* of Jesus by Mary, the miracles attributed to Jesus, or the Resurrection. Jefferson's version ends with Jesus's burial. Jefferson told one correspondent that the material he discarded was all "ignorance . . . , superstitions, fanaticism, and fabrications." The material he chose is mainly composed of parables and sayings that focus on the morals and ethics Jesus preached and demonstrated. According to one scholar, Jefferson "made a Socrates out of Jesus."

3   Jefferson never intended for anyone to see this new version. However, it was discovered in 1886 and published by the Government Printing Office from 1904 to 1957. The book was distributed to all new congressional members during that time. In 2001, the book was reissued by Beacon Press as *The Jefferson Bible: The Life and Morals of Jesus of Nazareth.* Since its publication, some scholars and religious leaders have denounced Thomas Jefferson's revision of the New Testament as "sheer audacity." These critics object to Jefferson's project of cutting and pasting together what he considered to be the best and most authentic passages of Scripture. They say his tampering with a sacred work mocks the Christian faith.

4   Although understandable, this criticism of Jefferson is not really fair. Jefferson did not rewrite the Bible; he merely selected those passages that were, to him, most meaningful. What Jefferson did was no different from highlighting, underlining, or annotating the Bible to mark favorite passages, something many Christians have done for years in their personal copies. Furthermore, Jefferson did not intend for his version of the Bible to be published. He intended to keep it to himself for private study and reflection. Remember it was discovered and printed only after his death.

5   The point is that Jefferson did not try to convince anyone else to accept his personal beliefs. Throughout his career Jefferson fought for religious freedom for all Americans, and we still possess this freedom today. Therefore, it's not fair to attack Jefferson for exercising the same right we enjoy. On the contrary, we should view his version of the Bible as an important historical document, one that helps us better understand this very important and influential founding father.

---

*immaculate conception: According to the Bible, the Virgin Mary conceived without the stain of original sin.

a. The author's bias would probably not inhibit her from recognizing and fairly evaluating an opposing point of view.

b. The author's bias is so strong she might have a hard time fairly evaluating an opposing point of view.

2. Hunters Are Wildlife's Best Friends

1   I am a hunter. I feed my family with the game I kill. All Americans eat dead stuff, but our meat is better, and it is harvested with a responsible connection to the Earth. This is true conservation—the wise use.

2   Our time-honored tradition continues because, in the face of global habitat destruction, those of us who cherish wildlife have demanded restrictions on its harvest, based on a sound and proven scientific equation of sustained-yield management.

3   We save and guard habitat and manage wildlife not for our freezers or shooting opportunities but rather for the future of this most valuable resource. The condition of wildlife and the ground that supports it are a barometer by which the quality of our lives is based.

4   Read this very carefully, because these game laws and restrictions are self-imposed, insisted on, policed and financed by us hunters to the tune of billions of dollars a year.

5   The lies of the animal rights freaks are perpetrated for the single cause of greed. They are to animals what Jim Bakker* was to religion. After deceiving millions of Americans out of millions of dollars, they have yet to save any animals.

6   Look closely at their shameful agenda and track record. These zealots* hate Americans who eat turkey on Thanksgiving. They are also extremely dangerous, having bombed medical testing labs, destroyed family-run farms, and even been convicted of animal abuse on occasion, grandstanding their lies at the expense of real animals' welfare. They recently committed their most repulsive act yet when one group proclaimed that the heinous crimes charged to accused mass murderer Jeffrey Dahmer were the exact same crimes as the preparation of a chicken for the grill. No clear-thinking American could possibly stand behind such statements.

---

*Jim Bakker: a television evangelist who served time in prison for improper use of funds collected for religious purposes.
*zealots: people so committed to a cause they lack all reason or compassion.

7   If you truly appreciate wild animals, these people must be stopped and hunters' dedicated efforts must be supported. Sure, we have bad guys. But those who conduct legal banking businesses should never be lumped together with bank robbers. Poachers are the bad guys, and hunters despise them as our number one enemy.

8   When responsible citizens are genuinely concerned about the well-being and future of wildlife, they do their homework and discover the truth. Our Ted Nugent World Bowhunters organization is dedicated to this truth and to sharing the wonderment of the great out-of-doors with our families and friends. (Ted Nugent, "Hunters Are Wildlife's Best Friends," *USA Today*, October 3, 1991.)

a. The author's bias would probably not inhibit him from recognizing and fairly evaluating an opposing point of view.

b. The author's bias is so strong he might have a hard time fairly evaluating an opposing point of view.

 ## Bias and Careless Logic

Writers whose bias keeps them from even considering opposing points of view are inclined to let their logic get careless. They don't do this because they're dishonest. They are just so certain of their own rightness they don't necessarily think about convincing others. Sure that they—and only they—are right, they fail to thoroughly explain their positions and fall back instead on flawed logic such as circular reasoning, slippery slope thinking, and personal attacks.

Circular Reasoning

The paragraph on page 490 about Jefferson's bible offers a good example of an informed opinion. Would you say the same about the next passage?

We Americans like to brag about progress, but, in fact, life was better in the nineteenth century than it is now. People were happier and more at peace with themselves. There just wasn't the same kind of anxiety and tension that there is today. If we had a chance, we would probably all get into a time machine and go backward rather than forward. All of our highly touted technological progress has not brought us an increased measure of contentment.

The author of this paragraph believes life was better a century ago. However, she—like our friend who prescribes garlic for headaches—offers no solid evidence to back up that opinion. The author could have quoted from journals, letters, or interviews; cited statistics; or even mentioned that there was hardly any divorce a century ago. But instead of offering support that might justify her opinion, the author simply makes the same claim over and over in different words. This tactic, called **circular reasoning**, is typical of writers given to promoting uninformed opinions. Lacking evidence, they rely on repetition. In response to circular reasoning, critical readers rightly become skeptical, or suspicious, of the opinion being expressed.

Slippery Slope

Writers who engage in *slippery slope* thinking insist that taking even one step in a particular direction will invariably lead to a series of steps that will end in disaster. Here's an example:

> If we ban handguns, the next step will be the banning of rifles, and then people who hunt for food will no longer be able to feed their families.

Writers who use slippery slope thinking assume that events similar in nature follow one another without reference to any specific context or condition. They ignore the fact that events usually arise in response to or as a result of particular circumstances. For example, many people want to ban handguns because statistics show a connection between handguns in the home and violent crime, both in and outside the home. That same connection does not exist between hunting rifles and crime. Thus it makes no sense to claim that banning handguns will automatically lead to banning rifles. Handguns and rifles are similar kinds of weapons, but they are used in very different ways and under very different circumstances.

Personal Attacks

Be wary of writers who respond to opposing points of view by personally attacking the opposition. In the following passage, note how the author attacks her opponent's character rather than his point of view.

Once again, David DeGrecco, columnist for the *New Jersey Sun*, has presented his tired old case for gun control. As usual, DeGrecco serves up the argument that gun-control laws can help eliminate some of the violence plaguing city streets across the country. Outspoken as usual, DeGrecco is curiously silent about his recent bout with criminal behavior. Less than two weeks ago, he and several others were arrested for demonstrating at the opening of a nuclear power plant. For one so determined to bring law and order to our streets, DeGrecco does not seem to mind breaking a few laws himself.

Here the author is obviously biased against the gun-control laws championed by David DeGrecco. That's certainly her right. Still, to be persuasive, she needs to challenge what the columnist claims— that gun-control laws can help eliminate violence. But instead of doing that, she attacks the man personally, pointing out that he was recently jailed. Yet DeGrecco's position on nuclear power has nothing to do with the issue at hand—gun control. This, then, is another instance of bias clouding the writer's ability to respond fairly and respectfully to opposing points of view.

EXERCISE 3 **DIRECTIONS** Each of the following selections expresses a strong bias for or against a particular position. But in some cases the author has fallen victim to one of the three errors in reasoning just described. Circle the appropriate letter to indicate an error. *Note*: Even the readings with errors may have some sound logic, so examine each paragraph individually.

1. No Sexual Harassment Equals No Soldiers

1 Over the years, there's been a good deal of attention focused on sexual harassment in the military, and rightly so. No one wants to see officers in charge of young female recruits abuse their power by sexually harassing those in their care. However, supporters of women in the military are making a crucial mistake when they try to eliminate sexism in the military and at the same time insist that women should go into combat alongside men.

2 To be a warrior means that a soldier has to revert to a more primitive mode of behavior and thought. It means that one has to assume a kill-or-be-killed mentality that allows little room for compassion or thought. It is very difficult, perhaps impossible, to encourage this mindset in men and at the same time expect them to fight side by side with women without reverting to a more primitive mode of behavior. As Fred C. Ikle, an undersecretary of

defense in the Reagan administration, expressed it, "You can't cultivate the necessary commitment to physical violence and fully protect against the risk of harassment. Military life may . . . foster the attitudes that tend toward rape, such as aggression and single-minded assertion."[†]

3   Viewed from this perspective, efforts to eliminate sexual harassment could have disastrous consequences during wartime, particularly if women are allowed into combat. Committed to being respectful toward women, male soldiers will also feel that they must rein in their aggression in the presence of women. As a result, they will hold back during combat training and eventually during combat itself. Our country will lose its military strength and its position as a world power.

a. The author uses circular reasoning.

b. The author uses slippery slope reasoning.

c. The author uses a personal attack.

d. None of the three errors is present.

2. Egg Donation May Not Be Such a Miracle for Donors

1 Because so many couples desperately want a child and can't have one, the search for women willing to donate their eggs for in vitro fertilization* has become a big business. Although many people consider in vitro fertilization a wondrous miracle, I must admit to being skeptical about the use of egg donors. The couple who gains a child, thanks to a donor, may be rightly jubilant; the donor, however, may be taking more risks than she realizes.

2   For starters, the egg donation process is not particularly pleasant. To prepare, women take daily hormone injections which force the maturation of ten to twenty eggs instead of the normal one or two. As a result of the injections, donors often suffer cramping and mood swings. Sometimes their ovaries become dangerously enlarged. At this time, there have been no signs of long-term side effects on donors, but it is possible that the injections may increase the possibility of ovarian cancer. No one really knows for sure what the long-term effects are mainly because in vitro fertilization hasn't been around for very long.

[†]Richard Rayner, "The Warrior Besieged," *New York Times*, June 22, 1997, p. 29.
*in vitro fertilization: *in vitro* literally means "in glass"; the term refers to the process of creating life in an artificial setting outside the human body.

3   Those who favor the use of egg donors argue that the women are being well paid for the risks they take. Unfortunately, the issue of payment only points to another objection. Some clinics pay donors as much as $8,000 for their eggs. In the face of such a sum, women who are young or poor—or in many cases both—can be lured by the money into ignoring the risks. As Diana Aronson, the executive director of Resolve, the national support group for infertile couples, points out: Large sums of money offered donors can lead to "inappropriate assessment of risk. If you're a college student, four cycles at $5,000 each may pay for . . . college"[†] and if you're a poor, unmarried mother, $5,000 will pay the rent for months.

4   Yes, egg donation may well provide infertile couples with the baby they so desperately desire, but someone else may be paying a terrible price for their joy. Couples desiring to use egg donation should ask themselves whether they are willing to let another woman take serious health risks so that they can become parents.

a. The author uses circular reasoning.

b. The author uses slippery slope reasoning.

c. The author uses a personal attack.

d. None of the three errors is present.

3. Attica Still Haunts Us

1   The worst prison insurrection in U.S. history occurred at the Attica Correctional Facility near Buffalo, New York, in September 1971. The atmosphere at the prison had been tense because of overcrowded and deteriorating conditions. Then, on September 9, a guard broke up a scuffle between two inmates, who were put into isolation cells as a result. A rumor that the inmates were being tortured spread throughout the facility. The next day, a group of inmates armed with baseball bats, pipes, chairs, and knives seized control of an exercise yard and took forty guards hostage. They demanded, among other things, better conditions and amnesty for crimes committed during the revolt. They also insisted that New York's governor, Nelson Rockefeller, come to the prison to address the problem. Governor Rockefeller refused. Three days after the riot began, he authorized state police to regain control of the facility by force if necessary.

[†]Marie McCullough, "Life for Sale: Market for Women's Eggs Is Heating Up," *Philadelphia Inquirer*, March 8, 1998, pp. A1 and A19.

2   On September 13, police armed with tear gas and shotguns stormed the prison, firing more than 2,000 rounds of ammunition in six minutes. Eleven hostages and thirty-two inmates were killed as a direct result of the police attack, although initially it was thought that the deaths were a result of prisoners' violence. When the prison's guards were again in control, they stripped, beat, and tortured inmates. They were especially brutal with the riot's leaders. In the first hours after regaining control of the prison, police also denied medical care to the wounded. As a result, in 1974, lawyers filed a class-action lawsuit on behalf of the 1,280 prisoners who were harassed during the attack.

3   But it wasn't until August 2000 that the State of New York finally settled the suit filed on behalf of the 1,280 prisoners incarcerated at the Attica Correctional Facility during the riot. Those men still alive received a group settlement of $8 million for the suffering they endured as a result of the prison insurrection. And make no mistake, they deserve every penny of that settlement, even a good deal more. Prior to the revolt, inmates had endured appallingly inhumane conditions at the facility. They had been permitted a shower just once a week and were allotted a roll of toilet paper just once a month. Their food was poor in quality and badly prepared. Requests for meals reflecting religious preferences were routinely denied. Because the prison's capacity had been exceeded by more than 40 percent, prisoners were also subjected to terrible overcrowding. When the inmates finally seized control of an exercise yard and took the guards hostage, Nelson Rockefeller flatly refused to address what were legitimate grievances. Determined to present himself as tough on crime and criminals, Rockefeller ordered a poorly executed assault on the prison, which left more than forty people dead.

4   Given the circumstances, it's impossible to understand the mind-set of critics who think the Attica settlement was fair. Its unfairness is indisputable, and those who think otherwise are refusing to look at the obvious. For what reason is impossible to say.

a. The author uses circular reasoning.

b. The author uses slippery slope reasoning.

c. The author uses a personal attack.

d. None of the three errors is present.

4. **Same-Sex Schools: Are They Really a Step Forward for Girls?**

1 On March 2, 2004, the Bush administration announced plans to relax restrictions on single-sex public schools and classrooms. The announcement came after almost thirty years of determined efforts by the federal government to enforce coeducation in public schools. Thanks to new regulations drafted by the U.S. Department of Education, it will be much easier to establish and maintain single-sex schools at taxpayers' expense.

2 This move on Washington's part will undoubtedly delight those who have been insisting, for more than a decade, that girls in particular would do better in school if boys were not present. The movement in favor of single-sex education for girls started in 1992 when the American Association of University Women published the report "How Schools Shortchange Girls." As the title indicates, the study strongly suggested that public schools do not do enough to ensure that boys and girls get equal treatment. Much was made of the fact that, according to the study at least, teachers tend to call on boys more often than on girls. For those educators convinced by this lone study, easing the restrictions on single-sex schools is an undisguised blessing.

3 However, there are at least two good reasons why single-sex schools, particularly for girls, are anything but a blessing. As Feminist Majority Foundation president Eleanor Smeal points out, the loosening of restrictions on single-sex schools offers no special benefit to girls. Like other feminists, Smeal believes that separating students by gender encourages sexism among boys and does not adequately prepare girls for jobs in integrated workplaces.

4 When it comes to preparation for the future, Smeal is 100 percent correct in her criticism. Girls need to have boys in the classroom. If they don't learn how to work and to compete with boys while in school, where the stakes aren't so high, how will they compete after graduation in the workplace? Imagine, for example, that a young woman, who has never been in intellectual competition with men, enters a management meeting where only men are present. Is she going to be able to hold her own, or is she going to become anxious and tongue-tied because her male colleagues don't use a "nurturing" style, purportedly employed more by women than by men?

5   Then, too, where does this isolation by gender end? Can we expect women who have gone to single-sex schools to demand that places of employment also be segregated? Probably. Once we agree that women should study only with one another, a segregated workplace can't be far behind.

a. The author uses circular reasoning.

b. The author uses slippery slope reasoning.

c. The author uses a personal attack.

d. None of these three errors is present.

5. Power and Prosecutors

1 In April 2007, the attorney general of North Carolina, Roy A. Cooper III, announced that he was dismissing all charges against three Duke University lacrosse players. The three young men had been accused of raping a young woman who performed at one of their parties. At the same time that he announced the dismissal of the charges, Cooper also rebuked Michael B. Nifong, the district attorney of Durham County, for rushing to accuse the young men while failing to thoroughly investigate the woman's allegations.

2   Cooper's public rebuke highlights a point made by Angela J. Davis in her new book, *Arbitrary Justice: The Power of the American Prosecutor*. Davis, a professor of law at American University Washington College of Law, argues that prosecutors all over the country have the power to direct and control the outcome of criminal cases, often with serious, even disastrous, consequences.

3   According to Professor Davis, Nifong, who has been accused of withholding exculpatory evidence favorable to the defense, is the rule rather than the exception. She insists that prosecutors intent on winning withhold evidence all the time, without oversight or penalty for their actions, and that our current judicial system, with its lack of transparency,* has no system in place for checking prosecutorial power. If anything, Davis argues, state legislatures have routinely passed laws that increase the power of prosecutors without worrying about the possibility that prosecutors might, unconsciously or intentionally, be corrupted by the extent of their authority. Victims of prosecutorial excess, she insists, are usually poor people who do not have the resources to mount a defense against prosecutorial injustice. Her hope is that the Duke case

---

*transparency: ease of visibility.

will shine a much-needed light on this problem in the American justice system and force a change.

4   Despite Professor Davis's detailed and often eloquent analysis of the failings inherent in the current judicial system, those ready to agree with her and demand a change in our justice system should remember that Professor Davis was once intimately acquainted with that very same system. Angela Davis first came to the public's attention when she was linked to the murder of Judge Harold Haley during an attempt to free a Black Panther defendant in a courtroom in 1970. Davis went underground, becoming the subject of an intense manhunt. After 18 months as a fugitive, she was captured, arrested, tried, and eventually acquitted in one of the most famous trials in recent U.S. history. Is it any wonder that she doesn't like prosecutors? (Source of information on Professor Davis's new book: Evan R. Goldstein, "The Power of the Prosecutor," *Chronicle of Higher Education*, May 11, 2007, p. B2.)

a. The author uses circular reasoning.

b. The author uses slippery slope reasoning.

c. The author uses a personal attack.

d. None of these three errors is present.

Check Your Understanding

Explain the errors in logic described in Chapter 9: circular reasoning, slippery slope thinking, and personal attacks.

_____

_____

_____

_____

_____

_____

**Allusion
Alert**

Pages 483–485 referred to the administration of President John F. Kennedy. One of the allusions you will see quite often in discussions of the Kennedy era is the reference to Camelot. In the legends surrounding King Arthur—who may have really existed as a sixth-century Welsh warrior—Camelot is the capital or center of Arthur's kingdom, a place where courage, beauty, and talent reign for a brief time despite a tragic ending. The musical about King Arthur, called "Camelot," was on Broadway when John Kennedy died. After his wife mentioned they loved the music, the Kennedy administration came to be known as Camelot, largely because of a line from the title song, "one brief, shining moment that was known as Camelot."

In addition to the Kennedy era, though, Camelot is also used to generally allude to a brief and wonderful time that passes all too quickly, as in this sentence about basketball great Larry Bird: "In Larry Bird's first eight seasons, he led the Celtics to three NBA titles and staged a battle royale with the phenomenal Magic Johnson of the Lakers. For basketball fans, it was Camelot time, and we haven't seen its like since."

Now that you understand allusions to Camelot, how would you paraphrase this sentence? "As handsome and charming as John F. Kennedy, some thought that when Bill Clinton arrived in office, Camelot would come back with him."

Paraphrase _____

_____

_____

To get more practice analyzing paragraphs, go to **laflemm.com** and click on *Reading for Thinking*: "Online Practice." Complete the interactive exercise on recognizing bias.

■ **DIGGING DEEPER**

LOOKING AHEAD As Heather Gehlert, the author of this reading, points out, the word *guys* is often used to refer to women as well as men. But is this any different from the days when we talked about newsmen to refer to male and female journalists? Nowadays the more accepted term is *journalists* or *newspeople*. Is the word *guys* somehow different? See what the author thinks and then see if you agree or disagree.

CAN THE TERM "GUYS" REFER TO WOMEN AND GIRLS?

1 Going out to eat with my father is always a tense affair. For the five or ten minutes it takes from the time the host or hostess seats us to the time our server comes to take our order, I sit quietly, feeling anxious and wondering how our waiter or waitress will greet us. Will she say, "How are you all doing today?" Or, "What can I get you folks to drink?" If we're near our hometown in the rural Midwest, there is a good chance she'll say the latter, but, more often than not, we hear: "Hi, my name is Jamie, and I'll be taking care of you guys today. Our specials this afternoon are smoked salmon, parmesan-crusted tilapia . . ." "Excuse me," my dad cuts in, his eyes narrowing to a glare, "but I only see one guy here." My stomach drops and I stare at the table in front of me, trying not to roll my eyes. The lecture never takes more than a minute, but it's still excruciating.* On rare occasions, a waiter or waitress will argue back, saying "guys" is a gender-neutral term. But, most of the time, he or she just stands very still, jaw dropped, looking stunned. Because this exchange never leads to a thoughtful discussion of gender and language, I long ago dismissed it as one of my dad's quirks—a one-person tirade* to laugh at and let go of. Besides, one of my father's biggest heroes is Bill O'Reilly—not exactly a portrait of feminist ideals.

2   Yet, for whatever reason, now that my dad and I live in different states and I see him only once or twice a year, I'm noticing how often men and women use the phrase "you guys" to refer to both sexes. It happens in restaurants, at council meetings—even in grade-school classrooms. And so, a voice in the back of my head is starting to say, Maybe he has a point. Maybe this isn't an

---

*excruciating: extremely painful.
*tirade: angry speech.

arbitrary* battle over an arbitrary word. A cursory* glance at blog postings shows that the use of the word "guys" is much more discussed and much more controversial than I had realized. Giving credence to my dad's argument, dozens of postings read something like this: Try walking up to a group of men and women and saying, "Hey, girls, how's it going?" The reaction won't be positive. The men in the group probably won't find the feminine label amusing—and certainly not arbitrary.

3   So why is the reverse acceptable? Why is "girls" gender-specific, but "guys" is not? "Is it because men are not considered gendered, like white people do not consider themselves a race or European-Americans ethnic?" writes Farrah Ferriell, an instructor at the Women's Studies Program at Western Kentucky University. "I say yes . . ." A few posts down on the same site, Kathy Ferguson, a teacher from Hawaii, writes, "You know, I think I find myself in the 'get a life' camp on these questions. . . . '[Y]ou guys' [can be said] with affection. Words don't have inherent meanings, after all; they have the meanings that usage gives them, and are not necessarily stuck in past patriarchal contexts. I also find that I have many more important struggles in my classrooms than these." Ferguson's point that words don't have inherent meanings is a good one. "He" could easily be a feminine pronoun and "she" a masculine word if we used them that way. However, "guys" is not a brand new term. And it's already gendered in many circumstances. "Guy" is masculine (e.g., That guy over there is really attractive). "The guys" is too (e.g., Will the guys in the room please stand up?) So, the distinction—and the controversy—seems to lie with the colloquial* phrase, "you guys."

4   That distinction makes me curious to know how many people consciously think "you guys" is gender-neutral and how many are just so used to hearing and saying it that they don't even notice its prevalence.* In my case, I had never consciously thought the term was gender-neutral; rather, I had just never carefully considered it until my dad brought it to my attention. Even if the majority of people really have thought deeply about this issue and still maintain that "you guys" is gender-neutral, why are generic* words always male? I have a hard time seeing any difference between "guys" and words like "mankind" or "Congressman." At

---

*arbitrary: determined by chance.
*cursory: quick, not thorough.
*colloquial: conversational.
*prevalence: commonness.
*generic: referring to a general category.

one time, those words, too, were considered generic. But now we know they're not—they're laden with meaning. They make women invisible by reinforcing the idea that men are the norm against which women are compared.

5   Why, then, would we want to risk repeating the same mistake? Especially when the solution is as simple as replacing "you guys" with "you all." True, this issue is not as pressing as, say, the war in Iraq or homelessness in San Francisco. But that does not mean it is not legitimate. Just because there's a war in Iraq, does that mean that the divorce someone is going through is any less real or painful? That being fired suddenly feels great? . . . Or perhaps a better example: Just because slapping a woman isn't as serious as raping her, does that mean we should ignore the former? On its face, using the term "you guys" seems harmless enough— gendered or not. But as the number of people who see it as gendered grows, so does the phrase's power to influence ideas about identity—to perpetuate the subtle yet damaging belief that being male is more valuable than being female. And the consequences of that extend far beyond the awkwardness of me having lunch with my dad. (Heather Gehlert, AlterNet: "Can the Term "Guys" Refer to Women and Girls?" February 28, 2007, www.alternet.org/ story/48527/.)

Sharpening Your Skills

DIRECTIONS Answer the following questions by circling the letter of the correct answer or filling in the blanks.

1. What is the main idea of the entire reading?

_____

_____

2. The main idea appears in what paragraph? _____

3. The author alludes to television talk show host Bill O'Reilly to tell readers about her father. The allusion implies her father

a. watches a lot of television.

b. is a radical when it comes to feminism.

c. is fairly traditional in his thinking.

d. is aggressive in conversation.

4. In paragraph 1, the author doesn't say why her father's lecture is *excruciating*. Readers are expected to infer that it is

   a. a reminder of a painful memory.

   b. embarrassing.

   c. long-winded.

   d. old news.

5. What does it mean for a word or phrase, in this case *guys*, to be gender-neutral?

   _____

6. Based on paragraph 4, it's logical to conclude that the author believes

   a. "you guys" is a gender-neutral expression.

   b. most people don't care if "you guys" is gender-neutral.

   c. most people have never stopped to seriously consider if "you guys" is gender-neutral.

7. Based on paragraphs 4 and 5, you can infer that

   a. the author thinks worrying about whether "you guys" is gender-neutral is a waste of time.

   b. the author believes "you guys" really is gender-neutral.

   c. the author thinks we should replace "you guys" with "you all."

8. The author's purpose is to

   a. describe how people commonly use the phrase "you guys."

   b. persuade readers that using the phrase "you guys" to refer to women has harmful effects.

9. The tone of the reading is

   a. concerned.

   b. comical.

   c. outraged.

   d. neutral.

10. Which statement accurately describes the role of bias in this reading?

    a. The author does not think using "you guys" to refer to women is an important issue.

    b. The author thinks using "you guys" to refer to women is an issue worthy of discussion.

    c. It's impossible to determine how the author feels about the subject.

Test 1: Recognizing Bias

DIRECTIONS Each of the following passages appears in a source where one would expect to find no evidence of bias. However, some of the passages do reveal a bias. Read each one. Then circle the appropriate letter to indicate what the passage does or does not reveal about the author's bias.

1. **Donoso, José (1924–1996)**   Born in Santiago, Chile, to a prominent family, José Donoso quit school at age nineteen and traveled in South America, where he worked on sheep farms and as a dockhand. Later, he went to school in the United States and received a B.A from Princeton University in 1951. Donoso spent the next decade working as a teacher and journalist in Chile, writing profusely. In 1955, Donoso published his first book, *Veraneo y otros cuentos* (*Summer Vacation and Other Stories*), which received the Municipal Literary Prize; one year later, he published *Dos cuentos* (1956; *Two Short Stories*), and in 1957 his first novel, *Coronación* (*Coronation*), appeared to much critical acclaim. *Coronación* describes the moral collapse of an aristocratic family, a recurrent theme in Donoso's work. Marrying Maria Pilar Serrano, a Bolivian painter, in 1961, Donoso began writing what is often considered his masterpiece, *El obsceno pájaro de la noche* (1970: *The Obscene Bird of Night*). He also renewed his friendship with Mexican novelist Carlos Fuentes, whom he had met in grade school. While spending some time at Fuentes's home, he completed *El lugar sin límites* (1966; *Hell Has No Limits*) and *Este Domingo* (1966; *This Sunday*), grim novels of psychological desolation and anguish. (Appiah and Gates, *The Dictionary of Global Culture*, p. 185.)

   a. The authors admire Donoso's work.

   b. The authors are critical of Donoso's work.

   c. It's impossible to determine the authors' personal feelings.

 2. **Christoph Gottwald (1954–),**   German novelist and poet. Because he got his start writing mysteries popular with everyone but the critics, Gottwald's emergence as a serious novelist has been shamelessly ignored. Yet his 1997 novel *Endstation Palma*, reminiscent of Heinrich Böll's early work, is worthy of serious critical attention. Using themes he probed previously in novels like *Cologne Crackup* (1980) and *Lifelong Pizza* (1994), Gottwald

again explores the inability of language to communicate our deepest needs, often with tragic results. Abandoning the comic detachment he used so brilliantly in his first two books, the novelist now assumes the voice of a man passionately committed to his subject and tortured by the strength of his own emotions. A conservative voice in a literary world desperate to be trendy, Gottwald may not get the audience he deserves, either in Germany or America. However, his fiction—in contrast to the work of his more highly praised and less talented contemporaries—will be read by future generations, long after more acclaimed novelists have been properly consigned to the trashbin of history. (Wordsmith, *Twentieth Century Comparative Literature*, p. 20.)

a. The author admires Gottwald's work.

b. The author is critical of Gottwald's work.

c. It's impossible to determine the author's personal feelings.

3. Litigation

Though it is expensive and time-consuming, litigation can bring about remarkable political change. Perhaps the outstanding example is the use of the courts by the National Association for the Advancement of Colored People (NAACP) in the 1940s and 1950s. In a series of cases, culminating in the *Brown v. Board of Education* decision in 1954, NAACP lawyers argued and the Supreme Court affirmed that school segregation was illegal in the United States. Women's groups, consumer groups, environmental groups, religious groups, and others have followed the lead of the civil rights movement in taking their causes to the courts. Corporations and trade associations have also engaged in litigation. However, the high cost restrains many groups. One interest group, the Women's Equity Action League, was unable to appeal a court ruling against it in an important case because it could not afford the $40,000 necessary to pay for copies of the trial transcript. (Gitelson et al., *American Government*, p. 228.)

a. The authors are supporters of litigation as an instrument of social change.

b. The authors are critical of litigation as an instrument of social change.

c. It's impossible to determine the authors' personal feelings.

4. Sigmund Freud

1 Sigmund Freud (1856–1939), the father of psychoanalytic theory, grew up in a middle-class Jewish family in Vienna, Austria, where he spent most of his life. As a young man, Freud received a medical degree and opened a practice as a neurologist. Among his patients were many cases of *hysteria*, an emotional disorder characterized by physical symptoms such as twitches, paralysis, and even blindness without any discernible* physical basis. Freud's work with these patients gradually led him to conclude that repressed memories and wishes underlie emotional disorders and that personality involves a perpetual conflict among forces within ourselves.

2 Freud's early writings were denounced by other scientists. In his later years, however, Freud began to receive the recognition he deserved for his courageous exploration of the human mind. When the Nazis invaded Austria in 1938, Freud was persuaded to move to England. He died a year later. (Rubin et al., *Psychology*, p. 395.)

a. The authors admire the work of Sigmund Freud.

b. The authors are critical of Freud's work.

c. It's impossible to determine the authors' personal feelings about Freud's work.

5. Jewish Refugees from the Holocaust

By World War II's end, about six million Jews had been forced into concentration camps and had been systematically killed by firing squads, unspeakable tortures, and gas chambers. The Nazis also exterminated as many as 250,000 gypsies and about 60,000 gay men. During the depression, the United States and other nations had refused to relax their immigration restrictions to save Jews fleeing persecution. The American Federation of Labor and Senator William Borah of Idaho, among others, argued that new immigrants would compete with American workers for scarce jobs, and public opinion polls supported their position. This fear of economic competition was fed by anti-Semitism. Bureaucrats applied the rules so strictly—requiring legal documents that fleeing Jews could not possibly provide—that otherwise-qualified refugees were kept out of the country. From 1933 to 1945, less than 40 percent

---

*discernible: visible to the eye or accessible to the understanding.

of the German-Austrian immigration quota was filled. (Norton et al., *A People and a Nation*, p. 543.)

a. The authors believe that World War II immigration restrictions were necessary at the time.

b. The authors are highly critical of World War II immigration restrictions.

c. It's impossible to determine the authors' personal feelings.

Test 2: Recognizing Careless Logic

DIRECTIONS Circle the appropriate letter to indicate which passages reveal one of the three errors in logic described in Chapter 9.

1. In the 1980s, using allegedly "recovered" memories as evidence of past child abuse was considered legitimate, and some therapists went to great lengths to make their patients remember the horrific childhood experiences that were destroying them as adults. Unfortunately, the therapeutic pendulum has swung in the other direction, and many current researchers and therapists echo the sentiments of Richard McNally, who suggests the following in his book *Remembering Trauma*: "The notion that the mind protects itself by repressing or dissociating memories of trauma rendering them inaccessible to awareness is a piece of psychiatric folklore devoid of convincing empirical* support."[†] It's hard to imagine how McNally, a widely respected clinical psychologist who has reviewed much of the experimental research and clinical evidence on recovered memories, could make this claim. After all, it is clear that recovered memories are real. We do, in fact, repress what is too painful to remember, and some of us have done so under conditions that need to be recalled, despite the pain the recollection might evoke. Repressed memories of child abuse need to be retrieved because the adults involved in them have done terrible things to children and need to be punished for their crimes. Recovered memories are more than real. They can also serve as evidence to punish those guilty of child abuse. We cannot consign them to the trashcan of psychiatric folklore. To do so is to add to the original crime that caused the repression in the first place.

   a. circular reasoning

   b. slippery slope thinking

   c. personal attacks

   d. no errors

2. Every five to ten years, it seems that someone decides that the Food and Drug Administration (FDA) is not doing its job, and currently there are, once again, calls for reform. This time around three former secretaries of the Department of Health and Human Services have created what they call the Coalition for a Stronger FDA, an organization

---

*empirical: based on observable evidence.
[†]In Carol Tavris and Elliot Aronson, *Mistakes Were Made*. New York: Harcourt, 2007, p. 111.

demanding agency reform. The goal of the group is to spend more tax-payers' money to increase food inspections and give the agency more regulatory authority. One of the group's spokespeople, Dr. David A. Kessler, a former FDA commissioner, bluntly says, "Our food safety system is broken." The question that has to be asked, though, is this: If the food safety system was so bad, why didn't Dr. Kessler fix it when he was commissioner? All too often, political officials, once they are out of the limelight, look for causes that will help them recover the public's attention. Jimmy Carter is probably the best example of this syndrome,* and David Kessler is another.

a. circular reasoning

b. slippery slope thinking

c. personal attacks

d. no errors

3. 1 When Jonas Salk, the creator of the polio vaccine, was questioned about patenting the vaccine, he replied, "Could you patent the sun?" But that was 1954, when scientists got their money from the government or independent funding institutions. It was a time, as bioethicist and scientist Sheldon Krimsky writes, when "it was considered unseemly for a biologist to be thinking about some kind of commercial enterprise while at the same time doing basic research." The two just didn't mix.

2 Unfortunately, that was then, and this is now, as the saying goes. Today many scientists serve on boards of industry, while universities have established offices of intellectual property to establish patents. Universities also provide incentives for faculty who are able to patent discoveries. The result is that disinterested scientists who work solely for the public good are becoming a rarity, and the public welfare is suffering because of it. For instance, among 161 studies purporting to analyze the possible adverse effects of new chemicals, investigators found that only 14 percent of the industry-funded studies claimed the chemicals could pose a threat. In contrast, 60 percent of the independently funded studies indicated that the chemicals might have dangerous side effects. Scientists may be telling themselves they can serve two masters, industry and the public, but there is a growing body of evidence suggesting this is just not true. (Source of information: Tavris and Aronson, *Mistakes Were Made*, p. 49.)

---

*syndrome: pattern.

a. circular reasoning

b. slippery slope thinking

c. personal attacks

d. no errors

4. 1 In May 2007, Jack Kevorkian, the advocate for assisted suicide, was released from prison after serving eight years of his ten- to twenty-five-year sentence for second-degree murder. While it is true that Dr. Kevorkian is seventy-nine years old and in poor health, it is also true that releasing him from prison sets a very bad example for all those who believe that assisted suicide is not murder. Currently, Oregon is the only state in the country that allows terminally ill patients to ask for and get what are, in fact, lethal amounts of medication. Most other states have rejected such legislation because they do not want to encourage assisted suicide. Yet in letting Dr. Kevorkian leave prison early, the state of Michigan, where Dr. Kevorkian was incarcerated, suggests precisely that, that helping people commit suicide is not a crime deserving the severest possible penalty. What the shortening of Dr. Kevorkian's prison term does is open the door for more people to follow in his footsteps, as indeed they will. After all, what is eight years to a fanatic committed to the belief that people have the right to choose the moment in which they die?

2 Given the reduction of Dr. Kevorkian's sentence, it would not be surprising to find more states allowing physician-assisted suicide. Once the idea of helping the terminally ill end their lives seems an acceptable and penalty-free practice, the time will quickly come when it's easier to argue that those on life support should be taken off, even if they have not, prior to being hospitalized, indicated that they refuse all attempts to keep them alive by artificial means.

a. circular reasoning

b. slippery slope thinking

c. personal attacks

d. no errors

5. 1 "Street View," the new feature Google has added to its map service, has stirred up a heated controversy. Type your address into the search box and what may well come up is a picture of your house; zoom in for a close-up and you can probably read the license plates on the cars parked in front of your house or, as happened to Mary Kalin-Casey, you might be able to see your cat sitting in the window. As Ms. Kalin-Casey pointed out in an interview with the *New*

York Times, "There is a line between taking public photos and zooming in on people's lives." Is the line a legal one? Probably not; at least not at this stage, no one is claiming that Google is breaking the law. What they are claiming is that some of the images on Street View are cyber versions of pictures a peeping Tom might take.

2   In one instance, users were asked for the "Best Urban Images" found on Street View. Among the images ranking near the top was a picture of two young women sunbathing on a rooftop and wearing bikinis. The women didn't know they were being photographed, and for many of us that is a clear invasion of privacy. While Google was careful to contact domestic violence shelters nationwide to make sure it did not include any shelter locations in its photographs, it did not contact everyone whose home is the object of a Street View. But until they do, Street View should stay in the planning stage because Ms. Kalin-Casey is not alone in thinking that a picture of her street is one thing, a picture of her home is another, and she does not want Google or anyone else peeping into her windows. (Source of information: Miguel Helft, "Google Zooms in Too Close for Some," June 1, 2007, www.nytimes.com/2007/06/01/technology/01private.html.)

a. circular reasoning

b. slippery slope thinking

c. personal attacks

d. no errors

Test 3: Taking Stock

DIRECTIONS Read the passage. Then answer the questions by filling in the blanks or circling the letter of the correct response.

Identity Theft

1. In 2001, Wanda, a 39-year-old Navy wife in Virginia Beach, received a call from a bank asking her to make a payment on a delinquent $15,000 loan. Wanda had never taken out a loan, but the bank had not made a mistake. As it turned out, a woman had stolen Wanda's personal information and used it to obtain credit. Wanda found out she had $17,000 in unpaid debts and a bad credit record. In short, she was the victim of "identity theft," a crime that involves pilfering someone's personal information and using it to obtain fraudulent credit cards and loans. Because identity theft is a growing problem with serious consequences, Americans need to change some of their habits or risk becoming victims like Wanda.

2. Stealing someone's identity is not all that difficult. Thieves just need to get their hands on an individual's name, Social Security number, and date of birth—the required information for getting credit. While the assumption is that criminals find this information on the Internet, they actually rely more on low-tech methods. The trash, for example, is a gold mine for documents containing personal information, so many identity thieves go "dumpster-diving" in search of discarded tax forms, legal documents, and hospital records. Others rob postal drop boxes to get information from individuals' correspondence. Some set up bogus websites that lure victims into providing personal data. Still others pay company employees to steal customers' records. As one identity thief put it, "All you need is some idiot, some young kid working at a hospital or bank who's not happy with his job, who's not making enough money. He'll sell you Social Security numbers." After gathering the necessary details, an identity thief can apply for a credit card, even listing his or her own name as an additional cardholder on the account. When the cards arrive, the thief begins spending.

3. According to the Federal Trade Commission (FTC), in 2002, about 7 million American consumers were victims of identity theft, and the number of complaints received by the agency has nearly doubled every year for the past three years. The growing number of such cases is producing severe consequences for both businesses and individuals. The FTC estimates that identity theft costs nearly $53 *billion* every year. Because federal law protects

them from fraudulent use of credit cards, consumers are usually not responsible for thieves' purchases. However, even if cardholders' liability is only $50, they may be forced to spend thousands more to undo the damage to their credit histories. Most victims of identity theft must devote many frustrating hours to sorting out the mess, dealing with angry creditors, and restoring their reputations as trustworthy consumers.

4   Businesses and government agencies have tried to combat this problem in a number of ways. Congress recently made identity theft a separate crime. The FTC created and maintains an identity theft database that provides information to law-enforcement agencies about perpetrators, victims, and potential witnesses. The three major credit-reporting companies—Equifax, Experian, and TransUnion—have begun sharing fraud notifications with each other. In addition, some state legislators are trying to pass new laws to limit the appearance of Social Security numbers on identification cards and other public documents. They are also seeking to double the maximum prison time, from 10 to 20 years, for identity theft.

5   However, everyone involved agrees that not enough is being done. Individuals and businesses criticize law-enforcement agencies for letting jurisdiction* issues hamper investigations and for focusing only on the larger cases while letting the smaller ones languish. As security issues analyst Avivah Litan points out, fewer than 1 in 700 instances of identity theft ends with the offender's conviction. Therefore, says Litan, many thieves have learned that identity theft is a "lucrative, low-risk crime."

6   Others, in contrast, blame organizations for not doing more to safeguard the information they collect. Hospitals and universities, for example, aren't required by federal law—as financial services and insurance companies are—to protect information. Still others blame credit card companies for their lax security practices. According to Ed Mierzwinski of the U.S. Public Interest Research Group, "There's so much money to be made that [credit card] companies don't care if they lose some money to identity theft." As a result, says Mierzwinski, "They don't have passwords that are changed often enough. They don't have audit trails,* . . . and they make credit too easy to get." He also criticizes the U.S. Congress, which "has made identity theft a crime for the criminal,

---

*jurisdiction: area of control or authority.
*audit trails: lists of documents that would allow the company to trace illegal credit back to the thief.

but it hasn't gone after the companies who aid and abet identity theft."

7 Then, too, consumers themselves contribute to the problem. In 1999, Americans made $1.1 billion worth of credit card purchases. The average American uses several cards and carries an average of $5,800 in credit card debt from month to month. The median total outstanding debt of households rose 9.6 percent between 1998 and 2001. In 2003, 1.6 million people filed for bankruptcy. Clearly, people are living well beyond their means, and most of them are teetering on the brink of financial disaster.

8 Still, consumers can take a few steps to protect themselves. For instance, if your Social Security number appears on your driver's license, have the state issue an alternate number. Also, don't print your Social Security number on checks, and do not share it with anyone unless absolutely necessary. Rip up the credit card solicitations you receive in the mail so that no one can get them from the garbage and fill them out. Before throwing them away, shred all documents that contain vital personal information. Obtain a copy of your credit report at least once a year to check for suspicious activity. Don't leave mail in your mailbox with the red flag up. As FTC Identity Theft Program manager Joanna Crane says, "To prevent [identity theft] from ever happening at all, you have to be extremely vigilant." (Sources of information: Stephen Mihm, "Dumpster-Diving for Your Identity," *New York Times Magazine*, December 21, 2003, p. 42; Neal Conan, "Analysis: Identity Theft," *Talk of the Nation (NPR)*, November 26, 2002.)

1. In your own words, what is the main idea of the entire reading?

_____

_____

2. Which statement best sums up the main idea of paragraph 2?

a. Dumpsters contain all the information an identity thief needs to commit crimes.

b. It is relatively easy to steal identities.

c. People can protect themselves from identity thieves in a number of ways.

d. Credit cards are much too easy to obtain.

3. How would you label the following supporting detail from paragraph 2? "The trash, for example, is a gold mine for documents containing personal information, so many identity thieves go 'dumpster-diving' in search of discarded tax forms, legal documents, and hospital records."

a. major

b. minor

4. In paragraph 4, the phrase "this problem" in sentence 1 is a stand-in for what phrase? _____

5. Which pattern or patterns organize the details in paragraph 4?

a. definition

b. simple listing

c. comparison and contrast

d. cause and effect

e. classification

6. What conclusion follows from the reading?

a. The thief who stole Wanda's identity was caught and sentenced to jail time.

b. The author of the reading considers identity theft a difficult problem that has no solution.

c. The author of the reading was once a victim of identity theft.

d. Currently, the best hope for avoiding identity theft is in the hands of the consumer rather than the government or legal system.

7. In paragraph 7, the author suggests that American consumers are part of the problem because they are so in debt. This criticism reflects what error in logic?

a. circular reasoning

b. personal attacks

c. slippery slope thinking

d. irrelevant evidence

8. From the information in paragraph 8, a reader might logically draw the conclusion that Joanna Crane

   a. believes very little can be done to stop identity theft.

   b. would support laws that make credit much harder to get.

   c. would probably agree that every business and household should have a paper shredder.

9. The author's purpose is

   a. to inform.

   b. to persuade.

10. How would you describe the author's bias?

   a. The author is critical of how little is being done by institutions to protect consumers from identity theft.

   b. The author thinks consumers need to take some responsibility for protecting themselves from identity theft.

   c. It is impossible to determine the author's personal bias.

C H A P T E R 10

Understanding and Evaluating Arguments

 In this chapter, you will learn

- why the ability to analyze arguments is a key critical reading skill.

- how to identify the essential elements of an argument.

- how to recognize some common errors that undermine or weaken an argument.

You may not realize it, but arguments are everywhere. The candidate who says "vote for me" offers an argument explaining why. The salesperson who wants to sell you a new DVD player is quick to describe the advantages of the latest models. Even a neighbor who wants to sell you her used car will try to convince you that you're getting a real bargain.

The point of these examples is simple: You need to be in a position to analyze and evaluate the competing arguments that confront you practically every day. Once you are able to do that, you can make informed decisions about which arguments are convincing and which ones are not. Then you can decide with confidence whether you want to share—or at least consider—the other person's point of view.

 # What's the Point of the Argument?

The starting point of an argument is the opinion, belief, or claim the author of the argument wants readers to accept or at least seriously consider. Whenever you encounter an argument in your reading, the first thing to do is decide what opinion, belief, or claim the author thinks you should share. In other words, you need to discover the main idea or central point of the author's argument. Discovering that point will be easier once you are familiar with the three kinds of statements—condition, value, and policy—likely to be at the heart of written arguments. What follows are the three types of statements, along with a description of the evidence they usually require.

Statements of Condition

Statements of condition assert that a particular condition or state of affairs exists or existed. Although these statements are based more on fact than opinion, they usually identify a state of affairs not likely to be well known by readers and thus in need of proof. The following would all be considered statements of condition.

1. Unlike most other crimes, drug offenses are subject to three jurisdictions: local, state, and federal.
2. The family as we know it has not been in existence for very long.
3. Although Henry David Thoreau celebrated solitude in his now classic book *Walden*, he actually spent very little time alone.
4. Romantic love is a very modern concept.

Although reasons are essential in any argument, statements of condition usually rely heavily on sound factual evidence.

Statements of Value

Statements of value express approval or disapproval. Frequently, they contrast two people, ideas, or objects and suggest that one is better or worse than the other. The following are all statements of value.

1. Among all the sports, boxing is the most dangerous and dehumanizing.
2. Lyndon Baines Johnson was a better president than most people realize.
3. The Electoral College has outlived its usefulness.
4. Given the outbreaks of mad cow disease, the government needs to do a better job overseeing the inspection of beef.

Although statements of value can and do require facts, they typically need examples and reasons as well. For instance, to talk about the "state of decline" in U.S. education, a writer would probably have to offer statistics proving an earlier superiority and more statistics or examples illustrating the current decline.

Statements of Policy

Statements of policy insist that a particular action should or should not be taken in response to a specific condition or situation. These policy statements often include words like *must*, *need*, *should*, *would*, or *ought*. The following are all statements of policy.

1. The Internet needs to be covered by strict censorship laws that protect children from access to pornographic material.
2. Shoeless Joe Jackson[†] should be admitted to the Baseball Hall of Fame.
3. College athletes who do not maintain a B average should be prohibited from playing any team sports.
4. Consumers should have the right to take legal action against HMOs that provide inadequate medical care.

With statements of policy, factual evidence is important, but sound reasons that answer the question *why* are also essential.

Can different types of argument statements be combined? The answer is most definitely yes. Here's an example: "Despite the cloud of

---

[†]Shoeless Joe Jackson: a famous baseball player who many think was unfairly implicated in the Black Sox baseball scandal of the 1919 World Series.

shame surrounding his name, Shoeless Joe Jackson was never convicted of any crime. As one of the most talented players in the history of baseball, he should be admitted to the Baseball Hall of Fame." In this case, we have a statement of condition (Jackson was never convicted of a crime). But we also have a statement of value (he was one of the most talented players in the history of baseball), and a statement of policy (he should be admitted to the Baseball Hall of Fame).

When you analyze an argument, look for statements that describe an existing condition, assign value, or urge a policy or action. Such statements, separately or combined, are usually central to an author's argument.

Check Your Understanding
Describe the three types of statements likely to be at the center of an argument.

1. Statements of condition _____

_____

_____.

2. Statements of value _____

_____

_____.

3. Statements of policy _____

_____

_____.

EXERCISE 1 **DIRECTIONS** Read each passage. Paraphrase the main idea or point of the argument. Then circle the appropriate letter to identify it as a statement of policy, value, or condition.

EXAMPLE

Does the Punishment Fit the Crime?

1 In 1984, lawmakers wanted to send a tough message on the sale of drugs. As part of a bill called the Sentencing Reform Act, Congress assigned mandatory minimum sentences for all drug

offenses taking place near schools. Offenders could get anywhere from five to twenty years based on the amount of drugs involved. With time, additional mandatory minimums became part of the legal system, including the "three strikes you're out" provision that specified life sentences for repeat drug offenders. While mandatory minimum sentences are still seen by some to be a solution to drug use in the United States, there are several reasons why the courts need to reconsider the effectiveness of mandatory minimum sentences.

2 Thanks in large part to mandatory minimum sentencing, jails are currently packed. A federal penitentiary like Leavenworth, built to house 1,200 prisoners, has occasionally housed as many as 1,700, creating overcrowded conditions that breed violence and riots. State correctional facilities are also overflowing, so much so that violent criminals are sometimes released to make room for nonviolent drug offenders. In 2003, the number of imprisoned drug offenders was an astonishing 330,000. This figure is larger than the number of people imprisoned for all crimes in 1970.

3 The group Families Against Mandatory Minimums (FAMM) regularly lobbies Congress for the repeal of mandatory minimums, citing cases like that of Michael T. Irish, a first offender sentenced to twelve years in federal prison for helping unload hashish from a boat, or Charles Dulap, imprisoned for eight years in federal prison for the crime of renting a truck used by a friend to import marijuana. FAMM was founded over a decade ago by Julie Stewart, who hadn't been particularly interested in the subject of mandatory minimum sentencing until her brother was imprisoned for five years after he was caught growing marijuana seedlings. It was Stewart who came up with FAMM's motto, "Let the Punishment Fit the Crime." (Source of information: Schlosser, *Reefer Madness*, pp. 53–55.)

a. In your own words, what is the point of the author's argument?

The courts need to change the laws requiring mandatory

minimum sentences.

b. That point is a statement of
   a. condition.
   b. value.
   (c.) policy.

EXPLANATION Because the author supports a particular action—the court's reconsideration of mandatory minimum sentences—*c* is the best answer.

1. Parents with a computer in the house should purchase software that filters, or blocks out, objectionable websites. Although most parents do not turn their kids loose in front of a computer and let them surf the Web on their own, even devoted parents cannot be with their children all the time. This means that impressionable kids can find their way to inappropriate, even dangerous websites. Kids can, for example, access websites featuring pornographic pictures and text. Children with access to the Web can also come into contact with people who want to seduce and abuse them. To avoid these very real dangers, parents need to purchase one of the many software programs that effectively locks kids out of all sexually explicit websites. There is also software that blocks access to expressly racist or anti-Semitic* sites. Parents might think about purchasing this type of software as well. While such websites may not endanger children's bodies, they can certainly harm their minds.

a. In your own words, what is the point of the author's argument?

_____

_____

_____

b. That point is a statement of

   a. condition.

   b. value.

   c. policy.

2. In far too many cases, students' grades have become so inflated that they're virtually meaningless. A whopping 83 percent of high school seniors who took the Scholastic Aptitude Test (SAT) in 1993 claimed to be A or B students, while only 28 percent of their 1972 counterparts made the same claim. It's nice to think that the nation's kids are just getting smarter. However, we'd have to overlook the fact that, during the same period, the average SAT score actually *fell* from 937 to 902. And what happens to all those stellar* students when they get to college? Well, they are likely to receive more inflated

*anti-Semitic: prejudiced against all people of the Jewish faith.
*stellar: excellent.

grades. The old "gentleman's C,"* earned by those who put forth only minimum effort, has become the "average person's B." Even elite, demanding schools like Harvard are doling out A's and B's to those who do little more than show up for class. The C grade no longer seems to exist. That's why graduate schools and employers have begun interpreting applicants' grade point averages much differently. They know that A sometimes stands for "average."

a. In your own words, what is the point of the author's argument?

_____

_____

_____

b. That point is a statement of

    a. condition.

    b. value.

    c. policy.

3. Retrieving Forgotten Heroes

1 Although some of the names of heroes of the civil rights movement have become household words—who hasn't heard of Martin Luther King Jr.?—others have remained relatively unknown, and it's time that attention be focused on their many contributions. Most of us know, for example, about Rosa Parks and how her refusal to move to the back of the bus and give up her seat to a white passenger helped spark the historic bus boycott in Montgomery, Alabama. Fewer people know that in 1944, a young black woman named Irene Morgan boarded a Greyhound bus in Gloucester County, Virginia, headed for Maryland. Weak from recent surgery, Morgan also refused to move to the back of the bus when told to do so. The police were called and she was arrested. Convicted of her "crime," Morgan appealed her decision and made legal history when Thurgood Marshall[†] argued her case before the Supreme Court and won.

2   Also relatively unknown is Fred L. Shuttlesworth. As pastor of the First Baptist Church in Birmingham, Alabama, Shuttlesworth organized the demonstrations and marches that helped win civil rights for African Americans. Shuttlesworth was a tireless organ-

_____

*gentleman's C: An old expression indicating that the sons of the wealthy or well-placed need not worry about achieving a grade higher than a "C," because they had money and position to back them up.

†Marshall later became the first African American to sit on the Supreme Court.

izer with superhuman courage. Racists bombed his house and beat him bloody numerous times, but Shuttlesworth was unstoppable. He provided shelter to civil rights workers and preached unending opposition to any form of discrimination.

3   Twenty-one-year-old student activist Robert Zellner was recruited to the civil rights movement by Martin Luther King Jr. himself. Zellner went on to become the first white field secretary in the largely black organization Student Non-Violent Coordinating Committee (SNCC). At demonstrations or sit-ins, Zellner always carried a Bible to indicate that his protests were meant to be peaceful, but that didn't save him from several brutal beatings. On one march to a voter registration office, Zellner was called a traitor to his race and beaten to the ground. In a sadly ironic twist, he was then jailed for being part of an "illegal" demonstration. A hero in his own right, Zellner never abandoned the cause of civil rights and he is still active as a speaker on college campuses. Yet his name is not widely known. (Source of information: Taylor Branch, *Parting the Waters: America in the King Years, 1954–63*, New York: Simon and Schuster, 1988, p. 513.)

a. In your own words, what is the point of the author's argument?

_____

_____

_____

b. That point is a statement of

    a. condition.

    b. value.

    c. policy.

4. *Empress of Ireland*

1   Most people know about the early twentieth-century maritime disasters the *Titanic* and the *Lusitania*. The *Titanic* was a British luxury ocean liner that accidentally hit an iceberg during its very first voyage from England to New York. When it sank on April 15, 1912, more than 1,500 of the 2,200 people on board lost their lives. The British ocean liner *Lusitania* was torpedoed and sunk by a German submarine off the coast of Ireland on May 7, 1915. When the ship went down, 1,198 died. Few people, however, realize that sandwiched between these two high-profile sinkings was a third one every bit as tragic. On May 29, 1914, the *Empress of*

Ireland, a luxury liner that made regular voyages between England and Canada, sank off the coast of Quebec. Of the 1,477 people aboard, 1,012 were killed.

2   On the day it sank, the *Empress of Ireland* had just left Quebec and was steaming down the St. Lawrence River toward open ocean water. Another ship, the Norwegian *Storstad,* was steaming downriver. The river was shrouded in fog; nonetheless, the two ships sighted each other at about 2:00 a.m. Aboard the *Empress of Ireland,* Captain Henry Kendall made adjustments to his ship's course, estimating that his changes would allow the ships to pass each other at a comfortable distance. Moments after Kendall altered his course, however, the *Storstad* completely disappeared in the fog. Concerned about the lack of visibility and the other ship's proximity, the captain blew the liner's whistle three times to indicate to the *Storstad* that he had ordered a reversal of the engines to slow his ship down. But when the Norwegian ship materialized again, it was heading straight for the side of the *Empress of Ireland.* Captain Kendall knew instantly that a collision was unavoidable, and he immediately ordered a sharp turn in hopes of reducing the *Storstad*'s impact to just a glancing blow.

3   Unfortunately, though, when the *Storstad* hit the *Empress of Ireland,* its bow went between the liner's steel ribs, delivering a fatal wound. Water poured in so fast that most of the liner's sleeping passengers had no chance to escape. Just ten minutes after impact, the ship lay on her side, with hundreds of passengers locked in her hull. Only fourteen minutes after the collision, the *Empress of Ireland* sank into the icy waters of the St. Lawrence. It was the worst disaster in Canadian history. (Source of information: www.pbs.org/lostliners/empress.html.)

a. In your own words, what is the point of the author's argument?

_____

_____

_____

b. That point is a statement of
   a. condition.
   b. value.
   c. policy.

Four Common Types of Support

Writers who want their arguments to be taken seriously know they have to do more than state their opinion. To be persuasive, they also have to provide their readers with support. In response, critical readers need to recognize and evaluate that support, deciding if it is both relevant and up to date. Four common types of support are likely to be used in an argument: reasons, examples and illustrations, expert opinions, and research results.

Reasons

Reasons are probably the most common method of support used by authors who want to argue a point. In the following passage, the author hopes to convince readers that cockfighting is a bloody and dangerous sport to support:

> Cockfighting, the pitting of two roosters in a ring to fight one another, often to the death, is illegal in all but one of the fifty states, Louisiana. In August of 2008, it will become illegal there as well. Unfortunately, the so-called "sport" of cockfighting continues despite laws forbidding it. Thus efforts to discourage participation must continue, and those who support the fights must be made to see what a violent, inhumane, and dangerous pastime it truly is. Cockfighting is one of the worst forms of animal cruelty. Participants strap razor-sharp spurs to two roosters' legs, feed them stimulants, and then toss the birds into a pit, where they tear each other apart until one dies a bloody death.
>
> Besides being cruel to animals, cockfights encourage illegal and violent behavior. They are notorious arenas of illegal gambling and drug trafficking, firearms dealing, and fighting. Shootings have even occurred when the violence in the ring spills over into the crowd. Raids of cockfights often result in many arrests. In a very real way, cockfights reinforce the idea that violence is a source of amusement. Perhaps worst of all, they send the same message to children whose parents allow them to witness these fights. The parents apparently consider them nothing more than good, clean fun.

To persuade readers to share her point of view, the author of this passage provides four specific reasons: (1) cockfighting is cruel to animals, (2) it encourages illegal and even violent behavior, (3) it reinforces the idea that violence is a source of amusement, and (4) it sends that message to children. By means of these four reasons, the author hopes that readers will begin to share, or at least to seriously consider, her point of view.

Examples and Illustrations

Particularly when arguing general statements of value—for example, boxing is dangerous, pesticides cause health problems, or Isaac Newton was an eccentric* genius—writers are likely to cite examples, illustrations, or even personal experiences as proof of their point. Look at how the following author uses examples to persuade readers that plastic litter is not just unsightly but also deadly.

> As litter, plastic is unsightly and deadly. Birds and small animals die after getting stuck in plastic six-pack beverage rings. Pelicans accidentally hang themselves with discarded plastic fishing line. Turtles choke on plastic bags or starve when their stomachs become clogged with hard-to-excrete crumbled plastic. Sea lions poke their heads into plastic rings and have their jaws locked permanently shut. Authorities estimate that plastic refuse annually kills up to two million birds and at least 100,000 mammals. (Gary Turbak, "Plastic: 60 Billion Pounds of Trouble," *American Legion Magazine.*[†])

Here's a case where the author piles example upon example in an effort to convince readers that plastic can be lethal.

Expert Opinions

In order to persuade, writers often call on one or more experts who support their position. In the following passage, for instance, the author suggests that cloning geniuses may not be a good idea. To make her point, she gives a reason *and* cites an expert.

> With the birth of Dolly, the first successfully cloned sheep, some have suggested that we can now consider the human gene pool a natural resource. We can clone a Nobel Prize–winning writer like Toni Morrison or a star athlete like Michael Jordan and thereby create a population of gifted and talented people. What could be wrong with that? Well, in the long run, probably a lot.

---

*eccentric: odd, weird.
[†]Also used in Rosen and Behrens, *The Allyn and Bacon Handbook.*

There's simply no guarantee that the clones would be everything the originals were. After all, genes don't tell the whole story, and the clone of a prizewinning scientist, if neglected as a child, might well end up a disturbed genius, no matter what the original gene source. As John Paris, professor of bioethics at Boston College, so correctly says on the subject of cloning, "Choosing personal characteristics as if they were the options on a car is an invitation to misadventure." (Source of information: Jeffrey Kluger, "Will We Follow the Sheep?" *Time*, March 10, 1997, p. 71.)

In this case, the author doesn't just let her argument rest solely on her own reasoning. She also makes it clear that at least one knowledgeable expert is very much on her side.

Research Results

In the same way they use experts, writers who want to persuade are likely to use the results of research—studies, polls, questionnaires, and surveys—to argue a point. In the following passage, for example, the author uses an expert and a study to support a statement of condition: There's a quiet revolution taking place among Amish women.

In a tiny shop built on the side of a farmhouse in Pennsylvania's Lancaster County, Katie Stoltzfus sells Amish* dolls, wooden toys, and quilts. Does she ever. Her shop had "a couple of hundred thousand" dollars in sales last year, says the forty-four-year-old Amish entrepreneur and mother of nine. Mrs. Stoltzfus's success underscores a quiet revolution taking place among the Amish. Amish women, despite their image as shy farm wives, now run about 20 percent of the one thousand businesses in Lancaster County, according to a study by Donald B. Kraybill, a professor of sociology at Elizabethtown College in Elizabethtown, Pennsylvania. "These women are interacting more with outsiders, assuming managerial functions they never had before, and gaining more power within their community because of their access to money," says Professor Kraybill, who recently wrote a book about Amish enterprises. (Timothy Aeppel, "More Amish Women Are Tending to Business," *Wall Street Journal*, February 8, 1996, p. B1.)

To make sure that readers seriously consider his position, the author cites a study and identifies the person who conducted the study, making it clear that his opinion is grounded in solid research.

---

*Amish: a religious group that generally avoids contact with the modern world and its modern machinery.

Check Your Understanding

Name the four types of support common to written arguments.

1. _____   3. _____

2. _____   4. _____

EXERCISE 2 **DIRECTIONS** Each group of statements opens with an opinion or a claim that needs to be argued. Circle the letters of the two sentences that help argue that point.

EXAMPLE Eyewitness testimony is far from reliable.

(a.) The testimony of eyewitnesses can often be influenced by the desire to please those in authority.

(b.) Studies of eyewitness testimony reveal an astonishingly high number of errors.

c. Eyewitness testimony carries a great deal of weight with most juries.

EXPLANATION Statements *a* and *b* both undermine the reliability of eyewitnesses and thereby provide reasons why eyewitness testimony cannot always be considered reliable. Statement *c*, however, is not relevant, or related, to the claim made about eyewitness testimony.

1. Uniforms should be mandatory* for all high school students.

a. Most students hate the idea of wearing a uniform.

b. Parents on a strict budget would no longer have to worry about being able to provide expensive back-to-school wardrobes.

c. If uniforms were mandatory in high school, students would not waste precious time worrying about something as unessential as fashion.

---

*mandatory: required or commanded by authority.

2. All zoos should be abolished.

   a. Zoos only encourage the notion that animals are on Earth for the amusement of humans.

   b. If all zoos were closed, no one has any idea what would happen to the animals now living in them.

   c. Although many zoos have improved the living conditions for the animals they possess, those animals still lack the freedom they have in the wild.

3. Because the deer population is sky-high, hunters should be allowed to shoot more deer per season.

   a. Desperate for food, deer are foraging by the roadside, where many are hit by cars, another indication that their population has to be reduced.

   b. With the exception of hunting, there doesn't seem to be any practical way to slow down the growth in the deer population.

   c. Most hunters have a great respect for the animals they kill.

4. Parents need to limit the amount of television their children watch.

   a. Unlike reading, watching television does not encourage a child to think imaginatively.

   b. Children who watch a lot of television are consistently exposed to violence and may well become too accepting of it.

   c. Programs for children dominate Saturday morning television.

EXERCISE 3 **DIRECTIONS** Read each passage. Then answer the questions that follow.

EXAMPLE Unfortunately, some people still believe that African Americans endured slavery without protest. But nothing could be further from the truth. In 1800, for example, Gabriel Prosser organized an army of a thousand slaves to march on Richmond. However, a state militia had been alerted by a spy, and the rebellion was put down. Prosser was ultimately executed for refusing to give evidence against his co-conspirators. In 1822, Denmark Vesey plotted to march on Charleston, but he, too, was betrayed by an informer. Probably the most serious revolt occurred in 1831 under Nat Turner. It resulted in the execution of Turner and more than a hundred black rebels.

a. What is the point of the author's argument?

It's simply not true that African Americans endured slavery

without protest.

b. Paraphrase the examples used to support that point.

1. *In 1800, Gabriel Prosser organized an army of slaves to*

march on Richmond.

2. *In 1822, Denmark Vesey plotted to take over Charleston.*

3. *In 1831, Nat Turner and more than 100 rebels revolted.*

EXPLANATION In this case, the author uses three examples to make her point: African Americans did not endure slavery without protest.

1. The fact that more women are lawfully arming themselves should be good news for everyone concerned with violence against women. Since the publication of Betty Friedan's *The Feminine Mystique*, feminists have been urging women to be independent and self-sufficient. What better evidence that women have "arrived" than that they no longer have to rely exclusively on the police (still mostly male) for protection? Feminists should applaud every woman who is skilled in handgun use. (Talk about controlling your own body.) Liberation from fear when walking on a dark street, driving on a country road late at night, or withdrawing cash from a bank machine is more important on a daily basis to most women than smashing any glass ceiling in the workplace. (Laura Ingraham, "Armed and Empowered," *Pittsburgh Post-Gazette*, May 19, 1998, p. E3.)

a. What is the point of the author's argument?

_____

_____

b. Paraphrase the reasons used to support that point.

_____

_____

_____

_____

2. All states should consider limiting tractor-trailer traffic on crowded highways. Over the past twenty years, the number of tractor-trailers on our nation's roads and interstates has doubled to 2.6 million, and that number is still increasing. By 2020, the number of trucks is expected to have doubled again. At the same time, though, the capacity of our roads and highways has either remained the same or expanded only a little. Put these two factors together and it becomes clear that the growing number of trucks is increasing the danger of accidents. Already, around 4,500 drivers and passengers die every year in truck-car accidents because smaller, lighter cars are easily crushed by the much bigger rigs, and that fatality rate will only continue to rise as the number of trucks increases. Obviously, the solution to this problem is to limit trucks to traveling in truck-only lanes and to prohibit them from traveling during rush hours. By restricting truckers in these ways, state officials can make the roads safer for everyone. (Source of information: Fred Bayles, "More Big Trucks Mixing with Cars Worries Officials," *USA Today*, February 9, 2004.)

a. What is the point of the author's argument?

b. Paraphrase the reasons used to support that point.

3. It's never too late to get physically fit. A 1999 study published in the *New England Journal of Medicine* showed that taking up weight training can reverse some of the effects of aging. In the experiment, nursing home residents ranging in age from eighty-six to ninety-five participated in a supervised, eight-week weight-training program. All of these elderly people increased their strength and improved their balance. Another more recent study conducted by the University of Pennsylvania Medical School has shown that elderly people who take up weight training can improve their bone density and reduce arthritic pain.

a. What is the point of the author's argument?

b. Paraphrase the results of the studies used to support that point.

_____

_____

_____

_____

4. Almost every college student has experienced prefinals terror—the horrible anxiety that puts your stomach on a roller coaster and your brain in a blender. Few escape those final-exam jitters because everyone knows just how much is riding on that one exam, often more than half of the course grade. Yet therein lies the crux* of the problem. Infrequent high-stakes exams don't encourage students to do their best work. More frequent tests—given, say, every two or three weeks—would be a much more effective method of discovering how well students are or are not mastering course concepts. With more frequent testing, students would be less anxious when they take exams; thus anxiety would no longer interfere with exam performance. More frequent testing also encourages students to review on a regular basis, something that a one-shot final exam does not do. Lots of tests also mean lots of feedback, and students would know early on in the course what terms or concepts required additional explanation and review. They wouldn't have to wait until the end of the semester to find out that they had misunderstood, or missed altogether, a critical point or theory.

a. What is the point of the author's argument?

_____

_____

b. Paraphrase the reasons used to support that point.

_____

_____

_____

_____

*crux: core; heart; key point.

Flawed Arguments

The preceding section of this chapter introduced four types of evidence likely to appear as support in an argument. In this section, you'll review two of the most common errors already covered—irrelevant reasons and circular arguments—and learn about four new ones.

Irrelevant Reasons

As you know from page 417, authors sometimes include reasons that aren't really relevant, or related, to their opinion or claim. Here, for example, is another argument that does not quite work because the author includes an irrelevant reason:

> The 1996 tragedy on Mount Everest in which eight people died in a single day is proof enough that amateurs should not be scaling the world's highest mountain. Even with the most skillful and reliable guides, amateurs with little or no mountaineering experience cannot possibly know how to respond to the sudden storms that strike the mountain without warning. Dependent on their guides for every move they make, amateur climbers can easily lose sight of the guides when a heavy storm hits. Left to their own devices, they are more than likely to make a mistake, one that will harm themselves or others. Besides, rich people—the climb can cost anywhere from $30,000 to $60,000—shouldn't be encouraged to think that money buys everything. As F. Scott Fitzgerald so powerfully illustrated in *The Great Gatsby*, it's precisely that attitude that often leads to tragedy and death.

The point of this passage is clear: Amateurs should not be climbing Mount Everest. In support of that claim, the author does offer a relevant reason. Mount Everest can be the scene of sudden storms that leave amateur climbers stranded, separated from their guides, and likely to harm themselves or others. But tucked away in the passage is a far less relevant reason: Rich people should not be allowed to think money buys everything. Well, maybe they shouldn't. Yet that particular reason, along with the allusion, or reference, to *The Great Gatsby*, is not related to the author's claim. Neither one clarifies why amateurs and the world's tallest mountain don't mix. This is the point that needs to be argued.

Circular Reasoning

As you know from Chapter 9, writers sometimes engage in circular reasoning. They offer an opinion and follow it with a reason that says the same thing in different words. Unfortunately, circular reasoning is not that unusual—particularly when an author is utterly convinced of his or her own rightness. In the following passage, for example, the writer believes that the United States' system of food inspection needs to be seriously overhauled. The author is so convinced he is right that he has forgotten to give us reasons why this change should occur, that is, what's the matter with the current system and why a different one would be better. Instead of offering reasons for his opinion, he keeps repeating it.

> Currently, our food supply is in danger of being contaminated from many different sources. When the very food we put in our mouths endangers our health, it is clear that we need to institute strict and regular inspections of food raised or grown in the United States, as well as food imported from other countries. We should be able to sit down to a meal and not worry that the food we eat will make us sick, but we won't have that sense of security about our food supply unless we improve our current system of inspections.

Hasty Generalizations

Generalizations, or broad general statements, by definition cover a lot of territory. They are used to sum up and express a wide variety of individual events or experiences. When generalizations appear in arguments, the rule of thumb is simple: The broader and more wide ranging the generalization, the more examples writers need to supply in order to be convincing. If an author generalizes about a large group on the basis of one or even two examples, you need to think twice before making the author's opinion your own.

In the following passage, the author makes a general statement about all HMOs. Unfortunately, that statement is based on one lone example, a fact that seriously weakens his argument.

> HMOs are not giving consumers adequate health care. Instead, budgeting considerations are consistently allowed to outweigh the patients' need for treatment. In one case, a child with a horribly deformed cleft palate was denied adequate cosmetic surgery because the child's HMO considered the surgery unnecessary, yet the child had trouble eating and drinking. (Source of information: Howard Fineman, "HMOs Under the Knife," *Newsweek*, July 27, 1998, p. 21.)

Unidentified Experts

In the passage about cloning on page 530, it makes sense for the author to quote a bioethicist in support of her opinion. After all, a bioethicist specializes in the study of moral and ethical issues that result from biological discoveries and applications. However, critical readers are rightly suspicious of allusions to unidentified experts, who may or may not be qualified to offer an opinion. Consider, for example, the "expert" cited in the following passage.

> Despite the doom and-gloom sayers who constantly worry about the state of the environment, the Earth is actually in pretty good shape. As Dr. Paul Benjamin recently pointed out, "Nature is perfectly capable of taking care of herself; she's been doing it for hundreds of years."

The author uses Dr. Paul Benjamin to support her claim that environmentalists anxious about the Earth's future are dead wrong. Yet for all we know, Dr. Benjamin might be a dentist, and a dental degree does not qualify him as an environmental expert. Without some knowledge of Dr. Benjamin's **credentials**, or qualifications, we shouldn't be swayed by his opinion. It also would help to know more about Dr. Benjamin's personal background and biases. If, for example, he's worked for a company cited for abuses to the environment, his ability to stay objective, or neutral, is suspect.

Inappropriate Experts

Occasionally, a writer might also attempt to support an argument by citing a famous person who doesn't truly qualify as an expert in the area under discussion.

> We should never intervene in the affairs of other countries. After all, didn't George Washington tell us to avoid entangling ourselves in the affairs of other nations? Even today, we should let his wisdom be our guide and steer clear of foreign involvements that drain our energy and our resources.

During the eighteenth century, George Washington may well have qualified as an expert in foreign affairs. But to cite him as an authority on modern problems is a mistake. It is doubtful that Washington could have imagined America's current status as an international power. Because his opinion could not be considered adequately informed, critical readers would not be impressed by references to his name and authority.

Unidentified Research

In the following passage, the author relies on some "studies" to prove a statement of policy: Pornography should be more strictly censored. But to be convincing as support, scientific research needs **attribution**; in short, readers need to know who conducted the research. References to unnamed studies like the one in this passage should arouse skepticism in critical readers.

> Because pornography puts womens' lives in danger, it must be more strictly censored. Studies have shown again and again that pornography is directly related to the number of rapes and assaults on women. As if that weren't enough, by repeatedly presenting women as sexual objects, pornography encourages sexual discrimination, a cause-and-effect relationship noted by several prominent researchers.

Authors may identify a study in the text itself or in a footnote that refers readers to a list of sources at the back of the book. Where a study is identified doesn't matter. What matters is that the author provides readers with enough information to check the source of the supposed evidence.

Dated Research

It also helps to know *when* the study was conducted; a writer who uses out-of-date studies rightfully runs the risk of losing readers' confidence. Take, for example, the following passage.

> The threat of radon gas is not as serious as we have been led to believe. In 1954, a team of government researchers studying the effects of radon in the home found no relationship between high levels of the gas in private dwellings and the incidence of lung cancer.

Here we have an author trying to prove a point about radon gas with a more than half-century-old study. To be considered effective evidence for an opinion, scientific research should be considerably more up to date.

Check Your Understanding

Complete the following chart by describing the types of errors that can occur in arguments.

Type of Support	Possible Error	Definition of Error
Reasons	Irrelevant reasons	
	Circular reasoning	
Examples and Illustrations	Hasty generalizations	
Expert Opinion	Unidentified experts	
	Inappropriate experts	
Research Results	Unidentified research	
	Dated research	

EXERCISE 4 **DIRECTIONS** Identify the error in reasoning by circling the appropriate letter.

EXAMPLE These days it's difficult to avoid the fact that the United States is in the grip of a serious health problem: More than 60 percent of the population is overweight. As a result, many men and women are at increased risk of serious diseases, ranging from colon cancer to diabetes. But if you count up the calories in, say, an oversized cheeseburger or a slice of double-cheese pizza, is it any wonder that obesity is a growing problem? Fast food companies arose to meet a real need; Americans were pressed for time and often needed to eat their meals on the run. But instead of making those meals healthy as well as profitable, the fast food industry decided it was better if they used cooking methods that shortened preparation time and, not incidentally, increased profits. Thus Americans were consuming, without their knowledge, high-calorie meals that didn't cost all that much in dollars but were actually very expensive in terms of health risks. No wonder people are suing fast food companies for obesity-related health problems. As Professor James Darwin has pointed out, when it comes to America's health problems, the fast food industry has a lot to answer for.

a. irrelevant reason

b. circular reasoning

c. hasty generalization

(d.) unidentified or inappropriate expert

e. unidentified or dated research

EXPLANATION In this case, *d* is the correct answer because the author uses the words of Professor James Darwin to support his case. We, however, know nothing about Professor Darwin's area of expertise. Thus we cannot tell if he is qualified to decide what the fast food industry does or does not have to answer for.

1. If you have a grass lawn surrounding your house, you are probably contributing to this country's environmental problems. For one thing, you could be using fertilizers and pesticides that can damage the soil structure, pollute wells, and kill wildlife. Homeowners with lawns actually use more fertilizers annually than the entire country of India puts on its crops. They also apply up to ten times more pesticides than U.S. farmers do. Unfortunately, research has proven that these chemicals wash off yards and pollute water supplies, thus contaminating the food chain. Lawn mowers cause another environmental problem. They produce as much air pollution in one hour as a car produces in a 350-mile drive. In addition, grass clippings are choking already overflowing landfills. Yard waste, most of which is cut grass, is the second-largest component of the 160 million tons of solid waste we dump into landfills every year. If that weren't enough, your lawn may be contributing to the destruction of plant and animal species. When developers building new houses bulldoze complex habitats and replace them with houses and grass, many plants and animals are killed or starved out.

a. irrelevant reason

b. circular reasoning

c. hasty generalization

d. unidentified or inappropriate expert

e. unidentified or dated research

2. The U.S. government needs to invest more money to improve and expand this country's rail service. In particular, Congress should commit to developing a national intercity network of high-speed trains. An intermodal transportation system (one that includes rail along with highways and airlines) is essential to keeping Americans moving in the event of a crisis. During a national emergency that disrupts one mode of transportation, the others should be able to absorb the traffic and allow people to continue to travel. For example, when airplanes were grounded for several days following terrorist attacks in September 2001, people relied on Amtrak passenger trains to get them where they needed to be. Without the trains, our nation would have been paralyzed. Furthermore, European countries such as France and Germany have excellent rail systems. Railroad transportation is an important public service, and it needs to be kept efficient and up to date.

a. irrelevant reason

b. circular reasoning

c. hasty generalization

d. unidentified or inappropriate expert

e. unidentified or dated research

3. Thousands of people who need organ transplants die every year because too few people agree to donate organs. Consequently, some people have begun to argue for tempting donors or their families with financial incentives in the form of either cash payments or tax credits. This is a terrible idea. Under no circumstances should we institute a system that permits the exchange of money for organs. Individuals or their families should not be allowed to gain financially from helping people who need transplants. Indeed, putting price tags on human organs is an appalling solution to the problem of an inadequate organ supply. We may need more donors to solve this crisis, but buying organs is just not the right way to address the shortage.

a. irrelevant reason

b. circular reasoning

c. hasty generalization

d. unidentified or inappropriate expert

e. unidentified or dated research

4. It just may be nature itself—not humans burning fossil fuels—that is causing global warming. Naturally occurring gases, such as water vapor, methane, nitrous oxide, and ozone, contribute to the so-called greenhouse effect that has raised Earth's temperature 30 degrees since the "Little Ice Age" of the seventeenth and eighteenth centuries. The oceans, too, seem to be partly responsible for the overall increase in our planet's temperature. From 1958 to 1978, Dane Chang and his colleagues at Hill Laboratories carefully studied the correlation between ocean temperatures and levels of carbon dioxide, the gas that causes global warming. These researchers found that increases in ocean temperature follow a rise in the atmosphere's carbon dioxide level. Such studies would seem to indicate that natural factors are producing our warmer climate.

a. irrelevant reason

b. circular reasoning

c. hasty generalization

d. unidentified or inappropriate expert

e. unidentified or dated research

5. A growing number of school districts are banning the childhood game of dodge ball from physical education classes and rightly so. The game is simply too aggressive and can cause serious harm. In one California incident, a child playing dodge ball was knocked to the ground by the ball's impact. Dodge ball is also not especially good exercise, particularly for those who are overweight. The slowest and heaviest children usually get knocked out of the game quickly. They then spend the rest of the game on the sidelines while the more athletic kids keep playing. It doesn't take a highly trained psychologist to realize that this experience cannot be good for an overweight child's self-esteem or self-image.

a. irrelevant reason

b. circular reasoning

c. hasty generalization

d. unidentified or inappropriate expert

e. unidentified or dated research

EXERCISE 5   **DIRECTIONS** Read each selection and answer the questions by circling the appropriate letters or filling in the blanks.

EXAMPLE

The Scopes Trial Revisited

1 The 1925 Scopes trial, also known as the Monkey Trial, got its name from John Scopes, a Tennessee high school teacher who

was tried and found guilty of breaking Tennessee's newly created Butler Act. The act forbade the teaching of Darwin's[†] theory of evolution, which argued that fossil evidence showed how humans had developed from lower forms of animal life—an idea that directly challenged the Christian view of creation. Ultimately, Scopes was charged with teaching theories that denied the biblical version of human creation.

2   Scopes's conviction was eventually overturned by the Supreme Court. Yet even before his conviction was struck down, his trial had done what seemed to be irreparable damage to the creationist notion that humans, unlike animals, were created by God. Scopes's defense attorney was the brilliant, witty, and eloquent Clarence Darrow, who mercilessly grilled his client's accusers. Darrow was particularly hard on the leading prosecutor, William Jennings Bryan, repeatedly posing questions that left Bryan embarrassed and stumbling for answers.

3   Regardless of the outcome of the Scopes trial, the controversy over how to teach human origins in the schools has never really gone away. Periodically it is stirred up again, as it was in Kansas in 1999, when the state school board removed the theory of evolution from the high school curriculum. It was reinstated in 2001, leaving some parents irate and determined to pull their children out of school and teach them at home. It would seem, then, that no school board's decision about how to teach the origins of humanity can leave everyone satisfied. Still, there is another possibility to consider: Schools could teach both theories so that neither group, creationist or evolutionist, feels slighted.

4   And there does seem to be some support for this more flexible position. A 1999 Gallup poll, for example, found that 68 percent of American adults believe children should learn both theories. Another poll came up with similar results. Then, too, don't parents have the right to determine what their children learn in school? Parents who want their kids to learn about creationism should not have their wishes denied; nor, for that matter, should parents who want their kids to learn about evolution. Both sides can be made happy if schools would present the evidence for both theories and let students decide which makes more sense to them.

5   An essential goal of education is to teach students to think critically. We want, that is, for them to know how to evaluate evidence

---

[†]Charles Darwin (1809–1882): the naturalist whose books *Origin of Species* (1859) and *The Descent of Man* (1871) scandalized the public by insisting there was concrete evidence to support the notion of humans' evolution from lower species.

and arrive at an informed decision. What better way to encourage critical thinking than to lay all the evidence for both sides of this controversy before students. Then they can decide which theory of human origins they choose to believe.

1. What is the author's point?

Schools should teach both evolution and creationism.

2. Identify the three reasons used to support that point.

a. *Polls suggest that a majority of parents want their children to learn both theories.*

b. *Parents should have the right to decide what their children are taught.*

c. *Teaching both theories would encourage critical thinking.*

3. Which of the following does the author offer in support of her conclusion?

a. specific illustration

(b.) results of research

c. expert opinion

4. Which error in reasoning can you detect in paragraph 4?

a. irrelevant reason

b. circular reasoning

c. hasty generalization

d. unidentified or inappropriate expert

(e.) unidentified or dated research

EXPLANATION In this example, the author presents readers with a statement of policy. To convince them, she identifies three reasons why her proposal makes sense. Her evidence, however, is a bit shaky. You can tell that by the presence of a rhetorical question in paragraph 4, where she doesn't allow for the suggestion that maybe parents shouldn't be permitted to determine and select curriculum. Even less convincing is her claim (paragraph 4) that "another poll" also found that a majority of adults want both theories taught. Unfortunately, who conducted the poll as well as when it took place remain a mystery. This is a good example of unidentified research.

1. Who Really Benefits from the Lottery?

1 In a recent editorial published in this newspaper, an argument was put forth in favor of a state-run lottery. According to the author of the editorial, there are many benefits to a state-run lottery and apparently no drawbacks. Now, the writer may honestly believe that a lottery would be a boon to everyone in the state, but I would argue that legalized gambling is a disaster waiting to happen.

2 Knowingly or unknowingly—and it doesn't matter which—state governments encourage addictive gambling when they promote lotteries. According to the American Psychiatric Association, addictive, or problem, gambling is a mental illness. Although treatable, it's still an illness, and it can lead to a host of social problems such as bankruptcy, theft, domestic violence, and job loss. Needless to say, these social problems can, in the end, prove costly to states hoping to benefit from lottery revenues. In promoting lotteries, the state, in essence, collects money from gambling with one hand and pays out double that amount in social services with the other. Advocates of state-run lotteries should consider that fact when they justify the lotteries by claiming they are a source of revenue for social programs. That logic may seem sound, but it doesn't add up on paper when the costs of addictive gambling are taken into account.

3 For example, a 1995 study by the Wisconsin Policy Research Institute estimated that each problem gambler cost the state around $9,500 per year in social services and business losses. The total loss to the state was about $307 million per year.[†] Another study indicates that around one in four problem gamblers has a history of substance abuse. This is yet another reason why state governments should not encourage gambling.

4 As Dr. Benjamin Martino has pointed out, legalized gambling blurs an important moral distinction: the distinction between honestly earned money and "ill-gotten" gains. Money from gambling is ill-gotten because it is not connected with any honest labor that benefits society. When we sanction* legalized gambling, we approve of bestowing wealth on people who have not worked for it. Given the number of ways in which legalized gambling hurts a society, how can any state government see fit to promote it?

[†]Chester Hartman, "Lotteries Victimize the Poor and Minorities," *New Haven Register*, August 3, 1998, p. 17.
*sanction: approve.

1. What is the author's point?

_____

_____

2. Identify the four reasons used to support that point.

a. _____

_____

b. _____

_____

c. _____

_____

d. _____

_____

3. In addition to these four reasons, which of the following does the author offer in support of his conclusions?

a. specific illustration

b. results of research

c. expert opinion

4. Which error or errors in reasoning can you detect in paragraphs 3 and 4?

a. irrelevant reason

b. circular reasoning

c. hasty generalization

d. unidentified or inappropriate expert

e. unidentified or dated research

2. Speed-Cams: More for Profit Than Safety

1 In nine states across the United States, law-enforcement officials have installed traffic cameras that photograph drivers who speed or violate other rules of the road. These devices, also known as "speed-cams" and photo radar, are controlled by a computer and a companion metal detector installed under the pavement. When the metal detector calculates that a car is moving too fast, it signals the camera to snap a photo of the vehicle's license plate. A

police officer then reviews these records and issues a citation to the driver. Although speed-cams have been used for more than thirty years in Europe, many Americans mistrust these "robocops" on our roads. In fact, several states have publicly decided *not* to implement this technology. States currently using these cameras should follow suit and remove the devices.

2   First, these cameras don't really deter speeders. Unless it's dark enough so that you see a flash in your rearview mirror, odds are you won't know you've been caught by a speed-cam until you get a summons in the mail. If you don't realize you've been caught, you're not likely to slow down. Then, too, there have to be other, less intrusive ways of ensuring motorists' safety. While some states photograph only the rear of the car, others—including Arizona, California, and Colorado—photograph the driver too. This type of electronic monitoring should concern every citizen of this country, and we should not allow our government to take pictures of us without our consent.

3   Unreliability is another reason to scrap the cameras. These technological marvels can, in fact, malfunction and fail. In San Diego, speed-cam sensors clocked drivers going much faster than they really were. As a result, the city disconnected its cameras in July 2001. This example conclusively proves that these machines are not reliable.

4   Opponents of speed-cams object to them because private companies handle the picture-taking with only a minimum of police involvement. More to the point, many of these companies base their profits on the number of tickets issued. Sometimes those profits amount to as much as $70 per ticket. Cities, too, are raking in increased revenues from fines paid by violators. In 2003, the British government pulled in more than $50 million in fines from one speed-cam. In the same year, Washington, D.C., issued $34 million worth of speed-cam–based tickets. This kind of revenue without a corresponding increase in human resource costs is certainly one of the technology's most attractive features, causing some critics to argue that city governments are more interested in profit than public safety.

5   But supporters of speed-cams also need to know that in 2003 the Australian government had to freeze $6 million in fines because of a speed-cam snafu. A truck was issued a camera-generated ticket for going twenty miles faster than the truck's engine could actually go. This kind of error suggests that speed-cams are prone to serious errors and cannot be relied on. (Source of information: www.iihs.org/research/qanda/speed_lawenforcement.html; www.thenewspaper.com/news/04/484.asp.)

1. What is the author's point?

_____

_____

2. Identify the three reasons used to support that point.

a. _____

_____

b. _____

_____

c. _____

_____

3. In addition to these three reasons, which of the following does the author use as support?

a. specific illustration

b. results of research

c. expert opinion

4. Which error or errors in reasoning can you detect in paragraph 3?

a. irrelevant reason

b. circular reasoning

c. hasty generalization

d. unidentified or inappropriate expert

e. unidentified or dated research

3. Grooming Counts or Does It?

1 Many companies have established rigid grooming standards for their employees. Walt Disney World, for example, insists that employees follow established guidelines for hairstyle, jewelry, makeup, and facial hair. Airlines also require flight attendants to meet certain weight restrictions. Federal Express (FedEx) and United Parcel Service (UPS), too, impose grooming standards that limit the length of men's hair. Currently, however, some of these policies are being justifiably challenged in courts by workers who claim that the standards infringe on their religious rights. At issue is whether employers have the right to enforce rigid grooming

rules on workers whose appearance expresses their religious beliefs or their cultural heritage.

2   According to the Equal Employment Opportunity Commission (EEOC), no company is allowed to prevent its employees from expressing religious beliefs through their appearance. The EEOC claims that forbidding such expressions of religious belief violates the Civil Rights Act. Both FedEx and UPS, for example, have fired drivers who refused to cut off their dreadlocks—long, thick strands of knotted or braided hair associated with Rastafarianism.* Similarly, several police officers employed by the Dallas Police Department were reprimanded or fired for wearing dreadlocks. In these cases and others, the EEOC and the Justice Department's Civil Rights Division have interceded on behalf of the employees.

3   The question of civil rights aside, employers also need to keep in mind that an employee's appearance seldom interferes with his or her ability to do the job. In other words, employers can afford to be more tolerant. Chris Warden, for example, was terminated from his job as a FedEx driver for wearing dreadlocks even though his manager's evaluations called him a superior employee. Warden's case proves that wearing dreadlocks does not affect an individual's job performance and therefore should not be a cause for dismissal.

4   As the multicultural population of the United States continues to grow, companies will be challenged more often for their insistence on strict grooming policies. It's high time employers embraced diversity and redefined outdated notions about what is "reasonable" and "acceptable." (Source of information: David France, "Law: The Dreadlock Deadlock," *Newsweek*, September 10, 2001, p. 54.)

1. What is the author's point?

_____

_____

2. Identify the two reasons used to support that point.

a. _____

_____

b. _____

_____

---

*Rastafarianism: a religious and political movement originating in the 1930s in Jamaica.

3. In addition to these two reasons, which of the following does the author use as support?

  a. specific illustration

  b. results of research

  c. expert opinion

4. Which error or errors in reasoning can you detect in paragraph 3?

  a. irrelevant reason

  b. circular reasoning

  c. hasty generalization

  d. unidentified or inappropriate expert

  e. unidentified or dated research

4. Could El Al Be a Model?

1   Officials of Israel's El Al Airline say that the four suicide hijackings that occurred in the United States on September 11, 2001, could never have occurred on their airplanes. They may be right. El Al has the most elaborate, thorough, and successful security system in the entire airline industry.

2   El Al's rigorous system of luggage screening prevents bombs and weapons from getting on board an airplane. Before being loaded onto an aircraft, all suitcases and bags are put into a pressurized box that will recognize and detonate any explosives inside. Bags transferring from flights are subjected to the same screening, and bags that cannot be matched to a passenger are not permitted on board. El Al also subjects passengers themselves to a time-consuming and controversial[†] screening process, used to ensure that potential terrorists will not board a plane. Even before a traveler arrives at the airport, his or her name has already been compared to a computerized list of terrorist suspects compiled by law-enforcement agencies around the world.

3   If a would-be hijacker manages to foil this system and board the plane, he or she faces still another security measure: undercover agents who travel on every flight. These armed agents, who look and behave like ordinary travelers, are stationed in aisle seats, where they watch for trouble. They are ready to defend passengers and protect the plane from a terrorist takeover. In addi-

---

[†]Critics of El Al's policies have complained that the screening process smacks of racial profiling.

tion to the presence of undercover agents, most of El Al's pilots are well educated and have advanced degrees.

4   El Al is based in a country torn for years by conflict and violence, yet it keeps travelers safe. In fact, the sole hijacking of an El Al plane occurred in 1968, at a time when the current security measures were not in place. (Source of information: Vivienne Walt, "Unfriendly Skies Are No Match for El Al," *USA Today*, October 1, 2001, p. 1D.)

1. What is the author's point?

_____

_____

2. Identify the three reasons used to support that point.

a. _____

_____

b. _____

_____

c. _____

_____

3. In addition to these three reasons, which of the following does the author use as support?

a. specific illustration

b. results of research

c. expert opinion

4. Which error or errors in reasoning can you detect in paragraph 3?

a. irrelevant reason

b. circular reasoning

c. hasty generalization

d. unidentified or inappropriate expert

e. unidentified or dated research

Identifying the Opposing Point of View

By definition, a solid argument includes a point of view or position and some form of support. However, arguments that revolve around a statement of policy or value are very likely to include both an opposing point of view and the author's response to it.

Here again is the article on mandatory minimum sentences (pp. 523–524), only now it contains an opposing point of view along with the author's response.

Does the Punishment Fit the Crime?

1   In 1984, lawmakers wanted to send a tough message on the sale of drugs. As part of a bill called the Sentencing Reform Act, Congress assigned mandatory minimum sentences for all drug offenses taking place near schools. Offenders could get anywhere from five to twenty years based on the amount of drugs involved. With time, additional mandatory minimums became part of the legal system, including the "three strikes you're out" provision that specified life sentences for repeat drug offenders. While mandatory minimum sentences are still seen by some to be a solution to drug use in the United States, there are several reasons why the courts need to reconsider the effectiveness of these mandatory minimum sentences.

2   Thanks in large part to mandatory minimum sentencing, jails are currently packed. A federal penitentiary like Leavenworth, built to house 1,200 prisoners, has occasionally housed as many as 1,700, creating overcrowded conditions that breed violence and riots. State correctional facilities are filled to overflowing, so much so that violent criminals are sometimes released to make room for nonviolent drug offenders. In 2003, the number of imprisoned drug offenders was an astonishing 330,000. This figure is larger than the number of people imprisoned for all crimes in 1970.

3   The group Families Against Mandatory Minimums (FAMM) regularly lobbies Congress for the repeal of mandatory minimums, citing cases like that of Michael T. Irish, a first offender sentenced to twelve years in federal prison for helping unload hashish from a boat, or Charles Dunlap, imprisoned for eight years in federal prison for the crime of renting a truck used by a friend to import marijuana. FAMM was founded over a decade ago by Julie Stewart, who hadn't been particularly interested in the subject of mandatory minimum sentencing until her brother was imprisoned for five years after he was caught growing marijuana

seedlings. It was Stewart who came up with FAMM's motto, "Let the Punishment Fit the Crime."

4   However, according to someone like Deborah Daniels, who was U.S. attorney in the Southern District of Indiana from 1988 to 1993, the punishment usually does fit the crime. This is so even in cases like that of nonviolent offender Mark Young,[†] who got a life sentence for playing the role of middleman in a drug-trafficking scheme. Daniels insists that mandatory minimum sentences are essential if the United States wants to encourage other countries to wage war on drugs. In her mind, mandatory minimum sentences set the right example.

5   Daniels doesn't seem to recognize that there is no proven cause-and-effect relationship between mandatory minimum sentences and drug trafficking in other countries, where drug exports rise and fall based on a variety of factors (e.g., government corruption, state of the economy, ease of access to drugs). All these factors have little or nothing to do with any sentencing example set by the United States.

6   What Daniels also doesn't acknowledge is how mandatory minimum sentences have been used to wring information from those threatened with stiff sentences. Because it is now the prosecutor, rather than the judge, who can demand a specific sentence, some prosecutors have used that power to get information about others allegedly involved in drug trafficking. Not surprisingly, the legal rewards for providing information have created a brand new black market—the buying and selling of drug deals. Thus a defendant who hopes to avoid lengthy jail time can buy, for the right amount of cash, information about alleged drug deals. In fact, some professional informers charge as much as $25,000 for a drug lead that might help diminish a lengthy mandatory minimum sentence. As members of FAMM regularly point out, mandatory minimum sentences are not only more than likely to be out of proportion to the crime, but they also encourage false testimony and the growth of an illegal market for drug information. (Source of information: Schlosser, *Reefer Madness*, pp. 95–100.)

In this illustration, the author's argument has expanded to include an opposing point of view—Attorney Deborah Daniels believes that mandatory minimum sentences set an example for other countries involved in a war on drugs—and a response. There's no evidence of a cause-and-effect connection between mandatory minimum sentences and the willingness of other countries to wage that war.

[†]Young had two prior convictions, one for trying to fill a fake prescription and one for possession of amphetamines.

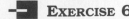 **EXERCISE 6** DIRECTIONS Read each argument. Then answer the questions that follow.

EXAMPLE

Home Schooling Isn't Really School

1 As a public school teacher, I have to admit I cringe every time I hear the phrase "home schooling." I know that many parents believe they are helping their children by teaching them at home. But in my experience, home schooling may do more harm than good.

2 Children who enter my class after a long period of home schooling usually have huge gaps in their education. True, they often read and write better than the average fifth grader, and their spelling is good. But they know very little about the social sciences, and science itself seems to be a foreign word.

3 In addition, children who have been schooled at home frequently have difficulty working with other children. Unused to the give-and-take of group interactions, they quickly show their discomfort or displeasure. Their response is understandable since they have spent years at home in a class of one or two at most.

4 I know that many parents believe that home schooling protects their children from dangerous or corrupting ideas and experiences. To some degree, they are probably correct in that assumption. Unfortunately, the protection home schooling provides may cost too heavy an intellectual price. In general, parents do not have the necessary training or background to give their children the wide-ranging and up-to-date education they need. And certainly parents cannot provide the kind of peer socialization found in schools outside the home.

1. What is the point of the author's argument?

Home schooling may do more harm than good.

2. What two reasons does the author give in support of that point?

a. *Children can end up with big gaps in their education.*

b. *Children schooled at home usually have difficulty working in groups.*

3. Identify the opposing point of view mentioned in the reading.

Parents believe that they are protecting their children from bad experiences and inappropriate ideas.

4. Paraphrase the author's response.

The protection costs too much socially and intellectually.

EXPLANATION As is often the case, the author states the point of the argument at the beginning of the reading—home schooling can do more harm than good—and then follows with two reasons for that position. Although the answer to a possible objection appears at the end, this is not necessarily standard. Answers to objections can just as easily be sprinkled throughout.

1. The Benefits of Home Schooling

1   Although it has been harshly criticized by many—often by those who have a vested interest* in supporting the status quo*—home schooling just may be the answer to our current educational crisis.

2   At home, children can learn one-on-one or in small groups. If they need some additional explanation or instruction, the home tutor can readily supply it. In public schools, in contrast, children often sit in classrooms with twenty or thirty other students. Such class numbers make it almost impossible for teachers to give students the individual attention they so frequently need. There are so many competing voices and questions, a teacher can't possibly respond to all of them. Someone has to go consciously unattended or unconsciously ignored.

3   Another advantage of home schooling is that it allows children to learn in a comforting, familiar environment, lacking in distractions. Any parent who has ever delivered a weeping child to the door of his or her classroom knows full well how terrifying some children find the classroom atmosphere with its noisy hubbub. Children who learn at home aren't distracted by their surroundings, nor are they inhibited by the presence of other children who might unthinkingly laugh at their mistakes.

---

*vested interest: having a special reason to promote or protect that which gives one a personal advantage.
*status quo: existing state of affairs.

4   Critics who claim that home schooling can't provide children with the breadth of knowledge they need always assume that the parents don't have the necessary qualifications. Yet of the parents I know personally who teach their children at home, two have a master's degree in physics, another a doctorate in psychology, and still another is a former elementary teacher with ten years of teaching experience to her credit. Parents who take on the responsibility of home schooling do not do so lightly. They know full well that they must provide their children with an education that prepares them for the world they will eventually enter.

1. What is the point of the author's argument?

_____

_____

2. Identify the two reasons used to support that point.

a. _____

_____

b. _____

_____

3. Identify the opposing point of view mentioned in the reading.

_____

_____

4. Paraphrase the author's response.

_____

_____

2. Teacher Performance Linked to Pay

1 In January 2004, The Teaching Commission, a blue-ribbon panel of nineteen leaders in government, business, philanthropy, and education that was chaired by former IBM chairman Louis V. Gerstner Jr., released its report on improving education in America's schools. Among the commission's conclusions was the controversial recommendation that each teacher's pay be determined by student performance. Although immediately opposed

by many teachers and teachers' organizations, this suggestion should be implemented in our schools. The recommendation makes sense for a number of reasons. For one, compensating teachers based on classroom results would replace an archaic, eighty-year-old system that pays a good teacher the same as a poor one. Currently, teachers' salaries are based only on years of experience, so an ineffective teacher who has taught for twenty years earns far more than a newer but far more effective one. According to The Teaching Commission, this system "does nothing to reward excellence." In other words, it would be fairer to the hardest-working teachers to reward them with bigger paychecks.

2   Opponents of performance-based pay argue that such a plan ignores the many factors affecting student performance, such as poverty or family background, that are outside teacher control. The commission, however, has recommended that teacher evaluations be designed to take such factors into account. What's more, commission members argue that many other professions use performance-based pay plans. Gerstner said, "Lawyers do it, engineers do it, business people do it. All professional people ultimately come up with methodology to judge the difference between great performance and mediocre performance. Just because it's hard doesn't mean we can't do it."

3   In fact, The Teaching Commission believes that tying teachers' salaries to performance will help raise their overall professional status. Unfortunately, teaching is often viewed as a second-rate occupation. The commission believes, though, that if teachers were compensated like professionals in other fields and were less limited by antiquated, experience-based pay scales, the highest-performing teachers would garner more respect for their efforts. Plus, bright and more talented individuals might be attracted to the profession.

4   The end result would be an increase in student achievement. Incentives could make teachers' work more difficult, but they would be rewarded for achieving better results. They would be more inclined to do whatever it takes to help their students learn; therefore, students stand to benefit the most. (Sources of information: The Teaching Commission, "Teaching at Risk: Blue-Ribbon Panel Calls for Overhaul of Teacher Education and Compensation to Recruit and Retain Talent in America's Public Schools," Press Release, January 14, 2004, www.theteachingcommission.org/press/2004_01_14_01.html; "Teacher Pay Tied to Student Progress?" CNN.com, January 14, 2004, www.cnn.com/2004/EDUCATION/01/14/teacher.salaries.ap/.)

1. What is the point of the author's argument?

_____

_____

2. Identify the four reasons used to support that point.

a. _____

_____

b. _____

_____

c. _____

_____

d. _____

_____

3. Identify the opposing point of view mentioned in the reading.

_____

_____

4. Paraphrase the author's response.

_____

_____

■ DIGGING DEEPER

LOOKING AHEAD The author of the reading on page 541 was convinced that the fast food industry had a lot to answer for when it came to the issue of obesity in the United States. The author of this reading has a different point of view.

EAT FRENCH FRIES AT YOUR PERIL

1 Flush from their victories against the tobacco companies, some lawyers and activists decided to take on what they claimed was another public health enemy—the fast food industry. The plan was to sue the companies selling the high-calorie foods that contribute to one of America's major health problems—obesity. Currently, 61 percent of the adults in the United States are overweight while the number of overweight children has tripled in the last twenty years. As some would have it, fast food is to blame.

2 From the point of view, for example, of John Banzhaf, a George Washington University law professor who helped wage war on the tobacco companies, the fast food industry, from McDonald's to Pizza Hut, has not adequately warned the public about the calories and fat their products contain. If it did, the logic goes, Americans would be more inclined to renounce fat-filled delicacies such as cheeseburgers with fries. Without doubt, Banzhaf's position earned some support from books like Marion Nestle's *Food Politics* and Eric Schlosser's *Fast Food Nation*. Both authors suggest that the way fast food companies manufacture and market products has contributed to the staggering increase in obesity. It should come as no surprise, then, that lawyers geared up to sue companies selling foods like pizza, french fries, and hamburgers, in the hopes of recovering the cost of treating diseases related to being overweight, like high blood pressure and diabetes. In addition to damages, lawyers hoped that the fast food industry would decide not only to decrease the amount of fat and calories in their products but also to increase prices. That way, it would not be so easy for consumers to grab a loaded-with-fat burger.

3 However confident lawyers proposing to sue the fast food industry may have been, they probably didn't reckon with the House of Representatives stepping in to prohibit litigation. Yet that is precisely what the House did in 2004 and 2005, when it passed what has come to be called "The Cheeseburger Bill." The bill explicitly targets lawsuits by obese patrons of fast food restaurants, who

say they became overweight by eating fast food. While the bill seems to have gotten stalled in the Senate, the idea has caught on with the states. Currently, nineteen states have passed so-called cheeseburger bills preventing such lawsuits. Similar legislation is pending in several other states. Even if lawyers find a way around the legislation forbidding their clients' from suing fast food companies, there are a number of reasons why such lawsuits will probably not have the same kind of success that accompanied lawsuits against the tobacco companies.

4   When it comes to showing a direct cause-and-effect relationship, those trying to pin their obesity on fast food will have a tough row to hoe. Obesity is considered to be 60 percent environmental and 40 percent genetic. In other words, obesity runs in families. What that means is that someone like fifty-six-year-old Caesar Barber, who at five ten and 272 pounds filed a class-action suit against McDonald's, Burger King, Wendy's, and KFC, will have a tough time proving his claim that eating fast food is the primary cause of his obesity and resulting health problems. Unless he can prove that key point, it may not matter that, as Barber said when interviewed on ABC's *Good Morning America*, "They [the companies] never explained to me what I was eating."

5   There is, however, no guarantee that suits against the fast food companies will have the same public support as lawsuits against tobacco companies had. For one thing, if the suits are successful, the fast food industry will undoubtedly change how it makes and markets its products. The industry will surely pass the extra cost on to consumers, who are unlikely to be grateful about this benefit of litigation. It's also true that some overweight people are tired of being told that "thinner is better." They might not look kindly on the notion that the fast food industry has inflicted obesity on the overweight consumer. They are more likely to argue that being obese should be an acceptable body type variation.

6   John Doyle, cofounder of the Center for Consumer Freedom, a restaurant industry group, has also made a compelling argument. Doyle's position is that people should be smart and savvy enough to recognize that foods like cheese, hamburgers, and french fries are high in both calories and fat. Doyle argues convincingly that people need to take responsibility for what they eat. After all, no one is forcing them to feast on french fries. Anyone who does is probably going to gain weight, and that's not the fault of companies who make and serve french fries. Doyle has a point. After all, does anyone really not know that a double cheeseburger is loaded with fat? (Sources of information: Geraldine Sealey, "Whopper of a Lawsuit: Fast Food Chains Blamed for Obesity,

Illnesses," ABCNews.com, July 26, 2002; Megan McArdle, "Can We Sue?" May 24, 2002, http://archive.salon.com/2002/5/24/ fastfoodlaw; http://money.cnn.com/2003/01/22/news/companies/ mcdonalds.)

Sharpening Your Skills

DIRECTIONS Answer the following questions by filling in the blanks or circling the letter of the correct response.

1. In your own words, what is the main idea of the entire reading?

_____

_____

2. What is the primary organizational pattern of the entire reading?

a. definition

b. cause and effect

c. comparison and contrast

d. classification

e. simple listing

3. What word or phrase is an important clue to the organizational pattern governing the reading?

_____

4. In the second sentence of paragraph 2, the pronoun *it* refers to

_____

5. In paragraph 4, Caesar Barber's lawsuit against several fast food companies is used to support which point?

a. Few people are willing to file a class-action suit against the fast food industry.

b. People who sue the fast food companies may have difficulty proving fast food was the sole source of their health problems.

c. More and more people are filing lawsuits blaming the fast food industry for everything from obesity to diabetes.

6. In paragraph 5, the first and second transition in the paragraph signal _____ and _____ .

7. The author offers four reasons why using lawsuits to attack the fast food industry may not be a good idea. Please paraphrase the first two.

a. _____

_____

b. _____

_____

8. What is the author's purpose?

a. to inform

b. to persuade

9. How would you describe the author's tone?

a. skeptical

b. neutral

c. outraged

d. friendly

10. Based on what the author says, you could draw which conclusion?

a. If consumers were disappointed after buying pills advertised as capable of making body fat melt away, the author would probably suggest that they sue the company who made the pills.

b. If consumers were disappointed by pills advertised as capable of melting away body fat and wanted to sue the company that made the pills, the author would probably tell them they should have known better than to buy the pills in the first place.

c. If consumers were disappointed after buying pills that were advertised as capable of making body fat melt away, the author would probably advise them not to expect results in so short a time.

Students who want to do an in-depth review of the steps in analyzing arguments should use *Getting Focused*, the web-based reading program accompanying this text. The program is available at **college.cengage.com/devenglish/flemming/getting_focused/1e/student_home.html**. Completing question 11 will provide you with a very thorough and complete review.

To get more practice analyzing arguments, go to **laflemm.com** and click on *Reading for Thinking*: "Online Practice." Complete the interactive exercise on analyzing arguments.

Test 1: Analyzing Arguments

DIRECTIONS Read each argument and answer the questions that follow by filling in the blanks or circling the letter of the correct response. *Note*: The author may or may not respond to opposition, and the argument may or may not include an error.

1. Kids and Sports

1   For many parents, competitive team sports like Little League Baseball and Peewee Football are an essential part of childhood. Thus they are anxious for their kids to try out and "make the team." Supposedly, competitive sports build physical strength. Even more important—or so the argument goes—playing competitive sports early on in childhood builds character. Still, parents intent on making sure their kids learn how to compete might want to rethink the notion that sports in which somebody has to win or lose are important to a young child's development. Competitive sports for preteen kids have some important disadvantages; these disadvantages need to be considered before parents push kids onto a playing field where the winner takes all.

2   Here's one thing that should be considered: Competitive sports can unduly stress a child's still developing body. Football, basketball, baseball, and even tennis are physically demanding. They put a very heavy strain on the body. This is particularly true if muscles or bones are still developing. Now, a ten-year-old who is just playing for the fun of it will probably not repeat a movement or motion that hurts, but what if that same child is playing for a trophy? Is he or she going to stop throwing that tough-to-hit curve ball just because there is a little pain involved? It's not likely. Unfortunately, the end result can be lifelong damage to a shoulder or an arm. Thomas Tutko, author of the book *Winning Is Everything and Other American Myths*, argues that kids should not be playing physically demanding sports before the age of fourteen. From Tutko's perspective, playing competitive sports before that age is simply too "traumatic," both physically and psychologically.

3   In his book *No Contest: The Case Against Competition*, author and researcher Alfie Kohn emphasizes that the psychological effects of competitive sports on those still too young to play them may be worse than the physical injuries that can ensue. Kohn's book summarizes the results of several hundred studies focusing on the effects of competition both on and off the playing field. Whether in the context of sports or the classroom, Kohn contends that competition "undermines self-esteem, poisons our relation-

ships, and holds us back from doing our best."[†] Clearly, Kohn would not support the notion of competition as a character builder for children. If anything, he sees it as a character destroyer, even if those competing are grownups.

4　　To be fair to those who insist there's no point to playing basketball, football, or baseball unless you keep score, these are games where the score counts. However, the position argued here is not that competitive sports should be abandoned; rather, they should be postponed until the child is ready to be not just a winner, but a loser as well. A fifteen-year-old is probably able to accept the simple fact that, at some time in life, everyone loses at something. But does a nine-year-old have to learn this lesson? In their early years, kids should concentrate on achieving their personal best. Are they running faster, jumping higher, or throwing faster than they did the last time around? Those are the questions they should be asking themselves, not who won and who lost.

1. What is the author's point?

_____

_____

_____

2. Identify the two reasons used to support that point.

a. _____

_____

b. _____

_____

3. Does the author include any of the following?

a. examples or illustrations

b. research results

c. expert opinion

_____

[†]A. Kohn, "No Win Situations," *Women's Sports & Fitness*, July/August 1990, pp. 56–58.

4. Does the author respond to any opposing point of view? _____
If so, fill in the blanks that follow.

Opposition   _____

_____

Response   _____

_____

5. Circle one or more of the appropriate letters to indicate the presence or absence of errors in the author's argument.

a. irrelevant reason

b. circular reasoning

c. hasty generalization

d. unidentified or inappropriate expert

e. unidentified or dated research

f. no errors

2. Access to Adoption Files

1 As of November 1, 2004, adoptees and birth parents living in the province of Alberta, Canada, got the legal right to obtain information about one another. Initially, either party had the right to veto access, but since 2005, neither has veto power over access to adoption records. With the exception of losing the right to veto, this policy should also be uniformly accepted in the United States, where access to adoption records is still hotly disputed with the dispute resulting in a hodgepodge of policies that vary from state to state. In some states, adoptees are allowed no information or "nonidentifying information." This information is limited to age, physical characteristics, talents, hobbies, and basic medical data. But the amount of even that information depends on the agency or court that releases it.

2   Over the years, many adoptees have rightly protested this situation, causing some states to modify their rules for access. For instance, even the most restrictive state laws allow for the opening of sealed files via court order. But the decision about access to adoption records should not be left up to the individual states. Instead, Congress should step in and enact legislation that gives adopted children the right to discover their parents and their history, both personal and medical. As many adoptees have pointed out, the sealed records policy may serve adopted children but become counterproductive when children grow up.

3   After all, restricting access to adoption files makes the search more difficult, but it does not necessarily stop adoptees—and less frequently birth parents—from searching. Those men and women desperate for information will, if they can afford it, hire a detective to find out what they are driven to know.

4   The truth is that many adoptees feel guilty about being put up for adoption. They assume that they did something wrong, something that made them so unlovable their parents were forced to give them up. These men and women need to know the real causes for their adoption. It helps an adoptee to know, for example, that his mother gave him up for adoption because she was too young to support him, not because she didn't love him. Such knowledge helps relieve the burden of guilt some adoptees carry around their entire lives.

5   There are also physical –rather than psychological—reasons why adoptees need access to their files. To take proper care of their health, they need to know what diseases they might have inherited. In more extreme cases, knowledge about biological parents can mean the difference between life and death. Sometimes adoptees are in need of an organ transplant, and they require an organ that comes from a natural relative. If all their relatives are unknown, these adopted men and women are at a terrible disadvantage—one that could cost them their lives.

6   Some parents who have given up their children for adoption resent the idea of opening up adoption files. They feel that their right to privacy will be threatened. Yet this objection is based on the assumption that adopted children want to hunt down their parents and intrude on their lives. But, as study after study shows, adoptees only want to know who their biological parents are. In some cases, they may even want to meet them, but they do not want to push their way into the lives of people who will not accept them. Giving the adopted person access to files does not mean that the parent or parents forsake all rights to privacy. It only means that the adopted child can attempt to make contact if he or she wishes, and the parents can refuse or accept as they see fit.

1. What is the author's point?

_____

_____

_____

2. Identify the three reasons used to support that point.

a. _____

_____

b. _____

_____

c. _____

_____

3. Does the author include any of the following?

a. examples or illustrations

b. research results

c. expert opinion

4. Does the author respond to any opposing point of view? _____
If so, fill in the blanks that follow.

Opposition   _____

_____

Response   _____

_____

5. Circle one or more of the appropriate letters to indicate the presence or absence of errors in the author's argument.

a. irrelevant reason

b. circular reasoning

c. hasty generalization

d. unidentified or inappropriate expert

e. unidentified or dated research

f. no errors

Test 2: Analyzing Arguments

DIRECTIONS Read each argument and answer the questions that follow by filling in the blanks or circling the letter of the correct response. *Note*: The author may or may not respond to opposition and the argument may or may not include an error.

1. Banning Peanuts

1   There was a time when the peanut butter and jelly sandwich was a staple of the school lunchbox. Often it was the one food that fussy children would willingly eat, and parents were grateful it existed, even if they personally found the combination distasteful. The popularity of peanut butter and jelly sandwiches, however, is a thing of the past as schools from New York to California have stopped serving them in the cafeteria. Many school officials have also asked parents not to put peanut products of any kind into their kids' lunches.

2   If the ban on peanuts sounds silly to you, then you obviously don't know an important fact: Based on 2000 U.S. Census data, the Food Allergy and Anaphylaxis* Network (FAAN) estimates that 1 in every 125 children is affected by peanut allergy. Other studies also strongly indicate that the number of children with allergies is increasing at alarming rates. The need for a ban on peanuts in the schools is not a trivial issue. It's a matter of life or death.

3   In November 1998, seventeen-year-old Mariya Spektor of Niskayuna, New York, died after she unknowingly ate some cereal that had peanut oil in it. In the very same month, twelve-year-old Kristine Kastner of Mercer Island, Washington, died after she ate a chocolate chip cookie that had finely minced peanuts in it. The reality is that children can and do die if they unwittingly ingest peanut products, and neither parents nor educators can afford to take the chance that this might happen.

4   Critics of the ban, among them some members of FAAN, worry that the peanut ban pits parent against parent, especially when desperate parents reduce the issue to "My kid's life or your kid's peanut butter sandwich." Still, opponents of the ban argue that there are other ways to handle the problem. They emphasize self-management on the part of the child along with special lunch zones where peanuts are, or are not, allowed.

---

*anaphylaxis: hypersensitivity to a foreign substance that, in some cases, can result in death.

5   Such suggestions, however, overlook a couple of crucial points. Labels don't always make it easy to discover exactly what's in the food being consumed. Then too, kids will be kids. Tell them to stay in one area of the cafeteria while avoiding another and they will do the exact opposite. Thus if peanuts in any form are allowed in school, there's always the possibility that a child with an allergy will ingest a snack that might prove deadly. Naturally, a child allergic to peanuts is not going to bite into a peanut butter and jelly sandwich, but that same child might well munch on a chocolate chip cookie containing peanuts, not realizing that nuts are in the cookie.

6   Parents of children allergic to peanuts are aware that many do not want peanut products banned from schools. One of those parents is Mark LoPresti of Grand Island, New York. LoPresti has a three-year-old son who is severely allergic to peanuts, and the father acknowledges the ban can create problems. Still he is fiercely determined that peanuts must be banned when his son is ready to go to school. As LoPresti puts it, "I'm not going to sacrifice my son's life for the right to have a peanut butter sandwich." It's hard not to sympathize with LoPresti's point of view. When it comes to the ban on peanut products in schools, an old adage seems to apply: "It's better to be safe than sorry." (Sources of information: Carrie Hedges, "Peanut Ban Spreads to Cafeteria," *USA Today*, December 3, 1998, p. 17a; www.canoe.ca/ Health9902/16_allergy.html.)

1. What is the author's point?

_____

_____

2. Identify the reason used to support that point.

_____

_____

_____

3. Does the author include any of the following?

   a. examples or illustrations

   b. research results

   c. expert opinion

4. Does the author respond to any opposing point of view? _____
If so, fill in the blanks that follow.

Opposition _____

_____

Response _____

_____

5. Circle one or more of the appropriate letters to indicate the presence or absence of errors in the author's argument.

a. irrelevant reason

b. circular reasoning

c. hasty generalization

d. unidentified or inappropriate expert

e. unidentified or dated research

f. no errors

2. Protecting Our Children from Pornography

1 In December 2000, Congress enacted the Children's Internet Protection Act (CIPA), which requires schools and libraries to have in place software filters that block computer access to sites featuring obscenity or pornography and are, therefore, harmful to minors. Libraries or schools that did not have such filters in place by 2002 faced the loss of government subsidies. This legislation seemed eminently sensible. It seemed almost impossible that anyone would quarrel with it. Yet, in fact, there was immediate opposition from the American Civil Liberties Union and, in particular, the American Library Association. Stranger still, a lower court actually sided with the American Library Association in a suit challenging the constitutionality of applying CIPA to libraries. Fortunately, on June 23, 2003, the Supreme Court struck down the lower court's ruling. But even though the issue has come to a legal resolution, the question remains: How is it that sensible people take it upon themselves to challenge legislation that does nothing more than protect innocent children?

2 More than 75 percent of the nation's public libraries offer Internet access. Thanks to that access, any twelve-year-old—unless filters are in place—can reach sites featuring hardcore sex scenes. Even worse, kids can get into chatrooms where they might make contact with sex offenders or child molesters. Children should not

be exposed to such websites or chatrooms. As Dr. Melanie Powers has pointed out, even one experience with a pornographic site can do irreparable damage to a child's psyche.

3   Opponents of the filters on library computers argue that they also block access to constitutionally protected free speech and unfairly infringe on the right of adults to have access to information not considered illegal in any way. But this complaint is sheer nonsense. Adults who want access to sites filtered out by the software can ask that it be temporarily dismantled. This is a right that is actually guaranteed by the CIPA legislation.

4   Libraries routinely enact the role of censor when they refuse to stock their shelves with pornographic books, magazines, or videos, and you won't find copies of *Hustler* or *Penthouse* tucked away in the magazine rack of your local library. Nor for that matter will you find a copy of *Deep Throat* in the video department. Yet no one claims that this act of censorship infringes on the right to free speech. Why shouldn't the same principle apply to the Internet? Libraries don't stock pornography; therefore, why shouldn't they exclude pornographic sites from their offerings to the public?

5   Our libraries need to be open to everyone. But by allowing children access to any website available on the Internet, we are turning our libraries into adult bookstores and doing what real adult bookstores cannot do for fear of legal retribution. Libraries that don't use software filters are exposing vulnerable children to pornographic material that might well do them terrible, even lethal, harm. (Sources of information: www.net/services/cipa; www.cnn.com/2003/law/06/24/scotus.internetporn.library.)

1. What is the author's point?

_____

_____

_____

2. Identify the two reasons used to support that point.

a. _____

_____

b. _____

_____

3. Does the author include any of the following?

    a. examples or illustrations

    b. research results

    c. expert opinion

4. Does the author respond to any opposing point of view? _____
If so, fill in the blanks that follow.

Opposition   _____

                  _____

Response   _____

                  _____

5. Circle one or more of the appropriate letters to indicate the presence or absence of errors in the author's argument.

    a. irrelevant reason

    b. circular reasoning

    c. hasty generalization

    d. unidentified or inappropriate expert

    e. unidentified or dated research

    f. no errors

3. Dangerous Self-Esteem

1   For years now, we have heard that high self-esteem is a prerequisite for achievement. As a result, many students work in classrooms where posters proclaim "we applaud ourselves." Exactly for what isn't always made clear. In some elementary schools, students complete sentences that begin "I am special because. . . ." According to what has become established educational wisdom, children who are praised, even for their mistakes, will become confident, successful adults. In response to that wisdom, some states (California for one) have established educational task forces on—you guessed it—promoting self-esteem. Yet now there is some evidence that self-esteem, if it's not backed by real achievements, might be dangerous.

2   As psychologist Brad Bushman of the University of Michigan puts it, kids who develop unrealistically high opinions of themselves can, when brought face to face with a more realistic version of who they are, become "potentially dangerous." Bushman, along

with Ray Baumeister of Case Western Reserve University, conducted a study of unrealistic self-esteem and found that students inflated by self-esteem not based on real achievement were likely to react with hostility or aggression when confronted by a world that fails to mirror their sense of importance.

3   The findings of Bushman and Baumeister have also been echoed by James Gilligan of Harvard Medical School. Gilligan, a long-time researcher into the causes of violence, agrees that inflated self-esteem with no basis in fact can be dangerous. Clinical psychologist Robert Brooks of Harvard concurs as well. According to Brooks, if teaching self-esteem is done inappropriately, "you can raise a generation of kids who cannot tolerate frustration."

4   Those who argue that the failure to teach self-esteem will cause a generation of children to grow up feeling worthless are missing the point. Schools and parents should continue to praise children for a job or task well done. No one is saying that they shouldn't. But self-esteem has to be based on real achievement, not on empty praise that encourages a child to believe everything he or she does is perfect, despite evidence to the contrary.

5   In the end, inflated self-esteem not based on any real accomplishment may well do more harm than good. Unfortunately, the tendency of some young people to become aggressive whenever the world does not reflect their own inflated sense of self-importance is proof positive that an entire generation of young people will never amount to anything. Raised by self-indulgent parents who threw traditional values out the window because they had to "do their own thing," these kids never had a chance to become responsible adults. One can only fear for our society once it is in their hands. (Source of information: Sharon Begley, "You're OK, I'm Terrific," *Newsweek*, July 13, 1998, p. 69.)

1. What is the author's point?

_____

_____

_____

2. Identify the reason used to support that point.

_____

_____

3. Does the author include any of the following?

    a. examples or illustrations

    b. research results

    c. expert opinion

4. Does the author respond to any opposing point of view? _____
If so, fill in the blanks that follow.

Opposition   _____

                 _____

Response   _____

                 _____

5. Circle one or more of the appropriate letters to indicate the presence or absence of errors in the author's argument.

    a. irrelevant reason

    b. circular reasoning

    c. hasty generalization

    d. unidentified or inappropriate expert

    e. unidentified or dated research

    f. no errors

4. In Praise of Bilingualism

1 Lack of English skills is the main reason why minority students fall behind in school. For those who care about the education of America's young people, that should be reason enough to promote bilingual education. But for those who are still not convinced, let me offer the results of some significant research and lay to rest commonly expressed worries about the effect of bilingual education on the acquisition of English.

2 Research on the effects of bilingual education shows that bilingualism does not interfere with performance in either language (Hakata & Garera, 1989). Thus it makes no sense to argue that non-native speakers should not have bilingual instruction because it will interfere with their acquisition of English. This claim is not grounded in any factual evidence.

3 Instead of discouraging bilingual education by trying to eliminate funding for it, we should encourage it because research suggests that the ability to speak two languages improves cognitive

flexibility* and the ability to think creatively (Diaz, 1983). This may be one reason why most other industrialized countries insist that their students master *at least* one other language. They know what we in the United States ignore: Bilingualism enlarges a person's capacity for understanding the world by giving him or her two different languages of interpretation. As linguist Benjamin Whorf established decades ago in his now classic article "Science and Linguistics," "We dissect nature along lines laid down by one native language. . . . The world's presented in a kaleidoscopic* flux* of impression which has to be organized by our minds—and this means largely by the linguistic systems in our minds."[†]

4   The child—or for that matter, the adult—who can speak two languages has more tools for understanding the world than we who are limited solely to English.

1. What is the author's point?

_____

_____

_____

2. Identify the two reasons used to support that point.

a. _____

_____

b. _____

_____

3. Does the author include any of the following?

a. examples or illustrations

b. research results

c. expert opinion

---

*cognitive flexibility: ease and quickness of thinking.
*kaleidoscopic: like a child's toy that constantly changes patterns and colors.
*flux: change; movement.
[†]Edward T. Hall, *The Silent Language.* New York: Anchor Books, 1973, p. 123.

4. Does the author respond to any opposing point of view? _____
If so, fill in the blanks that follow.

Opposition _____

_____

Response _____

_____

5. Circle one or more of the appropriate letters to indicate the presence or absence of errors in the author's argument.

a. irrelevant reason

b. circular reasoning

c. hasty generalization

d. unidentified or inappropriate expert

e. unidentified or dated research

f. no errors

Test 3: Analyzing Arguments

DIRECTIONS Read each argument and answer the questions that follow by filling in the blanks or circling the letter of the correct response. *Note:* The author may or may not respond to opposition and the argument may or may not include an error.

1. Double Punishment Not an Answer

1   The Higher Education Act (HEA) was signed into law over four decades ago by President Lyndon Baines Johnson. Its purpose was to make advanced education a reality for students who, without financial aid, might not be able to attend college. But since 1998 more than 140,000 students have not received any aid because they answered yes to question 35 on the application form: "Have you ever been convicted of possessing or selling drugs?" In 2003 alone, slightly more than 29,000 students found themselves without financial aid because of their response to that one question. For good reason, some members of Congress are sponsoring H.R. 685, a bill that would repeal the 1998 revision of the Higher Education Act.

2   For one thing, federal financial aid is not denied to people who commit far more serious crimes. The form does not ask about the applicant's overall criminal record, so those people who have been convicted of non–drug-related crimes can still receive financial aid. As one expert put it, "You can murder your grandmother and get financial aid, but you can't smoke a joint. You are denied aid even if you are convicted of a [drug] misdemeanor with no jail time. It is inequitable."

3   Furthermore, the criminal justice system has already punished the prospective student as a result of his or her conviction. Michael Cunningham, for example, was convicted of possessing a gram of marijuana. He paid the fine, completed his community service sentence, and now lives with the consequences of having a criminal record. Does it seem right that he was also forced to quit school because he was denied the $3,000 in financial aid he needed for his tuition? Mr. Cunningham's example is proof enough that this new legislation only serves to further penalize those who have already paid their debt to society.

4   Supporters of the law argue that it's a tough but necessary component of the war on drugs. They claim that the prospect of being denied financial aid will deter young people from getting involved with drugs. However, the law ignores the fact that people make mistakes but can still repent and change. Besides, most young people who experiment with drugs are just not thinking

ahead three or four years to when they might need funds for college. Chances are that the law's ability to deter people from drug use is being overestimated.

5   Finally, this law is not even what its sponsor wanted. U.S. Representative Mark Souder, a Republican from Indiana, said, "It hasn't worked out at all the way I intended." He meant for the financial aid denial to apply only to those who were convicted of drug use while either applying for or actually receiving assistance. He says he did not mean to penalize those who honestly admitted to a prior conviction.

6   Obviously, this law robs students of much-needed aid and should be eliminated. The war on drugs will not be won by throwing extra obstacles in the paths of people who seek to better themselves by attending college. (Sources of information: Michael Kranish, "Truth and Its Consequences," *Boston Sunday Globe*, September 9, 2001, pp. E1–E2; www.dailylobo.com/news/2003/02/21/opinion/ editorial.DrugPolicyLimits.A10.)

1. What is the author's point?

_____

_____

_____

2. Identify the four reasons used to support that point.

a. _____

_____

b. _____

_____

c. _____

_____

d. _____

_____

3. Does the author include any of the following?

a. examples or illustrations

b. research results

c. expert opinion

4. Does the author respond to any opposing point of view ? _____
If so, fill in the blanks that follow.

Opposition _____

_____

Response _____

_____

5. Circle one or more of the appropriate letters to indicate the presence or absence of errors in the author's argument.

a. irrelevant reason

b. circular reasoning

c. hasty generalization

d. unidentified or inappropriate expert

e. unidentified or dated research

f. no errors

2. More Homework May Not Pave the Road to Success

1 Local communities across the nation are pressuring schools to boost test scores so that kids can get into and do well in college. In response to that pressure, teachers are piling on the homework, starting in elementary school. A University of Michigan study found that in 1997, children ages nine to eleven were averaging three and a half hours of homework a week—a figure that is steadily increasing. At Farmland Elementary School in Rockville, fifth graders are being assigned up to an hour and a half of homework every day. Even six-year-olds are getting nightly homework assignments. Fortunately, more parents and education professionals are beginning to question the value of homework for younger children and are insisting that schools follow the PTA recommendation of ten minutes of homework per grade level.

2 First, it's clear that homework assignments for elementary school children do not improve academic performance. A 1999 study conducted by Sandra Hofferth, a scientist at the University of Michigan's Institute for Social Research, found no link between heavy homework assignments and improved grades. Harris Cooper, Ph.D., chair of the Psychological Sciences Department at the University of Missouri at Columbia, is one of the top authorities

on homework. Cooper claims that for kids in elementary school, "The effect of homework on achievement is trivial, if it exists at all."

3   While it's true that many parents and educators consider assignments that encourage creative thinking to be valuable, these are not the assignments children are getting for homework. Instead, they are being asked to complete dull textbook assignments that do not develop imagination or creativity.

4   Too much homework is also likely to generate angry, tearful battles at home because children dislike the dull assignments and try to avoid doing them. Parents, in turn, must force their kids to sit down and do the work, all of which creates a tension-filled home environment. In the long run, children will only begin to dislike school and schoolwork even more. Furthermore, Boston school board president General Francis A. Walker pointed out in 1900 that homework harms children's health. Around the same time, many educators believed that homework caused tuberculosis, nervous conditions, and heart disease in youth.

5   Excessive homework also interferes with extracurricular activities, which are just as important as academic studies. Many children today are involved in sports, hobbies, and music lessons. After-school assignments make it difficult for kids to engage in these activities, which teach valuable life skills that are just as important as formal academic knowledge. Children also need time just to be kids. They need to play with their friends and have leisure time with their families. As child psychiatrist Stanley I. Greenspan, M.D., points out in his book *The Irreducible Needs of Children*, a child needs a variety of nonacademic activities to grow into a whole person. That's why school districts should follow the lead of the East Porter County School Board in Indiana. In 1998, the board adopted a policy requiring school personnel to coordinate assignments so that students do not have to devote their entire evening to homework.

6   The drawbacks to homework outweigh the benefits. Let's stop pretending that it's helping kids achieve and keep schoolwork in the schools. (Source of information: Stephanie Dunnewind, "Homework Overload?" *Seattle Times*, November 16, 2002, p. 12.)

1. What is the author's point?

_____

_____

_____

2. Identify the four reasons used to support that point.

a. _____

_____

b. _____

_____

c. _____

_____

d. _____

_____

3. Does the author include any of the following?

a. examples or illustrations

b. research results

c. expert opinion

4. Does the author respond to any opposing point of view? _____
If so, fill in the blanks that follow.

Opposition   _____

_____

Response   _____

_____

5. Circle one or more of the appropriate letters to indicate the presence or absence of errors in the author's argument.

a. irrelevant reason

b. circular reasoning

c. hasty generalization

d. unidentified or inappropriate expert

e. unidentified or dated research

f. no errors

3. Serving the Nation: A Universal Call

1   Israel requires all of its young men to serve three years of mandatory military service. The Israeli Defense Force drafts women, too,

but not for combat positions. Sweden does not have a professional army. Instead, all of its younger men train for military service and then remain in the reserves until age forty-seven. The United States would do well to follow suit and require all of its young men and women to serve in the military for one or two years after leaving high school.

2   Opponents of compulsory service object, saying that universal conscription* would cost too much. They argue that Americans won't permit an increase in taxes to fund a significantly larger military. However, these critics forget that freedom is not free. All Americans should have the opportunity to serve their country. Also, learning to defend one's homeland is a patriotic obligation. Therefore, young people should be proud to devote a short time of their lives to fulfill an important civic responsibility.

3   This country needs compulsory military service in order to train its citizens to combat terrorism and to give them the skills to respond to threats and attacks of any kind. After World War II in 1945, President Truman noted that America's "geographic security is gone—gone with the advent of the atomic bomb, the rocket, and modern airborne armies." Yet fewer than 6 percent of Americans under the age of sixty-five know anything about military service. The rest of the population relies on a relatively small number of servicemen and women to protect them. This is a dangerous state of affairs given that the twenty-first century has ushered in a new age of warfare, one that often takes the form of attacks on innocent civilians. Americans can no longer be complacent or expect others to guard their safety. All citizens need to learn the specialized communication, emergency response, and civil defense skills necessary for combating various kinds of threats to the nation's security.

4   Mandatory military service would also help close the social gap that currently divides Americans from one another. According to journalism professor and naval reservist Philip Meyer, "One of the unplanned consequences of the military draft was a great leveling effect, where social-class distinctions were set aside." Unfortunately, once World War II came to an end, that leveling effect was no longer so powerful, and the country began to divide into separate and often unequal social groups. If all young men and women were once again required to serve together as equals, democratic ideals would be reinforced, and divisions between people of different classes would be narrowed.

---

*conscription: drafting for military service.

5   In an era when America is threatened by suicide bombers and bioterrorism, it makes sense for all citizens to participate in basic military training. One to two years of service is a small price to pay for a stronger defense and greater national unity.

1. What is the author's point?

_____

_____

_____

2. Identify the two reasons used to support that point.

a. _____

_____

b. _____

_____

3. Does the author include any of the following?

a. examples or illustrations

b. research results

c. expert opinion

4. Does the author respond to any opposing point of view? _____
If so, fill in the blanks that follow.

Opposition   _____

_____

Response   _____

_____

5. Circle one or more of the appropriate letters to indicate the presence or absence of errors in the author's argument.

a. irrelevant reason

b. circular reasoning

c. hasty generalization

d. unidentified or inappropriate expert

e. unidentified or dated research

f. no errors

4. **Information About Anthrax Helps Calm Panic**

1 In the autumn of 2001, a wave of anthrax contaminations raised the possibility that the United States might be the target of biological warfare. And it's certainly true that disease-causing microorganisms can be used as instruments of terror. Yet despite constant media speculation that our country's enemies might drop deadly anthrax bacteria from the skies or dump it into our waters, this particular biological weapon could probably not be used on a massive scale. Regardless of the media hype, there are three reasons why large-scale bioterrorism with anthrax would be difficult to achieve.

2 First, infecting large numbers of people would require specific types and large amounts of the deadly microorganism. Killer forms of anthrax, for example, must be manufactured in a laboratory by people who know which strains can be developed into lethal weapons. Then, once a fatal strain is actually produced, it must still be delivered in large enough quantities to infect a person. A toxic dose of anthrax is defined as 8,000 to 10,000 spores. Also, this quantity must be inhaled to fatally infect an individual. It has to be inhaled because anthrax-induced infections of the skin are fatal in only about 25 percent of cases.

3 Distributing anthrax on a large scale is another problem terrorists would face. For example, lethal anthrax spores would have to be ground finely enough to be inhaled. Each spore would have to be no larger than five microns. If the spores were dropped from airplanes, the wind would disperse them. This would make it unlikely that one individual could inhale enough to cause a fatal infection. Indoors, filters in buildings' ventilation systems would cleanse the majority of spores from the air.

4 Third, health care professionals can treat anthrax infections with an arsenal of antibiotics. As talk show host Oprah Winfrey has assured the public, "There are plenty of drugs that can be used safely and effectively." So far, she claims, no anthrax strains have shown any resistance to antibiotics like penicillin and the tetracyclines. According to former U.S. Secretary of Health and Human Services Tommy Thompson, eight staging areas around the country are each stocked with fifty tons of medical supplies, including vaccines, antibiotics, gas masks, and ventilators. These supplies can be moved within hours to the site of a bioterrorist attack.

5 Yes, the American public should stay informed about the possible dangers of a bioterrorist attack. But people should not panic or let fear restrict their movements. Biological weapons are a reality, yet the likelihood of a successful large-scale attack is very slight. (Source of information: www.thezephyr.com/anthrax.htm.)

1. What is the author's point?

_____

_____

_____

2. Identify the three reasons used to support that point.

a. _____

_____

b. _____

_____

c. _____

_____

3. Does the author include any of the following?

a. examples or illustrations

b. research results

c. expert opinion

4. Does the author respond to any opposing point of view? _____
If so, fill in the blanks that follow.

Opposition _____

_____

Response _____

_____

5. Circle one or more of the appropriate letters to indicate the presence or absence of errors in the author's argument.

a. irrelevant reason

b. circular reasoning

c. hasty generalization

d. unidentified or inappropriate expert

e. unidentified or dated research

f. no errors

Test 4: Taking Stock

DIRECTIONS Read the passage. Then answer the questions by filling in the blanks or circling the letter of the correct response.

The Sport of Boxing Needs a Fighting Chance

1 Boxing, according to fight promoter Lou DiBella, "is dirty from top to bottom. The sport is dying." It wasn't always so. At one time, boxing was very popular; throughout the early- to mid-twentieth century, when Joe Louis, Muhammad Ali, Joe Frazier, and George Foreman were fighting, it seemed like everyone was a boxing fan. People crowded around radios to hear announcers describe bouts, and boxers were admired for their skill and heroism. The sport has inspired many great writers (Ernest Hemingway, Jack London, and Joyce Carol Oates), filmmakers (*Rocky*, *Raging Bull*, and *Champion*), and even musicians (Bob Dylan). Today, however, even the best boxers are seen as celebrities who earn millions of dollars rather than superb athletes dedicated to their sport. The World Heavyweight title is no longer a position of respect and glory. One case in point is ex-champion and convicted rapist Mike Tyson, whose troubles with the law made him notorious and destroyed his career.

2   Of course, boxing still has die-hard supporters, who love the sport for its grace and excitement. "Boxing is the raw, narrative drama of physical conflict with a hero and a loser," said investigative journalist Jack Newfield. "On its rare best nights, fights like the ones between Ali and Frazier . . . reveal character and will and bravery that can be as uplifting as a symphony or a play." And many fans still agree with former heavyweight champion George Foreman that "boxing is the sport that all other sports aspire to be."

3   Yet even fans like Newfield have referred to the current state of boxing as a "slum" and a "sewer." They acknowledge that the sport is declining because of its corruption and its lack of uniform rules and standards. Cleaning up boxing and restoring it to its former glory days will require remedying two serious problems.

4   First and foremost, the sport must free itself of rampant corruption. For years, boxing has been plagued by bribes and fixed fights, and undercover FBI investigations have resulted in charges of money laundering, racketeering, fraud, conspiracy, and tax evasion. In a recent investigation, boxer Mitchell Rose told FBI agents that employees of Top Rank, boxing's second-largest promotional company, offered him $5,000 to throw his 1995 fight with Eric "Butterbean" Esch. When he refused the bribe and won the fight,

Rose was blacklisted. In 2001, a grand jury indicted Thomas Williams for accepting payment to take a dive against Richie Melito. Boxer Shelby Gross claims to have been offered $10,000 to lose to Melito, but he says he rejected the bribe.

5   Forged records and deliberate mismatches, too, have blighted the sport. Boxing's managers and promoters stand to make huge profits on events, so they are inclined to embellish boxers' records to generate more audience interest in a particular match. For example, when promoter Don King arranged Mike Tyson's first fight after Tyson's release from prison, he chose Peter McNeely, a boxer with a fake record of 36–1 to be Tyson's opponent. King's plan to engineer an explosive comeback for Tyson was almost too successful. McNeely was such a weak opponent, it took Tyson only ninety seconds to demolish McNeely in the ring, and matches that short are not crowd-pleasers. FBI stings have also produced forged medical records that have allowed boxers to continue to fight and earn managers and promoters large sums of money while sacrificing their own health.

6   Even when the fights are legitimate, boxing's judging is often disgraceful. While sports like basketball and baseball have quantifiable measures for winning, the outcome of a boxing match, as for a figure skating routine, is subjective—dependent on the opinion of those doing the judging. Jack Newfield claimed that, in many cases, promoters pay the judges, including their travel expenses. "[The judges] know which fighter is under an exclusive contract to that promoter. They don't have to be told that if they favor that promoter's employee, they will get future assignments from that promoter. Can you imagine a baseball owner picking and paying the home-plate umpire in a World Series game?" Lou DiBella, senior vice president of HBO Boxing and TVKO, agrees: "Judges know the unspoken agenda. It's the equivalent of George Steinbrenner picking the umpires for a playoff game with the Red Sox." Consequently, many decisions in championship fights are indefensible, and, not surprisingly, such biased and unfair decisions demoralize fighters.

7   To combat all these abuses, the U.S. Congress has enacted several laws, including the Professional Boxing Safety Act of 1996 and the Muhammad Ali Boxing Reform Act of 2002. In April 2004, the U.S. Senate passed a bill to establish the United States Boxing Administration (USBA). The bill's sponsor, Senator John McCain, said, "Without the adoption and implementation of minimum uniform federal standards, I fear that the sport of boxing will continue its downward spiral into irrelevance." Not everyone agrees with the idea of creating a national commission. Among

them is promoter Murad Muhammad, who says, "You can't change one hundred years of tradition." However, Mr. Muhammad has had charges of assault and battery and defamation of character filed against him, so his opinion doesn't merit serious consideration. Most fans agree that the USBA can strengthen and enforce existing boxing laws, reduce arbitrary practices, and provide uniformity in ranking criteria and contractual guidelines.

8   The USBA also needs to correct boxing's second major problem: the mistreatment of the boxers themselves. The USBA can establish and enforce uniform health and safety standards and create a centralized medical registry to protect boxers from injury or death. Since 1970, about fifty professional fighters have died in the ring. The most recent tragedy happened in 2003 when thirty-four-year-old Brad Rone, who had high blood pressure and was out of shape but needed money for his mother's funeral, was allowed to fight in Utah and ended up dying of heart failure after the first round. Clearly, better oversight for boxers' physical welfare is needed, and a national regulatory agency could demand that boxers like Rone pass complete physical examinations before entering a ring.

9   In addition to the creation of the USBA, boxers themselves should seize more power and authority by creating an association, or a union, to look out for their financial interests. Right now, a boxer's adviser and representative is his or her manager, which is akin to a baseball coach doubling as a financial adviser to a pitcher or an outfielder. It's no wonder that the majority of boxers make very little money and have no financial contracts, no pension plans, and no insurance. Just as baseball players have a union that negotiates on their behalf, boxers should organize themselves so that they can have similar protections.

10   In 2001, in an effort to resuscitate a dying sport, Jack Newfield created a Bill of Rights for Boxers that proposed, among other things, a national commission and a labor union to end the abuses. "Boxing has become like a gruesome car wreck," wrote Newfield. "I can keep watching only if I'm pulling a victim out to safety. . . . The best way I can display my respect for [boxers] is to try to clean up their polluted and toxic environment."

11   Newfield loved the sport of boxing. But his efforts to save it from itself have so far proved fruitless. Newfield died in 2004. Three years later, in July of 2007, the *New York Times* published an article in the sports section titled "In Boxing's Underbelly, a Blind Eye to Fighters' Health." As the title suggests, the boxing ring is still a "polluted and toxic environment," at least for those men and women who step into it. The managers, judges, and

promoters are undoubtedly still earning a profit at the fighters' expense. (Sources of information: Jack Newfield, "Should We Let Boxing Die?" *Parade*, May 2, 2004, pp. 6–7; Jack Newfield, "The Shame of Boxing," *The Nation*, November 12, 2001, www.thenation .com/doc.mhtml?i20011112&s=newfield; Rebecca Hanks, "McCain Gives Boxing Fighting Chance," U.S. Senate Committee on Commerce, Science, and Transportation Press Release, April 1, 2004, http://commerce.senate.gov/newsroom/printable.cfm?id=219936.)

1. Use context clues to define the word *rampant* in paragraph 4.

_____

2. In your own words, what is the main idea of the entire reading?

_____

_____

3. What word in sentence 2 of paragraph 1 is a substitute or stand-in for *boxing*? _____

4. What does the author's reference to Mike Tyson illustrate?

_____

_____

5. What pattern organizes paragraph 6?

_____

6. Which statement best sums up the main idea of paragraph 9?
   a. Boxers need a union to protect their interests.
   b. Boxers aren't very smart when it comes to financial matters.
   c. Boxers and baseball players have a lot in common.
   d. Boxers are not treated very well by their managers.

7. What opposing point of view does the author mention?

_____

8. What error in logic mars the author's response?

_____

9. From Lou DiBella's statement in paragraph 6, a reader might logically draw which conclusion?

    a. Lou DiBella wouldn't disagree with Jack Newfield's analogy comparing boxing to a "gruesome car wreck" (paragraph 10).

    b. Lou DiBella would be unlikely to support Senator John McCain's bill to create the United States Boxing Administration.

    c. Lou DiBella is probably one of the people responsible for the corruption in the sport of boxing.

    d. Lou DiBella is probably a good friend of boxing promoter Murad Muhammad, who is mentioned in paragraph 7.

10. What conclusion can you draw from the reading?

    a. Boxing promoters and managers want to reform boxing and make it a safer sport.

    b. Unlike boxing promoters, managers don't care whether boxing is made safer or stays exactly the same.

    c. Boxing promoters and managers will probably fight many of the changes reformers like Newfield want to make.

Putting It All Together

The four extended readings that follow are accompanied by discussion questions and writing assignments, which ask you to do what, until now, you've seen others do—argue a point of view. These questions and assignments are important because *Reading for Thinking* is not concerned solely with teaching you to understand and evaluate the ideas of others. Ultimately, its goal is to encourage you to confidently express and argue your own particular point of view.

■ **READING 1**

EXTREME PHILANTHROPY
Stephanie Strom

LOOKING AHEAD Human organs for transplant are in short supply, but if everyone had the attitude described in the following reading, the problem could be solved in a very short time.

1. Given that this selection is from a newspaper rather than a text-book, your pre-reading can be fairly quick. Get an overview by reading the first sentence of every paragraph.

2. Note the title and use it to focus your reading by asking, "What kind of philanthropy might be labeled extreme?"

3. Several different names are mentioned and repeated through-out. As you read, make sure you understand why the author describes these people and what they have in common.

WORD WATCH Some of the more difficult words in this reading are defined below. Watch for these words as you read. The number in parentheses indicates the paragraph in which they appear. An asterisk marks their first appearance in the reading. Preview the definitions before you begin reading and watch for the words while you read.

---

altruistic (2): thinking of others first

literally (2): in actuality

designations (6): specifications, restrictions

profile (6): description of specific characteristics

---

1 A LITTLE MORE THAN TWO YEARS AGO, HAROLD S. MINTZ, A salesman, gave one of his kidneys to a total stranger. "The first thing they do is send you to see a psychiatrist," said Mr. Mintz, who lives in the Washington area. "I thought that was hilarious, but it made sense. I mean, what kind of nut puts up his hand and says 'I want to give away body parts'?"

2 The number of organ donations from the living surpassed those from the dead, and has for the past two years. The vast majority of such good samaritans act to help a relative or close friend, but

transplant centers report an increasing number of "altruistic*
donors"—that is, people who want to give of themselves, literally,*
to whomever doctors decide is in need. Cathy Paykin, transplant
programs director at the National Kidney Foundation, said the
first publicly acknowledged instance of donor altruism occurred in
1999, when a nurse allowed doctors at Johns Hopkins University
to remove a kidney using the then new method of laparoscopy. . . .
The subject was in the news again after Zell Kravinsky, a Jenkin-
town, PA, real-estate developer obsessed with philanthropy—he
reportedly canceled his family's cable television service so he
could donate more money—gave away one of his kidneys. . . .

3   Nationally, more than 80,000 people are waiting for an organ—
a number that is expected to hit 100,000 by 2010. Two-thirds of
them, more than 55,000, are waiting for a kidney, and altruistic
donations are unlikely to shorten the line much, said Ms. Paykin.
"It is definitely increasing, but is it increasing to the point where it
will make a difference in the waiting list?" she said. "I doubt it."

4   The United Network for Organ Sharing, which tracks data on
organ donation, lists 134 altruistic kidney donors since 1998, and
eleven partial liver donors. Typically, less than 5 percent of those
who offer their organs are accepted. Most are rejected for medical
reasons. Since the University of Washington Medical Center in
Seattle started taking altruistic donors in 2001, for instance, it has
recovered organs from four. "It's really a very small percentage who
qualify," said Dr. Connie Davis, medical director of the kidney and
kidney–pancreatic transplant program at the university. "You have
to be in better than average shape mentally and physically."

5   Those who qualify must then go through a process that can
take several months. Christine Karg-Palreiro, a thirty-eight-year-
old civil engineer, had planned to donate a kidney to a colleague,
and went ahead with the surgery even after it turned out she was
not a match for him. The surgery took place two days after the
attacks of September 11, 2001, and today Ms. Karg-Palreiro has
five small scars to show for it, as well as an anonymous thank
you note from the recipient. "Giving a kidney is the coolest thing
I've ever done and if I had a spare, I'd do it again," Ms. Karg-
Palreiro said. She has long been a blood donor, as are many altruistic organ donors, and she has also signed up to donate bone
marrow.

6   Mr. Kravinsky also went through with his surgery, and his kidney was, as he wished, given to a black person, though experts
say federal laws would seem to prohibit such designations.*
Donors may specify a certain person they want to receive their

organs, but they are prohibited from discriminating against classes of people. "What they cannot do is say 'I don't want it to go to someone who's short or tall or skinny or fat,'" said Brian Broznick, president and chief executive of the Center for Organ Recovery and Education in Pittsburgh. "To me, what he reportedly asked for would be discrimination, and I don't think it should be allowed." Dr. Radi Zaki, the transplant surgeon who handled Mr. Kravinsky's surgery at Einstein Medical Center, said a five-member ethics committee had selected the recipient, not his patient. "The designation of the kidney was completely out of his hands," Dr. Zaki said. Mr. Kravinsky's kidney ended up going to a woman with much the same profile* he had demanded, but Dr. Zaki said that was because the hospital is in a largely African-American neighborhood.

7   Harold Mintz's kidney went to a refugee from Ethiopia who had settled in Washington and is an accountant. "We get together two or three times a year," he said. "I send my kidney a birthday card every year." Mr. Mintz, who is forty-five, attributed his desire to make such a personal gift to two things: the death of his father from cancer thirteen years ago and an encounter at a mall with an elderly couple who had set up a table with a sign taped to it asking for help in saving their daughter's life. "Their daughter had leukemia and they wanted people to go to their church to see if they could find a match," Mr. Mintz said. "So instead of chocolate and flowers, I paid $60 to get typed and tested." His blood type didn't match, and he later read the young woman's obituary.

8   Years later, after hearing about the Washington Regional Transplant Consortium, the first transplant organization to actively recruit what it calls "nondesignated" donors, he decided to volunteer a kidney, overcoming the resistance of his wife and his own concern about what would happen if his daughter ever needed a kidney and he was the only match in the family. Mr. Mintz said he does not expect his story to inspire legions of people to volunteer their kidneys to strangers, but he hopes that it might make more people willing to give up organs for friends and relatives. "When people hear what I did, they think I'm a hero or something, but that's not the case," he said. "I have good days and bad days like anybody, but if you can help somebody, especially somebody you know, I just want you to know that it's possible."

Stephanie Strom, "Ideas & Trends:
Extreme Philanthropy. . . ,"
New York Times, July 27, 2003.

PUTTING IT ALL TOGETHER **DIRECTIONS** Answer the following questions by circling the letter of the correct response or filling in the blanks.

Main Idea **1.** Which statement best expresses the main idea of the entire reading?

a. Although people who donate an organ to complete strangers are greatly admired, they are also viewed with suspicion. They are considered too good to be true, and some people wonder if they have taken altruism just a little too far.

b. More people should be willing to donate a kidney to strangers. If altruistic donors were more common, we could ease the suffering many people must endure while they wait for transplants, sometimes in vain.

c. Some people are so committed to the notion of helping others that they are willing to donate a kidney to strangers.

d. People who donate a kidney to strangers may one day regret their generosity if their remaining kidney malfunctions.

Inference **2.** In the second sentence of paragraph 3, the word *them* refers to

_____. In sentence 3 of the same

paragraph, the three *it* pronouns all refer to _____ _____.

Supporting Details **3.** Dr. Radi Zaki is mentioned to make which point?

a. Some people care more about others than they do about themselves.

b. An organ donor is prohibited from designating the recipient and discriminating against a particular group.

c. Altruistic donors will never be able to eliminate the organ shortage.

4. Why is the detail about Zell Kravinsky's canceling of his cable service included in paragraph 2?

_____

_____

Inference **5.** What connection does the author expect readers to make between the young woman who died of leukemia and Harold Mintz's decision to donate a kidney?

_____

_____

Purpose **6.** What is the author's primary purpose?

a. to inform

b. to persuade

Tone **7.** How would you describe the author's tone?

a. objective

b. concerned

c. skeptical

d. astonished

Allusions **8.** In paragraph 2, what Biblical allusion appears?

_____

_____

Drawing **9.** According to the reading, "The number of organ donations from the
Your Own living surpassed those from the dead, and has for the past two
Conclusions years" (paragraph 2). What does that suggest about the campaign
to get people to sign donor cards giving permission for organs to be
harvested after their deaths?

_____

_____

Bias **10.** Which statement best describes the author's position?

a. The author is skeptical of the motives behind altruists' donations of a kidney to strangers.

b. The author admires those willing to give a kidney to a stranger.

c. The author does not reveal any bias.

■ **VOICING** What do you think of altruistic donors? Do you consider their
YOUR actions admirable or crazy? Please explain your answer.
OPINION

_____

_____

_____

■ **THINKING THROUGH WRITING** Signing an organ donor card so that organs can be harvested after death is not a particularly difficult thing to do. But few do it. If doctors would ask next of kin to allow healthy organs to be used to save a life, the organ shortage might well disappear. Yet few doctors do. Write a paper explaining the following statement: "Although there are two relatively easy ways to remedy the shortage of human organs available for transplant, neither has become common practice." Begin by describing the two easy ways to remedy the shortage. Then explain why you believe neither has become a common practice.

■ READING 2

TALL TALES OF APPALACHIA
John O'Brien

LOOKING AHEAD The author of this reading was unhappy when he heard about the plan for a reality television program called *The Real Beverly Hillbillies*. From his point of view, such a show would encourage the stereotyping of Appalachia's inhabitants, something that he believed had already been done far too often with disastrous and painful results.

PRE-READING AND FOCUS STRATEGIES

1. This is an editorial from a newspaper. Adjust your survey accordingly, reading only the first sentence of every paragraph.

2. The title is an important clue to meaning. "Tall Tales" are stories that aren't true. As you read, try to identify exactly which tall tales the author has in mind. By the same token, pay close attention to any references to the real story behind the tall tales.

WORD WATCH Some of the more difficult words in this reading are defined below. Watch for these words as you read. The number in parentheses indicates the paragraph in which they appear. An asterisk marks their first appearance in the reading. Preview the definitions before you begin reading and watch for the words while you read.

> **vagaries** (5): changes; ups and downs
>
> **Gothic** (5): dark and horror-filled
>
> **marginal** (6): unimportant; on the sidelines

1 GREEN BANK, W.VA. — CBS IS DEVELOPING A REALITY TV SERIES modeled after *The Beverly Hillbillies*, the sixties sitcom. A poor family from a remote corner of southern Appalachia will be transported to a California mansion, the ensuing comic antics shown to America. Well, as a West Virginia farmer might say, that's a load of fertilizer. Having spent virtually my entire life in West Virginia, I can say with some authority that the strange, woebegone place called Appalachia and the hillbillies who inhabit it are a

myth—one devised a century ago to justify outsiders' condescension and exploitation.

2   In the 1870s, there was no "Appalachia." At that time, this mountainous stretch of the country from West Virginia to northern Georgia was one of the most prosperous agricultural areas in America. The people here drew upon their English, German, and Scotch-Irish roots to create a variety of vibrant, peaceful cultures. But in the 1880s that started to change. Outsiders came, ones who didn't care about the thriving farms. They wanted raw materials for their factories, and the mountains had them. Our mountains were covered with the largest and oldest hardwood forest that people had ever seen. The coal deposits were the richest in the world. Industrialization came here like a cyclone roaring through the mountains. People like my ancestors were bullied, threatened, and cheated out of their land. By 1920, timber companies had cut the entire forest. Most of the profits left the state along with the timber and coal.

3   As the mountains were denuded, the industrialists portrayed the families they were robbing as "backward people" and themselves as the prophets of progress. The missionaries who often accepted large donations from the industrialists exaggerated the "otherness" of these strange people. "Local color"** writers made brief visits to the mountains, then wrote fanciful books about the queer,** violent mountain folk. As realistic as Harlequin romances, local color books like Mary Murfree's In the "Stranger People's" Country were read and reviewed as journalistic accounts.

4   College professors began to use them as textbooks in sociology classes. The news media took its part with the infamous Hatfield-McCoy feud in the 1880s and 1890s—a conflict that as Altina L. Waller wrote in her book, Feud, was not really a family feud, but a war between coal mining interests and local interests. Corrupt politicians took isolated incidents and described them as a hillbilly feud. Reporters from the big cities wrote about "white savages" and "West Virginia barbarians." (The New York Times, for example, said of people in eastern Kentucky: "They are remarkably good shots and effective assassins," adding that they "are so accustomed to murder that they do not look upon it with the horror with which it is regarded in civilized communities.") Then, in 1897, the president of Berea College in Kentucky, William Goodell Frost, desperately trying to raise money for his

---

**local color: a literary movement that tried to preserve the customs and dialects of regions profoundly altered by the Civil War.
**queer: odd.

failing institution, created a fund-raising campaign based on the idea of saving the people in the Appalachians from themselves. In an *Atlantic Monthly* article, Frost described the southern Appalachians as our "contemporary ancestors" waking up from a Rip van Winkle-type sleep and in need of help in joining modern America. Frost's article made mythic Appalachia and its backward hillbillies a permanent fixture in America's imaginary landscape.

5   Many in the southern Appalachians are certainly poor, but the poverty grew out of the vagaries* of the coal market and outsiders' control of resources. Industrialists and others, however, blamed the people for their own poverty, and this myth continues because it is entertaining to the Americans beyond the mountains. Some of the region's middle-class writers continue to churn out Gothic* hillbilly tales, the descendants of local color stories.

6   This mythology has even been accepted by the people living here. Not long ago, one of the student counselors at West Virginia University told me that the most persistent problem she encounters is a lack of self-esteem. Bright, capable young men and women do not think they belong in college because they are hillbillies. I have taught at a small private college in West Virginia. Ninety percent of the students were from out of state. The few West Virginians on campus huddled together in their own corner of the student union. They had become marginal* people in their own state.

7   My own father spent his life backing up, apologizing for the space he took up in the world. He took the hillbilly stereotype to heart and all of his life believed that he was backward and inferior—a despair I, too, have been trying to escape all of my life. The reality show that CBS is considering not only exploits my part of the world, it also separates struggling Appalachians from the rest of the American poor. If a television network proposed a "real life" show treating poor African-Americans, Latinos, American Indians, Asians, or Jews as curiosities, they, and all Americans of good will, would be justifiably outraged. Many of us in the southern Appalachians are outraged too. That's why coal miners from the southern Appalachians plan to protest *The Real Beverly Hillbillies* outside the shareholders' meeting on May 21 of CBS's parent, Viacom. It's time the people of the southern Appalachians stood up for themselves.

John O'Brien, "Tall Tales of Appalachia,"
New York Times, May 10, 2003, p. A21.

PUTTING IT ALL TOGETHER   **DIRECTIONS** Answer the following questions by circling the letter of the correct response or filling in the blanks.

Context Clues **1.** Given the context, it's likely that *woebegone* in the last sentence of paragraph 1 means

    a. cheerful.

    b. pitiful.

    c. strong.

    d. lighthearted.

Main Idea **2.** Which statement most effectively paraphrases the main idea of the entire reading?

    a. The reigning stereotype of Appalachia hits too close to home to be funny.

    b. Television has seen to it that those who live in Appalachia are treated as comic figures worthy only of ridicule.

    c. The image of Appalachia as a weird place inhabited by backward people was created by late-nineteenth-century industrialists, who wanted to rob the region of its resources.

    d. No television program can adequately reflect the complexity of life in Appalachia; therefore, few creators of television fare even try to go beyond the traditional stereotype of the feuding hillbilly.

Transition **3.** Paragraph 2 contains a transitional sentence that signals both contrast and time order. Write that sentence in the blank.

_____

_____

Supporting Details **4.** Who was Mary Murfree, and why is she mentioned (paragraph 3) in the reading?

_____

_____

Allusion **5.** The author says that local color writers' descriptions of Appalachia were "as realistic as Harlequin romances." Harlequin romance novels are famous for being badly written and for reusing the same boy-meets-girl plot countless times. What does the author want to suggest by using this allusion?

_____

_____

6. In paragraph 6, the phrase "this mythology" refers to what idea in the two previous paragraphs?

_____

_____

7. In paragraph 4, the author describes how the president of Berea College in Kentucky alluded to "a Rip van Winkle–type sleep." Rip van Winkle is a character in a Washington Irving[†] short story about a man who goes to sleep and doesn't wake up for twenty years. When he does, he's shocked by all the changes in the world around him. What did the president of Berea College want to suggest by the allusion to Rip Van Winkle?

_____

_____

***Purpose* 8.** What is the author's purpose?

    a. to inform

    b. to persuade

***Tone* 9.** How would you describe the author's tone?

    a. angry

    b. ironic

    c. cautious

    d. objective

***Drawing* 10.** Suppose someone said to the author, "Oh for goodness sake,
Your Own lighten up. It's only a reality television show." Based on the read-
Conclusions ing, how do you think the author would respond?

_____

_____

_____

_____

_____

[†]Washington Irving (1783–1859): American writer; author of such famous short stories as "Rip Van Winkle" and "The Legend of Sleepy Hollow."

■ **VOICING YOUR OPINION** Having read this editorial, do you think you would be comfortable watching a program that made fun of "hillbillies," or would you be likely to boycott it and encourage your friends to do the same? Please explain your answer.

_____

_____

_____

■ **THINKING THROUGH WRITING** Write a two-part paper in which you first summarize John O'Brien's reasons for protesting a planned television program that makes fun of life in Appalachia. Then express your opinion as to whether this makes sense, being sure to give reasons why you feel as you do.

■ **READING 3**

ANONYMOUS SOURCE IS NOT THE SAME AS OPEN SOURCE
Randall Stross

LOOKING AHEAD — The popular online encyclopedia known as Wikipedia is free, updated constantly, and filled with extensive information on more than a million topics. Despite these strengths, however, historian Randall Stross argues that Wikipedia has one fatal flaw.

PRE-READING AND FOCUS STRATEGIES — To support his main point, the author compares Wikipedia to traditional encyclopedias. As you read, look for comparisons of the two, and when you finish, see if you can paraphrase the differences.

WORD WATCH — Some of the more difficult words in this reading are defined below. Watch for these words as you read. The number in parentheses indicates the paragraph in which they appear. An asterisk marks their first appearance in the reading. Preview the definitions before you begin reading and watch for the words while you read.

epistemological (1): related to the branch of philosophy that studies the nature of knowledge

collectivity (2): group or community

dint (2): force; power

conventional (2): usual or customary

credentials (2): qualifications

putative (3): supposed

egalitarian (3): promoting equality

Nobel laureate (3): winner of a Nobel Prize for outstanding achievement

vouch for (3): support; stand behind

jargon (3): specialized language

lay (3): nonprofessional

epistemic (3): related to or involving knowledge

recourse (7): access

burnishing (7): polishing

pecuniary (9): related to money

accolades (9): praise

candid (9): honest

taxonomy (9): ordered
system of
classification

wistful (12): filled with
sad longing

beta test (13): trial run
to eliminate errors

1   WIKIPEDIA, THE FREE ONLINE ENCYCLOPEDIA, CURRENTLY
serves up the following: Five billion pages a month. More than
120 languages. In excess of one million English-language articles.
And a single nagging epistemological* question: Can an article be
judged as credible without knowing its author? Wikipedia says
yes, but I am unconvinced.

2   Dispensing with experts, the Wikipedians invite anyone to pitch
in, writing an article or editing someone else's. No expertise is
required, nor even a name. Sound inviting? You can start immediately. The system rests upon the belief that a collectivity* of
unknown but enthusiastic individuals, by dint* of sheer mass
rather than possession of conventional* credentials,* can serve in
the supervisory role of editor. Anyone with an interest in a topic
can root out inaccuracies and add new material.

3   At first glance, this sounds straightforward. But disagreements
arise all the time about what is a problematic passage or an
encyclopedia-worthy topic, or even whether a putative* correction
improves or detracts from the original version. The egalitarian*
nature of a system that accords equal votes to everyone in the
"community"—middle-school student and Nobel laureate* alike—
has difficulty resolving intellectual disagreements. Wikipedia's
reputation and internal editorial process would benefit by having
a single authority vouch for* the quality of a given article. In the
jargon* of library and information science, lay* readers rely upon
"secondary epistemic* criteria," clues to the credibility of information, when they do not have the expertise to judge the content.

4   Once upon a time, *Encyclopædia Britannica* recruited Einstein,** Freud,** Curie,** Mencken,** and even Houdini** as contributors. The names helped the encyclopedia bolster its
credibility. Wikipedia, by contrast, provides almost no clues for

---

**Albert Einstein: physicist who revolutionized theories of space and time.
**Sigmund Freud: the Viennese father of psychoanalysis.
**Marie Curie: scientist who studied radioactivity.
**H. L. Mencken: famous editor and critic.
**Houdini: perhaps the world's most famous magician.

the typical article by which reliability can be appraised. A list of edits provides only screen names or, in the case of the anonymous editors, numerical Internet Protocol addresses. Wasn't yesterday's practice of attaching "Albert Einstein" to an article on "Space-Time" a bit more helpful than today's "71.240.205.101"?

5   What does Wikipedia's system offer in place of an expert authority willing to place his or her professional reputation on the line with a signature attached to an article? When I asked Jimmy Wales, the founder of Wikipedia, last week, he discounted the importance of individual contributors to *Britannica*. "When people trust an article in *Britannica*," he said, "it's not who wrote it, it's the process." There, a few editors review a piece and then editing ceases. By contrast, Wikipedia is built with unending scrutiny and ceaseless editing. He predicts that in the future, it will be *Britannica's* process that will seem strange: "People will say, 'This was written by one person? Then looked at by only two or three other people? How can I trust that process?'"

6   The Wikipedian hive is capable of impressive feats. The English-language collection recently added its millionth article, for example. It was about the Jordanhill railway station, in Glasgow. The original version, a few paragraphs, appeared to say all that a lay reader would ever wish to know about it. But the hive descended and, in a week, more than 640 edits were logged.

7   If every topic could be addressed like this, without recourse* to specialized learning—and without the heated disputes called flame wars—the anonymous hive could be trusted to produce work of high quality. But the Jordanhill station is an exception. Biographical entries, for example, are often accompanied by controversy. Several recent events have shown how anyone can tamper with someone else's entry. Congressional staff members have been unmasked burnishing* articles about their employers and vandalizing those of political rivals. (Sample addition: "He likes to beat his wife and children.")

8   Mr. Wales himself ignored the encyclopedia's guidelines about "Dealing With Articles About Yourself" and altered his own Wikipedia biography; when other editors undid them, he reapplied his changes. The incidents, even if few in number, do not help Wikipedia establish the legitimacy of a process that is reluctant to say no to anyone.

9   It should be noted that Mr. Wales is a full-time volunteer and that neither he nor the thousands of fellow volunteer editors has a pecuniary* interest in this nonprofit project. He also deserves accolades* for keeping Wikipedia operating without the intrusion of advertising, at least so far. Most winningly, he has overseen a

system that is gleefully candid* in its public self-examination. If you're seeking a well-organized list of criticisms of Wikipedia, you won't find a better place than Wikipedia's coverage of itself. Wikipedia also provides a taxonomy* of no fewer than 23 different forms of vandalism that strike it.

10   It is easy to forget how quickly Wikipedia has grown; it began only in 2001. With the passage of a little more time, Mr. Wales and his associates may come around to the idea that identifying one person as a given article's supervising editor would enhance the encyclopedia's reputation. Mr. Wales has already responded to recent negative articles about vandalism at the site with announcements of modest reforms. Anonymous visitors are no longer permitted to create pages, though they still may edit existing ones.

11   To curb what Mr. Wales calls "drive-by pranks" that are concentrated on particular articles, he has instituted a policy of "semi-protection." In these cases, a user must have registered at least four days before being permitted to make changes to the protected article. "If someone really wants to write 'George Bush is a poopy head,' you've got to wait four days," he said.

12   When asked what problems on the site he viewed as most pressing, Mr. Wales said he was concerned with passing along the Wikipedian culture to newcomers. He sounded wistful* when he spoke of the days not so long ago when he could visit an article that was the subject of a flame war and would know at least some participants—and whether they could resolve the dispute tactfully. As the project has grown, he has found that he no longer necessarily knows anyone in a group. When a dispute flared recently over an article related to a new dog breed, he looked at the discussion and asked himself in frustration, "Who are these people?" Isn't this precisely the question all users are bound to ask about contributors? . . .

13   There's no question that Wikipedia volunteers can address many more topics than the lumbering, for-profit incumbents like *Britannica* and *World Book*, and can update entries swiftly. Still, anonymity blocks credibility. One thing that Wikipedians have exactly right is that the current form of the encyclopedia is a beta test.* The quality level that would permit speaking of Version 1.0 is still in the future.

Randall Stross, "Anonymous Source Is Not
the Same as Open Source,"
New York Times, March 12, 2006, p. 3.5.

PUTTING IT ALL TOGETHER

DIRECTIONS Answer the following questions by circling the letter of the correct response or filling in the blanks.

Main Idea and Paraphrasing

1. Which statement best expresses the main idea of the entire reading?

    a. Wikipedia and traditional encyclopedias are both alike and different.

    b. Wikipedia's success will not last as more people discover how inaccurate the entries are.

    c. Wikipedia's credibility would increase if the accuracy of each article were verified by a named expert or experts.

    d. Wikipedia articles are created and updated in a process composed of several steps.

2. How would you paraphrase the main idea of paragraph 6?

_____

_____

3. What is the implied main idea of paragraph 9?

    a. Wikipedia is not a money-making operation.

    b. Wikipedia and its founder are admirable for several reasons.

    c. Because Wikipedia is maintained by volunteers, vandalism is a constant problem.

    d. Wikipedia differs significantly from commercial websites.

Supporting Details

4. Why does the author mention the changes made by Congressional staff members and Jimmy Wales in paragraphs 7 and 8?

    a. They illustrate the idea that anyone can contribute to Wikipedia articles, regardless of their level of expertise.

    b. They are examples of how "flame wars" can undermine the credibility of information.

    c. They support the point that information in Wikipedia articles is rarely 100 percent accurate.

    d. They illustrate the point that people can tamper with information posted in Wikipedia entries.

Pattern of Organization

5. Paragraph 5 is organized mainly by what pattern?

    a. time order

    b. comparison and contrast

    c. classification

    d. cause and effect

Paraphrasing **6.** How would you paraphrase this brief passage, using your own words? "Disagreements arise all the time about what is a problematic passage or an encyclopedia-worthy topic, or even whether a putative correction improves or detracts from the original version. The egalitarian nature of a system that accords equal votes to everyone in the 'community'—middle-school student and Nobel laureate alike—has difficulty resolving intellectual disagreements."

_____

_____

_____

_____

_____

Inference **7.** Why does the author mention Einstein, Freud, Curie, Mencken, and Houdini? What do allusions to these people mean to suggest?

_____

_____

8. How does Jimmy Wales, Wikipedia's founder, respond to criticism that his site is subject to spreading inaccurate or false information because it doesn't use qualified experts?

_____

_____

_____

Purpose **9.** What is the primary purpose of this reading?

    a. to inform

    b. to persuade

Tone **10.** How would you describe the author's tone?

    a. amused

    b. sarcastic

    c. skeptical

    d. neutral

■   **VOICING YOUR OPINION** Have you ever used Wikipedia to write a paper? If so, do you think it is a good source of information? Why or why not?

_____

_____

_____

■   **THINKING THROUGH WRITING** Summarize the reading in no more than one paragraph.

■ **READING 4**

FIVE WAYS TO DEAL WITH CONFLICT
Roy Berko, Andrew D. Wolvin, and Darlyn R. Wolvin

LOOKING AHEAD   This reading describes five different methods of responding to conflict. As you read, see if you recognize yourself in any of the descriptions.

PRE-READING AND FOCUS STRATEGIES

1. Because you, like most people, probably already know something about conflict and the different ways of dealing with it, pre-read only the first sentence of every paragraph.

2. The title tells you that there are five approaches to conflict. It is an obvious signal that you need to read the text in order to identify and to describe each approach.

3. The authors make it easy for you to identify the five approaches by printing the names in boldface. As soon as you spot them, slow down and pay close attention to how the authors define each approach. Jot your own version of the definitions in the margins.

WORD WATCH   Some of the more difficult words in this reading are defined below. Watch for these words as you read. The number in parentheses indicates the paragraph in which they appear. An asterisk marks the first appearance in the reading. Preview the definitions before you begin reading and watch for the words while you read.

---

ramifications (1): consequences

habitual (1): regular; automatic

status quo (2): existing situation

equitable (7): fair

---

1   PEOPLE REACT DIFFERENTLY IN DEALING WITH CONFLICT. SOME people pull back, some attack, and others take responsibility for themselves and their needs. Most of us use a primary style for

confronting conflict. Knowing your style and its ramifications* can be helpful in determining whether you are pleased with your conflict style. If you are not, you may need to acquire the skills to make a change in your habitual* pattern. The styles of conflict management are (1) avoidance, (2) accommodation/smoothing over, (3) compromise, (4) competition/aggression, and (5) integration.

Avoidance

2　Some people choose to confront conflict by engaging in **conflict avoidance**—not confronting the conflict. They sidestep, postpone, or ignore the issue. They simply put up with the status quo,* no matter how unpleasant. While seemingly unproductive, avoidance may actually be a good style if the situation is a short-term one or of minor importance. If, however, the problem is really bothering you or is persistent, then it should be dealt with. Avoiding the issue often uses up a great deal of energy without resolving the aggravating situation. Very seldom do avoiders feel that they have been in a win-win situation. Avoiders usually lose a chunk of their self-respect since they so clearly downplay their own concerns in favor of the other person's. Avoiders frequently were brought up in environments in which they were told to be nice and not to argue, and eventually bad things would go away. Or they were brought up in homes where verbal or physical abuse was present, and to avoid these types of reactions, they hid from conflict.

Accommodation/Smoothing Over

3　People who attempt to manage conflict through **conflict accommodation** put the needs of others ahead of their own, thereby giving in. Accommodators meet the needs of others and don't assert their own. In this situation, the accommodator often feels like the "good person" for having given the other person his own way. This is perfectly acceptable if the other person's needs really are more important. But unfortunately, accommodators tend to follow the pattern no matter what the situation. Thus, they often are taken advantage of, and they seldom get their needs met. Accommodators commonly come from backgrounds where they were exposed to a martyr who gave and gave and got little but put on a happy face. They also tend to be people who have little self-respect and try to earn praise by being nice to everyone.

4　　A form of accommodation known as **conflict smoothing over** seeks above all else to preserve the image that everything is okay. Through smoothing over, people sometimes get what they want, but just as often they do not. Usually they feel they have more to say and have not totally satisfied themselves.

5   As with avoidance and accommodation, smoothing over occasionally can be useful. If, for example, the relationship between two people is more important than the subject they happen to be disagreeing about, then smoothing over may be the best approach. Keep in mind, however, that smoothing over does not solve the conflict; it just pushes it aside. It may very well recur in the future.

6   Those who use this technique as their normal means of confronting conflict often come from backgrounds in which the idea was stressed that being nice was the best way to be liked and popular. And being liked and popular was more important than satisfying their needs.

Compromise

7   **Conflict compromise** brings concerns into the open in an attempt to satisfy the needs of both parties. It usually means "trading some of what you want for some of what I want. It's meeting each other halfway." The definition of the word *compromise,* however, indicates the potential weakness of this approach, for it means that both individuals give in at least to some degree to reach a solution. As a result, neither usually completely achieves what she or he wants. This is not to say that compromise is an inherently poor method of conflict management. It is not, but it can lead to frustration unless both participants are willing to continue to work until both of their needs are being met. Those who are effective compromisers normally have had experience with negotiations and know that you have to give to get, but you don't have to give until it hurts. Those who tend to be weak in working toward a fair and equitable* compromise believe that getting something is better than getting nothing at all. Therefore, they are willing to settle for anything, no matter how little.

Competition/Aggression

8   The main element in **conflict competition** is power. Its purpose is to "get another person to comply with or accept your point of view, or to do something that person may not want to do." Someone has to win, and someone has to lose. This forcing mode, unfortunately, has been the European-American way of operation in many situations—in athletic events, business deals, and interpersonal relations. Indeed, many people do not seem to be happy

unless they are clear winners. Realize that if someone wins, someone else must lose. The overaggressive driver must force the other car off the road.

9   The value of winning at all costs is debatable. Sometimes, even though we win, we lose in the long run. The hatred of a child for a parent caused by continuous losing, or the negative work environment resulting from a supervisor who must always be on top, may be much worse than the occasional loss of a battle. In dealing with persons from other cultures, European Americans sometimes are perceived as being pushy and aggressive. Many sales, friendships, and relationships have been lost based on the win-at-all-costs philosophy. Many of the aggressive behaviors in the personal lives of professional athletes are directly credited to their not being able to leave their win-at-all-costs attitude on the athletic field.

Integration

10   Communicators who handle their conflicts through **conflict integration** are concerned about their own needs as well as those of the other person. But unlike compromisers, they will not settle for only a partially satisfying solution. Integrators keep in mind that both parties can participate in a win-win resolution and are willing to collaborate. Thus, the most important aspect of integration is the realization that the relationship, the value of self-worth, and the issue are important. For this reason, integrative solutions often take a good deal of time and energy.

11   People who are competitive, who are communication-apprehensive, or who are nonassertive find it nearly impossible to use an integrative style of negotiation. They feel that they must win, or that they cannot stand up for their rights, or that they have no right to negotiate. In contrast, people who tend to have assertiveness skills and value the nature of relationships usually attempt to work toward integration.

12   Avoidance, accommodation, and smoothing over are all nonassertive acts; the person's needs are not met. Competition is an aggressive act in that the person gets his needs met at the expense of another person. Integration is assertive since the objective is to get one's needs met without taking away the rights of someone else. Compromise, depending on how it is acted out, can be either nonassertive or assertive.

13   *Apologizing.* Have you ever angrily said something to another person? Have you offended someone by being sarcastic or joking around when your remark was perceived to be serious and not

funny? Have you ever acted inappropriately toward someone whom you really like? If the answer to any of these is "yes," the question is, what did you do about it?

14   We all have said or done something we know has hurt or offended a personal friend, a significant other, or even a stranger. For many people brought up in the culture of the United States, one key to getting along with people is knowing when and how to **apologize**, to say you are sorry. How we react to having offended someone has a great deal to do with our background. If you've been brought up to fight for being right, not to give in, or to hold a grudge, you are not likely to consider apologizing. If you've been brought up to believe that the feelings of others supersede your own feelings, then making an apology is probably an automatic reaction.

15   Questions arise as to when it is appropriate to apologize and how to do it. For many people it is both hard to know when to apologize and difficult to apologize. You may be ashamed of your negative actions or have too much pride to admit to another that you did something wrong. Sometimes, even though you may want to apologize, you just may not know how. But remember that apologizing often solves the small problems and keeps them from getting bigger.

16   Traditionally, an apology basically has three stages. First, the person who has done the wrong should state exactly what he or she did. For example, the person could say, "I yelled at you after you told me that the idea I had presented at the meeting was wrong." Second, the perpetrator explains why he or she took the action. For example, the person could say, "I spent a lot of time on that solution, and I felt I had to defend myself." Third, a statement of remorse is made. For instance, the person could say, "I was upset, but I shouldn't have yelled. It didn't do anything to help deal with the task on which we were working." The reason the second step is optional is that you may not know why you took the action, or an explanation may incite further anxiety. If either of these situations is the case, it may be wise to skip that part of the process.

17   Does the process sound too formulaic or unnatural? It may well be, especially if you aren't in the habit of apologizing, but it lays out a pattern for verbalization that can and does work. Once you adopt the style, you may make adjustments to fit your own personality and situations, but at least you now have a format for the apology process.

18   The person who has been wronged may reject your apology. That is not your problem. If you offer an apology, and the apology is sincerely worded and felt, then whether the other person accepts or rejects the action is not the issue. You have fulfilled your obligation. You have recognized that what you did or said was wrong and have taken an action to let the other person know that you are remorseful. You can only be responsible for one person's actions, your own. You cannot make the other person act as you would like him or her to act. Therefore, acceptance of the apology is out of your hands. Don't go into the process of apologizing to receive forgiveness. Go in accepting that you are doing the right thing and that's your purpose.

19   Here are some additional tips that may make it easier to say you're sorry:

Take responsibility. The starting point of any change of behavior is self-admission. Admit to yourself that you have offended someone. You may know this right away, the other person's reaction may let you know you have done something hurtful, someone else might alert you to the situation, or you may realize it yourself at a later time. However you find out, you must admit that you have done wrong and accept responsibility for your actions or you won't be prone to take action.

Explain. Recognize that your actions caused a problem for the other person. If you can do so, and it is appropriate, explain why you acted as you did. For example, if you were angry and blurted out something, you might say, "I was really having a bad day, and what I said wasn't really aimed at you. I was mad at myself, and I took my anger out on you. I'm sorry."

Show your regret. The other person needs to see that you are aware that what you did was wrong. That is, if you think you were wrong, say that you are sorry or ashamed with a statement such as "I felt bad the minute I told your secret. You trusted me, and I betrayed your trust. I shouldn't have done that." This, of course, is only appropriate if you are regretful. If not, the apology will sound phony and may cause a bigger conflict.

Repair the damage. To be complete, an apology should attempt to correct the injury. If you damaged someone's property, offer to fix it. If the damage is emotional, you might ask, "I'm really sorry. What can I do to make it up to you?" There may be nothing concrete you can do, but the offer is usually enough and shows your sincerity. You might follow up by saying something appropriate, such as "I'll try to keep my mouth shut in the future. In the meantime, let me buy you a cup of coffee."

Use good timing. If possible, apologize right away for little things. For example, if you bump into someone, say you're sorry right away. However, if you have done something more serious, like insult a friend out of anger, you may need some time to figure out exactly what to say. A quick apology might not give you time to realize what you've done, why you did it, and what the ramifications might be.

Choose an appropriate conduit. What's the best conduit for an apology? Letters, e-mail, voice mail, the phone, and speaking face to face are all message channels that are available. The first three are definitely impersonal. Using them may be easier and might save you from facing the person directly, but they are usually not as effective as other channels. Resort to using them only if there is no way to meet face to face. If a person lives far away, then there may be no choice. If that's the case, using the phone is probably a better alternative than a written presentation. At least hearing the tone of your voice can be a clue to the honesty of your message. If you do apologize by voice mail, [one authority advises that] "it is best to plan exactly what you want to say, and keep it to thirty seconds, never more than a minute." Long, rambling messages quickly lose their impact.

20   A face-to-face apology is often best because you can display your honesty. It can be a humbling experience as you must see the other person's expressions, show yours, and probably hear a verbal reply. As one expert states, it is worth the anxiety since "you will be respected by the person [whom] you are addressing as well as by yourself more if you are able and willing to make your apology in this manner [face to face]. Smiles, laughter, hugs, handshakes, and other displays of appreciation and affection are added benefits for both parties that are all possible when apologizing this way!"

21   *It's not about who "won" or who "lost."* Remember, life is not a war unless you or the other person makes it a war. Stubborn pride often leads to a loss of friends and can result in physical confrontations. "An apology is a tool to affirm the primacy of our connection with others."

Roy Berko, Andrew D. Wolvin, and Darlyn R. Wolvin, *Communicating.*
Boston: Houghton Mifflin, 2004, pp. 185–192.

PUTTING IT ALL TOGETHER

Answer the following questions by filling in the blanks or circling the letter of the correct response.

Main Idea and Paraphrasing

1. Paraphrase the two main ideas developed in this reading.

a. _____

_____

b. _____

_____

2. Paraphrase the authors' explanation of conflict avoidance.

_____

_____

3. In your own words, what's the drawback commonly associated with compromise as a response to conflict?

_____

_____

Supporting Details

4. Would you call the detail about professional athletes (paragraph 9) a major or minor detail? _____

Explain your answer. _____

_____

Pattern of Organization

5. Which overall pattern organizes the information in paragraph 19 of the reading? _____

Drawing Your Own Conclusions

6. Frank and Evelyn are arguing over Frank's failure to complete his part of their shared research paper. Frank is insisting that his share of the paper was much more than Evelyn's and therefore he can't be blamed for not getting it done on time. Evelyn listens to his explanation and says, "I know I yelled at you and I shouldn't have, but I was anxious about the paper and your behavior seemed irresponsible. Perhaps I overreacted, but I'll lose my scholarship if I don't get an A on this paper." Frank responds by saying, "You shouldn't have yelled at me. I am overworked as it is and I'm doing more than my fair share." Frank is engaging in _____

behavior while Evelyn is trying to _____ .

7. Make up an example of someone engaging in conflict accommodation.

_____

_____

_____

_____

_____

Purpose **8.** What is the authors' purpose?

a. to inform

b. to persuade

Connotation **9.** In which direction does the authors' language lean?
and
Denotation

a. The authors' language leans toward the highly connotative.

b. The authors' language leans toward the highly denotative.

c. The authors strike a balance between connotative and denotative language.

Bias **10.** Do the authors seem to favor any one style of conflict management over the other? _____

Explain why you answered yes or no.

_____

_____

■ **VOICING** How would you describe your own style of dealing with conflict? How
YOUR does your style match the authors' descriptions? Does it fit right in,
OPINION or do you need a new category?

_____

_____

_____

■ **THINKING** Using question 6 as a model, write 5 different descriptions of peo-
THROUGH ple in conflict. Each one should illustrate a different method of
WRITING dealing with conflict.

CHAPTER

America Under Stress, 1967–1976

29

INTRODUCTION

1 The 1960s began with a wave of optimism and confidence in the ability of individuals and government to improve society and promote American interests abroad. For many, that optimism did not last throughout the decade. By 1968, American efforts to mold the emerging nation of Vietnam, to reshape American society along more egalitarian lines, and to banish poverty seemed either a lost cause or a venture that was flawed from the beginning. The Supreme Court under Chief Justice Earl Warren had in a series of controversial decisions expanded the rights of individuals while limiting the power of the state. Its rulings protected those accused of crimes, separated church and state, and expanded the legal right of privacy. But by the end of the decade, the Court was undergoing change as new justices replaced those leaving the bench. Activists like César Chávez, however, continued to believe that group and individual efforts could persuade government and society to promote social and economic justice, improving not only the lives of minorities and the poor but the overall quality of American life.

Like African Americans, many Latinos and 2 American Indians were encouraged by the 1960 election of John Kennedy, who promised increased government activism and social change. Also, like African Americans, Latinos and American Indians recognized that continued grassroots organizing and the mobilization of public opinion were needed to prod governmental action. To varying degrees these groups were successful—gaining national visibility; forcing local, state, and federal governments to respond; and providing paths for further gains.

In 1963, President Kennedy's assassination 3 brought Lyndon Baines Johnson to the White House. Johnson's political skills enabled him to go beyond the New Frontier to fight a war on poverty and to formulate his Great Society. Johnson was

*Words marked with an asterisk are defined at **laflemm.com**, *Reading for Thinking*: "Additional Materials."

comfortable dealing with domestic affairs, but foreign affairs were a different matter. In that arena Johnson seemed content to continue Kennedy's policies as he understood them, especially in Vietnam, where he was determined that the United States would not be beaten by a "two-bit" nation like North Vietnam. Johnson agreed with his advisers that the commitment of American forces was the only effective solution to defeat the Communists.

4   Certain political circumstances initially made that commitment difficult. A sudden buildup could weaken support for Johnson's domestic program and might drive the Chinese and the Soviets to increase their support of North Vietnam. To Johnson, the best choice seemed a carefully controlled, gradual escalation of American forces that would convince the North Vietnamese that the cost of the war was too high. The administration expected that the North Vietnamese would then abandon their efforts to unify Vietnam and that an American-supported South Vietnam would prevail.

5   The strategy failed miserably. North Vietnam chose to meet escalation with escalation until many Americans turned against both the war and Johnson. In 1968, watching opposition to the war mount, Johnson chose to break the momentum of escalation and started peace negotiations with North Vietnam. Unexpectedly, he also announced his withdrawal from the presidential campaign. The turbulent 1968 Democratic convention symbolized the outcome of Johnson's presidency—a divided nation and an end to liberal optimism.

6   Republicans rallied behind Richard Nixon, who, they said, would provide the leadership necessary to restore national unity and global prestige and reassert the traditions and values that had made the nation strong. Nixon's call for unity played on the uneasy expectations of a society that was fragmented by the Vietnam War, urban and campus unrest, and an array of groups clamoring for political, economic, and social changes.

7   Despite their unity rhetoric, Nixon and the Republicans inflamed social divisions to ensure their victories in 1968 and in 1972. They wanted to construct a solid political base around a Silent Majority—composed largely of middle-class white Americans living in suburbs, the South, and the West—who supported the war, opposed antiwar protesters and "hippies," and rejected justifications for urban riots and campus demonstrations. Promising a new, pragmatic conservatism that accepted legitimate government activism, Nixon's first administration achieved generally successful results. Nixon improved relations with the Soviet Union and the People's Republic of China and

withdrew American forces from Vietnam. Domestically, his policy choices showed flexibility, expanding some Great Society programs and following Keynesian guidelines to confront inflation and a sluggish economy.

Nixon, despite his successes, was not satisfied. 8 He wanted his political enemies ruined, and this desire contributed to the illegal activities surrounding the Watergate break-in at the offices of the Democratic Party National Committee. Watergate produced a bitter harvest: not only the unprecedented resignation of a president but a nationwide wave of disillusionment with politics and government.

Vice President Gerald Ford assumed the presi- 9 dency after Nixon's resignation in 1974. The first unelected president, he faced a floundering economy and a cynical public disgusted with politics. Regarded by many, even fellow Republicans, as an interim* president, Ford gained few domestic or foreign-policy victories. Nevertheless, after a sharp challenge from within his own party, he won the Republican Party nomination at their 1976 presidential convention.

Liberal Forces at Work

■ In what ways did the Supreme Court work to expand and protect rights of individuals during the 1960s? How did its decisions restrict the actions of local and state governments?

■ What problems did Hispanics and American Indians face in American society, and how did they organize to bring about change?

■ How did the federal government respond to the needs of Hispanics and American Indians?

The 1960s provided many groups in American society with hope that they, together with the federal government, might successfully challenge inequities* and expand their rights in American society. The civil rights movement demonstrated how grassroots activism could gain support from the federal government, especially from the Supreme Court and the executive branch, to achieve change.

The Warren Court

Until joined in the 1960s by the executive branch, 10 the Supreme Court—the **Warren Court**—was at

> **Warren Court** Term applied to the Supreme Court under Chief Justice Earl Warren; during this period the Court was especially active in expanding individual rights, often at the expense of state and local governments.

the forefront of liberalism, altering the obligations of the government and the rights of citizens. The Court's decisions in the 1950s redefined race relations and contributed a legal base to the 1964 Civil Rights Act. Also in the 1950s, the Court's *Yates v. the United States* (1957) ruling began a reversal of earlier decisions about the rights of those accused of crimes and started to require that states accept many of the protections accorded individuals under the Bill of Rights. For the next decade and a half, the Court expanded freedom of expression, separated church and state, redrew voting districts, and increased protection to those accused of violating the law.

11 In the *Yates* case, the Court released American Communist Party officials from prison who had advocated the overthrow of the American government but had not taken any actions to support their rhetoric: actions, not words, constituted a crime. Between 1961 and 1969, the Court issued over two hundred criminal justice decisions that, according to critics, hampered law enforcement. Among the most important were *Gideon v. Wainwright* (1963), *Escobedo v. Illinois* (1964), and *Miranda v. Arizona* (1966). In those rulings the Court declared that all defendants have a right to an attorney, even if the state must provide one, and that those arrested must be informed of their right to remain silent and to have an attorney present during questioning (the *Miranda* warning).

12 The Warren Court's actions involving church and state also angered many. In *Engel v. Vitale* (1962) and *Abington v. Schempp* (1963), the Court applied the First Amendment—separation of church and state—to state and local actions that allowed prayer and the reading of the Bible in public schools. Both decisions produced outcries of protest across the nation and from Democrats and Republicans in Congress. Governor George Wallace of Alabama stated, "We find the court ruling against God." Congress introduced over 150 resolutions demanding that reading the Bible and praying aloud be permitted in schools. Still, the Court's decisions remained the law, and communities and classrooms complied.

13 Critics also complained that the Court's actions not only undermined the tradition of religion but, perhaps worse, condoned and promoted immorality. The Court's weakening of "community standards" in favor of broader ones regarding "obscene" and sexually explicit materials in *Jacobvellis v. Ohio* (1963) was compounded in the 1964 *Griswold v. Connecticut* decision. In the latter case, the Court attacked the state's responsibility to establish moral standards by overturning Connecticut's laws that forbade the sale of contraceptives,

arguing that individuals have a right to privacy that the state cannot abridge.

14 The Court's rejection of statewide gerrymandering, or redrawing voting districts so as to favor one party, was less controversial but equally lasting in importance. It was the 1962 *Baker v. Carr* ruling that established the goal of making congressional districts "as nearly as practicable" equal in population—"one person, one vote." Two years later in *Reynolds v. Sims* the Court applied the same rule to state election districts. Still, by 1966, the Court's judicial activism had earned growing opposition. One poll found that 52 percent of the public considered the Court was doing a poor job. But for minorities and women and other groups outside the economic, social, and political mainstream, the Court remained a valuable ally.

The Emergence of *La Causa*

15 The roots of *La Causa*, as the farm workers' movement came to be called, preceded the 1960s. In the 1920s and 1930s, Latino activists had attempted to organize Mexican American workers in the fields and factories. With varying degrees of success, organizations such as the League of Latin American Citizens and the American GI Forum turned to the government and the court system to gain political, economic, and social legitimacy. Still, Hispanics and Latinos remained a largely ignored minority mired near society's lowest levels of income and education. Kennedy's candidacy, however, brought hope. Kennedy had initiated the "Viva Kennedy" movement to mobilize the Hispanic, especially the Mexican American, vote. This resulted in new organizations, like the Political Association of Spanish-Speaking Organizations (PASO), that worked to increase Hispanic political representation and recognition of Hispanic issues.

16 Initially expectant, Hispanic leaders soon were disappointed. The Kennedy administration named few Hispanics to government positions and seemed little interested in listening to their voices or promoting their civil rights. Johnson was seen as more of an "amigo." He quickly gained praise for appointing several prominent Mexican Americans to the administration and for guaranteeing that programs established under the War on Poverty and the Great Society reached into Hispanic communities. The praise became muted by 1966, however, as many Mexican Americans believed they were still being ignored, particularly in the West and Southwest. There, federal agencies appeared to defer to local and state governments that frequently opposed increased Mexican American political power and activism. Despite being the

largest minority in the western states, they were still, according to one Mexican American leader, the "invisible minority."

17 Encouraged by Kennedy and Johnson, but unwilling to wait for Anglo politics or the federal government, many Mexican Americans turned to more direct action. For many the beginning of the "revolution" came in 1963 when the Mexican American majority in Crystal City, Texas, toppled the established Anglo political machine and elected an all–Mexican American slate to the city council. Despite claims that they were Communists who wanted to create a "little Cuba" in South Texas, Crystal City was the product of a growing grassroots militancy among Mexican Americans, especially among young adults, who called themselves **Chicanos.** They stressed pride in their heritage and Latino culture and called for resistance to the dictates of Anglo society.

18 By the mid-1960s, many Latinos were becoming more visible. In the urban Northeast, the Puerto Rican population had increased to about a million. At the same time, however, especially in New York City, economic opportunities declined as manufacturing jobs, especially in the garment industry, relocated. The Puerto Rican Forum attempted to coordinate federal grants and to find jobs, while the more militant Young Lords organized younger Puerto Ricans in Chicago and New York with an emphasis on their island culture and Hispanic heritage.

19 In the West, similar actions were taking place. In Colorado, Rodolfo "Corky" Gonzales formed the Crusade for Justice in 1965 to work for social justice for Mexican Americans, to integrate Colorado's schools, and to foster pride in the Mexican heritage. In New Mexico, Reies Lopez Tijerina demanded that Mexican Americans be allowed to enjoy the rights, including land grants, promised under the Treaty of Guadalupe Hidalgo (which had ended the Mexican War in 1848) and to that end formed the Alianza Federal de Mercedes (the Federal Alliance of Land Grants). The nationalistic Brown Berets, formed in Los Angeles in 1967, expressed a militant view that rejected assimilation* into the Anglo world: "We're not in the melting pot. . . . Chicanos don't melt."

20 For most Mexican Americans, however, it was education, jobs, and wages—not assimilation or land grievances—that were key issues. They argued that discrimination and segregation still barred their children from a decent education; school districts needed to provide better educational opportunities for Hispanics and to offer programs that would meet special needs of Hispanic students, including bilingual education. Raul Ruiz

mobilized Mexican American students in Los Angeles in 1967: "If you are a student you should be angry! You should demand! You should protest! You should organize for a better education! This is your right!" He called for students to walk out of class if schools did not meet their demands. "Walkouts" spread in California and Texas.

In November 1968, Mexican American students 21 walked out of the high school in the small South Texas school district of Edcouch-Elsa. The activists demanded dignity, respect, and an end to "blatant discrimination," including corporal punishment— paddling—for speaking Spanish outside Spanish class. The school board blamed "outside agitators" and suspended more than 150 students. But as in other school districts, the protests brought results. The Edcouch-Elsa school district implemented Mexican American studies and bilingual programs, hired more Mexican American teachers and counselors, and created programs to meet the peculiar needs of migrant farm worker children, who moved from one school to another during picking season. In 1968, as Title VII of the Elementary and Secondary Education Act, bilingual education in public schools was approved. It required and provided funds for schools to meet the "special educational needs" of students with limited English-speaking ability. The act, which expired in 2002, aided education not only for those speaking Spanish but also for those speaking other languages—minorities for whom the dominant language spoken in the home was not English.

Cries for dignity, better working conditions, and 22 a living wage were also heard in the fields, where many of the poorest Mexican Americans worked as laborers. Trapped at the bottom of the occupational ladder, not covered by Social Security or minimum wage and labor laws, unskilled and uneducated farm laborers—nearly one-third of all Mexican Americans—toiled long hours for little wages under often deplorable conditions.

Drawing from a traditional base of farm worker 23 organizations, especially in Texas and California, in 1962 **César Chávez** created the National Farm

---

Chicano A variation of mexicano, a man or boy of Mexican decent. The feminine form is Chicana. Many Mexican Americans used the term during the late 1960s to signify their ethinic idenity; the name was associated with the promotion of Mexican American heritage and rights.

César Chávez Labor organizer who in 1962 founded the National Farm Workers Association; Chávez believed in nonviolence and used marches, boycotts, and fasts to bring moral and economic pressure to bear on growers.

Workers Association (NFWA) in the fields of central California. Chávez's union gained national recognition three years later when he called a strike against the grape growers. The union demanded a wage of $1.40 an hour and asked the public to buy only union-picked grapes. After five years, the strike and the nationwide boycott forced most of the major growers to accept unionization and to improve wages and working conditions. Chávez emerged as a national figure promoting *La Causa*, not only for farm workers but for all Latinos and other exploited minorities. Eventually, California and other states passed legislation to recognize farm workers' unions and to improve the wages and conditions of work for field workers, but agricultural workers, especially migrants, remain among the lowest-paid workers in the nation.

American Indian Activism

24 American Indians, responding to poverty, federal and state termination policies, and efforts by state government to seize land for development, also organized and asserted their rights with new vigor in the 1960s. In 1961, reservation and nonreservation Indians, including those not officially recognized as tribes, held a national convention in Chicago to discuss problems and consider plans of action. They agreed on a "Declaration of Indian Purpose" that called for a reversal of termination policies* and better education, economic, and health opportunities. "What we ask of America is not charity, not paternalism* . . . we ask only that . . . our situation be recognized and be made a basis . . . of action."

25 Presidents Kennedy and Johnson recognized the plight of the American Indian and took steps to ensure that they benefited from New Frontier and Great Society programs. Johnson, in 1968, declared that Native Americans should have the same "standard of living" as the rest of the nation and signed the Indian Civil Rights Act. It officially ended the termination program and gave more power to tribal organizations (see p. 865).

26 Kennedy's and Johnson's support for an increased standard of living and tribal and individual rights was a good beginning, but many activists wanted to redress* old wrongs. The National Indian Youth Council, founded shortly after the Chicago conference, called for "Red Power"— that is, for Indians to use all means possible to resist further loss of their lands, rights, and traditions. They began "fish-ins" in 1964 when the Washington state government, in violation of treaty rights, barred Indians from fishing in certain areas. Protests, arrests, and violence continued until 1975, when the state complied with a federal

In 1973, over two hundred Sioux organized by the American Indian Movement (AIM) took over Wounded Knee, South Dakota, the site of the 1890 massacre, holding out for seventy-one days against state and federal authorities. The confrontation ended after two protesters were killed and the government agreed to examine the treaty rights of the Oglala Sioux. In this picture, AIM leader Russell Means receives a blessing and symbolic red paint during the siege. *Dirck Halstead, Time and Life Pictures/Getty Images*

court decision (*United States v. Washington*) upholding treaty rights. Indian leaders also demanded the protection and restoration of their water and timber rights and ancient burial grounds. Museums were asked to return for proper burial the remains and grave goods of Indians on display. But for most, the crucial issue was self-determination, which would allow Indians control over their lands and over federal programs that served the reservations.

27 In 1969 a group of San Francisco Indian activists, led by **Russell Means,** gained national attention by seizing **Alcatraz Island** and holding it until 1971,

Russell Means Indian activist who helped organize the seizures of Alcatraz in 1969 and Wounded Knee in 1973.

Alcatraz Island Rocky island, formerly a federal prison, in San Francisco Bay that was occupied in 1969 by Native American activists who demanded that it be made available to them as a cultural center.

when, without bloodshed, federal authorities regained control. Two years later, in a more violent confrontation, **American Indian Movement** (AIM) leaders Means and Dennis Banks led an armed occupation of Wounded Knee, South Dakota, the site of the 1890 massacre of the Lakotas by the army. AIM controlled the town for seventy-one days before surrendering to federal authorities. Two Indians were killed, and over 230 activists arrested, in the "Second Battle of Wounded Knee."

28   While President Nixon opposed AIM's actions at Wounded Knee, he agreed with many of the activists that more needed to be done to improve tribal and individual lives. He doubled funding for the Bureau of Indian Affairs and sought to promote tribal economies. He condemned the termination program and supported acts that returned 40 million acres of Alaskan land to Eskimos and other native peoples. He also supported the restoration of the Menominees as a tribe after it had been terminated in 1953. In 1974 Congress passed the **Indian Self-Determination and Education Assistance Act,** which gave tribes control and operation of many federal programs on their reservations

29   As federal courts asserted Indian treaty rights in the 1970s, an increasing number of tribes found new economic resources in commercial and industrial ventures operated on reservations. Among the most lucrative and controversial were casinos, which started to open in the 1990s. The profits from such enterprises greatly improved the conditions of life of those involved. As Native Americans enter the twenty-first century, they remain among the nation's most impoverished and poorly educated minority, but there are reasons for optimism. Disease and mortality rates are declining, and Indian populations are increasing. Tribal and pan-Indian movements have sparked cultural pride and awareness; Indian languages are being revived and taught to the younger generations. "We're a giant that's been asleep because we've been fed through our veins by the federal government," stated a Navajo leader. "But now that's ending, and we're waking up and flexing muscles we never knew we had. And no one knows what we're capable of."

Johnson and the War

■ How did foreign-policy decisions made by Kennedy influence Johnson's decisions regarding Latin America and Southeast Asia? In what ways were Johnson's policies different from Kennedy's?

■ What considerations led Johnson to escalate America's role in Vietnam in 1965? How did the North Vietnamese respond to the escalation?

Suddenly thrust into the presidency by Kennedy's 30 assassination, Lyndon Johnson moved quickly to breathe life into Kennedy's domestic programs and to launch the more extensive Great Society. He was comfortable dealing with domestic issues and politics. In foreign policy, however, Johnson relied more heavily on his advisers—the "wise men," as he called them. Johnson was determined not to deviate significantly from past policies or allow further erosion of American power. Two regions of special concern were Latin America and Vietnam, where, like his predecessors, Johnson was determined to prevent further Communist inroads.

In the Western Hemisphere, Castro and his de- 31 termination to export revolution remained the biggest issue. Johnson agreed to continue Kennedy's economic boycott of Cuba and the CIA's efforts to destabilize the Castro regime. Concerned about instability in Latin America and the growth of communism, Johnson refocused Kennedy's Alliance for Progress. Stability became more important than reform. Assistant Secretary of State Thomas Mann told Latin American leaders that political, social, and economic reforms were no longer a central requirement for American aid and support. This new perspective, labeled the **Mann Doctrine,** resulted in increased amounts of American military equipment and advisers in Latin America to aid various regimes to suppress those disruptive elements they labeled "Communist."

The new policy led to direct military inter- 32 vention in the Dominican Republic in 1965. There, supporters of deposed, democratically elected president Juan Bosch rebelled against a repressive, pro-American regime. Johnson and his advisers decided that the pro-Bosch coalition was dominated by Communists, asserted the right to protect the Dominican people from an "international conspiracy," and sent in twenty-two thousand American troops. They restored order; monitored elections that put a pro-American president, Joaquin Balaguer, in power; and left the island in

American Indian Movement   Militant Indian movement founded in 1968 that was willing to use confrontation to obtain social justice and Indian treaty rights; organized the seizure of Wounded Knee.

Indian Self-Determination and Education Assistance Act   Law passed by Congress in 1974 giving Indian tribes control over federal programs carried out on their reservations and increasing their authority in reservation schools.

Mann Doctrine   U.S. policy outlined by Thomas Mann during the Johnson administration that called for stability in Latin America rather than economic and political reform.

mid-1966. Johnson claimed to have saved the Dominicans from communism, but many Latin Americans saw the American intervention only as an example of Yankee arrogance and the intrusive uses of its power.

Americanization of the Vietnam War

33 Kennedy had left Johnson a crisis in Vietnam. The South Vietnamese government remained unstable and its army ineffective, and the Viet Cong, supported by men and supplies from North Vietnam, were winning the conflict. Without a larger and more direct American involvement, Johnson's advisers saw little hope for improvement. Johnson felt trapped: "I don't think it is worth fighting for," he told an adviser, "and I don't think we can get out." "I am not going to be the president who saw Southeast Asia go the way China went," he asserted. But in 1964 he was focused on domestic issues and the upcoming election. Increasing the American role in Vietnam would come only after more strategic planning, increased covert raids against North Vietnam, and a public awareness campaign to generate support for a larger American role there. Aware of the need for more direct American involvement, the White House awaited an event that would allow asking Congress for permission to use whatever force would be necessary to defend South Vietnam.

34   The chance came in August 1964 off the coast of North Vietnam. Following a covert attack on its territory, North Vietnamese torpedo boats skirmished with the American destroyer *Maddox* in the Gulf of Tonkin on August 2 (see Map 29.1). On August 4, experiencing rough seas and poor visibility, radar operators on the *Maddox* and another destroyer, the *C. Turner Joy*, concluded that the patrol boats were making another attack. Confusion followed. Both ships fired wildly at targets shown only on radar screens. Johnson immediately ordered retaliatory air strikes on North Vietnam and prepared a resolution for Congress. Although within hours he learned that the second incident probably had not occurred, Johnson told the public and Congress that Communist attacks against "peaceful villages" in South Vietnam had been "joined by open aggression on the high seas against the United States of America."

35   On August 7, Congress approved the **Gulf of Tonkin Resolution,** allowing the United States "to take all necessary measures to repel" attacks against American forces in Vietnam and "to prevent further aggression." It was, in Johnson's

Unlike previous wars, Vietnam was a war without fixed frontlines. In this picture, marines work their way through the jungle south of the demilitarized zone (DMZ) trying to cut off North Vietnamese supplies and reinforcements moving into South Vietnam. *Larry Burrows/Time and Life Pictures/Getty Images.*

terms, "like Grandma's nightgown, it covered everything." Public opinion polls showed strong support for the president, and only two senators opposed the resolution: Wayne Morse of Oregon and Ernest Gruening of Alaska.

     The resolution gave Johnson freedom to take 36 whatever measures he wanted in Vietnam, but he remained unsure about what course of action to take and when. His advisers recommended committing American combat troops and bombing North Vietnam. To do nothing, Secretary of Defense Robert McNamara warned, was the "worst course of action" and would "lead only to a disastrous defeat." Johnson agreed and decided to limit the American commitment to air attacks on targets in North Vietnam. A Viet Cong attack on the American base at Pleiku on February 7, 1965, that killed eight Americans provided a hoped-for provocation for unleashing the air assault.

> **Gulf of Tonkin Resolution**   Decree passed by Congress in 1964 authorizing the president to take any measures necessary to repel attacks against U.S. forces in Vietnam.

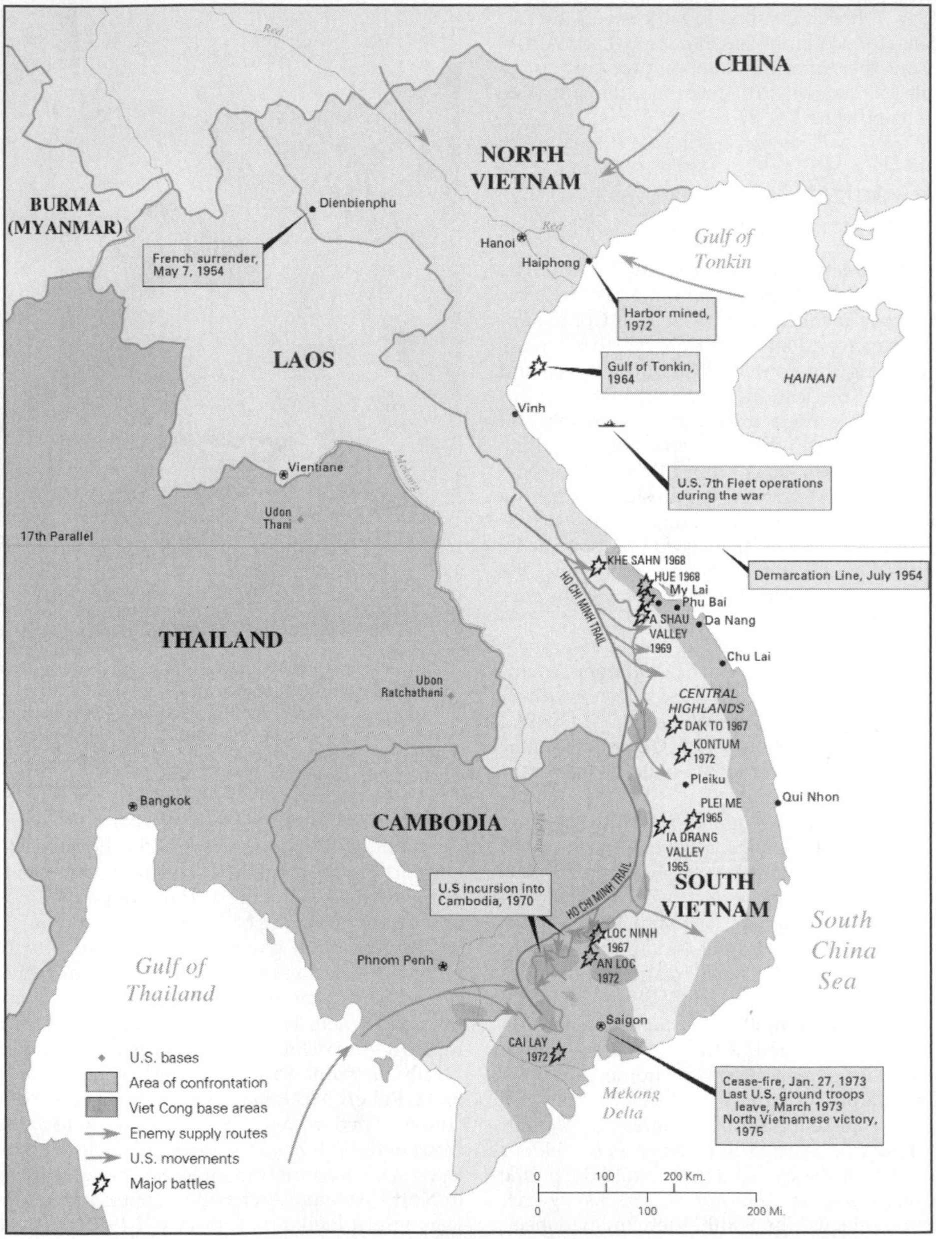

CHINA

NORTH VIETNAM

BURMA (MYANMAR)

Dienbienphu

French surrender, May 7, 1954

Hanoi

Haiphong

Red

Gulf of Tonkin

LAOS

Harbor mined, 1972

Gulf of Tonkin, 1964

HAINAN

Vinh

Vientiane

Udon Thani

U.S. 7th Fleet operations during the war

17th Parallel

KHE SAHN 1968

HUE 1968

My Lai

Phu Bai

Demarcation Line, July 1954

A SHAU VALLEY 1969

Da Nang

HO CHI MINH TRAIL

THAILAND

Chu Lai

Ubon Ratchathani

CENTRAL HIGHLANDS

DAK TO 1967

KONTUM 1972

Pleiku

Bangkok

PLEI ME 1965

Qui Nhon

CAMBODIA

IA DRANG VALLEY 1965

U.S incursion into Cambodia, 1970

HO CHI MINH TRAIL

SOUTH VIETNAM

South China Sea

LOC NINH 1967

AN LOC 1972

Phnom Penh

Gulf of Thailand

Saigon

CAI LAY 1972

Cease-fire, Jan. 27, 1973
Last U.S. ground troops leave, March 1973
North Vietnamese victory, 1975

Mekong Delta

◆ U.S. bases
▢ Area of confrontation
▢ Viet Cong base areas
→ Enemy supply routes
→ U.S. movements
✪ Major battles

| 0 | 100 | 200 Km. |
| 0 | 100 | 200 Mi. |

MAP 29.1 The Vietnam War, 1954–1975   Following the French defeat at Dienbienphu in 1954, the United States became increasingly committed to defending South Vietnam. This map shows some of the major battle sites of the Vietnam War from 1954 to the fall of Saigon and the defeat of the South Vietnamese government in 1975.

37   Operation Rolling Thunder began on March 2. On March 8, the 3rd Marine Division arrived to take up positions around the American base at Da Nang. By July, American planes were flying more than nine hundred missions a week, and a hundred thousand American ground forces had reached Vietnam. Near their bases, American infantry and armored units patrolled aggressively, searching out the enemy. Johnson's strategy soon showed its flaws. As the United States escalated the war, so too did the enemy, which committed units of the North Vietnamese army (NVA) to the fighting in South Vietnam. The U.S. commanding general in Vietnam, **William Westmoreland,** and others insisted that victory required taking the offensive, which necessitated even more American soldiers. Reluctantly, Johnson gave the green light. Vietnam had become an American war.

38   Westmoreland's plan was to use overwhelming numbers and firepower to destroy the enemy. The first major American offensive was a large-scale sweep of the Ia Drang Valley in November 1965. Ten miles from the Cambodian border, the Ia Drang Valley contained no villages and was a longtime sanctuary for Communist forces. The goal was to airlift in units of the air cavalry and search out and destroy the enemy.

39   The initial landing went without incident, but soon the Americans came under fierce attack from North Vietnamese troops. One soldier recalled that his "assault line [that] had started out erect went down to . . . a low crawl." The battle raged for three days with air and artillery supporting the outnumbered Americans. "There was very vicious fighting," North Vietnamese commander Nguyen Huu noted. The "soldiers fought valiantly. They had no choice, you were dead if not."

40   Both sides claimed victory and drew different lessons from the engagement. Examining the losses, 305 Americans versus 3,561 Vietnamese, American officials embraced the strategy of search and destroy—the enemy would be ground down. *Time* magazine named Westmoreland "Man of the Year" for 1965. Hanoi concluded that its "peasant army" had withstood America's best firepower and had fought U.S. troops to a draw. The North Vietnamese were confident: the costs would be great, but they would wear down the Americans. Both sides, believing victory was possible, committed more troops and prepared for a lengthy war.

41   Thus the war spiraled upward in 1966 and 1967. The United States and the North Vietnamese committed more troops, while American aircraft rained more bombs on North Vietnam and supply routes, especially the **Ho Chi Minh Trail** (see Map 29.1). The strategic bombing of North Vietnam produced great results—on paper. Nearly every target in North Vietnam had been demolished by 1968, but the North Vietnamese continued the struggle. China and the Soviet Union increased their support, while much of North Vietnamese industrial production was moved underground. It seemed that the more the United States bombed, the more North Vietnamese determination continued to increase. By mid-1966, it appeared to some in Washington that the war had reached a stalemate, with neither side able to win nor willing to lose. Some speculated that any victory would be a matter of will, and feared that growing opposition to the war in the United States might be a deciding factor.

The Antiwar Movement

42   Throughout 1964, support at home for an American role in Vietnam was widespread. Most Americans accepted the domino theory* and predictions that horrible reprisals against non-Communists would follow a Communist victory. The escalation of the war in 1965 saw a largely college-based opposition to the war arise—with Students for a Democratic Society (SDS) the prime instigators. The University of Michigan held the first Vietnam "teach in" to mobilize opposition to American policy on March 24, 1965. In April, SDS organized a protest march of nearly twenty thousand past the White House, and by October its membership had increased 400 percent. But by mid-1966, SDS was losing its leadership of the movement and was only one of many groups and individuals demonstrating against the expanding war.

43   Those opposing the war fell into two major types who rarely agreed on anything other than that the war should be ended. Pacifists and radical liberals on the political left opposed the war for moral and ideological reasons. Others, as the American military commitment grew and the military draft claimed more young men, opposed the war for more pragmatic reasons: the draft, the loss of lives and money, and the inability of the United States either to defeat the enemy or to create a stable, democratic South Vietnam. A University of Michigan student complained that if he were drafted and spent two years in the army, he would lose more than $16,000 in income. "I know I sound

> **William Westmoreland**   Commander of all American troops in Vietnam from 1964 to 1968.
> **Ho Chi Minh Trail**   Main infiltration route for North Vietnamese soldiers and supplies into South Vietnam; it ran through Laos and Cambodia.

selfish," he explained, "but . . . I paid $10,000 to get this education."

44   Yet college students and graduates were not the most likely to be drafted or go to Vietnam. Far more often, minorities and the poor served in Vietnam, especially in combat roles. African Americans constituted about 12 percent of the population but in Vietnam sometimes made up to 50 percent of frontline units and accounted for about 25 percent of combat deaths. Stokely Carmichael and SNCC had supported SDS actions against the war as early as 1965, but it was Martin Luther King Jr.'s denouncement of the war in 1967 that made international headlines and shook the administration. King called the war immoral and preached that "the Great Society has been shot down on the battlefields of Vietnam." He stated that it was wrong to send young blacks to defend democracy in Vietnam when they were denied it in Georgia.

45   Johnson labeled King a "crackpot," but he knew he had to win the struggle at home to successfully win the war in Vietnam. Watching the antiwar movement grow and public opinion polls register increasing disapproval of the war effort, the administration responded with **COINTELPRO** and **Operation Chaos** actions, in which federal agents infiltrated, spied on, and tried to discredit antiwar groups. FBI reports showing antiwar groups in league with Communists were leaked to the press and counterdemonstrations planned. Nevertheless, opposition to the war swelled. A "Stop-the-Draft Week" in October 1967 prompted more than 10,000 demonstrators to block the entrance of an induction center in Oakland, California, while over 200,000 people staged a massive protest march in Washington against "Lyndon's War."

46   The administration itself was torn by increasing disagreement about the course of the war. Hawks supported General Westmoreland's assertions that the war was being won, that by 1968 half of the enemy's forces were no longer capable of combat, and that more troops were needed to complete the job. Yet by late 1967 some of Johnson's wise men were taking a different view. In November, Secretary of War Robert McNamara recommended a sharp reduction in the war effort, including a permanent end to the bombing of North Vietnam. Johnson rejected his position, and McNamara left the administration. Still, Johnson decided to consider a "withdrawal strategy" that would reduce American support while the South Vietnamese assumed a larger role. But first it was necessary to commit more troops, intensify the bombing, and put more pressure on the South Vietnamese to make domestic reforms. "The clock is ticking," he said.

Tet and the 1968 Presidential Campaign

■ What were the political, social, and military outcomes of the Tet offensive?

■ What key issues shaped the 1968 campaign? What strategy did Richard Nixon use to win?

47   Johnson was correct: the clock was ticking—not only for the United States but also for North Vietnam. As Westmoreland reported success, North Vietnamese leaders were planning an immense campaign to capture South Vietnamese cities during **Tet**, the Vietnamese lunar New Year holiday, a maneuver that would catch American intelligence agencies totally off-guard.

The Tet Offensive

48   In January 1968, the Viet Cong struck forty-one cities throughout South Vietnam, including the capital, Saigon. In some of the bloodiest fighting of the war, American and South Vietnamese forces recaptured the lost cities and villages. It took twenty-four days to oust the Viet Cong from the old imperial city of Hue, leaving the city in ruins and costing more than 10,000 civilian, 5,000 Communist, 384 South Vietnamese, and 216 American lives.

49   The Tet offensive was a military defeat for North Vietnam and the Viet Cong. It provoked no popular uprising against the South Vietnamese government, the Communists held no cities or provincial capitals, and they suffered staggering losses. More than 40,000 Viet Cong were killed. Tet was, nevertheless, a "victory" for the North Vietnamese, for it seriously weakened American support for the war. Amid official pronouncements of "victory just

> **COINTELPRO**   Acronym (COunterINTELligence PROgram) for an FBI program begun in 1956 and continued until 1971 that sought to expose, disrupt, and discredit groups considered to be radical political organizations; it targeted various antiwar groups during the Vietnam War.
>
> **Operation Chaos**   CIA operation within the country from 1965 to 1973 that collected information on and disrupted anti–Vietnam War elements; although it is illegal for the CIA to operate within the United States, it collected files on over 7,000 Americans.
>
> **Tet**   The lunar New Year celebrated as a huge holiday in Vietnam; the Viet Cong–North Vietnamese attack on South Vietnamese cities during Tet in January 1968 was a military defeat for North Vietnam, but it seriously undermined U.S. support for the war.

around the corner," Tet destroyed the Johnson administration's credibility and inflamed a growing antiwar movement. The highly respected CBS news anchor Walter Cronkite had supported the war, but Tet changed his mind. He announced on the air that there would be no victory in Vietnam and that the United States should make peace. "If I have lost Walter Cronkite, then it's over. I have lost Mr. Average Citizen," Johnson lamented.

50 By March 1968, Johnson and most of his "wise men" had also concluded that the war was not going to be won. The new secretary of defense, Clark Clifford, admitted that four years of "enormous casualties" and "massive destruction from our bombing" had not weakened "the will of the enemy." The emerging strategy was to place more responsibility on South Vietnam, send fewer troops than Westmoreland had asked for, and seek a diplomatic end to the war.

Changing of the Guard

51 Two months after Tet came the first presidential primary in New Hampshire. There, Minnesota senator **Eugene McCarthy** was campaigning primarily on the antiwar issue. At the heart of his New Hampshire effort were hundreds of student volunteers who, deciding to "go clean for Gene," cut their long hair and shaved their counterculture beards. They knocked on doors and distributed bales of flyers and pamphlets touting their candidate and condemning the war. Johnson had not entered the New Hampshire primary, but as McCarthy's antiwar candidacy strengthened, Johnson's political advisers organized a **write-in campaign** for the president. Johnson won, but by only 6 percent of the votes cast. Political commentators promptly called McCarthy the real winner. New York senator **Robert Kennedy's** announcement of his candidacy and his surging popularity in the public opinion polls added to the pressure on Johnson. Quietly, Johnson decided to not run for the presidency.

52 On March 31, 1968, a haggard-looking president delivered a major televised speech announcing changes in his Vietnam policy. The United States was going to seek a political settlement through negotiations in Paris with the Viet Cong and North Vietnamese. The escalation of the ground war was over, and the South Vietnamese would take a larger role in the war. The bombing of northern North Vietnam was going to end, and a complete halt of the air war would follow the start of negotiations. At the end of his speech, Johnson calmly made this announcement: "I shall not seek, and I will not accept, the nomination of my party for an-

other term as president." Listeners were shocked. Lyndon B. Johnson had thrown in the towel. Although he later claimed that his fear of having a heart attack while in office was the primary reason for his decision not to run, nearly everyone agreed that the Vietnam War had ended Johnson's political career and undermined his Great Society.

The Election of 1968

53 There were now three Democratic candidates. McCarthy campaigned against the war and the "imperial presidency." Kennedy opposed the war, but not executive and federal power, and he called on the government to better meet the needs of the poor and minorities. Vice President Hubert H. Humphrey, running in the shadow of Johnson, stood behind the president's foreign and domestic programs.

54 By June, Kennedy was winning the primary race, drawing heavily from minorities and urban Democratic voters. In the critical California primary, Kennedy gained a narrow victory over McCarthy, 46 to 41 percent, but the victory was all too short. As the winner left his campaign headquarters, he was shot by Sirhan Sirhan, a Jordanian immigrant. Kennedy died the next day. His death stunned the nation and ensured Humphrey's nomination.

55 McCarthy continued his campaign but did not generate much support among party regulars. By the time of the national convention in Chicago in August, Humphrey had enough pledged votes to guarantee his nomination. Nevertheless, the convention was dramatic. Inside and outside the convention center, antiwar and anti-establishment groups demonstrated for McCarthy, peace in Vietnam, and social justice. Radical factions within the Students for a Democratic Society promised physical confrontation and threatened to contaminate the water supply with drugs. Chicago mayor Richard Daley, determined to maintain order, called in twelve thousand police.

Eugene McCarthy Senator who opposed the Vietnam War and made an unsuccessful bid for the 1968 Democratic nomination for president.

write-in campaign An attempt to elect a candidate in which voters are urged to write the name of an unregistered candidate directly on the ballot.

Robert Kennedy Attorney general during the presidency of his brother John F. Kennedy; elected to the Senate in 1964, his campaign for the presidency was gathering momentum when he was assassinated in 1968.

Violence erupted during the 1968 Democratic National Convention in Chicago. Using nightsticks, police attacked antiwar and anti-establishment protesters in Grant Park, near the convention hotel. The violent confrontations in Chicago did little to quell similar protests, unify the Democratic Party, or help Hubert Humphrey's chances for election. *AP Images.*

56 By August 24, the second day of the convention, clashes between the police and protesters started and grew more belligerent every day. Protesters threw eggs, bottles, rocks, and balloons filled with water, ink, and urine at the police, who responded with tear gas and nightsticks. On August 28, the police responded with force, indiscriminately attacking protesters and bystanders alike as television cameras recorded the scene. The violence in Chicago's streets overshadowed Humphrey's nomination and acceptance speech—and much of his campaign.

57 Many Americans were disgusted by the chaos in Chicago and saw it as typical of the general disruption that was plaguing the nation. The politics of hope that had begun the 1960s was losing its appeal by 1968. From both the political left and right came criticisms of the social policies of the Great Society and the foreign policies that mired the nation in the war in Vietnam.

58 Representing growing dissatisfaction with liberal social policies within Democratic ranks, Governor **George Wallace** of Alabama left the Democratic Party and ran for president as the American Independent Party's candidate. He aimed his campaign at southern whites, blue-collar workers, and low-income white Americans, all of whom deplored the "loss" of traditional American values and society. On the campaign trail, Wallace called for victory in Vietnam and took special glee in attacking the counterculture and the "rich-kid" war protesters who avoided serving in Vietnam while the sons of working-class Americans died there. He also opposed federal civil rights and welfare legislation. Two months before the election, Wallace commanded 21 percent of the vote, according to national opinion polls. "On November 5," he confidently predicted, "they're going to find out there are a lot of rednecks in this country."

59 Richard Nixon was the Republican candidate, having easily won his party's nomination at an orderly convention. He also intended to tap the general dissatisfaction, but without the antagonism of

> **George Wallace** Conservative Alabama governor who opposed desegregation in the 1960s and ran unsuccessfully for the presidency in 1968 and 1972.

the Wallace campaign. He and **Spiro Agnew,** his vice-presidential running mate, focused the Republican campaign on the need for effective international leadership and law and order at home, while denouncing pot, pornography, protesters, and permissiveness. Nixon announced that he would "end the war and win the peace in Vietnam" but refused to comment further. Nixon won with a comfortable margin in the Electoral College although he received only 43 percent of the popular vote. Conservatives were pleased. Together, Nixon and Wallace attracted almost 56 percent of the popular vote, which conservatives interpreted as wide public support for an end to liberal social programs and a return to traditional values.

Nixon Confronts the World

■ How did Richard Nixon plan to achieve an "honorable" peace in Vietnam?

■ How did Nixon's Cold War policies differ from those favored by earlier administrations?

60 As 1969 started, Nixon declared himself a happy man. He had achieved the dream that had been denied him in 1960. As president, he was determined to be the center of decision making, using a few close and loyal advisers to make policy. For domestic affairs, he relied on John Mitchell, his choice for attorney general, and longtime associates H. R. "Bob" Haldeman and John Ehrlichman. In foreign affairs, he tapped Harvard professor **Henry Kissinger,** as his national security adviser, and later made him secretary of state.

61 Repeating his campaign pledges, President Nixon promised to work for national unity and to promote minority rights. But he also wanted to consolidate a new conservative majority that linked long-term Republicans with those recently dissatisfied with protests, the Great Society, and the "liberal" attacks on traditional American society. While he presented himself as a pragmatic politician who could balance liberal and conservative views, his close circle of advisers knew that Nixon had little desire to incorporate liberal views with his own. Instead, he would court what he called the **"Silent Majority."**

Vietnamization

62 Nixon took office and faced not only a Democratic Congress but the looming specter of Vietnam. Vietnam influenced nearly all other issues—the budget, public and congressional opinion, foreign policy, and domestic stability—and Nixon needed

a solution before he could move ahead on other fronts. No one in the administration questioned whether American troops would be withdrawn, but there was considerable debate over the exit speed and how to ensure that the government of Nguyen Van Thieu remained intact. There was also the issue of international credibility. If the United States just left Vietnam, Nixon believed, it would harm American relations with its friends. "A nation cannot remain great, if it betrays its allies and lets down its friends."

63 The product was **Vietnamization.** As American troops left, better-trained, better-led, and better-equipped South Vietnamese units would resume the bulk of the fighting (see Figure 29.1, p. 638). In direct support of the South Vietnamese, the United States would provide increased air support, including if necessary the resumption of bombing North Vietnam. Changing the "color of bodies" and bringing American soldiers home, Nixon believed, would rebuild public support and diminish the crowds of protesters. Expanding the theme of limiting American involvement, in July Nixon developed the **Nixon Doctrine:** countries warding off communism would have to shoulder most of the military burden, with the United States providing political and economic support and limited naval and air support.

64 Nixon publicly announced Vietnamization in the spring of 1969, telling the public that 25,000 American soldiers were coming home. At the same time, he convinced some in the media to alter their coverage of the war. ABC's news director instructed his staff to downplay the fighting and emphasize "themes and stories under the general

---

Spiro Agnew Vice president under Richard Nixon; he resigned in 1973 amid charges of illegal financial dealings during his governorship of Maryland.

Henry Kissinger German-born American diplomat who was President Nixon's national security adviser and secretary of state; he helped negotiate the cease-fire in Vietnam.

Silent Majority Name given to the majority of Americans who supported the government and did not protest or riot; a typical member of the Silent Majority was believed to be white, middle class, average in income and education, and moderately conservative in values and attitudes.

Vietnamization U.S. policy of scaling back American involvement in Vietnam and helping Vietnamese forces fight their own war.

Nixon Doctrine Nixon's policy of requiring countries threatened by communism to shoulder most of the military burden, with the United States offering mainly political and economic support.

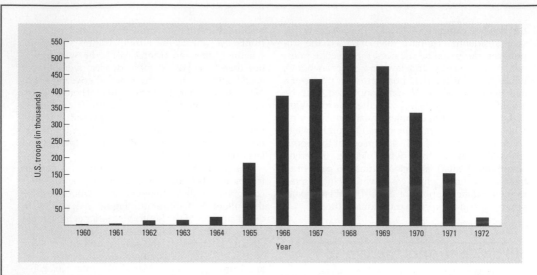

FIGURE 29.1 **Troop Levels by Year** For America, the Vietnam War went through two major phases: Americanization from 1960 to 1968 and Vietnamization from 1969 to 1972.

heading: We are on our way out of Vietnam." By the end of the year, American forces in Vietnam had declined by over 110,000, and public opinion polls indicated support for Nixon's policy.

65 The other dimensions of Nixon's Vietnam policy, however, were unknown to either the public or the press. Quietly, Kissinger and Nixon began work to improve relations with the Soviets and Chinese and to encourage them to reduce their support for North Vietnam. More significantly, the United States expanded its air war in two directions: targeting enemy bases inside Cambodia and Laos and resuming the bombardment of North Vietnam. The secret attacks on Communist sanctuaries inside Cambodia (Operation Menu) began in March 1969, with air force records being falsified to aid in official denials of stories about any such strikes. The intense air assault was part of a "madman strategy" that Nixon designed to convince the North Vietnamese to negotiate. Nixon said he wanted Hanoi "to believe that I've reached the point where I might do anything to stop the war." "We'll just slip the word," Nixon told his advisers, "that 'for God's sake, you know Nixon. . . . We can't restrain him when he's angry—and he has his hand on the nuclear button.'"

66 The strategy did not work. The North Vietnamese appeared unconcerned about Nixon's "madness," the increased bombing, or decreasing support from China and the Soviet Union. They believed that victory was only a matter of patiently waiting until America was fed up with the war.

Consequently, **peace talks** between Kissinger and the North Vietnamese in Paris produced only bitter feelings. Despite such setbacks, Nixon continued his strategy, and in 1970 ordered American troops to cross the border into Cambodia and destroy Communist bases and supply areas. Nearly eighty thousand American and South Vietnamese troops entered Cambodia and demolished enemy bases and large amounts of supplies. The mission, however, failed to halt the flow of supplies or weaken North Vietnam's resolve.

67 As Nixon assumed office, antiwar protests heated up as protests occurred around the nation, culminated by the March on Washington in 1969. In 1970 news about the invasion also refueled antiwar protests across the United States, especially on college campuses. Demonstrations at Kent State University in Ohio and at Jackson State University in Mississippi resulted in the deaths of six protesters. An angry Senate repealed the Gulf of Tonkin Resolution, which had provided the legislative foundation for the war, and forbade the further use of American troops in Laos or Cambodia.

68 Also adding to a broad opposition to the continued American role in Vietnam were reports of

---

peace talks Began in 1968 under the Johnson administration and continued by Nixon's; they produced little agreement until 1972 when Kissinger and North Vietnamese foreign minister Le Doc Tho began to work out a final accord that was signed in 1973.

On May 4, 1970, Ohio National Guard troops opened fire on a crowd of Kent State students protesting the American incursion into Cambodia, killing four of them. Here, a student screams in horror as she hovers over the body of one of the dead students. In outrage, campuses throughout the nation closed and students flocked to Washington to protest the war. *John Filo/Hulton Archive/Getty Images.*

American atrocities around the village of **My Lai** and the release of the **Pentagon Papers.** In 1968, American units, including a platoon commanded by Lieutenant William Calley, had killed over 500 hundred men, women, and children in and around the village of My Lai. The death toll would have been greater if army helicopter pilot Hugh Thompson and his crew had not rescued eleven civilians about to be killed by American soldiers. "It had to happen then, Thompson said, "'cause they were fixin' to die." Later, an official evaluation stated that some units and officers were "eager participants in the body-count game." The massacre, stories about drug use, **fragging,** and seemingly mindless slaughter strengthened the belief that the war was unraveling the morality of American soldiers. As Thompson explained, "This is not what the American soldier does." The moral fiber of American leadership also was questioned with the unauthorized publishing of secret documents (the Pentagon Papers) that indicated that American administrations from Truman to Nixon had not told the truth about Vietnam to the American people.

69 Despite public opinion polls indicating that two-thirds of the American people wanted to get out of Vietnam, Nixon's determination to maintain his policies never wavered. His resolve, however, was matched by North Vietnam. With peace discussions in Paris stalemated, the North Vietnamese in March 1972 launched its "Easter Offensive."

Pushing aside Army of South Vietnam (ARVN) troops, Communist forces advanced toward Saigon. A livid Nixon ordered massive bombing raids against North Vietnam and Communist forces in South Vietnam. By mid-June 1972, American air power had stalled the offensive and enabled ARVN forces to regroup and drive back the North Vietnamese. With their cities under almost continuous air attacks, the North Vietnamese became more flexible in negotiations. By October, with both sides offering some concessions, a peace settlement was ready. "Peace is at hand," Kissinger announced—just in time for the 1972 presidential election.

South Vietnamese president Nguyen Van Thieu, 70 however, rejected the plan. Reluctantly, Nixon supported Thieu and ordered the Christmas bombing of Hanoi and North Vietnam. One goal was to put additional pressure on Hanoi. Another was to convince Thieu that the United States would use its air power to protect South Vietnam. After eleven days the bombing stopped, and Washington advised Thieu that if he did not accept the next peace settlement, the United States would leave him to fend for himself. On January 27, 1973, Thieu accepted a peace settlement that did not differ significantly from the one offered in October. Nixon and Kissinger proclaimed peace with honor, and Kissinger shared the 1973 Nobel Peace Prize with his North Vietnamese counterpart.

The peace settlement imposed a cease-fire; re- 71 quired the removal of the twenty-four thousand remaining American troops, but not North Vietnamese troops; and promised the return of American prisoners of war. The peace terms permitted the United States to complete its military and political withdrawal, but the pact did little to ensure the continued existence of Thieu's government or South Vietnam. The cease-fire, everyone expected, would be temporary. When Haldeman asked Kissinger how long the South Vietnamese

My Lai Site of a massacre of South Vietnamese villagers by U.S. infantrymen in 1968. Of those brought to trial for the murders, only Lieutenant William Calley was found guilty of murder. Originally sentenced to life in prison, he was paroled in 1974.

Pentagon Papers Classified government documents on policy decisions leaked to the press by Daniel Ellsberg and printed by the *New York Times* in 1971. Efforts to block the papers' publication was rejected by a Supreme Court ruling.

fragging An effort to kill fellow soldiers, frequently officers, by using a grenade. It may have accounted for over a thousand American deaths in Vietnam.

government could last, Kissinger answered bluntly, "If they're lucky, they can hold out for a year and a half."

72 As expected, the cease-fire soon collapsed. North Vietnam continued to funnel men and supplies to the south, but substantial American air and naval support for South Vietnam never arrived. Neither Congress nor the public was eager to help Thieu's government. Instead, Congress cut aid to South Vietnam and in November 1973 passed the **War Powers Act.** The law requires the president to inform Congress within forty-eight hours of the deployment of troops overseas and to withdraw those troops within sixty days if Congress fails to authorize the action. In March 1975, North Vietnam began its final campaign to unify the country. A month later, North Vietnamese troops entered Saigon as a few remaining Americans and some South Vietnamese were evacuated by helicopter—some dramatically from the roof of the American embassy. The Vietnam War ended as it had started, with Vietnamese fighting Vietnamese.

As North Vietnamese forces entered Saigon in April 1975, the last American evacuees left by helicopter. Here, they scramble to the roof of the Pittman apartments in Saigon; others left from the roof of the American embassy. Henry Kissinger asked the nation "to put Vietnam behind us."
© *Hubert Van Es/Bettmann/Corbis.*

Modifying the Cold War

73 Ending the Vietnam War was a political and diplomatic necessity for Nixon and was part of his plan to reshape the Cold War. In his first inaugural address, Nixon urged that an "era of confrontation" give way to an "era of negotiation." To this end, he pursued **détente,** a policy that reduced tensions with the two Communist superpowers. China, with which the United States had had virtually no diplomatic contact since the end of the Chinese civil war in 1949, was the key to the Nixon-Kissinger strategy. The Soviets and Chinese had engaged in several bloody clashes along their border, and the Chinese feared a broader border war. Wanting American technology and believing that better relations with the United States would help deter Soviet aggression, the Chinese were ready to open diplomatic discussions with Nixon.

74 Nixon believed that American friendship with the Chinese would encourage the Soviets to improve their relations with the United States, leading to détente, and opening a great potential market for American producers. Sending a signal to China, Nixon lowered restrictions on trade, and in April 1971 the Chinese responded by inviting an American Ping-Pong team to tour China. A few months later, Kissinger secretly flew to Beijing to meet with Premier Zhou Enlai. The result would, as Kissinger phrased it, "send a shock wave around the world": Nixon was going to China. In February 1972, Nixon arrived in Beijing and met with Communist Party chairman Mao Zedong and Zhou. Suddenly the "Red Chinese" were no longer the enemy but "hard-working, intelligent . . . and practical" people. The Cold War was thawing a little in the East.

75 Nixon's China policy, as hoped, contributed to détente with the Soviet Union. Kissinger followed his secret visit to China with one to Moscow, where he discussed improving relations with President **Leonid Brezhnev.** Nixon flew to Moscow in May 1972 and told Brezhnev that he believed that the two nations should "live together and work together." Needing to reduce military spending, develop the Soviet domestic economy, and increase American trade, Brezhnev agreed. The meeting was a success. Brezhnev obtained increased trade with the West, including shipments of American

---

War Powers Act Law passed by Congress in 1973 to prevent the president from involving the United States in war without authorization by Congress.

détente Relaxing of tensions between the superpowers in the early 1970s, which led to increased diplomatic, commercial, and cultural contact.

Leonid Brezhnev Leader of the Soviet Union (first as Communist Party secretary, and then also as president) from 1964 to his death in 1982; he worked to foster détente with the United States during the Nixon era.

grain, and the superpowers announced the **Strategic Arms Limitation agreement** (SALT I), which restricted antimissile sites and established a maximum number of intercontinental ballistic missiles (ICBMs) and submarine-launched ballistic missiles (SLBMs) for each side. It seemed as if Nixon was reshaping world affairs.

76   However, in some areas, America's traditional Cold War stance was unwavering. In Latin America, Nixon followed closely in Johnson's footsteps, working to isolate Cuba and to prevent any additional Communist-style leaders from gaining power. Borrowing from Eisenhower's foreign policy, he used covert operations to disrupt the democratically elected socialist-Marxist government of **Salvador Allende** in Chile. For three years the CIA squeezed the Chilean economy "until it screamed," producing food riots, numerous strikes, and massive inflation. Finally, in September 1973, Chilean armed forces bombed and stormed the presidential palace, killing Allende. Kissinger denied any direct American role in the coup and quickly recognized the repressive military government of General Augusto Pinochet, who promptly reinstated a free-market economy.

Summary

77   When President Johnson assumed the presidency in 1963, the forces of liberalism that had given substance to the Kennedy administration continued their efforts to reform society. Encouraged by Johnson's Great Society and War on Poverty, Hispanics and American Indians organized, demonstrated, and turned to the government—especially the federal courts—to further their causes. The activism associated with the Warren Court intensified as the Court continued to issue controversial decisions that expanded individual rights and protections.

By the mid-1960s, however, liberals increasingly were divided and critical of the Johnson administration. At the heart of a growing disillusionment was the war in Vietnam.

Johnson continued Kennedy's foreign policies, 78 expanding commitments to oppose communism around the world. Unable to find options that would save South Vietnam and reduce the American role, Johnson eventually implemented a series of planned escalations that Americanized the war. The expectation that American military superiority would defeat Ho Chi Minh's Communists proved disastrous. As the United States escalated its efforts, North Vietnam forces kept pace and showed no slackening of resolve or resources. Within the United States, however, as the American commitment grew, a significant antiwar movement developed. The combination of the Tet offensive and presidential politics cost Johnson his presidency, divided the Democratic Party, and compounded the divisions in American society.

But more than the debate over the war divided 79 the nation. By 1968, the country was aflame with riots in urban centers, and an increasing number of groups were seeking better social, economic, and political choices. Those advocating social reforms, however, faced a resurgence of conservatism that helped elect Nixon. Hoping to find a strategy for withdrawing from Vietnam, Nixon implemented a policy of Vietnamization. He also wanted to restructure international relations by working to improve relations with the Soviet Union and China.

> **Strategic Arms Limitation agreement** Treaty between the United States and the Soviet Union in 1972 to limit offensive nuclear weapons and defensive antiballistic missile systems; known as SALT I.
>
> **Salvador Allende** Chilean president who was considered the first democratically elected Marxist to head a government; he was killed in a coup in 1973.

 Quizzes on this chapter are available at **laflemm.com**, *Reading for Thinking*: "Additional Materials."

Acknowledgments

Ronald Bailey. "The Pursuit of Happiness" by Ronald Bailey from *Reason* magazine, December 2000 print edition. Reprinted by permission of Reason.

Carol Berkin et al. From *Making America*, 4th ed. Copyright © 2006. Reprinted by permission of Cengage Learning Company.

Roy Berko, Andrew D. Wolvin, and Daryl Wolvin. From *Communicating*. Copyright © 2004. Reprinted by permission of Cengage Learning Company.

Douglas A. Bernstein. *Psychology*, 6th ed., pp. 566–567. Reprinted by permission of Cengage Learning Company.

Douglas A. Bernstein and Peggy W. Nash. *Essentials of Psychology*, pp. 274–276. Reprinted by permission of Cengage Learning Company.

Paul S. Boyer. *Promises to Keep*, p. 206. Reprinted by permission of Cengage Learning Company.

Paul S. Boyer et al. *Enduring Vision*, pp. 779a–b. Reprinted by permission of Cengage Learning Company.

Joseph DeVito. From *The Interpersonal Communication Book*, 10th ed. Published by Allyn and Bacon, Boston, MA. Copyright © 2004 by Pearson Education. Reprinted by permission of the publisher.

Harold Evans. From *The American Century*. Copyright © 1998 by Harold Evans. Used by permission of Alfred A. Knopf, a division of Random House, Inc., and Janklow & Nesbit Associates for the author.

Heather Gehlert. "Can the Term 'Guys' Refer to Women and Girls?" by Heather Gehlert from *Alternet*, February 28, 2007. This article is reprinted with permission from AlterNet.org and the author.

Google. Google results pages for Earl Warren. (http://www.google.com/search?hl=en&q=the+warren+court&btnG=Search).

Richard J. Hardy. From *Government in America*, p. 502. Used by permission of McDougal Littell Inc., a division of Cengage Learning.

Janet Shibley Hyde. From *Understanding Human Sexuality*, p. 524. Copyright © 1994. Reprinted by permission of The McGraw-Hill Companies.

Jeffrey Nevid. *Essentials of Psychology*, 2006, pp. 135, 288, 306. Reprinted by permission of Cengage Learning Company.

Jeffrey Nevid. From *Psychology: Concepts and Applications*, pp. 229–233, 496–497. Copyright © 2003. Reprinted by permission of Cengage Learning Company.

Mary Beth Norton et al. From *A People and a Nation*, 5th ed. (1993), pp. 492–493, 766. Reprinted by permission of Cengage Learning Company.

Mary Beth Norton. From *A People and a Nation*, 7th ed., p. 535. Reprinted by permission of Cengage Learning Company.

John O'Connor. "Tall Tales of Appalachia" by John O'Connor from *The New York Times*, Opinion Section, May 10, 2003, page A21. Copyright © 2003 The New York Times Co. Reprinted by permission.

William M. Pride, Robert J. Hughes, and Jack R. Kapoor. From *Business*, p. 480. Reprinted by permission of Cengage Learning Company.

Zick Rubin. *Psychology*, pp. 68–69. Reprinted by permission of Cengage Learning Company.

Kelvin L. Seifert. From *Lifespan Development*, p. 488. Reprinted by permission of Cengage Learning Company.

Stephanie Strom. "Extreme Philanthropy" by Stephanie Strom from *The New York Times*, Week in Review Section, July 27, 2003, p. 3. Copyright © 2003 The New York Times Co. Reprinted by permission.

Randall Stross. "Anonymous Source Is Not the Same as Open Source" by Randall Stross from *The New York Times*, March 12, 2006. Copyright © 2006 The New York Times Co. Reprinted by permission.

Alex Thio. From *Society: Myths and Realities, An Introduction to Sociology*, 1st ed., p. 211. Published by Allyn and Bacon, Boston, MA. Copyright © 2007 by Pearson Education. Reprinted by permission of the publisher.

Wikipedia.com. Wikipedia results page for Earl Warren. (http://en.wikipedia.org/wiki/Earl_Warren).

James Wilson and John J. Dilulio. From *American Government*, pp. 284–285. Reprinted by permission of Cengage Learning Company.

INDEX